Praise for

TOUGH LOVE

"As President, I leaned on Ambassador Rice's experience, expertise, and willingness to tell me what I needed to hear. In her memoir, *Tough Love*, you'll see why. It's a tribute to American leadership—and a unifying call for us to do our part to protect it."

—President Barack Obama

"In her candid memoir *Tough Love: My Story of the Things Worth Fighting For*, Susan Rice does something she says she couldn't as U.S. ambassador to the United Nations or as President Barack Obama's national security adviser: tell *her* story. And she does, in a personal and honest manner. . . . In many ways, this memoir is an ode to public service. . . . A student of history, she knows the U.S. has had past periods of strong divisions—the Civil War, the civil rights riots, Vietnam—but America emerged whole and, eventually, stronger. The choice is ours. It's the kind of tough love we could all use at the moment."

—NPR

"With her signature candor and incisive analysis, Rice tells behind-the-scenes stories about the events that have shaped our country and in the world, including the Edward Snowden leaks, the U.S. response to the Rwandan genocide, the Syrian genocide, and Russia's interference in the 2016 election. . . . The book weaves the personal and the public together to tell a compelling story of Rice's life."

—Essence.com

"Rice recounts, very briskly, her triumphs in the classroom and the playing field, the pain of her parents' divorce, her rapid ascent up the ladder of power, and the inevitable dangers to family life of a career in national security policymaking."

—Foreign Policy

"Former national security advisor Susan Rice recounts her untold story, from the West Wing to the day in Libya that changed her political career, sharing her triumphs and growing pains along the way."

—Marie Claire

"A stellar debut . . . Rice writes of juggling work and motherhood, and of the importance of being one's own advocate. Rice's insightful memoir serves as an astute, analytical take on recent American political history."

—Publishers Weekly (starred review)

"The daughter of up-by-their-bootstraps Jamaicans and African Americans, Rice achieved early success through disciplined hard work, intellectual brilliance, and friendships with the likes of Madeleine Albright. . . . Rice is able to look back on her experiences with pride, gratitude, and bracing realism."

—Booklist (starred review)

"A hard-hitting and candid *New York Times* best-selling memoir of a tough woman no longer confined by talking points, who shares her whole voice, her family history, her perspective, and her insider's take on a host of national security crises over the past three decades."

—Ibram Kendi, New York Times bestselling author of
Stamped from the Beginning, in *The Atlantic*

"Susan Elizabeth Rice is one of the most gifted, tenacious, and influential foreign policy voices of our times, and in her revelatory new memoir *Tough Love*, she takes us to the seats of power she's occupied, from the State Department to the United Nations to the West Wing of America's first black president, whom she served as national security advisor. In reading these pages, it's easy to see why President Obama would trust her to give him the clearest assessment of the facts on any day, at any moment, and to offer him unvarnished counsel on how best to keep the country safe. At the core of Rice's story, and brilliant career, is a fearless commitment to the truth and an unwavering devotion to the lessons she inherited as the descendant of Jamaican immigrants in Maine and enslaved Africans in South Carolina: to prize education as the path up to the American Dream and to have the confidence to be herself. In this remarkably honest examination of the opportunities and struggles confronting those charged with national security, Rice has given us an inspiring autobiography while making a critically important addition to the history of U.S. foreign policy."

—Henry Louis Gates Jr., *New York Times* bestselling author of
Stony the Road

"This is a breathtakingly honest account by a true American patriot about what it's like to grow up with tough love and then deploy those values on behalf of our nation's foreign policies. Weaving together the personal and the professional, Susan Rice describes how her upbringing in a distinguished but at times struggling family helped prepare her to be a fierce champion of American interests and survive the unfair attacks on her in the aftermath of the Benghazi tragedy. This book will not only inspire you about the true sources of America's greatness, it will also provide some lessons in empowerment, tenacity, and fearlessness."

—Walter Isaacson, *New York Times* bestselling author of
Leonardo da Vinci

"Susan Rice's intellect, strategic prowess, and integrity are unrivaled among today's national security leaders. I have seen firsthand how she has achieved vitally important results for American interests and values. *Tough Love* finally reveals who Susan Rice really is, much of which has been lost or misunderstood in public portrayals of her. The fearless, compassionate, funny, and selfless woman whom I have known since she was a child emerges as she shares with bracing honesty her challenges with family, motherhood, and leadership in the most demanding of male-dominated fields."

—Madeleine Albright, former Secretary of State

"In *Tough Love*, Susan Rice provides a compelling look at what it is really like to work in the inner sanctums of the White House and what it really means to walk the corridors of power. In a gripping display of humor and grace, Susan invites us all to share in her triumphs and her failures—and she teaches some important life lessons along the way. Reading *Tough Love* is like taking a master class in how to be a powerful woman. It is also a classic American tale, relatable to anyone who has ever dreamed of success. I was riveted from the first page to the last."

—Shonda Rhimes

"*Tough Love* is a must-read for leaders and their teams. A brilliant, courageous woman with a remarkable personal story, Susan Rice provides a riveting and moving account of rising to the highest ranks in national security and diplomacy along with unmatched insight into the most complex global challenges. She offers a master class for all who aspire to excellence, with invaluable lessons about high-performance leadership and effective management of complex teams in unforgiving circumstances. Her powerful, hopeful appeal to our shared values as Americans and all that we stand to gain by coming together is profoundly inspirational and more urgent than ever."

—Indra Nooyi, former chairman and CEO, PepsiCo

TOUGH LOVE

TOUGH
LOVE

―――

My Story of the Things
Worth Fighting For

SUSAN RICE

SIMON & SCHUSTER PAPERBACKS
New York · London · Toronto · Sydney · New Delhi

Simon & Schuster Paperbacks
An Imprint of Simon & Schuster, Inc.
1230 Avenue of the Americas
New York, NY 10020

Copyright © 2019 by SERice LLC

First Simon & Schuster trade paperback edition August 2020

SIMON & SCHUSTER PAPERBACKS and colophon are registered trademarks of
Simon & Schuster, Inc.

For information about special discounts for bulk purchases, please contact
Simon & Schuster Special Sales at 1-866-506-1949 or business@simonandschuster.com.

The Simon & Schuster Speakers Bureau can bring authors to your live event.
For more information, or to book an event, contact the Simon & Schuster Speakers
Bureau at 1-866-248-3049 or visit our website at www.simonspeakers.com.

Interior design by Dana Sloan

Manufactured in the United States of America

10 9 8 7 6 5 4 3 2

Library of Congress Cataloging-in-Publication Data is available.

ISBN 978-1-5011-8997-5
ISBN 978-1-5011-8998-2 (pbk)
ISBN 978-1-5011-8999-9 (ebook)

To my parents, Lois Dickson Rice and Emmett J. Rice,
who gave me all I needed and much more,

To my husband and life partner, Ian, without whom
none of this would be possible,

To our beloved children, Jake and Maris, who have
taught me what matters,

And to my brother, Johnny, who has never let me get
away with anything.

Contents

Prologue: Farewell to the Moral Universe   1

PART ONE: FOUNDATIONS

  1 Service in My Soul   17

  2 Coming Up   40

  3 Growing Up Too Soon   59

  4 Twice As Good   76

  5 Go West, Young Woman   94

  6 Busting Out   107

PART TWO: FUNDAMENTALS

  7 Rookie Season   129

  8 Always Africa   154

  9 Storming State   166

 10 "I Remember When I Too Was a Young Assistant Secretary"   186

 11 Going Global   205

PART THREE: THE BIG LEAGUES

12	Represent	237
13	High-Stakes Diplomacy	261
14	The Arab Spring Comes to New York	278
15	*Star Wars* Cantina	295
16	Benghazi	306

PART FOUR: COMING BACK

17	Running the Table	341
18	The Furies	362
19	Point Guard	384
20	Putting Points on the Board	411
21	The Fourth Quarter	426
22	"He F#%@ing Won?"	453
23	Bridging the Divide	466
	Afterword to the Paperback Edition	483
	Acknowledgments	491
	Notes	497
	Index	511

TOUGH LOVE

Prologue

Farewell to the Moral Universe

WASHINGTON, D.C.

JANUARY 20, 2017

I t starts like every other day, even though it is the last.

My intelligence briefer waits in the Secret Service vehicle outside my house to hand over the classified iPad containing the last President's Daily Brief of the Obama administration. We ride downtown together, as usual, but on this day the streets are eerily empty. Gray overcast skies, promising a good chance of rain, weigh on the city as we drive past familiar landmarks— Georgetown, the Kennedy Center, the State Department, and the Federal Reserve.

Outside the temperature is an unseasonable 43 degrees and rising, and I'm relieved to be wearing just a comfortable black, fitted jacket and black pants with a gold short-sleeved top underneath. No heavy winter clothing on what would typically be a frigid day.

There are five of us in the black armored SUV. My briefer and I sit behind two Secret Service agents who man the front seats. Between us is a red and black secure phone that comes in handy when I am on the road and the White House Situation Room needs to reach me. Often it's Secretary of State John Kerry on the line. Behind me in the back row of seats, where my kids normally ride, is *my husband, Ian, who is coming to help me carry away my last boxes and, more importantly, to share in the nostalgia of closing this chapter of our lives.*

As we pull into the White House complex, my briefer passes me a gift bag containing a very nice bottle of scotch—a totally unexpected parting present—which he says presciently, "may come in handy some days down the road."

Because the driveway separating the White House from the Old Executive Office Building is packed with two motorcades—one for President Obama and one for President-elect Trump—we have to jump out of the car and walk through the final exterior gate with Secret Service agents trailing behind, rather than drive up to the door of the West Wing basement to disembark, as we always do.

It's 9 a.m. on Inauguration Day: Friday, January 20, 2017. It feels more than a little strange.

Almost all of the White House staff is gone. The most senior worked through January 19. Only a handful remain. As national security advisor, I am on duty—until 12:01 p.m. when the forty-fifth president takes the oath of office. If, God forbid, there is a terrorist attack before noon on the Capitol where almost the entirety of the U.S. government is collected, I will be expected to respond as I would on any other day during the prior three and a half years. Assuming that no such crisis will occur, I plan on spending the final hours of my tenure tying up some loose ends, relinquishing the remaining documents that must go to the Archives, packing the last personal items in my office, and saying goodbye to those few colleagues I've yet to bid farewell.

My feelings are all jumbled up. I am sad to leave, knowing that I will mightily miss working with such good people and close friends every day. To a person, the senior staff of this White House, Obama's second-term team, are committed, kind, collegial, and selfless. It is them and my extraordinary National Security Council (NSC) colleagues I will miss the most. For years, through all kinds of trials, we hung together in battle on behalf of what we believed was right for our country, on behalf of a president we respected and loved. I will miss seeing President Obama every day and receiving his customary smart-ass ribbings about my shoes, my short stature, or my tennis game, which he claims without any evidence (and much to the contrary) that he can best. I will miss the thrill and the import of serving my country at the highest levels and working on issues of utmost consequence. I can't imagine that anything hereafter will compare.

Yet I am also excited to be free. To be back in charge of my life. To be responsible primarily to my loved ones and myself. To wake up when I want, exercise as much as I wish, wear yoga pants every day if I feel like it, spend quality time with my kids, and refresh the romance with the love of my life. Most immediately, I am looking forward in two days to running off to a faraway island with Ian (and no kids) for almost three weeks!

At one point, I might have worried about surviving devoid of the ongoing adrenaline rush that is a life of service, particularly in the White House. Not now. Sixteen years earlier, at the end of the Clinton administration, I made the transition from an intense government job to private life. Over the course of my fifty-two years, I had learned how to drive myself at varying speeds—from fifth gear to second gear—and am confident that I remember how to downshift.

Three hours left.

Curious, Ian and I walk around the first floor of the West Wing. Tall, lanky, as handsome and almost as youthful-looking as when we first met in college, my husband—who worked for years in television news, most recently as an executive producer—has his phone camera at the ready. All the jumbo photos of Obama and his family and staff have been removed from the walls. Empty wooden frames await Trump photos to fill them.

"Susan—" I hear the unmistakable voice of Ben Rhodes, deputy national security advisor and one of my closest friends, calling to us. I know I'm about to get one of the best hugs in the world. Ben is compact, with short-cropped hair and an impish demeanor. No one can beat him for loyalty, devotion, or dangerous tandem moves on the dance floor. I turn and see him approaching with Anita Decker Breckenridge, the striking blond, appropriately fierce deputy White House chief of staff, who carries a bottle of Veuve Clicquot champagne. We follow her like she's the Pied Piper to find Ferial Govashiri, the president's unfailingly warm and upbeat assistant. She is standing vigil in the outer Oval Office, making sure that as long as Obama is president, nothing untoward is going down on his premises.

Inside the Oval, the scene is surreal—the final stage of the presidential transition in all its banality, speed, and extraordinary professionalism. A crew of moving men is ripping down the old Obama curtains and putting up Trump gold. The Resolute Desk behind which President Obama sat—made of wood taken from the Arctic explorer HMS Resolute, and used by almost every presi-

dent since Rutherford B. Hayes—will soon be Donald Trump's. It is lying upside down in the center of the Oval with wires and cords hanging out, as the communications systems are reconfigured. The crew is changing out the Obama carpet, on which the famous quotation attributed to Martin Luther King Jr. is woven along its edge: "The arc of the moral universe is long, but it bends toward justice."

We do not linger. It is painful to witness the literal dismantling of Obama's White House. With a full appreciation of the irony of drinking champagne on the morning of Trump's inaugural, Anita pops the cork, and the five of us share the bottle. Without much in the way of words, we drink to our friendship, to the privilege of public service, to the pride we share in the accomplishments of the Obama administration, and to our prayer that the country is strong enough to endure whatever is to come.

Ian and I meander back to my suite, diagonally across from the Oval Office in the compact West Wing. I settle down at my desk for the last time to tackle the loose ends. Despite the press of end-of-administration responsibilities, I want first to act on a letter that I received from a former State Department employee who was gravely injured in the 1998 East Africa embassy bombings. We originally met when he was being treated at the Army's Landstuhl Regional Medical Center in Germany. His son wants to go to the Naval Academy, and he wrote to ask if I could help. Though I doubt I can be of much assistance, I want to make the effort on his behalf. I call a senior career staffer in the vice president's office, someone who will stay behind after Joe Biden departs, to ask if he can please try to help the son of a man who sacrificed immeasurably for his country. The vice president's office can nominate candidates for the service academies, and my hope is that the permanent staff can lend apolitical support to this family. I then call my former State Department colleague to relay that, while I am not optimistic, I made the request.

I shift gears to clean out the remaining items in my desk and finish up with the final boxes. It's a little after 11 a.m., and time is running out. The last weeks of the administration, not surprisingly, have been even more intense than usual. On top of the crush of enduring issues—the counter-ISIS campaign, North Korea, Afghanistan, Syria, Libya—I have had to spend many hours on additional tasks: briefing my successor as national security advisor, Lieutenant General Michael Flynn (Retired); coaching NSC staff who are leaving government on how to think about their futures; moving mountains of final paperwork to be signed by the president; and overseeing my team's yeoman efforts to archive my documents.

In the midst of those undertakings, came the sudden loss of my mother, Lois Dickson Rice. Her passing on January 4, 2017, left me shocked and bereft but also demanded a significant share of my time. Even though my younger brother, Johnny, took on many of the tasks that are invariably part of losing a loved one, it fell to me to obtain the death certificate, complete paperwork for the funeral home, schedule her memorial, pay severance to her caregivers, host grieving relatives, and ensure that her obituaries were both worthy and published in the right places.

There was no time to grieve. Too much was happening to allow myself to succumb to the undertow of pain inside me.

As these final days flew by, I left to the end one last email—a memo for the record, requested by our White House counsel's office. I knew I must get it done, but it wasn't urgent. It didn't seem to matter much when I wrote it. So it fell to the back of the jammed queue. The email was to memorialize a brief meeting that President Obama hosted on January 5 with Deputy Attorney General Sally Yates, FBI director Jim Comey, Vice President Biden, and myself. This discussion followed a larger meeting in which President Obama was briefed on the highly classified version of the Intelligence Community report, "Assessing Russian Activities and Intentions in Recent US Elections."

In this follow-on meeting that the White House lawyers had asked me to document, President Obama sought the Justice Department leaders' judgment of whether there was any reason that he should instruct me and other senior administration officials to be careful in how we briefed incoming Trump administration officials on Russia. Obama was explicitly not seeking to inject himself into any law enforcement business and, as always, he insisted that we proceed "by the book" to avoid any inappropriate White House involvement in Justice Department matters. Rather, from a national security vantage point, Obama wanted to know if there was any risk in fully sharing information related to Russia with the incoming Trump team. Comey offered his best judgment, which remains classified, and agreed that, if anything changed, he would let the president know. This is what I hurriedly write up as a summary of that brief conversation. I email it to myself in order to record, at the White

House counsel's request, that this discussion should not subsequently be mis-construed as the president improperly injecting himself into a matter under Justice Department purview.

The clock's minute hand inches past 11:15 a.m.

Time to turn on the television in my office to watch the inaugural proceed-ings.

Before saying goodbye to cherished colleagues in the Situation Room and the NSC front office, who will stay behind, I ask Ian if I should pen a note to my successor, Michael Flynn, who will take over my desk later that afternoon.

Over the last two months, Flynn and I have spent over twelve hours to-gether. He is a wiry, taut man, fit with a chiseled angular face and military-cut dark hair. In my presence, he seemed quite a different person than the fiery partisan who led the "Lock Her Up" chant at the Republican National Conven-tion. With me, Flynn seemed subdued, even daunted by the tasks ahead. He was civil and respectful, hungry for advice on how to do the job of national security advisor, if not so much for my views on policy matters. At the end of our final meeting, after I wished Flynn all my best, I started to extend my hand to shake his. He surprised me by asking, "Can I have a hug?"

Flynn seemed to understand what a tough assignment he was embarking on and recognized that I had done my best to help him succeed. I had, despite my misgivings. Though unexpected, I provided the requested hug—which was awkward, if a little touching.

In this context, a note seems somewhat superfluous, but Ian and I agree it is the patriotic and professional thing to do. On a White House stationery card, I reiterate my best wishes for his success in a job so crucial to the nation's security. I offer to help him, if ever I could, which is a duty and a creed among former national security advisors, regardless of party affiliation. I had always been grateful for the wisdom and generosity of my predecessors—from Henry Kissinger to Sandy Berger, from Tony Lake and Tom Donilon to Condi Rice and Steve Hadley. I would, of course, return the favor to anyone who came after me.

I leave the note on top of the desk and take one last look around the wholly sanitized national security advisor's office, burning into my mind's eye the image of the spotless walls, empty shelves, and, for once, a completely clean desk. Gone are the photos of my children and family. The wall is bare where the massive, gorgeous, reputedly $5 million Willem de Kooning painting entitled

. . . And the Cat (Untitled XI) *had hung, which was loaned to my offices at the U.N. and the White House by the de Kooning Foundation courtesy of the Foundation for Art and Preservation in Embassies. Gone too are the painted purple and blue wooden sign with a green handprint made by my daughter, Maris, at summer camp that greeted guests at my front office door with "Susan E. Rice's Office, National Security Advisor"; the placard with my signature mantra "Get Shit Done," which was strategically placed on my bookshelf to spur me on over the years; and the wooden carved desk plate emblazoned with "United States of America," which I liberated from the 2015 Camp David Summit with Gulf Arab leaders. The only remaining color in the room comes from the television set still playing the lead-up to the oath of office.*

Ian snaps some final pictures of my former office and captures me as I walk out one last time. The clock above the door reads 11:52. Time to go.

As I head out, I gather my beloved colleagues senior advisor Curtis Ried and special assistant Adam Strickler, who sit outside my office. Curtis is dressed to the nines as usual—in a perfectly tailored suit, funky colorful socks, and expertly coiffed hair. Adam is ready, as always, with his sweet smile, sparkly brown eyes, and unfailingly even demeanor, which have helped soothe me and several of my predecessors through countless storms. The four of us head down the stairs and out the door of the West Basement back to the driveway separating the White House from the Old Executive Office Building. We all pile into the Secret Service black armored Suburban. Before we pull away, I see John Fitzpatrick, NSC senior director for records and access, across the driveway. I jump out of the car and hustle over to give him a hug goodbye and thank him. An experienced career civil servant in his fifties, John has the enormous, ongoing job of overseeing the transfer of all Obama-era NSC records to the Archives.

As we roll out of the White House gates for the last time, my lead Secret Service agent, Tom Rizza, leans back and says, "Ma'am, I need to ask you for your White House cell phone and your badge." I hand them over dutifully, with a combination of sadness, finality, and relief.

The radio is tuned to the inauguration and, shortly after we leave the White House complex headed to Joint Base Andrews, President Trump takes the oath of office, concluding: "So help me God."

I'm thinking to myself, Please God, help us all, especially President Trump.

I struggle to persuade myself that his presidency will be better than his campaign and transition. Surely, the weight of the office will sober and steel him. It couldn't possibly be as bad as some fear.

Trump's speech is unpleasant, if unremarkable, until he utters words that seem to make the armored vehicle shudder: "This American carnage stops right here and stops right now."

We all look at each other, stunned.

"Did he just say 'carnage'? In his Inaugural Address?" I ask no one in particular. I really wasn't sure I heard him correctly.

Seated behind them, I sense the agents wince almost imperceptibly. No one is prepared for the cynicism and ugliness of "American carnage." We ride the rest of the way to Andrews in near silence.

When President and Mrs. Obama depart the Capitol after the swearing-in, they will helicopter to Andrews in order to fly to their destination in Palm Springs, California, on the plane that we think of as Air Force One (but isn't because Obama is no longer president). But before they depart, there will be one last goodbye.

Two months earlier, in November 2016, on our final overseas trip with the president, I suggested to Anita Decker Breckenridge that we organize a proper send-off for the Obamas at Andrews. I recalled fondly the moving and emotional goodbye for the Clintons staged in a big hangar with staff and cabinet, active duty military personnel, an honor guard, and military band. It was a great way to bond the team at the end of the administration and put a bow on eight years of triumph and tribulation—to say goodbye and thank you. I thought the Obamas deserved the same and knew how much it would mean for staff to be together with them one last time. Anita made it happen, as she did so much over the years.

We pull up to the packed hangar in time to hustle inside, make our way up to the front, and position ourselves close to the podium alongside the rest of the senior staff. Conversations are muted and abbreviated as we wait together for former President Obama and the first lady to arrive and speak to us assembled one last time.

When that moment comes and the president begins, "Michelle and I, we've really been milking this goodbye thing, so it behooves me to be very brief," someone calls out, "No, no!"

"Yes, yes!" he says, and continues from there.

As if to comfort the bereaved, he reminds us all that our jobs are not over. Democracy, he tells us, is "not the buildings; it's not the monuments; it's you being willing to work to make things better, and being willing to listen to each other and argue with each other and come together and knock on doors and make phone calls and treat people with respect. And that doesn't end. This is just a—just a little old pit stop. This . . . is not a period. This is a comma in the continuing story of building America."

He tells us all how proud he is of us, that he can't wait to see what we do next and, he concludes, "And I promise you, I'll be right here with you.

"All right?

"God Bless you. Thank you, everybody.

"Yes, we did. Yes, we can.

"God Bless America."

Then, too soon, it's time for them to leave. Former president and Mrs. Obama each give me and Ian farewell embraces and deliver many others. It is a fitting send-off for a president who had done so much good, with such humility, and who made his whole team proud every day he served.

Rain falls as the Obamas walk outside along the red carpet, up the stairs to the plane door, then turn and wave one last time. Many of us stay behind to share memories, comfort one another, and promise to stay in touch. The Secret Service has kindly agreed to take their former protectees home, including me and White House Chief of Staff Denis McDonough and his family, rather than leave us curbside at Andrews. The four of us cram back into my agents' SUV, plus my (now former) chief of staff Suzy George, and we head to my house.

Outside our home, Ian and I thank my four Secret Service agents from the bottom of our hearts. The bond of gratitude and trust you form with men and women who would give their lives to protect you is hard to convey.

After we take a few final pictures, I ask them, "Where do you go from here?"

"Well, ma'am," one says with a hint of trepidation, "we are going to pick up Kellyanne," the incoming White House counselor to President Donald J. Trump.

Stoically, I reply, "Good luck and thank you again," and turn to walk into the house with Ian and my team.

As soon as the door slams shut, overwhelmed by a flood of mixed emotions, I burst into tears.

———◆———

NOVEMBER 2012

FIVE YEARS EARLIER

"Honey, can you tell the doctor what's happening?"

"First, it was voices. And now it's like people, real people, but I can tell they aren't real . . . they are coming out of the walls. And they move toward me and talk."

"Are they scary? Do they threaten you?"

"No, not really scary, but it's creepy. They come at bad times like in class at school, or when I was at Frannie's house for a sleepover. And I don't know when to expect them, and it really bothers me."

"Do you recognize them?"

"No, it's mostly a man. I don't know him, but he is very real."

This was the recurring conversation my daughter, Maris, my husband, Ian, and I were having with various doctors at Children's Hospital in Washington, D.C. It was November 2012, and our beautiful, happy, seemingly healthy eight-year-old was suddenly having frequent and unpredictable hallucinations. She was bothered, and we were terrified.

Over a span of three weeks, a phalanx of neurologists, psychiatrists, ophthalmologists, and radiologists pummeled Maris with MRIs, needles, exams, and repetitive questions. The doctors said the most likely cause was a brain tumor. Other possibilities included schizophrenia, a visual disorder, abuse, or psychological stress. I was flying back and forth from New York, where I was serving as the United States ambassador to the United Nations, to attend these various appointments and to comfort Maris.

Eventually, the tests ruled out the worst possible explanations. No tumor, no mental disorder, no physical trauma or abnormality. Still, no explanation. The episodes continued for almost a year, albeit with diminishing frequency after January 2013. Over time, her doctors concluded that Maris was experiencing a stress reaction to watching her mother being assailed for my role in characterizing the Benghazi attack.

While serving as U.N. ambassador, I had appeared on five Sunday shows in mid-September 2012, just days after four Americans, including Ambassador Christopher Stevens, had been killed in a terrorist attack on the U.S. compounds in Benghazi, Libya. Speaking from talking points prepared by the Intelligence Community, I provided their initial assessment of what had happened. Rapidly thereafter, I became the target of right-wing commentators and Republican members of Congress who falsely accused me of incompetence and, worse, of lying to the American people about the circumstances surrounding the tragedy.

Still a young child, Maris had internalized the distress that had infused our household. In hindsight, Ian and I realized we had failed to turn off the television quickly enough and to keep it off at home, before it was too late. Maris was hurt and angry. She couldn't understand what was happening or why. But she was damn sure of two things: she loved her mother intensely, and she despised Senator Lindsey Graham. She wanted nothing more than to call his office and tell him so.

We didn't let her make the call, but we were sorely tempted.

Washington's politics of personal destruction don't come free of cost. They damage and destroy the lives of innocents who neither signed up for the public spotlight nor can comprehend vicious character assassinations of the ones they love.

Our son, Jake, then thirteen years old, managed to distance himself from the uproar that swept through our lives like wildfire. Or, at least at the time, he seemed better able to compartmentalize his feelings—something I know a little bit about too.

In addition to Maris, I worried a great deal about my seventy-eight-year-old mother, Lois. Brilliant, accomplished, and elegant, my mother was stuck at her Embassy Row town house in Washington, D.C., recovering from her third surgery in her battle with cancer, rather than enjoying the first of fall foliage in her home state of Maine, as she normally would in September.

My mother warned me: I should never have gone on the Sunday shows.

Until she passed, on appropriate occasions, Mom would remind me, with a gentle smile, of her advice unheeded.

In those early days, it was hard to grasp the depth and force of the reaction to my appearances. It was harder still to imagine that it would endure, not only through the entirety of the 2012 presidential campaign, but long thereafter. I became a household name and the poster child for bilious

Obama-haters on Fox and in right-wing social media. For months, it was relentless. And though it ebbed, it has never ended.

I have always viewed myself as a professional, a patriot, a dedicated public servant. I do not much mind if some people don't like me. And some don't. Never before, however, had I been accused of being stupid or, worse, dishonest. None of which mattered when, on September 16, 2012, I became and remain, as one commentator on MSNBC said, "the right-wing's favorite chew toy." Or at least one of them.

Ever since my name became synonymous with Benghazi, I have wanted to tell my story. Almost overnight, I went from being a respected if relatively low-profile cabinet official to a nationally notorious villain or heroine, depending on one's political perspective and what cable news channel you watch.

I am neither. The portrayals of me on both sides are superficial and uninformed by who I am and where I come from, by what motivates and truly defines me.

I could not tell my own story—until I left government. When I was a senior official who spoke publicly, I was speaking on behalf of the United States of America and our president. For the five years after Benghazi until I returned to private life, I was compelled to allow myself to be defined by others—something I never had to do before or otherwise would have tolerated. It's hard to convey how frustrating that feels, especially when the public portrayal is false or demeaning. Now I am free to not only tell my own story but also what I have learned over the course of my life in service.

Recently, the renowned professional tennis coach Nick Bollettieri watched me hit a few strokes on the court and said: "I can tell what you are. You are fiercely competitive and a sore loser." My younger brother, Johnny, and I laughed uproariously. Ten minutes into our first encounter, Bollettieri had nailed me. My hope is that I have grown more gracious in both winning and losing over time, but neither I nor Johnny was prepared to argue this point with Nick. He was more right than wrong.

For over four decades, I have been sprinting. Running as far and as fast as I can—through whatever pain—to try to exceed expectations, in school, at university, in my work, and as a daughter, wife, and mother. I've had little time to absorb and reflect on what I have discovered about myself, my family, my hometown of Washington, D.C., or the extraordinary professional experiences I've had. From my first job on the White House National Security Council staff, starting in the Clinton administration at age twenty-eight to becoming the youngest ever regional assistant secretary of state, from representing our country at the United Nations to wrestling as national security advisor with the toughest threats we face, I have been privileged to participate in making many of the most complex and consequential decisions the U.S. has confronted over the last twenty-five years.

I haven't had time to breathe. Until now. In retracing my steps and reclaiming my voice, it was necessary to revisit the foundations of who I am—to study my family history and build on the knowledge imparted to me in disconnected snippets over decades. To recall the myriad blessings I have been given, and to renew my vows to fulfill the responsibility that comes with such blessings. To relearn the fundamental lessons my parents taught me about race, resilience, equality, excellence, education, and overcoming adversity.

I am a direct person. You will find that what you see is what you get. I'm not pulling my punches, even when they land on me or the ones I love most. That's part of the tough love way I was raised. I also can't tell you absolutely everything. There are too many important issues on which I have worked over the years to recount them all. By necessity, I have been selective, since this is a personal story, not a comprehensive diplomatic history, yet one that I hope will elucidate how American foreign policy is customarily made. There are some matters—personal, professional, classified— I will keep to myself and take to my grave. Tell-all books, which sell copies at the expense of others, are tacky and not my style. But I am giving you all I can, the best I can, straight-up, with whatever wisdom I can add for good measure.

In the earlier chapters ahead, I've opened each with reflections on my time leading up to and including the Obama years. This nonlinear approach links my more recent past with my childhood and young adulthood, when I learned many lessons that would help shape me as a leader. From then, as I delve into my time in the Clinton and Obama administrations, I have opted for openings that typically go to the heart of the chapter to come.

Reflecting on our current complex and disconcerting times, I recognize that many Americans are questioning our leadership role in the world. Many also doubt the relevance of the American dream to huge segments of our society who have been left behind and locked out of the kinds of privileges that I've been fortunate to enjoy. My mother used to look back on her amazing life and say, "Not bad for a poor colored girl from Portland, Maine." We need more Lois Dickson Rices who can overcome the odds and win in tomorrow's United States.

Almost by definition, I am an optimist, or I couldn't stay sane while doing the intense and sometimes terrifying work of national security. I am a big believer in our country, which has given so much to me, my family, and to so many others with far less than what my grandparents had, who were both immigrants and descendants of slaves.

Yet, I am not naive. I know that it's *works* that matter—not words, not hope, not even the most powerful dreams. We each have agency and responsibility. We can't be passive bystanders, victims, or vigilantes. We must each commit to unify and to heal. We must fear none, especially our fellow Americans.

I still believe that the arc of the moral universe bends toward justice, but nobody is going to do the hard bending, if not you and me. It's our choice, and I have always believed we must choose each other.

My sincere hope in telling my story is that others may find in it inspiration and empowerment, perhaps a source of strength and fearlessness. If nothing else, I aim to share what I have learned along the way: the importance of always doing your best; picking yourself up and dusting yourself off; and driving down the court to the bucket—all while maintaining grace under fire.

Finally, I hope that you will see the value of my father's core doctrine. Emmett J. Rice, who overcame Jim Crow, the segregated armed forces, and pervasive employment discrimination to rise to the top of his field, hammered something essential into me and my brother: "Don't take crap off of anyone."

PART ONE

Foundations

1

Service in My Soul

My *first contact with Barack Obama came in a phone call from him in the summer of 2004.*

At the time, I was serving as a senior foreign policy advisor for the Kerry/Edwards presidential campaign, while on leave from my job as a senior fellow at the Brookings Institution. My primary responsibilities involved helping craft policy positions, supporting Senator Kerry in debate preparation, and managing our small foreign policy team. I also served as a television surrogate on foreign policy matters and liaised with our senior outside advisors.

Earlier that summer, Tony Lake asked me if I would be willing to speak to Obama, a state senator who was then running for the U.S. Senate from Illinois. Lake had been President Bill Clinton's first national security advisor and my first boss in government. Both a mentor and a close friend, Tony has a puckish smile, piercing blue-gray eyes, and a quick, dry wit. He may seem self-effacing, in part because he shuns the public spotlight, but he is tough and those people who think they can roll him will be sorely surprised.

Tony explained that he had been asked by his old friend Abner Mikva, a former White House counsel and member of Congress, to talk to Mikva's young former colleague on the faculty at the University of Chicago Law School. Behind the scenes, Tony had recently begun advising Obama on foreign policy issues and encouraged him to talk to me about Darfur, Iraq, and other salient issues. This would enable Obama to stay connected to the foreign policy side of the Kerry campaign—so that, as a candidate for Senate, he could make delib-

erate determinations as to whether he wished to align himself with, or depart from, the party nominee's positions. Glad to assist, I talked to Obama a couple times that summer by phone.

Like most Americans, my first real exposure to him came on the Tuesday night of the 2004 Democratic National Convention in Boston. Stuck at the Kerry/Edwards makeshift office in an unimpressive downtown hotel, my colleagues and I were on deadline, working through the campaign's response to the just released 9/11 Commission Report, and unable to make it to the convention center for the keynote address. Frustrated by having to miss the action at the arena—which we enjoyed every other night of the convention—we hustled downstairs and pitched ourselves in front of a television in the cramped and loud hotel bar.

When Barack Obama took the stage, we listened intently.

His speech was tremendously powerful and compelling, but for me it was much more. It drew me beneath the television set, where I looked up. As I watched, tears silently streamed down my face. I was amazed. For the first time, I saw an African American political leader of my generation who was passionate, intelligent, principled, and credible. He was neither an icon of the civil rights era nor a "race-man" (as my father used to call those who viewed the world primarily through the prism of race). He was a new American leader—for all. Like my children, he was both black and white, a role model for my son, Jake. Young and visionary, he spoke movingly of one America—"Not a liberal America and a conservative America, there's the United States of America." For the first time in my life, I had found a political leader to whom I could completely relate and who excited me.

In September, John Kerry spoke at the annual gala dinner of the Congressional Black Caucus Foundation—a must do for any Democratic presidential nominee. Kerry was well-received, but the star of the evening was the magnetic Barack Obama, who was on track to be the next senator from Illinois.

By chance, I was talking with the Reverend Jesse Jackson and other Illinois heavyweights as Obama dutifully made his rounds at the front tables. He stopped by the Illinois crowd to pay his respects and, as I turned from Jackson and stood up to see what the commotion was about, I found myself face-to-face with the senator-to-be. I introduced myself. He said he knew who I was and thanked me again for talking foreign policy with him on the phone back in the summer. I wished him good luck, and he moved on.

Following the election, in early 2005, Obama was sworn in as the junior senator from Illinois and tapped to serve on the Senate Foreign Relations Committee. Tony Lake and his dynamic, effervescent wife, Julie, hosted a dinner at their home in Washington to introduce the freshman senator to a small group of Obama generation national security experts, including me and my good friend Gayle Smith, with whom I had worked closely during the Clinton years. At the dinner table, Obama and I sat next to each other and found that our instincts on many issues were closely aligned. He was wicked smart, confident, and well-versed on foreign policy, but also funny and personable. Thereafter, he called me occasionally and invited me to meet with him and his team to discuss policy matters or planned travel.

In 2006, Senator Obama asked me to speak on a panel at his Hope Fund conference in Chicago and to comment on the foreign policy chapter in his forthcoming book, The Audacity of Hope. *After reading it, I gave him my unvarnished opinion, saying, "You're giving too much credit to Ronald Reagan and George H. W. Bush, while being comparatively ungenerous to Bill Clinton."*

There was a pause and then he asked me to continue.

As we talked through my critique, he acknowledged the imbalance and ultimately made some minor adjustments, giving greater weight to Reagan's failings (like Iran-contra) while treating Clinton's tenure more analytically and less subjectively. Most revealing during our exchange was the extent to which, much like me, Obama was by nature a pragmatist—more a foreign policy "realist" than a woolly eyed idealist. Yet his pragmatism neither rendered him cold nor tempered his high aspirations for America's capacity to do better at home and abroad. Barack Obama's fervent belief in our fundamental equality as people and in the goodness of our nation is what I think led him to community organizing, teaching, and ultimately to public service.

This is the same America in which my family, the Dicksons and the Rices, believes. These are the values that my parents and grandparents instilled in me. They raised me to remember where we came from. To honor the richness of my inheritance, value myself, do my best, and never let others convince me I can't. With good fortune came responsibility, they taught me; therefore, my duty was to serve others, in whatever way best suited my talents.

—•◆•—

It seemed like the biggest car ever. A massive, yellow Pontiac Bonneville station wagon, which our family drove each summer in the late 1960s and early 1970s for ten long hours from Washington, D.C., all the way up to Portland, Maine. For my younger brother, Johnny, and me, these trips were much anticipated and never disappointed.

We piled into the station wagon stuffed with our luggage and some toys. Dad drove. Mom issued instructions, often without finesse, and smoked cigarettes constantly as we plied the endless route, elongated by the New Jersey Turnpike with its smelly refineries and countless rest stops. If we got lucky, we could persuade our parents to stop at one of several Howard Johnson's for burgers or hot dogs and fries. By Boston, we could begin to see the light at the end of the tunnel. And finally, in Portland, when we arrived at Grandma and Grandpa Dickson's house, we were rewarded with the incomparable smell of Grandma's signature square-shaped molasses and sugar cookies that wafted through their big, old, musty, beautiful house.

We referred to my grandparents' home by its address, 51 Melrose Street, a place that looms large in my memory as the summer gathering spot for my mother's family. In the early 1960s, before my brother and I were born, my grandparents, with help from their children, managed to purchase this spacious, off-white, clapboard New England house with big porches and a widow's walk. It was close enough to "Back Cove" to smell the saltwater and, when the winds were unkind, the unrivaled stench of a nearby paper mill.

My childhood summers there were carefree. If Johnny and I weren't chasing our older cousins through the nooks and crannies of the antique house or poring over old photographs and mementos we found stashed in the attic, we were playing outside. My Grandpa David, a believer that children should be seen and not heard, would guide us through the tall corn of his prolific garden plot that spanned the lot just across the street. My uncle Leon and aunt Val taught us how to bait our hooks and cast to catch both small fry in Sebago Lake and bigger Atlantic fish off the rocks at Two Lights State Park on Cape Elizabeth. Johnny always seemed to reel in the foot-long, heavy fish while I'd fume over my puny haul of two-inchers—an early sign of my relentless competitiveness.

We swam in the frigid ocean at Crescent Beach, built sandcastles with our cousins, and marveled as my octogenarian grandfather—despite his Jamaican origins—braved the North Atlantic chill. We played kickball on the side lawn, and my right elbow still bears the keloid scar of a bad cut I sustained backpedaling to catch a fly ball. We rode bikes to Deering Ice Cream on Forest Avenue where I always got my Maine favorite: colorful, creamy rainbow sherbet.

In the evenings, we had lively family dinners, often with friends like "the boys," Chester and George, the kind gay couple up the street who kept close watch on my elderly grandparents during the harsh winter months, and with Aunt "Moo-Moo," an overly perfumed, colorful woman, another rare émigré from Jamaica. At these dinners, Johnny and I learned the rich family lore and how to consume the entire contents of a lobster, leaving no portion unmolested. We listened rapt, if a little cowed, during the high-decibel battles my father and my mother's brothers would get into over just about everything. My father and living uncles were highly educated black men who first crossed paths in the segregated Army Air Force during World War II at Tuskegee, and they each carried the rarefied arrogance and wit of those proud black men of their generation who achieved way more than society expected or appreciated.

Their intense arguments, peppered with "God dammits!" and pithy ad hominem zingers, were about all manner of issues, particularly race and politics. Hearing their raucous debates taught me the merits of fierce, often cocky contention. Arguing with a firm command of the facts, combined with dead certainty, whether feigned or real, I would discover, was an effective means of besting your opponent. My elders' bull sessions, along with constant debates at the dinner table, bequeathed me an early comfort with verbal combat and a relish for righteous battle. Raised not to fear a fight or shy away from advocating for a worthy cause, this aspect of my upbringing often (but not always) served me well in later years—whether on political campaigns, in policy debates, or during difficult negotiations with foreign adversaries.

More than anything, I was fascinated by the stories heard around my family tables—both in Maine and during trips to South Carolina to visit my dad's family. I grew up infused with the legacies of my elders—parents, grandparents, great-grandparents. Despite their very different histories and experiences—the immigrants on one side and the descendants of slaves on the other—the Dickson and Rice families shared common values, high expectations, and the compulsion to rise. As people who came from humble roots, their professional accomplishments outdistanced any constraints that institutional bias aimed to place on them, and they never failed to inspire me. They were New Englanders and southerners, Democrats and Republicans, who made great strides—with each generation exceeding the achievements of the last.

There was no single path for all, though two elements run consistently through my family tree: education and service. For my family, education is of utmost importance, worthy of every sacrifice, because it is the key to upward mobility and to securing the American Dream. (There was never any question as to whether my brother and I would go to college and graduate school. In our household, it was mandated, if not preordained.) The corollary to education—service—was embedded in my genes and seared into my soul. My forebears on both sides heeded the call to serve, to pay back far more than they were grateful to receive.

With a good education, economic stability, and physical security, my parents assured me I had everything needed to thrive—if not always a happy family life. Given these blessings, rare for many, but particularly for an African American girl, I was expected to give back, especially to those less fortunate than myself. Service could take many forms. It needn't be in the military or government. It could be in the nonprofit world, journalism, law, academia, medicine, business, or elsewhere. But I had to do for the larger community, the many, not just myself—as my parents, uncles and aunts, grandparents and great-grandparents had long exemplified.

———

My recollections of our earliest trips to Maine are mostly impressionistic, many of them crystallizing in my memory around the age of seven. But I vividly recall how my grandparents—gentle yet imposing—towered over our extended family, despite being notably small of stature. From my petite grandmother Dickson, I inherited my five-foot-three-inch frame, even though my parents were much taller and my brother dwarfs me by a full foot.

My grandfather David Dickson was a man of few words, but those he spoke carried weight. Though kind and restrained with his youngest grandchildren, in his prime he was a strict disciplinarian who wielded a razor strap, a swath of leather, to beat his boys. For lesser offenses, my uncles had to go fetch a switch—a thin tree branch—for their own whipping. Years later, whenever any of us kids were behaving badly, my mother would warn half in jest, "Don't forget Grandpa's razor strap is still hanging in the pantry."

As much as our grandfather appeared to be the ultimate authority in the family, my grandmother really called the shots in their household of five children—four sons, born between 1913 and 1921, and one daughter, my mother, Lois Ann, born in 1933. Ever warm, cheerful, and talkative, Grandma Mary Dickson was the salve that soothed the wounds and calmed tempers when they flared. To her children, Mary taught culture and refinement, making sure each played musical instruments, learned the details of their Jamaican heritage, and were thoroughly steeped in the Episcopal faith. She was also there for her children in more simple ways—like the times she'd wait up for Lois to come home from her dates in high school, to ask how they went, offer a snack, and tuck her into bed.

For her success in rearing five accomplished children, my grandmother was named "Maine State Mother for 1950" by the American Mothers Committee of the Golden Rule, and thereby a candidate for the national "American Mother" award. In a full-page, photo-filled spread in the *Portland Sunday Telegram*, Mary Dickson was lauded for her industriousness, piety, skills as a cook and gardener, and, above all, devotion to her children. On that same page, my seventeen-year-old mother wrote a tribute to Grandma Mary:

> *Mother has a quiet, unassuming but unshakeable faith in God's beneficence. She has an assurance, frequently put to the test, that if she and her family lived as best they knew in keeping with the will of God they would be protected against all adversity and find true happiness and peace of mind.*

Beyond the love I always felt from my grandparents and the fun I had visiting Maine every summer, what sticks with me about Mary and David Dickson is how much they made out of so little. They came to this country as immigrants with nothing but faith, pride, and a strong work ethic. Here, they raised a tight-knit family, educated their children, built a nest egg, and gave back to their community without ever forgetting where they came from. As my uncle David wrote of my grandparents in his memoir: "They were Republican in politics, conservative in spending, dedicated to clean living, the gospel of hard work, home owning, the family unit and very proud of the freedom and economic opportunity of the U.S.A."

Their story epitomizes the American Dream.

———

As an adult, I have come to realize how profoundly my grandparents' and parents' journeys have shaped my own.

Grandpa David Augustus Dickson was born in 1887 in Mandeville, Manchester Parish, Jamaica. With little formal education, managing only to complete a few years of secondary school, my grandfather was trained as a cobbler and worked as a clerk in the British woolens department at Sturbridge's clothing store. His frustration with his limited educational opportunities fueled his determination to do better, especially by his eventual children.

Grandma Mary Marguerite (Maude) Daly was born in 1890 in St. Elizabeth Parish, Jamaica. One of eight children, Mary was the daughter of a well-heeled Irish landowner and a mother who, according to family lore of uncertain reliability, was born in Calcutta, India. My great-grandfather Daly died at fifty, when my grandmother was ten, leaving his large family in economic peril and subject to the exploitation of his stingy millionaire brother. Mary was shunted off to live with distant cousins, the Millers, and perform menial tasks in their household. She never received much education beyond middle school and always resented that her circumstances were far inferior to that to which the Dalys' wealth should have entitled her.

David and Mary met at a confirmation class at the Mandeville Parish Anglican Church, and a committed courtship began. My grandfather would pedal his bicycle six miles uphill to visit with Mary on the front porch or walk her through the local market square. The Millers were not fans of my grandfather, because he was darker-skinned than they and hailed from the countryside rather than the more refined town.

Lured to the U.S. by an American hotelier who offered him a job in Harpswell, Maine—promising him the fruits of the American Dream—David set out by ship for Portland, Maine, and arrived in New York on May 16, 1911. David never made it to Harpswell, instead finding his first work in Portland as a janitor. A severe injury to his hand prevented him from plying his Jamaican trade as a cobbler.

Once he was settled, Grandpa David sent for Mary. Defying the Millers, in October 1912 my grandmother boarded a ship bound for Boston. A major hurricane interrupted the voyage, forcing her to disembark in Philadelphia and make her way alone to Portland. I still wonder at the bravery and resolve that would propel my tiny grandmother, at age twenty-two, to leave the only family she knew, sail alone, and find her way hundreds of miles across a strange land to reach her fiancé.

Devoted Anglicans, David and Mary were married on Christmas Day 1912, in the Emmanuel Chapel of their beloved Cathedral Church of St. Luke in downtown Portland. After sixty-six years of marriage, their funerals, which I would attend, would be held two years apart in the same chapel.

Hardworking and penny-pinching, my grandparents managed to eke out a decent living. Mary labored as a seamstress and laundress for affluent families. For nearly four decades, David worked as a porter, janitor, piano refinisher, and shipping clerk at Cressey & Allen's music store in Portland. He also moonlit as a bartender. Later, after the company went out of business, Grandpa would work another fifteen years as a janitor until age eighty at the Blue Cross and Blue Shield building.

To improve his lot, David took courses at Gray's Business College in Portland. Despite his innate intelligence and additional schooling, race prevented his advancement even to becoming a clerk at the music store. The owner, George Cressey, came to respect David deeply and told him years later that, had he been white, he would have enabled him to buy a share in the business and become a partner.

David read voraciously, with a passion for history and poetry, insisting his children do the same. In public, Grandpa always wore a well-tailored suit and tie. He made sure his kids had the finest clothes, if few to their name. A man who tracked every dime spent, he never bought a car, declaring that public transportation would suffice; yet he stocked the household with the highest quality of food—meat, fish, fruit, and, on special occasions, Maine lobster.

Soon after their arrival in America, Mary and David managed to become naturalized U.S. citizens and later buy a three-story, two-family home in a working-class area on Portland's Munjoy Hill. The neighborhood in which my mother grew up was inhabited by a mix of Irish, English, Jewish, and a cluster of black families, including several from the West Indies. Maine has long had very few blacks—according to the 1930 census, there were just 268 blacks in Portland (or 0.4 percent of the city's population). In that era, the Ku Klux Klan was active and the local NAACP chapter fledgling. For decades, my grandparents aspired to move into a better neighborhood, but realtors consistently refused to sell to blacks. My very light-skinned grandmother would sometimes be shown nice places, but when my brown-skinned grandfather showed up, suddenly none was available.

As Jamaican émigrés of different hues, my grandparents had complex views on race. My grandmother, while fully conscious of her second-class status as "colored," knew she had little discernible African blood. Half Irish and a quarter East Indian, with gray-blue eyes and faintly olive skin, she appeared only to the acute eye something other than typically white. Yet she identified as black, not least because her husband and children were unmistakably black. Like most West Indian immigrants, my grandparents were steeped in the British/Caribbean racial caste system, in which the *whiter* you were the *better* you were and the more opportunity you would likely have. Upward mobility was everything to them, and they viewed darker skin as a drag on one's future prospects. Because of their Jamaican origins, it seemed to me that my grandparents felt superior to darker American blacks and those, like my father, who descended from slave stock. I detected that subtle prejudice in them early on and perceived that they instilled in their own children at least a small measure of the same condescension.

Paradoxically, I also knew that the Dicksons were proud of their race and committed to its advancement. My grandfather founded and chaired Portland's "Negro Community Forum," which brought distinguished speakers to Sunday meetings and dinners in the Dickson home. David was active in the local NAACP and helped establish the USO Marian Anderson Club for "colored" troops stationed in Portland during World War II. After the war, he hosted Anderson in Portland and fought for blacks to be granted equal access to the white USO facility.

As a child, I didn't fully appreciate the extraordinary lengths to which my grandparents went to ensure that their children went to top colleges, but over the years, with each telling of their remarkable story, I came to admire their sacrifices and the seriousness with which they approached their duties as parents. Their kids were going to excel—whether they liked it or not.

As soon as his first son was born, Grandpa David purchased an endowment policy to fund his first year of college. My grandfather later learned of Bowdoin, Maine's preeminent private college, from his boss, Mr. Cressey, a Bowdoin graduate, who helped him obtain extra work there as a server at weekend parties. David saw Bowdoin's beauty—its eighteenth-century buildings, classic grassy quadrangle, and clapboard fraternity houses—and knew the caliber of its graduates. When I first visited Bowdoin many years later, I could immediately see why my grandfather resolved that his sons must go there.

Like many New England colleges and universities in the post–Civil War era, Bowdoin admitted very few African Americans. While known as the college that graduated one of the first black students, John Brown Russwurm in 1826, Bowdoin's record on integration was otherwise poor. It did not have another black graduate until 1910.

To raise additional funds to send his sons to Bowdoin College, my grandfather rented out the other apartment in his house and remortgaged their residence. After each of my four uncles graduated from Portland High School, all went to Bowdoin, working part-time jobs to help pay their tuition and support the education of their younger siblings. My grandfather, reputedly the first man to have four sons attend Bowdoin, was proud when years later Bowdoin's Class of 1912 made him an honorary member—the year that he would have graduated, had he attended college.

My uncles all lived up to their parents' expectations, if sometimes fit-fully and dramatically. Each achieved professional success—two became doctors, one an optometrist, and the other rose up through the academy to become a university president.

My uncle Leon, the firstborn, was dominating and charismatic. After a stellar record at Portland High School as an Eagle Scout, concert mas-ter, and chess champion, he graduated Phi Beta Kappa from Bowdoin in 1935, as only its ninth black graduate. He went on to Howard University Medical School, having been denied admission to Harvard because, he was told, there was no other black man with whom he could room.

A rebel against his parents' almost puritanical child-rearing, Leon got away with misdeeds that only a cherished firstborn son could. After my grandfather took out a loan to fund his medical school tuition, Leon blew his entire stipend gambling with friends. With no other option, my grandfather—furious, embarrassed, but determined—pleaded for and was granted another loan on the basis of his character and credit. My favorite part of this story is that Leon's gambling buddy, who had taken his tuition money, confessed on his deathbed to cheating my uncle that night and over the years.

During and after World War II, Leon served at the Tuskegee Veter-ans Hospital, where he established a reputation for being outspoken about "Southern prejudicial practices." He railed against the Veterans Adminis-tration and successfully resisted their efforts to send him to Waco, Texas, to work in what Leon called "mixed, Jim Crow facilities as flunkies for cracker heads." Leon later established a highly regarded family medical practice in Detroit with his wife, Val, a nurse. A committed Republican who was deeply involved in the Detroit NAACP, Leon believed he could best serve his community by charging his patients, mostly black factory workers, the same fees in the 1990s, when he retired, as he had when he started practicing in the 1950s.

My second uncle, Audley, left Bowdoin after two years, completed his degree in optometry at Columbia University, practiced in New York for thirty years, and married but had no children. I remember him from my early childhood as a sweet, selfless man whom all the Dicksons adored. A longtime smoker, he died of throat cancer in 1969, after enduring a permanent tracheotomy for years. Deemed the glue that kept the family close, his loss was an enormous blow to his parents and siblings.

By his own description, my third uncle, David—the family historian and a kind, humble man—was a sickly, socially awkward child who buried himself in history and literature library books. An accomplished debater and valedictorian at Portland High School, Uncle David was a phenomenon at Bowdoin. Only the second student ever to receive straight As in every subject over four years, he was honored as junior Phi Beta Kappa, summa cum laude, and valedictorian of the Class of 1941. His record of achievement aside, David felt ostracized at Bowdoin. As a black man, he and the few Jewish students were barred from joining fraternities and, as he wrote years later, the "psychological impact of that kind of arbitrary, completely undemocratic, un-Christian, and anti-Semitic exclusion was overpowering."

After obtaining his PhD in English literature from Harvard and becoming commanding officer of the medical unit of the 2143rd Army Air Field Base Unit at Tuskegee, Alabama, Uncle David decided to pursue a career in academia—a struggle, it turned out, at a time when only a handful of black professors taught at white institutions. When his own alma maters, Bowdoin and Harvard, refused to hire him, David turned to a favorite professor, who helped him secure an appointment as assistant professor of English at Michigan State University. David's long career took him to Washington, D.C., Long Island, and Montclair State University in New Jersey, where he was president from 1973 to 1984. I enjoyed getting to know him well, along with his sweet wife, Vera, and my three cousins, starting when they lived near to us in Washington.

Though I never met my uncle Frederick, the baby boy of the family, I reveled in the legendary stories about him. Fun-loving, exceptionally handsome, and a playboy fancied by all, Freddy was a three-letter varsity athlete and football star at Bowdoin. After serving in World War II, Freddy earned his medical degree at the University of Rochester and returned to military service in Japan during the Korean War. Back stateside, Freddy joined his brother Leon's medical practice in Detroit. Tragically, he died of a cerebral aneurysm on Thanksgiving night in 1957, at just thirty-five.

Devastated by the premature loss of their youngest son, my grandparents sought to make the best use of Uncle Freddy's $10,000 GI life insurance payout, a massive sum for a family that had never earned more than $5,000 a year. Instead of keeping the money, they gave it to Bowdoin as an annuity in Freddy's honor, which after my grandfather's death became the Mary M. and David A. Dickson Scholarship Fund to assist low-income students from Maine to attend the college. The fund has multiplied over the years and still thrives as testament to my grandparents' commitment to education and their love of Bowdoin.

————

My mother, Lois Ann—a surprise, long-awaited girl—arrived in the wake of her highly accomplished brothers. Back then, my forty-four-year-old grandmother had good reason to fear she might not survive another pregnancy or, if she did, that her child would be developmentally disabled. However, my mom emerged healthy and hardy, to the delight of her parents and her four older brothers. Eleven years junior to her youngest brother, Lois grew up effectively an only child. Although she was "the little princess" of the family, Lois was not to be outdone by her siblings.

By the time my mother was born in 1933, my grandparents were more established financially, and Lois enjoyed nice clothing and private piano lessons—without the need to work, as her brothers had during their school years. Still, her parents' ambitions for their daughter were no less than for their sons, and Mom felt the same responsibility, if not pressure, to excel—even at a time when few women went to college, much less on to professional accomplishment.

By every measure, Lois set the bar exceedingly high for those, like me, who came behind her. She was the star of the Portland High School Class of 1950: valedictorian, student council president, a concert pianist, and a champion debater. Her accounts of those days were also filled with memories of an active social life, dates with good-looking college guys, and lasting friendships. As her daughter, I was always awed by how easily my mother connected to others. She had a real knack for adopting strangers and making them feel as if they belonged.

Lois and her brothers grew up socializing mainly with white kids, because blacks in Portland were so few. Still, my grandmother, despite her own mixed background, drew the line for my uncles at interracial dating.

Mary viewed America as less racially tolerant than Jamaica and thought interracial marriage would ruin her sons. She told her Dickson boys to stay away from white girls, assuring them, as Uncle David recalled, that they would eventually find "Colored girls of beauty, charm and intelligence, in shades like the rainbow or a garden of beauty." Mary was highly judgmental about my uncles' choices in women, undermining those relationships she thought unworthy and pressuring each boy to marry either Jamaican women or light-skinned black Americans. And while I don't recall her saying so in my presence, I suspect Grandma was unimpressed with my mother's choice of my mahogany-brown father.

When it came time for Lois to attend college in 1950, my grandparents were flummoxed. My grandfather dreamt he could persuade Bowdoin to take women, or at least one, but Bowdoin would not accept women until 1971. Her brother, my uncle David, ultimately saved the day, recommending Radcliffe College in Cambridge, Massachusetts. It wasn't Bowdoin, but it was conjoined with Harvard, where David had received his doctorate, and thus would suffice.

My mom's college plans were jeopardized by a catastrophe that struck in September 1948 during the start of her junior year in high school. "That was the time," she told me over the years, "that Grandpa fell down the elevator shaft at the music store." He broke his back and shattered his feet. As a kid, I used to wonder how Grandpa could have failed to notice the elevator was missing. Then, one day as an adult, it hit me—as a janitor, he must have backed into the open elevator out of habit, pulling a cart or something with him. While Grandpa was hospitalized for over nine months without a salary, my grandmother returned to work as a maid to help compensate for their losses.

Soon, the family's modest savings for Lois's college tuition were exhausted. Number one in her class at Portland High, my mother was entitled to the State of Maine Radcliffe Club Scholarship; but it was denied to her by the chair of the selection committee. This white woman explained to my mother that the scholarship recipient was expected to return to Maine and "move in proper circles" where she might raise funds for Radcliffe. As a Negro, she claimed, my mother could not meet those expectations. Furious and offended, Mom was determined to obtain support. Fortunately, her high school principal and debate coach shared her outrage. They appealed to Radcliffe directly, which awarded Lois a $500 scholarship, $200 more than she would have garnered from the state fund. Mom also received $400 in supplementary financing from the National Scholarship Service and Fund for Negro Students (NSSFNS) for her first year and $300 for her second year. Never forgetting the value of this crucial support, Mom later devoted her career to helping others receive sufficient college assistance.

At Radcliffe, Lois Dickson came into her own, refusing to acknowledge any limits on her personal or professional ambition. Despite being an African American woman in the early 1950s, she clearly was going places.

———

As my mother finished college, my father was completing his PhD in economics at the University of California at Berkeley and laying his future path.

Emmett Rice was a brilliant, handsome, charming, yet complicated man whose background was quite different from that of Lois Dickson. My father was born in segregated South Carolina to parents who were the children of slaves. Despite the proximate legacy of the Civil War and the backlash against Reconstruction, my paternal grandparents, and even my great-grandfather, were college-educated.

Walter Allen Simpson Rice, my great-grandfather, was born a slave in South Carolina in 1845. At the age of eighteen, following the Emancipation Proclamation of 1863, Walter joined the Union Army during the last bloody years of the Civil War, serving with the Massachusetts 55th Volunteer Regiment. With the support of his benefactor, Lieutenant Charles F. Lee, Walter Rice completed his primary education in Massachusetts. Upon his return to Laurens County, South Carolina, Walter became a Freedmen's Bureau public school teacher and entered local politics. Shortly after being elected county clerk, however, his tenure ended in his exile from Laurens County when, as my father recounted, great-grandfather Walter faced death threats from the Ku Klux Klan and fled to New Jersey. Walter went on to obtain his divinity degree at Lincoln University in Pennsylvania and eventually became a presiding elder in the New Jersey branch of the African Methodist Episcopal (AME) Church.

Even more than his rare education, what impressed me most about my great-grandfather was his deep commitment to the advancement of former slaves. Rev. Walter Rice spent ten years collaborating with fellow black faith leaders in the New Brunswick area on the founding of the Manual Training and Industrial School for Colored Youth, more commonly known as the "Bordentown School." Sometimes dubbed "the Tuskegee of the North," the Bordentown School opened in 1886 with just eight students in a two-story frame house on West Street. Its ranks gradually filled with additional students, many of them homeless or abandoned children and some whose working parents could not find an appropriate school to house them. With limited funds to support his growing institution, but a grant of $3,000 from the state, Walter Rice was able to lease seven small buildings scattered across Bordentown.

In 1897, the school was bequeathed a highly coveted thirty-three-acre estate, which gave it a greatly expanded campus with panoramic views overlooking the Delaware River. At the same time, Bordentown began to receive sustained state support and eventually became part of the New Jersey public school system.

On our way to and from Maine, Dad would point out the exit off the New Jersey Turnpike for Bordentown, explaining to me and Johnny with pride how the school epitomized his family's devotion to education and the socioeconomic advancement of blacks. Though we never stopped to visit the dilapidated former campus, Dad described how Bordentown eventually became a highly successful, four-hundred-acre coeducational boarding institution, which taught its approximately 450 students technical skills such as farming and cooking, as well as a full college preparatory curriculum, ranging from Latin to physics. For generations, the school produced leaders in the African American community, while welcoming such luminaries to campus as Booker T. Washington, Mary McLeod Bethune, Eleanor Roosevelt, Albert Einstein, and Duke Ellington. Ironically, Bordentown was compelled to close in 1955, after the *Brown v. Board of Education* decision rendered the all-black, state-supported institution legally unviable.

Great-grandfather Walter Rice died in 1899 at fifty-four years old, the father of six children by two wives. One of those children—from his first marriage—was my grandfather, Ulysses Simpson Rice, who followed his father's path, first to teaching and later to the ministry. With a divinity degree from Lincoln University, Ulysses returned to South Carolina and married my grandmother, Sue Pearl Suber. They had four children: Ulysses Simpson Jr., (known as Suber), Gladys Clara, Pansy Victoria, and the youngest, my father, Emmett John Rice.

Born in 1885 in South Carolina, Sue Pearl, my grandmother, whom I remember as warm and dignified, was the daughter of a successful farmer and former slave, Pratt Suber. Chairman of the Laurens County Republican Party and county commissioner of education in the 1870s, Pratt was reputedly forced out of those roles by angry whites. As a public official, Pratt faced nearly constant harassment from whites who resented black gains during Reconstruction. In 1880, he was badly beaten while attending a large meeting of Republicans that was broken up by a white Democratic mob.

Two generations later, my father was born to Sue Pearl and Ulysses Rice on December 21, in either 1919 or 1920. (Various documents record his birth date differently.) Like my mother, Dad was a final child and happily unexpected. His elder sisters, Pansy and Gladys, were nine and ten and a half years older, respectively, and his brother, Suber, twelve years his senior. Emmett enjoyed a comfortable early childhood in Sumter, South Carolina, where his father was a widely liked, respected pastor and community leader. The family lived in the Mt. Pisgah AME church parsonage house, a well-appointed large clapboard. At seven, Emmett's idyllic life was upended by the sudden death of his father. My grandfather, Rev. Ulysses S. Rice, died in November 1927, at age fifty-one, from an undiagnosed heart condition. This shocking loss of his beloved father wounded my dad, leaving him vulnerable and lacking a strong male role model.

Shortly after my grandfather's death, my grandmother Sue Pearl lost the privilege of living at the parsonage house and faced almost immediate economic hardship. To support her family, she went back to school at age forty-two, using what savings she could muster. Having already attended Scotia Seminary, a North Carolina normal school equivalent to two years of college, Sue Pearl enrolled at Morris College in Sumter to get her bachelor's degree in teaching. As a teacher, Grandmother Sue Pearl became a rare working mother, in contrast to her peers who were mostly housewives. My father always told me how much he admired his mother's determination to provide for her family and professed complete comfort with women working outside the home. (In later years, Dad supported my career every step of the way, even though he struggled to apply the same standard to my mother.)

Sue Pearl moved her family from South Carolina to New York City around 1933 to join her eldest son, Suber, and to attain higher pay and a better education for her children, particularly Emmett. Having spent his first thirteen years in South Carolina, my father subsequently moved back and forth between New York and South Carolina until he graduated from high school. For Emmett, New York held the theoretical promise of a desperately desired respite from the daily humiliations of segregation. Indeed, my father never knew a white person well until he moved north. Unfortunately, New York sorely disappointed, as Emmett found his geographic boundaries circumscribed to Harlem and the few establishments, like the neighborhood YMCA, that allowed blacks.

At seventeen, Emmett enrolled at City College of New York (CCNY), one of the few affordable colleges in the city that catered to immigrant and working-class students. An urban, all-commuter school, CCNY was impersonal; my father found his professors aloof and little to bind him to the campus. While his classes were integrated, my father recalled, "There was a great deal of prejudice. White students . . . didn't have very much to do with me. I was pretty much isolated in college. . . . There weren't many black students," and those there were were "so scattered that I never had another black student in a class."

By college, Emmett knew he did not want to become a third-generation minister. Dad shared with me and Johnny that, as a young boy, he caught his father and other ministers cheating at a competitive game of croquet. My father reasoned that, "If men of God could cheat, then something must be wrong with the church." After that, Dad had no time for organized religion.

Instead, to his mother's initial disappointment, Emmett decided to take a less-trodden route at CCNY, attaining his BA in economics in 1941 and his master's in business administration (MBA) in 1942. As my father later explained to an oral historian at the University of California, Berkeley, he was "a child of the Depression. There was a lot of suffering. Twenty-five percent of the country was unemployed. I wanted to understand an economy which allowed this to happen. I wanted to see if there was anything that could be done to alleviate some of the poverty . . . pain and suffering, social unrest that I saw." In his early professional years, my father thought that one could change the world through policy; later, he concluded that the key was not economic policy but economic power.

Like my maternal uncles, and his brother, my uncle Suber, Emmett was drafted into military service at the height of World War II and spent four and a half years in uniform, first as an enlisted man and ultimately as an officer with the rank of captain. Called up by the Army Air Force, he was sent to a two-part officer training program, which began in Miami and was completed at Harvard Business School—where he learned "statistical control" and "quantitative management," a specialized form of accounting in an unusual program designed to build on his business background.

Emmett eventually deployed to Tuskegee, Alabama, where he joined the famed Tuskegee Airmen, the nation's first black fighter pilot unit, which distinguished itself in combat in Europe. My father was not a fighter pilot, though he learned to fly, but a staff officer who ran the newly created Statistics Office, which performed management analyses for commanding officers. He earlier served a stint at Godman Field adjacent to Fort Knox, Kentucky. There, segregation meant that he was denied access to the white officers' club. To add insult to injury, he saw German prisoners of war being served at restaurants restricted to blacks. His time in Tuskegee and Kentucky was a searing reintroduction to southern segregation, both in the military and the confines of off-base life.

Still, socially and intellectually, Dad's Tuskegee years were formative. He met an elite cadre of African American men who would later disproportionately comprise America's postwar black professional class, among them my mother's brothers, Leon and David. Dad's Tuskegee friends and acquaintances formed a network he maintained throughout his life. What was it, I have often wondered, about those Tuskegee Airmen and support personnel that seemingly enabled them to become a vanguard of black achievement? Perhaps the military preselected unusually well-educated,

capable men for Tuskegee, or some aspect of their service experience propelled them as a group to succeed. To my lasting regret, I failed to take
the opportunity to study this topic in depth before almost all those heroes
passed away.

Following D-Day, my father was sent to the West Coast to prepare to
deploy to the Pacific theater. He was spared combat by President Harry
Truman's decision to drop atomic weapons on Hiroshima and Nagasaki,
provoking the Japanese surrender. My dad's service to our nation has long
been a source of pride for me, particularly his affiliation with the celebrated
Tuskegee "Red Tails" who defied every expectation of their skill and patriotism.

But not for my father. He suffered from no such romanticism. Until his
death, Dad remained bitter about segregation in the military, profoundly
objecting to the insult and irony of being made to fight for freedom for
all but his own people. As offensive to him was the idea that blacks had to
prove their worth to whites. As he explained, "Many black pilots thought
that by serving in the Air Force they were proving that they could fly just
as well as white pilots. I, on the other hand, resented this notion, believing . . . we had nothing to prove." In the same vein, Dad taught me—*You
don't have to prove anything to anyone but yourself. Never doubt that you are more
than good enough.*

It was well after Tuskegee and his graduate education at Berkeley, as
a professional in the 1960s, that Dad developed a strong philosophy on
how to cope with pervasive discrimination. He grew certain that carrying
around the "consciousness of being black continuously is a psychological
burden." He noted, "You cannot bring your best performance to bear as
long as you have this additional drag on you. You have to free yourself of
this in order to work to your full potential and be able to compete fully."
Somewhat counterintuitively, my father insisted, much like my mother,
that we cannot allow ourselves to be defined or bound by race. As hard as
it might be and as unrealistic as it may seem, in my dad's view, it's always
better to try to act, work, and perform as if there were no such thing as
discrimination.

My father distilled his hard-won experience, acquired over the years,
into foundational "life lessons," as he called them, which he methodically

instilled in me and my brother. Dad summarized another key lesson on race as follows:

> *I concluded that I am only one person. I am only human, and I cannot carry the burdens of the world around on my shoulder . . . and at the same time function. So, I was going to be myself, and I was not going to be constantly . . . on my p's and q's because people expected me to. If my being black caused a problem, it was not going to be to me; it was going to be to other people.*

As I replay these words in my head, I am struck by how fully I have embraced my father's philosophy about race (and gender) as my own. My own refusal to allow what I look like to be *my* problem, one which gets into my head, is fundamental to the mind-set that has helped me succeed. Equally, I internalized Dad's message that I should never doubt my own abilities. This combination—being a confident black woman who is not seeking permission or affirmation from others—I now suspect accounts for why I inadvertently intimidate some people, especially certain men, and perhaps also why I have long inspired motivated detractors who simply can't deal with me.

Notwithstanding my dad's remarkable professional achievements, culminating in serving as a governor of the Federal Reserve, the lingering effects of southern segregation and decades of racial discrimination in the North scarred him deeply. My father chafed as he recalled the closed doors, the low expectations, and being told for so many years what he couldn't do. He couldn't eat at a lunch counter outside the base in Alabama. He couldn't sleep at a hotel when he drove with my mother through the South. He was expected to fight and die for his country, but his country didn't regard him as a full man. Remarkably, Dad waited to share these frustrations with me and Johnny until we were grown. He shielded us, determined that we never feel constrained by the limitations that tortured him.

Despite all this, my father was a deeply patriotic American. He traveled the world extensively and recognized the exceptional nature of America, its democracy, its values and its institutions. He knew that only in America could he have reached the highest levels of his field and served at the pinnacles of government. Only in America could he raise his black children to believe that we faced no insurmountable hurdles to our success.

Until he died at ninety-one, in 2011, however, my father's life was a mission to prove America wrong about race. He set out to show that, regardless of the barriers, he could fulfill his God-given potential. And, struggle by struggle, he did. The pain of racist indignities dissipated over time, but never evaporated.

My mother's experience with race was quite different from my father's, but their philosophies largely converged. As the daughter of immigrants, raised in an almost all white New England environment, Lois suffered fewer bald and brutal manifestations of discrimination than did my dad in the segregated South. Yet my mother was always a lonely minority and a woman, an outsider striving, never fully accepted into the elite circles in which she ran. Her experiences, less searing but still powerful, left Mom also determined to prove the doubters and denigrators wrong. From Radcliffe to her career as a champion of access to higher education for the disadvantaged, from the halls of Congress to corporate boardrooms, Lois would so excel, blowing away all (white) competitors, that no one could deny her worthiness. As she always told us, "never use race as an excuse or an advantage." Just best them all.

Emmett and Lois Rice raised me and my brother unburdened from the notion that we *couldn't*. They taught us that we should be who we are— without apology or regret—and become what we set out to be. The only constraints we faced were our own ambition, effort, and skills (which they assured us were considerable). Still, we had to be about more than making money. We were expected to make a meaningful difference in the lives of others, in whatever way suited us best. Our job was clear—work hard and excel. My parents' lessons were plain yet powerful:

Don't take no for an answer when the question is: *can I?*

Family comes first and must stand together.

Don't forget where you come from.

2

Coming Up

Through my interactions with him, by early 2006, I came to believe that Obama could run for president as early as 2008. I also saw a path to his potential victory. Conventional political wisdom aside, the timing felt like it might be opportune.

The Iraq War was intensifying and becoming increasingly unpopular. Over two thousand Americans had already been killed since the war began in 2003; the prisoner abuse scandal at Abu Ghraib rocked global public opinion; and President George W. Bush belatedly admitted that the war was predicated on false intelligence, even as he maintained the fight was worth it. That past summer, Hurricane Katrina left over 1,800 Americans dead, substantially as a result of rank government incompetence, and Bush seemed out of touch with New Orleans's suffering.

In this context, I sensed a hunger for change—for capable leadership, for unquestioned integrity, for what Obama came to call "turning the page." As an anti–Iraq War, young, optimistic candidate, Obama was an antidote to the times—refreshing, hopeful, and consistently principled. In my estimation, it was still too soon for another Clinton. After John Kerry's defeat in 2004, I believed it was time to move beyond the Vietnam generation, and many of my peers felt the same. Obama could energize youth and galvanize the African American community. It was time to show that America could renew itself, and Obama's election would be irrefutable proof of that.

An Obama victory, however remote it then seemed, represented the po-

tential for America to fully embrace the principle of equality, to show its resil-
ience in overcoming the debilitating legacy of race, and to validate the worth
of education, hard work, and integrity as the keys to succeeding on the merits
in this country.

A man of mixed race, of African and Irish heritage, raised primarily by
his white Kansan working-class grandparents, Obama embodied unity. Insist-
ing that what Americans hold in common far exceeds what divides us, he of-
fered hope that our future could be brighter than our past. I was drawn to his
optimism and shared his belief that we could forge alliances across political,
racial, and religious boundaries. Indeed, that had been my experience growing
up in Washington, D.C.—in a mixed black and Jewish neighborhood, in school
with Republicans and Democrats, and shaped by parents who had broken
countless barriers.

———•◆•———

They *never* talked about it. Strangely, my brother and I know almost nothing about my parents' courtship or their wedding, a second marriage for
each. And, somehow, we never asked, maybe because they had such a difficult relationship.

Though fourteen years apart, my parents each came into their own in
the 1950s—my mother while an undergraduate at Radcliffe and my father
after the war during his formative years as a graduate student at Berkeley.
By the time they met in New York in the early 1960s, both were rising in
their chosen professions.

At the all-women's Radcliffe College, despite its academic excellence,
my mother found that accomplishment was defined not in professional
terms but rather as marrying a Harvard man and raising your sons to go to
Harvard. Women were admonished to be prissy and prim, while adhering
to "the forbidden six: no slacks, no shorts, no blue jeans, no sprawling in the
buildings or on the steps, no smoking in any Harvard building . . . and no
bicycle riding in the Harvard Yard (Harvard men can't ride there either)."
Dating was encouraged. To my amazement, the 1951–1952 Radcliffe *Red
Book* advised young women: "Cambridge is a well-stocked hunting ground,
and it's a wide-open field. There are enough men to go around (recent tab-
ulations tabbed the man-woman ratio at five to one). Just remember, no

pushing and shoving." To reward the successful, "The first girl in each class to be married following graduation is presented with a set of Radcliffe China by other members of the class," and "the first baby girl to be born . . . is presented with a silver spoon and becomes the mascot of her mother's class."

My mother was one of only a handful of black women at Radcliffe. In her first year, her roommate was determined by race, and she was placed with Dorothy Dean, one of three black women in her class. The other, Jane Bunche, who later committed suicide, was the daughter of Ralph Bunche, the Nobel Prize–winning American U.N. diplomat.

Lois Dickson and Dorothy Dean could not have been more mismatched. Eccentric and hard-drinking, Dean later became known for her roles in various Andy Warhol films and as a fixture in New York gay men's circles. Mom shared with me her impression that Dorothy was "truly crazy and aimed to drive me equally nuts." For her sanity, Lois requested a different roommate her second year but was refused, because there were no other black girls with whom she could room. Moreover, as a scholarship student, she was not eligible for a single.

Characteristically relentless, Lois took her protest to the top of the college's administration and, ultimately, was rewarded with a coveted single room. I always admired and sought to emulate my mom's readiness to stand up and fight for herself. My mama wasn't going to let either Dorothy or Radcliffe kill her; she would torture them into submission first.

A natural advocate for others as well as for herself, Lois joined the Radcliffe Association for the Advancement of Colored People to press the concerns of black students on campus and in the greater Boston area. Despite being a rare minority, Mom swiftly emerged as a leader at Radcliffe, first elected to student council her freshman year and then president of her sophomore class. She ultimately won a hotly contested battle for student body president her senior year. (Remarkably, her distant cousin, Clifford Alexander, another child of Jamaican immigrants, was elected the following year to head Harvard's student government.)

As a student, Lois accumulated numerous academic awards, graduating Phi Beta Kappa and magna cum laude in history and literature. As well as Lois performed at Radcliffe, she fell a bit short of her own expectations, lamenting that she failed to achieve Phi Beta Kappa during her junior year or to graduate summa cum laude, as her brothers had. Her self-doubt not-withstanding, Mom was selected as Marshall of her Class of 1954, leading the commencement procession, and made several dear friends whom she kept until her death.

Moved by the politics of the day, the Cold War, McCarthyism, and the 1954 *Brown v. Board of Education* Supreme Court decision, Lois left Rad-cliffe determined to do much more than marry and raise children. Despite being an African American woman in the early 1950s, or perhaps because of it, Lois was going places far beyond what was asked or expected of her. Soon after graduation, she enrolled in graduate school at Columbia University as a Woodrow Wilson Fellow in English literature; but, after one year, Lois concluded that academia didn't inspire her.

Instead, she worked avidly on Adlai Stevenson's 1956 presidential campaign. Mom bragged about being "a Stevenson girl" who proudly served in various capacities, including as a campaign surrogate in local debates where she argued passionately that Stevenson uniquely had the commitment and the ideals to capitalize on the *Brown* decision and make America more equitable. His loss, a major disappointment to her, may have persuaded Lois to trade politics for other avenues of service.

Mom's first full-time job out of college reflected her personal mission to expand access to the transformative power of higher education, a calling that animated her entire career. As director of counseling services at the National Scholarship Service and Fund for Negro Students, the organization that had helped support her through Radcliffe, Mom provided counseling, as well as admissions and financial support, to qualified African American students to help them attend predominantly white colleges and universities.

One of my favorite stories from Mom's tenure at NSSFNS involves a trip she took as the organization's counselor to check on the sole black student in a class of four hundred at DePauw University in Indiana. Mom asked the young man how he was doing. He cheekily reported: "I am fine, except I'm lonely and need a date with an attractive young black woman. You wanna go out with me?" According to both sides, Lois remained resolutely professional and demurred, despite her suitor's arresting good looks. Thus began a lifelong, flirtatious friendship between my mom and the famed civil rights activist and Washington lawyer Vernon Jordan. To my knowledge, my mother never succumbed to his considerable charms, but I couldn't have blamed her if she had.

In 1959, Lois moved to the New York–based College Entrance Examination Board (CEEB), now the College Board, which administers the SAT and AP tests. With the exception of two brief sabbaticals, she stayed there until 1981.

Like many of her peers, Lois did marry right out of college—to the much older James Theodore "Ted" Irish, a classmate of her brother Fred's at Bowdoin. Irish was an interior designer who worked at the Corn Exchange Bank of New York City. Lois's parents hosted a lavish wedding for them in New York City in September 1954. Mom's first wedding was amply covered in the social pages of *The New York Times*. She would enthusiastically relate the details of her elaborate church wedding and reception at the Essex House Hotel, which her parents hosted despite their limited means. In her glamorous wedding photos, Lois Ann Dickson Irish was the quintessential bride—svelte and gorgeous in her long-sleeve silk and lace dress with a full train and intricate bouquet.

Back in those days, Mom lived in Harlem and led an active social life among the close-knit, young black professional community centered around the Riverton Apartments. In contrast to her depictions of their picture-perfect wedding, Mom spoke little about her marriage to Ted Irish, which ended in divorce in 1960. She portrayed Ted as kind, but rather shiftless, their marriage as a benign mistake but by no means a disaster. My sense from her, though never explicit, was that Mom may have concluded that Ted was gay, which rendered an uninspiring marriage untenable. In subsequent years, Mom searched for a more suitable life partner, falling hard at least one time before ultimately meeting my father.

———

After the war, Emmett Rice, having completed his undergraduate and master's degrees, decided to pursue his PhD in economics. Friends he met in the military had assured him that race relations were more open in California. Though skeptical, he enrolled at the University of California at Berkeley, where in the late 1940s and early 1950s, blacks comprised less than one percent of the student body.

At Berkeley, Dad was fortunate to live in International House (known as I-House), a predominantly graduate residence of almost four hundred students, roughly two-thirds foreign, mainly from Europe and Asia. He found the I-House experience broadening, stimulating, and enjoyable. As a former I-House staff member recalled, "Both foreign and American friends sought linkage with Emmett's social and intellectual orbit. . . . Discussions with him tended to be philosophical rather than confrontational. The result was that there was more light than heat, and people were drawn to him. Many remember the impact these discussions had on them."

Though in many ways a deeply serious man, my father always knew how to have fun. He had a deft charm and broad smile that rarely failed with women. He loved music, dancing, drink, and laughter. With his closest Berkeley buddies, Dad bought a convertible and shared a funky penthouse apartment on the roof of an old warehouse, where the parties were frequent and legendary. He went crazy for jazz while at Berkeley, taking in as many concerts and clubs as his studies allowed, and later instilled in me and Johnny his deep appreciation for jazz and its greats.

My father regaled us with stories of his years at Berkeley, calling them "the best times of my life." He made lasting friendships and had more than his share of girlfriends, some white—which was highly unusual in this era, even in California. Dad imbibed the nascent counterculture movement and suffered through the painful McCarthy-era loyalty oath controversy, which bitterly divided the faculty and graduate students. Above all, Emmett proclaimed, he felt liberated: "It was the first living experience . . . where I did not feel the constant pressure of being black. And the first time I had the experience of people relating to me, not so much as a black person, but as another person."

The labor market was a different story. In my father's experience, "It was much harder to get a job on the West Coast than it was to get a job on the East Coast. There was great reluctance to pass laws out here governing fair employment." He spoke out vocally on campus about the need for fair employment laws, drawing the ire of the director of I-House, Allen Blaisdell, who reproved him for "making statements like that to foreigners who might not understand." Years later, Blaisdell dimed out my father to the FBI for disloyalty during one of his initial background checks for work in the U.S. government.

Emmett initially faced workplace discrimination in California when he moonlighted while a graduate student as a fireman at the Berkeley Fire Department. The first black man to integrate the force, he started as a line fireman, without training, but soon was given the more suitable task of a fire alarm operator and dispatcher. Dad described the reaction of the white firefighters to his arrival: "They did not like the idea of having to have blacks in the department, because firemen live a fairly intimate kind of existence. Still, they seemed to take the view that it was not my fault. After all, they could not blame me for trying to get a better job."

My dad's favorite fireman story involved a little known near catastrophe that threatened the Berkeley cyclotron. One of his proudest and least-heralded successes, which Dad liked to recall for us, was the crisis that occurred when the grass in the Berkeley Hills caught fire near the nuclear reactor. "It was my job," Dad said, "to decide what resources were needed to fight this serious fire—how many men and trucks would go. Within a few hours, the fire was under control. We had saved the nuclear facility and the town of Berkeley."

Guided by great teachers and mentors at Berkeley, Emmett became fascinated by the economic transformation of underdeveloped countries and selected India as the subject of his thesis. Awarded one of the early Fulbright Scholarships to support his doctoral research from 1951 to 1952, Dad flourished in Bombay. As a brown-skinned man in a brown society, he was a foreigner but no longer a visible minority—an experience that afforded him great psychic relief. India's social hierarchy was structured more by caste than color, and my father was not immediately deemed inferior due to his race. Dad's strong conviction that race is an irrelevant indicator of a person's worth was further reinforced by seeing people of various dark hues run a major country.

Back from India, my father successfully defended his dissertation in 1955, becoming Dr. Emmett J. Rice, and embarked on a new profession as an academic—although he knew his was not a path to prosperity. In the mid-1950s, the constraints imposed by persistent prejudice barred him from opportunities in industry and government. "I could not have worked in the [U.S.] Treasury at that time. I could not have worked at the Federal Reserve," he observed. Getting a good academic job, however, turned out to be almost as tough, especially on the West Coast. Much to his frustration, "It was possible for a black person to get a job teaching at a major university in the East. But I could not get a job at San Francisco State."

So, leaving California, Dad landed his first job at Cornell University in Ithaca, New York, as an assistant professor of economics in 1954, teaching money and banking and corporate finance. My father was Cornell's first black economics professor and was hired upon the recommendation of a Berkeley academic who omitted mention of his race. Cornell was surprised and none too happy to discover when Emmett arrived that he was unmistakably black. Despite this inauspicious start, my father enjoyed his nearly six years at Cornell.

———

Though we were never told much about how they met, I do know that Emmett and Lois first crossed paths in the early 1960s, after Dad had taken a leave from Cornell to work at the Federal Reserve Bank of New York as a staff economist. Apparently, the two met at a dinner for the New York Fed. Each had recently ended childless first marriages, and both were moving up in their respective fields. They married in New York on November 4, 1962, in what I have gathered was a modest civil ceremony, witnessed by a couple of close friends, and followed by a party.

Almost immediately after their wedding, my parents moved to Lagos, Nigeria, where Dad had been sent by the U.S. Agency for International Development (USAID) as a research advisor to help establish the Central Bank of Nigeria in the wake of the country's independence. Mom took leave from the College Board and worked for the Ford Foundation as an educational specialist for West Africa. Their two years in Nigeria, punctuated by travel around West Africa and Europe, were, by all accounts, enjoyable. They amassed an impressive collection of Nigerian art, including valuable wooden sculptures that were a visual fixture of my upbringing.

I was conceived in Nigeria. Toward the end of their stay, Mom became pregnant with me, and I have long amused myself with the hypothesis that my origins in Nigeria, combined with my Irish and Jamaican ancestors, explain a lot both about my temperament and attraction to all things international.

Dad, who had made it known early on that he did not want kids, greeted the news of Mom's pregnancy with something far less than enthusiasm, suggesting that Mom had tricked him into fatherhood. My mother hotly disputed this assertion, but in Dad's view this pregnancy was among the first things to undermine trust in their marriage, which mutually dissipated over time. Complicating matters, Mom discovered she was bearing twins, a girl and a boy. To the limited extent my dad had any interest in fatherhood, he wanted a boy. As my parents made their way back to the U.S. to ensure Mom delivered the babies on home soil, they transited through Paris. Their TWA flight from Paris-Orly to New York-JFK on May 29, 1964, was more eventful than anticipated.

On takeoff, the Boeing 707's front tire blew out. The pilot aborted before reaching full speed, veering off the runway to the right, and crashed the plane nose down into the grass. Dad and Mom (bearing two four-month-old fetuses), along with the 101 other passengers and crew, managed to evacuate safely but were more than a little shaken.

Back in Washington, the remainder of my mother's pregnancy grew more difficult, as she was confined to bed with nursing assistance for the last two and a half months. Finally, I was born on November 17, 1964, at George Washington University Hospital in Washington, D.C.

My first brother was stillborn.

By the time it was confirmed for me that I was a twin, around the age of twelve, my relationship with my mother had begun to suffer from more than the typical mother-daughter tension. In a rented condominium in Aspen, Colorado, where my younger brother, Johnny, and I had accompanied Mom to a conference, she and I were in the midst of an argument, when I jabbed with something like, "I always knew you didn't love me as much as the others . . ."

Looking freaked out by this oblique comment, which, combined with previous ones, suggested to her that I had some subliminal knowledge that Johnny was not my only sibling, Mom blurted out: "How long have you known you were a twin?"

Baffled, I said, "What are you talking about?"

Realizing she had spilled the beans and that my intuition, if any, was totally unconscious, she recovered to explain calmly, "We didn't want you to know until you were much older, but you had a baby brother who died in the womb. It was very sad for your father and me, but we were very glad to have you emerge healthy."

Anger dissolved into tears as I softly asked, "What happened?"

"We don't really know," my mother replied. "It could have been the trauma of the plane crash. I never liked our first obstetrician—he was always dismissive of my concerns, and I suspect he could have missed something important. Or maybe the baby wasn't very strong compared to you and couldn't consume adequate resources. . . . We just don't know."

These last words landed like a punch in the stomach.

Is she saying I might have killed my brother? Does she blame me? Am I to blame? I never dared utter those questions aloud but ever since have felt a tinge of guilt. Perhaps from the very start, I was too strong, and Mom never quite forgave me for it? In my mind, this was a question unstated that hung over our relationship for years to come.

———

Back from Nigeria, my parents settled in Washington, D.C., rather than return to New York, because in the spring of 1964, my dad was named deputy director of the Office of Developing Nations at the U.S. Department of Treasury—a plum senior civil service position that paid $16,000 (more than the Federal Reserve Bank of New York). It also afforded my father a direct role in advising the secretary of treasury on U.S. financial policy toward the countries of Africa, Asia, and the Middle East. Taking this job meant effectively closing the door on a return to academia, a choice he never regretted. Mom also quickly jumped back into her career, returning to work just a few months after I was born. From the outset, I had a mother who worked in a professional capacity outside the home—not because she *had* to work, but because she *wanted* to work.

When I was twenty-one months old, my brother, John, was born, on September 1, 1966. Dad got his long-awaited, healthy baby boy. Mom once told me that, "Emmett finally made me feel worthy, by giving him a boy," allowing her to sense that she had at least partially compensated for whatever he viewed as her earlier failure. It was never clear to me whether that meant having children in the first place or losing their first son.

I was not so forgiving. When Mom returned from Sibley Hospital, she followed the best parenting advice at the time: *Go immediately to the older child and pay no evident attention to the newborn.* Even before I recall meeting the little interloper, Mom came to greet me in my crib. I stood up to welcome her—by biting her squarely on the nose. It was very painful, by Mom's frequent telling, and she responded reflexively by slapping my little face.

Soon enough, I came to see the merits of having a baby brother. With time, Johnny proved to be a mostly sweet and willing playmate. With chubby cheeks, engrossing brown eyes framed with ridiculously long lashes, and soft tufts of afro, he charmed our parents and made easy friends.

In the same year Johnny was born, my father was appointed by President Lyndon Johnson to be alternate U.S. executive director at the World Bank, a Senate-confirmed role in which he served until 1970, after his stint as deputy and later acting director of the Treasury Department's Office of Developing Nations.

My now complete immediate family moved to the leafy, predominantly Jewish Forest Hills neighborhood of Northwest Washington, as I finished the last months of preschool at the prestigious National Child Research Center, NCRC. My parents applied to send me to the Beauvoir School next, hopeful that, if admitted, I would begin my formal education with the best start the city could offer. Though my parents did not qualify for scholarship funds, paying full tuition would prove challenging on their government and nonprofit salaries. Highly competitive and expensive, Beauvoir is a pre-K through third grade, coed Episcopal school affiliated with the Washington National Cathedral. Like its sister and brother schools, St. Albans School for boys and the National Cathedral School for girls, Beauvoir is located on the Cathedral's fifty-nine-acre campus, known as "the Close," and enjoys beautiful, sweeping vistas of Washington from its perch atop Mount St. Alban, the highest point in the city.

My admissions interview got off to a rocky start when Mom took me to Beauvoir for the obligatory testing in a small building at the bottom of a big hill. According to my mother, I was unusually disengaged and diffident during the diagnostic examination. When she walked me slowly up the hill to meet the principal, Mom calmly asked me to be nice and act comfortably. I did not.

The principal, Mrs. Frances Borders, tried to draw me into conversation. I simply stared at her. She talked with my mother, who, hiding her panic and shame, tried to assure her that I was just being shy but could excel at Beauvoir. Mrs. Borders was polite and surely pretended to be understanding, but Mom knew I had flunked my interview.

As we were walking out of Mrs. Borders's office, I paused to observe her big fish tank and noticed a corpse floating on top. Turning around, I shot back, "Hey lady, your fish is dead!"

Apparently, that blunt, if impolite, insight was enough for them to grant me a spot in the Beauvoir Class of 1973.

––––

Soon after I began at Beauvoir around age four, when Johnny was still a toddler, my parents took us for the first and only time to Jamaica. The vacation was also an opportunity to track down some of Mom's relatives. Urban Jamaica was a loud, colorful, chaotic conflagration for the senses, one I found both exciting and overwhelming.

We stayed mostly on the coast but traveled inland up into the mountains to visit my mom's first cousin, known as "Uncle Cyril." As we pressed our way up the muddy, rutted mountain road, the old rental car labored with increasing difficulty. Finally, it quit with a sudden bang as the front hood flew open and smashed into the windshield. We were stuck in the mud on a desolate mountain road. I don't recall who rescued us after some hours, but it felt like we had been stranded forever.

Somehow, we managed to make it to our destination, a tropical mountain hollow where my relatives lived proudly among banana trees and flowers in a remote hovel that revealed poverty of the sort I had never seen. I was struck by the incongruity of meeting blood relatives who lived in a rickety wooden structure with a corrugated metal roof and ate from a modest garden plot. Without words, my parents were continuously teaching me about our good fortune.

The time our family spent enjoying the more urbane and touristy parts of Jamaica left us with lasting happy memories. Johnny had long feared swimming pools and any large bodies of water, due to an early encounter with a freezing-cold pool. Yet in Jamaica, he played happily in the sand and impulsively ran without warning into the soothing warmth of the Caribbean waters. Rushing in and out with abandon, Johnny finally ran up to my parents and begged, "Mommy, will you buy me an ocean?" That query has endured as a reliable laugh line in our family, reflecting both Johnny's adorable naïveté and the sense our parents gave us, even as young children, that nothing was beyond our reach.

———

The influence of my hometown of Washington, D.C., and those rapidly changing times, which were punctuated four months before I was born by the passage of the Civil Rights Act of 1964, proved almost as important to my personal development as family and schooling. Just as my political consciousness began to form, all hell broke loose in my city and across the country—protests, riots, and killings. My parents made sure Johnny and I faced the world as it was. They wanted us to see and absorb the tumult of that era, even if we could not fully comprehend it.

When I was three and a half, my mother sat me in front of the television with her to watch the train carrying Robert F. Kennedy's coffin make the slow journey from New York to Washington. Another great man was gone, and we were mourning. I barely understood assassination, but its consequences were inescapable. Dr. Martin Luther King Jr. had been shot two months earlier. Though I hardly grasped why he was so important, I could sense the profundity of Dr. King's loss.

The proximate evidence for me was that my hometown was engulfed in flames, looting, and chaos. The four days of riots in Washington and in cities across the nation following Dr. King's murder brought armed troops onto the streets. Smoke blanketed the skies downtown, as the 14th Street corridor and much around it was incinerated. The violence was far removed from our neighborhood, yet my parents made me watch it on television and visit its aftermath when calm returned.

Mom and Dad also rolled my eighteen-month-old brother in his stroller and held my hand as we walked through the muddy, mass camp that was Resurrection City, a tent town on the National Mall established to memorialize the late Dr. King's Poor People's Campaign. It was a weekslong protest in horrible conditions that dramatized the racial and economic discontent that pervaded our city and larger society.

The old genteel, safely segregated Washington was gone. A new, brutal, bitterly divided carcass of a city replaced it. The shards of burned-out

Washington haunted my childhood, as it took well over a decade—what seemed to me like forever—to repair the worst ravages of the riots and for the city's open wounds to seal into rough keloids.

Walter Cronkite narrated this crisis and every other major event throughout my childhood, memorably concluding each evening's broadcast with his signature closer: "And, that's the way it is." In the bygone era of just three national television networks, our news was delivered unvarnished and un-spun, although with little diversity of sources and presenters. Back then, Americans were blessed with a common fact base, rather than self-selected stories that reinforce our personal preconceptions. This enabled serious and productive debate.

Avid consumers of both broadcast and print news, my parents made sure our dinner table conversations resembled a debate hall. The greatest sin we could commit as children was to cause a delay that made my father miss the lead story on the nightly news. In this time before digital recording devices, when that occurred, we had hell to pay.

Nothing was more arresting for me as a child than the first images of man walking on the moon. On July 20, 1969, my parents called us into their bedroom to watch on their black and white television as *Apollo 11* landed and out walked American astronauts Buzz Aldrin and Neil Armstrong. Piloting the command module was Michael Collins, the father of Michael Jr., one of my contemporaries in school.

Then there was Vietnam—the open sore that bled nightly on our television screens. I was not spared its most dramatic images. As a child, I witnessed film of napalm attacks, air raids, close combat, Cronkite's nightly body count, the full brutality of war. I also saw the violent protests it inspired back home, on campuses, in my city, and around the world.

President Johnson declined to run for reelection. The Kennedys were gone. Hubert Humphrey was our candidate, and I sported "HHH" political buttons at three years old. The Democratic convention in Chicago devolved into riotous chaos. Nixon won handily, and the war intensified.

In later years, our dinner table remained a stage for a lively discussion club shaped by reports on the nightly news. Johnny and I learned to be assertive and, when necessary, *loud*—in order to get a word in edgewise. Alliances shifted among the four of us, depending on the issue; but, again, reinforced by lessons from our visits to Maine, we grew up being comfortable with verbal jousting, expressing our views with confidence, and engaging in worthy battle.

We lived history as a family, like the later events of August 8, 1974, when I came running into the kitchen breathlessly to report to my parents that there was breaking news on television: Nixon had resigned! They were shocked and thrilled. A robust family conversation ensued.

Watergate was not just a national phenomenon; it was a personal trauma, hitting us like a tidal wave. As the revelations unfolded and the prosecutions persisted, two of our schoolmates' parents, G. Gordon Liddy and Jeb Magruder, were sent to jail.

All the violence, the fractious debates, and the Washington political dramas gripped me as a child. I could never wish, nor would I be able, to ignore my city, my nation, or the world. My parents refused to give us that luxury—to allow us to think that public issues were somehow remote from us. They steeped us in the tumult, forced us to confront our relative privilege, and taught us explicitly that we had both agency and responsibility—the ability to effect change and the expectation that we must.

———

Beauvoir in those days was barely 10 percent black, if that. Of those, about half came from far across Rock Creek Park, the verdant barrier that separated much of Washington's white minority from the black neighborhoods that most D.C. residents inhabited. Fittingly, after we moved to Shepherd Park, we grew up right in the middle, safely enmeshed in our mixed Jewish and black neighborhood—where we moved not long before I started at Beauvoir. The first (and only) house my parents owned together was on tree-lined Myrtle Street in upper Northwest. With her exquisite taste, Mom turned that dark, imposing, large stone edifice into a warm and elegant home with beautiful art, quality furniture, and a lovely garden, which she personally tended.

As children, we roamed freely throughout our neighborhood, riding bikes, playing basketball and football, hopping between families who felt no need to check on their kids' whereabouts. Our neighbors were professionals—doctors, judges, businessmen, and academics—plus colorful figures like the musician Van McCoy, who wrote and recorded "Do the

Hustle," and Ron Brown, who years later became my senior colleague when he served as commerce secretary in the Clinton administration.

Our closest neighbor friends were the Cornwells, who had three daughters and three sons, all older than us except their youngest, Michael, who remains close to Johnny. Their mother, Shirley Cornwell, stayed tight over the years with my mom; and Dr. Edward Cornwell, a stout, proud, and loud surgeon, was a good friend of my father's.

My dad, Dr. Cornwell, and the other men-folk would sit around on weekends smoking cigars, drinking, and laughing raucously to Richard Pryor's profanity behind closed doors. As kids, we would sneak up and listen for hours to hilariously inappropriate albums, most memorably *Bicentennial Nigger*, marveling at how Pryor made foul-mouthed cussing and dangerous drug use seem almost unremarkable. I can still impersonate Pryor delivering many of his lines, like: *"You know, I first met GOD in 1929. I never will forget this. You see, I was walking DOWN the street. . . . I was not running. I was WALKING down the street eating a tuna fish san-wich!"*

Our other neighborhood buddies came from families with whom we carpooled to Beauvoir. They, like us, lived where our school's buses would not travel. For my working mother, the carpool was a constant and significant source of stress, as she relied on other families to share the burden of taking us to and from school. Carpool challenges were the main reason Mom chose to join the Board of Trustees of Beauvoir School (on which I served many years later). She arrived on a mission to make the school buses accessible to kids beyond the traditional white neighborhoods from which Beauvoir drew most of its students. As a champion of equality, Mom was deeply frustrated that she had to do carpool duty while wealthier, white moms who mostly didn't work, simply waited for their kids to be picked up and deposited at their doorstep.

I remember vividly the lengths to which Mom went to make her case. One day, at around age six, I walked in to find Mom creating what appeared to be a major art project. Puzzled, I asked, "Mom, what are you doing? That looks really complicated." Carefully affixing pins and string to a massive mounted street map of Washington, she patiently explained, "I'm making this poster to show the Beauvoir board how they could easily reroute the school buses so that kids who live east of the park can also ride to school. See, each of these different-colored strings shows a possible new bus route, and the pins indicate where Beauvoir families live." Never knowing my mom to be particularly arts-and-crafty, I was amazed by the rigor and detail of her project. When Mom set out to marshal data to argue her case, she was deadly serious.

Ultimately, she failed in her bus crusade, but Mom became deeply invested in our school and made good friends on the board, like chairwoman (later Secretary of State) Madeleine Albright and Douglas Bennet, who subsequently served as USAID administrator, NPR president, and eventually turned out to be another close colleague of mine in the Clinton administration. My dad regularly played doubles on Sundays with Madeleine's then-husband Joe Albright. After tennis, the Albright and Rice families would often gather at Hamburger Hamlet for foot-long hot dogs, thick shakes, and steak fries. It was in that era that Madeleine dubbed me "little Susie Rice," a diminutive I have always disliked but which she occasionally employed with humor when we worked together, just to remind me of how long she had known me.

———

An inveterate tomboy from the start, I spent my discretionary time getting dirty, playing sports, cheering the Washington Redskins against Johnny's Dallas Cowboys, trading coveted Sunoco football stamps, and avoiding all prissy, girly activities. My close friendships were with both boys and girls. But one thing was clear: you would not find me with dolls, princesses, fairies, or anything pink. To my mother's everlasting dismay, I also acquired a fully formed vocabulary of curse words, which for lack of a better explanation I blame on hanging out with the boys.

By graduation from third grade at Beauvoir, my intellectual and physical confidence was well-established. I had a strong sense of who I was, combined with a readiness to assert myself, even in elementary school. My third-grade teacher, Mrs. Kvell, a hard-ass from Estonia, pointedly advised me to "Stay strong," but, "try to be more gentle and less impatient with the other kids." Her admonition resonated with me, because she aptly identified a challenge that I have faced ever since—whether in dealing with school friends or work colleagues.

For as long as I can remember, my mother has been a key role model for me. In these years, she was promoted to head the College Board's Washington office, and we would often visit her after school, playing on the electric typewriters and distracting her staff. Even as a young child, I appreciated how unusual it was to have a professional working mother, as almost all of my friends had stay-at-home moms. It seemed cool that my mother wore stylish Ultrasuede dresses to work and traveled frequently to New York. Plus, despite the demands of her job, Mom remained deeply involved in our daily lives—often cooking family dinners and driving us regularly to and from school. As we grew older, she continued to check on our homework, oversee our social plans, and cheer at our sports events.

Madeleine Albright and my mom, along with their fellow Beauvoir board member and friend Alice Rivlin (who became the founding director of the Congressional Budget Office and later of the White House Office of Management and Budget as well as vice chair of the Federal Reserve), were among the few highly accomplished professional women I knew while growing up. Their dual success as mothers and top leaders in their fields made a powerful impression on me, demonstrating that career and family need not be a binary choice for women. Still, much as I admired Mom's career and understood that it entailed tradeoffs, I confess to having occasional moments of regret that Mom had no time for, nor little interest in, greeting us after school with freshly baked chocolate chip cookies or delicious fudge pie, like my friend Hutchey's mom, Muffett Brock, used to do.

To help at home, my parents employed a housekeeper who cleaned, watched us kids, helped cook, and served us weekday dinners. Mrs. Elizabeth Jennings—Mrs. J, as we called her—was a major figure in my upbringing. She was a strong, sturdy woman from Northeast Washington, with a dignity and self-assurance that exceeded her role in the household. To my mother's annoyance, Mrs. Jennings kept the television on constantly as she cleaned, and I became fluent in the plotlines of *All My Children* and *General Hospital*. Without any hesitation, she called my mother "Lois," and Lois called her "Jenny" or "Beth."

Mrs. Jennings took absolutely no crap from my mother, who could dish it liberally. A typical argument might begin with my mom complaining in the morning that Mrs. Jennings was behind on the ironing and laundry. Mrs. J would retort: "Loyce, don't start with me this morning. I am ver-rry ti-ired." Undeterred, my mom might reply, "Beth, I don't care how tired you are. I'm not paying you to rest!' It was then *game on*, before their banter—at once annoyed and affectionate—petered out.

Over these same years, Dad played a traditional paternal role, bearing little, if any, share of the household responsibilities. He enjoyed spending time with me and Johnny, contributing mainly by teaching us chess, poker, and tennis and playing each game with us frequently. These were "Dad things," and we cherished them for their intimacy and rigor.

With time, however, Dad grew increasingly frustrated with Mom's long work hours and travel, insisting that she was neglecting the family. Although he professed support for working women, citing his beloved mother, when it came to his own family he was ambivalent at best and, more often, resentful. This tension was among the factors that sorely strained my parents' marriage.

Around age seven, my parents' relationship began to deteriorate rapidly. Up until that point, I mostly ignored, even sublimated, the undercurrent of unhappiness in my household, holding fast to the good times when my parents got along—and bracing myself for the uncertainty of what might come. For fleeting moments, I could breathe and dare to hope they could resolve their differences—like the time when my parents announced they were traveling together to Rio de Janeiro with other members of the TWA Board of Directors. Their wish, and mine, was that this trip would light a spark that could salvage their tattered marriage. It was a fun visit, by both accounts, but failed to reverse their mutually destructive dynamic.

Arguably, my parents were never well-suited. My dad was not only brilliant and charming, but quick-tempered, impatient, and at least somewhat chauvinistic. My mom was beautiful, ambitious, and smart, but also high-strung, domineering, overtly powerful but latently insecure. Ultimately, they agreed on little, except politics, some friends, and their love for their children.

Despite that essential plot of common ground, for the next decade of my formative years, I grew up in the middle of something akin to a civil war battlefield.

3

***

Growing Up Too Soon

"**I**'*m all-in,*" *I answered without hesitation at the end of a phone call with Senator Obama in January 2007, a month before he officially announced his candidacy on that freezing cold day in Springfield, Illinois.*

The previous fall, senior staff in Obama's Senate office—who were quietly preparing for his presidential run—had been in touch to gauge my interest in joining their effort.

Barack Obama was the only potential 2008 candidate I found compelling, so when he personally asked me to partner with Tony Lake and recruit and lead his team of outside foreign policy advisors, I pledged my full support.

Keenly aware of the professional cost of burning bridges with the Clintons, proud to have served in the Clinton NSC and State Department, and knowing that Hillary was the Democratic Party's likely nominee, I was nonetheless confident that supporting Obama was the right choice for me. While we came from very different backgrounds, Obama and I were close in age, and had classmates and friends in common. Above all, we had shared ambitions for our country. Never before had I felt more affinity for a political candidate.

Win or lose, Obama's candidacy for me portended the fulfillment of my generation's dreams of service and the unrealized potential of this country that I love. If America could elect a black man with intelligence, dignity, and principles who didn't use race as an excuse or a crutch, as my parents taught me, then this was my fight.

I knew the Clintons wouldn't understand; and they didn't. For almost four-teen years, I had known, liked, and respected President Clinton and was grate-ful to serve our country under his leadership. I also admired Hillary, whom at the time I knew less well, but appreciated her kindness to me and her candor—including a memorable conversation on a long flight back from Africa when she shared some of her personal views about marriage at a difficult time for her. Though I questioned whether the country was ready for another Clinton so soon, I believed Hillary would make a good president. But Obama repre-sented so much more than a strong candidate. He embodied my dreams for our country.

I don't think the Clintons saw Obama coming. They assumed that Hillary would be the nominee and failed to imagine, until much later, that Obama posed a credible threat. They were slow in building their stable of foreign policy advisors—assuming, I suspect, that everyone who had served in the Clinton administration, which amounted to the bulk of the policy expertise in the party, would undoubtedly support Hillary—whether out of obligation, ambi-tion, affection, or fear.

In late January, before Obama formally announced his candidacy, former national security advisor Sandy Berger called me at home. Sandy had become my good friend and mentor over eight years of close collaboration. He was deeply committed to the Clintons, going back decades. Sandy surprised me by asking, "Would you like to lead Senator Clinton's campaign foreign policy team?"

I replied, "Sandy, I'm truly honored. I wasn't expecting this." After taking a deep breath, I continued, "Please thank Senator Clinton for me. I have enor-mous respect for her, but I have already committed to help Obama in a similar way."

The silence on the other end of the line seemed interminable. Having gath-ered himself, Sandy said calmly, "Are you sure? You know he can't win, don't you?"

I explained how I felt about Obama's candidacy, concluding, "This is not a choice against the Clintons, to whom I'll always be grateful. It's a decision in favor of Obama. And, yes, I'm sure."

Stunned, Sandy said without rancor, "You realize, don't you, that you are making a foolish, potentially career-ending move?"

The conversation ended civilly, and my relationship with Sandy never suffered. He remained a committed friend. Not everyone on the Clinton team felt the same way, even though in the grand scheme of the Clinton-Obama battle for talent, I was not a very senior defection.

Looking back, I do not recall a time, even as a child, when I was shy about speaking my mind, afraid of what others might think of me, or was even fearful of another person. My parents reinforced my sense of self and stoked my innate confidence. At home, we argued energetically over policy and politics, so I learned early on how to hold my own in debates, marshal strong arguments, and present them forcefully. In the Rice household, one could not afford to be intimidated by loud voices or shy away from vigorous disputes.

Yet there did come a traumatic period, when the fighting between my parents became deeply personal, and it was clear there was no road to reconciliation. In that painful process, I learned how to compartmentalize conflict, protect myself emotionally and psychically, and bounce back from adversity— all capacities that, ideally, I would not have needed as a child but would serve me well over the long haul.

———•◆•———

Our house became a tinderbox. My parents fought ugly and often, and it only seemed to get worse with time.

Johnny and I would come home from school fearful of what the night would bring. I eavesdropped on many arguments. They seemed to range from money to Mom's travel, their drinking, and, eventually, an affair. Their recriminations ran the gamut, with each side blaming the other: *Why are you home so late? Just leave me alone. That's a lie, and you know it! Don't you dare talk to me like that.*

The screaming and yelling seemed almost constant. Sometimes they scuffled, pushed and shoved, or threw objects at each other—hairbrushes, lamps, small statues.

"Be quiet, I can't sleep!" I'd yell. One night I lurked in the hallway just outside the kitchen where they were fighting. As I poked my head in to demand that they stop, I saw a wooden object fly through the air and hit the wall without harming either of them.

On occasion, they would wake me late in the evening to witness and presumably condemn the bad behavior of the other. The violence I saw was not terrible, but it was terrifying, because I never knew how far and how fast things might escalate. When I heard loud, angry voices, I would get up from bed, my heart racing, and steal downstairs to assess the severity of the fight—ready to intervene, if necessary. It got so bad that Johnny and I stopped inviting friends for sleepovers, since we couldn't predict when an embarrassing fight would ensue. I was constantly on pins and needles and furious at my parents for doing this to me and our family. Their screaming was bad, but the unpredictable violence and my foreboding that someone might get seriously hurt was far worse.

I heard my mom implicitly threaten suicide more than once, declaring, "I've had it. I can't take this anymore." I could not adequately assess whether she meant it or was just trying to manipulate my dad. But she had enough problems at the time—a neck injury (origins unknown) that landed her in traction for a short period, high stress, and unpredictable behavior—to make me doubt her will and ability to live. I feared that my mother might try to kill herself.

One day, Mom returned from the hospital with numerous stitches in a bad injury to her wrist. My understanding was that she punched through a windowpane in fury. I am not sure why, or even if that was a truthful story, but it underscored to me her irrationality and vulnerability. And it left me even more frightened.

Never before or since those years have I felt such shaking, stomach-wrenching fear—the kind that possesses you and eats through your soul.

Still I had no choice but to cope. I could not sit on the sidelines as my family burned with the risk that the conflagration would consume me and my little brother. Instead, I steeled myself and ran into the fire in hope that I might save something of their marriage, or if not, the ones I loved. Fearlessly, if foolishly, I offered myself as a sounding board for my parents' grievances against one another, trying to talk them toward calm, if not comity. As the older child, and in the absence of any alternative, starting at seven years old, I appointed myself chief firefighter, mediator, and judge, working to defuse arguments, broker compromises, and bring rationality to bear when emotion overwhelmed reason. In the process, I developed innate toughness, calm under fire, and an intuitive sense of when conflicting parties might be able to reconcile. These elements of my character endured and afforded me an unconscious reservoir upon which to draw, when much later, in my chosen career, I found myself again trying to put out other people's fires and forge common ground.

I learned far more than I wanted to know about my parents' marriage—that their unhappiness had deep roots, if unclear origins. That their trust was gone, and Dad had hired a private investigator to spy on my mother. That my mother clandestinely installed recording devices in our house to entrap my father. That they really didn't like each other and maybe rarely had.

The proximate catalyst for their breakup was the revelation that my mother was having an affair. Dad was able to confirm his suspicions using the detective. But my parents' discontent and disagreements well preceded Mom's affair.

Mom and Alfred Fitt likely met at a conference on higher education when Mom was working at the College Board, and Alfred was a special advisor to the president of his alma mater, Yale University. Their relationship convinced my mother that she wanted to divorce my dad and marry Alfred. The challenge was how to extricate herself and still retain equal access to her children in an era when the courts (and society) readily punished women for adultery.

In reaction to my parents' impending breakup, I behaved both maturely and angrily. Maturely, as I sought in earnest to hear each side out, appreciate their perspectives, and soothe their differences. Angrily, as I yelled at them to stop the fighting and be responsible adults. Once, I was so furious at my mother that I pinned her to the bed and slapped her face, screaming that I hated her for having an affair and ruining our family. Stunned and hurt, she offered little resistance, as if she understood my fury. Yet, on most occasions, she would argue back, insisting that I treat her with respect.

Generally, both parents seemed to appreciate that my acting out was a healthier means of expressing my anger than suppressing it. Still, I gave them plenty of grief, sometimes running away from home for hours at a time. Never putting myself in danger, I'd disappear to a friend's house or to remote places in the neighborhood, long enough to worry Mom and

Dad. One time, feeling left out, I timed my disappearance to ensure my dad and brother missed their plane to the Super Bowl. They were (and remained) furious with me for years (even though they made it to California with plenty of time to see the game).

On Johnny's seventh birthday, I drove with him and my mom to pick up his cake at a nearby bakery. Angry in general, and now especially annoyed that he was getting all the attention and I was relegated to the backseat in deference to the birthday boy, I plotted my revenge. Nobody noticed as I slid over and nonchalantly sat on the bakery box before moving back to my spot. When we arrived home and Johnny came to retrieve the box, he was hysterical to discover it was flat as a pancake.

My mother and father had the good sense to take both me and Johnny to a child psychiatrist to be evaluated. The doctors assessed that because I was expressing my feelings forcefully, I was coping adequately. Ever since, I have been a believer in not hiding emotions and expressing discontent, even anger, directly. With me, it's easy to know where you stand—for better or worse. To a fault, I hold myself and others to high standards, expecting the most out of those with whom I am closest, and continuously struggle to mask my impatience with shortcomings—mine and theirs.

My parents were more worried about Johnny, who the shrink assessed was repressing his emotions and denying our family reality. Much to his enduring frustration, Johnny was sentenced to about a year of therapy, forever resentful that I somehow managed to escape the same fate. Yet in slogging through the trauma of our parents' divorce together, Johnny and I evolved into fellow survivors, each other's constants, and became closer than ever. For years, I played the role of big sister—more mature, strong, secure—until as a late teenager Johnny came into his own. With quiet wisdom and confidence, he grew to support and advise me in equal, if not greater measure, such that as adults, he is as much my big brother as I am his elder sister.

———

As our family approached the breaking point, in the summer of 1975 when I was ten years old, my mother whisked me and Johnny away to Aspen, Colorado, where she was attending a conference. Two of her colleagues helped smuggle us to the airport, and we found ourselves unexpectedly on a plane to Denver. The whole thing had a faint whiff of cloak-and-dagger but, at the time, it didn't seem so strange. Mom had taken me and Johnny on work-related trips before without Dad. We happily returned from Aspen two weeks later, and it was only as adults that we came to realize we'd been kidnapped, albeit briefly, without my father's knowledge or permission.

Not to be outdone in their escalating parental competition, Dad took me and Johnny to Europe for the first time later that same summer. As a member of TWA's Board of Directors, Dad was entitled to free first-class travel for his immediate family and cut-rate stays at TWA-owned Hilton hotels. So we enjoyed a lovely, luxurious two-week trip to Paris, Rome, Madrid, and Marbella, Spain, on the Costa del Sol.

It was our first experience spending extended time alone with our dad. We had great fun visiting museums and historic sites, walking the streets, eating good food, playing tennis, and horseback riding. Johnny and I thoroughly enjoyed having so much uninterrupted time with Dad but had little idea that he was auditioning for his imminent debut as a single parent.

Then, suddenly, on September 24, 1975, soon after the academic year started, Johnny and I came home from school to eerie quiet and utter emptiness. Without warning, we found our house, now just Dad's house, was no longer home. We knew their separation was coming, but that knowledge failed to lessen the shock. Mom had moved out and taken most of the furniture and all of the charm with her. The house was a cavernous, tasteless, almost unfurnished shell of its former self, improved only by the arrival of our first color television.

The split followed a bitter battle involving their lawyers over a separation agreement, which would govern financial arrangements, custody, and visitation. The sticking points between my parents included how to divide their property and, in the unique case of their cherished Nigerian sculpture, how to fashion a swapping arrangement over time. But mostly, they couldn't agree on how to share us kids.

Mom was prepared (with great anguish) to concede custody to my dad, but she insisted on fifty-fifty visitation rights. Dad promised her orally, at least once in my presence, that he would allow equal visitation but refused to put it in a binding written agreement. He wanted control and argued simply that she should trust him. Understandably distrustful, Mom held out for months to get the pledge in writing until, ultimately, she realized she was screwed. She couldn't afford a court battle, wanted to marry Alfred, and needed a no-fault divorce. But she had initially lied under oath about the affair. Though she promptly corrected her story, my father's divorce lawyer had all the ammunition needed to dictate the divorce terms. Desperately hoping Dad would keep his word on equal visitation, Mom signed the separation agreement in January 1976.

Their separation meant that the fighting and my constant fear were blessedly over. If a caring adult or a close friend would ask how I felt about my new life, however, I would answer, point-blank, "It sucks." We all had to start from scratch: two houses, two single parents, shuttling between them.

Near school, Mom's new house was much smaller than our original family home and lacked charm. Of course, almost on Day One, Mom had it fully furnished in the good taste she brought to everything; still, it wasn't home. My hunch is that with only her modest nonprofit salary, Mom struggled to support herself and pay her half of our expenses, along with her legal bills.

My parents' separation ruined more than our nuclear family. It caused major rifts within our extended family and even friends, with everyone taking sides. Uncle Leon outright trashed my father. When we went to South Carolina to visit Dad's sister Aunt Pansy, an important figure in our lives, she had nothing good to say about Mom. Everything that once felt normal and secure seemed lost.

———

For five years after their separation, and long beyond their divorce in May 1977, Johnny and I remained in the middle of my parents' relentless tug-of-war. Neither parent could resist poisoning our perceptions of the other. Despite their best efforts to influence us, Johnny and I understood that, while flawed, neither parent was as the other portrayed. We knew each loved us unconditionally and never doubted their commitment to us as parents.

For the first two years, we did split our time equally between my parents' households, until Dad realized that we were sometimes exposed to my mother's new partner. When Dad warned Mom to stop seeing Alfred at all in our presence, she protested that they were getting married and that Dad's demand was unfair and irrational. Dad insisted and, for periods, Mom complied. Yet once Dad concluded that Mom would not consistently oblige, he curtailed our visitation to the letter of their legal agreement—every other weekend during the school year and half of all vacations, plus a few additional days when Dad traveled out of town.

Living in two households was stressful, especially until my parents worked out a minimally disruptive rhythm—one that allowed us to move on the weekends and avoid the humiliation of dragging our suitcases to school. In the interim, my friendships began to suffer, as some at school called me out for being moody and even combative. From classmates' offhand comments or cold shoulders, I realized that I was unconsciously antagonizing people. Finding myself increasingly isolated, I struggled to moderate my behavior and repair frayed friendships. With time, I got my act together at school, taming my temper and treating friends more gently.

Eventually, living under two roofs and commuting between them became a routine like any other, and we grew inured to the emotional and physical disruption. As in all aspects of our new reality, Johnny and I learned to tough out the hard stuff and make the most of what we had— each other, two devoted parents, safe places to live, good friends, and a great education.

As a single father, Dad went from the parent present mainly for the fun stuff to being omnipresent. At the outset, my father had almost no experience running a household. He could cook only steak and make instant coffee. He had never driven a carpool. He had to hire and manage his own housekeeper (rather, a series of them, each of whom lacked the constancy and refinement of our beloved Mrs. Jennings, who remained with my mother). Yet Dad managed to figure it out pretty fast, even if it wasn't exactly pretty.

Up in the morning long before us, he'd muster me with a cup of hot coffee, make us breakfast, and cook dinners that included a broadened repertoire of not only steak but chicken and tater tots and a handful of dishes in the other food groups. Almost daily, my father drove us to and from school, often in his prized gray 1964 Mercedes-Benz 190c with a red leather interior and ivory steering wheel. He had bought the car in Germany, when he and Mom traveled back to the U.S. from Nigeria shortly before my birth. Over decades, that old Mercedes never lost its intense leather smell or its historic charm. Riding in that car with my dad was one of the happy constants of these years. He kept it until after I went to college, repainting it a steel blue and ensuring it ran well, until a massive piece of ice fell off our roof, shattering the windshield and badly damaging the body of the car.

I came to see the essential Emmett Rice in the sacrifices he chose to make to be fully present for us, while continuing to be the best at what he did. To tackle huge stacks of paper he brought home from the office, Dad stayed up late working at the kitchen table after dinner, sometimes dozing off but determined to be prepared for the next day's meetings. Though he admonished us not to "burn the candle at both ends"—hounding us to get to bed if our homework dragged on too late into the night—he didn't always heed that lesson himself.

Originally, many of our peers had seen Dad as aloof, even intimidating—like Johnny's friend who would only enter the house after asking "Is your dad home?" and making sure the answer was no. Yet swiftly, our friends got to know Dad well, realizing that he was actually a cool parent who took small groups to Washington Bullets basketball games or concerts like Earth, Wind & Fire and the Commodores. His dramatic transformation in the midst of an otherwise dark time was a lasting gift to Johnny and me.

Even as my parents' marriage crashed, my father's career had taken off. He left the Treasury Department in 1970 and went on to head the D.C. Mayor's Economic Development Committee. Three years later, he transitioned to private banking. Named senior vice president for planning and development at the National Bank of Washington, then D.C.'s third largest bank, Dad was the first African American to serve in a senior management position at a major commercial bank in Washington. Dad's stint in the private sector, however, was relatively short-lived, because in 1979, President Jimmy Carter appointed Dr. Emmett J. Rice to the Federal Reserve Board, as only the second African American governor. I proudly held the Bible at Dad's swearing-in ceremony at the White House.

An eligible bachelor, Dad dated a couple of women seriously but ultimately chose to stay single—probably to give Johnny and me maximal stability and attention. Though brilliant, funny, and a connoisseur of good wine and music, I doubt Dad would have made an easy husband. While I admire my father more than anyone else, he possessed some less laudable characteristics, several of which I struggle with myself. Dad was opinionated and could be argumentative and quick-tempered. He was competitive, occasionally self-righteous, and utterly incapable of suffering fools. He would directly confront those he deemed subpar—whether an obnoxious journalist or an errant cab driver. Unlike me, Dad was also a very private person, almost secretive, and slow to trust those he did not know well.

There were additional sides to Emmett Rice that I got to see on full display as we grew older, particularly how he never wasted a teaching opportunity. Every time a word was uttered in conversation that we didn't know, Dad would say, "Go look it up in the dictionary." Feeling cheated that his father had died young without passing on his wisdom, Dad was determined to impart to us everything of importance he had learned. This, he hoped, would spare us from making unnecessary mistakes, as he had done. From Dad's perspective, our role was to listen carefully and take free advice respectfully, since it came from, as he said, "Someone who has your best interests at heart."

Dad's method of discourse was sometimes to be the devil's advocate, usually employed with a hearty sense of humor disguised by his serious quasi-scowl or a look that combined a smile with an air of disdain or, occasionally, a chiding remark. If someone had done something stupid that just lacked common sense, he would shake his head, as if to say, "C'mon, man," and then employ a common refrain, "Don't you know when to come in from out of the rain." Above all, he consistently insisted, *"Don't take crap off of anyone"*—that is, don't let anyone demean you, limit you, or define you.

Learning to live with divorced parents and their individual idiosyncrasies was one thing. Adjusting to my mom and her marriage to a different man was quite another.

———

With considerable trepidation, Johnny and I walked into Mom and Alfred's new town house on Embassy Row in Washington. As we passed through the vestibule and the front parlor, I glanced back at my little brother to see if he was okay. Wearing a pained, if brave, expression, he followed me into the melee.

As cold as it was outside on this January day in 1978, it somehow felt even less comfortable inside. Mom and Alfred had just gotten married on the grounds of the Washington Cathedral, and the house was crowded with family and friends celebrating at their wedding reception. The crowd included my grandparents, Mary and David, Uncles Leon and David, various cousins, my brand-new stepbrothers, Ben and Craig, and stepsisters, Cate and Ann (all grown), and countless invited guests. Food and drink were plentiful and elegant, as at all my mom's affairs, yet it wasn't festive to us. We didn't really want to be there but felt we had little choice.

As soon as Mom spotted us, she hurried over, hugging us in delight. Our presence was the product of a carefully orchestrated compromise over how to approach this day. Dad was immensely bitter about Mom's marriage to Alfred, while Johnny and I were highly skeptical of this new man in our lives. We viewed their union as tainted by arising from an illicit affair, which sounded the death-knell for our unitary family. The fact that Alfred was a WASP was tolerable from my perspective, but for my dad, I believe, losing his wife to a white man added insult to injury. He pressed us hard to boycott the entire event—wedding and reception. Mom, of course, desperately wanted us at both momentous occasions, as her joy would have been sorely dampened by our absence. By necessity, Johnny and I had become adept at balancing their competing demands. Looking to thread the needle, I decided that Johnny and I should attend the reception but not the wedding. No one was happy, but everyone dealt with it—the hallmark, I would later learn, of a sustainable solution to an intractable conflict.

My stepfather, Alfred Bradley Fitt, a graduate of Yale College and Michigan Law, and a World War II veteran, served most of his career in government. Before his stint on the staff at Yale, he was assistant secretary of defense for manpower during the Vietnam War, general counsel of the army, and deputy assistant secretary of the army for civil rights. In 1975, Alfred was named general counsel of the newly created Congressional Budget Office.

Clearly devoted to my mother, Alfred exerted largely a calming influence on her and also took a kind interest in me. He later taught me to drive stick-shift, helped type some of my term papers, and advised me on my college applications. Trying to temper some of Mom's excesses, at least those she took out on me, Alfred healthily reinforced my own sense of self.

However, it soon became evident that my stepfather had a drinking problem. Mom too could become petulant and impulsive when inebriated. Alcohol came to exercise an outsize influence on their household, creating a stressful dynamic that restored a measure of unpredictability to our lives when we so craved stability.

To make matters worse, Alfred clashed with Johnny. Those battles almost rivaled the ones I had with my mother. From the time I was ten to almost thirty, my mother and I were mutually combustible.

Mom was a complex character whose strengths and weaknesses were strikingly juxtaposed. Lois, as I sometimes called her (in part to annoy), was super-smart, highly intuitive, even prescient, as well as a talented cook, gardener, floral artist, and an elegant decorator. Extremely generous, she adopted strangers and made them her lifelong friends—bank security guards, waitresses, manicurists, workmen, and caregivers. Once she was your friend, my mother protected you mercilessly. Possessing a rare inner strength, toughness, and resilience that was evident from her stand-out academic success to her steely battle with six consecutive cancers, my mother was ultimately my biggest booster and fiercest defender.

But no one could cut me down to size faster or more harshly. For most of my teenage years, Mom and I picked at each other, seizing on each other's weaknesses and exploiting them. Typically, it would begin in her kitchen with something like:

"Susan, you really need to watch it. Your behind is getting too big. And you are not helping yourself with the butch way you dress—baggy pants, tasteless tops, and everything."

"Mom, I don't need this from you. Just stop," I'd rejoin, trying to end it.

"Well, if I don't tell you the truth, I don't know who will. You have the potential to be a pretty girl, but that afro is no help and you need to start 'putting your face on.'"

Incensed, I would escalate, "I don't know why you always have to be such a bitch. Maybe if you drank less you would be easier to tolerate."

Indignant, she would say, "Don't you talk to me like that! I'm your mother. You had better show proper respect."

"I will when you earn it," I would say, delivering the coup de grâce and storming out of the kitchen and upstairs to my room.

Neither of us meant to be as hurtful as we were, but ours had become an unhealthy dynamic. I had indeed lost a certain measure of respect for my mom, given the knowledge that she deceived my dad and left him for another man. I resented that she sometimes drank too much and lost a measure of her self-control. In my view, she had to own those failings, as they were inescapable; thus, the power balance in our naturally fraught mother–teen daughter relationship tilted more than normal in my favor. I smelled weakness and went for the jugular—in ways both overt and subconscious—an instinct I have learned to temper with age.

While letting Mom know I saw her flaws, I struggled not to expose my own insecurities. She harshly criticized my appearance, undermining my body image, such that I long doubted my attractiveness and remain sensitive about my weight. By contrast, Mom reliably reinforced my confidence in all other realms, particularly my intellect and integrity. Once into adulthood when our relationship blossomed (and I dressed better), Mom frequently told me that I was beautiful and helpfully contributed to selecting my wardrobe, even if she never quite gave up on my hair and, when deserved, my behind.

Despite all her strength, beauty, and style, Mom suffered from a nagging insecurity. Especially before she aged, Mom could be defensive, quick-tempered, and even dissemble. She never dwelt on the sources of her uneven self-esteem, but I suspect she always felt she didn't quite belong in the rarefied circles in which she traveled. At root, Mom still viewed herself as "a poor colored girl from Portland, Maine." She also repeatedly speculated that her own mother, Mary, having risked her life to bear such a late child, somehow resented or may not have truly wanted her. Mom regretted failing twice at marriage and was candid about the myriad professional challenges she faced as an early, lonely woman in white male executive suites and boardrooms.

Outside the home, Mom hid her self-doubt adeptly and largely overcame it as she rose professionally. Her passion remained education and equal opportunity for poor and minority youth. Over thirty years at the College Board, Mom lobbied strenuously to make college affordable for all. She worked closely with Senator Claiborne Pell to establish Basic Education Opportunity Grants, later renamed Pell Grants, which provide federal financial aid for low-income students. I am deeply proud that Lois D. Rice is widely lauded as "The Mother of Pell Grants" for her work in launching and sustaining this critical program, which has supported approximately 80 million Americans to attend college since 1973. Later, Mom would serve as senior vice president for government affairs at Control Data Corporation and as a director on eleven major publicly traded corporate boards, bringing her knowledge of Congress and public policy as well as her passion for equality to the private sector.

––––––

After marrying Alfred, Mom decided to sue for equal visitation rights, concluding that Dad was never going to honor his fifty-fifty pledge once Alfred became a permanent fixture. Their legal war involved high-priced, nasty lawyers on both sides, along with a judge who was the husband of a senior administrator at my school and also taught one of my classes. I wished he had recused himself; instead, for years, I felt like our family business was out on the street.

My parents' lawyers had the brilliant idea to call me and Johnny to testify before the judge as to which parent we preferred to live with. We were mortified by the notion of being forced to takes sides publicly against our parents. We loved them both dearly and did not want to lose either by choosing. Moreover, we were outraged that they and their lawyers were so consumed by winning that they failed to appreciate the impact on me and Johnny.

Thankfully, we had our own (pro bono) lawyer. In 1976, we became close to an angel named Peggy Cooper Cafritz. Peggy was the aunt of Casey Cooper, a close friend of Johnny's and mine whom we had met at Sidwell Tennis Camp.

Peggy was a lawyer by training, an activist, and pioneer in the D.C. arts community who cofounded the Duke Ellington School for the Arts. Peggy—hip, not quite thirty, and no BS—adopted me and Johnny as her godchildren, like she later did for scores of kids who needed help over the years.

When Peggy heard we had to testify, she invited us over to her house to conspire. "I have an idea," she said. "Why don't you write the judge and tell him how you feel about your parents and explain that you don't want to testify?" Impressed by her brilliance and deviousness, we lay on Peggy's floor to compose individual letters to the judge. Not accidentally, we neglected to tell our parents what we had done—blindsiding their flabbergasted lawyers and, for once, seizing the advantage in the case.

The judge had the decency to heed our wishes, so we never had to appear in court. In writing, we both proclaimed we loved our parents, though Johnny added that he just wanted to see his parents "on an equal basis." I steered clear of the issue at hand. Ultimately, the judge ruled in favor of my mother, granting her equal visitation rights.

My father appealed, and the appellate court reversed the decision, ruling 2–1 in favor of my dad. Mom was crushed. Even as Johnny and I sympathized with her loss, we were mostly relieved that the legal saga had finally ended—just as I was completing tenth grade.

Spanning almost ten years, my parents' prolonged fighting, brutal divorce, and lengthy court battle were my first major searing trauma. I was disgusted by my parents' inability to put their children's interests first and seethed with a rage that overrode my sadness and sense of loss. Forced to grow up faster than I should have, I resented that my parents had stolen a piece of my childhood.

Their divorce also left me wary of commitment in relationships with men, skeptical of the desirability and durability of marriage, and fearful of failing like my parents. Though I remained angrier at my mom than my dad, as an adult I have come to understand their actions and motives more clearly, and I am substantially more sympathetic to my mother's plight than I once was.

Unable to sway the outcome of their marriage, I turned my focus to what I could control—school, friendships, sports—and willed myself not to be undone by my parents' drama. Understanding the difference between what I could influence and what I could not proved an important survival tool for the future. From this ordeal, I began learning how to nurture my relationships rather than take them for granted, to channel my frustrations into constructive effort rather than letting my anger fester. Discovering that I had the ability to steady myself, even in the eye of a storm, I emerged with greater confidence and inner strength. The onslaught had shown me I could take a bruising hit and keep running. Instead of being a victim, I counted my perseverance as a personal triumph.

Painful as it was, the divorce gave me steel and grit, an early taste of adversity, and what I came to know as its corollary: resilience.

4

Twice As Good

By early 2007, we were off to the races.

Having cast our lot with Obama, Tony Lake and I sped to assemble the best possible stable of foreign policy experts to assist the campaign. There was little competition, as it turned out. Clinton relied, initially, on the most senior advisors like former secretary of state Madeleine Albright, Sandy Berger, and former U.N. ambassador Richard Holbrooke. She had lots of bosses but few workhorses.

We took a different approach, targeting younger, thirty-, forty-, and fifty-somethings—experienced but not cabinet-level former officials—who would do the thinking and writing we needed, not just offer sage advice. My colleagues at the Brookings Institution were ripe for the picking, and many of them were our best early recruits. My dear friend Gayle Smith, who had also worked for President Clinton and was much closer to him than I was in his post-presidency, signed on with Obama at the outset, as did my former NSC colleagues Richard Clarke and Randy Beers, who were both then retired from government and brought unparalleled counterterrorism and homeland security experience. Some prospective additions needed convincing that Obama had a prayer of winning, but most were excited by his powerful personal narrative, oratorical skills, and compelling policy views.

Tony and I swiftly assembled a large team of energetic, experienced talent who were able to support Obama across all issue areas. We also led a steering group of about a dozen core supporters, several of whom Obama involved *in speech preparation, drafting articles, debate prep, formulating key policy positions, and occasional conference calls. As the campaign matured, Obama built out his paid campaign staff, and colleagues like Ben Rhodes, Denis Mc-Donough, and Obama Senate staffer Mark Lippert took on the day-to-day policy leadership, drawing upon our external team for expertise as needed.*

My campaign appearances at house parties, fundraisers, public panels, rallies, churches, and get-out-the-vote (GOTV) events consumed a lot of travel time but were among my favorite activities. Over the course of the primary season, I journeyed from Iowa to New Hampshire, from South Carolina to Utah, New Mexico, South Dakota, Florida, Michigan, Georgia, Ohio, Virginia, Pennsylvania, North Carolina, and Indiana, often paired up with elected officials or celebrities, to talk to voters about why I believed Obama was the right person at the right time. Sometimes my pitch was generic; at other times I would speak in depth on his foreign policy credentials and positions.

The excitement on the hustings for Obama was palpable—from rural midwestern communities to big cities and suburbs, among people of all ages and races. Obama was tapping into a vein that was hungry for the kind of "hope and change" he represented.

One of my favorite trips was to New Hampshire in early January 2008, because I was joined by my ten-year-old son, Jake, who campaigned with me in the frigid, snow-covered southwestern corner of the state. From the bar in a modest hotel in Keene, New Hampshire, Jake and I watched television with friends as Obama was declared the winner in the hard-fought Iowa caucuses.

The victory was gratifying not only because it was the first contest of the primary season, but because, for Obama, everything depended on Iowa. Adjacent to his home state of Illinois, Iowa was the place where Obama bet the farm, gambling the bulk of his early money and field organization. It was no small feat for an African American to triumph in such a white state, where both his main opponents, Hillary Clinton and John Edwards, had long histories and faithful followers.

Buoyed by the prospect that we could replicate the Iowa victory in New Hampshire, Jake and I spent several days knocking on doors in Keene where voters craved substantive discussion with campaign representatives. To maximize our efficiency, Jake and I sometimes split up and went to houses individually, since one knock could result in being invited into the owner's living room for warmth from the deep snow, a hot beverage, sweets, and extended conversation.

Jake, who began his political journey as a lefty Dennis Kucinich supporter and has since migrated to the other extreme, was then a knowledgeable and persuasive Obama spokesman. At an Obama rally later in the week, I met charmed residents who gushed about how impressed they were with young Jake's confident command of Obama's policy positions and how polite and persuasive he was.

As the primary approached, I headlined events in Manchester, phone-banked, and served as a press surrogate in the pre- and post-debate spin room at Saint Anselm College. After days of rallies, debates, and GOTV activities, the primary outcome seemed uncertain. The Obama campaign remained hopeful, despite the negative impact of Obama's dismissive comment in the debate that Hillary was "likable enough" and, thereafter, of Hillary fighting back tears while in conversation with women voters at a local diner. As I canvassed in Manchester on primary day, the mood didn't feel great, and I worried that the night might end badly.

When the votes were counted, Obama indeed fell short. Even though I had hints of the outcome, the loss still felt like a breath-seizing blow. Obama's concession speech was graceful and featured the introduction of his signature rallying cry, "Yes, we can!" That night, at the New Hampshire staff party, which ended like a wake, we all realized we were in for a long, tough primary battle.

Even then, I sensed the New Hampshire loss may have been a blessing in disguise. We had to be able to take a punch and correct course; and the campaign needed time to test and season our candidate. Had the road to the nomination been quick and easy, I believe Obama may not have been as well prepared to take on the Republican nominee.

After Clinton won the next contest in Nevada by 5 percentage points but split the delegates almost evenly with Obama, the campaign was essentially tied going into South Carolina, an important southern bellwether and indicator of how African American voters would choose between their long-standing affinity for the Clintons and the potential historic opportunity presented by Obama.

At my first stop in a rural black church near Greenville, I arrived to learn that Michelle Obama, the scheduled headliner, would not make it due to plane *trouble. I was suddenly required to fill in as the main event, along with my former Clinton administration colleague, Ertharin Cousin, a Chicagoan with ties to the Obamas. I got up and mustered as much spirit and soul as I could to explain why I had picked Obama over Clinton. My rap probably sounded something like this: "Obama is about the future, our future. He is about change that we all can believe in. This choice is not about loyalty or passing the torch from one member of a dynasty to the other, however much we loved Bill Clinton. This is about the future and who has the ideas, the energy, the vision to understand your needs and make your lives better."*

For about a week, I traversed the far corners of South Carolina, my dad's home state, where I had spent time over the years visiting my aunt Pansy, who had died just the year before. I went to university campuses and Democratic Party breakfasts, knocked on doors, and helped staff the statewide headquarters. The Clintons fought hard in South Carolina, knowing that a loss there would be costly and bode ill for their ability to galvanize the black vote.

Despite a race-tinged campaign, Obama won handily. The victory was especially sweet, given the bitterness of the fight, and set the battlefield for the rest of the contentious primary season. "All-in," I remained devoted to helping Obama win the nomination, even though I realized that with each television appearance or super-delegate converted, I was digging my grave deeper with the Clinton machine. Yet this kind of dedication to mission, committing myself completely to what I believe in, came easily to me. It reflects who I am—indeed, who I grew into being at my demanding Washington, D.C., high school.

After Beauvoir, I attended the National Cathedral School for girls (NCS) from fourth grade until high school graduation, on the Washington Cathedral Close. Daily, as I greeted the ever-cheerful crossing guard while traversing Woodley Road, I looked up in awe at the immense, gray stone gothic Cathedral. Having attended services there since nursery school, I knew its massive flying buttresses, powerful tolling bells, meticulously carved gargoyles, and breathtaking stained glass windows—one containing a moon rock retrieved by the Apollo astronauts—with almost the same intimacy as my own home. To presidents and statesmen whose inaugural events and funerals are held there, the Washington Cathedral is the national house of worship. To me, it was my first church—its pulpit a familiar perch, its nave a path I regularly processed, its repertoire of hymns as much second nature as the Lord's Prayer. On these hallowed grounds is where I was most challenged, learned invaluable lessons, made friends for life, and became who I am.

Mom and Dad didn't agree on much, but they sent me off to NCS with a frequent refrain of my upbringing: "Always do your best, and your best will be good enough." That meant they would not tolerate half-assed effort by me or Johnny, because we had all the skills we needed to excel. And if we truly tried, even if we failed, they would be proud of us—no matter the result. At the same time, they counseled us never to use race as an excuse or a crutch. Undoubtedly, my parents warned, we would face racial discrimination and must call out and fight bias wherever we encountered it. For many, they stressed, pernicious prejudice remains an enormous obstacle. Yet, Johnny and I were fortunate to have an excellent education and other rare opportunities; therefore, we would be wrong to blame race for our own failures or use race unfairly to our advantage. Our parents taught us, quite matter-of-factly, that we needed to be *twice as good* as the next (white) kid, because that is what it would take to be considered almost equal. At NCS, I came to understand exactly what they meant and held fast to that wisdom everywhere I went.

After a solid, if not exceptional, start, I kicked into high academic gear between eighth and ninth grade, once the worst of my parents' divorce was behind me. In this period, I seriously considered leaving NCS for boarding school at someplace like St. Paul's or Andover in New England. I had friends who loved these places and was excited by the prospect of a fresh start—an escape from the turbulence of my family life. My dad urged me to stay. His voice mattered, but it was another that ultimately swayed me. In the English Department office where we often talked after school, my public speaking and American literature teacher, Jim Tibbetts, was relentless. Using the nickname given me by my basketball teammates, which was short for "Sportin," Mr. Tibbetts argued, "Spo, you are loved and will knock the lights out here at NCS. You have too much to contribute and too much to gain to leave. Don't do it."

In his late thirties, Mr. Tibbetts was jovial, heavyset, and frequently bearded, playing Santa Claus at Christmas and fitting the part. He became a mentor and a close friend whose door was always open, a kind and supportive male figure who was not a parent but understood me and what I was going through at home. The amount of time we spent together raised some eyebrows, but our friendship was one truly of respect, trust, and humor—lasting through college, graduate school, and well beyond.

Having taken Tibbetts's advice, I stayed at NCS, benefiting enormously from excellent teachers and coaches who perceived my potential before I did.

Ruth Ann Williamson was a legend at NCS who had been teaching Medieval History for at least thirty years. Smart, demanding, and eccentric, Mrs. Williamson pushed us hard. One day at the end of seventh grade, she pulled me aside and said, "Susan, you are a talented young woman. If you apply yourself, and work for it, I believe you can win The Flag." Her conviction that I could actually win the coveted American flag that flies adjacent to the National Cathedral—the prize given annually to the senior class valedictorian—was catalytic. Surprised that she thought I could do it, and even more startled that she bothered to tell me, I tucked the thought away until high school, when I resolved to do my true best.

History was my favorite subject, and John Wood, who taught eleventh-grade modern European history, helped cement my fascination and build my skills, readying me for the inimitable Anne Macdonald. "Annie Mac," as we called her, taught AP U.S. history in twelfth grade. Her course was tough and riveting, requiring us to conduct primary research at the Library of Congress, where I prepared my thirty-page paper on poverty in Appalachia. Mrs. Macdonald wrote me the most generous letters of recommendation, warranting that I had rare talents as a scholar, leader, and potential politician. An old-school Republican, she may have been the first person to tell me I should be president of the United States.

Mrs. Macdonald's words struck a chord with me, because at the age of ten, I had made up my mind that I wanted to become a U.S. senator.

I knew several senators and members of Congress; they were the parents of my friends, many of whom came from across the aisle. In that long-lost bipartisan environment in which I grew up, relationships were not constrained by politics but rather forged in compatibility and shared interests. Starting at Beauvoir, my classmates and I took field trips to Capitol Hill and toured the offices of members of both houses, including Senator Bill Brock (R-TN) and Representative Richard Ottinger (D-NY), the fathers of two of my closest early friends. I saw what senators did—make speeches, meet constituents, work on important issues. Politics was hot, and my hometown was hopping with the electricity of government.

———

Coming of age in D.C. in the late 1970s and early 1980s, I was steeped in models of leadership and exemplars of public service.

Vividly, I recall watching Egyptian president Anwar Sadat wave triumphantly as he walked into the Egyptian embassy across the street from my mother's house on Massachusetts Avenue. Secret Service snipers had requisitioned her roof. Sadat had just signed the 1979 Egypt-Israel Peace Treaty, ably negotiated by President Carter. It was a moment powerfully imbued with history, made more memorable by the fact that, just three years later, Sadat paid the ultimate price for daring to make peace with Israel, cut down in Cairo by assassins' bullets.

Soon after began the torturous 444 days during which we, like all Americans, feared and prayed for our fifty-two hostages seized in the takeover of the U.S. embassy in Tehran. Held by student revolutionaries backed by the extremist Iranian regime, these American hostages were public servants, mainly diplomats and military personnel, captured and tormented in the line of duty. On the January day in 1981 when they finally came home, cruelly released just after Carter left office, our nation rejoiced and honored the hostages with a huge parade down Pennsylvania Avenue. Yellow ribbons hung everywhere, and standing along the parade route I felt the enormous sense of collective relief.

Thereafter, I was swiftly reminded that the risks incurred by our country's public servants are not limited to those stationed overseas, nor to rank-and-file officials. In March 1981, shortly after taking office, President Ronald Reagan was shot and nearly killed outside the Hilton Hotel, just blocks from my mother's house, and we heard the sirens as they whisked him to George Washington University Hospital. Americans were shaken by such a brazen assassination attempt in our capital city. While I strongly disagreed with Reagan's policies, he was our president and an honorable man who had nearly given his life in service to our country. To me, his sacrifice, that of those injured, and of the diplomats, development officers, military personnel, and intelligence officers who operate daily in harm's way, was emblematic of the nobility of public service.

Within one city, I was exposed to consequential events from the local to the global that reinforced in me the importance of competent leadership, effective government, and wise public policy. The business of Washington was fascinating, and I wanted to be part of it.

My enthusiasm was tempered only by the realization that I lived in the one place on the American mainland that had *zero* U.S. senators. Washington, D.C., had no voting representation in Congress, and we still do not. As I argued passionately for the liberal side to my conservative colleagues at one of our weekly Government Club debates: "D.C.'s disenfranchisement is one of the major injustices of our political system. Over seven hundred thousand people pay full federal taxes. They can be conscripted into war but have no right to elect leaders whose votes count in Congress." This purgatory appears all but permanent, given that change would require a constitutional amendment, and Republicans have long wished to deny heavily Democratic D.C. a full voice in Congress.

When I decided to become a U.S. senator one day, I knew all of that, so I was an early and strenuous advocate of D.C. voting rights, even as I considered adopting a home state in adulthood. My teenage plan was to run for the House of Representatives before eventually trying for the Senate. To me, both chambers were interesting and important, but back then the Senate seemed more stable, sober, and collaborative than the rough-and-tumble House. As I set out to learn as much as possible about Congress and public policy, my path after college seemed clear: go to law school, practice law, get established locally, and, at the right moment, run for Congress.

My first job in life was as a Democratic page in the U.S. House of Representatives. In the summer of 1979, having just completed ninth grade, at fourteen I was thrilled to earn $600 per month. My mom got me the position through a member of Congress she knew from her work on educational policy. Like many congressional jobs then, a House page was a patronage appointment, one doled out by members based on seniority. Even without a home state and an influential representative to importune,

I, like several of my NCS and St. Albans peers, was able to get a summer job in Congress, because my mother had juice.

As pages, we all wore white shirts and blue pants, and our job was to deliver internal mail and packages between House offices. Given excessive freedom and independence, the only mortal sin we could commit was to throw our parcels into the regular mail. Democratic and Republican pages mingled and socialized, as many lived together at Thompson-Markward Hall, a dormitory on Capitol Hill. With a shared passion for politics, they came from all over the country, though very few were minorities. As a locally based page, I lived at home and rode the Metro to and from the Capitol.

Back then, there was virtually no adult supervision of this large summer posse of teens, aged fourteen to nineteen. In an era when young people partied hard and the drinking age in D.C. was eighteen, fellow pages smoked pot even in the garage of the Rayburn House Office Building. Weekend parties were routine, and I attended my share.

One Saturday night, I rode to a party in Virginia with a group of pages. The driver was Rebecca Moscone, a lovely, fun college freshman who six months earlier had lost her father, San Francisco mayor George Moscone, to assassination at City Hall. Living that summer at the home of Congressman John Burton, a friend of her father's, Rebecca had borrowed his car.

We left the party before midnight, and none of us, including Rebecca, was significantly intoxicated. Merging onto the highway, suddenly we heard the screech of metal on metal and watched in horror as our car ground into the side of a fast-moving Exxon oil tanker. Only an extended sideswipe, our car was damaged, but we were all okay. Our biggest fear was the reaction of the famously explosive congressman to news that we had wrecked his car. When Rebecca reported the accident the next morning, with all due contrition, his response was abbreviated and pointed, "Aaaah, fuck it," he said. Crisis averted.

Members of Congress were generally friendly and courteous to pages—joking, teasing, and telling us stories. Despite subsequent allegations of sexual misconduct by members with pages, I never saw or heard of anything untoward.

Still, as a fourteen-year-old page, I had my earliest and most jarring experience with sexual harassment. The twenty-two-year-old perpetrator worked as a doorman who controlled access to the House floor, a patronage job he landed courtesy of a family member. As I passed through his door, he would make flirtatious, sometimes outrageous comments. I would generally ignore him and keep walking into the House chamber. Then, one day after work, when I was waiting on the Metro platform at the Capitol South station, he approached me. Getting extremely close, he told me how he planned to do unprintable things to me with his tongue. Shocked and scared, I told him forcefully to leave me alone. He did not bother me again, but to this day I cannot forget how demeaning and disgusting he was.

Unfortunately, I have seen him multiple times since, though I always keep my distance. Now an elected official, he would likely deny any wrongdoing and may not even remember his offensive actions, but I pray he has never again sexually harassed or assaulted anyone. As jarring as his abusive behavior was, I am lucky. After I demanded he stop, he relented, and the experience did not scar me in any lasting way. Fortunately, in all my subsequent years of working in male-dominated environs, I never experienced other disturbing instances of sexual harassment beyond crude jokes, loose hands, and obnoxious comments, which I managed to parry or deflect.

Despite that doorman, I returned to Capitol Hill for each of the next three summers, taking on increasingly challenging assignments that deepened my knowledge of policy and the legislative process. It was my privilege to be sponsored by the wise and kind Representative Augustus "Gus" Hawkins (D-CA), one of the most senior African American members and chairman of the House Education and Labor Committee. Bald, compact, gentle, and soft-spoken, Mr. Hawkins quietly but effectively championed civil rights, employment and training, and education legislation, while serving as a model of civility. He was the outstanding member who served tirelessly for the greater good, not personal advancement.

My admiration for Mr. Hawkins, combined with those four summers on Capitol Hill, fueled my drive to serve in Congress, even as I became increasingly aware of its shortcomings. Legislative stagnation and many members' unabashed egotism injected a measure of realism into my idealized view of Congress—and this at a time when the House and Senate functioned comparatively well, and bipartisan cooperation was not an oxy-moron!

———

Summers exposed me to policy and politics, with the former becoming my calling, but as soon as September came, I dove back into the usual stuff of high school—academics, sports, extracurricular activities, and my social life.

Through varsity tennis and basketball, I learned how to be a team player, play to win, and eventually lose with grace (which I did frequently as a mediocre point guard). My first high school basketball coach had a profound impact on me. A hard-ass—raw, rough-edged, and barely out of college—she was the opposite of our typically refined teachers. Coming from a big, Catholic, working-class family in New Jersey, she had little patience for the pretentious, coddled girls at NCS, whom she ribbed mer-cilessly as soft little rich kids. To toughen us up, she kicked our butts, mak-ing us run more full-court suicides than any of us could endure.

Coach also took our team to a new level of play and cohesion, giving us each detailed individual feedback. She advised me to play with more confidence on offense—using my legs and putting more arc and backspin on my shot, concentrating on the square above the basket when executing driving lay-ups, and honing my ball-handling skills. We learned how to push ourselves and play real ball, not the effete game that many of her con-temporaries favored. We all loved our coach, and she came to love us back.

So I was surprised one day at practice when in conversation with the team on the sidelines of the gym, for no apparent reason and without ran-cor, she looked me in the eyes and called me "Nigger."

Reflexively and immediately, I replied, "Fuck you."

That was the end of that conversation. My teammates were stunned into silence.

I was shocked but not hurt. We both moved on. While I've never for-gotten her epithet, I never blamed her for it. And she never blamed me for responding in kind. I understood that the N-word was likely one she heard growing up. It came out involuntarily and not maliciously, but I also knew it could not go unanswered. Cussing out a teacher was something I have not done before or since.

Unfortunately, she stayed at NCS only for my freshman and sophomore years before leaving to marry and coach at the college level. Basketball was never as fun without her, but she kept in touch, following our team's progress and writing letters to me and other students long after she was gone. In them, she offered me thoughtful tips about setting personal goals in basketball, not letting myself get wrapped up in other people's expectations, whether athletic or academic, and insisted that I "be Susan Rice always."

Some thirty-five years later, during the 2012 Benghazi drama when I was regularly reviled on cable television, Coach sent me another handwritten letter, in which she apologized for ever hurting me, thanked me for my service to our country, and said she was inspired by me and would keep praying for me. I cherish that letter and keep it close.

Sports taught me to be fearless—even to use my body as a weapon. While enduring the frustration of sitting on the bench, I reveled in the success of my teammates. Playing point guard taught me how to lead a team in which everyone adds value, and my optimal contribution is not as an individual but is in eliciting the best performance from all the players in unison. Undoubtedly my approach to leadership in the years to come was forged not only in academia but also on the court.

Off the court, I devoted much of my energy to student leadership. As president of the school government in my senior year, I developed early political skills—public speaking, persuasion, and constituent service. My responsibilities also included helping the headmaster and senior faculty manage disciplinary cases and revise and enforce the honor code. I found the added stress of these adult obligations to be considerable—especially in combination with a rigorous course load and sports. While I relished serving my fellow students and being trusted by the faculty, I couldn't be serious all the time.

Like most teenagers, I found refuge in good friends and was closest to a trio of girls who later were my bridesmaids and remain besties. Laura Richards is kind, soft-spoken, sympathetic, and blessed with both intelligence and unusual common sense. Trinka Roeckelein is a high-octane, beautiful, and sensitive artist with multiple creative talents. With Andrea Worden, an excellent student and athlete (and far better basketball player than I was), I shared family difficulties, plus an enduring interest in China and human rights issues.

Over the years, I have stayed close to several other cherished NCS classmates, including Hutchey Brock, my first close Republican friend. The Brock family lived near the house my mother rented after the separation. When I was angry, sad, or needed a respite, I ran to Hutchey's house where I always found a welcoming safe haven. Their gentle Tennessee warmth and cohesive, loving family were a powerful antidote to the wreckage of my parents' marriage and a proximate example of a healthy home.

Given the racial composition of my school—there were about six black girls in my class of sixty-three students—most of my NCS friends were white. My social circle outside of school was little more diverse, because our parents insisted that, just as we would not join white elite dance societies or country clubs (even if we could), the Rices would not retreat within the walls of exclusively black kids' clubs. That applied especially to the D.C. chapter of Jack and Jill, a selective national social club for black children, which our parents refused to allow us to attend. When one of us questioned this edict, my parents' response was: "We may be relatively well-off blacks, but are not going to be 'bougie,' self-important, social-climbing Negroes."

At NCS, I never felt that race infused or affected my relationships with my white friends. My classmates knew and respected me for who I was, including the fact that I was African American, and they did not treat me differently than others. Not so all their parents, many of whom were quietly unreconstructed southern conservatives who belonged to segregated country clubs. (I emphatically exclude the Brocks from this category.)

At our Episcopal school, there were also few non-Christians, only a smattering of foreign students, and a small but robust cadre of Jewish girls. These friends generously invited me to Passover seders and to synagogue for special occasions, teaching me to love the decency and moral clarity of Judaism, particularly the socially conscious tradition of Tikkun Olam—repairing the world.

These insights came in handy when, at fourteen, I traveled with my dad and brother on a TWA Board of Directors' trip to Egypt and Israel.

It was late March 1979. We arrived just as the Egypt-Israel Peace Treaty was signed in Washington and six months after the Camp David Accords. In Egypt, we cruised down the Nile River Valley from Luxor to Aswan, exploring the major tombs and historic sites. In Cairo, we visited the Antiquities Museum and the Great Pyramids at Giza.

From Egypt we flew to Israel on the first-ever direct flight between the two countries. We stayed at the King David Hotel in Jerusalem and visited the Old City, Temple Mount, and the Holocaust memorial, Yad Vashem. Traveling east to Jericho and south to climb Masada, we floated in the Dead Sea and visited a working kibbutz. I loved Israel, with its energy, bustle, and idealism, and I felt later on, as a diplomat, that I was returning to a familiar place. In that fleeting moment in 1979, in contrast to my many later visits, Israel seemed like one of the most hopeful places on earth.

My own religious education came almost entirely from school, not home. While Dad had firmly rejected organized religion, Mom held on to her Episcopal faith mostly for purposes of weddings and funerals. From Beauvoir through graduation, I was steeped in the Episcopal Church, attending Friday services in the Cathedral and an additional chapel service during the week. Our parents left religion entirely to our own choice. While I was baptized Episcopalian as a baby, Johnny was not baptized at all. My mother confessed she felt badly about having left Johnny hanging but not enough that she rectified it. The Reverend John T. Walker, bishop of Washington through most of my time on the Cathedral Close, was a brilliant, socially committed, progressive African American leader, who helped draw me to the Episcopal Church. My faith deepened as I progressed in school such that, in eleventh grade, I decided to be confirmed.

Despite my confirmation, I can lay no claim to being a dutiful child of the cloth. Throughout high school, I continued to travel in the social crowd, seeking fun and a release from the pressures of family, school, and the wider world. Our partying became more frequent, and my friends and I became increasingly adept at hiding our escapades, even as we drank plenty of alcohol, smoked pot occasionally, and worse, drove intoxicated. Once, after our last exam of senior year, a large group of us celebrated by going drinking. After roaming the neighborhood, we returned to school where, overcome by nausea, I surreptitiously puked my guts out. Unable to make my own way, my friend Laura (who had not been drinking) drove me home in the late afternoon and deposited me in bed before Dad could discover what was up. I was never caught by my parents or teachers, nor do I think they even suspected me of wrongdoing.

Conscious at the time that I was living one step from catastrophe, I took risks in high school that back then seemed manageable, if slightly foolish. In retrospect, through the eyes of a mature adult and parent, I am struck by my own irresponsibility. Much as I still love a good throw-down and have used dance parties to break diplomatic ice, I look back on my teenage recklessness with due remorse.

This Washington, D.C., private school social life later became infamous during Brett Kavanaugh's Supreme Court confirmation hearings. Though I never met Kavanaugh in high school, he was my contemporary, and we have friends in common. Watching the testimony was traumatic, bringing back uncomfortable memories of this dangerous period filled with "BEER," unauthorized parties, and sex. Neither I nor (to my knowledge) any of my good friends experienced sexual assault in high school, but we easily could have been assailed by drunken boys in much the same way as Dr. Christine Blasey Ford recounted, or worse. But for the grace of God . . .

In a separate matter, I deliberately lagged the crowd. Several friends chose to lose their virginity before graduation; I did not. Though I had high school boyfriends, I took my mother's wisdom to heart without argument or question. "Susan," she would say, "always treat your body as a temple. There is nothing more important than your self-esteem, and the quickest way to ruin it is to have cheap sex with someone you don't really care for." Her message was especially powerful, because she made sure I knew that she always had my back. "Please use birth control, but if something ever goes wrong, I'm here for you and you must come to me." That was her mantra, and I heeded it.

————

In our highly competitive small school, college admissions were substantially a zero-sum game. Only two or three girls could expect acceptance to Harvard or Yale, which for many parents was the gold standard. Against this backdrop, I sensed that some parents of my classmates had suggested to their daughters, that because I was black, I would likely do well—better than I should—in the college admissions process. Their assumption that I would benefit from affirmative action, rather than succeed on the merits, stung and underscored these parents' fundamental belief that I was less worthy than their daughters.

Touring colleges, I was drawn to Yale's intellectual and social climate and decided to apply there "early action," which would enable me to learn of their decision before Christmas but not have to commit until the regular admissions process played out in late April.

Pleased and relieved to receive an acceptance letter from Yale over the Christmas holiday, I decided also to apply to Stanford. Mom had taken me and Johnny to visit Stanford years earlier, and I recalled fondly the great weather, beautiful campus, and the whacky marching band whose albums I was given as a child by Fred Hargadon, the legendary dean of Stanford admissions. My mother did not share my attraction to Stanford, which she dismissed as too far from home and inferior to Harvard, her own alma mater. Indeed, in the early 1980s, except in California, Stanford was not yet widely viewed as being quite as good as the best Ivy League schools. Mom insisted that, if I were to apply to any more schools, I must also try at Harvard.

In mid-April, I faced what is fairly called a "high-class dilemma." To help me decide, I visited Stanford again for the first time in years. I loved it—the sun, the fun, the easygoing attitude but serious academics—and didn't care that it was not an Ivy League or far from home.

On the way back, my plane got diverted to Nebraska because of an April snowstorm in the East. I had to spend the night on the frigid floor of the Omaha airport, while I wondered all night—*How am I going to forgive myself if I choose to go to New England and freeze my ass off from November through April?* It also seemed like time for a break from the East Coast preppiness and pressure I had lived with all my life—a chance for fresh perspective and less stress.

Mom, however, was dead-set against what she and Alfred derisively called "Leland Stanford *Junior* University." The heat was mounting from her, and it wasn't pleasant. Dad was cool either way and could see the merits of Stanford, given his love of Berkeley.

Yale wisely gave me space to decide, but not Harvard. I kept receiving increasingly harassing calls from the local alumni interviewer of prospective applicants. He had recruited me for Harvard and, apparently, it was his responsibility to land this fish. In our last call, after hearing me explain that I was seriously considering Stanford, he reiterated how superior Harvard was. Finding me unmoved, he shouted into the phone, "How can you not go to Harvard??!!"

Amazed, my response was brief and sharp: "Watch me." I then held my tongue, though I really wanted to add—*How? Because of arrogant assholes like you.* Instead, I packed up and moved to my godmother Peggy's house for the duration of the college decision period, both to escape my mom and Mr. Harvard.

The day our decisions were due coincided with the annual joint National Cathedral School–St. Albans Cum Laude Cathedral Service, when the top students in both schools are inducted into the honor society. That morning, in the shower, I decided to go to Stanford. It felt right, and I was sure of my choice. At the start of the processional at the Cathedral, I spotted my college guidance counselor and gave her the news, asking her to stay mum, since I hadn't yet told my parents.

After the service ended, I approached my mother and Alfred, who were sitting in the front of the Cathedral, with Dad nearby. Calmly, I said, "Mom, I've thought this through, and I've decided to go to Stanford."

My mother's face registered shock as she looked up at the immense stained glass window in the front of the nave and burst audibly and sloppily into tears, which both appalled and embarrassed me. Alfred comforted her. My dad congratulated me and moved on to dissociate himself from this insanity. To compound the trauma, the Harvard-educated father of a Harvard-bound classmate hugged my mother, consoling her with the words, "Oh Lois, I am so sorry." As if her daughter had died. I walked away in disgust. Mom remained inconsolable.

Only years later did she concede the wisdom of my decision.

———

My senior year at NCS ended on an early June weekend devoted to Flag Day, the honors ceremony, and graduation. Rain had forced the traditional Flag Day ceremony from the beautiful grassy lawn into the cavernous Ca-

thedral. All the graduating seniors assembled in the crossing of the Cathedral wearing long white dresses, each carrying a dozen red roses. My
parents sat somewhere in the nave, proud and satisfied that I had done my
best—with or without any final honors. As I prepared to leave the Cathedral Close after fourteen years of intense and powerful education, I felt
both exhausted and fulfilled, yet confident I had developed the skills and
the character to weather whatever might come next.

At Flag Day, I expected to win a couple of awards, maybe for history
and for citizenship, but not The Flag. As the ceremony wound down, I
had garnered some five awards, well exceeding my expectations. So, with
little stress, I awaited the announcement of the last award, The Flag. I was
surprised to hear "Susan Elizabeth Rice" announced as the winner, along
with my classmate, Catherine Toulmin, whom I was betting would win it
solo. It would not have occurred to me to aim quietly for The Flag, if not
for Mrs. Williamson's direct challenge in seventh grade.

That victory was sweet, especially because I imagined it would shut
down the parents of some of my white classmates who were telling their
daughters that I had gotten into the best colleges mainly because I was
black. Their ease at dismissing my capabilities infuriated me and also engendered some dichotomous feelings about affirmative action. Now, it
was clear: I may be black; but objectively by their standards, I was also the
best. They had to deal with that.

My father's daughter, I decided to let race be their problem, not mine.

5

Go West, Young Woman

*L*ate in 2007, I took a lengthy leave from the Brookings Institution to serve full-time as an unpaid policy advisor, surrogate, and spokesperson for the Obama campaign.

One hotly debated issue arose around the same time, when Obama and his senior advisors wrestled with a proposal that the candidate make an extended foreign trip. The campaign had long seen the potential benefits of a major tour abroad, which was high-risk but, if successful, high-reward. It was an opportunity for Obama to show his command of foreign policy issues and to be seen as presidential overseas, while also demonstrating his popularity abroad to American voters at home, particularly those who lamented America's diminished global leadership following the Iraq War.

The political strategists on the campaign originally argued for a European trip in late 2007, before the Iowa caucuses. Tony Lake and I thought the trip was a great idea but that the proposed timing was a major mistake. In those days, Obama had no standing, not yet having won a single primary. He was behind in the polls, still relatively unknown abroad, and unlikely to be taken seriously by foreign counterparts. On a conference call with Obama and his senior advisors to debate the timing of the trip, I interjected at the end: "Senator, the trip is a good idea, but you should go next year after securing the nomination. Going now is like running the 1982 Berkeley lateral play through the Stanford Band at halftime rather than in the last seconds of the game."

There were enough college football enthusiasts on the line for my point to land its punch. Folks were silenced for a short spell. Whether it was the effect of the analogy or surprise that the only woman on the call offered it, my logic seemed to prevail. Ultimately, Obama decided to wait until the summer of 2008 to take the trip.

Even once Obama was the nominee, such a trip promised to be a public relations and logistical high-wire act, especially without the policy support and infrastructure of the U.S. embassies. With campaign policy staff, my role was to help ensure that Senator Obama was prepared in substance for all of his bilateral meetings and that we got the policy right, while others coordinated our advance teams, transportation, and the large traveling press corps.

Following an official visit to Afghanistan and Iraq in his capacity as a U.S. senator, Obama continued on a campaign-sponsored swing through Jordan, Israel, Germany, France, and the U.K. I joined him throughout the campaign portion, mindful that, above all, we could not afford to make any mistakes.

In Israel, which was the trickiest leg of the journey, Obama deftly balanced his meetings with Prime Minister Ehud Olmert and opposition leader Benjamin Netanyahu in Jerusalem, and with Palestinian president Mahmoud Abbas in the West Bank town of Ramallah. To underscore his concern for Israel's security, Obama visited the southern Israeli town of Sderot, where Hamas rockets from Gaza regularly and cruelly rained down on Israeli homes. He paid his respects at Yad Vashem, the Holocaust memorial, and placed a personal message in the Western Wall. Despite arriving just after a horrific bulldozer terrorist attack in Jerusalem, Obama's visit proceeded smoothly.

In Germany, Obama delivered a major policy speech to a massive crowd of Berliners assembled at the Victory Column in the Tiergarten, where he stressed his commitment to work collaboratively with our European allies. I joined him as he met for the first time with a rather quizzical, if not skeptical, Chancellor Angela Merkel, who seemed unsure what to make of her wildly popular visitor. In France, its flamboyant president Nicolas Sarkozy all but endorsed Obama at a press conference set up as if for a visiting American president. In London, Obama met with Prime Minister Gordon Brown and opposition leader David Cameron in a more staid set of discussions, leavened by Cameron's hip gift to Obama of a box of CDs, underscoring their generational parity.

The trip ended without a hitch. Obama hit it out of the park, and the cam-

paign had substantially deflated the arguments of those who insisted that Obama was not ready to be president.

Upon our return in late July, the campaign's focus turned to the convention, debate preparation, and soon, transition planning. In addition to my other responsibilities, I was assigned to co-lead the national security transition team.

Throughout that fall, I felt like we were entering uncharted territory. There would be a new president, but we didn't know who or whether America had an appetite for real change. He would have to cope with a massive recession, but no one knew quite how deep or long-lasting it would be. At a personal level, I would either be staying at Brookings through the start of yet another Republican administration or returning to government in some unknown capacity.

That same sense of uncertainty and anticipation, tinged with hopefulness, recalled another fall during a much earlier turning point in my life—when I first left home for college. Heading west to Stanford, I was finally escaping the confines of the familiar and the constraints of other people's expectations, feeling free at last to forge my own way.

———•◆•———

Just before I left for college, Dad took me to a quick dinner at McDonald's to give me some parting advice. To underscore his seriousness, after we started eating, he pulled out a couple small pages of handwritten notes. I didn't recall his prior lectures coming with crib notes, so I listened with extra attentiveness. When he finished, I asked, "Dad, do you mind if I keep those notes?"

"Sure." Dad grinned, and handed me his scribbles, which I have preserved to this day.

On this occasion, when I think Dad felt a special duty to send his firstborn off as well-equipped as possible, his teachings were unusually pithy and wide-ranging. Dad's notes, just jots, condensed his advice into five numbered points:

1. Use of Time: Time is my "most valuable asset." I must "plan its use and manage it wisely."
2. Work: I must have high standards for my work and "learn to enjoy it, plan it, set goals."
3. Trust: "Trust is very tricky. There is no substitute for good judg-

ment about people." I must "know what I think at any given time but be flexible and prepared to change my mind—to upgrade or downgrade my judgments, including of people, without waiting for a crisis or confrontation." He also insisted: "In love, trust is an essential element. Be careful."

4. Take Care: I must "take good care of my mind and body," manage stress and care for my "mental and physical hygiene."

5. Philosophy: For my soul, I needed to formulate a "comforting, persuasive, pervasive philosophy of life."

While Dad made sure I packed his wisdom, it was Mom who ensured I actually made it across the country with all of my stuff together. I was very appreciative that she came with me out to Stanford to help me get settled at the start of my freshman year. Following the fiasco in the Cathedral, Mom had tried to be more supportive, not necessarily of my college choice, but of me. Before she left, Mom gave me a big hug and, as she always did, made a point of stressing, "You know how much I *adore* you," reminding me how proud she was of me as her daughter.

Despite requesting an all-freshman house, which I thought would be more fun, I was placed in a more sober four-class coed dorm. Still, I made good friends in both my dorm and beyond; for the first time, my social set came from various racial and socioeconomic backgrounds—fully reflective of the diversity of California and the larger country.

And then, there were boys! Coming from an all-girls school, I relished a coed environment where smart and attractive men were plentiful. It was like gazing at an all-you-can-eat buffet! In my first weeks, I went to plenty of fraternity parties, football games, and freshman events, meeting several guys who piqued my interest, but I was in no hurry.

Barely into my first week, however, I met a nice, cute senior at an ice cream social thrown by upperclassmen for freshmen in our dorm. He was tall and thin with gorgeous curly brown hair, soft eyes, and a great smile. I will always remember every detail of our first encounter.

He introduces himself and asks me where I am from. I announce proudly, "Washington, D.C." (because out west, you need to specify your Washington).

I ask him where he is from, and he says, "British Columbia." I pause to wrack my supposedly well-educated brain, thinking—*Where the hell is British Columbia?* I quickly deduce: Colombia is in South America. There is British Guyana and French Guyana. Maybe there is also a British Colombia.

So, I hazard: "Is that in South America?"

He looks at me quizzically like I am the biggest idiot he has met at Stanford. "No," he replies dryly, "it's in western Canada."

Almost four decades later, my husband, Ian Cameron, has never stopped giving me a hard time about our first encounter. In fact, he got more mileage out of that story the higher I rose in the diplomatic ranks.

After failing my geography test, I next encountered Ian a few days later at the first Stanford home football game. To this sunshine, bikini, and shorts affair, Ian and his buddy Paul Fisher had brought a cooler of gin and tonics, perfect for the hot weather. By the third quarter, I was feeling good enough—and Ian was looking good enough—for me to drape my arms around his neck and shoulders (while standing one step above him in the bleachers, since he is over a foot taller than me). I can't remember if Stanford won or lost, but I do recall going fountain-hopping with Ian and the Stanford Band (a postgame tradition when there is no drought).

At the start of November, then fully smitten, I called my mom to share that, "I met this guy. He's wickedly funny and extremely nice. It might be starting to become something. He sent me a dozen red roses—for Halloween!"

With November comes Big Game, the annual Stanford-Berkeley football contest that consumes the Bay Area. The 1982 Big Game, my first, was at Berkeley, so Ian and I made the trek across the Bay to Memorial Stadium. This time, I remember all too well what happened.

The game was tight throughout. With just a few minutes left in the fourth quarter, it was Cal 19, Stanford 17. Stanford quarterback John Elway threw a 29-yard pass on fourth down and 17 yards to go, from the Stanford 13-yard line. He managed to get the team into field goal range, and Stanford nailed the field goal with 8 seconds left. 20–19 Stanford, with 4 seconds on the clock. Our side was going crazy in the stands, and we incurred a 15-yard penalty for unsportsmanlike celebration on the kickoff.

Stanford started from its own 25-yard line and strangely opted for a squib kick. Cal fielded the ball and proceeded down the field. When the clock ran out, Stanford thought the Cal ball-carrier had been downed, and the Stanford Band along with many of our players swarmed the field in elation. But Berkeley kept moving downfield with a bizarre series of five consecutive laterals, plowing through the Stanford Band into the end zone and scoring by flattening a Stanford trombone player.

After tense deliberations, the referees ruled that the laterals were legal, and no Cal man was down. It was touchdown Cal! *WTF???!!* The 85th Big Game was awarded to Cal 25–20, on one of the craziest plays in college football history. We were stunned, then pissed, then devastated. "The Play," as it came to be called, was a low point of my Stanford experience, but years later provided a useful analogy with Barack Obama.

———

Academically, I found Stanford stimulating but not difficult. I have often marveled, truthfully, that "Nothing in life has seemed hard since NCS." High school had sapped nearly every ounce of initiative out of me. I came to Stanford exhausted, as the demands of academics, sports, and serving a voracious school administration as school government president had taken a toll on me. During my freshman year, I lacked the motivation to do much beyond the minimum—take classes, make friends, watch my soap operas, and spend time with Ian.

After graduating at the end of my freshman year, Ian stayed in Palo Alto and started his difficult search for an entry-level job in broadcast journalism. Eventually, he was hired by the tiny CBS affiliate in Eureka, California, as a reporter, producer, cameraman, weatherman, and weekend sports anchor. We managed to see each other on occasional weekends, when he or I could make the five-hour trek along the coast.

From Eureka, Ian moved to Ottawa, Ontario, to obtain his master's degree in journalism and later to work as a local TV news reporter in Canada's capital. We exchanged visits when we could and hoped our relationship would endure extended separation. By my junior year, Ian made clear that he hoped we might share a lifetime together, but we both realized how improbable it was—given how young we were and how much of life would intervene before either of us was ready to marry.

Not surprisingly, I was wary of committing to the first man I truly loved, worried about feeling trapped and never experiencing alternatives. Deeply skeptical of the sustainability of a happy, monogamous partnership, I confessed to Ian that I needed more than one data point—as it were—before getting married. In one of our many written exchanges of these years, I explained, *"I am a hyper-rational, super-empirical person. . . . I don't trust myself to rely solely on suspicion in making the biggest commitment of my life. My experience with my parents' divorce has made me scared and determined not to fail. What I seek is confidence, the confidence to believe my decision is an informed, correct one. I am not looking for someone or something better. I can't even imagine such a person. What I seek is confirmation of my suspicion that you are the person for me—and vice versa."*

The rational solution, we agreed, was that while we were living apart, we would remain a couple but could also date other people if we wanted. We adopted an explicit policy that equated to "Don't ask, don't tell." To this day, I have not asked what Ian did, but I took selective advantage of this freedom, which in my view probably enabled our relationship to survive years of long-distance.

———

After NCS, I was tired of student politics but wanted to deepen my knowledge of real-world issues. As a Washingtonian immersed in current events, I regretted that many very smart fellow Stanford students seemed uninterested in the major issues of the day. For me, Stanford was a constant reminder of how fortunate I was, including having a top-quality education when so many like me did not. Then, as now, structural inequality in the public education system, which persistently fails to serve poor students, means that most minorities will never have a true shot at social mobility. Like Mom, I felt driven to contribute to reducing educational disparities.

That passion led me to spend two summers working at the Black Student Fund (BSF), a nonprofit in Washington, D.C., that provides scholarships and support services to talented, low-income black students attending D.C.-area private schools. There, I wrote a guidebook for teachers seeking to incorporate black history and culture into their curricula. As a tutor/advisor, I also visited incoming students at their homes in the most distressed neighborhoods of the city, where crime, poverty, drugs, and parental neglect conspired to defeat or even kill these young people before they ever enrolled. Steeped in the economic and social stresses of low-income, inner-city students, I came to appreciate even more the crucial role, yet evident limitations, of government policy and dollars in ameliorating the causes and consequences of poverty.

Back on campus, I delved into several of these issues through my studies. As a history major, I took courses spanning Europe, the U.S., China, the Soviet Union, and Africa. A stand-out for me was "America in the 1960s," a class taught by Professors Barton Bernstein and Clayborne Carson (who later curated Dr. Martin Luther King Jr.'s papers at Stanford), in which we studied Vietnam, the civil rights movement, the Great Society, and the women's movement. It was a fascinating look at activism during a period I'd witnessed through a child's eyes, too young to understand. I was also energized by several political science courses, including Southern African Politics with Professor David Abernethy, which fueled my interest in Africa, and was able to explore areas outside my major, like poetry writing. A vehicle for introspection and emotional renewal, poetry for me was a space removed in which to observe and absorb the world around me, to feel whole. At Stanford, I was fortunate to study with leading poets, including the award-winning Denise Levertov and Peter Levi.

During my junior year, I got a respite from the nonchalance of the West Coast when I spent my winter and spring quarters at Stanford's newest overseas campus in Oxford, England—a great place to delve further into history and literature. I was enthralled by London—going to plays, concerts, and museums.

On one occasion, I attended a reading by the novelist, poet, and "womanist" Alice Walker. I had revered Walker for publishing her first book of poetry at twenty-four years old and winning the Pulitzer Prize for *The Color Purple*. So I waited in a lengthy, slow-moving line to ask her to sign my book. When I reached the front, I eagerly told her, "I really admire and respect you. I have dreamt for many years that I might equal your literary success at such a young age. It's a huge honor to meet you." Her terse, dismissive reply left me shocked and disappointed. I have never forgotten that deflated feeling and, in years since, even when under pressure or tired, I've tried to be kind to young women who come to me, as I did to Walker, to convey their admiration.

Overall, I had a blast during my junior year at Oxford: cooking elaborate dinners with friends in the intimate but well-equipped Stanford House on the High Street in Oxford; imbibing the English pub life; and traveling throughout Europe. Still, the distance of an ocean plus a continent between me and Ian was difficult in the era before email and cell phones. This was the period when Ian and I got into the habit of writing lengthy letters, which we cherish as a rare record of the evolution of our romance.

———

Not long after my return to Stanford for my senior year, I was delighted to host my brother for his first visit to campus as a college student. Following a challenging phase of his childhood in which he was hobbled by our parents' divorce and suffered as a skinny athlete at an all-boys school, Johnny had come fully into his own while at St. Albans. A handsome, popular boy, he became a top student, an outstanding athlete who played football, basketball, and baseball (plus tennis in the summers), and a confident, happy young man.

Though I had tried my best to woo him to Stanford, Johnny chose Yale, where he became the starting point guard on the varsity basketball team and distinguished himself as a successful student, Latin American Studies major, and mentor to young black fathers in New Haven. To my chagrin (as a committed nonjoiner), Johnny also became a proud member of Kappa Alpha Psi, a prominent black fraternity, as well as a Yale secret society. There, Johnny also met the wonderful woman he would eventually marry, Andrea Williams. As we grew into young adulthood, Johnny and I developed complementary strengths and weaknesses, such that we were able to elicit the best out of each other, while providing unvarnished criticism as needed.

In one important respect, Stanford gave me the opportunity to catch up to Johnny, who, as a child, had developed greater comfort and clarity about race. For me, college marked an important, if belated, step in the evolution of my own racial identity. Socially, I made a number of good black friends and enjoyed parties at Ujamaa (the black theme house), while also becoming involved in the campus anti-apartheid movement, which attracted many black students, among others.

One of my most powerful experiences was an unusual class called

"Group Communication." It involved no reading, only intense and very personal discussion among roughly thirty students about their experiences with race and ethnicity. I heard the stories of Alaskan natives, students who grew up in the East Los Angeles barrio, boat kids from Vietnam, biracial kids who didn't know whether they identified as black or white. Learning of their experiences exposed me to more complexity about identity than I had ever before understood. Standing before my classmates, who were open but not uncritical, I sucked up my courage to admit, "I'm uncomfortable with the fact that, intellectually, I fully understand and appreciate what it means to be black—our history, our burden, our responsibility. But socially and culturally, because I've spent most of my life in white environs, I feel behind the curve. Uncertain and uneasy."

There was still some distance to go to close that gap, and Stanford sped the process for me. In the past, I had occasionally been ripped by black kids for being an "Oreo"—black on the outside but white on the inside. I hated that insult mostly because it was racist and self-hating, but also because it failed to describe me accurately. In reality, I was more black inside than I knew how to be outside.

In parallel, my intellectual focus began to shift increasingly toward international issues: the legacy of colonialism, the obscenity of apartheid, the potential of Africa, the impact of superpower competition and the proxy battles of the Cold War, and the still real threat of nuclear annihilation. Looking to the future, I continued to aim for public service, having received a Truman Scholarship awarded to approximately one hundred top college sophomores committed to careers in government. To serve effectively as a U.S. senator, it was not enough to be knowledgeable about domestic and economic issues, I needed to be fluent in international affairs and adept at assessing global threats and opportunities.

This awareness is partly what inspired me to apply for the Rhodes Scholarship my senior year. As I told the selection committees, before attending law school my hope was to obtain a two-year master's degree in international relations from Oxford, gaining a unique perspective on international policy from studying on foreign soil. As a NATO ally, European Union member, and former colonial power, the U.K. promised to be a fascinating vantage point from which to dissect global issues.

With strong support from Stanford, I navigated two rigorous rounds of Rhodes interviews, the first at the state level for D.C./Maryland, and at the regional level for the Mid-Atlantic. When it was over, I emerged as among the four Rhodes Scholars selected for the Class of 1986 from the Mid-Atlantic. Two of the other three men, Elliott Portnoy and Joe Torsella, became my roommates in Oxford and lasting friends.

Late in my senior year, knowing I would soon study international relations in Oxford, I throttled back academically, setting aside my honors thesis, and became more active politically by ramping up my involvement with the campus anti-apartheid movement. By then, white Zimbabwe had yielded to majority African rule (in 1980). The apartheid government's crackdown on black dissidents in South Africa was in full force. President Reagan continued to resist the imposition of sanctions by Congress against the apartheid regime, when Archbishop Desmond Tutu delivered a galvanizing speech to a packed auditorium at Stanford. Tutu insisted that black South Africans "Don't want their chains polished; we want them removed." Incremental reforms were not enough; rather, the whole inhumane apartheid system must end. The college campus divestment movement was sweeping across the nation, but Stanford was engaged only tangentially and politely in the debate.

In 1986, Stanford boasted three of the thirty-two American Rhodes Scholars, an unusually high yield. Michael McFaul (political science and international relations major), Bill Handley (English major), and I were those selected. We became friends who shared an interest in the anti-apartheid struggle, even as the hypocrisy of accepting Cecil Rhodes's money, stolen from black Southern Africans, was not lost on us. We were not righteous enough to renounce our Rhodes Scholarships, but together we devised a plan to increase pressure on the university to divest in a smart, but nonconfrontational way.

With a top law firm, we established a nonprofit alternative endowment fund for Stanford alumni who wished to donate to the university but did not want to do so while Stanford continued to hold stocks in companies that invested in apartheid South Africa. The funds held by our nonprofit were to be available to Stanford, once it divested or apartheid ended. If neither occurred within ten years of the fund's establishment, the money would be donated to educational charities for black South Africans.

We launched the Free South Africa Fund at graduation in 1986—timed perfectly to ensure that Stanford president Donald Kennedy was mightily pissed. Kennedy, a wiry, balding, bespectacled biologist, had been a relatively popular president among students. Yet I came to see another side of him when he hosted graduating seniors and their families at his residence for Class Day. As my parents and I greeted President Kennedy in the receiving line, which wound along his broad lawn, he paused to berate me and condemn our initiative as destructive to the university. Pleased and surprised that he was so impressed with the potential power of our fund, I was not in the least flustered. My parents gave me "atta-boys" after we got out of Kennedy's earshot, proud that I was kicking up some righteous dust on my way out the door.

As it happened, the university never fully divested, but nine years later the Free South Africa Fund was dissolved in 1995, after apartheid had ended and Nelson Mandela had been elected president. The board of the Free South Africa Fund designated its remaining resources to a charity established in memory of a Stanford graduate and Fulbright Scholar who was murdered while doing research and volunteer work in South Africa. The Amy Biehl Foundation initially provided grants to Stanford students conducting scholarly research in South Africa. Looking back, the Free South Africa Fund was a potent political statement, though it never really threatened the university's fundraising efforts.

Graduation weekend was also memorable because my family came to Stanford—Johnny, Dad, Mom, and Alfred—and they all behaved civilly as they celebrated my achievement. After the commencement ceremony in the stadium, I returned with them to the History Department for my diploma ceremony. There, I was surprised to be granted my diploma not only "with distinction" as expected, but also with "Departmental Honors." This was strange, I thought, because I never completed my honors thesis. After the event ended, I intercepted a senior member of the History faculty to inquire, "I assume that a mistake has been made. My diploma says 'with honors,' but I didn't complete my thesis." She replied, "We know, but we thought that the body of your work in the major still warranted honors." I've always felt a little guilty about that.

My four years at Stanford really were a liberating, broadening experience—a time of intellectual stimulation, fun, and personal growth. Unburdened by the stresses of home life, I learned the extraordinary self-discipline that can only come from studying outside on the grass in beautiful weather while muscled, shirtless men play Ultimate Frisbee all around you. With Ian, I forged a mature relationship and gained confidence in my appeal to men, finally shedding much of the baggage of my mother's critiques of my appearance. Stanford was as close to heaven as I have ever come, and I often fantasize about going back to do another four years as an undergraduate.

6

Busting Out

On Election Day 2008, Ian and I rose early to get to the polls well before school started. Like many voters that morning, we took our children, Jake and Maris, then ages eleven and five, because we wanted them to experience the excitement of the moment and learn the importance of voting.

As we drove to our polling station in our neighborhood recreational center in the Palisades area of Northwest D.C., I could not help reflecting on the hard work and tough decisions that brought me and all of America to the point where we had the opportunity to cast our presidential ballots for Barack Obama.

Standing in the long and exuberant line at the polls on that crisp November morning, I was struck by how distant the past summer's foreign trip seemed as did all the hard work that preceded Election Day. None of it would matter unless Obama won. Although the polls were encouraging, I had learned from hard experience, most recently on the Kerry campaign, that polls are often wrong. In this case, I worried such surveys might be more wrong than usual, because no one could accurately assess how voters would truly feel about an African American candidate, once safely ensconced in the privacy of their own polling booths. It was white-knuckle time.

Ian, my Canadian-born husband, was not yet an American citizen, so he could not vote. That meant I had a crowd of three spectators looking intently over my shoulder as I marked my ballot, making sure I didn't mess up. After we dropped the kids at school, Ian flew up to New York to help manage ABC

News's election night coverage, and I headed alone to Loudoun County, Virginia, to knock on doors and encourage likely Obama voters to get out to the polls. It was the most important work that could be done that day, but also a healthy return for me to grassroots politics, which I had done little of since the early days of the campaign.

After I knocked on the last door that time would allow, I drove hurriedly back to Washington. Satisfied. Proud. Hopeful. Resolute in the knowledge that, win or lose, I had given everything to a mission I believed in deeply, now like every American I could only wait for the ballots to be counted and the results revealed.

———·◆·———

Multiple apprehensions loomed.

Having lived in Oxford for several months as a Stanford student, I understood that attending the university as an enrolled graduate student and a foreigner, outside the physical and psychic comfort of an all-American bubble, was sure to be a totally different experience—and not necessarily a good one. I was uncertain what would await me.

Leaving Ian to move across the Atlantic for at least two years was a far more consequential choice than studying abroad for a few months. We were hopeful about our future, but not ready to subordinate career and educational opportunities to our relationship, despite recognizing the considerable risk that, over time, one of us might be tempted away.

Another concern before first meeting the thirty-two American and eleven Canadian Rhodes Scholars on October 6, 1986, in New York City, was that I would dislike them—that as the "chosen ones" they would act as such: arrogant, pretentious, competitive, self-impressed, and determined to get what they wanted at others' expense.

The send-off luncheon hosted by the North American leadership of the Rhodes Trust only reinforced my fears. We gathered at the Harvard Club in New York the afternoon before we were to depart via British Airways for London-Heathrow. The setting was intensely formal. Men were required to wear business attire, and one of my new Rhodes colleagues, an unassuming young man from the Midwest, arrived without a coat or tie. Rather than offer him spare clothes, the doorman prevented him from joining our departure event.

Similarly, the parade of luncheon speakers assured us we were the cream of the elite. We should go forth and conquer, they said, acting as arrogantly as we wished—because we can and are worthy of it. It was breathtaking to witness, in the belly of the Harvard beast, how the most privileged actually perceive themselves—reminding me how glad I was to have selected Stanford.

Thankfully, my fellow Rhodes classmates far exceeded my expectations. Most were bright, humble, friendly, and self-effacing. Relieved, I wrote in an early letter to Johnny, "the asshole quotient" was blessedly low. Many of my colleagues came from modest backgrounds and over half were scientists, which suggested to me that they were unlikely to be ruthless, politically ambitious backstabbers. Over a third of my class were women, and four of the thirty-two Americans were African American. As time affirmed, this was a good group among whom I made lasting friends.

Our flight over to Oxford was a boozy but abbreviated voyage, a far cry from the long passage of prior years when scholars sailed on the *Queen Elizabeth 2*. The bus from Heathrow to Oxford dumped us randomly on the curb in small groups. We were expected to find our own way to our respective colleges scattered throughout the city. This was indicative of the whole Oxford experience—sink or swim. No briefing, no orientation, no coddling. You were expected either to know what to do or to figure it out. Fortunately, I recalled my way to New College, one of the more than thirty residential colleges that comprise Oxford University, and could guide a few colleagues to their destinations as well.

New College was unwelcoming. When a small group of us arrived exhausted and disoriented, we were met by the college porters who handed us our keys and merely waved in the direction of our dorm. "Over there, mates," was all the assistance we received. Wandering lost along the vague trajectory indicated, we eventually came upon the hideous Sacher Building, the residence for first-year graduate students. Most of our peers in other colleges were assigned to stately wood-paneled rooms in lovely old college entryways, while at New College we were consigned to a "modern," 1960s-era three-story concrete block, the antithesis of a traditional Oxford building.

Despite its familiarity, the contrast between Oxford and Stanford was jarring. Oxford was cold, damp, and dark—not just physically but also psychically and emotionally. The beautiful gothic spires, pristinely manicured gardens, and glorious ancient churches stood in contrast to the dirty, trash-infested streets, coal-laced soot that lightly blanketed outdoor surfaces, and the drunken dregs that emerged from local pubs promptly at eleven at night.

Until I made real friends, created comfort in my surroundings, and found my bearings academically, I felt fragile, even at times depressed. Much to my surprise, I discovered that among New College's some five hundred students, I was the only black person. There were a few dozen sprinkled elsewhere around the university, but at one of the biggest colleges, I was alone.

This realization should not have hit me so hard. Yet it left me feeling lost and bereft, searching for other faces of color. Eventually, I did find a small but committed cadre of black Oxonians, drawn from my American cohort of about a dozen to fifteen, plus several from the Caribbean and Africa, though no British blacks. Among this larger group, there were enough of us to gather informally for meals and games, dubbing ourselves the BBT (black brain trust).

In time, I adjusted to Oxford's gothic gloom: the biting, wet cold; the ancient buildings without central heating; and the stodgy, carbohydrate-laden, cooked-to-death food. The physical discomforts were minor inconveniences, which were counterbalanced by the considerable charms of the place—the historic libraries and Harry Potter–style dining rooms. The accessibility of the compact city, around which we biked everywhere even in the driving rain. The pubs; high tea with clotted cream and scones; sherry-, wine-, and port-laden dinners on "high table"; floating down Oxford's scenic rivers in small flatboats called punts; eating at Oxford's signature Jamaican, Indian, and Chinese restaurants (then the only consistently reliable cuisines); and frequent visits to London for the theater and better food.

Quickly, I made wonderful and soon-to-be-close friends, especially among the American and Canadian cohort of Rhodes and Marshall Scholars, and also with colleagues from Africa, the Caribbean, Australia, and New Zealand. Generally, however, British students had little time for us foreigners. Our collection of expatriates was close-knit, even though we were spread among various academic programs and colleges. Among my closest friends were three men—my housemates, Elliott and Joe, who cared for me like brothers, and Lance Bultena. Having traveled to Spain together, Lance and I bonded—over politics, philosophy, and a shared appreciation for poetry. A committed Republican from rural South Dakota, Lance is one of the smartest people I have ever met. We would stay up to all hours fiercely debating political philosophy and sharing stories of our disparate backgrounds. Everything in Oxford moved slowly by American standards and even more so by today's, but that snail's pace facilitated intimate conversations, leisurely walks, unhurried meals, and deep friendships.

The Oxford academic year consists of three terms from late September through June. My course of study was a two-year M.Phil (master's) degree in international relations, requiring core courses in political theory, history, and economics. To earn the degree, one had to pass a qualifying exam after spring break the first year, submit a thesis, and pass final exams at the end of the second year. In the meantime, our cohort of roughly fifteen master's students from all corners of the world attended weekly seminars, occasional lectures, and met one-on-one with our college tutors.

In both the seminars and tutorials, I was required to write and defend lengthy papers. The tutorial sessions were challenging, and I endured some pretty brutal criticism of my writing and analytical skills, something that temporarily shook my confidence, as I'd never felt academically inadequate in the U.S. It took me months to crack the code and write papers in the unique style that the Oxford faculty rewarded. I also struggled to be productive when I had so much free time. Though initially unimpressed by me, my New College tutor, Dr. Martin Ceadel, was patient and experienced with retraining Americans. He eventually managed to sort me out.

Despite Dr. Ceadal's best efforts, I almost flunked out of Oxford. In order to remain in the master's program, I had to pass the spring qualifying exam. Unlike at American universities where there is some compassion and flexibility, Oxford's rules cannot be bent or broken. If the exam is on date X at time Y, you must be there. No excuses. Not for being sick, dead, or otherwise indisposed. You miss it, you fail.

I had come back to the U.S. over spring break to be a bridesmaid in the wedding of my close high school friend, Laura Richards. Following the Saturday night wedding, my exam was set for Monday afternoon. I had booked myself on one of the few daytime flights from the East Coast to London, so I could arrive Sunday evening, get a good night's sleep, and be ready for the exam on Monday. After the reception, I came home Saturday night around 11 to finish packing and get ready to leave.

When gathering my valuables, I couldn't find my passport. Ian and I turned my mom's house upside-down looking for it. No luck. At 1 a.m., we drove across town and tore up my dad's house. No passport. Anywhere. I could not for the life of me imagine where the hell it could be. I only knew that we had to find it, or I would not make it back to Oxford in time. A passport could be obtained at the passport office Monday morning, but that would be too late for the exam. I panicked. *This could be the end of my Oxford experience.*

Just as freaked out, my mother kicked into high gear. At 3 a.m., she started going through her considerable Rolodex, calling various members of Congress to request their intervention to somehow get me a passport.

"Mom, please, stop. This is embarrassing and undignified. You can't keep waking up people all over Washington," I pleaded.

Undeterred, Mom then lit upon Mort Abramowitz, the assistant secretary of state for intelligence and research. Without any better idea, and seeing at least some hope of success, given that he was an actual family friend and worked at the right department, I relented and let her wake up the Abramowitzes. Mort was puzzled by the urgency but didn't argue.

He called the State Department Operations Center and miraculously managed to get the D.C. passport office to open for me on Sunday morning. The next day, Mort told my mom that he had an overnight house guest whom we had also awakened. Knowing Oxford well, their guest corroborated that making this exam was indeed critical.

A grumpy but obliging civil servant, Mr. Michael Persons, met me at the passport office. He directed me to where I could get a photo taken and issued me a passport on the spot, demanding only, "Let me know how that do-or-die exam goes." I am indebted to Mr. Persons but even more so to Mort and his wife, Sheppie, for saving my (academic) life.

I flew to London Sunday night, suffering a poor night's sleep in a cramped coach seat, but made it back in time for the exam. Wearing my short black exam gown, I eventually found my desk among the scores arrayed in the large wood-paneled exam hall. Relieved just to be present, if not in top form, I did not ace the exam but scored well enough to continue toward my degree. Though I have always been a little uncomfortable with my mother's readiness to importune the most powerful names in Washington, this time my mother's chutzpah saved me. I could not help but admire her long tentacles and willingness to use them on my behalf. It was an object lesson in networking.

———

I completed my M.Phil. degree with no further drama. My first two years at Oxford were my favorites, giving me the chance to try rowing crew, join an African American–led gospel choir, and play on the Oxford women's varsity basketball team. My game had improved considerably since high school—with more ball control and greater ability to see the whole court to set up plays. As the sole point guard, I started consistently and played throughout most games. Three of my teammates had been American college players, so we were pretty good, especially compared to the all-British teams.

I was pressed into performing in a major dramatic production of *For Colored Girls Who Have Considered Suicide/ When the Rainbow Is Enuf* by Ntozake Shange, produced by my good friend Terri Sewell. Terri convinced me I should play "The Lady in Blue." A bad-ass role with a lot of lines, it allowed me to tap in to my dramatic side. The cast and crew became some of my best friends in Oxford. Terri has since taken her organizing talents to Congress where she represents the 7th District, known as the Black Belt, in Alabama. Bonnie St. John, a para-Olympian skier, parlayed her extraordinary resilience into a career as a motivational speaker and author, while Lisa Cook, an esteemed professor of economics, became another daughter to my parents and a devoted auntie to my children.

Back in the day, however, it was arguably Robyn Hadley who impressed me most with her total unabashedness. My favorite example was our dueling interest in a particularly attractive American guy. Robyn made it simple. In her North Carolina drawl, she laid down her terms: "I'm giving you *FIVE* weeks. If you ain't on it, I'm ON it!" Appreciative of her grace, I suspected she probably knew she had me outmatched in guts. Sure enough, I was too reticent to hit on this man promptly and directly, and the weeks evaporated. Literally, five weeks to the day, Robyn was "on it," and they dated for several months.

That small but tight-knit circle of African American women formed the closest thing I ever had to a sorority, which I otherwise shunned. For the first time, I became fully at ease with who I am as a black woman. Finding that core group of African American friends (men and women) at Oxford was gratifying and more than a little ironic, since England was also the place where I faced some of my most overt encounters with racism.

Racial animus in Britain then was bald, without the refinement and comparative subtlety of America's version at the time. In this respect, living in England in the 1980s felt like the U.S. at least a generation prior. At New College where I lived and was a "member," I was afforded full dining and library privileges, a tutor, and a single room cleaned daily by a "scout." The "porters" manned the college gates and ensured that only members of the university and known guests were allowed to enter. Porters also handled mail, packages, and the pigeon post. In my early months, I had difficulty being deemed a rightful member of College. It was hard to discern the precise reason for this disparate treatment, because being black, female, or American alone could each test the reserve of the more snobbish Brits in Oxford. Representing all three rendered me a rare version of lower caste. The porters initially balked at handing me my mail, pretending that I did not (and could not) belong "to College." The bursar (treasurer) was slow to allow me to charge items to my bill, known as "battles," like any other member of College.

It was only after belatedly realizing I had to speak *their* English language—to harness the British class hierarchy to my benefit—that they stopped ignoring me and started treating me with respect. When next refused my mail, I finally spoke up in a clear, firm voice: "I am Susan Rice, a graduate member of this College. You will acknowledge my membership and ensure I get all my mail and other support from now on." I did not add a "please" or "thank you," because the implicit message I had to convey, however uncomfortable and unaccustomed, was "you are here to serve me." It worked, and thereafter I never had difficulties at New College.

The outside world was another story. While most English people I encountered were pleasant, or at least civil, there were some notable exceptions, like the Oxford city bus driver who slapped my hand sharply and chastised me loudly for taking my coins out of what was apparently the wrong side of the till: "You wait until I move the coins to the other side," he snapped. I was so surprised that I failed to react with appropriate indignation; yet I was sure he would not have struck a "typical" Oxford student.

———

Off the basketball court and outside the library, I stayed involved in the anti-apartheid movement. At Oxford, I had the great fortune of joining forces with black and white students from South Africa who had firsthand knowledge of the fight we were waging. Back home, over the summer, I brought my activism to my "other mother" Peggy Cooper Cafritz's dinner table in the Hamptons. Peggy's stimulating gatherings often included artists, actors, and other celebrities.

One night, Johnny and I joined her when she hosted the musician Paul Simon, who had recently released his album *Graceland*, which was partially recorded in South Africa. The album drew heavily on the musical talents of Ladysmith Black Mambazo and other black township artists who were relatively unknown in the U.S. *Graceland* was spectacular, and no one did more to expose Western audiences to South African musicians than Paul Simon.

At one point there was a lull in the conversation, and I dared to raise the issue of his decision to violate the cultural boycott, when many artists, performers, and companies of conscience were avoiding apartheid South Africa. With a hint of indignation, I asked, "Why did you have to record inside South Africa and bring tax revenue and legitimacy to the Boers?" Obviously sick of this critique, he responded civilly but impatiently, stressing the prominence he brought to South African artists.

I persisted, "Why couldn't you have flown the same South African artists abroad to record the whole album outside the country?" My willingness to provoke a debate and readiness to stand up for what I believe in, without regard for the consequences, made for an uncomfortable patch in the dinner, though nothing irreparable. Not persuaded by his argument, I still love that album.

From Oxford, I traveled widely throughout the U.K. and to Spain, Portugal, and Greece. In June 1987, a small group of Oxford friends and I also visited Moscow and Leningrad. The Soviet Union was still classically communist, and student trips were highly regulated, circumscribed experiences. We saw the Kremlin, Lenin's tomb, Red Square, Saint Basil's Cathedral in Moscow, and enjoyed the Hermitage and the midnight sun in Leningrad. On the streets, we bought old-style Stalinist posters and comrade clothing. It was a fascinating glimpse of the ruthless Soviet system before it collapsed.

Later that same summer, Ian and I backpacked through China for a month, which had barely begun opening to the West, the only tangible evidence being an inaugural Kentucky Fried Chicken restaurant off Tiananmen Square. There were few cars. Bikes and Mao suits were omnipresent. Little kids peed on the streets, squatting effortlessly in their bottom-less pants, and adults blew their snot onto the sidewalks as they speed-walked.

We began our low-budget journey in Hong Kong, flew to Beijing, and then made our way through much of the country by train, bus, plane, and boat. Arriving late at night at Beijing's airport without a hotel reservation, we were saved by puzzled Chinese eager to practice snippets of English and tell us where we could sleep. In Beijing, we visited the Forbidden City, the Summer Palace, Temple of Heaven, Tiananmen Square, Mao's mausoleum, and the Great Wall. Staying in cheap guesthouses and hostels, we traveled to Xi'an, Shanghai, Guilin, and Guangzhou.

With only a few words of poor Chinese to deploy, Ian and I patiently managed with gestures, our fascination with the country far outweighing our frustration. We came across numerous Chinese whose English was passable and were eager to engage an unusual short brown person coupled with a giant, skinny white guy. In this way, we encountered the Beijing Work Unit women's basketball team, who invited us to shoot hoops, discuss education, and take photographs. We found rural residents eager to show us around their villages. Naively, I wrote to my dad in a postcard, "Everything seems so open. It's very easy to forget you are in a communist country—no omnipresent military or police. People are open and helpful."

After four weeks, Ian had to leave, and I spent my final week visiting my close friend from National Cathedral School, Andrea Worden, who was teaching English in Changsha, Hunan province. Accustomed to few U.S. visitors, Andrea was delighted to welcome me to her small apartment, to play basketball with her students, and show me "normal" Chinese life off the beaten tourist path.

Our China trip was eye-opening, exposing us to rural and urban poverty of the sort we had not before seen, to China's profound history and culture, and to its seemingly long distance from achieving its evident potential. Ian and I proved that our relationship could endure the stress and intensity of a challenging trip and that, after years apart, we still enjoyed being together. Traveling rough in a deeply unfamiliar place with no language facility and little money was invaluable for building my confidence that I could go almost anywhere, adapt, and even thrive in very foreign lands.

Back at Oxford for my second year, Ian came to study for his master's degree in international relations at the London School of Economics, getting to know my Oxford friends. My return visits enabled us to explore London together. My Oxford years marked a significant chapter in my intellectual and social development. Had Ian and I not been able to share considerable portions of that experience, I wonder if our relationship would have endured.

At the end of my second year, I faced a major decision: should I return to the U.S. and attend law school, as planned; or stay at Oxford and convert my master's thesis into a doctoral dissertation on the role of the Commonwealth in the transition of Rhodesia to Zimbabwe? I was interested in doing more primary research, interviewing as many of the living protagonists as possible, and learning about how majority rule can emerge through peaceful means after a long, armed struggle, mindful of Zimbabwe's potential lessons for South Africa. I had taken the LSAT and still envisioned becoming an advocate for racial, social, or economic justice in the U.S. International relations was meant to broaden me, not become my destination.

———

"How many black lawyers do you know?"

"Tons," I replied, as I looked over my plate at Eleanor Holmes Norton. I was fortunate to be having lunch with Eleanor, who was then professor of Law at Georgetown University and since has been D.C.'s delegate in the U.S. House of Representatives.

She pressed on: "And how many black PhDs in international relations do you know?" I couldn't come up with any on the spot.

She continued to march me methodically through her logic. "How much do you enjoy your research?" Swiftly, I replied, "I love the topic and would welcome the chance to go to Zimbabwe to pursue field research."

"And, how old would you be when you are done with your dissertation?"

"Twenty-five," I said, expecting to be able to complete it within two more years.

"Well," Eleanor concluded, "if you love it, you should do it. Black PhDs in your field are rare. Black lawyers are a dime a dozen. If you finish your doctorate and still want to go to law school, you will only be twenty-five and have plenty of time to do so. I'd recommend you stay and get your degree."

Sold. I would get my doctorate in international relations. It seemed a minor deviation on my path at the time. But it turned out to be consequential.

At Oxford, I encountered plenty of ambitious Americans, several of whom wanted political careers. Though admiring their chutzpah, with time for self-examination I realized that I was not among them. Despite caring deeply about policy, I didn't have the patience or obsequiousness to run for office and was not keen on compromising my principles. Already disgusted by the growing role of money in politics and not good at asking others for help, I could not see constantly fundraising for myself rather than for a good cause.

Nonetheless, I took a few months' break from Oxford to work on the 1988 Democratic presidential campaign. Having completed my master's degree, I contacted Madeleine Albright, who had been kind to me since childhood. In the intervening years, she had obtained her PhD, worked for Senator Edmund Muskie, and served in the Carter White House on the NSC staff. Now a senior foreign policy advisor to presidential candidate and Massachusetts governor Michael Dukakis, Albright helped me get a job as a foreign policy aide on the campaign's Issues Staff, covering Africa,

Latin America, Ireland, parts of Asia, and aspects of international trade. My role was to liaise with outside experts, write policy papers and press guidance, fill out questionnaires from interest groups, and draft briefing memos for the candidate.

It was on the Michael Dukakis–Lloyd Bentsen campaign that I first worked with friends who would remain colleagues for the next twenty-five years: Gene Sperling, who later became national economic advisor; Sylvia Mathews (now Burwell), a close Oxford friend who rose to director of the Office of Management and Budget and secretary of health and human services; Michael Barr, another Oxford buddy who served as an assistant secretary of Treasury; and Nancy Soderberg, who went on to be staff director of the Clinton National Security Council and later alternate representative at the U.S. Mission to the U.N.

Together, we suffered through a depressing campaign marked by the racist Willie Horton ads run by Vice President George H. W. Bush and by a Democratic nominee who made memorable mistakes like riding as a short man in a tank with an oversized combat helmet. As November approached, it became clear we were going to lose badly. The campaign manager cleared out the headquarters, sending almost all of us away to get out the vote. I stumped in Prince George's County, Maryland, near home, enduring my first, but not last, soul-crushing losing campaign. While laid up in bed with a vicious flu for almost three weeks after our defeat, I cemented my view that electoral politics were not my thing. I would do policy.

————

After the campaign, I returned to Oxford and completed my PhD within two years, in December 1990. I delved into rich archival collections in Oxford and London and spent over a month doing field research in Zimbabwe, interviewing protagonists from both the government and opposition. I loved Zimbabwe, a spectacularly beautiful country with its red Flamboyant and lavender Jacaranda trees, impossibly balancing rocks, and a near perfect climate. In 1989, Zimbabwe was still comparatively prosperous and well-run, as its venal president Robert Mugabe had not yet become a complete autocrat who ruined the economy through extreme corruption and by seizing land from white farmers.

I was fortunate to have a fantastic thesis advisor, a renowned Oxford historian of Africa named Anthony Kirk-Greene. He was expert especially on Nigeria but had served as a British election official in Zimbabwe during the period I was studying. He guided me deftly through the dissertation process, which was leavened by his friendship, good wine, and convivial dinners at home with his lovely wife, Helen.

The advice Eleanor Holmes Norton gave me was excellent. Completing my dissertation is still the closest thing to giving birth I have experienced. Carrying the baby is often harder than the delivery, but the sense of joy and accomplishment when it comes is enormous. To add to the gratification, my thesis, "The Commonwealth Initiative in Zimbabwe, 1979–1980: Implications for International Peacekeeping," won the 1991 Chatham House–British International Studies Association Award for the most distinguished doctoral dissertation in international relations in the U.K. Once finished with my PhD, I was ready to be done with academia, including law school. I often wonder where I would have ended up had I continued on my original path. Sometimes I still think I missed my calling as a litigator.

My research trip to Zimbabwe, my first to Sub-Saharan Africa, whetted my appetite for more. After defending my dissertation, Ian and I set off in January 1991 on a month-long trip to Senegal, Niger, Ghana, and Côte d'Ivoire. As in China, we backpacked on a limited budget, but the infrastructure and accommodations in West Africa were far more rudimentary. The exception was Niger, where we stayed with my cousin, Valerie Dickson-Horton, who was the mission director for the U.S. Agency for International Development.

Niger—the arid land of the mysterious indigo-dyed, turbaned Tuareg traders—was fascinating. In Senegal, we traveled from Dakar and Goree Island to the Casamance in the south and to the Parc des Oiseaux on the northern border with Mauritania, where we were when the Gulf War began. Travel, which was mainly by bush taxi, was rough, and the poverty in Saint-Louis, the major city of the north, still stands out as among the worst I've seen. Raw sewage poured through trash-clogged streets, and most houses were made only of rickety sticks and mud.

In colorful, vibrant Ghana, we visited Accra, the slave castles on the Gold Coast, as well as the Ashanti heartland in Kumasi. Then the crown jewel of the former French West African empire, Côte d'Ivoire's economic capital, Abidjan, boasted fresh baguettes, the fancy Hotel Ivoire with its indoor ice-skating rink, and wealthy Frenchmen. Throughout our travels, we bought art that still adorns our house—batiks, metal and wooden sculpture, kente clothe, and Tuareg silver. The trip was the most interesting and taxing we have taken and reaffirmed that Ian and I could still manage together in challenging and unfamiliar circumstances.

West Africa marked a fitting conclusion to my Oxford years, a period of accelerated growth and maturation. I left feeling my independence was fully established, confidence strengthened, relationship with Ian solidified, and my circle of friends diversified and deepened, even as my ambitions remained unchecked. Oxford was a tremendous launching pad for whatever might come next.

———

Though still hoping that one day I might make public policy, with President George H. W. Bush in power, there seemed no proximate route for me into the executive branch (nor would I have wished to serve in his Republican administration). After Oxford, I decided to take yet another detour that would broaden my experience and develop different skills.

McKinsey & Company, a leading management consulting firm, had recruited me. Back then, McKinsey hired most of its associates out of the top business schools but reserved a few slots for Rhodes Scholars and others from nontraditional backgrounds they deemed strategic thinkers they could train in the necessary analytical tools.

Despite my atrophied quantitative skills, in early 1991 I joined McKinsey in Toronto, a comparatively small, collegial office that had a track record of molding non-MBAs, including roughly ten of my contemporaries from Oxford, into highly successful consultants. Better yet, Ian was in Toronto, having completed his one-year master's at the London School of Economics and landed a plum job as a producer at the Canadian Broadcasting Corporation's flagship nightly television news magazine, *The Journal*. My two years at McKinsey were both challenging and interesting, even if it wasn't high policymaking. Still, helping Canadian companies adjust to a changing global economy was important work. It was also great training for policy development, when down the road I would again need to digest vast quantities of information, formulate options for decision makers, execute implementation strategies, and make concise, compelling presentations to senior officials, not least the president of the United States.

More than eight years into my relationship with Ian, over half of which we had spent apart, the timing could not have been better for us finally to decide whether we would stay together. Through a process that combined personal maturation with something akin to comparative analysis, I had gotten many doubts out of my system. Yet, even with the right man, I feared my ability to sustain a relationship forever.

One fall Sunday in 1991, Ian and I were lazing in bed late into the morning. We started to argue about something insignificant. Our fights were not infrequent, but rarely consequential or lasting. This morning was no different.

To defuse the moment and declare an end to our dispute, Ian reached into a bedside drawer and pulled out a small box. Opening it, he revealed a diamond ring and then blindsided me by asking, "Will you marry me?" Melting into tears, after a few moments, I managed a muffled but determined "yes."

My parents were thrilled that Ian and I had decided to marry. To my occasional annoyance, my mother always viewed Ian as near perfect. If something were wrong between us, in her view, it was undoubtedly my fault (which was often true but not always so). Dad had finally acknowledged that Ian was good enough even for his little girl.

Ian's parents were equally supportive. I was no longer so young—his mom's original complaint—and had amply demonstrated my abilities and potential. Seeing that Ian and I were well-suited, race was not an issue for them, not least because Ian's older brother had already married a black woman. Clearly, however, they would have wished that I were Canadian rather than American. Foreseeing the likelihood that Ian and I would make our lives in the U.S., they preferred that their son stay in Canada. Beyond wanting her son to remain in closer proximity, Ian's mother sensed that my career might take precedence over Ian's in the U.S., limiting his assent and all but ensuring we might never return to Canada. His parents also had more mundane concerns. Ian's father, Newton Cameron, had made his fortune in the British Columbia plywood industry and sold his company at the right time to Canadian Pacific, a leading national conglomerate. The Camerons regretted that Ian's share of the family's wealth would be diminished under U.S. tax laws.

Ian and I planned to marry on Memorial Day weekend 1992, in Washington, D.C., at the Little Sanctuary, an intimate, charming stand-alone chapel on the grounds of St. Albans School. Our luncheon reception would be held at my godmother Peggy Cooper Cafritz's lovely house, replete with a rare collection of the best African American art, and large enough to support an indoor wedding, if weather necessitated, but perfect for an outdoor party on her expansive porch and lawn.

Shortly before the invitations were to be printed in February, I freaked out. My terror about commitment resurfaced with a vengeance. To get some perspective, I moved out of Ian's town house and into a monthly rental apartment downtown near Lake Ontario. Then I started seeing a therapist to help me confront my fears with their obvious origins in my family's collapse.

Ian let me go, without resistance or anger. Disappointed but stoical, even clinical in his assessment, he said, "You need to work through these issues. And, if you cannot, it's best that you figure that out *before* we get married." We postponed the wedding indefinitely, and I lived a life of monastic introspection. Soon after I left, Ian was sent by the CBC to South Africa to cover the referendum on ending apartheid. Throughout Ian's four weeks there, we did not communicate—partly so I could see what life without him might be like. I found it tolerable, but empty.

On the morning that Ian was to fly home from Johannesburg to Toronto, I awakened as usual to CBC Radio news. The lead story jolted me: Barbara Frum was dead of cancer. The nationally beloved anchor of CBC TV's national news magazine and Ian's boss and friend, Barbara had been a huge champion of our engagement.

I rose crying and sobered. Barbara's death delivered to me what one of my favorite writers, Virginia Woolf, called "a moment of being." In that instant, on that morning, I suddenly knew with clarity what needed to happen.

But first, I had to contact Ian in South Africa about Barbara. I reached the authorities at the Johannesburg airport and had Ian paged to call me on one of those white courtesy telephones. When he phoned, I said, my voice breaking, "Honey, I wanted to catch you before you got on the plane. I've got very sad news: Barbara Frum has died. I didn't want you to hear this and be shocked when you arrived. Also, I want you to know that I have been thinking a lot. I love you more than the universe, and I really do want to marry you. Will you take me back?"

He wept, buffeted by mixed emotions about Barbara and me, and said, "Yes." When he arrived in Toronto, I met him at the airport, and I have never contemplated being without him since.

———

We rescheduled our wedding for September 12, 1992—a clear, warm but not hot day with no humidity. It felt like God was cheering our journey together. Sadly, my stepfather had recently died after a long struggle with cancer. I was with Alfred and my mom in the hospital when he passed. Among his last words to me, both in seriousness and jest, were: "Susan, you had better be good to Ian and appreciate how special your relationship is, or I will come back and haunt you."

Not everyone was so sanguine about our marriage, and a few were bold enough to convey it. I had known Whalen McClellan, an older African American man and my father's neighbor on Myrtle Street, from the time I was four. One afternoon over the summer, he approached me as I got out of the car outside our house. Without any preface or apology, but genuine concern, Mr. McClellan said to me, "Are you *really* going to marry that white man? What are you going to do when he wakes up one day and calls you 'nigger'?" I was too shocked to respond. It seemed such a ridiculous question, but it shook me as a crass reminder of the racism and skepticism that Ian and I must be prepared to face as spouses and parents, even in liberal Washington, D.C. It also required me to acknowledge that prejudice against interracial marriage was as much or more a black thing as a white one. Sometimes I joke with Ian that I am still waiting for that fateful morning when "he wakes up and calls me 'nigger.'" To my surprise, rarely have Ian and I faced raw racism directed at us as a couple—in D.C. or elsewhere.

Our wedding was perfect. One hundred twenty-five friends and family members. A relaxed, but traditional Episcopal ceremony with unorthodox touches. My father walked me down the aisle. My brother, Johnny, was my maid of honor, holding the bouquet with some trepidation and dutifully performing all the typical functions. My bridesmaids were my three close friends from high school: Andrea, Laura, and Trinka. Ian's best man was a woman, a dear friend from high school, Barbara Arneil, while his two brothers and another high school friend served as groomsmen. We flew Canadian and American flags inside the church, gave praise for our love through "Resignation," a favorite Nikki Giovanni poem, and danced to James Brown's "I Feel Good" after we exited the church.

It was our ceremony, exactly as we wanted it.

Dad secured the wine and a New Orleans jazz band for the reception. Mom ensured the food, flowers, and decor were Lois-level impeccable. And Peggy kept my parents on their best behavior, making sure their lingering antagonisms in no way infused our special day.

Marrying Ian is the best decision I have ever made. I cannot imagine life without his unqualified love and rock-solid support, even when I least deserve it.

With Ian, I have never felt alone.

PART TWO

Fundamentals

7

Rookie Season

Everything changed for the Rice-Cameron family one evening in November 2008, as I was reading my five-year-old daughter, Maris, a bedtime story.

Not many nights earlier, together with millions of Americans, we had watched history being written with the election of Barack Obama. Early on in our pre-transition process, I had been asked to fill out the voluminous paperwork required for a senior administration position. Apparently, I had been the first potential appointee to be fully vetted for nomination, even though no one had indicated what position I was being vetted for. Whatever it was, days passed after the election before I heard anything.

Then, just as Maris and I had finished getting snuggled up in her bed and I'd begun to read, the phone rang. I excused myself and got up to answer in the adjacent study.

Picking up, I was surprised to hear President-elect Obama on the line. He said, "Hi. It's Barack. I hope I'm not interrupting anything important."

"No, I was just reading Maris a bedtime story."

"That's important," he said. "Call me back when you are done."

When I called back, with Maris in the next room in not quite certain slumber, President-elect Obama said, "I would like you to serve as my U.N. ambassador."

I thanked him profusely, before adding, "That's a great job, but I was very much hoping that you might also consider me for your national security advisor."

Obama demurred, explaining he planned to give that job to someone who *would be widely perceived on Day One as an experienced, steady hand at a time when he would be consumed by saving the economy. He said he intended to appoint retired four-star-general Jim Jones as national security advisor but would be prepared to consider me for that position down the road. In the meantime, he thought the best place for me was in New York, at the U.N.*

"Do you intend for your U.N. ambassador to be a member of the cabinet and participate fully in the NSC Principals Committee?" I asked. That had been the tradition in many prior administrations, but not during the George W. Bush–Dick Cheney years, and I believed it was important that the U.N. ambassador participate in the policymaking process at the highest levels. While Obama didn't acknowledge as much, he sounded as if he were not aware of that history. But he promptly said yes, that was his conception of the job. And, later, he made his decision stick, even when some White House advisors tried to walk it back. The president-elect concluded our discussion by recommending that I talk to Madeleine Albright, who he knew was my longtime mentor, as well as a former U.N. ambassador before she became secretary of state in the Clinton Administration. After you talk to Madeleine, he said, "Call me back tomorrow."

Before he hung up, Obama asked one final question: "What do you think of the idea of Hillary as secretary of state?" Given their hard-fought campaign, I was a bit taken aback, but replied, "If you are prepared to do that, I think it's a very good idea."

The next morning, I called Madeleine. As I had done many times before, I asked for her unvarnished advice. "Obama suggested I call you," I opened, "though I would have anyway. He has offered me the U.N. job. He's not ready to make me national security advisor. I suppose I could ask for deputy NSA. What do you think?"

Direct as always, Madeleine responded, "U.N. ambassador is a great job. You should take it without hesitation. You'll learn a lot, have a great deal of autonomy, and it often leads to higher places."

Enough said.

When I called Obama back to thank him again and say I would be honored to serve as his U.N. ambassador and a member of his cabinet, he seemed pleased. To myself, I noted with satisfaction that Obama appeared unfazed by my directness the night before in asking for the NSA job. We had a candid enough relationship for me to do so, and I had learned along the way that sometimes you need to be willing to advocate for yourself. Though I'd frequently seen my white male peers do the same without hesitation, often women tend to hang back. I was gratified but not surprised that Obama would expect no less from me.

I have not always so readily accepted the jobs that have been offered me— even very good ones. Long before Obama asked me to become U.N. ambassador in the fall of 2008, I began my journey in government following a very different phone call and a decision that would define my career.

———•◆•———

In December 1992, I was contacted by the Clinton transition team and asked to interview for two prospective positions on the new White House staff. At that time, I'd been at McKinsey for almost two years and wasn't in a rush to leave; I still had much to learn from consulting.

The month prior, Bill Clinton beat George H. W. Bush for the presidency and, although I had sat out this election season working at McKinsey in Toronto, several of my colleagues from the Dukakis team had worked on the Clinton campaign and were tasked with helping staff the new administration. Nancy Soderberg, a former Hill aide who had been my immediate boss on the Dukakis foreign policy team, was the first to find me and ask, "Susan, any interest in interviewing for the National Security Council staff?"

I didn't hesitate in answering, "Absolutely."

Shortly thereafter, Gene Sperling, my brilliant and sometimes disheveled economic policy colleague from the Dukakis campaign, called to inquire about my interest in joining the newly constituted National Economic Council (NEC), the economic policy analogue to the NSC. Surprised, I was delighted to be remembered by both Gene and Nancy and deemed worthy of their consideration.

On a weekend before Christmas, I flew down to D.C. from Toronto for two interviews. One was with Robert Rubin, who would chair the National Economic Council, and the second was with Tony Lake and Sandy Berger, who would run the National Security Council.

Rubin, a piercingly smart, wiry former cochairman of Goldman Sachs, met with me first, one-on-one. He tried to assess my interest in and suitability for some sort of role at the NEC. It was not clear to him (or me) where exactly I might fit, but he seemed interested in utilizing me somewhere in domestic economic policy.

My next interview marked my first encounter with Tony Lake, the national security advisor–designate, and his deputy, Sandy Berger. Lake was relaxed and loquacious, expounding on his interest in Africa and asking about my dissertation on Zimbabwe. Mindful of time and the need to conduct these interviews efficiently, Berger was all business and clearly impatient with Tony's digressions. Sandy tried to steer us back to the subject at hand, explaining that they were considering me for the role of one of two special assistants (or right hands) to the national security advisor and deputy national security advisor. This was not a policy role but a staff support job, where organizational skills, writing capacity, discretion, and judgment were key. I would have a bird's-eye view of all the issues with which the national security team grappled—but no line responsibility.

Both the NEC and NSC offered me jobs. Finding both options attractive, I wrestled with the decision. I liked the idea of having policy responsibility but felt that, even after McKinsey, my readiness to take on an economic job was questionable. My academic foundation in international relations—combined with my foreign policy work on the Dukakis campaign—better prepared me for the NSC role. Then again, at only twenty-eight years old, with no prior executive branch experience, I would be starting from behind most of my colleagues in either capacity. However, since my role at the NSC would be to support the national security advisor and not directly make policy, I thought my preparation was probably sufficient.

Additionally, on a gut level, I found the high-stakes, sometimes life-and-death nature of national security policymaking more stimulating. As a pragmatist, I also calculated (perhaps inaccurately) that if, later on, I wanted to make the leap back to economic or domestic policy, there would be more opportunities to do so than if I tried to jump from the domestic to the international side, where the established experts would more likely doubt the applicability of my experience.

After deliberating, I accepted the job as special assistant to the national security advisor, turned down Bob Rubin, and gave notice to McKinsey. My bosses at McKinsey were supportive and understanding, as was Ian. I would be moving home to D.C. just months after our wedding, and he would remain in Toronto at the CBC until he could find an attractive journalism job in Washington. Long-distance, again!

In my last weeks at McKinsey, I continued to commute to a small town in rural Quebec where I worked for a manufacturing client. On Monday mornings, I would awaken early for the flight and drive, returning Thursday or Friday evening. At about 1:30 on a Monday morning in early January 1993, my phone rang, rousing me from sleep. Picking up, still groggy, I heard Sandy Berger identify himself. Without any niceties, he announced that I no longer had an offer to be his and Tony Lake's special assistant. They had determined that they only needed one, not two assistants, and they were going to keep the guy who had worked with them on the campaign. Jolted, I was now properly awake. Sandy then said that I could still come to the NSC, if I wanted to be a director for Africa on the NSC staff.

Offered a real policy job that should have been quite appealing, I nonetheless took no time before giving him my reply. "No, thank you," I said, "I'm not interested in working on Africa. I would prefer another portfolio." No doubt put off by the arrogance of a twenty-eight-year-old neophyte, Sandy abruptly ended the conversation without clarity as to whether or not it would be our last.

It wasn't that I was uninterested in Africa, but as an African American woman in a very white male field, if my first job in government were focused solely on Africa, I feared I could get pigeonholed and never be viewed as someone who could work on wider issues. In retrospect, I marvel at my own chutzpah but am glad I refused to be typecast. Even though I understood that Tony and Sandy had no such intention, I recognized that other people's perceptions could become my reality. I was comforted by knowing that McKinsey would welcome me staying and Bob Rubin might still have me at the NEC.

About ten days later, after hearing only vaguely from Nancy Soderberg that they might be able to work something else out at the NSC, I got another call. This one, equally abrupt, was from some guy I had never heard of: Richard Clarke.

Clarke was the senior director for global issues and multilateral affairs at the NSC and a former assistant secretary of state. Clarke barreled ahead, "Lake and Berger told me to interview you for a role as a junior director in my office. I told them I don't want any junior directors. Either you are good enough to be a director, or I don't want you. So they told me to consider you for director for international organizations and peacekeeping. When are you coming down?"

"I'm very grateful for your interest," I replied and let him know I could be back in Washington by early February. Quickly, I added, "Thank you, and I look forward to meeting you."

"Thank Tony and Sandy, not me." With that, he hung up.

Later, I learned that Dick Clarke is legendary for his unforgiving demeanor and his skills as a "bureaucratic Samurai," or interagency knife-fighter.

The interview went well, and I was hired. As it turned out, I could not have asked for a better first boss in government. Dick's office covered everything from counterterrorism to counter-narcotics, humanitarian relief to U.N. affairs, peacekeeping to refugees. My portfolio, the United Nations and peacekeeping, was a busy one, and it meant I would work closely with my mentor Madeleine Albright and her team, since she was to be ambassador to the U.N. Even though Dick didn't want any baby directors, he also didn't want any screwups. He had brought back his very good friend and longtime partner at the State Department, Rand Beers, to be his deputy. Among Randy's responsibilities were to mentor me until I could safely fly solo.

Randy is a redheaded, ruggedly handsome former Marine, whose hearing was diminished while fighting in Vietnam. A devoted father and husband, avid runner, and gentle soul, Randy had served for decades at the State Department and the National Security Council. Like Dick, he was highly regarded in both Republican and Democratic administrations; but, unlike Dick, he always managed to play nicely with colleagues. Randy would go on to serve in various higher offices in subsequent years, including as acting secretary of homeland security under President Obama.

For about six months, Randy taught me the ropes—everything from how to write coherent, persuasive memos to the president and national security advisor, to how to run an effective interagency policy meeting. One of his most valuable pieces of advice, understood by too few foreign policy experts, was, "Follow the money." By that, Randy meant learn the national security budget inside and out; he explained: "Where there is money, there is real potential policy impact. If you can grasp the budget and figure out where to vacuum up underutilized funds, you will run circles around your interagency colleagues." This lesson served me well for the next twenty-five years.

Randy also taught me how to deal with Dick Clarke when he was being difficult. His advice was to be firm and clear in response to any stray voltage Dick directed at me—in other words, "Don't take crap." Before long, Randy concluded I had earned my wings, and I was soon treated like the other more experienced directors and advanced to reporting directly to Dick.

Dick is a hard-ass—gruff, sarcastic, whip-smart, someone who pulls no punches—but also a generous, endearing, loyal man, who would become a lasting friend to me and my family. He is beloved by the legions of younger people he has mentored and trained. Though highly respected by his bosses in the Reagan, Bush 41, and Clinton administrations for his exceptional competence and candor, many of his peers at the White House and in the agencies disliked him, some intensely. Dick didn't suffer fools. While chairing interagency meetings, he could shut people down with a dismissive retort designed to highlight their stupidity, and he would mow over obstacles to accomplish his aims. Following the terrorist attacks on 9/11, Dick ran afoul of the Bush 43 administration after he publicly criticized them for paying insufficient attention to the Al Qaeda threat.

At the start of my four and a half years on the NSC staff, Dick taught me how to "get shit done," which became my mantra. From watching Dick I also learned the pitfalls of behaving with unnecessary aggressiveness, while mastering the nuts and bolts of making policy and moving the interagency bureaucracy.

Intimacy and collegiality were the hallmarks of what was then a relatively small NSC staff, consisting of some 150 policy experts. We all knew each other, and when we needed to hunt down a colleague—to talk through a problem or air a policy dispute—we just walked down the long, high-ceiled, marble corridors of the Old Executive Office Building adjacent to the White House and rang their bell. Email was not yet the main mode of communication among NSC staffers; we spoke face-to-face. Moms and dads brought their kids to the office on weekends where they played with makeshift toys or paper clips as their parents toiled long and unpredictable hours. National Security Advisor Lake and his deputy Sandy Berger were accessible, and we would go directly to their office or occasionally they to ours when we needed to hash out a pressing matter.

The NSC sat at the nexus of the national security agencies, coordinating policy formulation and implementation, cajoling the State and Defense Departments to embrace or at least acquiesce to President Clinton's agenda. In the early years, it was difficult having to follow the well-liked and highly experienced George H. W. Bush with a young president who had no federal government or military experience. The agencies tested and resisted us, as is normal in any new administration, but with time and after our share of missteps, the bureaucracy came along.

My U.N. portfolio meant that, along with my regional colleagues who had direct policy responsibility, I tracked the hot conflict issues of the day, including Bosnia, Haiti, Cambodia, Mozambique, Angola, Somalia, and Rwanda. This was an era when peacekeeping was growing rapidly as a tool of conflict prevention and resolution and when, in the wake of the end of the Cold War, civil wars seemed to be proliferating. With Clarke, I also coordinated the interagency process on peacekeeping issues, multilateral sanctions policy, development, and human rights issues that involved the United Nations.

———

At the very outset of the Clinton administration, I was thrown into the deep end of the crisis pool. President Bush had decided in December 1992, as he was leaving office, to send 28,000 U.S. forces to Somalia to help restore order and enable the delivery of food and relief supplies to victims of the war-induced famine then ravaging the country. This massive humanitarian intervention, known as Operation Restore Hope, was laudable in its initial aims but left the incoming Clinton administration with the complex challenge of managing a large military mission in a remote, poorly understood corner of the world. Just days before Clinton took office, the

U.S. suffered its first combat death in Somalia. Thus began a cycle of increasingly deadly confrontations pitting U.S. and U.N. forces against the notorious warlord Mohammed Aidid's clan militia.

America's strategy, as inherited from the Bush administration, was to hand off responsibility for the U.S. military operation as soon as possible to the United Nations. After some delays, in May 1993 the U.N. finally established its largest peacekeeping force to date (28,000), taking over from the U.S.-led multinational force. There were roughly 4,000 American troops attached to the initial U.N. force, including 1,300 who remained outside of U.N. command and formed a helicopter-mobile Quick Reaction Force. The U.N. mandate was to provide security sufficient to enable the delivery of humanitarian relief; but in practice, given the running armed conflicts between warlords and their clans, the mission required trying to disarm and disable recalcitrant militia, most prominently Aidid's. In other words: combat.

One Saturday morning in early June 1993, I received an urgent call at home from the White House Situation Room. Wearing weekend casual clothes, I dashed to my office at the Old Executive Office Building—a ten-minute drive from our house in the Adams Morgan neighborhood—to deal with my first major policy crisis: twenty-four Pakistani U.N. peacekeepers had been killed by Aidid's forces in several attacks across the Somali capital, Mogadishu. It was the second worst loss of peacekeepers' lives in U.N. history, a major blow to the nascent U.N. force and to the perceived ability of the U.S. to provide sufficient backup to U.N. forces under attack. In Dick Clarke's office, we scrambled to issue press statements, ensure the right people in the agencies called the Pakistanis, and coordinate the dispatch of instructions to the U.S. Mission to the U.N.

The U.N. Security Council was set to meet in emergency session, and Ambassador Albright and her team needed swift guidance on the pending Security Council resolution condemning the attack and threatening justice against the perpetrators. The final resolution, which was unanimously adopted, called for the arrest and punishment of the perpetrators. It was widely perceived as a declaration of war against Aidid.

Despite being unfamiliar with Somalia, my bosses remained convinced of the righteousness of America's humanitarian mission. Instinctively, they refused to get punked by some two-bit warlord; so they decided the U.S. should double down on the mission to eliminate the threat from Aidid. This seemed like the obvious policy choice, and I had no misgivings when President Clinton first ordered Marines and Army Rangers to hunt down Aidid and his henchmen, and to raid his home, weapons depots, and radio station. The population of Mogadishu, which had initially supported the U.S. mission, however, largely turned against us and the U.N. Aidid's supporters chanted "Down with America!," and Aidid vowed to remain on a "collision course" with the U.N. and U.S.

While the mission's objective remained humanitarian, the U.N. and the Clinton administration concluded we needed to use whatever force necessary to restore order. Over the summer and early fall of 1993, the U.N. suffered further casualties, and U.S. losses mounted as well. Our European allies opposed the intensified U.N. combat role, and Congress passed nonbinding resolutions aimed at curtailing the U.S. military mission, calling for it to be authorized by Congress if it were to be extended beyond its November 15 mandate.

On Sunday, October 3, 1993, I received another unexpected call from the Situation Room: two U.S. Black Hawk helicopters had been shot down by Aidid militia. Several U.S. servicemen were dead, captured, or missing. Reaching the office, I was disgusted and horrified to see on television the bodies of U.S. soldiers being dragged through the streets of Mogadishu. As we watched the on-screen desecration of our own Special Forces, I knew, as I had learned from Dick Clarke, that when crisis hits, there is no time for emotion. We needed to steel ourselves, focus, remain unflustered, execute, and deliver.

By the time that nightmare was over, eighteen American servicemen had been killed and seventy-three wounded. Suddenly, everything changed for the new administration, as it confronted its first major national security crisis and accompanying political trauma.

————

Even with both houses of Congress under Democratic control, in the wake of these shocking losses, President Clinton faced extraordinary congressional pressure to immediately withdraw U.S. forces from Somalia. Secretary of State Warren Christopher and Secretary of Defense Les Aspin tried valiantly to argue with Congress for time and space to finish the mission with dignity. I vividly recall the stunned realization in the White House that their efforts had backfired spectacularly. It must have been one of the most brutal spankings of cabinet officials before members of a Congress led by their own party. Congressional Democrats and Republicans then turned their ire on President Clinton and the rest of his senior national security team. On the verge of mandating the near immediate return of U.S. forces, Congress was set to force a sudden and humiliating retreat that would have set back security in Somalia, eroded the credibility of America's military commitments globally, and undermined the authority of the commander-in-chief.

To avert such legislation, President Clinton pledged that all U.S. military would leave Somalia within six months. He also announced interim plans to reinforce the U.S. military presence in Somalia and offshore by inserting a total of twenty thousand troops to protect U.S. personnel. Congress then voted to bind the president to his stated timeline by setting March 31, 1994, as the cut-off date for funding military operations in Somalia—an extraordinary, rare rebuke of executive authority. I have never forgotten this harsh reality: Congress can effectively constrain the commander-in-chief when its will is sufficient.

On March 26, 1994, the last U.S. forces left the shores of Somalia in amphibious vehicles. It was a low-key, even ignominious departure that, thankfully, occurred without incident. Back at an anticlimactic ceremony on the White House Lawn, President Clinton thanked our military for their service and sacrifice, closing the book on one of the most ill-fated military missions in recent U.S. history.

This first major crisis I faced in government was searing, and Somalia would shape my own perspective as well as U.S. policy for decades to come.

While the U.S. and U.N. operations definitely helped ameliorate the dire humanitarian situation in Somalia, saving an estimated one million lives, by almost all other measures U.S. involvement there was a failure. Thirty U.S. servicemen were killed in action and 175 were wounded as the mission crept well beyond its original humanitarian parameters.

From my vantage point, the U.S. had underestimated the complexity and dangers of humanitarian intervention and overestimated the capacity of the U.N. to conduct complex peace enforcement missions. The U.N. suffered from an unachievable mandate, insufficient forces, lack of coordination, and ineffective command and control. Individual peacekeeping units, including the Americans', took orders from their national capitals rather than from the U.N. commander on the ground or headquarters in New York. To exacerbate matters, the U.S. under-resourced its own contingent within the U.N. force and got sucked into "nation building."

As many of my more senior colleagues would later admit, the Clinton administration failed to prioritize a political solution over an elusive military outcome—before it was too late. In targeting Aidid, the U.S. and U.N. personalized the mission and turned large segments of the Somali population against us. Neither the U.S. nor the U.N. developed the capacity nor had the humility to try to comprehend the extraordinary political complexities of Somalia's clan structure and fiercely independent culture. We also failed to engage Somalia's neighbors early enough to learn from their far greater knowledge of the country.

Without relevant doctrine or experience, the U.S. found itself enmeshed in what was effectively a sectarian civil war, bogged down in urban counterinsurgency operations against a smaller but more agile enemy—a challenge we would face again years later in Iraq. U.S. policy ran far afield of public and congressional sentiment, leaving the president with little support when things went badly wrong. I also observed that the NSC Principals, the cabinet-level committee that sets U.S. national security policy, were insufficiently involved in decision making, leaving too much to their deputies; moreover, for too long, there was no senior point person clearly accountable for driving policy formulation and implementation. Somalia provided me an early, real-world case study of what not to do.

At the peak of my youthful outrage after Black Hawk Down, as the events came to be known, I confessed to some good friends at a dinner party, "If I had my way, we would turn Mogadishu into a parking lot." At the time, the notion that we could send U.S. forces to a faraway land to save innocent lives only to have our own lives taken was infuriating and bewildering. Only with greater experience and maturity would I come to understand that, despite my occasional inclination to flatten our opponents (especially two-bit warlords), escalation and the use of overwhelming force against locals, particularly when it entails high civilian casualties, will almost always boomerang and undermine the mission—whether humanitarian, counterinsurgency, or counterterrorism.

The Somalia crisis also taught me to be skeptical of Congress's capacity to play any constructive role in addressing real-time national security crises. While bipartisan sanity prevailed to prevent a vote to force Clinton to withdraw U.S. forces immediately, politicization instincts ran deep, especially among Republicans like Senators John McCain and Phil Gramm, who seemingly wished to undermine President Clinton by arguing (uncharacteristically) that the U.S. ought to cut and run as soon as we accounted for our POWs and MIAs. Likewise, I discovered the serious political and operational limitations of the U.N., especially to succeed in real combat missions, even with strong U.S. backing.

Personally, I never fully got over my own frustration with Somalia; for the next two decades, I maintained a studied ambivalence to conflict resolution there. Knowing well the costs of failure, I would struggle with whether the potential benefits of reengaging in the thankless task of trying to help Somalis reconcile and rebuild were worth the enduring risks. The greatest cautionary tale for me was how essential it is for the cabinet-level officials to remain hands-on in decision making whenever U.S. forces are engaged in combat. Their deputies, however skilled and effective, need full support when crises occur. These hard-learned lessons from Somalia stuck with me through the following twenty-five years, as I rose through the ranks of national security policymaking.

———

Wrestling with the explosion of complex U.N. missions globally, the new Clinton administration sought to define and codify a rational and sustainable basis for U.S. support to U.N. peacekeeping operations. We believed in the value of the U.N. and wanted peacekeeping to endure as a vital tool of conflict resolution. We recognized the need to do our part but refused to become the world's policeman and bear a disproportionate share of global costs and risks. Congress was deeply skeptical of U.N. peacekeeping and, after Somalia, any remaining public tolerance of perceived U.S. overreach had evaporated.

Early in the administration, President Clinton signed a directive mandating that we develop a new U.S. policy on U.N. peace operations—defining how and when we should decide to vote for, support, fund, and terminate them. As the NSC director responsible for U.N. affairs, I played a central role in crafting that policy along with Dick Clarke and Randy Beers. It was a complex bureaucratic "goat-rope," a term Dick used to describe the challenge of corralling and reconciling the competing views of the various government agencies with much at stake in the outcome.

The Pentagon wanted as little to do with the U.N. as possible and viewed peacekeeping as an unworthy sissy mission. The State Department and U.S. Mission to the U.N. favored more robust U.S. support for the U.N. and saw peacekeeping as a comparatively low-cost way to share the global burden of preventing and resolving regional conflicts. My personal instincts aligned largely with State's but, as an NSC director, my role was to be the honest broker, to try to find common ground and forge compromise.

It took months to develop the policy and months more to build interagency support for its key elements. As we did, we were constantly buffeted by unfolding world events—the U.N.'s challenges in Bosnia, Haiti, Cambodia, Somalia, and eventually Rwanda. From each, we learned different yet valuable, and sometimes competing, lessons. We worked to refine the impending peacekeeping policy, incorporating our learning in real time. The result was Presidential Decision Directive 25 (PDD-25): "U.S. Policy on Reforming Multilateral Peace Operations," issued May 3, 1994, almost a year and a half after the policy review process began. It was a comprehensive, thoughtful, and well-conceived document, of which I remain proud. It has endured as standing U.S. policy through at least three administrations—Clinton, Bush 43, Obama—and remains, at the time of this writing, on the books.

PDD-25 recognized the strengths and limitations of U.N. peacekeeping and mandated increased U.S. support to improve the U.N.'s capacities, while placing wise and appropriate constraints on U.S. involvement. Yet in many ways, it was a conservative, cautious document, tempered in its initial enthusiasm by the weight of hard-won experience. It was meant to ensure we did not allow the U.N. or ourselves to overreach or misalign U.N. mandates with resources. In that, it was largely successful. Inadvertently, it also served to constrain our imagination and hinder our ability to react swiftly to the unforeseen. In a tale of unintended consequences, PDD-25 may have contributed to one of the Clinton administration's most difficult and controversial decisions. Or, more precisely, lack of decision.

———

To this day, I am haunted.

When I stepped off the helicopter, I had no idea what I was about to see. It was December 1994, and I was among a small party of Washington officials who accompanied National Security Advisor Anthony Lake to a church and adjoining school in rural eastern Rwanda. A few yards from the landing site, the ground became thick with decomposed corpses. They were jammed so tight that it was treacherous to walk without stepping on one. Grown bodies. Children's bodies. Babies in mothers' arms. Shot up. Hacked up. Decaying faces. Frozen in the position they fell. All over the churchyard. In the church. Across the school grounds. Dead bodies everywhere. Hundreds, if not thousands. And the putrid smell, though ebbing, remained.

This was one of countless massacre sites across this verdant, hilly, densely populated Central African country the size of Vermont. Ground zero of the Rwandan genocide. Up to one million killed in a preplanned slaughter of ethnic Tutsis and moderate Hutus at the hands of their fellow citizens—extremist Hutus and those they forced into violence. The primary killing machine was the simple but lethal machete. They murdered each other *by hand* with long knives at close range. It was unspeakable cruelty that left me without words or even tears for many, many hours after we left the church site.

———

This brutal question still loops in my brain: *How did we, the U.S. and the international community, let the genocide happen?*

I remember the news flash, April 6, 1994, just one week after the U.S. military withdrawal from Somalia, another report from the White House Situation Room: the plane carrying the presidents of Rwanda and Burundi was shot down near the airport in Kigali, Rwanda. As the U.N. director on the NSC staff, I knew this was ominous. Rwanda was already on a knife's edge, and neighboring Burundi had endured its latest spasm of

Hutu-Tutsi violence just months earlier in October 1993, when an estimated fifty thousand Tutsis were killed after Tutsi soldiers had murdered Burundi's Hutu president.

Still, few predicted precisely what happened next.

Immediately after the plane went down, the Hutu-dominated Rwandan army carefully targeted their first victims. The next day, April 7, the rampant killing began. Radio Mille Collines—a hate radio outlet with government links—bombarded the airwaves, inciting Hutu to massacre Tutsi ("exterminate the cockroaches"), even identifying locations where those hiding could be found. The army went house to house, slaughtering. Hutu extremists murdered Rwanda's acting prime minister in cold blood and then mutilated ten Belgian U.N. peacekeepers who were assigned to protect her. Kigali was a massive killing field. Within days, the entire country became a bloodbath.

The U.S. government's first priority in such a crisis is always to evacuate American embassy personnel and other U.S. citizens. The French and Belgian militaries flew in to rescue their nationals. The U.S. military, which had pulled its last personnel out of Somalia barely a week earlier, was nowhere near in position to mount a swift airlift or NEO, noncombatant evacuation operation. U.S. Marines would have to come from ships in the Indian Ocean and could not arrive in time to make an immediate airlift feasible. Our embassy personnel would have to try to escape overland by convoy to Burundi, without dependable security.

Given the killing that engulfed the countryside, this was an extremely dangerous evacuation. Back in Washington, we were all gripped by the fear that we would lose our colleagues. The State Department, which had the lead in ensuring the safe departure of its personnel, set up a round-the-clock crisis task force within its Operations Center. Working long hours from the low-ceiling, bottom section of our double-decker office in the Old Executive Office Building, which had been vertically subdivided by a previous occupant (the notorious, if industrious, Oliver North), I pestered the task force and the Africa Bureau frequently for the latest updates. President Clinton drove over from the White House to State to show solidarity and buck up the duty officers on vigil. When, after two long days, all American embassy personnel were safely evacuated, the collective sigh of relief we emitted in Washington was deep but short lived. Unfortunately, U.S. personnel were not able to evacuate our Rwandan embassy employees, and we later learned many of our local staff were killed in the ongoing massacres.

With no official Americans on the ground, we lost our primary eyes and ears. There was little real-time, formal information on what was happening, just anecdotal reporting mainly from nongovernmental organizations, the NGOs, and limited flows from the U.N. force (the United Nations Assistance Mission for Rwanda, or UNAMIR), which was hunkered down in defensive positions after the Belgian peacekeepers were killed. Within a week, countries began withdrawing their contingents from the U.N. force, greatly reducing its size and efficacy and turning it into a bystander as the killing raged. It was not until a couple of weeks later, when the international press corps arrived, that American officials gained a fuller appreciation of the extent of the horror. As the nightly news carried nauseating footage of masses of bodies rushing down choked Rwandan rivers, it became increasingly clear that we were in the midst of a full-blown genocide, and neither the U.S., Rwanda's neighbors, the U.N., nor its member states were prepared to halt it.

In Washington, after the very proximate trauma of Somalia, neither senior U.S. officials, nor I, ever contemplated sending U.S. forces back to an even more remote and unknown part of Africa for another humanitarian intervention. No one in the Clinton administration argued for direct U.S. military involvement. No one in Congress did. No major U.S. editorial board did either. This was a case when the most obvious option was beyond the realm of the conceivable. In addition, the utility of the greatest military on earth in stopping thousands of people from killing their neighbors with knives was questionable. We had just failed to stop a warlord equipped with machine guns mounted on SUVs—unsophisticated "technicals," as they were called—from killing U.S. servicemen in Somalia.

In hindsight, what still strikes me most is the lack of discussion or debate. In those early weeks, we were reeling and did not have the customary policy meetings to decide what to do next. I, we, never proposed what seemed unthinkable—U.S. military intervention. It wasn't that President Clinton decided not to intervene. As the genocide unfolded, the president never asked for, nor did his senior advisors present him with any decision to make on the matter.

Four years later, on his first visit to Rwanda, in 1998, President Clinton apologized for the international community's failure to respond swiftly enough to the genocide. In subsequent years, Clinton called Rwanda his "personal failure" and his "biggest regret" as president. In 2013, on one of many subsequent visits to Rwanda, where his foundation is active, President Clinton mused that, if he had deployed even ten thousand U.S. troops, the U.S. might have "saved at least a third of the lives that were lost." I don't know on what basis he came to this assessment, but perhaps with a sizable U.S. military intervention joined by an even greater complement of American-led international forces, we could have made a difference, even if at great risk and cost.

Yet, in reality, so soon after eighteen American service members were killed in Somalia while assisting U.N. peacekeepers, Congress would likely have refused to support another U.S. military intervention in an African country that most Americans had never heard of. Had President Clinton actually deployed U.S. forces into Rwanda, Congress might have terminated funding for the U.S. intervention and perhaps all U.S. financial support for U.N. peacekeeping.

In the moment, as events unfolded, many of the policy choices that the U.S. government did actually make seemed logical. But in hindsight, they were unacceptable in the aggregate.

The first major choice came roughly two weeks after the genocide began. Once their peacekeepers were slaughtered, the Belgians decided to withdraw their battalion from the 2,500-person U.N. force. They appealed to the U.S. as a NATO ally to back their decision at the U.N. by giving their withdrawal some diplomatic cover. This meant agreeing that the U.N. mission, with its limited size and mandate, was incapable of addressing the killing and should withdraw for its own safety and credibility. The U.N. secretary-general, Boutros Boutros-Ghali, gave the Security Council three options: a) substantially augment the U.N. force and strengthen its mandate; b) reduce the force to 270 and limit its mandate to brokering a cease-fire and assisting as it could with humanitarian relief, while trying still to provide some meager measure of protection to civilians who had taken refuge with the U.N.; or c) withdraw UNAMIR entirely, recognizing that it was unsuited to the dramatically worsened context.

In deference to the Belgians, and consistent with the rigorous criteria of PDD-25, Washington instructed the U.S. Mission to the U.N. (USUN) to go with Option C: insist that UNAMIR withdraw. Meanwhile, African members at the U.N. and others argued to increase the force dramatically but offered no capable or ready troops to do so. In addition to the Belgians, the Bangladeshi and Ghanaian battalions were also withdrawing, leaving a minimal presence. Thus, Option A was a pipe dream in practice and, after the Somalia debacle, unimaginable to many even in principle.

The Security Council coalesced around the middle option of reducing the force, leaving the veto-wielding U.S. alone in supporting full withdrawal. I recall listening on the line when Ambassador Albright called Dick Clarke. She was as livid as I have ever heard her. Albright told Dick, in effect: "I have just stepped out of the Security Council. We are totally isolated. No one else agrees we should completely withdraw the force. Plus, my instructions from Washington are just plain wrong. The U.S. can't be responsible for completely abandoning Rwanda. I need new instructions. Now." As a result of her willingness to fight a bruising internal battle, Ambassador Albright ultimately received authority to join the consensus in the Council on the U.N. drawing down to 270 troops. Human rights groups and many others criticized this action as cowardly and deadly, given that the small, remaining U.N. presence was powerless to stop the killing or even to protect those whose had taken refuge among U.N. personnel. But the only option that could have made a difference—augmenting the force—was not feasible, because no country had both the will and the capacity to provide the necessary troops swiftly enough.

Another dilemma was whether to employ U.S. military assets to jam Radio Mille Collines. National Security Advisor Tony Lake rightly pressed the Pentagon to develop this option, but in a May 5 memo from Undersecretary of Defense for Policy Frank Wisner to Deputy NSA Sandy Berger, DOD concluded that, in the Rwandan context, "jamming is an ineffective and expensive mechanism that will not accomplish the objective the NSC Advisor seeks." That memo effectively ended internal discussion over the utility of shutting down the hate radio broadcasts.

The horror of the killing sparked another active debate in May and early June—whether to label what was transpiring in Rwanda a "genocide." For many weeks, major press outlets, including *The New York Times*, referred to events generically as a "civil war," which in part it was. Along with the press and many analysts outside the human rights community, U.S. policymakers were slow to recognize the organized, systematic, ethnic-based nature of the killing. The U.S. government crept up to the designation, as State Department officials were eventually allowed to acknowledge gingerly that "acts of genocide may have occurred." Typically, the secretary of state is responsible for making formal genocide determinations. The issue ultimately fell to the elder statesman Warren Christopher, a venerable and exceedingly cautious lawyer. He and some of his staff worried about the implications of the genocide designation, fearing that saying the word would create political pressure on the administration, if not a legal obligation, to intervene.

National Security Advisor Lake repeatedly characterized events in Rwanda as "genocide" in meetings with human rights groups, a judgment with which I agreed, given the scale and intent of the killing. Still, it was not until June 10 that Secretary Christopher publicly and reluctantly conceded: "If there's any particular magic in calling it genocide, I've no hesitancy in saying that."

As the extraordinary scope of the killing in Rwanda grew more obvious by early May 1994, pressure mounted at the U.N. and in Washington to do more—and fast. The U.N. secretary-general proposed to assemble an all-African force to fly into Kigali and move outward into the countryside to protect civilians. U.S. military planners thought this concept was madness, given the dangers of inserting any sizable force by air into a hot war zone, much less a U.N. force of limited capacity. Along with others in the administration, I supported a counterproposal for a different concept of operations wherein U.N. personnel would enter Rwanda from the neighboring countries and establish safe zones along the border where civilians could be protected. For weeks, U.S. and U.N. planners argued over the right course. Eventually, lacking support for our concept, the U.S. relented, and Boutros-Ghali won agreement gradually to establish UNAMIR II, which would base itself in Kigali and work its way out of the capital.

Several African governments committed to participate, but their contingents were very slow to arrive, in part because the U.S. insisted on a phased approach tied to conditions on the ground, and in part because they were unable to deploy without external assistance and lacked basic equipment from radios to armored personnel carriers (APCs). To try to expedite their deployment, Dick Clarke and I pressed the Pentagon to lease forty-six APCs to the U.N. to enable the Ghanaian battalion to become operational. As one of the most capable contingents and a friendly nation, Ghana was a prime candidate for U.S. assistance. We pleaded with colleagues on the Joint Staff, "You can spare less than fifty APCs. It's not going to affect military readiness."

Still, the Pentagon hated the idea of relinquishing its vehicles and transporting them to Rwanda; above all, strangely, the Department of Defense balked at painting their APCs white, as was necessary to identify them as neutral U.N. vehicles. Dick and I spent countless hours battling with DOD, insisting, "You can easily repaint the APCs back to Army green when the lease is over." Eventually we wore them down, and they agreed to send the APCs. Some months later, my NSC colleagues and I were deeply chagrined (but also mildly amused) to learn that at least some of our American APCs were being used as chicken coops!

After the establishment of UNAMIR II, it took months for sufficient U.N. forces to arrive. In the meantime, the killing raged on, and hundreds of thousands of refugees spilled into Rwanda's neighboring states. Frustrated by the lack of international response, and keen to protect their Rwandan government Hutu allies from Tutsi rebels led by Paul Kagame, the French government decided to send its own troops to Rwanda. France's defense minister, François Léotard, in seeking U.N. support for what they dubbed "Opération Turquoise," maintained that their mission would be to "protect threatened civilians, not for war operations or military assistance."

I, among others, doubted that claim. France had long armed and supported the Rwandan army, which included the Hutu extremists who orchestrated and conducted the genocide. Therefore, the French government's impartiality was dubious, and its objectives in this instance were highly suspect. Secretary Christopher argued strenuously however that we should vote at the U.N. to endorse the French mission, in part out of loyalty to an ally.

As an NSC director, my status was equivalent to that of a State Department deputy assistant secretary, four ranks below the secretary of state. Nonetheless, convinced that supporting the French mission would compound our strategic mistakes, I argued passionately to Sandy Berger that we should oppose the French force. Given France's ignoble history in Central Africa of propping up friendly, if unsavory governments and picking sides in ethnic conflicts, I smelled a rat in their motives. Still, for all my opposition, I had no viable alternative to offer. Indeed, it would have been very difficult politically and diplomatically for us to block the French deployment without ourselves being willing to intervene. In the end, we went along with the French.

Over the next two months, French forces not only set up a safe haven in southern Rwanda to protect civilians but also gave military cover and tacit support to enable the Hutu ringleaders of the genocide to escape unscathed into neighboring Zaire, disappearing amidst the hundreds of thousands of refugees. For years to come, long after Kagame's rebels ended the genocide by routing the Rwandan government forces in July 1994, and took power, those refugee camps and ringleaders continued to threaten Rwanda.

The final consequential decision U.S. policymakers faced came as the genocide was ending and hundreds of thousands of mainly Hutu refugees poured into Zaire, creating massive cholera colonies and the greatest humanitarian relief requirement in decades. What would the U.S. and international community do to address this mass suffering? Having failed even to consider trying to halt the genocide, feeling guilty for the human costs of that failure, and facing on average well over one thousand additional refugee deaths a day, the Clinton administration finally decided to deploy the U.S. military.

At its peak, Operation Support Hope involved over 2,350 U.S. military personnel spread across Central Africa to airlift and supply enormous quantities of food, medical supplies, tents, and water purification equipment to assist the roughly two million refugees who flooded Goma, Zaire. The U.S. military has extraordinary capacities and talents, including its lesser known ability to mobilize massive resources quickly to respond to disasters, however remote, whether natural or man-made. Operation Support Hope saved thousands of lives. It also enabled policymakers to feel like we had at least done *something*. However, that post-facto humanitarian relief operation, while appropriate, hardly mitigated my enduring anguish over the U.S.'s and international community's collective failure to respond to the Rwandan genocide.

How could humans do that to one another? How can you hate any group that much? How can one live with such culpability? How can a nation recover from such insanity?

These questions endure. Rwanda has recovered remarkably, if imperfectly. No one there *speaks* anymore of ethnic groups. There are no Hutus and Tutsis, out loud. In public, there are only Rwandans. Paul Kagame, whose rebel forces ended the genocide, still rules Rwanda today, having taken effective power shortly after the violence ended. Kagame governs both with laudable vision and an iron fist. In Rwanda, political opponents often disappear or die. The press is muted. Political parties are stifled. Rwanda invaded neighboring Congo (as Zaire was renamed) multiple times, ostensibly to free refugees and combat the perpetrators of genocide. But its forces slaughtered thousands of innocent Congolese, especially ethnic Hutu, toppled the government, and exploited Congo's considerable mineral wealth. Kagame has extended his term repeatedly under the theory that he is uniquely capable of leading his fragile country.

By contrast, Kagame has also kept the country together, substantially healed its wounds, grown its economy rapidly, and made Rwanda a leader in Africa. He has brought health care, internet connectivity, and agricultural innovation to every corner of the country. Women comprise over 60 percent of the legislature. Rwanda pioneered local reconciliation and forgiveness courts, known as *gacaca*. Kagame banned plastic bags, and you will hardly find garbage anywhere. Rwanda is now akin to the Singapore of Africa, a far cry from that churchyard and the hundreds like it across the country.

It's hard to convey the myriad ways in which the Rwandan genocide affected me. It was a personal trauma, a source of nightmares and deep regret. Though I was not a senior decision maker, I was still a working-level participant in a massive policy failure. I carry the guilt with me to this day. It made me perhaps overly sympathetic to Rwanda, its people and leaders. It also rendered me hyper-vigilant in our efforts to try to prevent and resolve recurrent conflict and ethnic violence in Central Africa, not just in Rwanda, but also Burundi and Congo.

The Rwandan genocide left me hungry for mechanisms that could help prevent or mitigate the consequences of such a policy failure again. Later, as assistant secretary of state for African affairs, I championed the creation of the African Crisis Response Initiative, through which the U.S. trained and equipped six thousand African peacekeepers to be ready to respond more quickly when a future need arose. I strongly supported the Great Lakes Justice Initiative, a Clinton second-term effort to build regional capacity for the rule of law and reconciliation, which could help torn societies prevent conflict and heal their differences. At the same time, the administration fully backed the International Criminal Tribunal for Rwanda and similar justice mechanisms in West Africa.

Several months after I left the Clinton administration, I picked up my home phone and was surprised to receive a cold call from a young journalist I had never heard of before: Samantha Power. She was writing a book on genocide, including Rwanda, and wanted my reaction to what she was planning to report. She said she was told that I had worried aloud in an interagency meeting about the domestic political implications of using the term "genocide." I told Samantha emphatically that what she heard was not true. Samantha insisted she had it from two separate sources. I reiterated that I did not (and would not) inject political considerations into a policy decision, particularly as a junior NSC staffer.

Nonetheless, in her 2002 book, *A Problem from Hell*, Samantha wrote: "Susan Rice, a rising star on the NSC who worked under Richard Clarke, stunned a few officials present when she asked, 'If we use the word "genocide" and are seen as doing nothing, what will be the effect on the November [congressional] election?'" To my dismay, Samantha had completely ignored my protestations.

The words she attributed to me did not reflect how I thought or how I spoke in interagency meetings. The question she alleged I posed would have been wildly out of left field and fundamentally off-topic. Moreover, it would have been ridiculous for a working-level staffer entirely disconnected from the White House's political operation to ask midlevel, career civil servants and military officers to offer a complex political judgment well outside their realm of competence.

Despite telling Samantha that I had no recollection of any such discussion and was confident I had never said such a thing, I decided not to deny it on the record, fearing my denial would not be deemed credible. Rather, I chose to dismiss (and try to defuse) the accusation by commenting for attribution: "If I said it, it was completely inappropriate, as well as irrelevant." That was my mistake. In subsequent years, this urban legend gained traction, becoming an enduring stain on my public record and my first real taste of being grossly mis-portrayed in the press. Despite my lasting frustration and outrage, this dispute did not ultimately impede my ability later to work well with Samantha and become friends.

Of course, it was the human cost of the Rwandan genocide that has haunted me ever since. It left me determined to go down fighting, if ever I saw an instance where I believed U.S. military intervention could be at once feasible, effective, and make a critical difference in saving large numbers of human lives at an acceptable risk to U.S. interests. However, as I rose to more senior roles, I came to realize that such conditions are rarely fulfilled.

During the Obama administration, I assessed they pertained in Libya, but not in Syria, despite the extreme human toll. In both instances, I may have been wrong. Such calls are never black and white; in actuality, they are fraught with uncertainty and prone to miscalculation. Failure, as I discovered early, is an inevitable result of policymaking. We did fail; we will fail. Our aim must be to minimize the frequency and the price of failure, while learning from our mistakes—and hopefully not the wrong lessons.

8

Always Africa

One day in February 1995, I was riding in an official vehicle to the White House from Capitol Hill with National Security Advisor Tony Lake. As the NSC's U.N. director, I had accompanied Tony to meetings with senators we were trying to persuade to fully fund the administration's budget request for U.N. peacekeeping and to agree that the parameters we had placed on U.S. support for U.N. peacekeeping were wise and sufficient. Even the Democratic-led Senate was highly skeptical of the U.N. in the wake of Somalia and Rwanda. Tony, nonetheless, felt these Hill meetings had gone well, and he was in a relaxed mood.

He turned to me and said, "What is the capital of Tanzania?"

"Dar es Salaam," I replied.

"What is the capital of Botswana?" he continued.

"Gaborone," I shot back. Tony validated my answer but dutifully corrected my pronunciation.

"Burkina Faso?"

"Ouagadougou," I countered, feeling pretty good about my answers but bewildered as to the purpose of this pop quiz.

"Good," Tony said. "How would you like to be the NSC senior director for African affairs?"

I was flummoxed. Knowing he was playing with me, I still marveled that the national security advisor was promoting me to the NSC's top job on Africa on the basis of a capitals quiz. I asked for a night to consult with Ian and think about it, which he granted.

This time, though still a bit hesitant to get pigeonholed in Africa, I felt I could accept an Africa job with less risk. I had demonstrated my chops in a global portfolio, performed well enough to be selected for promotion at an early stage, and relished the opportunity to run my own office. In accepting this post, I would be Dick Clarke's peer, just two years after being christened his baby director. I would have a regional portfolio, making me the coordinator of U.S. policy for the forty-eight countries of Sub-Saharan Africa. This was preferable to having a "functional," or geographically cross-cutting portfolio, like the U.N. or nonproliferation or intelligence, because I had line responsibility for a defined portion of the planet. And, after two years under Dick's rigorous tutelage, I felt ready for whatever might come next.

I also had to admit to myself that, on some level, I began in Africa and never left. Conceived in Nigeria, raised amidst the wooden sculpture of the Yoruba and Igbo, student of the complex history of Africa and its diaspora, activist against apartheid, scholar of Zimbabwe's struggle for independence, intrepid backpacker, and bush taxi vagabond, I am ever steeped in Africa. Always. It remains an inextricable part of me.

The next morning, I told Tony that I would be honored to accept, and for the duration of the Clinton administration my work centered on Africa.

————•◆•————

As I started in this new role, I felt proud to focus on Africa and come back to the region of my graduate studies. Believing deeply in Africa's importance and potential, I resented the prejudice and shortsightedness that historically had relegated the continent to the bottom of America's national security priorities. The U.S., I had come to appreciate, has a profound national interest in expanding prosperity in this important emerging market, improving livelihoods, resolving conflicts, bolstering security, and advancing democracy and respect for human rights. Now it was my job to insist that the people and countries of Africa be deemed as worthy and deserving of America's attention and resources as any other region.

Several issues dominated my tenure from 1995 to 1997 as special assistant to the president and senior director for African affairs. Among them were: Burundi, which remained an ethnic tinderbox after Rwanda; South Africa, whose brand-new democratic government led by Nelson Mandela we had a deep interest in supporting; Angola, where the lengthy civil war had resumed; Liberia, the war-wracked West African nation with the closest historical ties to the U.S.; and Nigeria, Africa's most populous country, which was suffering under a brutal military dictator.

Africa was gaining prominence on President Clinton's foreign policy agenda, as a region to which he was becoming increasingly drawn. Moreover, Tony Lake, his national security advisor, was himself originally an Africa hand. In addition to preventing and responding to conflicts and crises, President Clinton sought a positive partnership with countries in Africa, based on mutual respect and enhanced engagement. He was especially committed to promoting economic growth and opportunity and confronting Africa's security challenges, including the burgeoning threats of disease, notably HIV/AIDS, and terrorism.

———

It was terrorism that elevated Sudan to a place of unusual prominence on the Clinton administration's agenda, making it a consistent focus of my attention throughout my tenure at the NSC and State Department. In February 1993, shortly after President Clinton took office, terrorists led by Omar Abdel Rahman, known as "the Blind Sheikh," detonated a truck bomb under the World Trade Center in New York City, killing six and wounding over one thousand. I was barely three weeks into my first job at the NSC, and my boss Dick Clarke had lead responsibility for counterterrorism at the White House. I observed closely as he tracked events and worked through the FBI and Justice Department to bring the perpetrators to justice and foil additional attacks.

Not long after the World Trade Center was bombed, an FBI informant revealed another plot orchestrated by Abdel Rahman to assassinate public figures and attack multiple landmarks in New York, including U.N. Headquarters, hotels, office buildings, the Holland and Lincoln Tunnels, and the George Washington Bridge. As the bombers were mixing their explosives, federal and local officers busted in and arrested them on June 24, 1993. Five of the eight perpetrators entered the U.S. on Sudanese passports, and there was compelling evidence that two officers at the Sudanese Mission to the U.N. had offered to assist the plotters, including by providing diplomatic license plates and vehicles to enable the perpetrators to access the garage at U.N. Headquarters. As a result, in 1993 the U.S. designated Sudan a State Sponsor of Terrorism and imposed sanctions for its role in supporting terrorism both abroad and on U.S. soil, for its close ties to Iran, and for its continued provision of a safe haven inside Sudan to various Palestinian and other terror organizations, as well as their financiers and leaders, including Carlos the Jackal, Abu Nidal, and Osama bin Laden.

The Clinton administration's concern about Sudan's support for terrorism only heightened in 1995 when Sudan was involved in a failed attempt to assassinate Egyptian president Hosni Mubarak. Egyptian gunmen shot up Mubarak's armored car as his convoy was driving from the airport to the Organization of African Unity (OAU) Summit in Addis Ababa, Ethiopia. I was alerted promptly by the White House Situation Room and informed that Mubarak escaped unharmed. His motorcade diverted immediately to the airport, enabling Mubarak to return safely to Egypt. We later learned that the gunmen had traveled to Ethiopia on Sudanese passports and used weapons shipped into Ethiopia on Sudan Airways. Two of the perpetrators fled on Sudan Airways back to Sudan, where they conveniently disappeared. When Sudan refused to hand over the suspects, the U.S. led moves at the U.N. Security Council to impose diplomatic and airline sanctions on Sudan.

Sudan's sustained support for terrorism, combined with the dangerous environment in its capital, where U.S. officials had been threatened, subjected to harassing surveillance, and twice attacked, led the administration to consider closing the U.S. embassy in Khartoum in February 1996 and relocating the reduced embassy staff to Nairobi in neighboring Kenya. The final straw was an attack by Sudanese agents on a U.S. embassy vehicle that seriously wounded the official inside.

I favored closing the embassy for security reasons, as did the CIA and my bosses at the NSC. The secretary of state, however, ultimately makes such decisions, and the ever-cautious Warren Christopher faced significant pressure from the Africa Bureau and, in particular, the new American ambassador, Tim Carney, to keep the embassy open. Carney, a mustachioed, bespectacled, professorial diplomat who had just secured his first ambassadorship, quickly revealed himself to be more sympathetic to the government of Sudan than most U.S. decision makers. In the Principals

Committee meeting where the issue was debated, Carney argued strenuously to keep the embassy open; he saw merit in maintaining close communication with Khartoum. Secretary Christopher ultimately decided to
close the embassy, necessitating that Carney vacate his post in Khartoum
and perform his ambassadorial duties from a rump office in Nairobi. I
believe that Carney always blamed me for that decision.

My view was that the regime in Khartoum, then led behind the scenes
by the radical Islamist cleric Hassan al-Turabi, was plainly opposed to the
U.S. and our national interests. The indisputable evidence included its
active support for terrorism, gross violations of human rights—particularly against the people of southern Sudan and later Darfur—and efforts
to destabilize friendly neighboring states. Add to that the regime's long-
standing support for the brutal Lord's Resistance Army, which for decades
has terrorized northern Uganda.

On a bipartisan basis, U.S. policy in both the administration and Congress was supportive of the people of southern Sudan and hostile toward
Khartoum. As I testified before Congress in July 1998, we viewed Sudan
and its National Islamic Front government as "the *only* state in Sub-Saharan
Africa that poses a direct threat to U.S. national security interests." This
determination led the Clinton administration to adopt a policy aimed at
pressuring the regime in Khartoum to fundamentally change its behavior.
Rather than a policy of regime change, this was one of pressure, isolation, and containment. In keeping with our growing concerns, I directed
the interagency process that resulted in the administration's imposition of
comprehensive economic sanctions on Sudan in November 1997, freezing all Sudanese assets in the U.S, banning all investment and most trade
with Sudan. These sanctions were swiftly backed by Congress and codified
into law.

I had argued for a complete trade ban, including a prohibition on the
U.S. continuing to import gum arabic from Sudan. A rare product found
only in trees that grow throughout Africa's Sahel region, gum arabic is a
key ingredient in sodas, newspaper print, and prescription drugs. Senator
Robert Menendez from New Jersey, the geographical heart of the pharmaceutical industry, vehemently objected to sanctioning gum arabic, even
though it was Sudan's largest export to the U.S. A force on the Senate

Foreign Relations Committee, Menendez was typically tough on human rights and terrorism; in this case, however, he sought an exception for his home-state industry. Viewing his proposed exemption as a gutting measure, I argued strenuously that Secretary Albright should resist his demand. Admittedly, my vehemence may have been excessive. In retrospect, my doggedness reminds me of my refusal as a child to cede any ground during dinner table battles when convinced of the righteousness of my position.

To douse my fervor, Albright enlisted her counselor and close advisor, Wendy Sherman, who knew the Hill extremely well, having served as assistant secretary of state for legislative affairs. Wendy sat me down in her seventh-floor office to explain that Secretary Albright had to be pragmatic. When you are responsible for U.S. policy toward the whole world, not just one continent, as Wendy patiently reminded me, you must choose your battles carefully. This was a fight that mattered greatly to the powerful Menendez, who could hold more important administration priorities hostage. I was rolled—politely but firmly. For me, this was a resounding policy defeat.

As part of our toughened approach, we supported neighboring states' efforts to counter the regime in Sudan and helped them defend against rebels backed by Khartoum. Through the Frontline States Initiative, the U.S. channeled $20 million in nonlethal, defensive military aid to Ethiopia, Uganda, and Eritrea starting in 1996. We also signaled our support for the independence aspirations of the Sudan People's Liberation Movement (SPLM) of southern Sudan, which was fighting for the right of self-determination or, failing that, for a new government in Khartoum. In later years, when Sudan launched its bid for one of the rotating African seats on the U.N. Security Council in 2000, the U.S. organized a rare and surprisingly successful campaign to deny Sudan its anticipated seat, substituting Mauritius, a friendly, democratic market economy, in its place.

The enduring challenge we faced, as we aligned U.S. policy with that of Sudan's neighboring states, was casting our lot with undemocratic leaders. We had to weigh competing imperatives. On the one hand, a core pillar of our policy toward Africa was the promotion and consolidation of democracy and defense of human rights; on the other, our top priorities in East and Central Africa were counterterrorism, reducing ethnic conflict, and preventing another genocide. As a result, there were times when regional cooperation to advance U.S. security interests took precedence over democracy promotion. For a period, I and others in Washington (outside the human rights community) saw potential in several of the relatively "new" or up-and-coming African leaders. To overgeneralize, Meles Zenawi of Ethiopia, Isaias Afwerki of Eritrea, Paul Kagame of Rwanda, and Yoweri Museveni of Uganda, each in his own way seemed in the early to mid-1990s to be intelligent, straightforward, independent-minded, self-reliant, and economically astute leaders who were willing to work with Washington to address security threats and conflicts in Somalia, Sudan, and later in Congo, formerly Zaire. At the time they stood in contrast to the calcified leaders-for-life in places like Mobutu Sese Seko's Zaire, Mugabe's Zimbabwe, and José dos Santos's Angola; and, for a while, they seemed willing to collaborate in the service of goals we shared.

Later, in 1998, when their mutual cooperation openly frayed, these so-called "New African Leaders" turned their guns on each other and, in some instances, their own people. The unsavory compromise we had made of prioritizing American security interests over our values became ever more costly and difficult to stomach. Human rights activists and some journalists leveled substantial criticism at the Clinton administration and me personally for our perceived coziness with these deeply flawed leaders. We erred, in retrospect, in heralding their leadership as "new" and as a departure from the norm. I do not regret our cooperation over issues of mutual interest, such as Sudan, but believe we would have been wiser to explain our approach in terms of national interests, while avoiding praise for individual leaders and speaking out more forcefully about their failings and abuses.

By the time President Clinton and his cabinet-level advisors approached the end of his first term, they had brokered a landmark peace agreement in Bosnia and defused a political crisis in Haiti. As their confidence in executing national security policy grew, they came to see beyond Africa's multiple crises to perceive its long-term potential. In Washington more broadly, attention to Africa was rising. It was a rare foreign policy arena in which partisan differences were few, and cooperation was the norm.

The Clinton administration was eager to seize opportunities to build a genuine U.S.-Africa partnership. Anthony Lake spearheaded this focus, including by taking personal leadership of U.S. diplomacy to prevent another genocide in Burundi. For a national security advisor—whose responsibilities include every continent and region of the world—Tony devoted uncommon attention to Africa.

Other senior officials followed suit, and I joined several of them on various trips across the continent. Ambassador Albright's U.N. responsibilities required sustained attention to Africa—addressing conflicts in Angola, Mozambique, Sudan, and Central Africa—and I traveled with her on all three of her official African visits. In 1995, Commerce Secretary Ron Brown famously declared in Senegal that "the era of America ceding the African market to the former colonial powers is over," shaking France to attention. And, in early 1997, First Lady Hillary Clinton made her first of two solo trips to Africa, visiting West, Southern, and East Africa to promote democratic progress and increased U.S.-Africa trade and investment. I found it gratifying to be working on an area that was attracting top-level interest and where I felt we could paint policy on a virtually blank canvas.

Following President Clinton's reelection in November 1996, attention turned to who would lead the national security team in the second term. Christopher, Lake, and most of the other Principals departed, and Clinton decided to elevate Deputy National Security Advisor Sandy Berger to national security advisor and U.N. ambassador Madeleine Albright to secretary of state. They, in turn, moved to restock the NSC and State Department with their chosen team.

In early December 1996, I was called to meet privately with Berger and Albright in the White House Situation Room. As my mother's old friend, Madeleine and Mom had conspired over the years to guide me on various issues—from important professional decisions to tedious judgments about my hairstyle, which they both suggested I should change to look more mature. During Clinton's first term, of course, Ambassador Albright and I had worked together intensively on U.N. and African matters. Sandy had also become a valued colleague and friend, as we labored through myriad tough issues together.

Once we settled into our seats, I realized that this was to be a conversation about my future. Madeleine said she would like me to serve with her at State as an assistant secretary, a promotion that Sandy enthusiastically backed, even though it meant me leaving the NSC. Questions followed. "Do you want to move to State? What policy areas would be of most interest to you?" We discussed the Bureaus of International Organizations, which oversees U.N. affairs; Democracy, Human Rights, and Labor; and Intelligence and Research. Each was a functional bureau with important but relatively discrete mandates. They also raised the Bureau of African Affairs, which seemed to be their preference.

Secretly, I felt trapped. Africa seemed a bridge too far for me. Not because I was unprepared in substance, but because I knew something no one else except Ian did: I was two months pregnant. Ian and I had barely digested the implications of our decision to start a family and had not told even our parents, much less any friends or colleagues. I wanted to wait at least until the end of my first trimester—past the period of highest risk for miscarriage. Also, such an announcement didn't seem conducive to constructive consideration of my next career move. So I hedged, implying that Africa may not be the best fit for me. They seemed puzzled. The unprecedented opportunity at age thirty-one to lead a regional bureau should have been highly attractive to me, and while I was capable of running these other bureaus, Africa was squarely in my wheelhouse.

Boxed in, with great trepidation, I confessed, "What I am about to tell you, I have not even told my mother. Madeleine, knowing Mom, you especially will appreciate how hurt she would be if she knew you learned this before her. But I don't think we can have a meaningful conversation unless you know: I am pregnant." They were surprised, yet totally supportive, finally grasping my hesitation. I continued, "I worry that I won't be able to travel to the extent that the Africa job requires if I have an infant. I also would need a first-rate deputy to help me hold things together in the bureau when I do have to travel. Recognizing that I am young and have no prior experience at State, I would want a heavyweight with me."

They got it—assuring me that they would support me as a new mother, their expectations regarding travel would be calibrated accordingly, and I could have any deputy I wanted.

"I know exactly who I would want," I said.

"Who?" they asked.

"Johnnie Carson."

They knew Johnnie. He was one of the most experienced and respected career officers, our ambassador to Zimbabwe and previously to Uganda, and among the foreign service's most senior African Americans. He was someone I admired and trusted to provide wisdom and ballast to the bureau. "Done," they said, which I was not sure would be welcome news to Johnnie, since he would have to leave a plum ambassadorship in Zimbabwe and return to a tough bureaucratic job at main State.

Madeleine and Sandy reiterated that they thought I would be the best person for the Africa job, given my demonstrated ability to digest the issues and drive Africa policymaking, my unique understanding of Clinton's preferred approach, my closeness to them, and my passion for putting Africa far higher on the nation's foreign policy agenda.

"We really hope you accept this offer," Madeleine said, as Sandy nodded in accord.

"Thank you both very much for your confidence in me. Can I have a day or two to talk with Ian?" I replied, rising to my feet and gathering my things.

Together, Ian and I weighed the benefits and downsides, pretty easily concluding that it was an opportunity I should not pass up. We had family in Washington to support us. We could afford a nanny, and, to ensure our family was intact, Ian would move back from Canada, where he was working. The next day, I accepted the job and told my parents, but I never revealed to Mom that Madeleine knew before she did that I was pregnant with Jake.

I remained as senior director for Africa at the NSC well into 1997, as my nomination was formalized, and I awaited my confirmation hearing. Senator John Ashcroft, the evangelical Christian and staunch, if genteel, Republican chairman of the Senate Subcommittee on African Affairs, seemed in no hurry to meet me or set a hearing date.

Months passed, and the administration's legislative affairs staff tried to figure out why Ashcroft wouldn't give me the time of day. They ultimately divined that he was reportedly uncomfortable with, and perhaps opposed to, the notion of a young pregnant woman serving as assistant secretary for Africa. Finally, in late July 1997, just as I was due to deliver, Ashcroft agreed to meet me—the prerequisite for a hearing.

Our meeting was set for July 22, and though I was mindful that seeing me in the fullness of my pregnancy would do little to assuage his concerns, I was looking forward to sitting down with Ashcroft and getting the confirmation ball rolling. As fate would have it, at about 4 a.m. on the 22nd, almost a week after I was due, I started feeling the unmistakable pangs of labor. For some hours, they were tolerable, early-stage pains, and I thought—*Why not carry on working through much of the day, as I had every day up to that point of my uneventful pregnancy?*

Around 11 a.m., Ian and I concluded it was time to brave the blistering heat and humidity to make our way to George Washington University Hospital, where my mom met us. Lois decreed emphatically that I needed to call Ashcroft's office and postpone our meeting. I objected, arguing that I may never get another chance to see him. She said: "Look, if you go up there and your water breaks in that meeting, you truly will never see him again." The voice of reason. I called.

Ashcroft graciously agreed to meet me a bit later in the summer, so I ceased worrying about that and focused the remainder of the afternoon on the fact that my epidural wasn't working to mask my increasingly intense labor pains in a discrete but significant patch of my belly. Some eight hours later, our son, Jake, arrived with what we would later come to recognize as his customary flair for the dramatic, necessitating extraction with the unwelcome use of forceps. Like all new parents, we found our lives had changed forever—for the better.

While in the early stages of my three-month maternity leave from the NSC, Ashcroft finally met with me. He was cordial and forthright in our introductory meeting in his Senate office. Over heavily sweetened iced tea, Ashcroft explained that he chaired three subcommittees and, frankly, Africa was of least interest to him. Nonetheless, he promised to schedule my hearing for September after the Senate returned from summer recess.

My parents and Ian accompanied me to the hearing, and I also carried in a bassinet our six-week-old son. As per custom, at the start of my opening statement, I introduced my family members present, including young "John David Rice-Cameron," who, although we called him "Jake," coincidentally had the same given names as the subcommittee chair. John David Ashcroft welcomed us, duly noting his namesake's presence. I privately wondered if Ashcroft worried that Jake's quiescence might be short-lived and I might luck into a shorter than usual hearing.

Indeed, the session was not prolonged, extended only by the late arrival of the ranking member of the Senate Foreign Relations Committee, Joe Biden, who apologized for his tardy Amtrak train from Delaware. Senator Biden was effusive, praising my nomination and stressing that he for one had no reservations whatsoever about my comparatively tender age (implying that others may). He recalled at length how he began in the Senate at twenty-nine years old as the single father of two boys, cheerfully recounting how he had done just fine. It was a generous salve, and it also helpfully chewed up the clock. After a nominal quantity of questions, Ashcroft adjourned the hearing before Jake even stirred.

On October 9, 1997, I was unanimously confirmed by the Senate as assistant secretary of state for African affairs. Three months to the day after Jake was born, when my maternity leave expired, I moved to the State Department.

9

Storming State

ABUJA, NIGERIA
JULY 7, 1998

To this day, many people in Nigeria think I killed him.

    In early July 1998, I traveled to Nigeria with Undersecretary of State for Political Affairs Tom Pickering, who was then among the most senior career Foreign Service Officers. As assistant secretary of state for African affairs, I had gotten to know Pickering, my immediate boss, as a wise, fast-talking, and deeply knowledgeable diplomat. Having served as ambassador to six major countries and the United Nations, Pickering had seen and heard almost everything. The purpose of our trip to Nigeria was to encourage a responsible political transition. The nasty former dictator, Sani Abacha, had died a month earlier in the company of prostitutes. Viagra was reportedly involved. His interim successor was a moderate military leader, Abdulsalami Abubakar, who hoped to shepherd Nigeria through a democratic election to select its new leader.

    A primary objective of our visit was to meet the wrongfully imprisoned opposition leader, Moshood Abiola. He was the presumed winner of Nigeria's 1993 election, but the results were annulled, and he was later arrested. We hoped to negotiate his freedom so that he could participate in the upcoming election.

    Along with Pickering and U.S. ambassador to Nigeria Bill Twaddell, I met Mr. Abiola in an austere government guesthouse on the vast presidential com-

pound in the capital, Abuja. A large and imposing man, Abiola came with his minder shortly after we arrived. Pickering, a former U.S. ambassador to Nigeria, knew Abiola from years past and greeted him warmly. Abiola, robust and happy to see us, sat on the couch and began to tell us how poorly he had been treated during his four years in prison. He was wearing sandals and multilayered, traditional Nigerian dress. I noted that his ankles were swollen.

About five minutes into the conversation, Abiola started to cough, at first mildly and intermittently, and then wrackingly with consistency. He said he was hot, so I asked his dutiful minder, "Please turn up the air-conditioning." Noticing a tea service on the table between us, I offered Abiola, "Would you like some tea to help calm your cough?"

"Yes," he said, with appreciation, and I poured him a cup. He sipped it, but continued coughing. Increasingly uncomfortable, Abiola removed his outer layer, leaving one layer on top. I shot Pickering a worried glance.

The coughing became dramatic. I told the assembled men, "I think we better call for a doctor." No one argued. The minder immediately placed the call.

Abiola asked to be excused and went into the bathroom off our meeting room. When he emerged, he was bare-chested and sweating profusely, barely able to talk. He lay down on the couch writhing and then rolled facedown onto the floor. The doctor arrived promptly, took a quick look at him, and declared that Abiola was having a heart attack and must be transported to the hospital immediately. The men labored to lift the heavy Abiola into a small car, and we rushed to the nearby, rudimentary presidential hospital. I grabbed his eyeglasses off of a side table where he had left them, his only belonging, thinking of his daughter Hafsat in the U.S., whom I'd met before we left.

The doctors worked on him furiously, but within an hour they pronounced him dead.

We braced for violence. Abiola's sudden and mysterious death would hit like a bombshell in Nigeria's political tinderbox. Conspiracy theories would spread like metastatic cancer. Serious unrest throughout Nigeria was possible. Washington would hyperventilate, since it's not every day that a major figure drops dead in a meeting with senior U.S. officials. His family would need to be told. And, urgently, Nigeria's acting president would have to hear directly from us, even though his minister was present at the hospital and knew how it went down.

Ambassador Twaddell panicked and urged me and Pickering to rush to the airport and leave the country immediately. "Hell no," we said. This delicate situation required deft management, not a hurried exit in a cloud of suspicion.

Right away, I called National Security Advisor Sandy Berger, my former boss, briefed him, and dictated a White House press release. Then we went to the Nigerian presidential palace to relay the entire drama to the acting president. We urged him to issue a careful statement and to announce the establishment of an independent autopsy by international experts, in order to quell rife speculation and limit the potential for violence. The acting president did both.

Next, Pickering, Twaddell, and I went with former Nigerian foreign minister Baba Kingibe to see Abiola's wives and daughters. All of us walked in together, but soon I realized that I was effectively alone in the room with these distraught women. The men had hung far back and left the job to me—just like the pouring of the tea. I proceeded to explain that their husband/father was dead. He had died of an apparent heart attack that began in our meeting. The doctors did all they could to save him but could not. The ladies' wailing was so intense, it haunts me to this day.

We briefed the press, and I returned to the U.S. embassy to write the official cable to report exactly what had happened. As a senior official, I almost never wrote up cables summarizing meetings, but in this case there was no more efficient way to ensure we got this very important history straight.

As I was typing, I heard in the distance on CNN a familiar voice of indignation. It was none other than the Reverend Jesse Jackson, then serving as President Clinton's special envoy for the promotion of democracy in Africa. Reverend Jackson served capably in this role, and with good intentions; but on this occasion, I could have throttled him. He was riffing about how Abiola died under suspicious circumstances in a meeting with U.S. officials. I could not believe my ears—our own guy implying we were killers! Immediately, I placed a call to his longtime aide Yuri and asked him to shut the Reverend down. "Please, just get him off the set." That happened, even as I was still watching the segment.

We stayed overnight in Nigeria to try to calm things, offer any needed assistance to the government, and make an orderly departure. Fortunately, despite deep public upset, no significant violence occurred. The autopsy eventually confirmed the cause of death as a heart attack. Nonetheless, it was Nigeria where

conspiracy theories abound. The most popular, which still has currency over
twenty years later, is that I killed Abiola by pouring him poisoned tea.

From that experience, I found that being a woman policymaker comes
with unique hazards. The men would not have offered, much less thought, to
pour the tea. They may not have swiftly called for a doctor. They may not have
been able to break the bad news to the wives. Not for the last time, it was I, not
they, who took the public fall for a crime nobody committed.

––––

At the time of our ill-fated meeting with Abiola in Nigeria, I had been
assistant secretary of state for African affairs for just under nine months.
Even before settling into my spacious, wood-paneled sixth-floor office at
the State Department, my first order of business had been to assemble a
top-quality team of senior and experienced deputies, including Ambassadors Johnnie Carson and Vicki Huddleston, and Witney Schneidman,
the only other political appointee. I had received invaluable advice from
Ambassador Prudence "Pru" Bushnell, a smart, intuitive, straight-shooting
career diplomat, whose toughness was belied by her slight stature and unassuming manner. Pru had served as a deputy assistant secretary in the Africa Bureau before being dispatched to Kenya as ambassador. She warned
me unsparingly of the skepticism I would face as a young female political
appointee in the pinstriped culture of the State Department. She counseled
me to focus on policy outcomes and not to let the bureaucracy weigh me
down.

Yet the best gift Pru gave me was the recommendation to hire Annette
Bushelle as my personal assistant, a veteran of the office and Pru's former
secretary. Annette was a godsend, not only an extremely competent administrator, but an ever-attentive mother to me at work, who advised and
protected me like my own mom, but without any of the attendant friction
or frustration.

From the start, the AF Front Office, as it was known, was welcoming
and supportive, but the rest of the bureau seemed to have been less certain
what to expect.

The forty-three ambassadors and half dozen office directors who reported directly to me were mostly white, male, career Foreign Service Officers (FSOs) who ranged in age from roughly fifty to sixty-five. They were

experienced Africa hands, mainly cautious, conservative in temperament and style, who viewed me as inexperienced, way too young for the job, and perhaps especially unsuited as a new mother. Some were silently dismissive. Many were passive-aggressive. A few were open-minded. Among the handful of female and African American ambassadors there was a slightly greater degree of acceptance, but they too were taking a wait-and-see approach.

My reputation from the NSC, as I was about to discover, had preceded me. From what I was eventually told by close colleagues, I was perceived as smart, dynamic, decisive, bureaucratically skilled, and tough, but also brash, demanding, impatient, hardheaded, and unafraid of confrontation. Some had also dubbed me imperious, autocratic, micromanaging, and intolerant of dissent. Though it was clear (and probably resented) that I had strong backing and top cover from the White House and the seventh floor (the secretary's suite) at State, the open question was whether I could translate my access and relationships into policy success and increased respect and affection from the veterans of the Africa Bureau. At the outset, I estimated that about two-thirds of my direct reports were hostile or leaning negative toward me, and about one-third were open or leaning favorable. My aim was to flip that balance over the course of my tenure, fully recognizing that there were some who would never be fans.

Like many political appointees, I felt from the start that I was playing beat-the-clock. We had just over three more years in which to advance and entrench the president's agenda, and I was not one to waste time. I came in with a clear vision of what I wanted to focus on. Within my first weeks on the job, I convened a conference of all the Chiefs of Mission serving in Africa. Each of our ambassadors returned from their posts to gather on the Eastern Shore of Maryland to discuss our priorities. In addition to the staples of conflict prevention and resolution, promotion of democracy, and human rights, I championed a "New Partnership with Africa for the 21st Century," grounded in spurring economic growth and development through increased trade, aid, and investment.

Another theme I consistently stressed was that U.S. policymakers need to better understand and address the range of transnational security threats that incubate in and can emanate from Africa, including terrorism, international crime and drug flows, and infectious disease. To deepen our collective knowledge, I asked the Intelligence Community to provide two briefings to the ambassadors on international criminal flows and the terrorist threat in Africa; obliging, they noted it was the first time they had been asked to compile that information for senior policymakers. In 1997, I was surprised to discover that the terrorist threat in Africa was underappreciated by many; I made it a top priority to heighten awareness—especially among these ambassadors.

That first Chiefs of Mission conference was somewhat awkward. In substance, it went well enough, but I felt the weight of the ambassadors sizing me up. Not there to make friends or win a popularity contest, I refused to apologize for having my baby at the conference so I could breastfeed him. My direct style did not endear me to every one of those seasoned diplomats. What I cared about was that I was granted the respect and cooperation necessary to "get shit done." And, if I did, I knew those many who cared foremost about outcomes might eventually accept me on the merits.

The other potentially tough audience I was mindful to try to tame was the African leaders—ambassadors, ministers, and heads of state—with whom I would work directly as their principal interlocutor. Secretary of State Albright talked to African leaders when the stakes were especially high, or she was visiting their country. The president would engage African leaders when he traveled, they visited the White House, or if the stakes were huge. But I was the official who, on a daily basis, needed to be able to pick up the phone and talk to President X or travel to meet with him. Most African leaders accepted that disparity in rank, understanding that dealing with the United States was unique and especially important. A few older, very long-serving and corrupt leaders, like Robert Mugabe of Zimbabwe and José dos Santos of Angola, would sometimes play hard to get and occasionally make themselves unavailable at the last minute. Mostly, however, I was easily able to represent the U.S. at the highest levels of government in Africa and get the audiences I needed.

Interestingly, if the African leaders had reservations about my youth or gender, they hid them well. On occasion, I would encounter someone whose jaw dropped when they first met me. One civil society leader in Nigeria blurted out something like: "We thought you were sixty years old, two hundred and fifty pounds, and six feet tall," based on media impressions. When the Sudanese ambassador to the U.N., Elfatih Erwa, with whom I had tussled remotely, first met me at the General Assembly, he exclaimed, "Oops, you're beautiful, I always thought you were a monster." By contrast, some journalists, especially a few retrograde, white South African writers, like Simon Barber, were fixated on the length of my skirts.

Still, I never had any African leader balk at dealing with me. Soon I realized that it was because they had no choice: I represented the USA whether they liked it or not, and they had to deal with the USA whether they liked it or not. Nonetheless, over time, I formed excellent working relationships with many leaders across the continent, including Meles of Ethiopia, Kagame of Rwanda, Museveni of Uganda, Obasanjo of Nigeria, Chissano of Mozambique, Mogae of Botswana, and Rawlings of Ghana, all of whom were unfailingly respectful and appropriate in their dealings with me.

Within six weeks of my arrival at State, in December 1997, I accompanied Secretary Albright on the first of her four trips to Africa as secretary of state. She visited Ethiopia, Rwanda, Uganda, the Democratic Republic of Congo, Angola, South Africa, and Zimbabwe. Secretarial trips are grueling, complex enterprises that require careful design of the itinerary down to each meeting, and massive preparation of briefing memos, speeches, and press materials. The embassies and support staff in Washington handle the logistical feat of smoothly and safely transporting the secretary, staff, security detail, secure communications gear, and traveling press corps via a U.S. Air Force plane.

Albright's first secretarial trip to Africa was largely successful, but for one unfortunate and unauthorized comment by a traveling staffer to the press. The staffer was quoted as saying, "We don't do Mary Robinson," a reference to the U.N. High Commissioner for Human Rights, which suggested we were disinclined to press the African leaders with whom we met on human rights. Understandably, Secretary Albright was furious and unloaded on a small group of us senior staff as we flew between stops on her plane, demanding to know, "Who on this plane, who among us could be so stupid and tone-deaf to say such a thing?"

We never did learn who the culprit was. Not only was this a damaging leak, but it played into an unwelcome critique that we were prepared to give the so-called "new African leaders" something of a pass on democracy and human rights, if they advanced our shared security agenda. Albright personally was offended, as she has always been an ardent defender of democracy. Plus, Mary Robinson was the respected former president of Ireland and an important interlocutor for the secretary.

Apart from this incident, for me the trip was most memorable as my first extended period away from Jake. He was barely five months old, and I was still breast-feeding. While traveling, I frequently became engorged, as I struggled to find time in the intense schedule to pump and dump my milk so that my supply could be sustained while I was away. In my absence, Jake drew down my stored reserves and drank formula as needed to supplement.

———

In Uganda, we traveled to the far north in Gulu to bear witness to the ravages of the Lord's Resistance Army (LRA), the mystical, bizarre Sudanese-backed rebel group that terrorized the region, stealing children and torching villages. We visited a hospital where children camped at night, hoping that strength in numbers would shield them from being kidnapped in rebel raids, and a rehabilitation center run by the NGO World Vision for those who managed to escape their abductors. World Vision introduced us to a young, roughly three-year-old boy whose family had recently been slaughtered on the side of a dirt road by the LRA. The boy and his one-month-old baby sister had been shielded by their mother who lay on top of them in the ditch. The mother was killed but the boy managed to climb out from under her and realized that his sister was also alive. He carried her for a full day as he walked to Gulu to seek assistance.

Looking into that little boy's eyes cut me to my core. I will never forget him or his sister, Charity, that beautiful baby girl who was younger even than Jake. As Secretary Albright cradled fragile Charity in her arms, I felt at once deeply grateful to be fortunate enough to raise a child in security, yet maddeningly powerless to help the orphaned child in front of me. As we left, my sense of guilt and betrayal was overwhelming.

Our last stop in Africa was Zimbabwe, a country I knew well from my doctoral dissertation. In the years since I studied there as a graduate student, Mugabe had become increasingly authoritarian and corrupt, wrecking the economy and allowing the country's once excellent infrastructure to deteriorate. On our final day, as we prepared to leave the hotel, I plugged my breast pump into the socket, using my normal AC/DC converter. The apparatus first sparked and then fizzled. Dead.

I was mortified. We were forty-eight hours from returning to the U.S., with a final stop on the way back in Brussels. My milk supply was reduced already due to the infrequency with which I had been able to pump. I was far from ready to give up breast-feeding, which was my unique and most intimate connection to Jake, one that neither his father nor his nanny could replace. It made me feel vital to his existence, when I was wrestling with my own insecurities about whether I could (and should) be trying to succeed simultaneously at my demanding job and as a first-time mother. Feeling prematurely defeated in that struggle and just exhausted, I broke down and cried. (Note to mothers: always bring a manual pump overseas as a backup.)

Before leaving Zimbabwe, I called Ian and asked him to order a new pump. I consulted older women, seeking advice on what to do. Someone said, "I've heard that drinking lots of beer and hot chocolate is good for your milk supply." It sounded like an old wives' tale, but who doesn't like beer or hot chocolate? In Belgium, I was blessed to be able to consume both in ample supply. Miraculously, it worked, and I was able to make it home in time to resume pumping and feeding before my supply totally evaporated.

I managed to continue breast-feeding Jake for another four months—until I had to join President Clinton on his first trip to Africa as president. Then I gave up, reluctantly conceding that if pumping on a secretarial trip had nearly done me in, the pace and unpredictability of a presidential tour with only a few hours of sleep every night would make pumping completely unsustainable.

———

Clinton's first Africa trip was alternatively a buoyant, somber, and jubilant wild ride. With his easy charm, gently graying full head of hair, and long-fingered, almost regal hands warmly greeting all he encountered, President Clinton bounded energetically through the twelve-day, six-nation tour.

The trip was an unprecedented multi-region, extended presidential visit to Africa. Clinton brought with him much of his cabinet (though as she often did, Secretary Albright stayed back, enabling me to take her place as the senior State Department official to join the president in every meeting and on every site visit). There were dozens of members of Congress, a huge traveling press corps, and ample staff support.

When the president of the United States travels abroad, the accompanying footprint is massive. When he travels to six countries in Africa, it becomes mind-boggling. First of all, six stops constitute an insanely long itinerary for any presidential trip. (When years later I was in a position to make such decisions, I would never have done that to Obama.) Then factor in the distances, security risks, and lack of adequate medical support in Africa, and it's a whole different order of magnitude. Hospital ships with helicopters on stand-by loiter offshore. Secret Service detachments flood each country. Military transport planes leap-frog armored limousines from location to location. Experts install secure communications packages housed in soundproof containers at every stop. For each destination, there is an evacuation plan. The competency and complex orchestration are a wonder to behold.

We began in Ghana, where the most amazingly thick and raucous crowds lined the streets for miles from the airport to Accra's Independence Square. There, a massive rally greeted President Clinton and his Ghanaian host, the frenetic, impulsive, but charming former military officer, President Jerry Rawlings. The greeting was the most extraordinary I have ever witnessed, befitting the first stop on the first-ever comprehensive presidential tour of Africa, in the first African country to achieve independence.

Next, in Uganda, the president visited a rural village and met with regional leaders in Entebbe. As I had urged, Clinton added a brief but moving stop in Kigali, Rwanda, where he met with survivors of the genocide, the president and vice president of Rwanda, and apologized on behalf of the U.S. and the international community for the failure to try to halt the genocide.

In South Africa, I joined Clinton as he visited Robben Island and toured Nelson Mandela's cell with the former prisoner, now president, as his guide. I was deeply moved to witness firsthand the tall, aging, yet still powerful

Mandela exhibit extraordinary dignity and a genuine lack of bitterness toward his captors, as he described dispassionately the harsh conditions of his twenty-seven years of imprisonment, eighteen of which he endured on Robben Island. Standing in the hot sun at the old prison quarry where he once labored, wearing a classic, colorful open-collared Madiba shirt, Mandela's telling of his incredible story took me back to my days as an anti-apartheid activist, when I refused even to consider traveling to South Africa. Now, I was America's senior diplomat for Africa joining my president in bilateral meetings with Nelson Mandela, president of a free South Africa.

The traveling press corps took full advantage of South Africa's wineries and culinary treasures, enjoying the comparative luxury of Africa's most developed country. The next stop was Botswana, where after quickly dispatching with official meetings, the Clintons decamped to the Okavango Delta in the north to enjoy some game watching. Then, in Senegal, the Clintons visited Goree Island, a last point of departure for many Africans during the slave trade.

The trip was a highly successful, fun, if exhausting journey, which sent the very clear signal that Africa was high among President Clinton's priorities. He was confident in Africa's potential and keen to reap the benefits of a U.S.-Africa partnership based on mutual interest and mutual respect. At the center of the agenda was his "Partnership for Economic Growth and Opportunity in Africa," which aimed to catalyze Africa's full integration into the global economy through increased trade, investment, debt relief, and development assistance. He championed passage of the landmark African Growth and Opportunity Act, which would open the U.S. market as never before to goods from Africa. And President Clinton sent the strong signal to his entire cabinet that each member was expected to invest his or her time and institutional resources in Africa, and he would be keeping track of their progress.

The high we all felt coming off that trip was intense and exhilarating, but it was short-lived.

————

Apart from President Clinton's trip to Africa in late March, 1998 was a year from hell. Murphy's Law prevailed. Everything went wrong.

Barely six weeks later, the shit hit the fan in the Horn of Africa. Ethiopia and Eritrea came to sudden blows. Their leaders had once been close partners in the struggle to overthrow the repressive Derg regime in Ethiopia in 1991 and in achieving Eritrean independence in 1993. More recently, tensions had been building along their lengthy common border, which had never been demarcated after Eritrea's independence. Economic frictions, exacerbated by Ethiopia's negative reaction to Eritrea's introduction of an independent currency in 1997, created a combustible environment. When Eritrean and Ethiopian border guards skirmished on May 6, 1998, it was clear that either the leaders would quickly defuse tensions, or things might spiral out of control.

In Washington, we were deeply concerned to see two friends of the U.S. fight each other, particularly after I and President Clinton had (prematurely) heralded them as "new African leaders." Personally, I was sickened to see Isaias of Eritrea and Meles of Ethiopia morph from collaborators to combatants. They were also important U.S. partners in addressing regional hot spots from Somalia, to Sudan, to Congo. The situation worsened in mid-May when Eritrea rolled tanks into the Badme area, a rocky, barren, lightly populated stretch along the border, administered since independence by Ethiopia. Eritrea also seized land in two other places along the border, asserting its territorial claims through the unlawful use of force.

When the call came for help, I was in Paris meeting with my French counterparts on a range of African issues. A wider war seemed probable, and I flew directly to Addis Ababa, the Ethiopian capital, with a mandate from Secretary Albright and the White House to try to ease the tension. A strong team of experts on East Africa came from Washington to meet me. The team included Gayle Smith, then a senior USAID officer who in her previous life had been a war correspondent covering the Ethiopian and Eritrean rebel movements that now led the governments in each country. Gayle had known both leaders well for years and understood how to get into their heads. David Dunn, a jovial and capable career diplomat, ran the East Africa office at the State Department, and Lieutenant Colonel Michael Bailey was an experienced Africa hand and U.N. peacekeeper from the Pentagon. Long-haired, intensely committed, and unaccustomed to the constraints of government, John Prendergast was an Africa director at the National Security Council, whom I had hired from the NGO world before I moved to State.

We arrived in Addis Ababa, Ethiopia, to find a very agitated Prime Minister Meles Zenawi nearly bouncing off the walls of his dark, spartan, yet spacious formal office. Extremely intelligent, normally cool and calculating, Meles was seething, almost shaking, with anger at Eritrean president Isaias Afwerki, whom he felt had betrayed him. Their last (and final) conversation had ended badly, and Meles was resigned to war. In our meetings, Gayle and I tried to calm him down and understand his position: he insisted that Eritrea withdraw from Badme immediately and unconditionally in order to restore "the status quo ante." He repeated reflexively, "*Not one rock!*" in the soil of Badme could be altered; everything must be exactly like it was before the fighting began. I could hardly believe we were facing a major war over a virtually valueless piece of barren land.

We knew Isaias would be an even tougher customer in terms of his willingness to compromise, but armed with Meles's bottom lines, we flew across the border to Asmara, the neat and orderly Eritrean capital, to explore Isaias's position. In normal times, Isaias was hot-tempered and mercurial, unpretentious yet canny. He was, by turns, brash and charming, engaging and infuriating, but above all unpredictable. In this moment of stress and uncertainty, he was a roiling ball of rage, egged on by his perennial sidekicks and closest advisors, two men both named Yemane.

In our initial effort at shuttle diplomacy, we were joined by a senior Rwandan delegation led by Vice President Paul Kagame, who was respected by both leaders and well-known to us. As anticipated, Isaias proved even more recalcitrant than Meles; worse, he insulted and dismissed our efforts to defuse the conflict. Isaias maintained that the land he seized belonged to Eritrea, that Ethiopia had initiated several previous rounds of fighting along the border, and that it wished to topple his government. All Eritrea had done, according to Isaias, was to retake what was rightfully theirs. There was, in his view, no need for mediation.

Kagame, angered by the disrespectful attitude of Isaias and convinced of the futility of mediation, returned to Kigali but deputized his minister in the Office of the President, Patrick Mazimhaka, and other close aides to continue working with us. Undeterred by the intransigence of both Meles and Isaias—and determined not to give up on my first real attempt at personal diplomacy and conflict resolution—I continued shuttling between the two leaders, looking for a way forward. Even though my responsibilities spanned the whole African continent and this intensive sort of diplomacy could not be my full-time job for long, I was convinced that only the U.S. could possibly apply the sustained diplomatic resources and attention needed to resolve this conflict. If we quit, no one else could fill the void. Moreover, our particular team, given its composition and relationships with the players, was uniquely suited to try.

But the risks were palpable. All commercial flights between the two capitals had been halted, so we were compelled to fly the long distance back and forth between Addis and Asmara in a small U.S. military prop plane and later a little leased plane that seated four passengers. As tensions escalated, the airspace over the disputed area also became a war zone, and we were forced to fly way out over the Red Sea to avoid being shot down, adding hours and additional stress to our travels. These rides were terrifying, white-knuckle journeys buffeted by high winds over mountainous remote areas. As a new mother, I chastised myself silently for taking such risks, but I figured—*what choice do I have?* Still, I couldn't help fearing that we might meet the same fate as revered former U.S. congressman Mickey Leland, who died in a 1989 plane crash over a remote part of Ethiopia as he tried to mitigate recurrent famine. Indeed, in 1999, Ethiopian forces downed a South African civilian private plane flying over the two countries.

With the help of the Rwandans, we drafted a framework of principles designed to end the conflict. Our proposal involved Eritrean withdrawal in accordance with international law, a cease-fire, monitors, and an internationally sanctioned process to delimit and demarcate the border.

Following one tense meeting in Asmara, Isaias demanded that he and I meet solo and kicked out my team. I protested but decided to stay in order to prove that I could take him one-on-one. Alone in his austere meeting room, decorated sparsely with the ugly, heavy wooden furniture typical of the ceremonial offices of some African heads of state, I heard him out. As usual, he was obnoxious, condescending, and offensive, arguing by turns that we were stupid, biased, and incompetent. Isaias insisted in effect that, "Eritrea had done no wrong. We are the victims. We are not moving an inch. Let there be war to teach the arrogant Ethiopians a lesson."

In response, I was forceful and perhaps even profane, countering, "This is the dumbest war I can imagine. It can and *must* be resolved peacefully." I told Isaias he needed to pull his forces back and work with us to address the underlying conflict. The meeting ended in an impasse, but I had demonstrated that neither I nor the USA would be cowed by him. Both buoyant and exhausted, I reported to my team that Isaias had challenged my "manhood," but I stood my ground and gave it all back to him.

After two separate rounds of intensive diplomacy culminated in early June, Ethiopia accepted our proposal. We pressed hard in Asmara on Isaias to relent, but he stubbornly refused, insisting instead on demilitarizing the disputed areas and direct talks with Ethiopia—a nonstarter. My next move was to travel with our Rwandan partners in four hops on our rickety small plane to Ouagadougou, Burkina Faso, where the leaders of the Organization of African Unity (OAU), which years later became the African Union, would convene for their annual summit. Our goal was to seek the OAU's endorsement of our framework proposal.

Shortly after we took off from Eritrea, Ethiopia launched a major air assault on the Asmara airport, sharply escalating the conflict. Eritrea responded by striking both military and civilian targets deep inside Ethiopia, including the densely populated historic city of Mekele, killing civilians on the street and hitting a school. The air war underscored the determination of the two countries to bloody each other badly and heralded the start of a sustained, deadly conflict. The U.S. drew down our embassy staff in Asmara to a bare minimum, while President Clinton personally interceded with the leaders to broker successfully an air strike moratorium after about ten days of intensive bombardment.

In parallel, we worked to mount diplomatic pressure on the parties to agree to a cease-fire and political resolution. In Ouagadougou, I became the first American ever allowed formally to address the OAU Council of Ministers. With Patrick Mazimhaka, I outlined the history of our efforts and the substance of our proposed framework, ending by asking for and receiving agreement from the OAU to endorse it and to commit to joining us in sustained diplomacy toward a resolution. We next set our sights on New York, where we obtained a U.N. Security Council resolution demanding that both sides cease hostilities, welcoming the air moratorium, and supporting the U.S. and OAU mediation efforts. At this stage, Rwanda handed off its role as our African negotiating partner to the OAU. Algeria later stepped in, proving to be a very capable partner.

Fighting died down after the air moratorium went into effect and the rainy season intensified. The parties were hardly through with hostilities; instead, they used the monsoon months to mobilize, train, and deploy large forces to the border area, dig trenches in World War I fashion, and purchase massive quantities of sophisticated weapons and aircraft from Russian, Eastern European, and Chinese arms dealers.

In September 1998, at my suggestion, President Clinton appointed my good friend and former boss, his former national security advisor Anthony Lake, as special envoy for Ethiopia and Eritrea. Tony would take over the negotiating team, assuming day-to-day responsibility for the shuttle diplomacy and liaison with the OAU, reporting to Clinton through me and Gayle Smith, now the new NSC senior director for African affairs. Gayle and I remained deeply involved in all aspects of our strategy and diplomacy, but with wide responsibilities and an African continent blowing up in multiple places simultaneously, we could not devote the necessary sustained attention to this critical conflict. Ever wise, deeply respected, and collegial, Tony was the perfect envoy to drive forward our negotiations in partnership with Algerian prime minister Ahmed Ouyahia and his team, making numerous trips to the warring capitals.

Over two and a half years, the U.S. never relented in its diplomacy, as the deadly war raged on. Whenever possible, I joined Tony on his missions to the capitals and to Algiers, where we coordinated with the Algerians and co-hosted "proximity talks," in which the parties spoke to the U.S.-Algerian mediating team, though never to each other, even as we all stayed in the same diplomatic compound. As we continued to try to narrow the differences between the parties, political pressure mounted in each country to finish the war.

One day in the spring of 2000—with economic costs soaring for two of the world's most impoverished countries and the rainy season fast approaching when the ground would turn into impossible mud—my office phone rang. When I picked up, there were no voices. All I could make out in the far distance was B. B. King singing "The Thrill Is Gone." After the song ended, a deeply frustrated Tony Lake, with John Prendergast, reported from Algiers that both sides remained as dug-in as ever. They were very near throwing in the towel. My job, easy by comparison, given their claustrophobic confinement in a bland Algerian diplomatic facility, was to talk them off the ceiling. I calmly implored them, "Take a break, find something to drink, then get some sleep. And remember the stakes." We could not give up.

As the Algiers talks reached a critical moment in early May 2000, it was not the warring parties but an American who blindsided all of us. U.S. ambassador to the U.N. Richard Holbrooke, who was leading a Security Council delegation to Africa, unilaterally diverted the U.N. mission to Eritrea. Holbrooke was not only a talented veteran diplomat with an outsized ego but also a contemporary and rival of Tony Lake's from the Vietnam era when they both served as young Foreign Service Officers. Over the objections of our negotiating team and without sanction from the White House, Holbrooke and seven U.N. diplomats dropped into Asmara with little knowledge of the leaders or the complex issues at play. Holbrooke, who bore a decades-long, personal animus toward Tony Lake and a strong, if more recent, disdain for me, decided to prove that he could do what we couldn't and broker an end to the war. He fell prey to Isaias's efforts to charm and mislead him about the history and balance of culpability in the conflict. Ignorant and emboldened, Holbrooke proceeded to Addis from Asmara, armed with Isaias's talking points.

Meanwhile, in Ethiopia, Meles—desperate for a way to hold off his own hard-liners, who were pressing for a final offensive to vanquish Eritrea—urged the U.S. to offer him a diplomatic lifeline. Instead, Holbrooke, refusing to consult Tony or others on the U.S. negotiating team, presented Meles with an Isaias proposal that had already been considered and rejected by Ethiopia. When Meles asked if this was the best and final U.S. offer, Dick said yes, misrepresenting the American position. Furious at what he perceived to be an eleventh-hour American effort to try to dupe him, Meles angrily refused Holbrooke's warmed-over scraps.

Holbrooke erupted, berating Meles as "the Milosevic of Africa." By convincing Meles that the Americans were no longer willing to play a constructive role, Holbrooke virtually ensured that the war would resume with Ethiopia launching its planned offensive. When within forty-eight hours, it did, the joke throughout the State Department was that Holbrooke's next book should be *To Start a War*, a sequel to his memoir entitled *To End a War*, which recounted his role in the Bosnia negotiations that resulted in the Dayton Peace Accords. Yet this last phase of the war was no joke. Of the up to 100,000 soldiers who died in the conflict, tens of thousands perished in this final offensive. Following his diplomatic failure, Holbrooke publicly lambasted the leaders, especially Meles, and surreptitiously spun up critical press stories and editorials blaming me and Tony for the failure of American diplomacy.

This time, Ethiopia routed Eritrea. The U.S. led the U.N. Security Council in imposing an arms embargo on both countries, a step many observers argued we should have taken earlier, but that until then, we assessed, would have made tough negotiations even more difficult. When the offensive ebbed, we were able to persuade the parties to return to Algiers for further proximity talks in early June. After a few weeks of additional negotiations, Tony and our team gained both sides' agreement to a formal cessation of hostilities and complex arrangements for separating and monitoring the opposing forces with a U.N. peacekeeping force. The parties also agreed to conclude a final and binding peace agreement that would define and demarcate the border, resolve all claims and disputes, and eventually restore ties between the countries. The Algiers Agreement was signed by the parties on December 12, 2000, and by Secretary Albright on behalf of the U.S. as a co-guarantor.

The deadliest inter-state conflict in the world had ended. The U.S. partnership with the OAU and Algeria to accomplish this goal was indispensable as well as unprecedented. The Clinton administration was given considerable credit for the eventual success of our negotiation by some of the same press outlets that had criticized us six months earlier. On behalf of President Clinton, for our work to resolve this horrific conflict, National Security Advisor Sandy Berger awarded Tony, me, and Gayle the Samuel Nelson Drew Memorial Award. This prize was deeply meaningful, as it recognized the sacrifice of my late NSC colleague, an Air Force colonel, who died in 1995 along with two other dedicated public servants, Joe Kruzel and Robert Frasure, in a fiery accident on a mountainside in Bosnia, while working with Richard Holbrooke to bring peace to the Balkans. Their loss is emblematic of the risks our unsung Foreign Service Officers and civil servants as well as our uniformed military, incur every day to bring peace and hope to the most dangerous parts of the world.

For over two years, our Ethiopia-Eritrea negotiating team was relentless in their high-stakes, high-stress diplomacy with two sides that needed and resented us in equal measure. I honed my skills as a negotiator, diplomat, and team leader, experiencing firsthand the extreme difficulty of trying to reconcile warring parties. I learned the immeasurable value of patience and persistence in a complex negotiation, the difficulty of overcoming the intransigence of stubborn leaders facing their own domestic pressures, and the importance of negotiating outside the glare of the public spotlight where positions only harden.

In this, as in many conflicts, U.S. diplomatic engagement was essential to achieving an agreement. No other country could have applied the resources, prestige, tenacity, and weight to press for resolution; yet, as we were repeatedly reminded, U.S. influence has limits. America cannot compel recalcitrant warring parties to make peace, even when they are poor and substantially dependent on us for assistance. While tireless effort is best exerted at every stage to try to end a war, I found that the breakthrough often only comes when one or both sides is exhausted and ready to relent. Until then, the conflict likely will not prove "ripe" for resolution through mediation.

In January 2001, shortly before the administration ended, I visited Eritrea for the last time. Over the prior three years, it had been Isaias who was most difficult throughout the negotiation, yet he was the one who insisted on taking me dancing at a popular nightclub in Asmara and out on the Red Sea in a small Eritrean military boat from the port of Massawa. Awkward, ironic, and in some ways gratifying, that visit would give me the chance to see him finally relax and revert briefly to his former jovial, if caustic, self. It would be the last time we had any fun together.

After the war concluded in December 2000, a long, cold peace ensued; but progress toward demarcating the border and normalizing relations between the two adversaries would remain frozen until 2018, when a new Ethiopian leader finally agreed to fully implement our original agreement unconditionally.

10

"I Remember When I Too Was a Young Assistant Secretary"

"**D**on't forget, it can always get worse."

Barely ten months into my job as assistant secretary of state for African affairs, on August 6, I was given memorable advice by Tony Lake as I struggled to juggle competing conflicts while establishing my leadership of the bureau. Tony—twenty-five years my senior—was just the person from whom I needed to get wisdom and perspective. Over dinner, I lamented the crush of crises, confessing it was starting to feel overwhelming. He listened intently, but instead of offering much needed reassurance, Tony warned quietly that more could still come.

Hours later, shortly after 3:40 a.m., the secure phone next to my bed rang. I answered to hear the familiar formality: "This is the State Department Operations Center with Ambassador Johnnie Carson for Assistant Secretary Rice."

"This is she," I said, rousing myself from a deep sleep.

My deputy, his voice laden with concern, reported, "There have been two near simultaneous attacks on our embassies in Nairobi and Dar es Salaam. It seems they were truck bombs. Ambassador Bushnell in Kenya reports numerous casualties."

I jumped out of bed. Within minutes, I was out the door and on my way to State. When I arrived ten minutes later, I went straight to the Operations Center on the seventh floor, the nerve center of the department, where watch officers answer calls from around the world, follow the news, cable traffic, and connect State personnel by voice- or videoconference to every embassy in the world and any department in Washington. I was pointed to a conference room, where a secure videoconference was already in progress.

My former boss, Dick Clarke, was on the screen chairing an emergency session of the Counter-terrorism Support Group, the interagency committee mandated to prevent and respond to terrorist attacks. He asked the military to transport U.S.-based civilian search-and-rescue teams to arrive as quickly as possible to recover victims from the wreckage. He directed the FBI to send teams immediately to Nairobi and Dar to investigate the attacks.

Early reports indicated that the bombings had all the hallmarks of Osama bin Laden's Al Qaeda—simultaneity, potency, American targets. In Kenya, twelve Americans—diplomats, family members, military and intelligence personnel—were killed, along with an estimated 200 Kenyan civilians, including over thirty who worked at the embassy, plus scores of passersby on the street. Thousands were wounded, many grievously by flying glass and debris. The building caved, the scene conjuring Dante's Inferno. In Tanzania, eleven Tanzanians were killed but no Americans.

Nairobi was the deadliest attack on a U.S. embassy in American history. We learned later that morning that Al Qaeda also planned to strike a third U.S. embassy at the same time in Kampala, Uganda. By a fluke of luck, however, Ugandan authorities stopped the truck carrying explosives at the border and averted that bombing.

—————— • ◆ • ——————

Never had I experienced a crisis of this magnitude—and right square in my chain of command. My colleagues had been killed. Our embassies across the continent remained at heightened risk. Many were vulnerable due to their proximity to roadways and their routine construction in the "pre-Inman" era (that is, before the 1983 Beirut bombing, after which most of our embassies were built to withstand such powerful blasts). Al Qaeda could strike again without notice. Families of Americans in Kenya were overwhelming the phones at the Operations Center seeking information and solace. We set up several twenty-four-hour task forces to support the embassies, monitor developments, and assist the families of victims. As we labored to save the injured, we evacuated many to U.S. military medical facilities in Germany and the U.S.

Throughout this ordeal, I was on the phone with our ambassadors in Kenya, Tanzania, and Uganda, trying to meet their requests for support and intelligence. My deputies and I sought to comfort staff who had lost embassy co-workers and friends, even as we were all compelled to keep working in overdrive, with little sleep, throughout the aftermath of the bombings.

Shortly after the attacks, I received an unsolicited visit from a psychiatrist in the State Department Medical Unit. He came, he said, because he was concerned about morale among the Washington-based staff in the Africa Bureau. With remarkable clumsiness for a shrink, he asked, "You understand, don't you, how much stress and trauma your colleagues in the bureau feel?"

Indignant and impatient with this seemingly pedestrian intrusion, I said, "Of course, I do." I thought, *what the hell is your point?*

He said he hoped that I could assist in reducing their anxiety by easing their workload and assuaging their fears.

Then I snapped, "We are all under stress. Understandably. We have just lost a dozen of our colleagues. They are not coming back. We are working around the clock to support their families and the embassy staff. I hardly see what you think we can stop doing at this stage. We are going to have to muscle through this as best we can. Thank you for your concern."

Opening the door to let him out, I all but slammed it behind him. I had no patience for his touchy-feely platitudes. With hindsight, I better appreciate that it was his job to show concern and try to alleviate our collective distress. My frustration with the doctor stemmed from failing to see how I or anyone else could have measurably eased the burden we all felt. Additionally, I now wonder if my ability to compartmentalize and plow through pain left me unable to fully appreciate how others may process grief differently.

Days later, I traveled with Secretary Albright to Dar es Salaam and Nairobi. We visited grievously wounded embassy staff in Nairobi's hospitals, several of whom had lost limbs and suffered life-changing injuries from glass and metal projectiles. We saw the shell of our destroyed embassy, a shocking monument to the potency of the blast. While mourning the Kenyans and Tanzanians killed and wounded, the secretary and I tried to lend emotional support to our country teams in both capitals. Throughout, I felt overwhelmed by loss, stricken by the power of evil, and submerged in the anger and grief of loved ones, especially as we flew eighteen hours back to Andrews Air Force Base in a C-17 military transport plane alongside the flag-draped coffins of our colleagues.

August 7, 1998, was the worst day of my professional life, as it was for many colleagues, from the secretary of state to desk officers in the Africa Bureau. Yet, our grief and devastation bore no comparison to that felt by Ambassador Bushnell, her brave team at Embassy Nairobi, and, above all, the families whose loved ones were killed. On that infamous day, terror took our foreign service officers. A Marine and airmen. Intelligence officers. Civil servants. An epidemiologist with the Centers for Disease Control. American public servants, all.

Susan Bartley lost both her husband and son. Julian Bartley Sr. was a senior embassy officer, and Julian "Jay" Jr. was interning at the mission over the summer. As with the others, Susan and her daughter, Edith's, immeasurable pain saddens me to this day. Each colleague lost, each family bereft, weighed on me with almost suffocating force. These dedicated professionals were patriots doing their utmost for their country on August 7, just like they did every day.

Two weeks after the attacks, President Clinton retaliated by sending scores of Tomahawk missiles into an Al Qaeda camp in Afghanistan and the Al Shifa pharmaceutical factory in Sudan. The decision to attack and the target selection were closely held within a small group of cabinet-level principals. Dick Clarke, as counterterrorism czar, was in those meetings, but I was not. The attacks were criticized by Clinton's political opponents as "Wag the Dog" distractions from the mounting Monica Lewinsky scandal. In fact, the U.S. reprisals were justified and barely proportionate responses to Al Qaeda's terrorism and a warning that we could strike their facilities inside Afghanistan at will.

The Sudan target was a more controversial choice. It was selected largely because a soil sample analyzed by U.S. intelligence revealed the presence of EMPTA, a precursor compound for VX, a deadly chemical agent of the sort Al Qaeda threatened to weaponize against American targets. Bin Laden, who lived until 1995 in Sudan, was also believed to have had some financial stake in the factory. But the Sudanese government and some others maintained that the plant had always been a purely civilian, commercial facility that had been gratuitously hit due to American animus toward the country. The Sudanese claims were never validated.

In the months that followed, we operated on high alert, given the potential that additional U.S. facilities in Africa would be hit by Al Qaeda. We faced an unyielding stream of threat information, much of it specific, revealing plots to attack targets across the continent. It was like playing whack-a-mole, trying to stay ahead of the enemy and thwart any future strikes. I led the Africa Bureau through a detailed assessment of the vulnerability of our diplomatic posts on the continent, with the aim of having a strong basis for seeking additional funds from Congress to harden or rebuild those facilities that needed it most. In the late 1990s, many of our African posts were deemed both "high threat," meaning we assessed there to be an Al Qaeda presence or ability to hit the target, and "high vulnerability." We felt like sitting ducks.

Secretary Albright successfully pressed Congress to appropriate supplemental funds to reinforce existing embassies, including with such basic measures as placing Mylar on windows to reduce blast impact and prevent glass flying and installing makeshift barricades to achieve additional "setback" from the street. Albright also obtained funds to rebuild our embassies in Nairobi and Dar es Salaam in safer locations and to accelerate the gradual pace of new construction to replace other vulnerable missions across Africa.

Within the Africa Bureau, our top priority was to avoid another attack, even at the expense of normal embassy operations. When one evening in December 1998 my principal deputy, Johnnie Carson, reported that we had multiple, credible, imminent threats targeting numerous U.S. embassies, I immediately ordered the shutdown of all our embassies in Africa for the following day. I then returned to the pressing issues at hand, working as usual late into the evening. The next morning, I received an early phone call from my immediate boss, Undersecretary of State for Political Affairs Tom Pickering. Uncharacteristically irate, he yelled, "How the hell do you close all the embassies in Africa and neglect to inform the Seventh Floor?"

Only then did it hit me: I had forgotten to inform him or any of my superiors that I had unilaterally shut down the entire continent—an unprecedented move. Letting Pickering learn of my directive from the morning press added insult to injury. Apologizing profusely, I took full blame, telling him, "This was entirely my screw-up, a major one, and it won't happen again."

I relearned an old lesson. Under sustained pressure from the cumulative crises and fear for our personnel, I had been moving too fast.

My failure to keep Pickering in the loop was hardly my only misstep. Two days before Christmas 1998, and just over a year since I began as assistant secretary, Howard Wolpe invited me to lunch at the Magic Gourd, a mediocre Chinese restaurant near the State Department. Howard was serving with me in the Africa Bureau as President Clinton's special envoy for the Great Lakes Region of Central Africa. His full-time role was to devote high-level effort to ending the conflicts in Congo and Burundi and trying to prevent further mass atrocities. Howard had served fourteen years as a member of Congress from Michigan. A PhD in political science specializing in African affairs, for a decade he was chairman of the House Africa Subcommittee and led efforts to enact legislation imposing sweeping sanctions on apartheid South Africa. A brilliant, principled, gentle man with a self-deprecating humor and goofiness that were incomparable, Howard was uniquely able to trip over his own feet, even fall, and then laugh hysterically at himself.

Twenty-five years my senior, Howard had decades of experience on me. As a respected elder and fellow political appointee, largely invulnerable to any potential vengeance, he gamely accepted the mission (I presume from my career deputies) to deliver some very tough counsel. Over sweet-and-sour something, he calmly explained how I had alienated most members of my team. "You are too hard-charging and hardheaded," he said. Rather than listen well, he said, "You are overly directive and intimidate others so much that you quell dissent and stifle contrary advice." He allowed that I was smart, but too brash, knowledgeable but immature. He warned me bluntly that I would fail as assistant secretary if I did not correct course. Yet Howard also made clear that he wanted me to succeed and his advice came from a place of respect and affection.

At first, I was knocked back, not expecting to be taken to the woodshed. As the seriousness of Howard's message sank in, I collected myself and listened carefully. Crushed by the weight of my own failure, I felt relieved— even in that very difficult moment—that I had someone nearby like Howard who was not afraid to administer the toughest kind of love. I asked clarifying questions, without defensiveness, fully understanding how important and urgent his message was. After thanking him profusely for his guts and generosity, I took the holiday to fully absorb and reflect on what he said.

I was hurt but sobered, chastened but not angry. He was right. I had to do better.

I needed to be more patient, have multiple speeds, slow down, and stop driving my team so hard and fast, as the State Department shrink had counseled. I had to listen and solicit competing opinions, build personal relationships, not simply direct but generate collective ownership of decisions. In addition, as my third-grade teacher had long ago advised, I had to learn to be more patient and forgiving of others and show more respect for the experience of my career colleagues.

Thanks to Howard, I was able to correct course before it was too late. Under his tutelage, I became a better leader and manager, as he kindly acknowledged. I also gained a deep appreciation and respect for the extraordinary talent and experience embodied in the career foreign service and civil service and have since done my utmost to help develop and promote the most promising officers. As assistant secretary and thereafter, I championed increased funding, enhanced security, and due appreciation for the service and sacrifice of the State Department's and USAID's career employees who often risk their lives in the line of duty but get a fraction of the public appreciation that our service members rightly receive.

Howard Wolpe, who became a dear friend and comrade in arms, will forever have my gratitude. In later years, when I needed to coach junior colleagues to be more effective policymakers, I often cited the value to me of Howard's intervention, which truly saved me from myself.

As special envoy, Howard Wolpe played a key role in resolving "Africa's First World War," the bloody battle for control of Congo that drew in numerous neighboring countries. During that same crazy summer of 1998, Congo's eastern neighbors, Rwanda and Uganda, invaded Congo to try to topple the young government of former rebel leader Laurent Kabila. One year earlier, these two governments had helped overthrow the decades-old, corrupt, repressive regime of Mobutu Sese Seko. But after Kabila reneged on his pledge to close the refugee camps housing Rwandan Hutu rebels, including many who had committed genocide, Rwanda airlifted rebel forces clear across the vast Congo to threaten its capital, Kinshasa. Angola, Zimbabwe, Chad, and Namibia rallied to save Kabila's government, embroiling seven foreign armies in a complex regional conflict. The fighting took on an ethnic cast, where the Congolese army targeted minority Tutsis, and Rwandan-backed Congolese rebels conducted brutal reprisal killings against Rwanda's Hutu adversaries.

Our fears of renewed genocide in this volatile region resurfaced, along with recognition that intensifying conflict in Congo, the continent's third largest country that borders nine other nations, would subsume much of Africa in costly warfare. Howard's job, in coordination with our ambassadors in the region, was to apply the full weight of America's diplomatic muscle, alongside African, European, and U.N. partners, to try to prevent mass atrocities and broker a peaceful resolution.

As with Tony Lake's work on Ethiopia-Eritrea, I backed Howard's efforts with my own diplomatic weight and relationships in the region. Together, we formulated our goals, strategy, and negotiating tactics; and, occasionally, we traveled together to the region. In late October 1998, when the multinational war was raging, we made a strong push for foreign forces to halt the fighting and withdraw from Congo, while pressing Kabila's government to enter serious negotiations with Congolese rebels. Along with my special assistant John Underriner, I embarked with Howard and Gayle Smith on a regional tour of the key countries involved in Congo, plus Mandela's South Africa, which was an important mediator.

Such trips were intense and exhausting, as we hopped between distant capitals on small private planes. Commercial airline connections in Africa were scarce, unreliable, and often dangerous. As an assistant secretary, rather than a cabinet official, I did not rate a dedicated military plane, so we often leased four- or six-seat propeller planes (jets were a rare luxury), which were vulnerable to weather and mechanical challenges.

On this trip, we flew in a small plane on what became a particularly memorable leg from Pretoria, South Africa, to Luanda, Angola, a 1,500-mile journey that required a refueling stop in rural Namibia. It was approximately a four-hour flight, so we left South Africa early in the morning to arrive in Angola by midday and go straight into meetings with senior officials. Along the way, as we plotted our message to the Angolans, the four of us sat close—almost toe to toe. Gayle and I faced forward, with John and Howard facing us, flying backward on our tiny plane. It made for convenient conversation, but soon was too intimate.

About an hour into the flight, I started feeling clammy and weak. As my perspiration increased, my stomach turned over, signaling it was quite discontent. I announced to my colleagues, "I'm not feeling well," and reached for the air sickness bag, which thankfully was handy. With muffled apologies, I opened the bag and threw up voluminously. Suddenly, to my horror, I felt my lap growing warm and wet. The bag had a hole in the bottom, and I was covered in puke. My lightweight, rayon blue dress with white polka dots, once ready for my meeting with the president of Angola, was ruined, and I would have no time to change before my meeting.

In a flash, I caught Howard and John sitting there slack-jawed in shock, but canny enough to gingerly pull back their feet to try to save their shoes from the vomit pooling beneath us on the floor. As soon as I finished being sick and realized the gravity of the situation, there was only one thing I could do: laugh hysterically. Kindly, as friends, they all joined me in howling at the insanity of the moment. But we still had the problem of the dress, and the leader of our delegation being a smelly, unpresentable mess.

We landed on a dirt patch in nowhere Namibia to refuel as planned. There was a single gas pump, a water hole with hose, and some rudimentary bathrooms. The men gave us some privacy, as Gayle turned the hose on me and my dress, spraying me down until I was thoroughly drenched in the desert. She and I then went into the bathroom to strip down and ensure we had washed away all signs of vomit. Confident we had succeeded, all that remained was for me to air-dry over the ensuing couple of hours.

As I have said countless times over the years: "Thank God for Gayle!" Starting when she was my colleague working for USAID in East Africa in the mid-1990s, Gayle quickly became and remains one of my very best friends. Tall and imposing, with a shock of short, spiky white hair, Gayle resembles a white Grace Jones. She is smart, irreverent, fearless, and fun-loving. We have found great strength and solace in each other for some twenty-five years. As partners in leading Africa policy during the latter years of the Clinton administration, we shared a rare bond of trust and common judgment that enabled us to be exceptionally efficient. Often, counterparts at State and the NSC suffer from rivalry, mutual suspicion, or even hot friction. In our case, we could divide and conquer, maximizing our ability to drive policy outcomes without ever doubting or questioning the other's motives or efficacy.

Our Congo-focused tour of the region was more memorable for the side-dramas than the policy outcomes. Despite our efforts, the Kabila government refused to negotiate with its rivals. Kabila's external backers extended their commitment to prop him up, and Rwanda, Burundi, and Uganda remained unyielding in their determination to rid Congo, by whatever means necessary, of those who had committed the 1994 genocide and still threatened Rwanda.

The war continued unabated until the summer of 1999, when Howard in partnership with Southern African leaders and other mediators negotiated the Lusaka Ceasefire Agreement, signed by all the countries involved in the Congo War. Unfortunately, disputes among the rebel groups delayed their signatures, and fighting persisted for a few months after the cease-fire was declared. Even after the fighting quelled, the issues of who would monitor and enforce the agreement and how to catalyze a political reconciliation within Congo remained unresolved.

Sensing another opportunity to best his bureaucratic rivals and perhaps to use Congo to cement his years-long bid for a Nobel Peace Prize, U.N. ambassador Richard Holbrooke entered the scene to prove that he could seal implementation of the deal that Howard had helped broker but not yet secured.

Over the preceding years, Holbrooke's career had spanned diplomacy, journalism, investment banking, and various nonprofit causes, but his unabashed goal was to become secretary of state, and he committed his full energies to that objective. Beginning as assistant secretary of state for East Asian and Pacific affairs in the Carter administration, he later served as U.S. ambassador to Germany and assistant secretary of state for European and Canadian affairs in Clinton's first term, when he played a leading role in brokering the Dayton Peace Accords, ending the Bosnian war. In 1998, Clinton nominated Holbrooke to be U.S. ambassador to the U.N., which Holbrooke likely anticipated would bring him within striking distance of becoming secretary of state, perhaps in a first Al Gore term.

Dick combined, in rare measure, impressive diplomatic skills with hubris, persistence, and an unmatched devotion to self-promotion. I'd never met him in person until one day—while he waited many frustrating months to achieve confirmation as U.N. ambassador—he showed up at my State Department office. I was on Capitol Hill in meetings when my assistant Annette Bushelle called my cell. She reported that Ambassador Holbrooke was in my office demanding to see me.

"Please tell him I am not there, and we can make an appointment to meet at a mutually convenient time," I said.

Seemingly anguished, Annette persisted, "He wants you to come back now to meet with him. He's not leaving."

"Tell him I am on the Hill meeting with members of Congress and will not return until my meetings are done." Annette agreed but predicted, "I think he will be here when you get back."

He was. Holbrooke camped out in my office for well over an hour. When I arrived, I sat down in my chair next to his encampment on my couch and asked what was so urgent?

"I wanted to meet you," he began. "You know, I dislike you already because you broke my record as the youngest regional assistant secretary."

I knew Dick had a well-established reputation, but I was truly surprised to see it demonstrated so amply in our first encounter. We went on to discuss various policy issues, with Holbrooke insisting that we would be working closely together, given that African affairs typically dominate the U.N. Security Council agenda. On this, he was correct, and the next two years proceeded on the course he set in our initial encounter.

Holbrooke, I discovered from our first meeting, was not only a seasoned diplomat but a classic bully: he dominated and abused those he could, but he respected, if demeaned, those he could not. To deal with him, I needed to heed my dad's advice: push back hard and "don't take crap off him."

Once Holbrooke was confirmed in August 1999 as the ambassador to the U.N., some fourteen months after his nomination, it was game on.

One of his first gambits was to embark on a tour of the Central and Southern African region, reprising over a year later the trip Howard, Gayle, and I had taken with the same aim of settling the conflict in Congo. Howard Wolpe accompanied Holbrooke on his whole journey, along with a dozen Holbrooke staffers and Holbrooke's wife, Kati Marton, while my schedule only allowed me to join for a few stops. Across broad swaths of Africa, Holbrooke bullied and charmed, blustered and berated heads of state, trying to compel them to yield by the sheer force of his personality. It was an impressive, if unsuccessful, display of effort and ego.

Undeterred by failure, Holbrooke tried again when he presided over the Security Council as president. Declaring January 2000 "the month of Africa" at the U.N., Holbrooke invited all the African heads of state involved in the Congo conflict to New York for a summit meeting chaired by Secretary of State Albright.

As the leaders began to arrive at the U.N. in advance of the summit, Holbrooke summoned me, our staffs, and my ambassadors accredited to the countries concerned to a Sunday meeting in his office. The discussion grew heated, as he towered over a cramped conference room table and argued that the mandate of the U.N. peacekeeping force in eastern Congo must not include disarmament of the Hutu militia and former Rwandan army elements who had committed genocide and continued to destabilize Congo's eastern neighbors. Howard and most of the ambassadors patiently tried to persuade Holbrooke that if the U.N. didn't take on this task (difficult as it was) no one would, and the region would remain a tinderbox. With each salvo, Holbrooke grew more convinced of the righteousness of his position.

When I weighed in forcefully in opposition to his position, Holbrooke, dripping with sarcasm and condescension, responded slowly, "Ah, I remember when I too was a young assistant secretary . . ." Whatever else he said thereafter, I didn't hear.

His aim was to emasculate me (or the female equivalent) in front of the older ambassadors who reported to me. It was a pivotal moment: if I let him get away with denigrating me in front of six of my ambassadors, I would be weakened thereafter as leader of the Africa Bureau and the decider on U.S. Africa policy. If I said anything further, the conversation would have devolved into an ugly shouting match. With no better idea on how to respond, I looked him square in the face, as he continued to speak, and raised my right hand prominently, prolonging the display of my middle finger. He kept talking. It was clear he saw my gesture, but he never acknowledged it.

While Wolpe and Prendergast were plainly amused, my ambassadors were uniformly shocked—some bemused and impressed, others horrified. As the discussion continued, I worried about two things. First, that our distinguished six-time ambassador now serving in Congo, William Swing, might have a heart attack. He was an older man, a genteel southerner with a divinity degree, who agreed with Holbrooke's position and surely never expected to see a senior official, an assistant secretary no less, address a superior as I just did. Second, I wanted to tell my bosses in Washington what happened before Holbrooke did.

For Swing, I simply prayed. For my bosses, I excused myself some minutes later and walked out into the hallway to reach Secretary Albright and National Security Advisor Sandy Berger. When I was connected to the secretary, I started, "I am calling to report that I just gave the finger to a member of President Clinton's cabinet." She laughed and asked for elaboration. I explained the back-and-forth, and she simply said, "Good for you!" Berger was equally amused and supportive. While I felt fully justified in my indignation with Holbrooke at the time and still do, if I had it to do over, with the benefit of age and experience, I might have found another way to convey the same message—with words and without profanity.

The Congo Security Council Summit was attention-grabbing and brought the region's leaders back together for the first time since Lusaka, when a cease-fire agreement had been brokered but not sufficiently respected; yet it yielded little tangible progress. Indeed, it nearly came off the rails before it started when Holbrooke offended the elderly, prickly Zimbabwean president Robert Mugabe, the senior African leader in attendance, who threatened to boycott and thus torpedo the meeting. Holbrooke pleaded with Secretary Albright to visit Mugabe on an emergency basis at his hotel in New York and try to soothe him. She obliged, reluctantly saving Holbrooke's signature summit.

In the months to follow, Holbrooke gradually lost interest in Congo, concluding both that there was little prospect for a high-profile diplomatic victory and the publicity value of the enterprise had been exhausted. Holbrooke moved on to other targets, including Ethiopia-Eritrea, and far more successfully the battle against HIV/AIDS, which he helpfully catalyzed by elevating it to the U.N. Security Council agenda. In a signal achievement, he negotiated the reduction of U.S. dues paid to the U.N. and, in turn, secured funds from Congress to pay off long-standing U.S. arrears to the U.N.

Holbrooke's retreat from the Central African field left it largely open again to Howard Wolpe. Through persistence, skill, and deft diplomacy, Howard played a critical role in implementing the Lusaka Agreement and fostering peace and reconciliation in neighboring Burundi.

Holbrooke's disdain for me endured until his untimely death in 2010 while serving in the State Department as special representative for Afghanistan and Pakistan. Over the years, Holbrooke had mastered the Washington influence game, cultivating influential members of the press by providing generous access and copious leaks and building an army of dedicated acolytes by nurturing talented young experts. As needed, he enlisted his faithful foot soldiers and journalist friends to aid his own ascent and trip up any perceived adversaries, myself included.

It took me years to understand why Holbrooke had seen me as a threat or some kind of competitor, starting even as far back as the late 1990s in the Clinton days. He was almost twenty-five years my senior and three levels above me in government. Yet, perhaps mindful that he himself had risen swiftly from an assistant secretary to the cabinet, Holbrooke and his posse deemed it necessary to work hard during the Bush years to undermine my prospects for higher office by disparaging me to my boss at Brookings and stoking negative press stories about my work on Africa. If it hadn't been for Barack Obama, whose rise Dick failed to foresee, Holbrooke might have succeeded. Instead, eight years after my most heated encounter with Holbrooke, Obama elevated me to U.N. ambassador.

———

During the two and a half years that we wrestled with resolving the Ethiopia-Eritrea war and Congo's conflagration, the U.S. faced numerous other serious challenges in Africa, which converged in the summer of 1998 shortly after President Clinton's historic trip to the continent. Nigerian dictator Sani Abacha died suddenly in June, enabling the start of a transition to democratic rule. Fierce clashes erupted in Liberia's capital, Monrovia, between government forces and rival militia, which enveloped the American embassy and forced the emergency drawdown of U.S. embassy staff in September 1998. In Angola, the tenuous 1994 peace agreement between the government and UNITA rebels disintegrated, plunging the northern part of that strategic, oil-rich country back into conflict. Simultaneously, war and famine in southern Sudan intensified.

As laser-focused as my colleagues and I were on resolving these and other conflicts raging across the continent—from Burundi to Sierra Leone—we still devoted significant energy to advancing the lasting, beneficial aspects of President Clinton's Africa agenda. The president's Partnership for Economic Growth and Opportunity, which I helped envision and later implement, aimed to spur economic reform and regional integration throughout Africa by combining a near 50 percent increase in development assistance with unprecedented debt relief and concerted steps to increase U.S. trade and investment in Africa. Most agencies were eager to rally to President Clinton's call to do more with Africa. Some, however, were less enthused, notably senior leaders at the Treasury Department, who were skeptical of granting many poor African nations debt relief.

At Treasury, Secretary Robert Rubin and later his successor, Larry Summers, at least initially viewed debt relief to most African countries as a costly moral hazard, which would encourage their further profligate spending. At State and the White House, we considered African countries' bilateral and multilateral debt to be an unsustainable drag on their prospects for economic reform and growth. The battle was engaged on the eve of President Clinton's first trip to Africa, after a meeting in the White

House's Cabinet Room where I had urged the announcement of a presidential push for international debt relief.

Bob Rubin, whom I like and deeply respect, grew furious at me as I pressed the issue. He launched into an uncharacteristic rage, concluding with a line that approximated "over my dead body!" Rubin's influence and importance far exceeded mine, so I assumed I was defeated on the spot, but the proposal gradually gained traction within the interagency, thanks in large part to the combination of Gayle's efforts within the White House and my persistence at State.

By 1999, when Larry Summers led Treasury, support had grown at the International Monetary Fund for the Heavily Indebted Poor Countries initiative (HIPC). Frustrated with the growing momentum behind the push for debt relief, and particularly any consideration of relief for Nigeria, which he considered especially undeserving given its history of corrupt military rule, Summers summoned my immediate boss, Undersecretary Tom Pickering, and my deputy for economic policy Witney Schneidman, to a meeting in his office. He pointedly excluded me. Witney returned to report that Summers began the discussion by angrily asking Pickering: "Can you control Susan Rice?" Pickering replied undramatically, "No." The meeting failed to thwart progress toward meaningful debt relief but underscored how much frustration greeted my tenacity in some quarters.

———

Among the Clinton administration's notable accomplishments was the enactment of the African Growth and Opportunity Act (AGOA) in May 2000, following years of intensive effort by the administration and allies in Congress to grant duty-free, quota-free access to the U.S. market for most goods exported from Africa. This landmark legislation, which I championed as a top priority, finally accorded Africa the same status as many other regions, like the Caribbean, and promised to catalyze substantial growth in the economic ties between the U.S. and the continent. With strong bipartisan support, AGOA was extended by Congress in the Obama era and endures as the cornerstone of the U.S.-Africa economic relationship.

With backing from the White House and secretary of state, during my tenure the Africa Bureau launched significant initiatives in Africa to improve education, especially for girls. We worked with the U.S. Department of Transportation to strengthen aviation safety and security. With the Defense Department, we established the African Center for Strategic Studies, a war college for African officials to bolster civilian control of the military, and strengthened African capacity to conduct peacekeeping operations in Sierra Leone and elsewhere.

Faced with the mushrooming HIV/AIDS crisis, President Clinton declared the pandemic a national security threat, vastly increased American investment in HIV drugs and treatment in Africa, and pressured the pharmaceutical industry to reduce prices and substantially improve access to life-saving drugs in Africa. Subsequently, President George W. Bush built on these efforts and established PEPFAR, a historic, large-scale program to fight HIV/AIDS globally that has endured with strong bipartisan support and saved countless lives.

The advance of democracy in Africa, ever fitful and nonlinear, scored two major wins in the 1990s, supported by large American investments of diplomatic attention and financial resources. In South Africa, after Nelson Mandela was elected president in 1994, the Clinton administration provided over $600 million in bilateral aid and established the U.S.–South Africa Binational Commission—co-chaired by Vice President Al Gore and South African deputy president Thabo Mbeki. This multi-agency commission helped spur bilateral cooperation across sectors ranging from sustainable energy to black economic empowerment. Through painstaking negotiations, the U.S. and South Africa also managed to resolve the notorious ARMSCOR case, which had prevented renewed bilateral military cooperation due to violations of U.S. export control laws by the apartheid regime. Though we struggled through disputes with South Africa over trade policy and HIV/AIDS, the Clinton administration managed to establish warm ties with South Africa's new black majority government and to cooperate in addressing conflicts in Congo and Burundi.

Nigeria marked this period's second major breakthrough for democracy in Africa. Following Abacha's death by heart attack and Abiola's untimely passing, the interim military leader kept his pledge to return Nigeria to democratic rule through free and fair elections. Thus, in 1999, the experienced and respected former president Olusegun Obasanjo was now elected president. Obasanjo is a wise, plainspoken former general, a devout

Christian, and a down-to-earth leader who personally eschewed corruption and endeavored to return Nigeria to its regional leadership role as a military and diplomatic heavyweight.

Obasanjo and I enjoyed an easy and candid relationship, which facilitated deeper bilateral ties and effective policy coordination. One evening when Obasanjo was visiting New York, he called me and Gayle over to his suite in the U.N. Plaza Hotel for consultations. When we arrived, Obasanjo was arguing amiably with his sassy wife, Stella, while munching on scrawny, roasted chicken wings. As we sat talking about conflicts in West and Central Africa, Obasanjo punctuated his message by nonchalantly hurling well-picked chicken bones—much to our amusement—backward over his shoulders across the presidential suite.

This warm and strategic relationship yielded the establishment of a U.S.-Nigeria Bilateral Commission chaired by the secretary of state; a visit by President Clinton to Nigeria in 2000 on his second and final trip to the continent; and crucial U.S. military training and equipment to enable the deployment of five Nigerian battalions to help restore order and stability in Sierra Leone, where civil war had raged since 1991 and the capital was repeatedly threatened by rebel forces.

As difficult as this period was for Africa, given the proliferation of conflicts, which underscored the mismatch between Africa's extraordinary potential and its proclivity for backtracking, during the Clinton era we accomplished much of which I remain proud. It was also a period of enormous professional growth for me, even if fitful and sometimes painful.

I learned that leadership is more like conducting a symphony than performing as a virtuoso player of any single instrument—often with multiple, potentially dissonant musicians and the need to achieve harmony among them. I also found that securing the buy-in and support of those career officials who will outlast any political appointee can be slow and cumbersome, but the extra effort and patience it takes to get there can pay lasting dividends. The most enduring outcomes are not always the swiftest ones; indeed, the best route from Point A to Point B is not always a straight line but could be a path with twists and turns.

Belatedly, I resolved to make enemies wisely: if it is not necessary to burn a bridge, don't. Enemies you thought you left behind on the side of the road have a nasty habit of getting back up, dusting themselves off, and trying to chase you down. Another lesson learned: some adversaries aren't worth the effort; they are better ignored or given the Heisman (a stiff-arm) than combated directly. Others merit combat. As a matter of temperament and morality, I always prefer to be direct, as my father taught me, and thus to launch a prompt frontal assault. But I have learned with time that sometimes patience is the best strategy for achieving the purest justice.

It was arguably a huge risk to give a thirty-two-year-old, breast-feeding, African American woman the job of assistant secretary for African affairs. If I were Madeleine Albright, knowing now what I didn't know then, I'm not sure I would have offered me the job at that age. She had my back, however, at every turn and believed in my abilities.

Winning the respect of African leaders, my superiors in the cabinet outside of the White House and State, the bulk of my ambassadors, and my Washington-based staff was a serious challenge. I met it, perhaps against the odds, because we were able, ultimately, to achieve significant policy results.

Despite tragedy and setbacks, for the first time American policy elevated Africa to a place of priority, not due to Cold War competition but rather mutual interest and mutual respect. By arguing strenuously that bolstering African security, prosperity, and democracy served both American interests and values, and by driving multiple complex policy initiatives and negotiations in tandem, my team and I helped enlist the whole of the U.S. government in concrete efforts to transform our economic and strategic relationship with this vast and rising continent.

Not only did I gain invaluable experience as a policymaker but also as a manager, diplomat, and spokesperson for U.S. policy. Through testimony before Congress, numerous speeches to wide-ranging audiences, television appearances, and press interviews, I grew adept and comfortable with the public-facing aspects of foreign policymaking. And I tasted both indisputable failure and harsh public criticism, arming me with the first layers of tough skin that I would need in greater thickness when the going got much rougher.

11

Going Global

*I*t was a crystal-clear September morning, comfortably warm but not hot or humid—as beautiful as the day Ian and I were married almost exactly nine years earlier. I was looking forward to celebrating our anniversary the next day. Driving into the office with the top down and radio turned up in my red Honda S2000 (my "premature midlife crisis," as I called it), the sunny skies and balmy warmth gave me one more reason to feel grateful for the latest developments in our lives.

Nine months earlier, on January 20, 2001, after eight years at the White House and State Department under President Clinton, I had left government, exhausted and ready to downshift. My son, Jake, was three and a half and had only known a mother who commuted to Africa with excessive frequency. Within a week after I left government, Jake said to me, "Mommy, I hated that job. I'm really glad it's over." Taken aback by his brutal honesty and self-awareness, I was also deeply grateful that he had the sensitivity to wait until after I left government to tell me how he really felt. One week earlier and I would have crumpled in tears.

It had taken me some time to reenter the real world. I had some immediate priorities: buy a cell phone for the first time; get my first personal email address; familiarize myself with using the internet, then a relatively new tool that I had ignored while in government; get a trainer and exercise regularly. Above all, I wanted to spend time with my son and try to have a second child. I knew I didn't want to go back to work right away. I wanted to sleep, travel, and reflect.

205

For much of 2001, I managed to decompress and tend to the home front. We moved from our compact townhome in D.C.'s hip Adams Morgan neighborhood in the thick of city life—where we would wake occasionally to find a knife, errant passport, or a homeless person in our front yard—to the leafy, spacious area called Kent, in the far western corner of the city. We bought and decorated our current house, a property with plenty of space and a backyard pool, large deck, and grassy play area.

It was then, shortly after this move, on an otherwise exquisite morning in September as I drove to Georgetown, where I briefly consulted part-time at a start-up, that our world was shaken to the core.

Without warning or premonition, NPR's breaking news caused me to accelerate inadvertently as my heart skipped a beat. At about 9:15 a.m., Bob Edwards interrupted the regularly scheduled Morning Edition *programming and reported that the Twin Towers of the World Trade Center had each been struck by an aircraft. Flashing back to the near simultaneous bombings of our African embassies in August 1998, I knew immediately it must be Al Qaeda. It was an attack on the heart of New York City and a far deadlier do-over of the same target the Blind Sheikh had hit in 1993 eight years earlier.*

Shortly before 10 a.m., after I arrived at the office, the first of the towers began to collapse, followed some thirty minutes later by the second. Already, the Pentagon had been struck. The State Department, White House, and Capitol were being evacuated for fear of yet another plane incoming to Washington. My mind immediately turned to my four-year-old son, Jake, who I was relieved to recall was safely at home with our nanny, Adela, since he only attended preschool in the afternoon. Ian was at the ABC News Bureau in Washington, and I realized he would probably be gone overnight as the networks would have to provide 24/7 coverage. I worried next about colleagues in the Pentagon and friends who were career employees at the White House and State, with whom I had worked intensively until just months ago. They all could be in the bull's-eye.

———◆———

Like every American, I was shocked, horrified, and furious but not entirely surprised. Al Qaeda was a formidable and committed adversary, as I had learned firsthand. What I, like many others, did not fully anticipate was the extent of their capacity to strike on American soil.

For weeks, planes stopped flying in and out of Washington. The border with Canada was shut. Bilateral trade, our shared lifeblood, ground to a halt. No one traveled. Muslims became targets of intensive, irrational ire. And we went to war in Afghanistan.

This first foreign attack on American soil since Pearl Harbor stoked outsize fear and unfounded suspicions. Still, I never anticipated it would touch me so directly. Until the Washington blame game began.

To deflect responsibility from the new Bush administration, its surrogates sought to blame Clinton administration officials and its holdovers who remained in government, notably my first boss at the NSC and counterterrorism czar, Richard Clarke, whom they falsely accused of failing to warn them adequately about the Al Qaeda threat. It got quite ugly, as Bush officials were blamed for ignoring intelligence warnings, Clinton officials were accused of missing opportunities to capture or kill bin Laden, and Congress established a joint investigative committee. Later, the independent 9/11 Commission was formed.

In December, a British freelance writer, David Rose, published an explosive article in the January 2002 edition of *Vanity Fair* entitled "The Osama Files." He falsely accused me, as well as Madeleine Albright and Sandy Berger, of essentially being responsible for the 1998 East Africa embassy bombings and the 9/11 attacks. When I first saw the article, my blood boiled and skin crawled. I found it an outrageously deceitful and irresponsible excuse for investigative reporting and couldn't believe *Vanity Fair* would publish such a hit job. The article began:

> *September 11 might have been prevented if the U.S. had accepted Sudan's offers to share its intelligence files on Osama bin Laden and the growing al-Qaeda threat. Recently unearthed documents reveal that the Clinton administration repeatedly rejected the help of a country it unwisely perceived as an enemy.*

Specifically, Rose alleged that I, with Berger's and Albright's assent, refused repeated offers by the government of Sudan to provide the U.S. government with Sudanese intelligence files that, had we only accepted, would have provided invaluable information about Al Qaeda operatives and their network. Thus, we would have been able to take down the terrorist organization. The accusation was basically that I refused the purported Sudanese offers or ordered others to refuse them, because of my irrational and implacable hatred of the Sudanese regime.

It was a wholly baseless and dishonest allegation, put forward by two self-avowed opponents of U.S. policy and of me personally, which benefitted the extremist government of Sudan. Nonetheless, given the breathtaking nature of the charge—that I was responsible for the deaths of over three thousand Americans in the worst terrorist attack on U.S. soil—it gained attention on CNN and elsewhere.

Albright, Berger, former undersecretary of state Tom Pickering, and I published a detailed rebuttal, the contents of which I also summarized on television shortly after the article was published. We wrote in the March 2002 edition of *Vanity Fair*:

> *The fact is members of the Clinton administration met* repeatedly *with Sudanese-government officials to seek their full cooperation on counterterrorism issues, both prior to the suspension of our full-time embassy operations in Khartoum in February 1996 and in the years thereafter.*
>
> *U.S.-government representatives met with Sudanese officials on terrorism issues on multiple occasions from 1996 to 2001 in venues ranging from Addis Ababa and Khartoum to Virginia, Washington, D.C., and New York. In none of those meetings, despite repeated U.S. requests for detailed information on bin Laden's network, finances, and operatives and on other terrorist organizations, did the government of Sudan [G.O.S] hand over its alleged files or provide detailed information deemed of significant operational value by U.S.-government counterterrorism, law-enforcement, or C.I.A. officials. . . .*
>
> *Since May 2000, the U.S. has had a full-time counterterrorism team in Khartoum for the precise purpose of obtaining detailed information from Sudan on terrorism. That Khartoum also apparently failed to share these alleged documents at any time prior to September 11, including with the Bush administration for more than eight months, suggests that Khartoum had no intention of sharing this information with the U.S. It seemingly did so only after September 11, fearing U.S. retaliation.*

As false and outlandish as the claims against me were, it was still hard to fathom them. Former U.S. ambassador to Sudan Tim Carney, who could never conceal his dislike for me and my Clinton administration colleagues, was a key, on-the-record accuser. Carney seemed to me to be seeking revenge for what he believed to be my role in closing his embassy in Khartoum in 1996 and for our disagreements over Sudan policy.

His sidekick was a Pakistani American businessman, Mansoor Ijaz, who had oil interests in Sudan. A generous donor to the Clinton presidential campaigns, he was apparently frustrated that he had failed to parlay his money into policy influence. Ijaz attempted to carry messages between the Sudanese leadership and the White House, and after the White House refused to utilize him as a private channel, I believe he became embittered enough to try to blame me and other Clinton officials for 9/11. Carney and Ijaz were joined in their defamatory allegations by a paid lobbyist for Sudan and senior Sudanese government officials. Sudan no doubt feared that President Bush might attack it again after 9/11 and therefore sought to absolve itself of any responsibility for harboring bin Laden by trying to shift culpability for their lack of counterterrorism cooperation to former U.S. officials.

In May 2002, almost six months after the *Vanity Fair* article, a reporter for *Elle* magazine, Ruth Shalit, published an investigative report "J'Accuse!" in which she interviewed me and several of my accusers. The article exposed the biases of Carney, Ijaz, and even Rose (whom I've never met) through their own on-the-record quotes, which revealed their desire to take me down personally. David Rose told Shalit that I was "a lying toad." Ijaz told her:

She had dreams of becoming the first African-American Secretary of State. To build her career, she was willing to ignore every single indication that the Sudan might be willing to come forward and become a member of the family of nations again. She used her blackness, *if I may put it that way, to climb a ladder that ultimately ran out of rungs. Never again! Never again should we allow a U.S. government official to allow her personal views on a country to enter into the policy-making realm.*

Similarly, Carney said to Shalit, "You've got people saying September 11 wouldn't have happened. . . . She [Rice] was seen as someone of enormous potential, but she's seriously damaged her prospects as a result of being so completely wrong on the Sudan question. There's no doubt about it." Shalit also revealed that former CIA operative Milton Bearden, a key unnamed source for Rose and a registered lobbyist for Sudan, was paid $1.35 million by another American, Anis Haggar, an honorary consul for Sudan. Carney was also shown to be close to Haggar and to have taken money from him for travel and expenses for trips to Africa.

Perhaps frustrated that "The Osama Files" had lost traction, Ijaz and Carney wrote an op-ed in *The Washington Post* in June 2002 that provided new fodder for right-wing attacks on Bill Clinton. In the *Post*, they again targeted me and others, recycling the "Osama Files" claims and falsely alleging that, in 1996, Sudan had offered to hand over bin Laden to the U.S., implying that Berger and others had failed to take up the offer.

Together, these men leveled an audacious and sustained assault on me and my superiors. Their attacks ultimately failed to rehabilitate Khartoum or to sink my career, but not before causing considerable pain. This was my first time in the barrel—my maiden national hazing—in which I faced a public assault on my integrity and competence. It was both shocking and painful to be the subject of vicious lies, and particularly to be blamed for such a horrific and deadly event. The depth of the hate reflected in the attacks on me left me reeling at first. Being publicly vilified was a new and bracing experience. Once I absorbed the blow, my pain turned to anger, as it often has since childhood, and then to resolve—to fight for the truth and press on. In the process, I began developing the emotional body armor I didn't know I would need in the future.

Fortunately, facts are facts (or they used to be). The 9/11 Commission examined the allegation that Sudan had offered to turn over bin Laden to the U.S. and concluded that it was unfounded. The Joint Congressional Inquiry into 9/11 specifically examined the *Vanity Fair* allegations that I and other Clinton Administration officials had refused Sudan's offer of intelligence files on Al Qaeda. According to a principal staffer on the Inquiry, Daniel Byman, "after many interviews and the review of numerous documents, the Joint Inquiry established that many of the claims in the article had little merit, including the allegation that Dr. Rice and other senior Administration officials refused an offer of serious cooperation. The Joint Inquiry's review also found no evidence that this supposed offer of help from Sudan in the late 1990s would have prevented the 9/11 attacks."

Carney and crew's smears lost steam for almost a decade, until my dedicated detractors seized a subsequent opportunity to try to block my ascent.

———

While in the Clinton administration, I poured the last dirt on the grave of my youthful political ambitions. I discovered that as an assistant secretary (of state or most agencies), one typically has more policy influence and decision-making authority than all but the most senior senators. With direct, line responsibility for distinct areas of policy, plus a budget and staff who carry out those policies, you have much greater ability to determine outcomes than through the cumbersome and uncertain legislative process, or even by exercising oversight responsibility. For a lot less pain, and far more gain, I could make policy without running for office, raising money, or compromising my principles.

At age thirty-six, I had already had significant experience in national security policymaking; but, down the road, I hoped to serve at more senior ranks—eventually at the cabinet level. To do that, I had to broaden my knowledge and expertise beyond Africa and be accepted as someone who could contribute on foreign policy globally. Making this transition would not be easy. Most former regional assistant secretaries of state continue to work primarily in their original area of expertise after they leave government—whether in the private sector, academia, or think tanks—seemingly content to stick with the region they know best.

I needed to forge a different path.

After a recuperative period of low-intensity consulting and speaking, in the fall of 2002 I decided to join the Brookings Institution, an esteemed, nonpartisan think tank, as a senior fellow in the Foreign Policy Studies program. From the time I left government, my mother had been pressing me to pursue the think tank life, arguing that it would grant me personal and intellectual freedom, good colleagues, a distinguished affiliation, a public platform, and a solid salary. She was right.

More importantly, Brookings enabled me to conduct scholarly research, write, and opine on a broad range of subjects, including but not limited to Africa. Long experienced with the menace of Al Qaeda, I was one of the very few scholars at Brookings to openly oppose the Iraq War. From the start, I viewed that war of choice as a dangerous diversion from the main objective of defeating Al Qaeda globally and in Afghanistan, one that would open a Pandora's box in the Middle East.

While at Brookings, I traveled to Asia and the Middle East, expanding my understanding of the policy challenges and opportunities these regions posed. My friend and former colleague in the Clinton administration Kurt Campbell, who had served in the Defense Department as the senior Asia policy advisor, invited me to travel with groups of experts to China, Australia, and Singapore. He also opened the door to my joining the Aspen Strategy Group, an annual bipartisan gathering of current and former senior officials who spend several August days delving deeply into complex policy issues.

Through Brookings, I joined working groups focused on Europe and the Persian Gulf. I wrote articles, policy briefs, and op-eds, and gave speeches, interviews, and congressional testimony on a wide range of subjects. My in-depth research focused on measuring state weakness as well as the nexus between fragile states, global poverty, and transnational threats to U.S. national security. This work drew on my experience working on Africa but applied it to global challenges. My years at Brookings enabled me to broaden my expertise, while allowing me flexibility to travel, serve on numerous nonprofit boards—including the U.S. Fund for UNICEF, the Beauvoir School (following in my mother's footsteps), and the National Democratic Institute—and, best of all, to grow my family.

———

To Ian and me, it felt that over the first five years of our marriage, circumstances continually conspired to separate the two of us. After moving from Toronto to Washington in 1993, when I joined the Clinton administration, Ian was able to work in the CBC's Washington Bureau; but by 1995 he had been called back to Toronto for a promotion as senior producer of *The National*. Most weekends, Ian made the trip to Washington and, occasionally, I returned the visit to Canada. Long-distance marriage was tedious but not unfamiliar to us after years of living apart. We didn't plan to tolerate a commuter marriage forever, but there seemed no obvious end in sight, as we both were doing professionally what we wished. Ian still liked the CBC, and despite several efforts had not been able to secure a comparable job at an American television network. Moving back to Canada was not an option I seriously considered so long as I had the opportunity to work at the White House. So, we resolved to endure the distance for the time being.

Then, in 1997, the Almighty, it seemed, intervened yet again. He sent Jake to save us from ourselves. Jake's welcome arrival accelerated our return to living under one roof. Just prior to Jake's birth, Ian moved back to D.C., making the first of many professional sacrifices and fulfilling another of his parents' fears about our marriage. The next year, Ian transitioned from the CBC to ABC News's Washington Bureau, where he worked as a producer for *World News Tonight*; yet it took several years to regain the seniority that he had given up at the CBC. Ian knew that for my career to reach its potential, I had to be in Washington. He also knew that his own career could thrive in the U.S. once he made the move to an American network. In effect, Ian generously made a long-term bet on me.

If marrying Ian is the best decision I ever made, Jake jump-starting our family is our greatest blessing. God has a sense of irony and humor, and Jake is proof. From birth when he had a reparable but delicate condition that required three surgeries and tricky postoperative care, to college where he became known for his outspoken leadership as a conservative, Jake has challenged us every step of the way.

Born jaundiced and skinny with gorilla-length arms, Jake developed unevenly as a child. He was plainly very smart, with a powerful memory and strong verbal skills. To this day, whatever he is fascinated by becomes an all-consuming passion. He absorbs everything there is to know about his passions—beginning when he was pre-verbal and pointed insistently with his middle finger at every ceiling fan in sight, to his serial obsessions with the Teletubbies, Thomas the Tank Engine, dinosaurs, the Revolutionary and Civil Wars, every living mammal, the U.S. presidents (which he could recite in order, forwards and backwards), polls and election results in almost every congressional district from 2008 to the present, world geography, and now finance, birdwatching, and the intricacies of various policy issues, foreign and domestic.

Jake's interest in world affairs began early, and I took advantage of my post at Brookings to expose him to events and people of interest. There was no one I was more keen to introduce him to than former South African president Nelson Mandela. When in 2005 a slower moving, yet still-sharp Mandela came to Brookings, Jake and I sat very near the front of the audience. In the middle of his discussion with Strobe Talbott, Brookings's president, Mandela suddenly paused and, for no apparent reason, interrupted himself. He looked directly at Jake (wearing his little coat and tie) and said in his distinctive South African brogue, "Young man, are you the president of this country?"

Taken aback but not knocked off his game, Jake replied, "No sir, not yet."

Mandela seemed amused by Jake's answer, which I too thought was cute at the time, but his ready retorts seem less so these days, given how my son's political views have evolved. After the event, Jake was thrilled to shake Mandela's hand before giving his first press interview at age nine to the French news service Agence France-Press about his reaction to meeting the great Madiba, which he likened to meeting Martin Luther King Jr.

We applied Jake to three top D.C.-area private schools for prekindergarten. At four, his first visit was to the Georgetown Day School, a progressive coed school with an excellent reputation, and he distinguished himself. Jake walked into the school for the "play group" interview and marched straight up to the director of admissions. No sooner had I introduced him than he blurted out with intensity, "I hate this school!" He spent the next half hour in the play group refusing to talk to anyone, totally disengaged. At that stage, the director of admissions gently suggested that perhaps we would prefer to come back another day.

I was livid. When we got outside the school, I gave Jake the harshest talking-to that he received from me until he reached maturity: "You don't have to like a place, but you are not allowed to be rude. If you pull that trick the next time at Sidwell Friends or Beauvoir, you will be in bigger trouble than you have ever been." Steaming, I marched him to the car and drove home furiously. As I calmed down, I recalled with some amusement that retribution is fair play: Jake had tormented me (with a little more spice) just as I had my mother when at the same age I refused to speak until the last seconds of my interview at Beauvoir. Jake pulled it together for his subsequent interviews, and now we both laugh at this episode.

In his early elementary years, Jake initially had difficulty with catching, throwing, and other gross motor skills. During youth soccer, Jake was easily distracted by birds and never much took to the game. Tennis finally caught Jake's interest around age ten, an attraction perhaps spurred more by the views of his libertarian coach than by any deep passion for the family sport.

In second grade, Jake's teachers at the Beauvoir School were puzzled and concerned by the gap they observed between his evident capacity in the classroom and his abysmal results on every standardized test. He had also been slow to read until a savvy teacher found some history books that grabbed him. The school recommended we get Jake tested professionally, and the results revealed that Jake had Attention Deficit Disorder (ADD) in addition to certain executive function and sensory processing challenges, the latter of which had affected his gross motor coordination.

In the context of this testing, Jake's pediatrician Dr. Amy Pullman decided out of an abundance of caution to require a cardiological exam before she prescribed any ADD medication, which is a stimulant. She worried, in part, that Jake (and possibly Ian), both tall and slender with long arms and legs, might have Marfan syndrome (aka Abe Lincoln disease), a genetic disorder that is characterized by their tall, lean body type and can cause the aorta, heart valve, and eyes to degenerate dangerously. The exams ruled out Marfan for both Jake and Ian but revealed by chance that Jake had another rare condition: Wolff-Parkinson-White (WPW) syndrome, in which the heart is wired with an extra electrical pathway that causes it to beat rapidly. In its most severe form, WPW can kill unexpectedly (often during the late teens or twenties), when the heart is stressed by physical exertion or stimulated by drugs like cocaine or ADD meds. Jake needed cardiac ablation, an invasive heart procedure to determine the severity of the WPW and to "zap" the extra electrical pathway in order to return the heart to normal function.

Bewildered and scared, I took Jake up to Boston Children's Hospital shortly after he finished second grade to be treated by one of the country's leading pediatric cardiologists. As it happened, Jake's doctors determined during the ablation that he had the worst form of WPW, placing him at high risk of death. To our enormous relief, they readily fixed Jake's heart, and he now has a normal life expectancy due to the hyper-vigilance of his extraordinary pediatrician.

After the heart scare, Jake's medical issues abated. With tutoring, physical therapy, medication, and extreme determination, Jake steadily overcame his challenges, blossoming as a high schooler at the Maret School into a top student, a leader among his peers, and a member of the varsity tennis team.

———

Maris was born on a snowy day in early December 2002. Jake's insistence on the previously unheard-of name "Maris" prevailed over our dithering indecision, after our OB-GYN, Dr. Sharon Malone, blew up our planned girl's name by casually mentioning that she had delivered three "Sophia's" in just one day the week prior. The day Maris arrived, I was scheduled to meet with the prime minister of Ethiopia, Meles Zenawi, along with Gayle Smith and Tony Lake. Meles was visiting Washington to meet with President Bush, and we had planned an informal visit, one of our first since the end of the Ethiopian-Eritrean War, two years prior, when most of our discussions were all business. When I had to cancel, the prime minister, Gayle, and Tony decided to drive through the snow to visit me at Sibley Hospital just two hours after Maris had emerged robust, ample, and charming from the start.

Five-year-old Jake, ever protective if sometimes smothering of his baby sister, objected when during Meles's visit the nurse came around to announce she was taking his sister away for a changing. He protested loudly, "Please don't CHANGE the baby!"

By Christmas, three weeks later, Maris had firmly established herself as a force within our family. Even as an infant, she exuded a wisdom and cool confidence that prompted my mom to predict that Maris would prove payback to me for my strong-willed challenges to her over the years. (Turns out, she was wrong about Maris but right about payback—belatedly, from Jake). Several friends, who first met Maris before she could even utter a word, observed that she gave the uncanny impression of "having been here before." Her facial expressions and body language spoke volumes before she could, revealing even her presidential preferences. When, at eighteen months in the summer of 2004, I said the words "George Bush," Maris would grimace and frown in mock anger. When I said "John Kerry," she would smile broadly, raise her arms, and clap in approval. I swear I didn't teach her that, but I can't pretend that I didn't encourage this display once I discovered her talent.

As a baby, Maris ate readily, slept through the night at an early age (unlike Jake), and rarely cried without reason. At her first medical examination at one week old, our pediatrician touched her hairline and matter-of-factly observed, "She's going to be blond."

Stunned, I blurted uncontrollably: "Get the fuck out of here!"

Dr. Pullman looked at me impassively, glanced over at Ian knowingly, and replied, "You should have thought of that when you married him."

Stung and ashamed by my stereotypical expectations, I let the discussion of hair drop. When Maris's hair started growing in earnest, to our surprise it was no-kidding red before changing to blond. I admit to hoping and assuming that I would have children who looked a bit more like me. Ian's genes skunked mine, twice over.

At Brookings, I had ample freedom not to travel and was able to breast-feed Maris much longer than Jake. When she was fourteen months old, I took my first extended trip away from her to a conference in Italy. While abroad, I continued pumping (this time I brought a backup, just in case) and returned home five or six days later, eager to resume feedings. When I greeted Maris that afternoon, she was a little standoffish, but I didn't make much of it. After a short period of reacclimation, I lay her down on my lap to breast-feed. She bit me so forcefully and unexpectedly that I screamed in pain. My scream caused her to cry, and we both were hot messes.

Rattled, I left it alone for several hours. That night, as usual, I took Maris upstairs to her room, and with the lights dimmed I held her closely on my lap in the rocking chair. After she relaxed, I offered her a bedtime feeding. After a few seconds of fussiness, Maris sat up erect on my lap, pulled down my shirt emphatically, pointed to her crib indicating that it was bedtime, and declared: "All Done!" To my surprise (and admiration), she was serious. Having so decreed, it was the end of breast-feeding.

Not since that hard bite has Maris caused me much pain. On the contrary, I can think of very few others with whom I enjoy spending time as much. Smart, sincere, self-assured, Maris gets along well with almost everyone unless you mess with her.

As younger children, Jake and Maris generally engaged nicely, despite their five-and-a-half-year age gap and their very different personalities and temperaments. As a mother, I learned early on that, with kids, like with birthday cake at a little friend's party, you "get what you get and don't get upset." In other words, I believe that kids come into this world precooked to a substantial extent, with the capacity to be molded and shaped, but with much of their nature established. That humbling conclusion came hard and powerfully to me, as someone who is a roll up your sleeves and take-charge kind of leader. Without question, parents, extended family, school, and other external influences play a critical role in shaping a child. That's why I have been a fairly hands-on parent. I have also seen how the same two parents in the same household can produce very different characters. To me, that's part of the great joy of parenting; it keeps you on your toes, and it's never boring. It's also forced me to develop more patience than I would have otherwise, though still not enough.

Since Jake was born, I have viewed being a mother as my most important and rewarding job. Motherhood, I believe, has also made me a better policymaker. It has given me a sense of priority about what matters most. It has invested me more deeply in the future and in the long-term consequences of policy choices. An issue like climate change is one that concerns me deeply in any case. Still, it becomes personal when I consider the impact of our action or inaction on my children and grandchildren.

Motherhood also gave me relief from the stress of work. Nothing offered a better sense of perspective than holding my child, reading him a bedtime story, cheering her at a soccer game, or worrying about his academic challenges. The kids have always provided me both comfort and opportunities to have direct and meaningful influence on things large and small, when the problems of the world seem intractable. Moreover, nothing puts a work or policy challenge into its proper dimensions like a child's health crisis or a very sick parent.

Ian and I have tried our best to raise healthy, self-respecting, curious children who care about others. Parenting any child is challenging but there can be additional challenges when raising self-aware, mixed-race children who must find their unique identities as white-looking black kids in privileged white environs within a majority-black city. I have wrestled with how best to imbue our kids with a sense of their history and responsibilities, when they have grown up mostly free from burden and another generation removed from the struggles of their ancestors. There are limits to what family history, book learning, travel, and service can teach. Without knowing the hurt of being serially doubted or discounted, without feeling what it's like to be judged reflexively on the basis of their appearance, there is a potent aspect of the African American experience that I cannot adequately impart to my children. This recognition leaves me feeling that I have fallen short in an important part of parenting that is peculiarly my domain.

In tackling these and all the other challenges of child-rearing, I am blessed to have an exceptional partner in Ian, who is an actively engaged, fully committed parent beloved by our kids. We share the same values and dreams for our kids, and we are mostly a good team, even though we differ in style. I am the more strict parent, less flexible and forgiving, quicker to discipline. When Jake attempts to hijack a family vacation by compelling us all to go birding in some distant, obscure location, or Maris begs to spend nearly a month (yet again) at summer camp in the middle of her high school years when working or traveling might be better preparation for college, I am the parent who is the heavy hand and readily says "No." Ian is gentler, more patient, and prefers to get to "yes," but even he has limits. The kids have learned not to push him too far, because when rarely their dad gets truly angry, it is a sight to behold. Together, Ian and I produced two smart, loving kids who know their minds and are unabashed in expressing their views. Still, they remain works in progress; our jobs are far from done.

———

Brookings was the ideal place for me to focus on family while also expanding my foreign policy horizons and developing a more global perspective. While there, I could also engage in political activity on the side and take leaves of absence as needed. In 2004, I assisted Governor Howard Dean's primary campaign as a very part-time outside advisor, because he was the only leading Democratic candidate to oppose the Iraq War. When he flamed out following his infamous shrieking speech after the Iowa caucuses, I sat out the rest of the primary season.

Still chastened by the crushing Dukakis loss, in the summer of 2004 I chose nonetheless to take a leave of absence from Brookings and accept a job on the Kerry campaign, because I was committed to defeating George W. Bush, particularly after his disastrous decision to invade Iraq. John Kerry was then, in my mind, a strong if imperfect candidate. His Iraq War stance was unsatisfying, mainly insofar as he claimed to be "for it before I was against it," while his understandable focus on Vietnam seemed dated and largely irrelevant to me.

Tall, lean, and carefully coiffed with thick gray hair and angular features, Kerry not only looked the traditional part of president but he was also deeply experienced, energetic, and eager to do battle. Working with my old friend Randy Beers, I contributed to crafting Kerry's policy positions, supported debate preparation, and co-managed our small foreign policy team. I also served as a television surrogate on foreign policy matters and liaised with our senior outside advisors. It was a far more significant role than I played on the 1988 Dukakis campaign and one that helped hone my political experience. At this stage, though I had no personal interest in running for office, I recognized that, as a political appointee, my best path back into a policy role was likely through a winning campaign.

On election evening 2004, like many campaign staffers, I flew from our headquarters in Washington up to Boston for the election night party. Unlike sixteen years before, the race this time was tight down to the wire, and the early exit polls looked good for Kerry. The Bush team, seeing the same exit polls, was reportedly downcast as they returned to Washington on Air Force One, and our side was buoyant—until about 9 p.m., when it started to seem the exit polls might be wrong. By midnight, Ohio hung in the balance and, without a come-from-behind-win there, Kerry looked cooked. In the light of morning, it was clear we had lost, and Kerry conceded.

Kerry's defeat was even more devastating than Dukakis's had been. This, my second outing on the team of a Massachusetts Democrat, was a far more successful campaign than my first, but it seemed to suffer from some of the same ills. These ranged from a failure to energize African American voters, a misplaced assumption that logic and integrity were sufficient for victory, and the lack of a consistent, strong counterpunch—whether on Iraq, the swift boat veterans who smeared Kerry unfairly, or charges that Kerry was a "flip-flopper."

Notwithstanding the loss, I didn't feel that my service on the Kerry campaign had been a waste of time or effort. It was a noble and necessary battle, fought ably on behalf of a laudable candidate, by good people. And, of course, it was during the 2004 contest that I came to meet the man, then a candidate for the U.S. Senate from the state of Illinois, who would enable me finally to say that I worked on a winning presidential bid.

After the Kerry campaign, I returned to Brookings to pursue my policy research and writing, especially on weak states and the impact of state fragility on U.S. national security, and I continued to deepen my understanding of other regions. When Senator Obama asked me in early 2007 to join his campaign and co-lead his outside foreign policy team, I had said "I am all-in," but didn't immediately envision how deep my involvement would become. Through 2007, I was able to balance my home life and my work at Brookings with my involvement on the campaign, which included fundraising, recruiting experts, and advising Obama on speeches, debate prep, and foreign policy matters. When the primary season began in 2008, I had to take unpaid leave from Brookings in order to serve additionally as a public surrogate and travel as requested by the campaign.

———

From the outset, advising Obama came easily to me. Our minds worked in similar ways (although, I hate to admit, his is keener than mine and that of any of our colleagues). Our policy instincts and values meshed almost completely; we respected each other's intellect and could communicate plainly without pretense or polish. We both were hands-on, detail-oriented thinkers who demanded high-quality analysis and output. As I grew to know him well, it seemed I could predict with almost uncanny accuracy what he was thinking about a particular issue and even how he was likely to say it. Keeping this odd intuition to myself, I puzzled at how natural it felt to me. Eventually, I realized that this was not prescience but the fact that, more often than not, what Obama would say was very much what I was thinking and would have said myself, sometimes almost verbatim. This instinct made serving as a surrogate on his behalf a whole lot easier.

To the task of building a bench of foreign policy experts, I brought my own prior experience in government and a network of seasoned colleagues—contacts who were not readily available to a junior senator running as an upstart candidate. Like all of the early Obama supporters, these recruits joined the team for the right reasons—not because they were angling for their next job, but because they believed in the message of the candidate and the type of change he intended to bring. This kind of camaraderie and selfless devotion to mission buoyed us through the rough pre-primary season throughout 2007, when Obama consistently lagged Clinton in national polls and took some punches in early debates. Clinton had tried to portray Obama as green, unprepared for the weight of the office, and unable to unite the party.

After coming in third place to Obama in Iowa, Clinton felt she needed to go on the offensive, personally and through surrogates. And for the Obama team, losing a heartbreaker in New Hampshire meant it was time to hunker down for a grueling battle, understanding that it wasn't going to be short or pretty.

Indeed, it got quite ugly very quickly. Clinton surrogates, including but not limited to BET founder Bob Johnson and former vice presidential candidate Geraldine Ferraro, used racially tinged language to denigrate Obama. They and others variously implied that he may have dealt drugs; attended an Islamist madrassa; was Muslim and/or a foreigner; had only gotten as far as he had because he was black; and could be assassinated if elected. Former president Bill Clinton dismissed Obama's candidacy (or, as he later insisted, Obama's opposition to the Iraq War) as "a fairy tale," which offended many African Americans. Following the South Carolina primary, Bill Clinton discounted Obama's twenty-nine-point drubbing of Hillary as the result of the black vote and suggested his victory would be as fleeting as Jesse Jackson's, saying: "Jesse Jackson won South Carolina in '84 and '88. Jackson ran a good campaign. And Obama ran a good campaign here."

After South Carolina, the contest became even more combative on both sides. Among other attacks, Senator Clinton and her surrogates regularly questioned whether Obama could garner the support of "working, hard-working Americans, white Americans." The race-baiting was shocking and very dispiriting to me, as one who had been (and remains) proud to have served President Clinton and had long viewed the Clintons as supportive of African Americans. It took me some while to get over my sore feelings; but, with time and in victory, I did.

Also challenging was politics within the Democratic Party, particularly the Congressional Black Caucus (CBC). Many CBC members initially strongly supported Hillary, out of years of loyalty to the Clintons. Some also viewed Obama as an upstart who had failed to wait his turn, a young Turk prematurely challenging the hierarchical black political establishment. The Clinton campaign's racial overtones prompted some misgivings, notably from Representative Jim Clyburn of South Carolina, but, like most CBC members, all of whom were also coveted super-delegates, he refrained from endorsing Obama until it was clear Hillary would not win the nomination.

I got firsthand insight into this dynamic when Eric Holder, then a former deputy attorney general, and I went to meet privately with New Jersey congressman Donald Payne in the spring of 2008 to seek his endorsement of Obama. Congressman Payne had long been a good friend and ally of mine, a close collaborator on African issues, and a respected senior member of the CBC. Eric and I labored for over an hour to convince Payne that Obama was the real deal, right on the issues, and likely to win the nomination. Payne, we argued, shouldn't miss the opportunity to be a relatively early supporter of this remarkable young leader we were convinced could become the first African American president. But Payne stonewalled us, returning variously to his commitment to the Clintons, his doubts about Obama's bona fides, and his deep resentment of these young, know-it-all, come-from-nowhere, elite, Ivy League–educated politicians like Obama and then–Newark mayor Cory Booker, who haven't paid their dues. It was several more months before Payne finally (and perhaps reluctantly) got on the Obama bandwagon. Our failure to win over Payne did not hurt my relationship with him, but it was an abject reminder of the complex racial politics that imbued the 2008 Democratic primary contest.

My parents were also interesting barometers for me to read.

In early 2007, when I told Dad that I was backing Obama, he balked. Concerned that a black man could not be elected president, he tried to dissuade me from leaving the Clinton camp. I told him I could see a path for

Obama to victory, but mostly, "He represents what I care about." I also felt it was too soon for another Clinton and argued that political dynasties, as with the Bushes, were getting tired. Plus, I wasn't nearly as sure as he was that a black man couldn't win the presidency.

This kind of robust but friendly argument epitomized my adult relationship with my father. Ever since childhood, the fundamentals between Dad and me were never shaken. We shared a strong intellectual connection, a fascination with the world and public policy, an unsparing sense of humor, a passion for tennis, and a readiness to stand up for what we believe without fear of others.

Our strengths and weaknesses closely aligned. We both were often accused of intimidating others, even when (mostly) that was not our intent. Dad appeared overly serious, walking around with what looked to be a frown on his face when really he was just driving himself intensely. Similarly, when not familiar with me personally, people frequently misread anger in my face when I am not smiling.

Despite his dedication to me and those he loved most, dealing with Dad was not always easy. He never shed his quick temper, inherent impatience, and fierce independence. Getting along with him required accepting the good with the difficult, though sometimes it was necessary just to fight it out and move on. Dad had an indomitable spirit.

I was deeply disappointed when, in 1997, shortly after Jake was born, Dad decided to move across the country. His timing couldn't have been worse. He was seventy-eight, and I wanted him close—especially now that his grandson had arrived. Yet, ever since his graduate school days at Berkeley, Dad had dreamt of returning to the West Coast. He was also sick of Washington after forty years and eager to escape the Mid-Atlantic, particularly its tedious winters with occasional treacherous ice storms and excessive summer humidity. Over several years, Dad had toured the Pacific Coast from British Columbia to Northern California, looking for the perfect spot. California, he concluded, was too expensive. He searched for a good view, nearby salmon fishing, reasonable cost of living, and proximity to a major airport.

Finally, he found his place: a comfortable house with an exceptional view of the Columbia River and Mount Hood framed spectacularly by his living room and kitchen picture windows. Camas, Washington, is just across the river from Portland, Oregon, and twenty minutes from its airport. Washington State has no state income tax, and Oregon has no sales tax. It was perfect for my frugal economist father. Initially, I agonized that he was heading to a strange part of the country as a single man, where he knew no one and would be lonely and vulnerable if he had a health crisis.

I was wrong to worry. Dad quickly immersed himself in Camas, making scores of new friends, including eligible women, through a group of active seniors called "The Ospreys." The group met most mornings for an hour-long walk in the woods and then coffee and breakfast at a nearby café. To my relief, he also found an excellent network of doctors. Whenever I visited him in Camas, he was happy, relaxed, and appreciative of his newfound life out west.

Thankfully, Dad came back east a few times a year for extended visits and always for the holidays. He also made regular trips to South Carolina to spend time with and care for his older sister Pansy, until 2007 when she died. In D.C., Dad enjoyed hanging out with his friends and resuming rituals like taking me and Ian to the annual Christmas ball for the Washington-area Boulé, a fraternity of accomplished African American professionals.

Dad loved to laugh, relished a loud party, and could boogie with the best until his final days. I will never lose the image of my dad at eighty-nine, rocking with Democratic strategist and television commentator Donna Brazile at my house just after President Obama's first inauguration. As his favorite dance song, Tom Browne's "Funkin' for Jamaica" blared and they circled each other on the floor, the party crowd chanted, "Go, Donna. Go, Donna." To this day, in our household, any subsequent true throwdown has been nicknamed a "Go, Donna."

Even from a distance, Dad remained active and present in our lives. When we were apart, Dad and I spoke frequently by phone. He would call to talk current events or comment on my television appearances. If I hadn't heard from him, I would call almost daily to check in, as I worried increasingly about him living alone far across country. Eventually, we installed a system where we could remotely monitor motion, his comings and goings, and detect anything unusual, but Dad resisted all forms of visiting nursing care. He barked and scared off all the caregivers that the local services sent over at our request.

Then, one morning, they cracked the code. Dad was home alone when the doorbell rang. When he opened it, there stood an exceptionally attractive, young African American nurse named Ticey Westbrooks. Without knowing why she was there, he opened the door wider and said, "Come on IN!" When she explained that she had been sent by the caregiver agency, he still didn't put her out. They clicked, and Dad finally had a visiting nurse he liked and we trusted.

On one of his return trips to D.C. in March 2007, I convinced Dad to give Obama a chance. Dad came to a fundraiser I co-hosted for the then still long-shot candidate. Finally, my father saw what I saw. From then on, Dad supported Obama sincerely, if skeptically, given my father's experience of race in America.

My mother was a different story. Like Dad, she attended the fundraiser and became a committed donor. Unlike Dad, she never questioned my decision to join Obama's campaign. She grasped immediately what animated my enthusiasm for him and would spend the rest of her life fretting and fawning over her favorite president.

By then, my relationship with Mom had evolved greatly.

Mom mellowed with age, and I matured becoming less impatient and more appreciative of my mom's many gifts. By my late twenties, we had become what she always said she wanted us to be: "best friends." It was Mom who lured me to the Brookings Institution in 2002, where she had been a Guest Scholar since the early 1990s after leaving the Control Data Corporation out of frustration that she was unfairly compensated relative to her male peers. At Brookings, Mom worked on education policy, higher education finance, and workforce diversity issues. She also found a new love and reconnected with friends from whom she had grown distant as she cared for Alfred while he battled cancer. She took great joy in spending summers at her lovely house on Penobscot Bay near Camden, Maine. Overall, her stress level came down considerably, which enabled her to leverage her many talents and temper her most evident flaws.

Johnny and I both benefited from the changes we saw in Mom. Like mine, his relationship with her improved with age and independence. After

Yale, Johnny worked at AT&T before attending Harvard Business School (finally giving Mom a Harvard grad) and thereafter at Disney and the NBA in Latin America and Japan. While at Harvard, Johnny conceived of a non-profit called Management Leadership for Tomorrow (MLT), which ten years later he turned into reality.

Management Leadership for Tomorrow prepares minority college students, largely from lower-income backgrounds, for coveted postcollege jobs and graduate schools that can help deliver true economic mobility for their families. Utilizing one-on-one coaching, mentorship, and connections, MLT supports over a thousand students and professionals annually to become senior leaders who can transform their organizations and communities.

Mom was a founding board member and avid fundraiser, viewing MLT as a much-needed addendum to her life's work of expanding access for minorities and low-income students to higher education. Both Mom and Johnny understood that, for the less privileged who grow up without the "social capital" that elites enjoy, merely graduating from college does not ensure full access to the American Dream. These students also need the targeted training, support, and relationships that will help them secure the best jobs and continue to rise.

Like Mom, Dad was proud that his son had chosen to carry on our families' tradition of service through education, which dates back to his grandfather's founding of the Bordentown School. Through MLT, Johnny has taken to scale my parents' commitment to helping others by partnering with over 150 corporations and universities to prepare more than seven thousand African American, Latino, and Native American "Rising Leaders" to excel in top companies and social sector organizations.

By contrast, Mom was slower to support Johnny's personal choices, particularly in women. After expressing some hesitation about most of Johnny's prior relationships, Mom finally embraced Andrea Williams, the woman he ultimately married. Having only half jokingly admonished Johnny while in college to "never bring home a white girl," Mom toasted the couple at their wedding rehearsal dinner by bestowing on the bride (a black woman) her highest possible compliment, "Most of all, Andrea reminds me of me."

Like Ian is to me, Andrea is exactly what Johnny needs—a calm, patient, devoted, and accomplished partner who balances Johnny's energy, intensity, and silliness. Andrea played varsity tennis at Yale and continues to compete formidably, rising to the number one ranked woman in America in the 50+ age group. After graduating from Stanford Business School at the height of the tech boom, Andrea worked for top investment banks as a highly regarded equity analyst of Silicon Valley companies. She has since devoted herself to various entrepreneurial ventures, along with their two children, tennis, and nonprofit work. Since Johnny and Andrea moved back to the Washington area from California in 2007, our families could not be closer.

Becoming a grandmother turned out to be Mom's greatest joy and also did more than anything to smooth out our edges and elevate our relationship to the high point we sustained over the balance of her life. She was there in the delivery room with Jake and almost every day thereafter, spending quality time with him and Maris throughout their lives.

Our friendship grew ever stronger over the years. From helping me improve my wardrobe to tutoring me in the fine points of preparing a worthy Thanksgiving dinner, Mom and I were able to cooperate and support each other with rare acrimony. As she battled cancer and other health challenges, from 2006 to her passing in 2017, Mom was deeply appreciative of the attention Johnny and I gave to her care. Her struggles brought us closer, underscoring just how much we loved and needed each other.

As I returned to the public spotlight, Mom remained fiercely protective of me, bristling at every criticism and bursting with pride at my success. Not at all tech-savvy, Mom could barely use a simple cell phone and had no phone alerts or internet access to track my activities. Instead, she watched CNN incessantly and cultivated a network among my staffers who would call to alert her to watch me on television. Following my public appearances, she would phone me to provide her unvarnished critique of how I looked and what I said.

————

By early 2008, Mom had lots of feedback to offer. At this point, in addition to my role as policy advisor and coordinating the outside experts, I had been tapped increasingly by the Obama campaign as a television spokesperson. A full-time volunteer, but not a paid staffer, I kept my base in Washington and visited headquarters in Chicago occasionally. Since Obama's time was spent mostly on the campaign trail, I had only intermittent contact with him and engaged mostly with the policy staff. At debate prep, debates, or meetings with the candidate, I also interacted with the political team, including David Plouffe, the wiry, puckish, and super-analytical campaign manager, and David Axelrod, the warm, jovial senior political guru. On and off the campaign trail, I also came to know well senior advisor Valerie Jarrett, one of the Obamas' closest friends and trusted aides. Valerie always offered me kind support and candid insights from inside headquarters.

The campaign regularly sent me out on cable television to represent Obama's positions on key foreign policy issues and sometimes to debate Clinton representatives or Republican opponents. In a hard-fought, sometimes bitter primary, I was confident on the air, a happy warrior unafraid to throw a punch as needed. Yet, as I discovered during the 2008 campaign, it is not hard to make the kind of mistake on television that gives your opponent an opening they can exploit, even if what you say is not technically inaccurate.

In early March 2008, I appeared on Tucker Carlson's MSNBC show, and the conversation went like this:

MR. CARLSON: So Hillary Clinton runs this ad, the famous red phone ad, that says when the phone rings at 3 o'clock in the morning, you know, who do you trust to make those snap decisions that could hold all of our lives in the balance? And the Obama campaign, I thought very wisely, came back and said, name one that you—you know name a situation where you've judged a foreign policy crisis, and she couldn't. I'm going to ask the same question to you. Where has Barack Obama been in a position where he has to make those kinds of decisions?

MS. RICE: He hasn't, and he hasn't claimed that he's been in a position to have to answer the phone at 3 o'clock in the morning in a crisis situation. That's the difference between the two of them. Hillary Clinton hasn't had to answer the phone at 3 o'clock in the morning. And yet she attacked Barack Obama for not being ready. They're both not ready to have that 3:00 a.m. phone call.

I continued:

> The question is . . . when that phone call is received for each of
> them for the first time, who's going to make the right judgment?
> On the critical foreign policy issues of the day, whether it was a de-
> cision to go to war in Iraq or the decision to give President Bush the
> benefit of the doubt and beat the drums of war with Iran, Hillary
> Clinton has made the same wrong judgment as John McCain and
> George W. Bush. Barack Obama has made a very different judg-
> ment. So, neither one of them, and nor John McCain for that mat-
> ter, have had that 3 o'clock phone call that others have had. And I
> think we have to be honest about that.

My comments were seized upon by opponents as a confession by a senior Obama spokesperson that Obama was not prepared to be president.
It made for an unhelpful and distracting story for several days. My main
point was valid—that no one has had the true experience of taking a crisis
call until they occupy the presidency, and what matters in a candidate is
good judgment. Still, if I could reformulate my answer, I would not have
used the word "ready" and said simply "neither has ever taken a 3 a.m.
call." Obama never mentioned this mistake to me, but thereafter without
ever being told so by anyone on the campaign, I was tacitly benched for a
few weeks and given only safer opportunities by the campaign to appear
publicly, until the furor died down.

My transgression, however, was rapidly eclipsed by fellow Obama
advisor Samantha Power, who called Hillary Clinton "a monster." While
Samantha had asked that her words be treated as off-the-record in an otherwise on-the-record interview, the U.K.'s *The Scotsman* published her
comment anyway. The Clinton campaign took great offense, whether real
or feigned, demanding Samantha's sacking. The Obama team acknowledged that the comment had gone a bit too far, and Samantha felt compelled to resign as an advisor to the campaign and apologize publicly to
Senator Clinton.

Thereafter, I rarely, if ever, ran afoul of the Obama campaign's sen-
sibilities and continued my active role as a media and in-person surro-

gate through the end of the general election. As our attention shifted from Clinton to Senator John McCain, the nominees' relative national security credentials became a persistent theme. The McCain camp portrayed Obama as soft and inexperienced, while we questioned McCain's policy judgment and temperament. In my press appearances, I criticized Senator McCain's tendency to "shoot first and ask questions later," arguing: ". . . it's dangerous, and we can't afford four more years of this reckless policy." I also noted that, "On critical, factual questions that are fundamental to understanding what is going on in Iraq and the region, Senator McCain has gotten it wrong and not just once but repeatedly." McCain, I said, "shot from the hip," and was "very aggressive, belligerent."

These jabs, it seems, got under McCain's skin. Whether it was the substance of my critique or the messenger, I am not sure. John Kerry, General Wesley Clark, and other surrogates had made similar arguments but, in subsequent years, many journalists speculated that McCain's outsize hostility to me derived in substantial part from my criticisms during the 2008 campaign. Perhaps the comment that most rankled McCain related to Senator Obama's upcoming trip to Iraq in the summer of 2008 (where McCain had visited earlier). Speaking of Obama, I said: "I think he wants to get out and do as much as he can. I don't think he will be strolling around the market in a flak jacket," an allusion to McCain's much touted, heavily guarded, brief walk in a Baghdad market in which he aimed to show how much security had improved. While I make no apology for my critiques of McCain's policy judgments, I do regret the "flak jacket" comment, since it was flippant and mocking, and it ran counter to my deep respect for McCain's service to our country and all he endured as a POW.

———

Following the highly successful overseas trip that Obama had taken to the Middle East and Europe to demonstrate his competence on the world stage, the last months of the general election were dominated by the convention, debate preparation, and transition planning. Against the backdrop of the crashing economy and McCain's missteps in the economic policy realm, Obama's star continued to rise. Foreign policy receded somewhat as a dominant campaign theme. During the last weeks of the campaign, the balance of my effort shifted to preparing for the transition, including establishing teams to coordinate with the outgoing Bush administration at the National Security Council and each of the national security agencies.

On election evening, I had chosen not to go to Chicago to be with the campaign team and the Obamas. For me, it was a moment that required the proximity of family. Win or lose, I needed to be with my mother and the kids to watch the election returns. Ian had to work from New York, and my dad stayed out west, but we all were in frequent telephone communication throughout the night.

Our first stop was to join Tony Lake and Julie Katzman at their home for a small (hopefully celebratory) gathering. It was a fitting coda to a journey that began with Tony four years earlier, when he first asked me to talk to then-Senate candidate Obama about foreign policy. Mindful of how wrong exit polls can be, and still somewhat skeptical that America could actually bring itself to elect a black man, I was taking nothing for granted. As the results began to come in with the Obama-Biden ticket winning several of the most contested states—Virginia, Pennsylvania, Ohio, Florida, even Indiana, North Carolina, and Colorado—it seemed that an election evening might *finally* go our way. After Tony's, we sped to a party at my brother's house and arrived shortly before the victor was declared.

As we awaited the results, Mom and I sat on the couches in Johnny's family room, glued to the big screen TV. I tried to concentrate on the television but found myself frequently gazing at my kids, five-year-old Maris and eleven-year-old Jake, and my nephew and niece, Mateo and Kiki. This historic evening seemed more about them and their generation's future than anything else.

The older kids and Johnny's guests milled around in muted anticipation. Then the announcement blasted across the airwaves: Barack Obama was the forty-fourth president of the United States! The campaign's signature song, Stevie Wonder's "Signed, Sealed, Delivered" blared like a triumphal anthem for the faithful as we all waited for Obama. When at last he took the stage, with his beautiful wife and two adorable daughters, along with Vice President–elect Biden and his massive family, it seemed real for the first time.

With my mom sitting very close to me and Maris crashed in my lap, I refrained from loud cheers and just cried copious tears of joy and relief.

It had actually happened. An incredible, historic, impossible dream come true. America had proved my dad and so many others wrong. Deep down, I too had doubted whether this moment would come in my lifetime. When it did, I couldn't stop crying—that night and all the next day.

For all the wisdom we had received from our parents, all their encouragement to reach for the pinnacle of possibility—as a family and as a nation—the aftermath of the election did not allow time to reflect on how we got there, thankful as we were for all that had brought us this far. Following the deluge of my tears, which lasted through Wednesday, it was time for me to look forward, to prepare for where we were all headed next. By Thursday, I had pulled myself together and showed up to work at Transition Headquarters.

PART THREE

The Big Leagues

12

Represent

On December 1, 2008, at a press conference on a cold Chicago morning, Obama made my nomination as U.N. ambassador official, while announcing the rest of his national security team.

For the last three weeks, the transition had been consumed by the full-blown economic crisis the new administration would face and by top personnel decisions. The national security transition team focused on engaging with Bush administration counterparts at the various agencies, supporting senior nominees preparing for their confirmation hearings, and considering lower level staff selections. We also readied the high-profile foreign policy choices we intended to make in the early days of the new presidency. Priorities included banning torture and codifying Obama's determination to close Guantánamo and reform detention policy. As my focus had necessarily shifted to preparing for confirmation, selecting key staff, and getting ready to hit the ground in New York, the press conference was the first time I allowed the reality and responsibility of where I was headed next to hit me.

I had flown out to Chicago with my parents, Ian, and the kids to be there as Obama, joined by Vice President–elect Joe Biden, took to the podium to speak to the seriousness of the moment—with his signature optimism.

Obama prefaced our introductions by providing an overview of the national security challenges facing the nation, calling them "just as grave—and just as urgent—as our economic crisis." As Obama had argued during the campaign, economic power went hand in hand with military might as foundations of our national power. Now, he stressed, "America must also be strong at home to be strong abroad."

Sharing his vision of the complex world he was about to inherit, President-elect Obama posited, "The common thread linking these challenges is the fundamental reality that in the twenty-first century, our destiny is shared with the world's. From our markets to our security, from our public health to our climate, we must act with the understanding that, now more than ever, we have a stake in what happens across the globe."

Clearly outlining the mandate of the team I was joining—along with Hillary Clinton as secretary of state, Robert Gates, who would remain as secretary of defense, Eric Holder as attorney general, Janet Napolitano as secretary of homeland security, and General James Jones as national security advisor—Obama declared: "We will show the world once more that America is relentless in the defense of our people, steady in advancing our interests, and committed to the ideals that shine as a beacon to the world: democracy and justice; opportunity and unyielding hope—because American values are America's greatest export to the world."

Obama, introducing me next to last, called me a "close and trusted advisor," and added that he saw the role of permanent representative of the United States to the United Nations as a crucial one. My job would be to represent the U.S. to the world at the only body that included all its 193 nation-states. "Representing" means showing up, being in charge, speaking with authority, and negotiating to advance American interests. Every word I uttered, every step I took, would be closely watched and judged, but I felt ready.

"As in previous administrations," President-elect Obama noted, "the U.N. ambassador will serve as a member of my cabinet and an integral member of my team. Her background as a scholar, on the National Security Council, and Assistant Secretary of State will serve our nation well at the United Nations. Susan knows the global challenges we face demand global institutions that work. She shares my belief that the U.N. is an indispensable and imperfect forum. She will carry the message that our commitment to multilateral action must be coupled with a commitment to reform."

At the press conference, each nominee gave short remarks. In mine, I repeated a line that I had used frequently, first in crafting Obama's remarks during the campaign and later in my own speeches: "To enhance our common *security, we must invest in our common humanity." It is a statement that still reflects my view of how America should best lead in the world, even after years of testing.*

In the conference room, where the nominees convened briefly with Obama and Biden before the announcement, I saw Hillary Clinton for the first time since the campaign began. I congratulated her and told her I looked forward to working with her. She was polite but a little cool, until after the event when it came time to greet my family. Then she could not have been more gracious, and I continue to prize a picture we all took together with a very small Maris posed adorably in front of Hillary, whom she already quite admired.

———

My next order of business was to be confirmed by the Senate as U.S. ambassador to the United Nations and to get ready for the Big Leagues. Like other nominees, I was given a small team of experts to help guide and prepare me for the hearing with massive briefing books and "murder boards"—intensive mock hearings where I was peppered with tough questions that could arise. They also set up obligatory meetings in advance of the hearing with members of the Senate Foreign Relations Committee, which turned out to be uneventful. Indeed, the whole confirmation process could not have proceeded more swiftly or smoothly. Senators Susan Collins of Maine and Evan Bayh of Indiana, both of whom I had known previously, kindly agreed to introduce me to the committee.

Senator Collins began, "The people of Maine are proud of what this remarkable woman has accomplished in her distinguished career of service to our nation, and we take special pride in her strong ties to our state." After detailing my family's history in Maine going back to the early twentieth century, she explained that we first met "when we were both participants in a series of seminars sponsored by the Aspen Strategy Group." Collins continued, "I was so impressed with her brilliance and nuanced insight as I listened to her discuss various foreign policy challenges. I knew at that time that she was a real star." Finally, she concluded, "I can think of . . . no better messenger than Dr. Susan Rice. I am honored to present her to this distinguished committee, and I enthusiastically endorse her nomination."

Collins's comments were so generous that committee chairman John Kerry quipped, "What a wonderful introduction. Remind me that if I am ever in need of an introduction, I want to put in my reservation right now. It does not get better than that." The rest of my hearing proceeded in the same vein, with Maris providing the only drama by silently frolicking and dancing in the aisle of the hearing room. Senators from both parties asked important and serious questions, but there was no rancor, and I committed no fumbles. One week later, on January 22, for the second time in my career, I was unanimously confirmed by the Senate. Three days later, I went to work at the U.N. on behalf of the American people.

———

Monday mornings began the same way for four and a half years.

A rushed awakening, shower, dress, kiss Ian and the kids goodbye, dash out the door to jump in the big armored SUV with just my briefcase and a small day bag, and speed to National Airport. For me and my Diplomatic Security (DS) agents—who protected me in both Washington and New York—the airport runs became an adrenaline-rushed game to see how close we could cut it and still make the shuttle to or from New York. Usually, I could leave home in D.C. at 7:30 a.m. and just make the eight o'clock shuttle to La Guardia. Once at the airport, we walked briskly (as heels made running inadvisable) around the security checkpoint, down the corridor, and straight onto the plane, with the gate agents variously scowling or hailing our just-in-time arrival.

Usually the last to board, with one DS agent accompanying me, I would settle into my coach seat and read my briefing materials and newspapers in preparation for the day ahead. The dash to the plane got my juices flowing and, barring a weather delay or a rare traffic impediment, we made it to New York in time for me to be in my office or the chair behind the "United States of America" plaque at the United Nations Security Council before the 10 a.m. session began.

Three days after President Obama's inauguration, and one day after I was confirmed, on January 23, 2009, I was sworn in to office. The following Monday, when I first arrived in New York to start my tenure as U.S. permanent representative to the United Nations, Ian and I began a whole new long-distance balancing act. He had recently been promoted to executive producer of the Washington, D.C.–based *This Week*, ABC News's

Sunday show, and the kids were well-ensconced in schools they liked—both factors that made moving the family to New York a nonstarter. In D.C., Ian had the support of my mom, who was a hands-on grandparent, and our indispensable nanny, Adela Jimenez. So, for four and a half years, I commuted, and our kids saw me mainly on the weekends. It's difficult to assess the impact of losing that time at home. I know how hard it was for me to be removed from the daily lives of Jake and Maris and fully appreciated how much my absence placed added burdens on Ian.

———

By the time I arrived in New York, I had assembled a small but first-rate team to help me run the U.S. Mission. Some, like my wise and savvy chief of staff Brooke Anderson and foreign service officer Erica Barks-Ruggles, my deputy who ran our Washington office, had been colleagues and friends since the Clinton administration. Others, like my senior advisors Elizabeth Cousens, a good friend since Oxford, and Salman Ahmed, whom I had not met before the transition, were deeply experienced experts who had worked for years in and around the U.N.

My principal deputy was Ambassador Alejandro "Alex" Wolff, whom I first met in the 1990s when he was executive assistant to Secretary Albright. A deeply experienced foreign service officer with an impish grin and an accompanying mischievous streak, he had also worked as deputy under my two immediate predecessors, Zalmay Khalilzad and John Bolton. Alex knew everything and everybody at the Mission and the U.N. and helped ensure I met the right ambassadors and U.N. officials in the correct order, and that I was well-briefed on their comparative strengths and weaknesses. Alex assisted me with plotting strategy on tough issues and managed the budget, day-to-day operations, and personnel at the Mission. This freed me to represent the U.S. in the Security Council, before the press, at events and receptions, and to lead the Mission through the most consequential debates and negotiations.

President Obama came to office with a clear vision of his foreign policy principles and priorities. My primary goal as U.S. ambassador was to advance his objectives through the United Nations. First and foremost, Obama had to deal with the complex challenges he inherited, chiefly: preventing a global economic meltdown; responsibly winding down major ground wars in Iraq and Afghanistan; and degrading Al Qaeda while bringing to justice Osama bin Laden, who remained at large.

On top of this, Obama set out to seize fresh opportunities and confront threats that would peak in coming decades. Asia, the emerging center of gravity for the global economy and geopolitical competition, is where Obama sought to rebalance U.S. resources and attention. To make the world more secure, he prioritized stemming nuclear weapons proliferation, locking down "loose" nuclear material and an arms reduction treaty with Russia, while envisioning "the peace and security of a world without nuclear weapons." Similarly, Obama invested in combating climate change, while strengthening our cyber defenses and global health security.

At a broader level, President Obama understood upon taking office that his overarching goal must be to renew America's global leadership. As we had agreed during our first substantive policy conversation over dinner at Tony Lake's house in 2005, Obama viewed America's strength and prosperity as inextricably linked to that of others; we do *not* live in a zero-sum world. When America cooperates and inspires, when we lift up others, we tap into common aspirations for dignity and opportunity, rather than stoke fear and disunity. That is how America best attracts others to our cause and tackles issues that matter most to Americans' security and prosperity.

Obama was adamant that the United States cannot and should not bear the burden of global leadership alone, especially not through military means. We needed to use all elements of our national strength, not only the best military but also the top diplomats and development experts in the world. America also had to resist the temptation to overreach and overcommit, because there are limits both to our resources and to our influence, particularly our ability to solve problems within other states.

Above all, Obama emphasized that the U.S. could not lead from a position of strength abroad if we were not strong at home. Facing the Great Recession, Obama focused early on jump-starting America's economic recovery, creating jobs, reforming Wall Street, and making health care accessible to all. Internationally, he worked to broker high-standards free trade agreements, including the Trans-Pacific Partnership Agreement, which would boost U.S. exports and employment while providing greater protections for labor and the environment.

To confront tough global issues effectively, we would build diplomatic coalitions to work with us. That's where the United Nations came in. The administration frequently sought U.N. Security Council authorization when it would enhance the legitimacy of our efforts and our ability to rally partners to our side. After the excesses of the "war on terrorism," America also needed to lead by example, including by banning torture, working to close Guantánamo, and standing firmly in support of American values—democracy, universal human rights, and the rule of law.

At the same time, Obama sought to bind recalcitrant states to their U.N. obligations and international law. With Russia and China, the U.S. was prepared to cooperate when mutually beneficial—from nonproliferation to climate change and global health. Yet we were resolved to confront U.S. adversaries with strength in order to deter and defeat aggression.

Against this backdrop, in President Obama's view, my job and that of my team was to bridge old divides, find common ground where possible, stand tough when necessary, and forge collective solutions that would help us confront the most intractable global challenges.

It was a tall order, especially since I arrived to find (unsurprisingly) that the U.S. was not in good standing at the U.N. We had lost ground due to bruising battles over the Iraq War and the bullying style of U.S. ambassador John Bolton, my predecessor once removed, who once famously said: "The Secretariat building in New York has 38 stories. If it lost 10 stories, it wouldn't make a bit of difference." Under President George W. Bush, the U.S. frequently opposed progress on issues of greatest concern to the majority of U.N. member states. From indigenous rights to access to food and clean water, from climate change to women's reproductive rights, the U.S. had been viewed as indifferent or even hostile to many issues that mattered most to developing countries.

I set out to change that. My principal initial challenge was to improve the perception of the U.S. at the U.N. by pursuing goals that served not only U.S. interests but those of most U.N. member states. In my early days, I often encountered resistance from some of the career officers at the Mission when I suggested that the U.S. should change its position on a particular issue. For instance, the U.S. had historically objected to language in U.N. General Assembly resolutions recognizing that people had a "right to food." I understood the institutional urge to resist the creation of new "rights," but for the new Obama administration to argue that people didn't have an existential need to eat seemed completely nonsensical. When I pressed on why we opposed something like this, I was told, "That's how we've always done it." That answer was tantamount to waving red at a bull. We would not object to the "right to food" and, henceforth, I insisted that we would need persuasive, substantive reasons to maintain such controversial positions. "How we have always done it" would not cut it.

More broadly, under my leadership, the U.S. Mission championed human rights and the fight against global poverty. We prioritized climate change as both a genuine threat to U.S. national security and an existential concern for small island nations. We recommitted to the basic bargain of the Nuclear Non-Proliferation Treaty, whereby those possessing nuclear weapons agreed to strive to eliminate them, as they concurrently stopped all others from acquiring them. The U.S. enthusiastically promoted the U.N. Millennium Development Goals, the advancement of women and protection of their reproductive rights, and finally signed the U.N. convention to support the rights of persons with disabilities.

I was especially committed to achieving progress on LGBT rights. While not a popular cause with many U.N. member states, I have long viewed this as the last major frontier in the battle for civil and human rights. With strong backing from Washington, over the course of four and a half years, I pushed the envelope as far as I could at the U.N. The U.S. joined the Core Group of countries at the U.N. committed to LGBT rights. We championed pro-LGBT resolutions at the U.N. Human Rights Council and the accreditation of the first LGBT NGOs by the U.N. We backed fair and equitable treatment of LGBT employees at the U.N. I am particularly proud that the U.S. demanded and, after some serious diplomatic combat, ultimately achieved the inclusion of LGBT persons as among those groups protected from extrajudicial killing in a landmark 2010 General Assembly resolution. On issues of human dignity and broadening economic opportunity, the battles we fought marked a clear departure from the positions of the previous administration.

In charting this new course, I had a few things working in my favor.

There was tremendous international excitement and goodwill toward President Obama. People at the U.N., as around the world, had high hopes and wanted him to succeed. Secretary Clinton and senior officials at the State Department were like-minded philosophically and supportive of me, despite occasional disagreements we had over particular policy issues. I was familiar with the U.N. from my prior tenure at the NSC and the State Department during the Clinton administration. The U.N. secretary-general, Ban Ki-moon, was generally favorably disposed toward the United States. And I was coming not too far on the heels of the infamous John Bolton.

At the same time, I enjoyed a high degree of latitude. President Obama made clear to his team at the White House and at the State Department that he had full confidence in my judgment and abilities. To most in Washington, New York was out of sight and out of mind, which afforded me considerable flexibility and breathing room. No one questioned me on day-to-day decisions or tactics and, if they interfered, their efforts typically failed. On big issues, such as the Middle East, Iran, and North Korea, or whether to join the Human Rights Council, I did need Washington's blessing on our approach; and then colleagues usually accepted our recommendations.

While Obama believed deeply in the utility of multilateral action, in truth he was not as enthusiastic about the U.N. as some perceived. When announcing my nomination, President-elect Obama signaled publicly his tough love approach to the U.N., stressing: "We need the United Nations to be more effective as a venue for collective action against terror and proliferation, climate change and genocide, poverty and disease." No romantic in any policy context, the president was rightly impatient with the sprawling and constipated U.N. bureaucracy and its capacity for waste and abuse. As ardent a proponent of U.N. reform as any of the institution's critics, Obama viewed America's role as to pressure and support the U.N. to become leaner, increasingly efficient, and worthy of American taxpayer dollars. As his permanent representative, I often felt that President Obama tolerated the U.N. more than he appreciated it, but he allowed me to do the necessary work to advance American interests. At the same time, Obama rightly insisted that the U.S. pay its U.N. dues in full and on time and succeeded in working with Congress to ensure our commitments were fulfilled—something that had been far more difficult in the 1990s during President Clinton's tenure.

Throughout my time in New York, I benefited from being perceived as close to President Obama and a reliable and faithful representative of the White House. I had the advantage of being in the president's cabinet and a member of the National Security Council Principals Committee (PC). This meant that I was not just spouting the president's line; I was intimately involved in the decision making and fully understood the rationale behind our policies. I had an independent voice and a vote at the PC table, which I attended via secure videoconference from New York, or in person in Washington when I could.

The inclusion of the U.N. ambassador in the cabinet is a tradition dating back to President Eisenhower when he appointed Henry Cabot Lodge. It endured, except under President George H. W. Bush, who had served as U.N. ambassador, and later George W. Bush, who both required the U.N. ambassador to report to the secretary of state through the assistant secretary of state for international organization affairs.

It is a tricky balancing act to play the dual role of member of the cabinet and the PC, reporting to the president on the one hand, while serving (at least technically) as an instructed ambassador reporting to the secretary of state (like all other ambassadors) on the other hand. As was the custom with most of my predecessors, I had an office with a small staff in D.C. This team led by my highly capable and, if necessary, sharp-elbowed deputy, Erica Barks-Ruggles, and later by the unflappable, efficient Rexon Ryu, worked the State Department bureaucracy to ensure that the instructions I received were ones I could execute in good conscience. When, occasionally, there were significant policy differences to resolve, such as whether the U.S. should rejoin the U.N. Human Rights Council, I could escalate the argument to the secretary of state or the White House if need be. It took some time and a bit of bureaucratic boxing to restore the U.N. ambassador's position from its subordinated role during the Bush years.

An early challenge was to establish my relationships with the other principals and, above all, with Secretary Clinton. Given the bruises of the primary season and my decision to join the Obama campaign, ours could have been a fraught, even contentious relationship. Initially, a couple of people on Clinton's personal staff seemed intent on punishing me through selective leaks to the press about my leadership style or relationships within the State Department. But Hillary herself was always a good colleague and effective partner.

We had a standing, half-hour, one-on-one Friday morning meeting in her office at State when we were both in town. Secretary Clinton would often begin the meetings by asking, "How's your family doing?" We would then turn to hot topics in New York and whether I needed help, which she never failed to provide, if requested. On one occasion early in the administration, I asked for her view on a leading candidate for a senior U.N. position, a person she had known previously as a high-ranking foreign official. Caustically, Clinton joked that the prospective candidate "would be the last cockroach to crawl out from underground after nuclear winter." I was impressed.

In our weekly meetings, we would also discuss issues on the Principals Committee agenda as well as personnel matters, and compare our takes on consequential meetings. She was always down-to-earth and forthcoming, civil, and friendly. The secretary was good to me over our four years, and I always admired and appreciated her professionalism. Beyond that, she was generous personally—especially with her concern about my parents' health challenges, how the kids were faring in my absence, and, later, how I was enduring after I came under attack for Benghazi.

One inclement Monday morning in February 2009, roads and runways in D.C. were extremely icy, and my flight to New York was canceled. By this point, I had more or less adjusted to the demands of the commute, and knew, when I stepped out of my house, that my intrepid Diplomatic Security detail would have an alternate plan to get me to my job on time.

As U.N. ambassador, the State Department assigned me a team of DS agents in New York and D.C. DS typically protects the secretary of state, visiting foreign ministers, and the U.N. ambassador, while Secret Service protects the president, vice president, their families, select White House personnel, the secretaries of treasury and homeland security, and visiting heads of state. Whether at work or at home, DS accompanied me *everywhere*. Doctors' offices, kids' schools, vacations. It could get awkward—particularly when the family was involved—to have extra people with us whether we wanted them there or not. After all, meting out discipline to a misbehaving child, getting annoyed with your spouse, or holding vigil at the hospital with a sick parent can be uncomfortable with an audience present. Yet the DS agents were always discreet, helpful, and supportive and, with time, they came to know my kids and parents well. Indeed, it became a too-frequent trauma when agents my kids loved were suddenly rotated off my detail—sometimes without the opportunity for a proper goodbye.

Even though I grew close to my agents, at the start of my tenure my lead agent in Washington proved to be a challenge. Opposed to any familiarity, old-school, from the tradition of not speaking unless spoken to, he had a distant, business-only demeanor and, as I later found out, forbade all other agents to talk to me. That wasn't going to work for me because, if I have to let unfamiliar men (or an occasional woman) into my most personal life, I want to know who they are, where they come from, and to engage with them as normal human beings. Early on, I realized this first lead agent in Washington was not a fit for me, but in that initial month I hadn't yet figured out how to solve the problem without breaking a lot of crockery at State.

On that February morning, when my flight was canceled, and I stepped outside, expecting to jump into the black Suburban, it was nowhere in sight. Instead, I spotted the lead agent gingerly walking down from the top of our street. When he reached me, he said, "Ma'am, because of the ice, we need to walk up to the intersection to meet the car." I didn't think twice about it, and we made our way to the car and off to Union Station for the nearly three-hour train ride to New York.

Later that day, my New York press team alerted me that a local Fox News crew was on my block in D.C. filming the aftermath of an accident involving Diplomatic Security. "What accident?" I asked. Alex Wolff, along with the chief of security at the U.S. Mission, kept everything matter-of-fact and to-the-point as he gave me the whole story. The Washington lead agent had instructed the DS driver that morning to pick me up in front of the house as normal. Instead of driving up from the bottom of my one-block icy street, they drove down from the top. The heavy, armored SUV lost traction and slid at some pace down the hill, crashing into a neighbor's Mercedes. The DS lead agent failed to tell me or my neighbors and took me to the train as if nothing happened. Somehow, Fox got wind, and it was a story before either I or Ian had even heard about it.

Incredulous, I immediately wanted to know, "Are you telling me that the lead agent withheld important information from me, failed to inform the police and our neighbors, and now has implicated me in leaving the scene of a crime?" Apparently so.

That was the last I had to deal with that lead agent, so one early problem was solved. When I returned from New York that Thursday night, I deposited a case of nice wine on my neighbor's doorstep. DS paid for repairs to their car. End of that story.

From then on, I never had anything but the best experiences with the dedicated DS agents, especially the only one, David Millet, who remained on my detail from the very start to the finish of my tenure.

———

Aside from travel concerns and adapting to a full-time security detail that followed me everywhere, I also had to adjust to certain challenges of living in two cities—starting with the basics of having clothing and toiletries in both places. The U.N. ambassador's residence for sixty-plus years was on the top (forty-second) floor of the Waldorf-Astoria Towers on Park Avenue, a fifteen-minute walk or five-minute drive to the U.N. When I first moved into the residence—known at the U.S. Mission as "the WAT"— I appreciated the impressive four-bedroom apartment, huge by New York standards, with soaring views, ornate high ceilings, a chef's kitchen, a large foyer, an expansive living room, and a dining room suitable for entertaining forty at a sit-down event.

As ambassador, I was able to give the residence my own touch by selecting beautiful works of art—thanks to the State Department's "Art in Embassies" program and the Foundation for Art and Preservation in Embassies, which place American artists' work in U.S. embassies. I chose to feature the dramatic and colorful works of prominent African American artists, primarily from the New York area, such as Carrie Mae Weems, Mickalene Thomas, and Whitfield Lovell.

The massive apartment was terrific for entertaining, accommodating over two hundred at a standing reception. As a single inhabitant away from my family, however, the place could feel empty and sometimes lonely.

Most Mondays through Thursdays, I stayed overnight in New York. When I did not have a dinner engagement—something I tried to limit in order to manage both my weight and sanity—I would come home to the residence and eat a solitary but healthy meal, ably prepared by the residence chef, Stanton Thomas, and served by the evening household attendant, Ana Barahona. The residence manager Dorothy Burgess was a wonderful, no-fooling woman from Barbados, who had seen some dozen U.S. ambassadors and their families come and go. The lovely staff became friends who cared generously for me and who ran the ambassador's residence with the utmost professionalism.

With so much underused space, I gladly invited family and friends to visit. Often when I was home on weekends in D.C., administration colleagues conserved government resources by staying at the WAT apartment in comfort and security with their families—including Vice President Biden and his wife, Jill, First Lady Michelle Obama and her girls, Valerie Jarrett, Denis McDonough, Ambassador Ron Kirk, and many others. I also welcomed my USUN colleagues to stay there as needed, including after Hurricane Sandy when many staff members who lived in lower Manhattan lost power for days.

My own family visited New York on occasion, enjoying memorable gatherings at the Waldorf. In 2009, Dad came back east again for the holidays. At nearly ninety, he was in tolerable health, despite contending with high blood pressure, congestive heart failure, and atrial fibrillation, which he managed with medication. He was still sharp, mobile, and self-sufficient. That first year, Dad and Mom joined our family for Thanksgiving in New York. We saw the Rockettes at Radio City Music Hall, a Broadway show, and took in the sights from the Empire State Building to the USS *Intrepid*. It was a great time for our kids and their grandparents, one which demonstrated the benefits of the détente my parents had reached years earlier.

Beginning with my wedding, when they were compelled to collaborate on everything from the menu to music, Lois and Emmett managed to interact more civilly. By the time Jake arrived five years later, my parents had grown accustomed to engaging each other with only rare fireworks. Becoming grandparents provided the balm that truly soothed their relationship, enabling us all to enjoy their company without worrying that they would go at each other. It's fair to say that they became friendly, if not quite friends.

For that transformation, I remain forever grateful. Over the span of almost twenty years, at the end of their lives, my parents gave us back our unitary family. Johnny's kids and mine have happy memories of their grandparents individually and together, with only historical knowledge of their previous antagonism. And Johnny and I finally experienced the peace and joy of many wonderful family occasions spent together with our parents.

Even the warmth of family, however, could not obscure the many defects of the Waldorf apartment. If you didn't live there, you would think it was the height of luxury. But the Waldorf-Astoria was an ancient and run-down hotel, as I would be reminded from time to time. Occasionally, I would turn on the tap in the morning and watch mud brown and foul-smelling water belch forth, precluding showering. After particularly fierce thunderstorms, because of the roof's disrepair, sizable chunks of plaster from the ceiling would crash onto the living room floor. The window unit air conditioners could not withstand high winds, and rain could pour in when the flimsy casings blew out. Roaches were not uncommon, even massive ones of the tropical variety.

The Waldorf charged the U.S. government a fortune in monthly rent for poor maintenance, so I eventually embarked on a search to purchase my successors a less expensive yet better residence. The Washington bureaucracy and the laborious appropriations process, which does not take into consideration basic financial concepts like net present value, reflexively stymied efforts to do American taxpayers a long-term favor. Only several years later, after the Chinese bought the hotel and the security implications of their ownership sank in, did the State Department allow my successor, Samantha Power, to sign a deal to move the U.S. out of the historic Waldorf-Astoria.

———

One of my primary responsibilities in New York was to build relationships with other permanent representatives. With 193 U.N. member states, I could not meet formally with each one individually, but over time I came to know most of my colleagues—some very well. The most important were those we had to do frequent business with: the other four of the five permanent members (P5) of the Security Council—the United Kingdom, France, China, and Russia; the other nonpermanent members of the U.N. Security Council (UNSC) who rotated on and off the Council in two-year terms; and important allies like Germany, Canada, Spain, Italy, Israel, Japan, South Korea, Australia, and New Zealand. I also prioritized knowing the African ambassadors, some fifty-plus who often voted en bloc in the General Assembly, and the Pacific Islanders—small nations that reliably supported the U.S. even on the toughest issues.

As part of our carefully choreographed series of initial meetings for me as the brand-new U.S. ambassador, I met the permanent representative of Israel on Day One. Israel is the focus of outsize attention at the U.N.—most of it unfair and excessively negative. My responsibility, as is traditional, was to stand up for and protect Israel against attacks on its legitimacy and security. It was a role I embraced with passion and played aggressively throughout my tenure at the U.N. I loathe anti-Semitism and racism. For me, it's personal. And too much of the anti-Israel vitriol at the U.N. stems from crass prejudice.

In my early years, my work in defense of Israel was greatly aided by having a first-rate partner in Gabriela Shalev, Israel's first and only female U.N. ambassador. An appointee of Foreign Minister Tzipi Livni (with whom I had become friends during the Bush years), Gabriela is a distinguished professor of law and a jurist. At our first meeting, she greeted me alone in her private office. In her heavy accent, Gabriela talked movingly about her love of Israel, the tragic loss of her husband in the 1973 Yom Kippur War, and her two beloved children whom she raised alone. Gabriela is a strong but slight woman with close-cropped graying dark hair, powerful eyes, and a warm intensity that immediately captivated me. Old enough to be my mother, she and I became close—sharing perspectives with brutal honesty, plotting ways to serve our shared goals, and lamenting the forces that made Israel a perennial target at the U.N. and the Netanyahu policies that gave near daily fodder to Israel's critics. To this day, Gabriela is my sister, a prized relationship forged as we fought together in the muddy trenches at the U.N.

Our battles seemed never ending. Throughout 2009, I used my constructive relationship with Ban Ki-moon, the cautious but principled and pro-American secretary-general from South Korea, to push from behind the scenes to keep the notorious Goldstone Report out of active consideration by the Security Council. The report summarized the conclusions of a U.N. fact-finding mission, which harshly condemned Israel's actions in the recent 2008-2009 Gaza War. Had the document been formally inserted on the Security Council's agenda for debate, Israel's opponents would have had a field day trying to censure Israel for what South African jurist Richard Goldstone alleged were potential war crimes.

The next year, after Israel conducted a raid on a Turkish flotilla seeking to break Israel's blockade of Gaza that turned deadly in international waters, Turkey and the Palestinians forced an emergency meeting of the UNSC. Pressure was high to strongly condemn Israel, but with Alex Wolff and our team, I managed to achieve a more measured statement that expressed "regret for the loss of life," condemned "those acts which resulted in the loss of life," and called for an "impartial and . . . transparent investigation."

By the end of my tenure, I had fought many such defensive battles—from pulling the U.S. out of the World Conference on Racism due to its anti-Israel bent to protecting Israel in the U.N. Human Rights Council against that body's deeply ingrained anti-Israel bias. I spearheaded efforts to prevent Palestine from being admitted prematurely to the U.N. as a full member state (a status it sought in order to bypass negotiations for a two-state solution), just as I worked to protect Israel from efforts to rebuke their nuclear program at the International Atomic Energy Agency (IAEA) and led the annual losing charge in the General Assembly against a litany of anti-Israel resolutions.

Most notably, upon instructions from Washington, I cast the sole veto of the Obama administration to block a 2011 Arab- and Palestinian-sponsored resolution that would have declared Israeli settlements "illegal." Like each prior U.S. administration for over forty years, Republican and Democratic, the Obama administration deemed Israeli settlement activity "illegitimate" and counterproductive to peace. Committed to doing our utmost to try to broker an ever-elusive Israeli-Palestinian peace agreement, we viewed U.N. intervention as an unhelpful diversion that could set back efforts to press the two parties to negotiate directly and forge a two-state solution. In an effort to maintain international unity, the U.S. counterproposed a softer rebuke of settlements through a lesser legal instrument of the U.N. Security Council—a presidential statement. When the Palestinians rejected that compromise offer and insisted on bringing their resolution to a vote, the Obama administration decided to oppose it. In my White House–drafted speech explaining the U.S. position after the vote, I stressed that "Our opposition to the resolution . . . should . . . not be misunderstood to mean we support settlement activity. On the contrary, we reject in the strongest terms the legitimacy of continued Israeli settlement activity," which "has undermined Israel's security and corroded hopes for peace and stability in the region."

Despite our extraordinary exercise of the veto in order to protect Israel and the peace process, I was surprised to find my statement criticized as harsh and gratuitous by some in the American Jewish community. The expectation that we were supposed to veto the resolution *and* sugarcoat U.S. opposition to settlement activity struck me as excessive, even though I agreed with the necessity to veto.

Throughout my time as U.N. ambassador, I was proud to fight hard for Israel's legitimacy and security. Historically, many U.N. member states have displayed a distinct bias against Israel, stemming in part from their anticolonial orientation. In its worst form, this bias is tinged by noxious, barely disguised anti-Semitism. Along with racism, homophobia, and other forms of prejudice, I was determined to battle anti-Semitism wherever it surfaced in the world body.

While at the U.N. I was grateful to receive the praise and thanks of many pro-Israel groups for my strong defense of Israel. Better still, throughout my time in the Obama administration, I could always rely on one phenomenal Israeli man to be in my corner: Shimon Peres. Former prime minister and president, founding father, visionary peacemaker, and global statesman, Peres became my cherished friend. I first met him in 2009 at a luncheon in his honor in New York hosted by the Conference of Presidents of Major American Jewish Organizations. I spoke briefly at that event, as did he. At the end, he held me by my shoulders, looked deeply into my eyes with his piercing blues, and thanked me for my words and my service.

Later that year, Peres invited me to Israel to speak at the annual Israeli Presidential Conference, called "Facing Tomorrow." I began my speech with a little Hebrew, "Todah rabah. Erev Tov"—thank you very much and good evening. I affirmed, "an essential truth that will never change: the United States of America remains fully and firmly committed to the peace and security of the State of Israel. That commitment spans generations and political parties. It is not negotiable. And it never will be negotiable." After the speech, President Peres pulled me aside to counsel: "That was a great speech, very well done," he said, "but you must pause long enough to allow the audience to exhaust its applause." Marveling at my comparative inexperience, I hugged him and thanked him warmly for such kind wisdom from a true veteran. Lesson learned.

In the coming years, Peres and I met in Israel, Switzerland, and the U.S. He would write or call when he sensed from afar that I might need moral support. Peres, who had met every U.S. president since Kennedy, loved President Obama like a son, and saw in him so many qualities of greatness, as he often told me. He worried about Obama's security and political fortunes and cared deeply for those of us close to him. He was generous with his incomparable wisdom and experience. Peres was warm, energetic, charming, funny, and, all told, the sexiest senior citizen I have ever known. I loved Shimon Peres like a father figure but can only imagine what a devil he might have been in his prime.

————

My first major test at the U.N. came from North Korea. The isolated Stalinist regime greeted President Obama with a ballistic missile launch on April 4, 2009, the day of his historic speech on nonproliferation delivered in Prague on his first overseas trip as president. North Korea has a habit of creating crises to test the reaction of new U.S. administrations. Ours came on a Saturday night, so the next morning after appearing on the Sunday shows, I dashed to New York from Washington to join the Security Council closed-door debate on how to respond. Obama had declared that fresh sanctions on North Korea were needed to build upon the regime of initial sanctions imposed in 2006 under the Bush administration. It was my job to obtain those sanctions as quickly as possible.

The task was complicated. Russia and China, which wield veto power, opposed any new sanctions resolution, fearing it would drive North Korea away from the (dormant) negotiations known as the Six Party Talks. In the UNSC, Russia and China also argued that the launch did not explicitly violate prior resolutions because it carried a satellite, not a missile. The U.S. view was that any launch using ballistic missile technology, as this launch did, was banned and must be punished. Japan and South Korea, which are directly threatened by North Korea, given their proximity, were deeply rattled and demanded their ally the U.S. achieve a strong result. Their insistence only hardened Chinese and Russian resistance.

After a week of haggling, we reached a compromise: we would adopt a presidential statement (known as a PRST), a less formal form of U.N. action than a resolution, but still a legally binding one, and use that vehicle in a novel way to impose fresh sanctions on selected North Korean companies and individuals. The statement also affirmed the U.S. position that any launch of any payload using ballistic missile technology, whether satellite or warhead, is a violation of U.N. resolutions and international law. The PRST was a clever threading of the needle that, while imperfect, was satisfactory and afforded me a dry run for the much tougher, more consequential negotiations to come.

In late May, after formally pulling out of the Six Party Talks, North Korea conducted its second nuclear test, conveniently timed to coincide with Memorial Day. I rushed up to New York yet again to attend an emergency meeting of the Council where, with little Russian or Chinese resistance, we swiftly condemned the North Korean test and agreed to work on a new sanctions resolution. Then the hard work began.

Negotiating high-stakes, high-profile resolutions under the persistent glare of the press, daily prodding from Washington to hurry up (while trying to manage their expectations), and the near hysterical anxiety of my Japanese and South Korean counterparts, made for a stressful mix. Not even six months into the job, enmeshed in intense negotiations at the U.S. Mission or small conference rooms at the U.N., I faced the toughest and most important test of my early tenure. I had to achieve a strong new sanctions resolution in the face of Chinese reluctance to hit their traditional ally with more than symbolic penalties. The Russians, ever potent opponents, traditionally joined the Chinese position on North Korea; so, the challenge was to move China while keeping our European and Asian allies on board, even as they chafed at largely being kept in the dark.

As always, my toughest customer was Russian ambassador Vitaly Churkin. When I arrived at the U.N., Vitaly, who started there in 2006, was an experienced veteran and a diplomatic force of nature who variously charmed and intimidated all comers. I was charmed, on occasion, but never intimidated. The two of us fought with legendary ferocity, variously with sarcasm, humor, or just pure venom; yet we also became friends. Vitaly was ever the worthy opponent—razor-smart, a skilled communicator, equally adept as an obstructionist and a problem solver, by turns maddening and great fun. I used to joke with my staff that a victory in the Security Council never felt fully satisfactory unless it involved besting Vitaly.

He and I tangled over issues large and small, publicly and privately. Vitaly was the only U.N. ambassador ever to object to my bringing my son into the U.N.'s nonpublic sessions. From age eleven onward, Jake loved these meetings and could sit for hours mesmerized by the debates. He was always silent and well-behaved, but Vitaly couldn't stand the idea of a child in the Security Council. He repeatedly threatened to halt the meetings and insisted on Jake's expulsion. We nearly came to blows one day after such a session, in Jake's presence. Vitaly yelled at me, "Do you allow your son to watch pornography?" "Of course not," I said. He rejoined, "Then why do you let him watch Security Council debates?"

On North Korean sanctions, at this early stage in 2009, Vitaly was a little more rational than he was about Jake. When it came to North Korea, however, my most important counterpart was the Chinese ambassador. I worked closely with Zhang Yesui on my first of several extended U.S.-China bilateral negotiations over North Korea. Ambassador Zhang is a measured, thoughtful man whom I found to be straightforward and true to his word. Unlike some Chinese counterparts, Yesui had a good sense of humor, an easy manner, and an earnest desire to do business constructively without superfluous bluster or drama. We spent countless hours in closed-door negotiations, usually with a small team of advisors on either side. When we reached the critical endgame, however, sometimes it was just the two of us—a format the Chinese typically avoid with Americans, preferring the protection from Beijing that a note taker provides.

As became a pattern over the coming years, the negotiation began with me presenting an ambitious menu of proposed sanctions and demanding that China accept them. China would balk, and after days of internal negotiations in Beijing, come back with a meager counterproposal. I would dismiss their offer as wholly inadequate and press for many of the most important measures on our original list. Days later, they would counter. And so on, until either we reached an acceptable outcome that Washington believed substantially increased the pressure on North Korea or fell short. If it fell short, and I felt I could not get any more out of the negotiation in New York, I had two tactical options: erupt with the Chinese ambassador in frustration and threaten to take a U.S.-drafted resolution straight to the UNSC and dare China to veto it (something it never wants to do on North Korea); or, I could ask President Obama to call the Chinese president and press our position at the highest level. If the first move failed, the latter course usually yielded some incremental give from Beijing, often enough to get us over the finish line.

This pattern repeated itself as we negotiated three major North Korea sanctions resolutions during my tenure. Each new resolution was harder and took longer to obtain than the last, as it had to exceed the previous in how much added pain it imposed on North Korea. China is North Korea's major trading and diplomatic partner, so each additional turn of the screw also adversely affected Chinese banking or economic interests and required difficult consensus building in Beijing.

However, this early North Korea negotiation was my most challenging. There had not been new U.N. sanctions imposed on North Korea since the first round in 2006. The Japanese and South Korean ambassadors were nervous, wanting in on the action but able to add little value. The Japanese press corps was in my face everywhere I went for two weeks, such that a DS agent had to get a bit physical with one particularly pushy camerawoman outside our office building. To make matters worse, I was not familiar with intense negotiations with the Chinese. I hadn't yet discerned the rhythm and style of their approach and how to assess if we were close to collapse or to comity.

For nearly two weeks, sleep eluded me as I worried much of the night about whether we would get where we needed to with China, whether I would disappoint Washington and fall short in the eyes of my new team. As the deliberations with the Chinese drew out, South Korean and Japanese anxiety grew. I could feel them wondering—*Is this new Obama team up to the job? Would the Americans sell us short? Can we trust them?* The U.K., France, and Russia, fellow veto-wielding members of the P5, are unaccustomed to being left out of the room in any consequential negotiation. Understandably, they hated being treated as afterthoughts who could be counted on to go along with whatever the U.S. and China agreed. Still, the Europeans understood that the outcome was going to be determined by Washington and Beijing; they would grouse but only balk (perhaps publicly) if they thought we cut a weak deal. More pressure to perform.

To keep all sides on board, I met bilaterally with each of the P5, plus South Korea and Japan, and hosted occasional negotiating sessions with all those players together. On one such occasion, I invited all six of the other delegations to meet with the U.S. team in our modest main conference room at the temporary U.S. Mission, which we occupied until the completion of our new, more secure building across the street from the U.N.

In this particular conference room, there were photographs hanging on the wall of every prior U.S. ambassador, in order of their tenure—as is customary inside U.S. embassies. As the difficult discussion progressed, things started to get heated. Russian ambassador Churkin was typically stubborn and obnoxious. The Chinese were hiding behind the Russians, opposing the tough proposed sanctions on our list. And the others were adding little value in moving us forward. Sensing an opportunity to shake up the negotiation and seize the initiative, I stood up suddenly, interrupting the conversation. I moved to my right and dramatically ripped a photograph off the wall. I sat back down and banged the framed photo on the table so that it faced my colleagues as I faux-raged: "We can either do this the nice way or the hard way. It's up to you. But we are gonna get this done."

The photo I had selected was of John Bolton, the most widely disliked of my recent predecessors. All my colleagues at the table knew who he was, and many had had the displeasure of working with him. My stunt first silenced and then lightened the room but made a clear point: I was not playing, and we were not going to tolerate a lame outcome.

In the end, after barely two weeks, we achieved a milestone resolution, codified as 1874. It strengthened the existing arms embargo, authorized a range of financial sanctions, granted states the authority to search, seize, and dispose of suspected banned North Korean cargo, and froze the assets of targeted North Korean officials and companies. This resolution significantly increased the pressure on North Korea and laid the basis for even more impactful sanctions in years to come. Its unprecedented elements, particularly the cargo inspection and financial provisions, also established a template for subsequent strong sanctions on other countries, including Iran and Libya.

Drama, I learned, can be a useful negotiating tool, if sparingly employed. More importantly, my intimate dealings with the Chinese over the course of my U.N. years gave me critical insight into how their system operates, what their interests and fears are, and how to negotiate with them effectively. I found that pushing back relentlessly in the face of Russian obstruction and Chinese resistance was the key to success in the Security Council. Particularly as a rookie and the only woman among the P5 ambassadors, I realized that I needed to consistently show confidence and resolve and never let them see me sweat. Thus, with the counsel and support of a first-rate team at USUN, I passed my first major test as U.S. ambassador, while gaining valuable experience and confidence as a negotiator.

13

High-Stakes Diplomacy

My first meeting with the Iranian ambassador began in broad daylight one afternoon in New York City but was meant to achieve maximum discretion. Rather than find a quiet corner at the U.N., which would raise eyebrows, or host him at the U.S. Mission, which was frequented by journalists, it was agreed I would visit him at his residence.

Diplomatic Security dropped off me and Puneet Talwar, the top Persian Gulf expert on the NSC staff, just around the corner from the Iranian residence, an elegant old town house on Fifth Avenue across from Central Park. We walked casually up to the door and rang the bell—as normal as can be. The ambassador's assistant answered, and the ambassador greeted us in plain sight at the bottom of the stairs. I stuck my hand out to shake his, as I did scores of times a day at the U.N., but he demurred, awkwardly placing his hand on his chest. Then I recalled, religious Iranian men won't shake a woman's hand. The same custom prevails with ultra-Orthodox Jewish men.

The Iranian ambassador was Mohammed Khazaie, a U.S.-educated former member of the Iranian parliament and representative at the World Bank. In public, he was a firebrand and perfectly apt representative of his neanderthal president; in private, the ambassador was soft-spoken, urbane, and respectful. To establish contact between us and open up the channel, Puneet, who had prior experience with Khazaie, joined me in our initial encounters.

In the numerous meetings that followed over the years, Khazaie and I met upstairs in his front parlor. Dates, pistachios, and fruit were proffered in abun-

dance. Coffee and tea as well. It was always civil, if formal. After the first few encounters, Puneet stopped coming to New York, and I met Khazaie alone, following up by providing back-briefings to a tight circle of White House and State Department colleagues. Conscious that I would be vulnerable should he attempt anything untoward, I was a bit wary of visiting his house solo, as were the DS agents, though they never interfered. Yet my instincts, which were validated, told me that he would not cross any lines.

While I came to trust my physical safety in Khazaie's presence, I was surprised to learn that the FBI did not trust me. Soon after I started meeting with Khazaie, the FBI came to the U.S. Mission to meet with my chief of security and with my deputy, Alex Wolff. They never asked to see me. In virtual whispers, the FBI told Alex that they had seen me go in and out of the Iranian ambassador's residence and were suspicious of what I was doing. While it is the FBI's job to conduct counterintelligence operations on U.S. soil and to be concerned about Americans who may be compromised, I was dismayed that they would think I might be among them. Alex told them to buzz off, assuring them that what I was doing was fully authorized. Fortunately, Alex was one of the very few people on my team who was read into this private channel. "Thank you for handling this as skillfully as you did," I later commended Alex, who laughed when I said something to the effect of, "Otherwise, I would have had the FBI all up in my grill for years to come."

Most of my visits and occasional phone calls with the Iranian ambassador were to deliver or receive a message between our capitals or to discuss issues of concern. I pressed for the release of three captured American hikers, who were eventually freed, and for the return of Robert Levinson, a former FBI agent who disappeared in Iran in 2007 and is still missing, believed to have been kidnapped by Iranian officials. I demanded an end to attacks committed by Iranian forces against U.S. military personnel in Iraq and conveyed the U.S. determination to retaliate. On behalf of the Department of Defense, I proposed the establishment of a U.S.-Iran military-to-military hotline to avoid unintended conflict in the Gulf, but Iran did not agree. At times, I was compelled to endure Khazaie's complaints about FBI surveillance of him and his personnel in New York. Frequently, we discussed Iran's nuclear program, and I warned that the U.S. was committed to halting it—by whatever means necessary.

On rare occasions when we passed each other in the U.N. corridors,

Khazaie and I acted as if we did not know each other. Once, we exchanged hot words at a distance in a large U.N. committee meeting over an issue related to the U.S. role as host nation of the U.N. But apart from my work to sanction Iran harshly, we rarely had occasion to cross paths publicly. Remarkably, for years our private channel remained unknown to most, save the FBI and, I imagine, the Israelis.

———•◆•———

Even as the U.S. government moved to increase pressure on Iran, we needed a way to communicate with the hostile regime. The Swiss embassy in Tehran, which we used for consular matters after we closed our own embassy in Tehran in 1979, was not suitable for sensitive political messages. Just as we have long had a discreet "New York channel" with the North Koreans, a backdoor way of exchanging messages utilizing their U.N. Mission in New York, we needed a confidential and reliable channel to Iran. Early in my tenure, due to my trusted role in the administration and my proximity to the Iranian ambassador in the relative discretion New York afforded, I was tapped by the White House to open an invisible line of communication with Iran.

Yet, even as we established a dialogue, relations between our two countries, long fraught, were about to become more strained. In addition to North Korea, the Obama administration had inherited the challenge of eliminating Iran's nuclear program. Unlike North Korea, Iran did not yet have any nuclear weapons, but it had the facilities to make fissile material and was stockpiling that material swiftly so that it could make a bomb within two to three months, if it so decided. From the outset, the Obama administration was committed to preventing Iran from obtaining a nuclear weapon, which would threaten U.S. forces in the region, Israel, our Gulf partners, and even Europe.

Our strong preference was to accomplish this objective through a combination of increased economic pressure and diplomacy, but President Obama remained ready to use force if other options failed. At the same time, Obama wanted to demonstrate respect for the Iranian people who suffered under an odious, repressive regime. To this end, President Obama began the practice of delivering an annual Nowruz (New Year's) message to the Iranian people. Out of pragmatism, we also signaled our willingness to engage in dialogue—sometimes blunt—with the Iranian government on its nuclear program, Iran's support for terrorism, and other matters of grave concern to the U.S.

Two developments in 2009, however, underscored the need for fresh sanctions on Iran. First, after declaring victory in Iran's presidential election, which was deeply marred by irregularities, Mahmoud Ahmadinejad, Iran's noxious incumbent president, ordered a vicious crackdown on civil society, beating and killing scores of peaceful protesters in the streets of Iran's major cities. Next, in September, the U.S. revealed the existence of a secret, undeclared, underground Iranian nuclear facility, which lent new impetus to our efforts to pressure Iran to come to the negotiating table.

Caught red-handed, Iran tried to get ahead of international pressure by agreeing to meet with the five permanent members of the UNSC plus Germany and the European Union (known as the P5+1) in Geneva to discuss its nuclear program. In October, Iran allowed international inspectors to visit the previously secret facility at Fordow and declared itself willing to ship most of its enriched uranium abroad to be converted into a scarce fuel for making medical isotopes, in order to buy time for real negotiations on its nuclear program. Iran, however, soon reneged on that bargain. The IAEA reported that Iran had enriched some uranium to 20 percent (close to bomb-grade quality) and continued working on warhead designs far longer than previously suspected. Iran's recalcitrance in the face of unprecedented U.S. willingness to negotiate on the nuclear program galvanized the Obama administration's push for much tougher sanctions.

Again, the ball was in my court: I had to deliver strong new sanctions, but this time there was less pressure to get it done fast. I was given time to maximize the impact of the outcome. In January 2010, I began negotiations with the P5 and Germany on a new sanctions resolution.

During my time as ambassador, I came to know my fellow P5 counterparts extremely well—their skills, weaknesses, temperaments, and idiosyncrasies. In this period, I spent far more time with each of these men than with my husband, and at times I felt that we were almost as familiar.

I enjoyed each of my counterparts to varying degrees and more so over time, but we all sometimes fought one another with a vehemence and a vengeance that only married couples could muster.

My British colleague, Sir Mark Lyall Grant, was likable and highly capable but the most fastidious of my colleagues. While Mark and I agreed on the substance of most matters, we sometimes differed on the means of achieving our goals. For instance, I grew impatient with Mark over Syria when he would allow negotiations with the Russians to drag on for months, make last-minute concessions, and then become indignant when, predictably, Moscow ordered Churkin to veto. We could have put forward tougher texts that fully reflected the frustration of the Council with the Assad regime and garnered the same result in far less time, but Mark kept hoping that he could potentially bring the Russians along.

French ambassador Gérard Araud eventually became one of my favorite colleagues, but only after we frequently butted heads, and he and his staff trashed me repeatedly to the press. Gérard is extremely smart, hilarious, acerbic, and was one of the few openly gay ambassadors in New York. He has zero patience for Yankee sophistry. He loves New York City, is a well-read scholar of history and literature, and views much of the world as beneath him.

In December 2010, I hosted Gérard and the entire U.N. Security Council for two days of meetings on Capitol Hill, at the State Department, and with President Obama. Ian and I kicked the occasion off with a reception for ambassadors and their spouses at our home in Washington. Thirteen-year-old Jake was already known to many of my colleagues (not just Vitaly) because of his passion for foreign policy, which had only intensified through many visits to the U.N. and conversations with U.N. representatives from around the world. Jake was a knowledgeable and poised interlocutor, but back then his views often diverged from official U.S. policy. For instance, the Arab ambassadors at the U.N. found charming Jake's strong sympathies for the Palestinian cause, which compelled me to limit his unsupervised conversations with them. (In the years since, Jake's views have migrated toward the opposite extreme of uncritical support for the Netanyahu government.) During this rare party in Washington, Jake engaged the ambassadors in erudite conversation. He opined to the Indian representative (against U.S. policy) that India ought to be a permanent member of the Security Council and later asked the Chinese ambassador's wife, "Why does China manipulate its currency?" eliciting a flummoxed response.

At eight, Maris was more reserved and committed no diplomatic faux pas. Attired in a fancy dress, she nicely greeted guests with a warm smile and friendly banter. When she came up to join me as I conversed with Gérard, she offered a cheerful hello. Gérard looked down contemptuously at her and sneered, "I don't like children." Maris was both shocked and unimpressed. I should have been outraged but was more amused. Gérard can be condescending; but as I learned, he is also a great ally in battle and can be charmingly self-effacing. I also came to like his partner Pascal very much, and when Gérard moved to Washington as French ambassador to the U.S., a posting he initially dreaded but came to like, we remained on good terms.

My second Chinese counterpart, Li Baodong, who once served as a low-level U.S. embassy Beijing employee and later China's ambassador to the U.N. in Geneva, replaced my friend Zhang Yesui as China's permanent representative in 2010. At first, Baodong didn't appear to have the heft, grace, or measured temperament of Yesui. Initially, he also seemed unsure of himself, or at least uncomfortable in English. With time, I got to know him better. He is, in fact, plenty canny and smart, and grew increasingly effective over time. By 2013, after a number of revealing one-on-one discussions about North Korea and our respective policies, I came to respect his skills and directness as well as to enjoy him as a colleague.

The P5 ambassadors worked intimately together for months as we negotiated on Iran sanctions. Employing the same tactic as on North Korea, I initially proposed a long list of powerful sanctions, aiming to drive the negotiation to its maximal outcome. Unlike North Korea, however, Iran was not an issue on which my European colleagues were prepared to defer to the U.S. For years, under President Bush, the U.S. had refused even to sit at the negotiating table with Iran, leaving the diplomacy as well as previous rounds of sanctions in Europe's hands. The Europeans—France, Germany, and the U.K. (EU-3)—expected to drive the push for strong new sanctions in New York. Ambassador Araud, who had previously been

France's chief negotiator on Iran, especially resented my determination to play a leadership role in the negotiation. Yet I was under clear instructions from Washington to ensure we got what we needed and thus to keep control of the negotiations. President Obama's policy and prestige were on the line, and we could not afford to outsource this effort. Thus, I had to balance Washington's anxiety with the Europeans' pride and deeper experience on this issue. To do so, I tried to ensure that the Iran negotiation was a truly collaborative effort with the EU-3, where we agreed initially on what we sought to achieve and worked together to maximize our success. Our comparative advantage was the U.S.'s superior ability to obtain agreement from the highly reluctant Chinese and Russians on a strong resolution.

President Obama met with Chinese president Hu Jintao in Washington in April 2010, on the margins of the first Nuclear Security Summit. Obama seized that opportunity to press Hu on tough new sanctions on Iran. China was a major trading partner of Iran, relied on Iranian oil, and had refused thus far to engage seriously in any concrete discussion of additional sanctions. But Obama's personal intervention opened the door to increased Chinese flexibility such that, following the meeting, Obama dispatched me to meet with my Chinese counterparts that same afternoon in Washington. The talks that followed over the subsequent weeks yielded considerable progress with the Chinese, which demonstrated to the Europeans the critical value of U.S. leadership, even if they didn't like to admit it.

Russia was the next target, and here Secretary Clinton played an important role in preparing the battlefield with Russian foreign minister Sergei Lavrov. Even more critically, President Obama had forged a collaborative relationship with Russia's young new president, Dmitri Medvedev, and used their tie to encourage Russia to accept more expansive penalties on Iran. With these openings, I was able to move the negotiation forward in New York so that, by May, we had a strong text that was broadly agreed upon among the P5 and Germany. We achieved that in part by providing Russia and China with Washington's assurances that the U.S. would not penalize their economic interests beyond what they had agreed to in the sanctions, a pledge that was honored more in the breach once Congress enacted intensified U.S. national sanctions.

Prior to the U.N. vote, we also needed to manage Congress carefully, which was chomping at the bit to impose unilateral U.S. sanctions on Iran and frustrated at the slow pace of the negotiations in New York. I had numerous discussions with senior Democratic members of the House and Senate. These exchanges generally followed the same line as with Howard Berman of California, the chairman of the House Foreign Affairs Committee, whom I repeatedly urged, "Please, please, give us more time. I'm confident that we'll get a good resolution out of the Security Council. But not if Congress acts first. If Russia and China see Congress go ahead and act unilaterally, including with penalties that hit them indirectly, I promise you we will lose them in New York. Russia and China will pocket congressional action as an excuse to avoid passing U.N. sanctions and turn around and argue that *we* acted in bad faith by targeting their economic interests." Berman understood that while the U.S. could always impose national sanctions, we needed a U.N. resolution for the European Union to act as well as to compel other countries to impose far more powerful multilateral sanctions. Getting the New York–Washington sequence right was critical and, ultimately, we managed to keep Congress onside.

Just when we were close to finalizing a P5 agreement and taking the text to the full Council, we encountered an unexpected obstacle. Brazil and Turkey—both rotating members of the UNSC with major business interests in Iran and egotistical leaders, Luiz Inácio Lula da Silva and Recep Tayyip Erdoğan, respectively—tried to derail the sanctions. They proposed that Iran commit to a lesser version of an aborted prior agreement, in which it would ship out of the country its low-enriched uranium in exchange for receiving a higher-grade uranium of the type that could only be used to make medical isotopes, not a bomb. Desperate to avoid sanctions, Iran suddenly embraced this gambit after the Brazilian and Turkish leaders made a last-ditch trip to Tehran. Suddenly, it seemed Russia might be swayed by the Turkish-Brazilian Hail Mary. So, I was relieved that Secretary Clinton intervened successfully with Foreign Minister Lavrov to keep Russia on board. Consequently, the day after Turkey and Brazil triumphantly announced their flimsy deal, the P5 jointly introduced our sanctions resolution for consideration by the whole Council. This move clearly signaled that the key powers were united in dismissing the Lula-Erdoğan bid as too little too late to halt new sanctions.

UNSC Resolution 1929 was adopted on June 9, 2010, with twelve countries, including all the permanent members, voting in favor, Turkey and Brazil opposed, and Lebanon abstaining. After six months of slogging, I felt gratified and relieved to achieve a considerable success—an exceptionally strong sanctions resolution that laid the predicate for even tougher U.S. and E.U. penalties to follow. The resolution's provisions included measures that authorized broad financial and banking sanctions and froze the assets of scores of Iranian entities involved in their nuclear program, including affiliates of the Islamic Revolutionary Guard Corps, a particularly notorious arm of the Iranian military. In addition, the Security Council authorized intrusive inspections of suspect Iranian cargo, banned the sale to Iran of eight categories of heavy weapons and all related military training, prohibited Iran from launching any ballistic missiles capable of carrying a nuclear warhead, and banned Iranian foreign investment in nuclear-related projects.

While many experts at the time doubted that this resolution would push Iran to enter into real negotiations, it ultimately had exactly that effect. Resolution 1929 paved the way to the Iran nuclear deal. After Hassan Rouhani defeated Ahmadinejad to win the presidency in 2013, having run on a platform of engagement with the West to achieve sanctions relief, it was obvious that stringent economic pressure had indeed compelled Iran to come to the negotiating table.

Notwithstanding the high-visibility nuclear challenges posed by Iran and North Korea, the bulk of the U.N. Security Council's agenda pertained to Sub-Saharan Africa, where conflicts persist, and the U.N. has deployed its largest and most complex peacekeeping and humanitarian missions. In my four and a half years at the U.N., I made eight official trips to Africa, most with multiple stops. Sometimes I traveled independently as an American cabinet official, but often as part of a formal UNSC delegation. The Council spent countless hours working to stabilize hot spots spanning from Somalia in the Horn of Africa, to Congo in Central Africa, to Côte d'Ivoire and Liberia in the west.

Council members were mostly unified on how to approach these conflicts, with two notable exceptions: Côte d'Ivoire, where Russia maintained a curious commitment to the discredited former leader Laurent Gbagbo; and Sudan and southern Sudan, where Russia and China reliably protected Khartoum from Western countries that strenuously opposed the genocidal regime and supported southern Sudan's right to self-determination.

Sudan, for me, was a familiar challenge, going back to the Clinton administration when we opposed Khartoum's support for terrorism and its violent repression of the people in southern Sudan during decades of civil conflict. The people of southern Sudan were black, Christian, and animist, with major cultural and historic differences from their predominantly Arab and Muslim rulers in the north. Southern Sudanese had sought independence for decades; in response, Khartoum employed starvation, aerial bombardment, including of hospitals and schools, and militia raids to terrorize and enslave the southern population and deny them self-determination. The conflict in the south cost an estimated two million lives and was among the deadliest in the world. On a bipartisan basis, the U.S. was united in support of the people of southern Sudan, and Christian groups were especially active on their behalf.

Late in my tenure as assistant secretary for African affairs, I took up a defiant challenge from Sudan's foreign minister to "Go see for yourself" whether there is slavery in southern Sudan, which Khartoum always vehemently denied. In November 2000, I flew unannounced on a small U.N. World Food Program aircraft from its hub in Lokichoggio, Kenya, to a barely visible dirt strip in southern Sudan. I met with women in the southwestern village of Marial Bai who had escaped slavery and rape at the hands of northern militia and visited an American missionary hospital in Lui that suffered regular bombing by Sudanese aircraft, including just hours after I left. Additionally, I spent the night in the town of Rumbek, a small hub of economic activity and base for U.N. agencies.

When I returned to Nairobi to report to the press the horrific personal stories of abuse I had documented, the Sudanese government protested vehemently that I had violated their sovereignty. I didn't care. The truth of their ongoing atrocities had to be told, and I was not going to be intimidated into silence. On the record, I sharply condemned Khartoum's rampant bombings of civilian targets and expressed my outrage after hearing firsthand accounts from women and children who were abducted, beaten, raped, tortured, enslaved—atrocities committed by militia at the direction or with the support of Sudan's government.

That trip in 2000 reinforced my abhorrence of the Khartoum regime and underscored the desperation, poverty, and oppression suffered by the people of southern Sudan. The region was the place that time forgot. It was almost biblical. No roads, no communications, no functioning economy beyond small-scale subsistence agriculture, no schools, no nothing. Southern Sudan's leader, John Garang, viewed by some as the George Washington of South Sudan, was an American-educated smooth talker. But his people suffered like none other on earth and his undisciplined, marauding Sudan People's Liberation Army were among those who most brutally victimized them.

The Bush administration properly sustained a focus on Sudan, investing significant effort in brokering the 2005 Comprehensive Peace Agreement, by which Sudan agreed to allow the south to conduct a referendum on independence in January 2011. This landmark agreement faced innumerable obstacles in implementation but laid the foundation for the eventual establishment of South Sudan. However, on another front, Khartoum turned its killing machine west to the Darfur region of Sudan, where dissident ethnic groups challenged central government authority. The ensuing genocide, directed by then-president Omar al-Bashir and conducted by the Sudanese army, took over 300,000 lives at its peak between 2003 and 2005. While Secretary of State Colin Powell rightly insisted that the U.S. call the killings "genocide," I argued as an outside policy expert that the Bush administration's response amounted mainly to hand-wringing. Instead, I urged that the U.S. consider an air campaign and a naval blockade to halt Khartoum's killing. In sum, my opposition to the cruelties of the Sudanese regime had continued unabated prior to taking up my post at the U.N.

Khartoum did not look forward to the arrival of the Obama administration. In addition to my own stance, as senators, Barack Obama and Joe Biden, as well as Hillary Clinton, had all taken tough lines against Sudan—especially on Darfur. Soon after I arrived in New York, the International Criminal Court indicted Bashir for war crimes and genocide in Darfur and issued arrest warrants, making him the first sitting head of state to face such charges. The Bashir regime responded by expelling thirteen international aid organizations that delivered well over half of the critical humanitarian assistance to the desperate millions of internally displaced persons in Darfur. The Security Council was paralyzed, unable to condemn Khartoum, because Russia, China, and Libya shielded Sudan from censure. It was an early low point that foreshadowed the divisions that would only deepen in the Council on Sudan.

In March 2009, President Obama appointed retired Major General Scott Gration as his special envoy for Sudan. I had come to know Scott during the campaign when he was an early Obama supporter and frequent campaign surrogate. An affable former Air Force general and the son of missionaries, Scott and I got along fine personally. Nonetheless it soon emerged that we had stark policy differences over Sudan. Scott favored a more accommodating approach to Khartoum, cast public doubt over whether genocide persisted in Darfur, and recommended in testimony before Congress that the U.S. preemptively ease sanctions and lift the State Sponsor of Terrorism designation. Referring to how to engage Khartoum, he said, "We have got to think about giving out cookies. Kids, countries, they react to gold stars, smiley faces, handshakes, agreements, talk, engagement." Gration's approach alarmed me as well as many in Congress and the NGO community.

As the administration conducted its first review of Sudan policy, I argued strenuously at the Principals' table that we should not give rewards to Sudan without concrete, irreversible changes in their policies and actions. Unfortunately, my differences with Scott were reported widely in the press, I trust through no fault of his and I know through none of mine. We were both loyal members of the Obama administration; neither of us had an interest in our dispute being aired publicly, which only heightened the difficulty for the president, who had to make the final decision. As the review progressed, I sensed that Secretary Clinton might be sliding into a more accommodationist camp, leaving me increasingly isolated as a proponent of maintaining a conditional, action-for-action approach. Unusually, I perceived that some in the White House may have been mischaracterizing my views on Sudan to the president. Thus, I took what was for me the rare step of invoking my privilege as a principal and member of the cabinet to write a memo directly to the president outlining my concerns about the direction of the policy review and explaining my recommended approach.

When the policy review concluded in October, and the president decided, I was satisfied with the outcome. No significant benefits would accrue to Khartoum unless their behavior on southern Sudan and Darfur changed substantially and irreversibly; moreover, we agreed to a significant list of penalties that would be imposed if Sudan's behavior persisted or backslid.

Gration continued to pursue a rhetorical approach that worried me, but he deserves credit for gradually improving humanitarian access into Darfur in the wake of the NGO expulsions, helping to end the conflict between Chad and Sudan, and then turning his focus in 2010 to the upcoming referendum on an independent South Sudan scheduled for January 9, 2011.

As the referendum approached, there were many reasons for concern. Six years after the Comprehensive Peace Agreement, none of the difficult issues between north and south had been resolved. Electoral arrangements were way behind schedule, and fears mounted that Khartoum would renege on its promise to allow the referendum to proceed. When U.N. Secretary-General Ban Ki-moon proposed a foreign-minister-level meeting on the margins of the annual gathering of heads of state at the opening of the General Assembly in late September 2010, I recommended that President Obama attend and elevate the meeting to an important summit just about one hundred days before the scheduled referendum.

Obama's presence attracted many key leaders from Africa and Europe and lent impetus to implementation of the Comprehensive Peace Agreement and the crucial January referendum. In his remarks, Obama warned of "more pressure and deeper isolation" for those who violate their commitments. But he also offered improved relations between the U.S. and Sudan, enhanced trade and investment ties, and the exchange of ambassadors—if Sudan fully and faithfully adhered to its commitments, ended the violence and the humanitarian crisis, and ensured accountability for war crimes in Darfur. Obama's intervention and the potential for improved relations with the U.S. most likely positively influenced Sudan's decision to allow the referendum to proceed.

Two weeks later, I led a Security Council delegation to southern

Sudan, Darfur, and Khartoum. The trip highlighted the continued suffering of the hundreds of thousands of displaced persons in Darfur, who were trapped in dusty, barren camps with insufficient food and water. Their makeshift villages were constantly threatened by Khartoum-backed militia who raided on horseback and burned the grass huts to the ground, killing as many as they could. In southern Sudan, we pressed the Sudan People's Liberation Movement leaders to prepare to govern in service of their people rather than in the insular, corrupt fashion to which they had already grown accustomed. Finally, our meetings in Khartoum enabled us to reinforce the necessity of allowing the referendum to be conducted unimpeded.

Almost miraculously, three months later, on January 9, 2011, millions of southern Sudanese came peacefully and joyfully to the polls to express their long-suppressed desire for independence, voting 98.6 percent in favor of establishing their own country, South Sudan.

———

The postelection euphoria was short lived.

In the six months after the vote leading up to official independence, the many issues that remained unresolved between north and south again came to the fore. In May, I led a second UNSC delegation to Sudan and South Sudan to try and defuse tensions and smooth the path to independence now just two months away. The challenge was exacerbated by the fact that Sudan remained a bone of contention between the U.S. and Russia. Most, if not all of the time, Russia vigorously protected the brutal Khartoum regime against economic and other pressures, while it readily dismissed southern Sudanese aspirations for independence and was studiously indifferent to the suffering of its people.

During one private argument on South Sudan, Russian ambassador Vitaly Churkin taunted me: "You think this new state will become independent, and all will be great. But I tell you, it will be stillborn and a mess for many years to come." Certain he was wrong, I strenuously objected.

While Vitaly was always reluctant to travel overseas with the Security Council, preferring to send a deputy, he especially hated going to Africa, which I think he felt was uncomfortable and beneath him. Churkin, French ambassador Araud, and other colleagues complained more intensely when

I led UNSC trips to the field, because I insisted that we get out of stifling meeting rooms in the capital and visit real people facing real challenges—in rural health clinics, desolate refugee camps, and remote villages that had seen recent conflict.

This time, since I was leading a particularly consequential and timely mission to Sudan, Vitaly made a point of coming along, I believe to try to check me. I knew Africa far better than he, so check me he could not, but bother me he did. One of my most vivid and not-so-cherished memories is of Vitaly walking barefoot past me down a long hotel corridor in Khartoum without speaking. He was wearing only a white hotel bathrobe that didn't close properly at the belly, exposing too much of his pale chest. Apparently, something had happened to his suit. An image once seen, it is impossible to forget.

In the midst of our visit to Khartoum, fighting broke out along the soon-to-be north-south border, with Sudanese forces seizing the disputed Abyei area and moving troops into the Blue Nile and Southern Kordofan regions—southern areas of Sudan that border what would soon be South Sudan and have populations that resist Khartoum's authority. Khartoum's aggressive actions enraged me and most other members of our delegation, prompting us to deliver very tough messages to our Sudanese interlocutors. Sudan's sustained bombing of these areas also led the U.N. to ramp up its efforts to defuse tensions and the U.S. to warn that improved relations were at risk if Sudan persisted. In the weeks just before South Sudan's independence, we successfully pressed the two countries to pull back their forces and accede to an Ethiopian-led U.N. border force to demilitarize and monitor Abyei.

Tensions subsided sufficiently for South Sudan's Independence Day, July 9, 2011, to be a raucous celebration. I was honored to be asked by President Obama to lead the U.S. delegation to the independence ceremonies. It was a distinguished group that included General Colin Powell—who as secretary of state had played an important role in paving the way for self-determination for the South Sudanese—along with Congressman Donald Payne, a fierce, longtime champion of the South Sudanese people, and General Carter Ham, the four-star general in charge of U.S. Africa Command. As head of delegation, I could bring one guest. I chose soon-to-be-fourteen-year-old Jake. My son has long been passionate about Africa—and not just the birds and the wildlife. We had visited Southern Africa previously, and he knew a lot about Sudan through me and his own study. He was thrilled to meet Colin Powell, ride on a U.S. Air Force jet, visit the U.S. military base in Djibouti, and talk Libya war strategy with General Ham.

In Juba, the South Sudanese capital, the U.S. delegation had a prime location in the shade near the stage, where I would speak along with several visiting heads of state and South Sudan's new president, Salva Kiir. At some point during the hours-long, scorching ceremony, as I would later learn, Jake wandered around to stretch his legs and get some water, carrying his trusty long-lens digital camera and tripod (essentials for the avid birder he had become). He was some distance removed from our delegation's seats when suddenly he was confronted by an angry security official who, as Jake would report, demanded, "You need to leave. No journalists allowed in the VIP section."

Jake explained, "I am not a journalist. I'm here as a guest, and my mother is the American U.N. ambassador, Susan Rice." But that explanation failed to satisfy the increasingly belligerent guard. Jake continued to protest politely to no avail. As the situation escalated into a near shouting match, with the guard preparing to take Jake into custody, a U.S. protocol officer arrived to plead Jake's case, again without success. Finally, Ezekiel Gatkuoth, a six-foot-six, three-hundred-pound South Sudanese official, who served as head of South Sudan's mission in Washington, saw what was happening. Recognizing Jake as my son, he intervened to validate his story and spare him a trip to Juba's finest jail.

The celebration in Juba was a wonder to behold—jubilant dancers, musicians, military parades, ululating women, back-slapping African leaders, and champagne and canapés for VIPs under air-conditioned tents—an extravagance that foretold problems to come. I returned to New York in time for the flag of South Sudan to be raised at U.N. Headquarters on July 14, as the world's newest country was admitted to the international body that helped birth it. The joy at the U.N. was almost as irrepressible as in Juba. That night, I hosted a loud, super-sweaty dance party on the twenty-second floor of the new U.S. Mission building where Americans,

South Sudanese, African delegates, and many others boogied long into the evening. In that miraculous moment, it seemed like the dreams of millions might in fact come true.

Alas, for the long-suffering people of South Sudan, who have been betrayed at every turn, lasting peace proved too much to hope for. Soon after independence, Sudan and South Sudan turned on each other. Fighting erupted along the border over disputed oil-rich areas. South Sudan, which owned 75 percent of the oil of the original undivided nation, still depended on pipelines, refineries, and ports in the north. The economy of each nation was linked directly to the other; yet, after fighting resumed, South Sudan took the self-defeating step of stopping oil production, sending both countries into an economic tailspin. Within South Sudan, ethnic-based political factions contested for power, while brutally abusing their people and robbing them blind through corruption. South Sudan's army raped, tortured, and killed many thousands of its own citizens. Salva Kiir, South Sudan's hard-drinking, do-nothing, demi-dictator president, who has little regard for the welfare of his people, later came to blows with his vicious, self-aggrandizing vice president, Riek Machar.

By December 2013, it was clear: South Sudan was, in fact, stillborn. One of my most bitter regrets is having to admit that Vitaly was right.

For the duration of the administration, I along with top U.S. officials, including President Obama, continued to try to help the people of South Sudan achieve the promise of their independence. Yet, so long as the population of South Sudan suffers under such leadership, there will be little the U.S., U.N., or others can do to enable them measurably to improve their lives.

When it comes to South Sudan's morally bankrupt leaders, I am reminded of the depressing adage, *"You can't help those who refuse to help themselves."*

14

———

The Arab Spring Comes to
New York

I t was St. Patrick's Day 2011.

As we milled about on the floor of the U.N. Security Council waiting for all members to arrive to vote, I chatted with staff and fellow ambassadors. Many were sporting green ties in honor of the Irish, while I wore a green wool jacket. The color was not deep but almost a lime green, similar in hue, coincidentally, to the Libyan flag. Within a few minutes, I noticed that the South African permanent representative, Baso Sanqcu, a bald compact man, was absent. I didn't want the vote to proceed without knowing how it would come out, so I dashed to the door of the Council to intercept Baso when he came in. Eventually, he arrived.

Presumptuously, I blocked his entry.

"Do you have instructions?"

"Yes," he replied, clearly somewhat exasperated.

"What are they?" I pressed.

"We will vote yes," he conceded but didn't seem happy about it. I thanked him and moved out of his way so he could enter the chamber.

———•◆•———

The subject of this crucial vote was Libya, a hot topic on the Security Council's agenda along with several other matters stemming from the regional uprising known as the "Arab Spring."

The convulsion in the Middle East began when a desperate street vendor set himself on fire in Tunisia in December 2010. Within two months, President Hosni Mubarak was deposed in Egypt, after three decades of both repressing his people and serving as a reliable regional partner of the U.S. In raging debates around the Principals Committee table about how the U.S. should respond to Mubarak's violent crackdown on peaceful protesters, Secretary Clinton, Defense Secretary Gates, National Security Advisor Tom Donilon, and Vice President Biden argued forcefully for standing by Mubarak, whom they had known for years. Younger officials, including Ben Rhodes, Tony Blinken, Samantha Power, and me, maintained that the U.S. should support the democratic aspirations of the youth in Egypt and across the Middle East.

President Obama ultimately decided to align America with the peaceful protesters in Egypt's Tahrir Square seeking to exercise their universal human rights. He urged Mubarak to step down, first privately, and when that failed, Obama reiterated his plea publicly.

The Arab Spring brought similar policy dilemmas from Bahrain to Yemen to Syria; in each instance, the administration's approach varied depending on the specific circumstances. America's traditional Sunni Arab partners, led by Saudi Arabia, were outraged that the U.S. would (in their view) betray a partner like Mubarak and were deeply unsettled by the unrest sweeping the region. But even as our Arab partners lamented Mubarak's departure in Egypt, they were eager to see Assad removed in Syria and Qaddafi gone in Libya.

Less than a week after Mubarak's resignation in mid-February 2011, Libyan dictator Muammar Qaddafi, who had brutally enforced one-man rule for over forty years, suddenly faced his own uprising. Across the country, Libyans, led by opposition elements in Benghazi, demanded Qaddafi's ouster. As their protests intensified, Qaddafi responded with escalating violence, unleashing his military against civilians and rebels alike. The Libyan army fired directly on unarmed protesters, killing five to seven hundred in February 2011 alone, according to estimates by the chief prosecutor of the International Criminal Court. The regime also arbitrarily arrested masses of opponents, committed torture and rape, forced disappearances, and indiscriminately bombed populated areas as the rebellion intensified. Given

Qaddafi's history of slaughtering thousands of his own people, we believed that he might stop at nothing to quell his opposition.

It was not just U.S., European, and Arab officials who comprehended the potential gravity of the situation. Qaddafi's own diplomats in New York saw the writing on the wall and, after years of loyal service to a pariah regime, they split with Qaddafi and joined the opposition. I had come to know Ambassador Abdurrahman Shalgham, the Libyan permanent representative and former foreign minister, and his deputy Ibrahim Dabbashi, because Libya had served as a nonpermanent member of the Security Council during my first year in New York. In private, they were tough but thoughtful individuals, who throughout this crisis demonstrated more of a conscience than they had let on previously—even bravely lobbying the Security Council to take forceful action against their own government.

As international outrage mounted, the Security Council moved to impose sanctions on the Libyan regime, including an arms embargo and asset freeze; in a rare move, the Council also referred Qaddafi and his henchmen to the International Criminal Court to be tried for war crimes. The U.S. froze over $30 billion in Libyan government assets, closed our embassy in Tripoli—bringing our diplomats out of harm's way—and moved warships from the Red Sea into the Mediterranean to show force and increase our optionality. Yet, despite these actions, Qaddafi intensified the killing.

By early March, the British and French had begun to lobby for the international imposition of a no-fly zone over Libya to protect civilians from Qaddafi's forces. In Washington, we agonized over how to respond. There was reluctance to get into a third war, after Afghanistan and Iraq, in yet another Muslim-majority country. Doing nothing, however, pierced the conscience of many of us. The no-fly zone seemed a half-assed response, like being a little bit pregnant. We would own the problem but not have the means to fix it. Merely preventing Libyan planes from flying and bombing would not stop the ground forces with tanks from seizing successive cities on the road from Tripoli to Benghazi. Moreover, we discounted the ability of the U.K. and France to sustain an effective no-fly zone on their own, despite their considerable bluster, and knew that they would not launch without the backing of the Security Council, which required our assent.

The calculation in Washington shifted when on Saturday, March 12,

2011, the twenty-two-nation Arab League adopted an unprecedented statement calling on the UNSC to impose a no-fly zone and protect civilians, while recognizing the Libyan opposition forces as the legitimate government. On Monday, Lebanon introduced a draft resolution to implement the Arab League decision. France and the U.K., which had for weeks been agitating for a no-fly zone, championed the text as well. The looming question was: *What would the U.S. position be?*

Washington continued to dismiss a no-fly zone as worse than nothing, and I had argued that case forcefully in closed-door, "informal" meetings of the Security Council. Because I so roundly rejected a no-fly zone, the U.K. and French ambassadors had concluded that Washington wanted to do nothing.

On early Tuesday evening, I stepped out of a vehement and inconclusive Council debate to walk back across First Avenue to our office at the U.S. Mission in time to join a meeting with President Obama and his national security principals via secure videoconference. Hillary was plugged in remotely from Paris. The issue—*what to do about Libya*—was the same one we were debating in the Council. Qaddafi's forces were moving steadily eastward down the coast capturing town after town from the rebels and closing in on the insurgency's stronghold in Benghazi, Libya's second largest city. Qaddafi had vowed to wipe out its residents, warning: "Prepare yourselves from tonight. We will find you in your closets."

The Principals debated back and forth, as the president listened intently and, per usual, asked probing questions. Gates, Biden, Donilon, and White House chief of staff Bill Daley argued we should not intervene. While taking the humanitarian risks into account, these colleagues stressed that, ultimately, we had no compelling national security interest in Libya and should not involve ourselves in another Middle Eastern conflict. Even though the Arab League had requested U.N. (and thus U.S.) involvement, my colleagues maintained that Libya was not our fight and, effectively, that the likely costs of letting Qaddafi take Benghazi and retain his iron grip were acceptable when compared with the risks.

I argued the opposite—we *should* try to save innocent lives. The Arab Spring would be killed in the crib if Qaddafi were allowed to wipe out his citizens. The country was important as a linchpin in central North Africa, tucked between volatile Egypt and Tunisia and a gateway both to Europe and Africa's terrorist-infested Sahel region to the south. Though not yet a genocide, mass atrocities were certain as Qaddafi brandished the means and the motive to kill thousands imminently. I maintained that President Obama should not allow what could be perceived as his Rwanda to occur—a moment when the world looked to the U.S. for leadership, and we blinked. A comparatively limited U.S. military commitment could make a meaningful difference. We should not agree simply to a no-fly zone. If we were serious, we needed a much wider U.N. mandate to protect civilians, and I believed there was a reasonable chance we could get one out of the Security Council.

Ben Rhodes, Tony Blinken, and Samantha Power joined me in advocating for action. To my surprise, so did Hillary Clinton. Having just visited Egypt, and now in Europe for consultations with Arab and European leaders, she changed her mind, morphing from reluctant to intervene to supporting U.S. involvement.

Obama was frustrated. We were under pressure to make a decision, and the only option he had been given was a feckless no-fly zone, which everyone agreed wasn't worth the candle. Why, he railed at his national security advisor and Pentagon team, were we not in a position to consider viable alternatives? He abruptly adjourned the meeting to host an annual dinner for the four-star combatant commanders and their wives. "We'll come back here in two hours. By then, I want some real options on the table," Obama ordered.

Meanwhile, at the U.N., the informal meeting on Libya had ended inconclusively. My team and I had prepared for various contingencies, including the possibility that we would be asked by the president to pursue a far more ambitious resolution of the sort I believed we needed. That draft was in my back pocket, just in case.

When the NSC meeting resumed, we discussed concrete options, including an approach that would entail first bombing Libyan air defense systems to gain exclusive control of the skies and then targeting Qaddafi's heavy weapons—tanks, artillery, aircraft—and any massing Libyan troops if they threatened civilian areas. All agreed this was a more logical approach if we were going to engage militarily, but the Principals still differed on whether or not to act. As he often did, President Obama polled not just the Principals at the table for their views but also the expert staff seated along the walls of the wood-paneled White House Situation Room. The staff generally favored action.

Having digested all the various perspectives and asked piercing questions, Obama spoke. He said he would favor U.S. military action, but only under several conditions: 1) that I could obtain UNSC authorization for a robust mandate to protect civilians; 2) that Hillary could get the Arab League countries to agree to participate; and 3) that the U.S. role would be limited—we would launch the attacks, take out Qaddafi's air defenses, and establish air superiority but after that the Europeans, especially the Brits and French, would have to carry the bulk of the load.

Biden reiterated his opposition but took some comfort in Obama's conditions, predicting that there was no way Russia would allow this resolution to pass. I offered my own assessment, "The Russian position so far is ambiguous, so the vice president could be right that they will veto any resolution. But I also think there is a decent chance we can get this resolution through. Mr. President, I will give it my best shot." Getting the Arabs to put real skin in the game, rather than just rhetoric, also seemed a significant hurdle. So, the meeting ended with us having marching orders but the outcome in doubt.

The next morning, I came to the U.N. with a head of steam and a tough, sweeping authorization in the form of a draft resolution at the ready. As soon as the Security Council meeting started, I asked for the floor. With the full force of emotion commensurate with the gravity of the situation, I laid out the U.S. position:

> *I spent most of last night in a series of meetings with my president and his national security team. I am now prepared to share the U.S. position. Our view is that the situation in Libya is dire; and, we have very little time to save lives. After considerable deliberation, the U.S. is prepared to back a strong resolution to protect civilians and strengthen sanctions on the Qaddafi regime. We will not support a simple no-fly zone, which will do nothing to stop the forces massing on the ground heading for Benghazi. With the robust mandate*

*we seek, we will take out Libyan air defenses, their heavy weapons—like
tanks, artillery, and aircraft—and halt advancing columns of soldiers. This
would need to be an unfettered mandate to protect civilians, and I don't want
any ambiguity about what we intend to do with it. This will be an air war to
save innocent lives. The U.S. is prepared to join militarily with like-minded
countries in a coalition to enforce the resolution to save innocents. The choice
is yours: you can vote with us; or, accept responsibility for another historic
failure of this Council to act to prevent a potential genocide, when the means
were available to do so. Your governments must decide which side of history
you will be on. Mine will be on the side of meaningful action to save civilians
and the population of Benghazi.*

Just before I said my last word and leaned back in my seat, my team moved
quickly around the room, handing out our draft resolution that would implement what I had outlined.

The Council was dead silent for several seconds after I finished. Everyone was somewhere between moved and shocked. Lebanon broke the
silence and signaled that it was on board with a stronger U.S. text. The
United Kingdom followed suit. France was flummoxed. My counterpart,
Gérard Araud, with whom I had a complex and not yet entirely friendly
relationship, balked. *Why raise the bar? Why not stick with a no-fly zone?* He
thought that we were bluffing. To the press, on background, he opined
that he suspected the U.S. was playing games—upping the ante so far that
we were trying to ensure our draft would fail, while allowing us to claim
credit nonetheless. It was a typically French conspiratorial view of events
that was not entirely unjustified, given the abrupt shift in the U.S. position.

Privately, I assured Gérard that we did not play that way: *What you
see is what you get.* We genuinely favored the more robust mandate as the
only approach we thought had merit, if we were going to act. My message
was—*So, let's work together to get this done.*

Russia, sensing an opening, offered its own alternative draft resolution
that simply called for a cease-fire in Libya with no enforcement mechanism. It was a last-minute gambit to derail our more robust text. The
Russian draft gained little to no traction in the Council and, uncharacteristically, Churkin dropped it without much of a fight. After France signaled

it would support the U.S. text, I "put it into blue," which meant the resolution was finalized, no further changes could be made, and it could be voted on—up or down—within twenty-four hours.

By the end of the day, as my team quietly polled Council members, it seemed we were in striking distance of enough votes. Russia and China, almost always hostile to U.N.-authorized humanitarian intervention, were question marks. They had no special affinity for Qaddafi, but also don't like giving the U.S. free rein, especially to use force. The three African members—Nigeria, Gabon, and South Africa—were also uncertain, as the African Union had long benefited from Qaddafi's largesse and hated to see the U.S. intervene in Africa with Arab forces rather than support African-led diplomatic and military efforts. Germany and Brazil made clear they were likely to abstain. We needed at least nine of fifteen Council members to vote yes, and no veto-wielding members to oppose.

That night, Gérard convened the P5 ambassadors at the French Mission to discuss the timing of the vote and next steps. Churkin pulled me aside for a private conversation. Without prelude, he said, "I believe Moscow will abstain on your resolution." That meant the veto-wielding Russians would not vote yes but also would not block passage of the resolution.

I looked at him quizzically. Moscow almost never signaled in advance how it would vote on a controversial text. It also struck me as very strange that the Russians, even under Medvedev, would so readily allow such a robust resolution to pass that would give us carte blanche on the use of force, impose exceptionally tough sanctions, and authorize a blockade of Libyan arms imports. I had thrown the whole kitchen sink into that resolution, larding it up with authorities that we had never previously achieved in other contexts like North Korea and Iran. Yet Churkin did not seem troubled by his instructions and appeared to relish sharing them in advance. I asked him what he expected the Chinese to do, knowing that Russia and China closely coordinate their U.N. votes on everything of consequence. He said he thought they too would abstain.

Now, I was suspicious. We had just surmounted the biggest hurdle to getting our text adopted, but something didn't feel right. The Russians, I surmised, were betting that we would get bogged down in Libya. I believe they figured we were making a major mistake, and they had decided to give us just enough rope to hang ourselves. Or maybe, Vladmir Putin, then Russia's prime minister, was giving his president Dmitri Medvedev, whom he would replace the next year, enough rope to hang himself.

I reported to Washington that the holdouts now seemed to be the Africans, whom we needed to vote in favor of the resolution in order for us to cross the nine-vote threshold. Gabon would not be a problem if we could get Nigeria. My hunch was that Nigeria seemed get-able with some effort, and Assistant Secretary of State for African Affairs Johnnie Carson, my former Clinton-era principal deputy, managed to secure Nigeria's support. But South Africa was a problem, given its typical prickliness and the governing African National Congress's revolutionary aversion to Western involvement in the continent's affairs.

With the vote scheduled for late afternoon on Thursday, March 17, President Obama called President Jacob Zuma of South Africa to press for his support. The NSC staff reported to my team that Obama sensed he had gotten a favorable response, but Zuma was not clear. Moreover, in New York we had not heard anything at all from the South African Mission. My staff was chasing them, trying to determine their position, but could not find out even if they had received instructions from Pretoria, much less what they were. That's why I staked out my South African counterpart at the entrance to the Security Council.

When the vote was called, ten members including all the Africans supported the resolution, and five (Russia, China, India, Brazil, and Germany) abstained. Raising my hand to vote yes, I unwittingly created an image that would gain fame in Libya. It was nighttime in Libya when the Council session concluded. The Libyan ambassador chased me down excitedly after the vote to hug and thank me, and he shared live footage on his phone of massive crowds in Benghazi cheering and celebrating the vote. The image of me in my green jacket, raising my hand to vote yes and scanning the large, circular Council table to verify that we had the needed votes, was played over and over again on a big screen in Benghazi's main square. Ironically, my homage to St. Patrick's Day led to the iconic picture that captured the moment for the Libyan people.

I got the U.N. vote and did all the press engagements that the White House requested in its aftermath. Secretary Clinton had worked skillfully to get the Arabs on board, particularly Qatar and the UAE. President Obama talked to French president Nicolas Sarkozy and British prime minister David Cameron and obtained their commitment to carry the bulk of the military load. The conditions had been met. Obama publicly warned Qaddafi one last time to halt his advance on Benghazi, but Qaddafi persisted.

———

A few days later, President Obama left for a long-planned official visit to Latin America with his family and the White House team. It was spring break for my kids, and we flew as planned to Anguilla in the Caribbean. We desperately needed this time away together. Separation from my family was always the most difficult part of my job at the U.N. The kids were six and eleven when I began in New York, and by the time I left would be ten and fifteen (almost sixteen). When we set off for the Caribbean that spring, eight-year-old Maris and Jake, almost fourteen, were each becoming the two very different individuals they are today. Maris, steady and still wise for her years, seemed to be adjusting to school and friends, while Jake had begun a more dramatic transition from boy to an independent-minded teenager. He and his dad fought frequently in my absence, as Jake tested his boundaries.

Ian had borne the brunt of caring for the kids when I was away—getting them ready for school, serving breakfast and dinner, carpooling, and overseeing homework. Just as I was wrapping up my week, his work at *This Week* was kicking into high gear, peaking every Friday through Sunday. By late 2010, Ian and I were forced to admit we were ships passing in the night, and the kids had serial parents rather than much collective family time. Given the strain on our family and his waning enthusiasm for the job, Ian decided to take a buyout offer in January of 2011. After leaving ABC, he looked forward to dedicating his talent and time to community service.

Selfishly, I worried that Ian would become a stay-at-home dad, making him the primary parent. My fears ranged from *Honey, I'm afraid the kids will see me somehow as less relevant in their lives and even more distant*, to *Ian, what if you feel unfulfilled as a stay-at-home dad or resent being seen by status-conscious Washingtonians as less respectable?* Ultimately, none of my concerns were justified. Ian loved life after ABC, and I was a huge beneficiary of his greater freedom and attention to the home front, including his invaluable assistance to my ailing parents.

Beyond the stresses of the Libya negotiation and our family separation, the time away for spring break would be welcome for another reason. On the morning of March 10, I had received a devastating call from Ticey Westbrooks, the wonderful young nurse who was taking care of my dad at his home in Washington State.

Over a year earlier, on Christmas Day 2009, my ninety-year-old father had suffered a stroke while he was staying with us in Washington for the holiday. He came upstairs to breakfast a bit wobbly, complaining that his vision was partially blocked. After a couple calls to some doctor friends, we hurriedly took him to nearby Sibley Hospital, where he was diagnosed and admitted. While in the hospital, he developed a bowel obstruction that required emergency surgery, which was itself very risky. He survived the surgery, but his blockage did not resolve, requiring a second surgery two weeks later. I spent weeks working out of corners of Sibley Hospital. After six weeks in hospital and rehab, a much weakened and very cranky Dad came home to live with us.

I hired and managed the 24/7 caregivers who helped him bathe, drive, and exercise, while Ian played an outsize role in keeping Dad company in my absence. For the kids, it was a blessing to have many extra months living with my dad. He used his time with Jake and Maris to impart his "life lessons" on race, duty, excellence, and self-esteem. They played chess together, and Jake and Dad spent hours discussing political philosophy.

After flying him back to Camas, Washington, in October and getting him settled in with Ticey, I managed to visit Dad twice. His health remained precarious but not critical, and his mind was still solid. We talked almost every day. In fact, we had spoken the night before the unexpected early morning phone call from Ticey—after I finished at the U.N. Dad was thrilled to hear about Jake's latest report card, which signaled a sustained improvement in his academic performance.

As usual, we ended the conversation with me saying, "I love you," and Dad replying in his warm, deep voice, "Honey, I love you too."

"Night, night," I said.

"Sleep tight," he replied, replicating our ritual from my childhood.

When she called that next morning, Ticey was in tears but managed to choke out that Dad had passed away peacefully in his sleep overnight.

Emmett Rice had always been the world to me and, suddenly, he was gone.

I had to break the news to my brother, Johnny, pulling him out of a business meeting. He happened to be in New York, and he hurried over to the Waldorf, where we hugged and cried together. President Obama called almost immediately to offer his condolences, as Johnny and I sat together for some while in disbelief and mourning. Before long, Johnny reminded me that I had work to do, "Dad wouldn't want you slacking now, with Libya and everything else on your plate." I had to keep going.

The memorial service in Camas would wait, and we would throw a party in Washington in Dad's honor some weeks later. Dad wasn't much of a planner, except in certain matters. He gave us clear instructions years before on how to handle his passing: a very short service with *no* long speeches; no church; good but inexpensive wine; and his carefully crafted playlist dictated for the occasion. Miles Davis. Duke Ellington. Louis Armstrong. Oscar Peterson. And, of course, Tom Browne's "Funkin' for Jamaica" to bring it all home.

———

Ten days later, I so badly needed this break in Anguilla to process Dad's passing as well as to comfort and be comforted by the kids and Ian. Soon after our arrival in Anguilla, the president gave the order to initiate air strikes in Libya. I was slowly starting to decompress, absorbing the sunshine and relative quiet.

On our third day, as I played my usual morning game of tennis with Ian, one of the DS agents came abruptly on the court, interrupting our rally to announce that the White House chief of staff needed to talk to me. That's strange, I thought—Bill Daley almost never called me. I had known the large, balding Bill Daley since he was commerce secretary in the Clinton administration. I left the court and climbed into DS's SUV to have cool and quiet for the call.

"Where are you?" Daley said as soon as he picked up.

"I'm in Anguilla with my family."

He shouted, "You start a fucking war and then you go on vacation to the Caribbean?"

Shocked to a chill, I replied evenly: "I am on a long-planned vacation. I am the U.N. ambassador. My part of this equation is done. I passed the resolution, and I did the press work. What else could I possibly do? I don't control any aspect of the military action."

"I can't believe you are away."

Incredulous, I asked, "Did President Obama ask you to call me?"

"No," he conceded.

"Well, Bill, thank you," and I politely ended the call.

Angry and upset, I was shaking and my heart was racing. He knew I was on vacation, and his only objective was to ruin it. The rest of the day was horrible until the evening when the phone rang again.

Valerie Jarrett's warm and steadying voice greeted me. She quickly asked, "Are you okay?"

"No, not at all," I confessed. Still incredulous, I relayed the conversation with Daley.

"Yeah, I heard he was really rough on you. Don't worry about it. It's not about you. He is under a lot of stress. The president is fine with you being away."

If not for her call, I wouldn't have recovered enough to regroup and make the most of the remainder of the week with my family.

The following Monday, President Obama made a short trip to New York to dedicate the new U.S. Mission building, which was aptly named after the late commerce secretary, my old neighbor and friend, Ron Brown. Obama greeted me in the elevator as we rode up with his agents to the top floor for the ceremony.

"Nice tan," he commented, laughing. "I hear my chief of staff had a bad day last week."

"No kidding."

He smiled and said apologetically, "Don't worry about it. We're cool."

My relief was complete, but my anger at Daley unabated. I went to see him a couple of weeks later to make sure he understood how I felt about our conversation. He acted like nothing had ever happened.

———

The operation to protect civilians in Libya accomplished its proximate goal. Benghazi was spared. So were countless thousands of civilian lives.

The Libyan army continued to fight rebels, but no major massacres of civilians were reported. Rebel forces steadily gained ground, buoyed by the persistence of NATO air strikes. No Americans were killed in combat, although two U.S. servicemen were safely recovered after their plane went down due to mechanical problems, having been assisted by Libyans grateful for the American intervention.

U.S. involvement in the air campaign lasted longer than expected, as our European partners proved unable to carry the load, despite their pledges. They lacked ordnance and sufficient combat aircraft to sustain the fight. As the mission stretched on for several months, the Russians and Africans quickly turned against the operation, blaming the U.S. and our allies for vastly exceeding the mandate given.

The mandate was extremely broad, but I had explained plainly before the Security Council how it would be used. Still, Russia resented that the mission lasted months and argued that the objective had seemed to morph from sparing civilians to removing Qaddafi. In fact, regime change was not the original objective of the mission, but Qaddafi would not relent. Consequently, the NATO-led bombing campaign ended only after rebels captured and killed Qaddafi on October 20. The Russians (and Putin in particular) have since tried to portray Libya, falsely, as proof of American duplicity and obsession with regime change. In Putin's warped mind, Libya is a key milestone on the road of deteriorating U.S.-Russian relations.

Initially, the mission in Libya seemed a triumph of good over evil. The United States was deeply popular, along with France and the United Kingdom. *The New York Times* reported in May 2011 that, "Many Libyan parents with newborn girls are reportedly naming them Susan, in honor of Susan E. Rice, the Obama administration's ambassador to the United Nations, for her vote in the Security Council in favor of establishing the no-fly zone"—the imprecise term the *Times* used to shorthand the totality of the U.S.-led military action.

When I visited Libya in November, less than a month after Qaddafi was killed by rebel soldiers in Sirte, his last stronghold, I was welcomed with more warmth and joy than I have experienced before or since as a representative of the United States on foreign soil. Massive crowds gathered in the central square in Benghazi to greet me, many by raising their right hands and moving their heads swiftly from side to side, mimicking my body language as I scanned the Security Council table to count the yes votes for the historic Libya resolution. On the walls of buildings surrounding the square were pictures of hundreds of young Libyan men murdered or missing under Qaddafi's rule. I was surprised to see a big sign captioned, "Fantastic Four—God Bless You All. Thanks For All," with large photos of U.K. prime minister David Cameron, French president Nicolas Sarkozy, President Obama, and me!

In the streets of Benghazi, men and women swarmed me, asked to shake my hand, and thrust their kids into my arms to hold. The large complement of Diplomatic Security and the rebel security guards who protected me seemed a bit nervous, but the tight crowds were clearly friendly, and I was never fearful.

As my team and I flew out of Benghazi, my wise, young special assistant and friend, Priya Singh, shared a message for me from one of our Libyan escorts. He said that for all the public displays of gratitude we saw that day, the people of Benghazi would never be able to thank the U.S. enough, because just before the U.N. vote and President Obama's decision to intervene, Qaddafi's troops were closing in on the city with orders to rape and kill. Without U.S. leadership, they would not be there to greet us. Deeply moved by his words, I confessed to Priya, "I feel like I could be done today. I feel I've done something."

Unfortunately, it was not enough and, before long, Libya's tide of joy began to recede. After some months, the interim Libyan government proved to be divided and ineffectual. The international effort to support the new government faltered for lack of strong leadership from the U.N., Europe, or the U.S. We underestimated the difficulty of establishing a unified, stable government in a country where there had never been actual institutions, only the writ and whim of one man. Wishfully perhaps, having internalized the lessons of Iraq, the administration sought to minimize U.S. involvement in Libya, while expecting our European allies to drive the state-building effort—a challenge they embraced in principle but lacked the capacity to meet. In New York, I gathered Arab, European, and

U.N. counterparts with some regularity to try to galvanize and concert our diplomatic and peace-building efforts. Meanwhile, in Washington, lingering ambivalence among some Principals about the original operation led the NSC to convene few Principals Committee meetings at a time when our efforts might have had maximum impact.

Then, in September 2012, Ambassador Christopher Stevens and three U.S. officials were killed in a terrorist attack on our diplomatic facilities in Benghazi. Heartbroken, my colleagues and I mourned the deaths of all four Americans. For me, it also brought back the trauma of the 1998 terrorist attacks on our embassies in East Africa. Yet, this latest assault was equally personal, as I had come to know Chris as a valued colleague in Washington. Warm, handsome, and fearless, Chris was deeply knowledgeable and committed to the Libyan people. He couldn't wait to get back out there as ambassador to a post-Qaddafi Libya. Like all who knew Chris, I was shocked and profoundly pained by his loss in a country he so loved and a city that so loved him. Benghazi and its highly politicized aftermath caused policymakers in Washington to shy away from Libya even more.

In the president's second term, as national security advisor, I tried to refocus and sustain senior-level attention on Libya in order to support a unified national government, stabilize what was increasingly becoming a failed state, and dislodge the ISIS terrorists who had filled the vacuum created by the Qaddafi government's collapse and the opposition's failure to install an effective replacement. While we did manage to reduce the terrorist threat in coastal Libya, extremists flowed through Libya to the Sahel, destabilizing Mali, Niger, and other parts of the region.

Libya remains a state without an effective government, and an exporter of refugees and instability. As in Somalia, I believe the U.S. intervened for the right reasons. We made fewer mistakes and paid a far lesser price for our success protecting civilians in Libya than we did in Somalia. And yet what we left behind is not dissimilar—a fractured state without an effective central government, continued factional fighting, a lingering terrorist threat, and a source of insecurity in the region. Though I remain conflicted, on balance I still think we did the right thing to intervene in Libya and save thousands of innocent lives. Libya was an urgent case, I believe, where the risks and costs of intervention to the U.S. were tolerable when weighed against the humanitarian benefit. That said, while we and our European partners won the war, we failed to try hard enough and early enough to win the peace. Whether it could have been won at all is a real question; but not having given it our best shot, we will never know.

15

Star Wars Cantina

I was groggy.

It was too early, even on a regular Sunday morning, for a call from the White House. But on this Sunday, after I had been out until the wee hours at the after-parties following the 2011 White House Correspondents' Dinner, the last thing I was prepared for was an order to get to the White House as soon as possible. John Brennan, the president's counterterrorism and homeland security advisor, needed to see me. I scrambled into the shower and tried to call my Diplomatic Security detail. They were supposed to accompany me everywhere I went, but in Washington they did not sit overnight outside my house. They came when they knew I planned to leave. Once in a rare while, however, I would need to leave home unexpectedly and would try to give them as much of a heads-up as possible. Without my detail, I jumped into my red convertible (which I never got to drive anymore) and sped to the White House. I parked on the street and made my way through layers of White House security, which I was accustomed to bypassing when driven into the complex by my agents.

Inside, I went directly to Brennan's basement office, a low-ceilinged, windowless cave downstairs from the Oval Office. Brennan and I sat at the small round table in his office, and he pulled out some photographs and maps. "The president and I want you to know that we are about to launch a surprise raid into Pakistan with the aim of capturing or killing Osama bin Laden," Brennan began with no ceremony. "We've been planning this for some time. Our intelligence seems solid, but we're not certain he is where we think he is."

Brennan outlined the various strands of intel that added up to their assessment of bin Laden's location. It was by no means a slam dunk.

We talked through the political and security risks of the mission and its timing. Like a few other principals, I had not been part of the small team involved in the decision making on the raid. It was exceedingly sensitive, and I fully understood that, without an operational role, I had no "need to know." Still, the White House did not want to blindside me or other NSC cabinet officials who would have learned about this in the press if not for our early Sunday morning briefing. After about a half hour, I was sworn to secrecy and sent on my way with the promise that I would be updated later when the outcome was known.

I went on with my day as planned—attending a brunch and playing tennis. With Ian and the kids, I maintained a studied nonchalance. My stomach was doing flips for hours, but on the outside, I was "maintaining my composure," as Johnny and I used to joke with one another. By well into the evening, I had heard nothing and was starting to worry.

Then the phone rang with the White House on the line. Deputy National Security Advisor Denis McDonough reported, "We got him." He explained that the raid became more complicated than anticipated when a helicopter crash-landed in the compound, but our troops had found bin Laden, killed him after he resisted, confirmed his identity, evacuated his body, got safely out of Pakistani airspace, and buried the mastermind of 9/11 at sea. Denis told me the president would make an announcement within an hour. "Thank you," was all I could think to say. My heart pounding, I turned on the television to see all the networks heralding the breaking news of a presidential announcement on a subject TBD.

I started yelling to the kids and Ian to come into our bedroom. They came fast. When the news broke, we all started screaming, yelling, and hollering with joy. I quickly hit the music and blasted a family favorite, "All Right Now!," the Stanford victory song as played by the Stanford Band.

The four of us danced with abandon, jumping as high as we could at the appropriate points, a move typically used to celebrate a touchdown. "All right now, baby it's all right NOW. . ." Perfectly appropriate song for the occasion. And, if I had a tinge of guilt about encouraging my kids to dance on someone's grave, it was instantly replaced by joyous relief that the man who had blown

up our East African embassies and killed three thousand souls on 9/11 was at
the bottom of the sea.

———•◆•———

Even as the bin Laden raid and Libya drama unfolded, upheaval in other parts of the Arab world kept spreading—notably to Syria. In mid-March 2011, Syrian dictator Bashar Assad's security forces fired repeatedly on unarmed civilian demonstrators, and what began as a popular uprising in four cities swiftly morphed into a rebellion that engulfed the capital, Damascus, and much of the country. After many months of rebellion and repression, as the regime relentlessly tortured, imprisoned, and killed its opponents, the violence in Syria escalated into full-fledged civil war, with the government employing helicopter gunships, barrel bombs, and chemical weapons to snuff out the increasingly pervasive opposition. Politically divided and operationally fractious, the opposition consisted of fighters ranging from bakers and doctors turned rebels to violent Islamist extremists, including some with ties to ISIS and Al Qaeda.

At the U.N., the U.S. and our Arab and Western partners labored for years to condemn the Assad regime's actions, impose sanctions, broker cease-fires, spur a political transition to a Syria without Assad, and investigate and punish the Syrian regime's use of chemical weapons. At every turn, from April 2011 to my departure from the U.N. at the end of June 2013, and for the entirety of the Obama administration, our efforts were consistently and callously thwarted by Russia (and its sidekick China). Russia had long-standing military bases in Syria and a broad strategic relationship with Assad and his principal backer, Iran. Particularly after Vladimir Putin returned as president in May 2012, Russia was determined to do everything possible to protect Assad diplomatically and ensure he eluded U.N. Security Council condemnation, sanctions, or significant pressure of any sort. The debates over Syria in the Security Council, both in public and behind closed doors, were the most acrimonious I experienced, with Russia (and to a lesser extent China) pitted against increasingly outraged U.S., U.K., and French delegations.

Russian ambassador Churkin frequently alleged that the West's aim in Syria was "a policy of regime change," citing Libya as a precedent. My

rejoinder was that the Libya analogy was bogus and a cheap ruse by countries that wanted to continue selling arms to Syria. In the Security Council,
declaring it a "dark day" in Turtle Bay, the neighborhood in New York
City in which the U.N. is located, I made clear, "The U.S. is disgusted" by
Russia and China's behavior, and lamented how "a couple members of this
Council remain steadfast in their willingness to sell out the Syrian people
and shield a craven tyrant."

Three times during my tenure, and twice more before President
Trump took office, Russia and China "double-vetoed" relatively mild
U.K.- and French-drafted resolutions to condemn Assad, maintaining dis-
ingenuously that they were "imbalanced," unhelpful, or designed to be the
camel's nose under the tent for regime change. Russia argued conveniently
(and falsely) that it got snookered on Libya and that the NATO operations
there, which resulted in Qaddafi's death, far exceeded the U.N. mandate.
Russia insisted that never again would it allow Western military intervention in the Middle East, and least of all in Russia's client state, Syria.

Though battles with Churkin were never more heated than over Syria,
Vitaly was in some ways my closest colleague. We admired each other's
skills and intellect, and we made each other laugh. Behind closed doors,
when the cameras were gone and voyeuristic members of the Security
Council absent, Vitaly often worked to find common ground, including
on North Korea and the Israeli-Palestinian conflict. I know he agonized
privately over Syria and tried within the P5 to broach compromises, which
he sought to sell to Moscow to avoid yet another Russian veto. To his obvious disappointment, he repeatedly failed to win over his bosses.

At the end of my tenure in New York, Vitaly was one of the only foreign ambassadors I asked to speak at my farewell party. Why him? Because
I knew he would make me and everyone else laugh raucously (at my expense). I had gotten him good some years prior, when in a December 2010
closed-door Security Council session, I put up on the screen a picture of
his face photoshopped into an image of the Grinch Who Stole Christmas.
(They bore a striking resemblance.) It was the perfect takedown of Vitaly,
who had stolen Christmas from so many U.N. diplomats every day of the
year, not to mention millions of suffering people around the world. At my
farewell party, Vitaly's roasting of me did not disappoint. He recalled our

many verbal battles, reprising his choice line that some of my most favored language "could not be found in the Oxford dictionary." He also left me with some gaudy Russia gear promoting the 2014 Sochi Olympics.

From the moment Ian met Vitaly's lovely and kind wife, Irina, the two struck up a warm rapport. After I left New York for Washington, Vitaly and I kept in touch, if infrequently. Ian and I hosted Vitaly and Irina for a private dinner at an elegant Washington restaurant in December 2015, as we had done occasionally in New York. But on this rare visit to Washington for them, it was bittersweet. The U.S.-Russia bilateral relationship had hit bottom over Russia's annexation of Crimea, invasion of Ukraine, military intervention in Syria, and U.S. and E.U. sanctions against Russia. I highly doubt Moscow would have approved of our meeting, since we were no longer colleagues and had no need to see one another. Instead, this was a social occasion, indicative of our enduring friendship and even mutual affection. I had no idea that would be our last meeting.

Over two years later, sitting at my kitchen table in Washington, I struggled to reread the February 20, 2017, tweet, making sure I understood it correctly: "BREAKING: Russian officials say their Ambassador to the United Nations, Vitaly Churkin, has died in New York City at 64." The tears flowed and flowed. Vitaly and I had a love/hate relationship like no other. And, I miss him.

———

In August 2011, during a relatively calm couple of days, I bared my comedy soul on *The Colbert Report*. Asked to describe the U.N., for the first time I acknowledged publicly that, "Sometimes it feels a little bit like the *Star Wars* bar scene where some of the most colorful dictators of the world will come and give their speeches." Stephen Colbert laughed, before I quickly added, "But most of the year it's actually a pretty serious place."

During my first year in New York, I became acquainted with the distinct rituals that had been adopted, in part, I imagine, to promote civility among diplomats from vastly different backgrounds. For starters, each month, one of the fifteen U.N. Security Council members assumes the rotating presidency of the Council on the basis of alphabetical order. For the permanent members, however, the Council presidency arrives like clockwork every fifteen months.

During my tenure, the U.S. chaired the Council three times, when it was my responsibility to set the month's agenda (in consultation with the U.N. Secretariat), preside over both formal and informal meetings, brief the press after each session of significance, and craft any special sessions, policy initiatives, or resolutions we wished to pursue. In addition, there is a social aspect to the role wherein the month's president hosts a start-of-the-month breakfast, a working luncheon meeting with the secretary-general, and an end-of-the-month cocktail reception. The president also presents each member of the Council with a gift unique to his or her country, and the president's spouse hosts a lunch for the other fourteen spouses and the secretary-general's wife. Ian took his duties as a U.N. spouse seriously and came up to New York each month for these lunches and other events, building a great deal of goodwill for his willingness to participate actively, despite being one of few men in the group.

Whenever possible, I used the U.S. rotating presidencies to lighten the mood and build camaraderie among Council members. I twice took the whole Security Council to New York Knicks games where they met former players and watched from the owners' box. I hosted the P5 ambassadors at the U.S. Open tennis tournament. And, during my first presidency, my gift to the Council was two tickets for each delegation to an Aretha Franklin concert at Radio City Music Hall. Spectacularly generous, Aretha hosted us backstage after the concert for Chinese food and photos with her. The ambassadors and their spouses loved it.

In 2009, the U.S. turn at the Council's presidency coincided with the annual opening of the General Assembly (UNGA) in September—when heads of state and foreign ministers converge for two weeks in New York City. Each head of state addresses the entire membership of the General Assembly from the green marble podium in the massive wooden chamber. The General Assembly hall is constructed as a gently sloping amphitheater containing almost two hundred three-person desks (and three chairs behind) with country placards prominently displayed. Each member state's physical placement in the General Assembly shifts over time but remains in alphabetical order by the countries' formal names.

Traditionally, the U.S. president always delivers the second speech on opening day, after Brazil. Visiting U.S. presidents also typically greet the staff of the U.S. Mission, host a large reception for the other heads of delegation, meet with the secretary-general and president of the General Assembly, and conduct a number of bilateral meetings. In addition, the president often convenes thematic meetings with selected countries to advance the U.S. agenda on issues of concern. During his tenure, President Obama hosted such meetings on U.N. peacekeeping reform, Sudan and South Sudan, refugees, the campaign against ISIS and violent extremism, and the Open Government Partnership.

For eight years, President Obama upheld every aspect of these customs, even when the annual ritual came to feel more like an ordeal. He took his UNGA speech very seriously and spent hours refining his themes and the final draft. That first year he chose to stay in New York for several days, which enabled him to add to his schedule a number of additional "side events." The centerpiece of his inaugural visit was chairing a first-ever presidential-level summit meeting of the UNSC on nuclear nonproliferation.

All of the P5 leaders attended the summit, and each of the fifteen countries was invited to speak for no more than five minutes. I was nervous about the time limits, knowing that: a) President Obama had a hard stop and would have to leave the session after two hours; and b) most presidents and prime ministers speak at length and generally can't be controlled when they're in front of a microphone, especially on the world stage. When Obama would have to leave the chair, Secretary Clinton would take his place, but it would be considered impolite for heads of state to have to speak with a lower-ranking official (even a foreign minister) presiding. I agonized over the time limits, concocting with my team an unusual timer and lighting system to signal to the heads of state when their time was up.

My biggest concern, though, was totally out of my control: that year Libya was a nonpermanent member of the Security Council, and Muammar Qaddafi (still in his dictatorial heyday), who would represent Libya at the summit, normally spoke literally for hours. The day before the summit, Qaddafi gave a legendary performance at the General Assembly, extending his fifteen minutes to one hundred minutes of vitriol and almost comical nonsense. That was when I was first struck by the theatrics of the U.N. Between Qaddafi and Iranian president Ahmadinejad's offensive rants, the national costumes and diverse customs, the U.N., especially at

General Assembly time, conjured for me the *Star Wars* cantina, where creatures of every type consorted unconstrained.

My fear was that Qaddafi would reprise that rant in front of the Security Council, with Obama as chair unable to cut him off politely, thus overshadowing an otherwise successful event. The evening before the summit I called my Libyan counterpart, Ambassador Shalgham. I pleaded with him to do whatever he possibly could to ensure that Qaddafi stayed on script and on time.

Shalgham calmly assured me, "It will be all right."

"How can you be so confident?" I asked.

He said, "Trust me. I promise we will stay within the time limits."

I thanked him for his assurances and pledged to deliver a very nice bottle of champagne if he succeeded. Usually a good sleeper even when under stress, I did not sleep well at all that night. The next morning, as the session began, I realized why Shalgham had been so confident. He had somehow managed to persuade Qaddafi that the summit was not worth his time, and Shalgham represented Libya in the meeting as the only non–head of state at the table. Enormously relieved and appreciative, I sent over to the Libyan mission that afternoon a bottle of my favorite, Veuve Clicquot.

Obama's UNGA visits involved certain rituals. The reception for heads of delegation usually occurred the evening before his major speech to the General Assembly. After the reception at about 9:30 p.m., the president, the national security advisor, secretary of state, speechwriter and Deputy National Security Advisor Ben Rhodes, senior director for the U.N. on the NSC staff, a few others, and I would decamp to the spacious living room in my apartment atop the Waldorf Towers. Stanton Thomas, our jovial chef, would prepare a copious spread of cheese, tortilla chips and homemade guacamole, salmon, and other hors d'oeuvres. He would also put out plenty of wine, beer, and liquor, and produce a single carefully crafted Grey Goose martini for the Boss. We would then review the UNGA speech, debating its contents, and hash out other issues, such as how to approach upcoming bilaterals with Netanyahu and Abbas on the Middle East peace process. These gatherings could go long, but with the speech in the morning and often major rewrites pending, Ben and the president (both night owls) prepared for an even later night.

After one such UNGA evening in 2011, Obama lingered behind after the others left, which indicated to me that he wanted to talk privately. As he often did, he asked how I was doing, how my family was bearing my absence, if the White House team was being supportive, and how I was holding up after the fairly recent loss of my father.

"Everything's fine," I answered, thanking him. "I do miss Ian and the kids."

He nodded with understanding, and then shifted gears. "Have you ever thought about being World Bank president? Would you be interested in that role?"

Somewhat caught off-guard, I did know it was time for the administration to put forward its candidate to succeed Bush's appointee, Robert Zoellick. In fact, I had been told by friends in the White House that Tom Donilon was floating my name for the position, perhaps, they said, in a bid to sideline me as a potential candidate for secretary of state or national security advisor in an Obama second term. If it were such a gambit, it was a clever one. The World Bank presidency is a coveted position, with great ability to influence global development efforts, and it would allow me to return home to Washington. Still, I was surprised and could only think about my late father, a former World Bank acting executive director and real expert in development economics. He would roll over in his grave if I accepted such an important role without further preparation and qualification. Apart from my knowledge of Africa and my more recent experience steeped in a complex multilateral institution, I was not then very well matched to the role. Another concern was not wanting to jump out of the national security realm, where I thought my skills and training were best utilized.

After a pause, I answered, "I appreciate you thinking of me. But if the United States can't come up with someone more qualified than me to run the World Bank, we ought to give up the presidency of the Bank."

Whether he was just checking the box to say he knew I was not interested, or if he really thought I might be intrigued, I couldn't tell. Obama just smiled, changed the subject, and never raised it again.

I was in no hurry to leave the U.N., which for all its serious intensity and sometimes feigned camaraderie was exceptionally rewarding. For what would ultimately be four and a half years, I enjoyed enormous freedom. So long as my great team and I took care of business at the U.N., and I responded when needed by email or phone, no one in Washington was breathing down my neck or tracking my every move. I loved running the U.S. Mission of 150 civil servants, foreign service officers, and handful of political appointees. It was an intimate enough staff that I knew most everyone, ties that were enhanced by annual basketball games at Chelsea Piers, where the U.S. Mission staff took on the U.N. security guards, and by righteous dance parties I loved to throw (with a party playlist my staff perfected over time). We twice hosted our annual Fourth of July party at the Central Park Zoo, bringing the beasts of the U.N. together with their caged counterparts. It was good fun.

———

Toward the end of my time at the U.N., the family and I joined with Johnny and his family for a trip to Mexico. With a third family, we rented a lovely house overlooking the ocean north of Puerto Vallarta. For the first several days, I had a relaxing time, lounging by the pool or on the beach, playing tennis, drinking margaritas, and chilling.

One afternoon, when most of the others were down the cliff on the beach, I stayed back at the house. My twelve-year-old nephew, Teo, Johnny's eldest and an excellent athlete like his parents, asked if I felt like tossing the football. Since my early tomboy years, throwing a football was one of my favorite things to do, and I prided myself on having a strong arm, good spiral, and never throwing "like a girl." We took the ball out onto the expansive lawn overlooking the landscaped gardens on top of the cliffs.

I was wearing a dress-length cotton cover-up over my bathing suit, flip-flops, and sunglasses—perfectly comfortable gear for a game of catch. After about ten minutes, we were well warmed up, and we each backed up to elongate our passes. Teo moved up the slope a bit, and I moved down. Teo threw a strong ball off to my right, which I assessed was within reach. To catch it, I jumped and laid out almost horizontally. I managed to snag it, sating my competitive instincts and demonstrating to my nephew that I still had game.

Except, I miscalculated. I had picked up steam heading downhill and overestimated how far removed I was from the bushes. When I landed, I was facedown in a large, vicious cactus plant still holding the football. The needles were triangular-shaped spears, the size of a fingernail, and they were embedded in every part of me. My scalp, face, arms, legs, bottom. Everywhere.

Teo rushed over to pull me up out of the bushes, and when I was upright, blood started streaming from the scores of holes where the cactus spikes were embedded. I looked like something out of a Halloween horror movie. To his enormous credit, Teo remained calm and started pulling needles out of me. My lead DS agent rushed over to join in the uncomfortable extraction, while other agents sent for a doctor. I was bloodied and in pain but apparently not too badly hurt, as we were able to ascertain once I got the needles out of my head and face. Thankfully, the sunglasses had protected my eyes, and my legs and arms suffered the worst damage, including some scars that lingered for a couple years.

Of all the risky ventures I took while U.N. ambassador—from traveling to war zones in Iraq, Afghanistan, and South Sudan to being mobbed in Libya and trudging through the slums of Delhi, the closest DS got to having to save me was when my lead agent kindly and carefully removed cactus needles from my booty in Mexico.

16

Benghazi

B
y the time I arrived at my mother's town house near Washington's Du-
pont Circle, I was spent from an emotionally exhausting day. It was
Friday evening, September 14, 2012—several years before my mom passed
away. I walked down the dark, narrow outside steps into her modern basement kitchen and kissed her, as she sat in her normal place at the head of her
small, polished wooden kitchen table watching CNN.

"How are you feeling?" I asked, mindful of Mom's fragility just three months
after she had suffered a stroke following yet another cancer surgery. While my
mother had recovered significantly, she was not at her full strength. Mom said
she felt okay and asked how I was faring, fully appreciating that this had been
an especially tough week for me and my colleagues.

I told her, "Today, I had my weekly conference with Secretary Clinton and
attended a Principals Committee meeting at the White House." But, much
more painfully, I continued, I had just accompanied President Obama, Vice
President Biden, Secretary Clinton, and other cabinet officials at a ceremony
where we met the grieving families and paid respects to the four Americans
killed three days earlier in the September 11, 2012, terrorist attack on the U.S.
diplomatic facilities in Benghazi, Libya.

In the hangar at Joint Base Andrews, we sat facing four flag-draped coffins
bearing the bodies of Ambassador J. Christopher Stevens, foreign service officer Sean Smith, and CIA contractors Tyrone S. Woods and Glen Doherty. These

brave men had made the ultimate sacrifice in service to our nation on a mission to build peace and protect American interests. The painful and powerful image of their four coffins each being loaded into four separate hearses is one I will never forget. We were all mourning. The event had left me drained and fighting flashbacks to the caskets I accompanied back to Andrews fourteen years before, following the 1998 East Africa embassy bombings.

Weakened but indomitable, Mom asked next, "What are your plans for the weekend?" I reminded her that on Saturday I had long-standing arrangements to take the kids to the Ohio State University, where I had delivered the commencement address in June, for a tailgate and football game against U.C. Berkeley. Then I added, "And on Sunday, I will be appearing on all five Sunday shows."

Mom gave me a skeptical look.

This was only three days after the Benghazi attack, as my mother knew from following the news closely. It was a week that began with the swarming of the U.S. embassy in Cairo, and a wave of anti-American protests directed at U.S. outposts across the globe. I reminded her that it was nine days before the annual opening of the U.N. General Assembly when President Obama and scores of world leaders would gather on my turf to discuss such issues as Iran's nuclear program, the Palestinians' bid for statehood status, and Syria. Israeli prime minister Benjamin Netanyahu was ramping up his U.S. public relations campaign to pressure the Obama administration into a military confrontation with Iran. These were issues that I addressed publicly with frequency. And, I added, as she well knew, the presidential election campaign was heating up. For all these reasons, I explained, the administration had to put out a senior foreign policy official on television.

Mom immediately pressed me, "Why do you have to go on the shows? Where is Hillary?"

"I think that Hillary is wiped after a brutal week," I said. "The White House asked me to appear in her stead and, even though this isn't how I wanted to spend my weekend, I'm willing to do my part."

She was unrelenting, "I smell a rat. This is not a good idea. Can't you get out of it?" Dismissively, I replied, "Mom, don't be ridiculous. I've done the shows many times before. It will be fine."

It wasn't.

———•◆•———

Even as the attack in Benghazi was still ongoing, Republican presidential nominee Mitt Romney had already politicized the tragedy in a statement issued on September 11. Romney blasted, "It's disgraceful that the Obama administration's first response was not to condemn attacks on our diplomatic missions, but to sympathize with those who waged the attacks." This cheap and misleading hit referred to a tweet issued from the U.S. embassy in Cairo about the violent demonstrations in Egypt's capital city, not about Benghazi. But it was a leading indicator of how crazy this all would get, and it may partially explain why my mother smelled a rat.

I appeared on the September 16, 2012, Sunday shows, all five of them—ABC's *This Week*, CBS's *Face the Nation*, NBC's *Meet the Press*, *Fox News Sunday*, and CNN's *State of the Union*. I was asked what had happened in Benghazi on September 11, when four U.S. government officials, including Ambassador J. Christopher Stevens, were killed in a terrorist attack on our diplomatic facilities. To explain, I shared the latest available unclassified assessment produced by the U.S. Intelligence Community (IC). These were the so-called "talking points" written by the CIA at the request of members of Congress who asked for information they could use publicly:

- The currently available information suggests that the demonstrations in Benghazi were spontaneously inspired by the protests at the U.S. Embassy in Cairo and evolved into a direct assault against the U.S. diplomatic post and subsequently its annex. There are indications that extremists participated in the violent demonstrations.
- This assessment may change as additional information is collected and analyzed and currently available information continues to be evaluated.
- The investigation is ongoing, and the U.S. Government is working with Libyan authorities to help bring to justice those responsible for the deaths of U.S. citizens.

Though I had no role in crafting the CIA's talking points, I did not blindly parrot their contents. As U.N. ambassador, on a daily basis—six days a week (except Sunday)—I received and thoroughly read a classified briefing provided to me and other top officials by the Intelligence Community. The CIA plus sixteen other agencies and parts of agencies comprise the U.S. Intelligence Community, which is led and coordinated by the director of national intelligence (DNI). The personnel of the Intelligence Community consist predominantly of apolitical, career professionals who do their utmost to keep our country and the American people safe.

My daily intelligence briefing, provided to me on Saturday, the day before the shows, had been fully consistent with the talking points that I was given. Therefore, I was comfortable that what I would say on Sunday morning reflected an up-to-date assessment.

In each television appearance, I drew squarely from the unclassified talking points provided by the Intelligence Community and made clear that I was providing our government's best *current* understanding of what had transpired. However, I repeatedly noted that our assessment could evolve as we gathered more information, particularly from the FBI investigation. As of early Sunday morning, September 16, when I taped the shows, the IC's latest assessment was that the attack on our compounds in Benghazi had evolved from demonstrations "spontaneously inspired" by the protests in Cairo into a direct assault on our Benghazi diplomatic compound. The Cairo protests were among the many instances of anti-U.S. demonstrations and violence that had erupted at several U.S. embassies across Africa, the Middle East, and South Asia that week following the widespread circulation on social media of *Innocence of Muslims*, a video that sparked anger in the Muslim world because it denigrated Muhammad, the Prophet of Islam.

Following the shows, I went home to change and join Ian at Maris's soccer game, and the rest of the day unfolded uneventfully. Over the coming week, however, controversy began to brew about what I said on the Sunday shows. At first, it was an isolated trickle stoked by partisan talking heads on Fox News, which I almost never watch and always pay little heed.

Fox started pushing the narrative on September 20 that the Obama administration, in Sean Hannity's words, was engaged in "a widespread cover-up based on flat-out lies, all aimed to protect a president who happens to be running for reelection." Hannity pointed to my comments on

Sunday as Exhibit A. The next day Fox aired an exchange that began with co-host Dana Perino saying, "She [Ambassador Rice] goes out, and she is the one who says this is all just the video, the information we have at the time. Three days later, we find out that is completely wrong. How does that happen?" Co-host Eric Bolling replied, "Honestly, Dana, looks and smells and probably is a cover-up. . . . Politically, it looks bad for President Obama. So they had to blame it on a movie. Anything but what it was. A terrorist attack."

On September 25, Republican senators John McCain, Lindsey Graham, Ron Johnson, and Kelly Ayotte wrote a letter to me taking issue with my comments, alleging, "You made several troubling statements that are inconsistent with the facts and require explanation." Following a selective and misleading parsing of my Sunday show statements, their letter concluded, "We look forward to a timely response that explains how the U.S. Ambassador to the United Nations could characterize an attack on a U.S. consulate so inaccurately five days after a terrorist attack that killed four Americans."

On September 28, Representative Peter King (R-NY) was the first to call for my scalp, telling CNN, "I believe she should resign." He elaborated, "This was such a failure of foreign policy message and leadership, such a misstatement of facts as were known at the time. . . . To me somebody has to pay the price for this." King's bald demand shocked me. I also understood it likely foreshadowed that the hits on me would continue and intensify.

Over the coming weeks and months, my Sunday show appearances were harshly criticized by Republicans who sought to discredit President Obama's strong record on fighting terrorism, including killing Osama bin Laden. As the senators' letter presaged, I was attacked primarily for four reasons.

First, the president's opponents claimed that I (and other administration officials) had tried to deny or downplay that the tragedy in Benghazi was a terrorist attack. In fact, I never suggested that the perpetrators were not terrorists or that the attack was not a terrorist attack, though I used the CIA-approved term "extremists," which in the IC's parlance (and mine) meant the same thing in the context of an attack. To the contrary, on CBS's *Face the Nation* I made plain that we understood the perpetrators to be extremists, of a variety to be determined, as my exchange with Bob Schieffer showed:

> BOB SCHIEFFER: Do you agree or disagree with him [the Libyan president] that al Qaeda had some part in this?
>
> SUSAN RICE: Well, we'll have to find . . . that out. I mean I think it's clear that there were extremist elements that joined in and escalated the violence. Whether they were al Qaeda affiliates, whether they were Libyan-based extremists or al Qaeda itself I think is one of the things we'll have to determine.

We later learned—once the Senate Select Committee on Intelligence investigation was complete—that the perpetrators included individuals affiliated with terrorist groups, including a Libyan-based Salafist extremist group called Ansar al-Sharia in Benghazi, and Al Qaeda branches in Africa and Yemen. The investigation did not confirm that the terrorist attack was ordered, directed, or orchestrated by Al Qaeda, as many Republicans had maintained (without firm evidence), despite the fact that it occurred on the anniversary of the September 11, 2001, terrorist attacks. Rather, the Senate Intelligence Committee found, "It remains unclear if any group or person exercised overall command and control of the attacks or whether extremist group leaders directed their members to participate."

Second, I was harshly criticized for saying that the attack was "spontaneous" and "not premeditated," as opposed to carefully planned well in advance. My statements were fully consistent in this regard with the CIA-drafted talking points approved by the Intelligence Community. Again, an excerpt from my discussion on *Face the Nation*:

> BOB SCHIEFFER: Madam Ambassador, he [the Libyan president] says this is something that has been in the planning stages for months. I understand you have been saying that you think it was spontaneous? Are we not on the same page here?
>
> SUSAN RICE: Bob, let me tell you what we understand to be the assessment at present. First of all, very importantly, as you discussed with

the [Libyan] President, there is an investigation that the United States government will launch led by the FBI, that has begun and—

BOB SCHIEFFER *(overlapping)*: But they are not there.

SUSAN RICE: They are not on the ground yet, but they have already begun looking at all sorts of evidence of—of various sorts already available to them and to us. And they will get on the ground and continue the investigation. So we'll want to see the results of that investigation to draw any definitive conclusions. But based on the best information we have to date, what our assessment is as of the present is in fact what began spontaneously in Benghazi as a re-action to what had transpired some hours earlier in Cairo where, of course, as you know, there was a violent protest outside of our embassy—

BOB SCHIEFFER: Mm-hm.

SUSAN RICE: —sparked by this hateful video. But soon after that spon-taneous protest began outside of our consulate in Benghazi, we believe that it looks like extremist elements, individuals, joined in that—in that effort with heavy weapons of the sort that are, unfor-tunately, readily now available in Libya postrevolution. And that it spun from there into something much, much more violent.

BOB SCHIEFFER: But you do not agree with him that this was some-thing that had been plotted out several months ago?

SUSAN RICE: We do not—we do not have information at present that leads us to conclude that this was premeditated or preplanned.

On September 16, and for days thereafter, the U.S. Intelligence Com-munity continued to assess that the attack was "spontaneous" and not pre-planned. However, on September 28, twelve days after my Sunday show appearances, the spokesman for the director of national intelligence issued an *updated* assessment of the Benghazi attack that offered their latest deter-mination that the terrorist attack had been "deliberate and organized" and that the initial assessment that I utilized had been revised:

As the Intelligence Community collects and analyzes more information re-lated to the attack, our understanding of the event continues to evolve. In the immediate aftermath, there was information that led us to assess that the attack began spontaneously following protests earlier that day at our embassy in Cairo. We provided that initial assessment to Executive Branch officials and members of Congress, who used that information to discuss the attack publicly and provide updates as they became available. Throughout our investigation we continued to emphasize that information gathered was preliminary and evolving.

As we learned more about the attack, we revised our initial assessment to reflect new information indicating that it was a deliberate and organized terrorist attack carried out by extremists. It remains unclear if any group or person exercised overall command and control of the attack, and if extremist group leaders directed their members to participate. However, we do assess that some of those involved were linked to groups affiliated with, or sympathetic to al-Qa'ida. . . . As more information becomes available our analysis will continue to evolve and we will obtain a more complete understanding of the circumstances surrounding the terrorist attack.

Some weeks later, the Intelligence Community again adjusted its position, reverting back to its original conclusion, as reflected in the talking points, that the attack was "opportunistic" and did not involve any significant advance planning. The Senate Intelligence Committee investigation completed in 2014 reached the same conclusion, that the attack was "not a highly coordinated plot, but was opportunistic."

Third, I was accused of blaming the incendiary video for the Benghazi attack rather than terrorists. That charge was widely repeated in the mainstream media and became urban legend. For instance, Reuters reported on September 16 that "The U.S. ambassador to the United Nations, Susan Rice, said on Sunday talk shows that the preliminary information indicated the [Benghazi] attack was a spontaneous reaction to the video." On October 15, *The New York Times* wrote, "But in the days after the [Benghazi] attack the Obama administration's surrogates said it grew out of a peaceful protest against the video."

What I repeatedly said, consistent with the best information available at the time, was that we believed that what happened in Benghazi had been inspired spontaneously by events in Cairo, where the anti-Muslim video had prompted violent protests against our embassy. In other words, the video was the precipitating factor *in Cairo*, and events in Cairo inspired Benghazi. I did not mean that the Intelligence Community had said that the video itself was the proximate spark in Benghazi. That was not the IC assessment. My comments on ABC, where I was interrupted in midsentence, unfortunately were imprecise. But I made the point clearly on CBS with Bob Schieffer and again on NBC's *Meet the Press* with David Gregory:

> *Our current assessment is that what happened in Benghazi was in fact initially a spontaneous reaction to what had just transpired hours before in Cairo—almost a copycat of—of the demonstrations against our facility in Cairo, which were prompted, of course, by the video. . . . Obviously, that's—that's our best judgment now. We'll await the results of the investigation.*

Despite my effort to be clear that the violence in Cairo stemmed from the video, reputable commentators and journalists elided my comments and established a public narrative that I blamed Benghazi on the video. It stuck.

Subsequent investigations, including by *The New York Times*, that took account of the motivations described by Libyans—who witnessed or were involved in the attacks—revealed that, contrary to what we thought at the time, the video did appear to have been a catalyst for the attack on the Benghazi diplomatic facility. Among those who reportedly said so was Ahmed Abu Khattala, who was convicted in U.S. court for his significant role in the attack.

Finally, I was lambasted for stating that there had been a protest or "demonstrations" at our diplomatic facility in Benghazi that evolved into a larger and violent attack. Hewing carefully to the talking points provided by the IC, which initially assessed that there had been "demonstrations" in Benghazi, that was the assessment I provided. This information turned out to be wrong, and days after my appearance, the IC revised its judgment to reflect their subsequent determination that there were no protests. This proved to be the main error in the original talking points.

As Undersecretary of State for Management Patrick Kennedy, a career foreign service officer, told Congress, "if any Administration official, including any career official, were on television on Sunday, September 16th, they would have said what Ambassador Rice said. The information she had at that point from the intelligence community is the same that I had at that point."

———

Throughout October, the attacks on me—some ferocious—were sustained. Romney himself gave a speech on October 8, in which he said, "This latest assault cannot be blamed on a reprehensible video insulting Islam, despite the Administration's attempts to convince us of that for so long." Senator Lindsey Graham said on October 11 that I was "either incompetent or untrustworthy—she's one of the two."

Once the DNI's statement was released updating its assessment on September 28, Democrats began coming to my defense. Senator John Kerry issued a statement saying, "I'm particularly troubled by calls for Ambassador Rice's resignation. She is a remarkable public servant for whom the liberation of the Libyan people has been a personal issue and a public mission. She's an enormously capable person who has represented us at the United Nations with strength and character." Senate Majority Leader Harry Reid insisted: "In order to inform the American people, the Obama administration, including Ambassador Rice, reported the preliminary information they had after the attack, despite the uncertain nature of intelligence in the fog of battle, and have responsibly updated the American public as new details have emerged."

After his brief visit to the General Assembly in late September, I didn't see much of President Obama for the duration of the campaign season. He was frequently on the road, and I was mostly in New York. But on October 12, shortly before the second presidential debate, National Security Advisor Tom Donilon invited me for lunch in his office at the White House. This was rare, if not unprecedented, so I suspected there was a larger reason for the invitation. Sure enough, in the midst of our meal, in popped President Obama.

No substantive discussion ensued; his purpose was simply to ask—*You okay?* He underscored his concern for me and his view that the attacks on me were all political gamesmanship. Obama had my back. "Stay strong, Susan," he assured me.

"I'll be all right," I said, "but I can't say the same for Maris or my mom." We didn't go into the details of the trauma that my daughter and Mom were experiencing. In these highly stressful weeks after my Sunday show appearances, Mom kept CNN blaring in her kitchen through almost all her waking hours, obsessed with what was happening to me. Like nine-year-old Maris, who was having batteries of tests to try to explain the frightening hallucinations she had recently begun to experience, Mom was traumatized. But unlike Maris, Mom understood what was going on. Still, she couldn't stand to see her daughter attacked, my integrity maligned. That stung her. And me.

Confessing that having Senator Graham denigrate my intellect and honesty was beyond galling, I told the president, "I will hang tough." I appreciated the Boss's very deliberate effort to buck me up. His private and public support helped sustain me through the heat of the October onslaught.

Just four days later, in the October 16, 2012, presidential debate, Governor Romney attacked President Obama on Benghazi. After Secretary Clinton had said that she "takes responsibility" for the thousands of State Department employees and their security, President Obama declared in the debate that the buck stopped with him: "Secretary Clinton has done an extraordinary job. But she works for me. I'm the president, and I'm always responsible, and that's why nobody's more interested in finding out exactly what happened than I. . . ."

Still, Romney went on the offensive: "There was no demonstration involved. It was a terrorist attack, and it took a long time for that to be told to the American people. Whether there was some misleading, or instead whether we just didn't know what happened, you have to ask yourself why didn't we know five days later when the ambassador to the United Nations went on TV to say that this was a demonstration. How could we not have known?"

Jesus, I thought, as I watched from home. *Now I'm in the middle of the presidential debate. This is nuts!*

Obama came back swinging, "The suggestion that anybody in my team, whether the Secretary of State, our U.N. Ambassador, anybody on my team, would play politics or mislead when we've lost four of our own, Governor, is offensive."

Boom. He sure did have my back.

Undeterred, Romney kept going, accusing Obama of refusing to call Benghazi an "act of terror" until fourteen days later, and was incredulous when Obama replied that he called it that right away, on September 12, the day after the attack.

CNN moderator Candy Crowley intervened, dutifully reading aloud the transcript of Obama's September 12 Rose Garden statement, in which he clearly used the words "act of terror." Romney appeared flummoxed and deflated. That was the last time Romney tried directly to bury Obama with Benghazi.

Over the remaining weeks of the campaign, I continued to be called all manner of things by Republican surrogates and pundits. It was incredibly frustrating to be publicly denigrated and not be able to fight back. As U.S. ambassador to the U.N., I spoke every day for my country and the president, not for myself, especially on a politically fraught issue in an election season. So I largely kept silent on the subject even as the attacks mounted.

I don't mind being disliked. I would always rather be respected than liked, if I had to choose. But to have my integrity impugned, to be branded a liar, hurt like nothing I had experienced before.

I fully understood that the attacks on me were a proxy for attacks on the president and, to some extent, that helped me not take it too personally during the election season. I also recognized that I was irresistible to Fox News, given my relatively high profile as Obama's U.N. ambassador and my perceived closeness to the president going back to his 2008 campaign. For the remaining weeks before the election, I viewed my role as to suck it up, take the hits, keep my head down, and survive to fight another day. It wasn't easy but putting mission first—continuing to represent the U.S. at the U.N.—made it a tolerable sacrifice.

October lasted an eternity. Feeling numb, I focused on my job and my family, reserving no space for my own emotions. Plowing through was an effective, if diversionary, coping mechanism, but I figured I could come to terms with my own emotions later.

Throughout this period, my incredibly loyal staff at the U.S. Mission to the U.N., wounded and appalled, worked crazy hours on top of their regular duties to defend me in the face of relentless media inquiries and congressional scrutiny. Only later would I learn how much they suffered on my behalf. Years after, when attacks against me resurfaced, or they were forced to relive the fall of 2012, they acknowledged to me their pain and stress. They had suffered to a degree that I had not, because I couldn't let it be about me. But they too put mission first, and their mission was to protect me when I couldn't and others wouldn't. My team performed thankless and lonely roles with enormous devotion and skill.

Strangely, in the halls of the U.N., it was as if nothing had happened. Few, if any, colleagues broached the subject of Benghazi. The U.N. press corps, which questioned me multiple times a week, never once asked me about the Benghazi controversy, until after the election. At the U.N., this was a non-story—a dishonest political attack not worthy of distracting from the real issues we were dealing with such as Syria and the push for Palestinian statehood.

By the third week of October, I briefly thought perhaps the tide was shifting. Several reputable press outlets, including CNN, *The New York Times*, and *The Wall Street Journal*, reported that I had relied on talking points which had been written by the CIA, not the White House, and had been approved by the Intelligence Community as a whole. It was plainly reported that, only after I was interviewed, did the IC receive information that changed their assessment. Despite the facts being widely disseminated, the attacks continued. I soldiered on, consumed by the responsibilities of representing the U.S. at the U.N. The weight of the job helped me stay focused and prevented me from wallowing too much in the assaults on my integrity.

———

Still, I wasn't prepared for the attacks on me *escalating* after the election. Naively, I had assumed that once the campaign was over and the president was reelected, the Republicans would see little continued utility in maligning me. During the campaign, White House chief of staff Jack Lew told me that the president wanted me to be vetted as a candidate for secretary of state. I had been thoroughly scrutinized in 2008 before being nominated for the U.N., but this was to be an updated and potentially even deeper vetting. I agreed and indicated my interest in the job, fully understanding that I was not the only candidate in contention. Senator John Kerry was also under consideration, and perhaps others. I had no firsthand reason to believe I was the president's preferred choice, despite a great deal of press speculation to that effect.

No sooner was the election over than Senators McCain and Graham, joined by New Hampshire senator Kelly Ayotte, launched their campaign to prevent me from becoming secretary of state. On November 14, McCain threw down the gauntlet, declaring: "Susan Rice should have known better, and if she didn't know better, she's not qualified. I will do everything in my power to block her from being the United States Secretary of State." For good measure, McCain accused me of "not being very bright." Graham also vowed to do his utmost to thwart my nomination, dutifully echoing McCain in his attack, saying, "I don't trust her. The reason I don't trust her is because I think she knew better, and if she didn't know better, she shouldn't be the voice of America."

That same day, President Obama was forced to respond to McCain's and Graham's comments at his first press conference after winning reelection. ABC News's Jon Karl asked for the president's reaction to their comments and "would those threats deter you from making a nomination like that?" Totally uncharacteristically, President Obama nearly erupted:

> *Well first of all I'm not going to comment at this point on various nominations that I'll put forward to fill out my cabinet for the second term. Those are things that are still being discussed. But let me say specifically about Susan Rice, she has done exemplary work. She has represented the United States and our interests in the United Nations with skill, and professionalism, and toughness, and grace. As I've said before, she made an appearance at the request of the White House in which she gave her best understanding of the intelligence that had been provided to her.*
>
> *If Senator McCain and Senator Graham, and others want to go after somebody? They should go after me. And I'm happy to have that discussion with them. But for them to go after the U.N. ambassador who had nothing to do with Benghazi? And was simply making a presentation based on intelligence that she had received? And to besmirch her reputation is outrageous. And, you know, we're after an election now. . . .*
>
> *But when they go after the U.N. ambassador, apparently because they*

think she's an easy target, then they've got a problem with me. And should
I choose, if I think that she would be the best person to serve America in the
capacity at the State Department, then I will nominate her. That's not a
determination that I've made yet.

I was in a luncheon for Security Council ambassadors at the Indian
Mission to the U.N. when my phone started blowing up. I excused myself
to find out what on earth was going on and ran smack into my assistant,
who was coming to pass me a note about the president's statement. Mortified that he was compelled to defend me yet again, I was also deeply moved
and gratified by the president's response. The force of his answer and his
rare display of public anger revealed how determined he was to make his
selection without regard for partisan political attacks.

For my detractors, it was showtime. Republicans launched a sustained
assault from multiple sides led by McCain and Graham. Nearly one hundred House Republicans joined the fray, writing a letter to Obama opposing my potential nomination:

Though Ambassador Rice has been our Representative to the U.N., we be-
lieve her misleading statements over the days and weeks following the attack
on our embassy in Libya that led to the deaths of Ambassador Stevens and
three other Americans caused irreparable damage to her credibility both at
home and around the world. . . . Ambassador Rice is widely viewed as hav-
ing either willfully or incompetently misled the American public in the Beng-
hazi matter. . . . We strongly oppose any efforts to nominate Ambassador
Susan Rice for the position of Secretary of State.

Soon it became a bench-clearing brawl. Democrats decided they had
had enough of what Senator Dianne Feinstein called "character assassination" and what Representative Eleanor Holmes Norton termed my record being "mugged." They went out in my defense. House Democrats,
led by the Congressional Black Caucus and women members, launched a
counter-letter praising me and supporting my nomination. House leaders,
including Nancy Pelosi previously, and Steny Hoyer, Adam Smith, and
Adam Schiff now came robustly to my defense.

No one did more to counter the attacks on my character and qualifications than Jim Clyburn, the third-ranking Democrat and senior member from South Carolina, who had known my dad as well as me. Clyburn took serious offense that a fellow South Carolinian, Lindsey Graham, was leading the attack on me and noted, as did Congressional Black Caucus incoming chair Marcia Fudge from Ohio, that by calling me "incompetent" and "not qualified," despite my evident academic and professional qualifications, they infused racial and sexist "code words" in their attacks. Clyburn said:

> *This had nothing to do with Susan Rice. Now we know from testimony of [former CIA director David] Petraeus . . . that the talking points she was given, she absolutely read from the talking points. . . . Now, if she had deviated in some way from the talking points, then they would have some issue with her.*
>
> *. . . You know these are code words. . . . These kind of terms that those of us, especially those of us who were born and raised in the South, we've been hearing these little words and phrases all our lives, and we get insulted by them. Susan Rice is as competent as anyone you will find. . . . Say she was wrong for doing it, but don't call her incompetent. That is something totally different.*

Senators, who I think would have preferred to stay on the sidelines until the president made his choice between me and their colleague John Kerry, felt compelled to swarm the field, because the attacks had continued after the election and gone too far. Democratic senators, led by Dick Durbin, Barbara Boxer, Carl Levin, and Feinstein, energetically debunked the Republican attacks on my qualifications and integrity, stressing my effective service at the U.N. and that I had done nothing but accurately convey the information provided to me. Editorial boards from the *Los Angeles Times* to *USA Today*, from *The Washington Post* to *The New York Times* blog, did the same.

The month of November was worse than October, because there was no end in sight to the incoming hits. While finally able to speak in my own defense, I was distressed initially to see little pushback coming from the White House, with the very notable exception of the president himself.

I could not have asked for more from Obama, but he could hardly make me his principal priority. I needed colleagues in the White House to assist from the podium in the press room and to provide support to my small press and legislative affairs teams.

One day, in utter frustration, I called Ian from my office at USUN and complained, "I feel I'm floating out here alone, without the necessary support. Like a piñata." Wondering how long I was going to have to put up with this crap, I confessed, "I don't know what to do anymore. I just don't know." Out of exhaustion and helplessness, I cried with him on the phone.

At the U.N., my press team and I concluded it was finally time for me to go on the record and speak for myself. On November 21, at the press stakeout following a Security Council discussion on the cease-fire in Gaza, a reporter asked me, "Explain your view of the controversy concerning your comments about Benghazi? And . . . is Senator McCain fair in what he has said?" Explaining that I had relied solely on the information provided to me by the Intelligence Community and made clear that it was preliminary, I continued:

I knew Chris Stevens. I worked closely with him and had the privilege of doing so as we tried together as a government to free the Libyan people from the tyranny of Qaddafi. He was a valued colleague, and his loss and that of his three colleagues is a massive tragedy for all of us who serve in the U.S. government and for all the American people. None of us will rest, none of us will be satisfied until we have the answers and the terrorists responsible for this attack are brought to justice.

Regarding McCain, I went on to say:

Let me be very clear. I have great respect for Senator McCain and his service to our country. I always have, and I always will. I do think that some of the statements he's made about me have been unfounded, but I look forward to having the opportunity at the appropriate time to discuss all of this with him.

Shortly after I spoke publicly, the White House finally kicked into gear. With the president's blessing, Deputy National Security Advisors Ben

Rhodes and Denis McDonough led the charge. Their aim was both to have my back and test whether the most vocal Republican senators who opposed my potential nomination could be defused or neutralized such that their opposition, if enduring, would not be too prolonged or costly to the president's second-term priorities.

To that end, the White House set up meetings for me with key senators in late November. They thought that it would be helpful to have Michael Morell, the acting CIA director, accompany me to the Hill, because the CIA had written the Benghazi talking points, which Morell had approved. He could validate that I was speaking only on the basis of what the IC knew at the time. Michael is a stand-up guy, and I appreciated his willingness to join me.

Over the course of two long days, we had several meetings. I met with Senator Joe Lieberman (an Independent who caucused with the Democrats), who was a close friend of McCain and Graham. Supportive and rational, Lieberman broke with McCain and Graham, telling Andrea Mitchell on MSNBC that he saw no reason to oppose my nomination or confirmation, adding "it seems to me that everything she said on those many appearances that Sunday morning were within the talking points that she had been given by the intelligence community."

Michael Morell and I then met at length with Senators McCain, Graham, and Ayotte. This meeting was contentious from the outset. McCain came out swinging. Bullying and blustering, he refused to let me answer many of his questions. He grew furious when Michael, in his effort to be helpful, mistakenly commented that the FBI had edited out the term "Al Qaeda" from an early draft of the talking points. McCain suggested that Michael was lying; of course, he was not. Michael corrected himself just a few hours later, clarifying that it was CIA personnel, not FBI, who made those edits before the points reached him. But once McCain got started, it was hard to stop him.

What I didn't fully appreciate at the time but have since come to believe, is that McCain was not interested just in punishing me for my words on Benghazi. There was likely more to it. Perhaps he also sought retribution for my closeness to the man who defeated him and for my own deprecating comments about him during the 2008 campaign. Graham piled on with his snarky, unctuous, and hyper-partisan outrage and later used Benghazi to fundraise and shore up his conservative credentials in expectation of a Tea Party primary challenger in 2014. Ayotte was the least aggressive but clearly opposed my potential candidacy.

As I said to the senators when we met, "I regret that the talking points provided to me by the Intelligence Community, and the initial assessment they were based on, were incorrect in one key respect: there were no protests or demonstrations in Benghazi. No one more than I wishes that we had had perfect information just days after the terrorist attack. But, as you know, it is often the case that the intelligence evolves. That's what happened here. Neither I nor anyone else in the Administration intended to mislead the American people at any stage in this process."

Despite acknowledging my error in our meeting, the senators' dismissive response made plain that they never intended to give me a fair hearing (nor even hear me or Michael at all). After our meeting, they issued harsh statements claiming they were even more "troubled" and "concerned" about the information I conveyed on September 16 than they had been before. Graham also pronounced himself "very disappointed in our Intelligence Community. I think they failed in many ways." The senators demanded much more information from the FBI and other agencies on what happened in Benghazi, as Graham said, "Before anybody can make an intelligent decision about promoting someone involved in Benghazi."

Senator Bob Corker, who was the ranking Republican on the Senate Foreign Relations Committee, met with me separately. He was more civil but equally dismissive of my prospective nomination, calling me a partisan flack who was better suited to serve as spokesperson for the Democratic National Committee. Publicly, Corker said, "I don't think people around here want in the secretary of state's office someone who's a political operative." Then, straining credulity, he added, "But, I'll give her a fair hearing." By contrast, in a private pull-aside with me after our formal meeting, he told me candidly: "Your problem is that you are just too *good*." As he implied then and on later occasions, I was a smart, powerful communicator, whom admittedly he quite "likes." In his view, I was too effective a spokesperson, one the Republicans had every interest in sidelining. It wasn't personal, in his mind. It was politics.

The most disingenuous meeting I had was with Senator Susan Collins of Maine. Four years earlier, she had kindly introduced me at my confirmation hearing for U.N. ambassador, heralding my qualifications and my strong family ties to Maine. In the intervening years, I had failed to pursue a deeper relationship with her. Now in public after she met with me, Collins said, "Frankly, I found her to be very defensive and not very forthcoming. I walked out of the meeting with a profound sense of disappointment." She also said, "I am concerned that Susan Rice's credibility may have been damaged by the misinformation that was presented that day."

The disappointment was mutual. Behind closed doors, Collins pressed me hard on why I went on the Sunday shows instead of Clinton, casting my decision as a self-serving audition for secretary of state. Despite my explanation to the contrary—that I agreed to do the shows, notwithstanding my long-planned Saturday travel with my kids, purely out of duty to the White House—she persisted in a nasty prosecutorial vein. She shocked me most by returning to the 1998 East Africa embassy bombings by Al Qaeda, suggesting that I was to blame for those attacks, despite the fact that the independent after-action report on the embassy bombings, which is required by law, found no fault with me. In the press, Collins tried to give lift to this latest smear, saying, "What troubles me so much is the Benghazi attack in many ways echoes the attacks on those embassies in 1998, when Susan Rice was head of the Africa region for our State Department. In both cases, the ambassadors begged for additional security." This attack was the lowest blow.

When the meetings were over, Collins made plain she remained unmoved. McCain and Graham sustained their offensive against me and expanded it unfairly to encompass Michael Morell. I had made no progress on the Hill and arguably suffered another public setback, as it became clear that most of these senators were resolved (no matter what I said) to deny Obama (seemingly out of vengeance for his reelection) the person they perceived to be his first choice for secretary of state.

The public battle over my non-nomination continued to mount into early December, but McCain and Graham stepped back a bit, content to let others take up the cudgels. McCain signaled his readiness to continue fighting, however, by announcing his intent to join the Senate Foreign Relations Committee, which would be responsible for screening the eventual nominee for State.

Meanwhile, GOP staffers conducted extensive opposition research against me, mining the historical record for new lines of attack, since the Benghazi assault appeared to be losing steam. They turned their focus to assailing my Africa record, sometimes with the help of long-standing critics of my tenure in the Clinton administration, including former ambassador to Sudan Tim Carney and committed loyalists of the late Richard Holbrooke, who seeded various negative press stories and opinion pieces, including one that resurfaced the false *Vanity Fair* allegations about Sudan and 9/11. Additional stories in *The New York Times*, *The Atlantic*, and elsewhere blasted me for being too close to Rwandan president Paul Kagame and protecting Rwanda from criticism at the U.N. I was also accused of being too sympathetic to autocratic "new" African leaders and indifferent to the extreme suffering in Congo.

Other press stories painted me as hotheaded, having a "personality disorder," "screeching," and being temperamentally ill-suited for the role of chief diplomat. A separate line of attack related to the bizarre claim that I was not actually opposed to the Iraq War (despite my early support for Howard Dean). Yet another vector was to assail my husband's financial holdings, including in TransCanada, a Canadian oil pipeline company, which detractors said should disqualify me, since the State Department would advise the president on whether to approve the controversial Trans-Canada pipeline. (This was a particular red herring, as all I would have needed to do was recuse myself, which I did as national security advisor.)

Even the Russian government piled on, publicly opposing my nomination because I was too "ambitious and aggressive." That condemnation I wore as a badge of honor, deeming it a backhanded compliment of my efficacy in battling Russia as U.N. ambassador. Taken together, it was clear I was facing an impressive multi-front assault fueled by disparate opponents from various stages of my career.

As harsh as the criticism was, I was heartened and deeply gratified by the sudden deluge of support. In Congress, Democrats in both houses were powerful advocates. Just one Republican publicly broke ranks to support me, Senator Johnny Isakson of Georgia, a kind, genteel man with whom I had worked closely on Africa issues. He used to send me Georgia peanuts and was always gracious. When asked about my potential nomination, Isakson told CNN, "What you don't want to do . . . is shoot the messenger. She read what she was told to read on those days and those five interviews. . . . She's become the focal point because she was put on the tip of the spear by the Administration. She is a very smart, very intelligent woman. I know this Ms. Rice, I think she's done a good job as Ambassador to the U.N."

Outside groups came to my defense—women, African Americans, and leaders of the American Jewish community who hailed me as a "gladiator" with "an unprecedented 100% pro-Israel voting record" in the U.N. Numerous colleagues—bosses, subordinates, and peers—rallied to my defense. From Madeleine Albright and Sandy Berger to former staffers at the NSC, including John Prendergast and Jeremy Weinstein, and (Republicans) Shawn McCormick and Jendayi Frazer, my Clinton administration contemporaries were outspoken. Michael O'Hanlon from Brookings also wrote many helpful articles supporting me. Secretary Clinton came to my defense in early December as well, calling me "a stalwart colleague," emphasizing, "Let me repeat what I have said many times. . . . Susan Rice has done a great job as our U.N. ambassador" and has "played an important role in what we've been able to accomplish in the last four years."

I was greatly buoyed by the depth and breadth of this outpouring of support when I needed it most. Yet, even as I appreciated their vocal defense of my integrity and my record, it was awkward for me, because I did not want to promote myself or campaign for the job of secretary of state. Instead, I wanted the decision to be the president's to make without external pressure (at least any generated by me). Moreover, I knew that Senator Kerry was a very strong candidate who was bound to enjoy the support of many of his Senate colleagues.

By mid-December, it became clear that the attacks on me were not going to abate. Moreover, a budgetary crisis, the so-called "fiscal cliff" was looming, and Congress needed to confront this pressing partisan battle. I didn't want a fight over my confirmation to add fuel to that fire or to delay and potentially derail top second-term priorities like immigration reform, to which I assigned enormous urgency and importance.

With Democrats controlling the Senate, I believed then (and still do) that I would have garnered more than enough votes to be confirmed, if not by a great margin and after an ugly fight. Senator Dick Durbin, the majority whip, agreed. When asked by the press on December 9 if he believed I would be confirmed if nominated, he said, "I do believe so. At the end, some of the criticisms against her have been unwarranted. Many have gone just too far. There's really a basic feeling of fairness. She's an extraordinary person. She's certainly well-educated and has really served our nation well as ambassador to the U.N."

Before the days of Trump, Betsy DeVos, Brett Kavanaugh, and our collective acquiescence to the narrowest of confirmation margins, I believed that the secretary of state (and other senior-most positions) should not be chosen along party lines. It is a role too important to our national security and international leadership to be used as a political football. That is still my view, though now it may seem quaint and antiquated.

After a couple of agonizing days of soul-searching and intense conversations with loved ones and a couple of my closest advisors, I made a decision. When I shared it with my mom—one early morning in the kitchen of my New York residence at the Waldorf, where she was visiting and drinking a cup of coffee—she must have spotted the resolve on my face as I walked in, still in my bathrobe. I joined her at the counter and gave her an extended hug.

"I've thought about this long and hard, and I've decided to pull out." Outlining my reasoning, I explained, "First, I don't think it is worth the demolition derby—to myself, our family, and the president's priorities. It's a manufactured controversy and a political hit job. But it isn't worth fighting just because I feel vilified. You know how much I *hate* to quit. Anything. Ever since I was a tomboy and a competitive athlete and student, you know I have always refused to give up. But you also taught me there are bigger things than my ego, my reputation, or even my perceived integrity. Things like our policy priorities and our country."

My mother was heartbroken, but I think also a bit relieved. We cried together for several minutes. Mom told me, as always, "You know how proud I am of you and how much I adore you." She understood the basis for my decision and respected it. It meant everything to me to have her there to support me, to hold me close as if I were still her baby, and to assure me it would all be all right.

Ian was disappointed but, as always, my rock. I later learned that he was much more upset and angry than he let me know at the time. My brother, Johnny, was deeply pained that I had suffered so much and furious that it was ending this way. He too hid much of his emotion from me, but I could sense his deep frustration. Maris was grateful this nightmare was about to be over and didn't hide her relief that we would soon put the ordeal behind us.

The person whose reaction I was least prepared for was Jake's. I flew home and sat with him in our yellow-painted living room in Washington. He was then fifteen. I explained to Jake that I was withdrawing from consideration, because the fight wasn't worth it for our family or the country. Jake had been dispassionate and strong throughout the whole Benghazi drama, but suddenly he broke down into tears. He begged me to change my mind: "Mom, you can't quit. You are not a quitter. You taught me all my life never to give up. How can you do this?"

I tried to explain, "Jake, this is not about me. Sometimes, you don't put yourself first. You put others first like your family, the president, and our country."

He insisted, "I will be okay. The family can handle it. We have already been through the worst. You can't let those people attacking you win." We went back and forth for a while like this until he realized I wasn't going to change my mind. I held him like my mom had held me and wept.

With my team, I devised a plan to roll out my decision. I spoke with the president and told him of my conclusion. It was a somber conversation. He said he was grateful for my continued service, deeply sorry for all I had been through, and respected my decision to withdraw. In my letter dated December 13, I wrote to him:

I am highly honored to be considered by you for appointment as Secretary of State. I am fully confident that I could serve our country ably and effectively in that role. However, if nominated, I am now convinced that the confirmation process would be lengthy, disruptive, and costly—to you and to our most pressing national and international priorities. . . . Therefore, I respectfully request that you no longer consider my candidacy at this time. . . . I am grateful, as always, for your unwavering confidence in me and, especially, for your extraordinary personal support during these past several weeks.

In response, the president issued a statement:

For two decades, Susan has proven to be an extraordinarily capable, patriotic, and passionate public servant. . . . I am grateful that Susan will continue to serve as our Ambassador at the United Nations and a key member of my cabinet and national security team. . . . I have every confidence that Susan has limitless capability to serve our country now and in the years to come, and know that I will continue to rely on her as an advisor and friend. While I deeply regret the unfair and misleading attacks on Susan Rice in recent weeks, her decision demonstrates the strength of her character, and an admirable commitment to rise above the politics of the moment to put our national interests first.

To break the news in my own voice, I gave an interview to NBC's Brian Williams, who anchored a weekly network prime-time news show, *Rock Center*. Before I left the U.S. Mission to head to Rockefeller Center to tape the show, President Obama called me again at my office. He reiterated his appreciation for how I handled everything. But his main message was what he said in closing: "Keep your cool. Don't let them see you angry. Listen to some Jay-Z in the car on the way over there." And, that's what I did, rocking to "Empire State of Mind," on my headphones.

After taping Brian Williams's show and finishing a couple more press calls at the Mission, I rushed to La Guardia Airport to catch the last shuttle to Washington. With my good friend and former deputy chief of staff Meridith Webster and a DS agent, we hurried through the airport to reach our gate. We arrived to find the US Airways gate agent slow-rolling the final boarding process to give us a few extra minutes. As we boarded, the flight attendant greeted us with a warm smile that said, *I've got your back*. My window seat was halfway to the back of the plane. As I made my way down the aisle, several people looked up. When I sat down, the passengers broke out into spontaneous applause. They had heard the news. *Wow*, I thought. To make it even better, shortly after takeoff, the flight attendant brought me a minibottle of red wine as a gift.

Once I made the decision to withdraw, I knew it was right—a weight off my shoulders. The extraordinary outpouring of support that flooded in from every corner of my personal and professional life moved me beyond words. The hundreds of emails, notes, and calls were overwhelming and left me feeling comforted and strengthened. The messages that meant the most came from scores of foreign service officers from the most senior to very junior expressing their admiration and disappointment that I would not be their secretary.

I truly had no idea I had so many supporters in their ranks. Thinking back to my earlier years as assistant secretary of state and the feathers I had unintentionally ruffled, I was deeply gratified to see that I had corrected course sufficiently to overcome much of the skepticism and hostility that I generated in my first year or two at State. With time and personal growth, I had apparently earned the respect and even affection of many with whom I was serving. That knowledge, above all, helped me to persevere. I was content to remain at USUN where I had a great team, lots of freedom, and the issues were never boring.

I also knew that I might still be asked to serve President Obama in another capacity that I would love, such as national security advisor. In any event, I could now focus fully on my family, my staff, and my job in New York. I would take stock and learn as much as I could from this shattering experience.

Just over a week later, President Obama announced he was nominating John Kerry to be secretary of state, a choice that was met with widespread and bipartisan approval in the Senate. I issued a statement saying: "America is fortunate that Senator John Kerry will be our next secretary of state. . . . Senator Kerry has served extremely ably and demonstrated selfless commitment to our country. . . . I have been honored to work with him in the past, and I look forward to working closely with him again on President Obama's national security team." Graciously, Kerry emailed me the next day to say, "Thanks so much for your tremendous statement yesterday . . . it bowled me over. Very generous and hugely appreciated." I felt confident that I could work at least as well with Kerry as I had with

Secretary Clinton, despite the awkwardness of being publicly portrayed as rivals for the same job.

Before Christmas in 2012, Secretary Clinton hosted a festive party at her Washington home for scores of senior State Department officials. Knowing that she would depart once her successor was confirmed, it was also something of a farewell party. Since the 2008 campaign, I encountered President Clinton only intermittently, and he was often cold to me upon initial contact. Once the conversation got going, however, he typically warmed up and seemed to forget that he bore a (hopefully) receding grudge against me. On this evening, at Hillary's party, he was right away his old self—voluble, intense, and warm.

President Clinton pulled me aside to commiserate kindly about Benghazi and its aftermath. He told me, in effect, "That was tough stuff, and you held strong under fire. You handled it very well." I was truly touched by his expression of concern and empathy. It meant even more coming from someone who had endured far worse. At the same party, Chelsea Clinton, who has always been lovely, engaged me in a more intimate conversation about how my kids were doing. She knew all too well how the politics of personal attack affect the families of those targeted, especially kids. I will forever be grateful for her sensitivity and warmth.

———

I always wondered—*Why me?* Why was I the one the GOP went after when I was a comparatively bit player in the actual Benghazi drama? Why not White House spokesperson Jay Carney? After all, Carney spoke about the Benghazi attacks almost daily from September 11 onward. He made more categorical statements than I—over a period of weeks. Like me, he was careful to rely on the Intelligence Community's assessment and not to make independent personal judgments. When the assessments changed, he updated his characterizations. Yet for some reason, I, not Jay, became the right-wing caricature of mendacity.

Why not Secretary of State Hillary Clinton (until later)? CIA director David Petraeus, whose agency had produced the talking points to begin with? Secretary of Defense Leon Panetta? National Security Advisor Tom Donilon? *How* was it that I became the bogey(wo)man of Benghazi?

To begin to answer that question, after I left government in 2017, I consulted a former producer at Fox News who worked there throughout the Benghazi period. He gave it to me straight.

My Fox friend explained that individuals make great villains, not organizations or institutions like the State Department. Individuals put a face on an issue for the audience and provide "a ratings bonanza." In going on five Sunday shows, I provided Fox "an opportunity to introduce a new villain" plus tons of video which provided "tremendous fodder" they could play over and over. They could not make Obama the perpetual target. They needed someone "fresh, unpredictable," and Jay Carney was not interesting. As a spokesman, the public expected him to be "a lying flack" (which he decidedly is not). My Fox friend argued that, if someone else had gone on those Sunday shows and said the same thing, that person would have become the fresh villain. When I asked pointedly, he maintained that it really wasn't about me personally or even about my race or gender. To bolster that point, he noted that "Bill Clinton was the original Fox villain" and later Barney Frank.

Secondly, he explained, Fox viewers were offended that I did not blame the attack on "radical Islamic terrorists" but rather appeared to be crediting a video created by an American, thus blaming America. By stoking the perception that I failed to blame Islam, Fox could grab and energize their audience. They also could use me to hammer Obama and make the case that we were misleading the public or withholding information for political purposes. All that was "red meat for our audience." Fox, he said, has an "unbreakable bond" with its viewers. They know what their audience gravitates toward, and Benghazi was perfect bait.

When I asked why Fox kept going after me once the election was over, he explained that there were "no other good scandals," and Fox and its viewers still objected to the fact that Obama would not use the term "radical Islamic terror." All they needed to do was continue to play the audio and video of me to get an angry reaction from the audience. Fox's goal, he said, is to wind up the audience every night and make them angry. Anger = ratings.

Finally, he elaborated, now that I am a "familiar villain," Fox will continue to use me. Any simple, quick sound bites "re-hit a raw nerve," and it's easy to brand me a "liar" or a "leaker" in perpetuity. A *recyclable* bogeyman.

This explanation about "why me" sounds logical (from the Fox News point of view), though I find it somewhat hard to believe that neither my race, my gender, nor my perceived closeness to the president made me a more attractive villain. Fundamentally, my Fox friend's insights underscore my mother's wisdom—I never should have gone on those Sunday shows that day.

———

After a much needed winter break with the family, I returned home in January 2013 to find that the dust had settled, and the spotlight had moved off me. Maris gradually improved. Eventually, after about a year, the episodes stopped entirely. My mom and the rest of my family moved on.

I too recovered. Painful as the whole experience was, I knew that I really only had two options—walk away or soldier on. To me, it wasn't really a choice. I never considered quitting, not least because I knew I hadn't done anything wrong. I would never give my detractors that satisfaction. As long as my family hung tough, I knew I could endure. My main coping mechanism was just to power through—by doing my job to the best of my ability, supporting my extraordinary USUN team who had suffered alongside me, and making jokes at my own expense. I lampooned myself at the U.N. Correspondents' Dinner just before Christmas and, later, in the spring of 2013, went on *The Daily Show* with Jon Stewart. I needed to laugh more than almost anything.

At the same time, I did some serious introspection about what went wrong and why. My team and I spent many hours in postmortem. I also consulted with Ian, Johnny, and outside allies who had deep experience with crisis management and could help me extract the leadership lessons I should take from this experience.

I realized several things.

First, again, my mother was right. It was a mistake to agree to appear on the Sunday shows, particularly in campaign season, even though my motives in doing so were selfless. In retrospect, while I don't think—as some have suggested (including my mom)—that I was set up, I do believe that Hillary Clinton and Tom Donilon appreciated what I did not. The first person to tell the public about a highly political tragedy was likely to pay a price. The opposition typically wants a scapegoat. Early information is almost inevitably wrong. That is not the Intelligence Community's fault or anyone else's. It's just that we learn more and gain better insight as time passes after a crisis.

I also acknowledge that there were some words and phrases I uttered on Sunday, September 16, that I wish I could restate with more precision, less certitude, or not have said at all. None of them materially changed the substance of what I said, but they offered fodder for my critics to pick at. Going forward, I have tried to avoid doing all five Sunday shows, the so-called "full Ginsburg," named after Monica Lewinsky's lawyer, William Ginsburg, the first to appear on all five. I learned the hard way that the more interviews you do, the more your comments are parsed, and the more likely you are to make a mistake.

In truth, had I refused to go on the shows, I would have felt guilty and selfish. Someone else would have had to go out. I am a team player, and I don't like shunting off on others what I am capable of doing. By deferring to that instinct, by putting the cause and the team first, I did myself a disservice.

My brother, Johnny, one of my closest confidantes, fiercest supporters, and bluntest critics, shared with me several additional insights. Sometimes Johnny's advice feels pedantic, but he knows me better than anyone and sees me in ways that I can't.

Johnny gave it to me straight: during Benghazi, I had "acted like a girl." (Ouch.) He meant that I put everyone else's interests above my own and that, after the election, I didn't promote or campaign for myself the way a guy would have. "With you," Johnny complained, "it's always mission first. That's your greatest strength, but it can also work against you."

I countered that it was inconsistent with my principles to gin up public pressure on the president to nominate me by generating carefully timed positive press coverage or encouraging constituency groups to lobby on my behalf. Johnny retorted that Senator Kerry, for example, had made it plain that he did not wish to be considered for secretary of defense, only state, thus denying Obama one way to have his cake and eat it too. I explained to Johnny that, girly or not, I would never be comfortable trying to box in the president.

Next, Johnny insisted that I needed to learn that being good and right is not enough. Up until Benghazi, I had always succeeded on the basis of merit, but "sometimes, merit isn't enough," my brother cautioned. "This lesson has come to you late, since really you have not had any major professional failures before."

"You need people who will go the extra mile for you," he continued. In reality, if there was a truth to be told or a fight to be had, I had never been afraid to stand up for what I believed. But as Johnny reminded me, I have always had difficulty asking others to do anything for me—even when I need it most. Johnny insisted: "You have to cultivate sponsors, champions, and 'rabbis' in advance." He explained that, "When people see that you are under fire, you need them to jump in fast and be willing to battle on your behalf." His comments made me realize that, on some level, I may also have suffered from lingering resentment among some career veterans in the State Department who recalled my assertiveness and relentlessness as a young assistant secretary for Africa. Maybe, had I more enthusiastic advocates among their ranks at the early stage of the Benghazi onslaught, they might have helped to quietly blunt some of the most unfair characterizations of my motives. While I am deeply grateful for all those who ultimately came to my defense, their support came late, after months of public pummeling. Still, that was on me for not having asked earlier, or at all.

Johnny, Ian, and many others also stressed that I had not spent enough time building relationships with the media and other D.C. playmakers who earlier on could have shot down a fabricated narrative before it spiraled out of control. They were right; I had neglected over the years to cultivate the press sufficiently. I needed friends and allies in the media—not for Holbrooke-style self-promotion, which I loathed—but to earn the courtesy of the benefit of the doubt. Before someone writes a nasty story about me, it is helpful if they bother to ask me to respond to the charge against me. Despite being married to a journalist and having a number of press acquaintances, I had few close contacts or friends in the press and appeared to them aloof and standoffish. I had to change that. I was not going to be a "source"—that's not my style. I despise leaks to the press and would not traffic in them. Yet, I could be more accessible, enjoy drinks or a meal, build relationships, and even make friends with journalists without giving away more than my time and candor. It was a realization I came to far too late, but this is a case of better late than never. Throughout the remainder of my time in government, I tried to engage more openly with the press, particularly the White House press corps when we traveled abroad, and through the occasional lunch or dinner in New York and Washington.

Finally, I also resolved to build stronger relationships with members of Congress, who I discovered belatedly can make a big difference with their support or silence. Most of my friends and interlocutors on the Hill are Democrats, but there are a few good Republicans who have been supportive since Benghazi. I won't out them, but they know who they are, and I am grateful to them.

———

In the years ahead, eight congressional committees investigated Benghazi. Appropriately, I was never called to testify publicly, since even Congress eventually came to understand that I was not a central player in the Benghazi tragedy. And, not one inquiry, even the longest and most politicized investigation chaired by Representative Trey Gowdy, concluded that I had deliberately misled the American people or acted improperly. Not one.

While the experience of being publicly pilloried was painful and temporarily knocked me off course, I came out of it stronger, tougher, and wiser. I emerged with an even fiercer resolve to never again let others define me. In a different context, Hillary Clinton once advised me, "Remember, revenge is best served cold." My revenge was simple: to continue serving my country undaunted and unbound.

Grandma Mary and Grandpa David Dickson emigrated from Jamaica to Portland, Maine, in 1912. Neither finished high school. Mary, a maid and seamstress, and David, a janitor, put all five of their children through college. *(Photo courtesy of Susan Rice.)*

Uncles Leon, Audley, David, and Fred Dickson graduated from Bowdoin College and became doctors, an optometrist, and a university president. This photo was taken in the early 1950s, after their service in World War II. *(Photo courtesy of Valerie Dickson Horton.)*

My mother, Lois Dickson Rice, with my grandmother Mary Dickson, who was named "Maine State Mother" for 1950 for raising four outstanding sons and my mother. Mom was valedictorian at Portland High School before graduating Phi Beta Kappa from Radcliffe College in 1954 as student body president and class marshal. *(Photo courtesy of Susan Rice.)*

My father, Emmett J. Rice (center), was born in South Carolina in 1919. During World War II, Dad ran the Statistics Department at Tuskegee Army Air Force Base. After the war, he completed his PhD in economics at U.C. Berkeley and became a professor at Cornell. *(Photo courtesy of E. John Rice Jr.)*

My parents, Emmett and Lois Rice, married in New York City in 1962, when my father was a staff economist at the Federal Reserve Bank of New York and my mother worked at the College Board. It was a second marriage for each. After their wedding, they moved to Nigeria for two years, where Dad helped establish the Central Bank and Mom worked for the Ford Foundation. *(Photo courtesy of Susan Rice.)*

I was born in Washington, D.C., in 1964. Here I am at around four months old, a happy, if drooly, baby. *(Photo courtesy of Susan Rice.)*

BELOW: By thirteen months old, I was already working the phones. *(Photo courtesy of Susan Rice.)*

From as early as I can remember, my dad never missed an opportunity to teach me and my little brother, Johnny, one of his life lessons. Dad often used to say, "Don't take crap off of anyone." This photo was taken when I was about three and Johnny was one. *(Photo courtesy of Susan Rice.)*

51 Melrose Street was the second home my grandparents owned in Portland, Maine, which I visited nearly every summer of my childhood. I have many cherished memories of fishing with my brother, rummaging through the old attic with my cousins, and riding my bike a few blocks to Deering Ice Cream for rainbow sherbet. *(Photo courtesy of Susan Rice.)*

Christmas 1971 will always be a cherished memory of a time when my family was happy and whole, without the rancor and turmoil that followed my parents' divorce. *(Photo courtesy of Susan Rice.)*

My third grade class at the Beauvoir School visited Capitol Hill and met with Senator Bill Brock (R-TN), who was the father of my good friend and classmate Hutchey. I grew up in a bipartisan environment with many fellow students whose parents were politicians and government officials. This early exposure helped spark my interest in public service. *(Photo courtesy of Susan Rice.)*

At the National Cathedral School (NCS), I played varsity basketball and tennis. My tennis has always been better than my basketball, even though this photo suggests I once had hops. Photo courtesy of the National Cathedral School.

In 1982 I graduated from high school as valedictorian and president of the school government. It was my honor to carry the cross in the processional at the Washington Cathedral, where I had been confirmed in the Episcopal Church and received my religious education. *(Photo courtesy of Susan Rice.)*

Four years later, when I graduated from Stanford University, my whole family was there to support me, despite my parents' bitter divorce and my mother's having remarried. From Stanford, I went to Oxford University on a Rhodes Scholarship and earned my PhD in International Relations. *(Photo courtesy of Susan Rice.)*

Dad's career spanned academia, the Treasury Department, the World Bank, commercial banking, and corporate boards. Dad served as a governor of the Federal Reserve from 1979 to 1986. *(Photo courtesy of Susan Rice.)*

BELOW: Mom was a true role model professionally and personally. As vice president of the College Board, Lois D. Rice became known as the "Mother of Pell Grants." Later she served as a corporate executive and on the boards of eleven public companies. She concluded her career at the Brookings Institution as a scholar and advocate for workforce diversity. *(Photo courtesy of Susan Rice.)*

I met my college sweetheart, Ian Cameron, during my first week at Stanford. We dated for ten years, often over long distances. This picture was taken shortly before our wedding. *(Photo courtesy of Susan Rice.)*

When we finally married, it was a beautiful and joyous September day in 1992. Our ceremony on the grounds of the Washington Cathedral combined the traditional and unorthodox, including my brother as maid of honor and James Brown blasting as we walked out of the church. After the reception, we threw a righteous dance party for our friends. *(Photo courtesy of Susan Rice.)*

In early 1993, at age 28, I landed my first job in government on the National Security Council staff. Here, as senior director for African affairs, I am pictured with National Security Advisor Tony Lake briefing President Clinton in preparation for a foreign leader call. It was a weekend, so he took the call upstairs in the White House residence. *(Photo by Bill McNeely, courtesy of the Clinton Presidential Library and Museum.)*

My longtime mentor and friend Secretary of State Madeleine Albright swore me in as President Clinton's assistant secretary of state for African affairs on October 22, 1997. This photo was taken just before the ceremony at the State Department. With three-month-old Jake in tow, I was beginning to learn about being a working mom. *(Photo courtesy of Susan Rice.)*

Our daughter, Maris, was born in a snowstorm in 2002. Hours later, this photo shows my dear friends, Tony Lake and Gayle Smith, greeting her, joined by Ethiopian Prime Minister Meles Zenawi, who was very happy to meet our baby. Meles and I got to know each other during negotiations to end the tragic war between Ethiopia and Eritrea. *(Photo courtesy of Susan Rice.)*

One of my mother's greatest joys was being a devoted "Nana" to her four grandchildren. She had a truly special bond with Jake, her oldest grandchild. When Jake was about three, they enjoyed a hearty laugh in my mother's kitchen. *(Photo courtesy of Susan Rice.)*

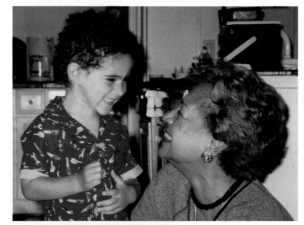

This is one of my favorite pictures with my daughter, Maris, when she was two. We are on a ferry in British Columbia, Canada, where we travel frequently to visit Ian's family. *(Photo courtesy of Susan Rice.)*

Many years after my parents divorced, Mom and Dad managed to bury the hatchet and enjoy much cherished time with Johnny's family and mine. This is Christmas 2004, one of the many happy holidays they enjoyed with all their grandchildren. Pictured at our house are me, Mom, Dad, Johnny, his wife Andrea, Jake, Maris, my nephew Mateo and niece Kiki. Ian was the photographer. *(Photo courtesy of Susan Rice.)*

In 2009, after President Obama's inauguration, I began serving as U.S. ambassador to the United Nations. In this role, I negotiated and advocated for U.S. interests at the U.N. Here, I am presiding over the U.N. Security Council as its rotating president—a monthlong role that I performed three times during my tenure. *(Photo courtesy of Susan Rice.)*

As U.N. ambassador, I lived and worked primarily in New York, but came home to Washington for meetings at the White House and State Department and to see my family on the weekends. During a relaxed moment in the Oval Office with President Obama in June 2009, we tossed the football before getting down to business. My years playing sports served me well throughout my career in a predominantly male world. *(Photo courtesy of Pete Souza.)*

In November 2011, I received an extremely warm welcome from the people of Tripoli and Benghazi, Libya, after I led efforts to pass a U.N. Security Council resolution authorizing military action to protect civilians from Qaddafi's ravaging army. The crowds in Benghazi were thick and warm with parents placing their children in my arms for hugs and photos. *(Photo courtesy of Susan Rice.)*

In my first month as national security advisor, on July 27, 2013, I faced my most stressful test: throwing out the opening pitch at Nationals Park. I couldn't afford to throw a dirt ball and be mocked on certain cable channels. From the mound, I threw a strike. What a relief! *(Photo courtesy of the Washington Nationals Baseball Club.)*

In late August 2013, President Obama chaired several NSC meetings on Syria to discuss Assad's use of chemical weapons. In this meeting, I was alone in arguing that we should proceed with military strikes in Syria without seeking congressional authorization. President Obama decided to seek Congress's approval, which was not granted, but he found a negotiated path to eliminating the bulk of Syria's chemical weapons stockpile. *(Photo courtesy of Pete Souza.)*

As national security advisor, I traveled with President Obama whenever he went abroad. In this photo, taken in the UK, I was laughing so hard because the president graciously insisted on carrying my purse as we got off Marine One, the presidential helicopter. My hands were indeed full, but it's highly unusual for the POTUS to carry anything when deplaning, except, in Obama's case, his cup of tea. *(Photo courtesy of Pete Souza.)*

During a 2014 trip to Israel as national security advisor, I was delighted to spend time with the late Israeli president Shimon Peres, one of the world's great leaders and a man I was proud to call my friend. *(Photo courtesy of Tsafrir Abayov / Associated Press. May 7, 2014.)*

In Alaska in 2015 to highlight the threat of climate change, President Obama and I donned toasty indigenous hats. *(Photo courtesy of Pete Souza.)*

Privately, President Obama called his all-female national security team "The Furies." On Saturday, December 5, 2015, Deputy National Security Advisor Avril Haines, Counter-Terrorism and Homeland Security Advisor Lisa Monaco, President Obama, and I were cracking up about a *New Yorker* cartoon depicting "The Furies 2.0." *(Photo courtesy of Pete Souza.)*

A serious moment, in October 2016, when I am briefing President Obama in the Oval Office on the threat to freedom of navigation off the coast of Yemen. *(Photo courtesy of Pete Souza.)*

It was painful to watch as White House engineers dismantled President Obama's Oval Office and prepared it for President Trump on Inauguration Day 2017. *(Photo courtesy of Ian Cameron.)*

Our family had a great evening in September 2018 enjoying *Hamilton* at the Kennedy Center in Washington, D.C. Together with our two very different children, Jake (21), and Maris (15), we all found inspiration in this phenomenal story of our founding and the value of our democracy. *(Photo courtesy of Susan Rice.)*

PART FOUR

Coming Back

17

Running the Table

"Let's try that again," called Tim Lea, the very fit Secret Service lead agent, after a mediocre practice throw I'd just let loose while warming up in the tunnel underneath the Washington Nationals' baseball stadium. It was minutes before the start of the Nats game against the New York Mets on Saturday, July 27, 2013.

For the last month I had been back at the White House in my new role as national security advisor. On Day One, I found myself smack in the middle of a maelstrom of crisis that would presage the next two years of nonstop crazy pressure. In just six months, we would grapple with Egypt, Edward Snowden, Syria, a wholesale internal review of our Middle East policy, the launch of secret negotiations with Cuba, and private talks with Iran, among other challenges.

Yet none of those critical issues and all-consuming demands caused me more stress than when I was slated to throw out the ceremonial opening pitch at Nationals Park before a capacity crowd.

For well over a month, I had been practicing sporadically with several agents, first from Diplomatic Security, and then from the Secret Service, which took over my detail when I moved from USUN to the White House. When the big day arrived, before it was time to head out to the field, Tim Lea and I made sure to warm up in the tunnel—where the two of us tossed long balls back and forth, and I fought back nerves.

Tim took my baseball debut very seriously. Like a brother, he had wor-

ried aloud that I could not afford to embarrass myself. I appreciated that he seemed almost as keen on protecting me from public humiliation as from any potential physical threat. Normally crowds don't faze me. I can easily give a major speech to a stadium-size audience, as I had done at the Ohio State University and Stanford commencements. Somehow, this felt different.

When I walked out into the massive stadium, my stomach flipped over. Ian, Jake, and Maris, along with Johnny and Andrea, my niece Kiki and nephew Mateo, all joined me on the first base line, offering last-minute encouragement. Johnny, typically less diplomatic than the others, warned, "Don't mess this up, Spo," employing the high school nickname given me by my basketball teammates.

I took the mound. The stadium erupted with a lot of friendly cheers but also some audible boos. Benghazi was not far in the past. Still a tomboy jock in my own self-image, I refused to take the girly way out by throwing from in front of the mound. I would try to throw the whole distance. The time between when the umpire told me to head to the mound and I had to pitch felt like a nanosecond. The pressure to throw immediately felt intense. Through my terror, I wound up and let it rip. It felt like it was going high, but the umpire yelled "Striiike!" and the catcher Wilson Ramos nodded with smug satisfaction.

Rarely, if ever, have I felt more relief. I didn't let womankind down. Fox wasn't going to be able to loop me throwing a dirt ball. I could come back to the White House and report to the president that I hadn't humiliated him or myself.

———◆———

Seven months earlier on a Sunday morning in January, I'd found myself unexpectedly sitting in the Oval Office, my back killing me. I could barely sit. The soft sofa adjacent to the president's chair was the last place I needed to be. That same day, I'd thrown my back out lunging for a backhand volley during my weekly tennis game with Karim Najdi, the coach at St. Albans School, who for years sacrificed his Sundays to help keep me sane as a service to his adopted nation. When President Obama's assistant called me that morning to ask if I could come to see the Boss, I had no idea what the topic was or why we needed to have a rare, off-the-calendar, private meeting in the Oval.

Trying to mask my severe pain, I appreciated that, as usual, Obama quickly got to the point. He noted that, for his second term, Deputy National Security Advisor Denis McDonough would take over as White House chief of staff, and he now needed to consider potential replacements for Denis. While Denis's successor would initially serve under the current NSA, Tom Donilon, Obama wanted my view, because, as he indicated, "It's important that you can work well with the new deputy—whomever it is I choose." He added matter-of-factly, "once you take over Tom's job." Back pain notwithstanding, I sat up a little straighter. This was the first direct confirmation from Obama that he intended to name me NSA, which I appreciated but let pass unremarked.

Over the past weeks after withdrawing from consideration for secretary of state, I'd been continuing in my role as U.N. ambassador—content to stay a while longer. The president had hinted earlier that he might choose me to be his second-term national security advisor. But anything can change, and in Washington you can never be certain.

The president floated two potential names for his principal deputy national security advisor. Though I liked and respected them both, I expressed my preference for the one he ultimately chose, Tony Blinken. Tony was Vice President Biden's national security advisor and his longtime aide from the Senate. We had served together in the Clinton administration and, under Obama, we had found ourselves frequently aligned on major issues at the Principals table. Tony was affable, formidably smart, and superbly prepared for the role but also a trusted friend with whom I enjoyed working. Funny and serious, nice but firm, and always unflappable, Tony would effectively run the crucial Deputies Committee, which is (normally) the hardest working team in Washington and reports to the Principals Committee, which I would chair.

Left unsaid by the president, but obvious, was that I was meant to keep this conversation in utter confidence, except from Denis. The time frame for my start at the NSC was unclear, but it appeared that the president might wish Tom to stay for the bulk of 2013 to provide continuity, since much of the rest of the national security team was turning over. No one on my USUN team knew if or when I might move back to Washington. Nothing is done until it's done, and folks needed to see me fully grounded at the U.N. until I was no longer. Following that confidential Sunday meeting in the Oval, it was back to New York first thing Monday morning to find a good doctor who could fix my back.

Strangely enough, when the president called in late May to tell me it was time to prepare to come home to Washington—in advance of Tom's late June departure—my private reaction was muted. I was pleased, not thrilled—gratified that this opportunity had finally come but sobered by the trials that had preceded it. Above all, I felt ready to step in, glad to be reunited with my family, and sad to leave my wonderful USUN team.

The president also sought my views on my successor at the U.N. He was inclined toward Samantha Power, then senior director for multilateral affairs at the NSC, whose portfolio during the first term included all U.N.-related issues. She and I had worked amicably and closely over my tenure, and I knew Samantha really wanted the job. I told the president I thought she would do well.

On June 5, 2013, in the White House Rose Garden, fully in bloom on a perfect Washington summer day, President Obama thanked Tom Donilon for his dedicated service and announced before our families and the assembled press corps that I would succeed Tom as national security advisor, effective July 1. Samantha would replace me at the U.N.

In his remarks, President Obama, recalling my role in his 2008 campaign, said: "I'm absolutely thrilled that she'll be back at my side." Perhaps as a subtle counterpunch to my Benghazi detractors, he called me a "consummate public servant—a patriot who puts her country first."

After reviewing my experience on the NSC staff and as assistant secretary of state, President Obama gave me (and Johnny) the highest compliment, "She is fearless; she is tough. She has a great tennis game and a pretty good basketball game. Her brother is here, who I play with occasionally, and it runs in the family—throwing the occasional elbow—but hitting the big shot." Pretty apt, I thought, at least as it pertained to Johnny and our elbows. Obama ended by acknowledging Ian, Jake, and Maris for their sacrifice and quipped that I would be "the first person ever in this job who will see their family more by taking the National Security Advisor's job."

During the rest of June, I split my time between New York and Washington, where I joined the customary daily meetings with Obama and spent hours with Tom, as he briefed me on the various sensitive issues he handled, many of which were not discussed at the Principals table. Smart, meticulous, and politically astute, Tom had served in every Democratic administration since Jimmy Carter's, including as deputy national security advisor from the start of Obama's tenure. He was steeped in both policy issues and the national security decision-making process. As we conducted a thorough handoff over the course of a month, I quickly realized that, while at the U.N. I had literally been covering the world, and in the Principals Committee we discussed a wide range of policy issues, the job of national security advisor was broader than both.

My additional responsibilities would span coordination and oversight of sensitive intelligence matters that I had not previously been read into, defense policy, military operations, counterterrorism and cyber security issues, and certain national security legal and law enforcement issues. I also had to master the national security elements of the federal budget, international economic issues from trade to sanctions to export controls, our nuclear policy and procedures, and continuity of government protocols in case of a major crisis.

I felt well-prepared for the NSA role, given that in my prior jobs I had seen the national security decision-making process from every vantage point. Having served as both a junior and senior NSC staffer, I understood the extraordinarily important role the staff plays in crafting policy options and coordinating the agencies. As a regional assistant secretary, I had joined the secretary of state and her deputies as a backbencher in countless Principals and Deputies Committee meetings and saw policymaking succeed and fail. Finally, as U.N. ambassador and a principal myself, I had an appreciation for what works from the perspective of the other senior policymakers around the table. Most valuably, I was walking in with an established relationship with the president, which was already grounded in mutual trust and respect.

My work in New York had afforded me a hands-on feel for the interests and attitudes of Russia and China, as well as valuable experience with other important global players—from the Europeans to India, Japan, South Korea, and Australia, from Mexico and Brazil to Israel and the Gulf Arab countries. And, Africa was well-known to me. In sum, I was confident in having the necessary grasp on the major countries with which I would do business.

Still, the job of the national security advisor is very different from that of U.N. ambassador. The U.N. role is outward-facing—representing the U.S. to the world, prominently speaking to the public, press, and Congress, negotiating with scores of foreign countries, traveling abroad frequently in service of U.S. and, as appropriate, U.N. business. The NSA role is primarily an inward-facing job—advising and supporting the president, formulating and coordinating policy among the agency heads, guiding strategy, and managing the NSC staff.

While the NSA gives some public speeches and interviews, he or she neither testifies before Congress nor customarily takes on such a high public profile as to risk overshadowing the secretaries of state or defense. I knew that I performed well in both types of jobs but soon would be reminded as I settled in the role of national security advisor that, temperamentally, I preferred being less in the public spotlight.

When I returned to the White House, I brought with me a deep and personal respect for the NSC staff, knowing firsthand how skilled and hardworking they are and how critical their role would be in enabling me to perform optimally. The staff consists mainly of career professionals assigned for a year or two from their home agencies (e.g., State, Defense, the Intelligence Community, USAID, Justice, Homeland Security). There are a few political appointees sprinkled throughout, but most are apolitical, highly talented career professionals.

The NSC gets its pick of the best, and that was what I worked to ensure we had. I brought just a couple of my great team from USUN to join me at NSC initially. Salman Ahmed, my brilliant, gentle, and wise USUN chief of staff, became my senior advisor and NSC senior director for strategy and planning. Taara Rangarajan, a young but trusted and mature personal aide in my Washington office, served as my special assistant and right-hand administrator. Later, I recruited a number of other staffers from USUN.

To enable a smooth transition and allow myself time to evaluate key members of the NSC staff, I made no immediate personnel changes. Only after months of observation did I move to swap in some players with strengths more suited to my vision. The staff had grown from about 150 people during the Clinton years to about four hundred by the time I became NSA. The increase was due mainly to the growth of the technology/systems staff and the international economic team, which is jointly shared with the National Economic Council, as well as the creation after 9/11 of the Homeland Security Council and its subsequent incorporation by President Obama into the "National Security Staff" (NSS).

I swiftly learned that my team detested being termed "NSS." Many shared the view that it was "demeaning," and ahistorical. In a small but not insignificant way, I sensed that it sapped their pride in serving at the White House. As a former NSC staffer, I too disliked the term "National Security Staff." We were the staff of the statutorily constituted National Security Council and should be so designated. So, once I was well-ensconced in the job, I asked President Obama to sign an executive order changing our name back to its hallowed original. Few things he did made the president (and me) more popular with the dedicated men and women of the NSC.

Similarly, while I came to the White House with a personal bias in favor of reducing the size of the unwieldy NSC staff, I waited a year and a half to launch an NSC "right-sizing and reform" process in order to pressure-test my hypothesis and to ensure that we made any changes gingerly and wisely so as not to disrupt our ability to serve the president. By the time I left, I was proud that I managed to shrink the NSC staff by 15 percent through attrition and rebalancing portfolios, without firing or curtailing anyone simply to cut positions.

When I started my tenure officially on July 1, 2013, it was hard to believe that twenty years had passed since I'd first gone to work in government as a twenty-eight-year-old entry-level staffer at the NSC. My early NSC mentors—Dick Clarke, Tony Lake, and Sandy Berger—had each helped me build a foundation and prepared me in the fundamentals of national security policymaking. Much had changed in the interim. Back then, the internet was not widely accessible, infant CNN was the only cable news network, and cell phones were the size of bricks. It was a different world entirely.

———

Despite all that I had learned in the intervening years, it was hard to feel ready for the full-blown shitstorm that hit me on Day One. In all those hours of pre-briefing, no one had warned me that Egypt would implode on my first day in office. On July 1, Tom was already gone. Obama was away, completing a major trip to Africa, and I was getting settled at my large wooden desk in my northwest corner office on the ground floor of the White House's West Wing. Home alone.

In Cairo, millions massed in the streets demanding the ouster of Egypt's first democratically elected president, Muslim Brotherhood leader Mohamed Morsi, who had taken office one year earlier. Thousands of counter-protesters rallied in support of Morsi, who remained defiant, refusing several opportunities to compromise with the opposition, including an appeal from Obama delivered in an urgent phone call from Tanzania. So far, there had been only sporadic violence, but the risk of civil conflict was real. The military, led by General Abdel Fattah el-Sisi, gave Morsi an ultimatum: make peace with his opponents within forty-eight hours, or else. President Obama urged Morsi to "Be bold," to be a leader for all Egyptians and to forge a unity government before it's too late.

Soon after Obama's call, I spoke by telephone with Morsi's foreign affairs advisor, Essam el-Haddad, to warn that the window for accommodation was quickly closing. I stressed that they needed to take urgent steps to deescalate the crisis and avert military intervention. While reiterating that the U.S. strongly opposed any extraconstitutional moves, I reinforced President Obama's point that the Egyptian military "is not taking direction from us."

By the time Obama returned from Africa late on July 2, Egypt was in the midst of a nonviolent, popularly driven coup stoked by Gulf Arab leaders that resented Mubarak's departure and feared Morsi's election. The next day, Sisi declared Morsi deposed, placed him under house arrest, installed an interim president, and pledged new elections. While many Egyptians had grown weary of Morsi's failed economic policies and his autocratic tendencies, a sizable portion of the population, including those sympathetic to the Islamists, insisted (correctly) that Morsi was legitimately elected and must continue to govern. The country was combustible, and the U.S. (always focused on the security of our personnel) ordered all non-essential embassy staff and their families to leave Egypt.

This crisis was the subject of the first Principals Committee meeting I chaired—on Day One as NSA. I would have preferred a few days to settle into the job, meet the staff, and read briefing materials before convening the Principals. In this instance, as in many others, crisis interceded to upend my best-laid plans. When Obama returned, he swiftly requested a meeting of his full National Security Council, in which he chaired the assemblage of cabinet Principals.

But first things first. It was July 4, and I had to uphold the family tradition of marching with our neighbors, the "Millwood Mob," in the Palisades Independence Day parade. After completing that duty and downing my annual hot dog, I showered and rushed to the White House to staff my first NSC meeting.

As NSA, I always sat to the immediate left of the president in these meetings—close enough to exchange notes or a quiet comment and to take his temperature with respect to the issues and my agency counterparts. Alternatively, as had long been the case, we were able to communicate without reliance on words.

On this day, it was plain from the outset that the Situation Room was not the place Obama wanted to be. July 4 is his elder daughter, Malia's, birthday, and the president was due to host not only a family birthday celebration but also thousands of military families and staff for the evening fireworks display on the White House lawn.

We quickly got down to business. The proximate issue was how should the U.S. respond to the military takeover in Egypt? On one level, the answer appeared obvious: a coup had occurred, and U.S. law requires that we halt all assistance to extralegal governments, like Egypt's new military-backed regime. Yet it wasn't so simple. Egypt was the second largest beneficiary of U.S. aid after Israel, receiving $1.5 billion a year, including $1.3 billion for the military. While corrupt, repressive, and undemocratic, the Egyptian military had long been a reliable partner for the U.S.—a bulwark against terrorism, a valued neighbor to Israel and our Gulf partners, and an important contributor to security in the Sinai and Suez. If we cut all assistance, the U.S.-Egypt partnership would grind to a halt. Moreover, we viewed the Morsi government as more than a disappointment, having lost our sympathy, if not its legitimacy. Still, it was hard to justify circumventing the coup designation.

Several principals, including Secretary of State John Kerry, Defense Secretary Chuck Hagel, and CIA director John Brennan argued we should not deem this a coup. Others, including Deputy NSA Ben Rhodes and Chairman of the Joint Chiefs General Martin E. Dempsey, emphasized the difficulty of pretending otherwise. The president listened intently, challenging the arguments on both sides, and then decided: *We will not call it a coup, nor will we say that it was not; we will remain silent on the question, thereby not invoking the law that would cut off all assistance and effectively acquiescing in the coup without saying so.*

It was an artful, if contorted, finesse, which I endorsed at the time. Yet the nondesignation both strained credulity and infuriated some members of Congress, like John McCain, who in this instance preferred legal orthodoxy (calling it a coup) over pragmatism. Reaching that fundamental decision sufficed for the moment on the 4th of July. It enabled me to take a break long enough to enjoy Malia's poolside birthday gathering and the fireworks with my family.

Yet the turmoil in Egypt continued to consume us. Days later, Morsi supporters took to the streets in large numbers demanding his restoration to power. The military responded by firing into crowds, killing over fifty people and wounding hundreds on July 9 alone. By August, when the president took his week-long vacation in Martha's Vineyard, the situation in Cairo was spinning out of control.

When the president travels domestically, he is always accompanied by a senior NSC staffer. Usually, I delegated that responsibility to a trusted colleague, but I made a habit of joining President Obama on Martha's Vineyard, as I had learned the hard way that bad things often happen in August (e.g., the 1998 embassy bombings). Being new in the job, I also felt obliged to limit my own vacation, so I tried to combine staffing him with family time. Ian and the kids joined me on the Vineyard, and I hoped to be able to work in the mornings and hang with family in the afternoons and evenings. It was a flawed plan, which in future years I did not replicate. Martha's Vineyard afforded a nice change of scenery, but since I was always on-duty it was no vacation.

Every morning during the president's so-called "vacation," I would get up early to send him a daily briefing memo and often visit or call him from our makeshift, secure NSC office across the island to discuss pressing matters. On August 14, the issue was the Egyptian military systematically slaughtering Morsi supporters in Cairo's streets. Up to a thousand were killed and thousands wounded by heavy weapons in a horrific display of bloody repression.

President Obama instructed me to convene his NSC by secure conference call. Outraged by the carnage, he ordered a full review of our assistance to Egypt. In a statement to the press the next day, Obama canceled the upcoming major annual U.S.-Egypt military exercise originally planned for September and set in motion a process that resulted in the suspension of both cash assistance and the delivery of heavy weapons systems, including fighter jets, helicopters, tank kits, and antiship missiles. The president allowed military training and counterterrorism support, as well as education and health programs, to continue.

Relations between the Obama administration and Sisi's Egypt never returned fully to normal. Sisi is a strongman, who craves power and crushes dissent. Obama remained distrustful of him and disappointed in his leadership. The president, my fellow White House staffers, Samantha Power, and I were more inclined than State, Defense, and CIA to punish Sisi and the Egyptian military for their myriad abuses, but most of us were also pragmatists who understood we could not afford to sever the relationship. For the remaining years, we sought to strike an awkward balance between demonstrating our discontent and forcing an irreparable breach. I always found this middle ground unsatisfactory but do not think the alternatives—fully breaking with the Egyptian military or failing to hold them at all accountable—were preferable.

———

I am not a morning person. Thankfully, neither is President Obama.

That made life easier than it could have been. Working for President George W. Bush, who reportedly started in the Oval Office before 7 a.m. and ended most days by 5 p.m., might have killed me. By contrast, Obama worked in the residence until late into the night, devouring his briefing materials and decision memos, sometimes calling or emailing with a question or concern. Luckily, I never had to wake him with a "3 a.m. phone call," because I knew that, if I emailed him even at 2 a.m. or later, he was likely to respond or call me back. Obama rose around 7 a.m., worked out religiously, ate breakfast, read his intelligence materials, and came down to the office usually around 10 a.m. That suited me just fine.

I woke up to NPR's *Morning Edition*—usually around 6 a.m. Most days, I would work out in our small basement gym, reading the newspaper on the elliptical machine while listening to the television. If I could stand it, I turned on *Morning Joe*. On those many days when their commentary risked raising my blood pressure even before 7 a.m., I would divert to the BBC. After showering and saying goodbye to the kids, I would jump into the Secret Service armored Suburban for the twenty-minute ride to the White House.

Waiting in the car was my intelligence briefer, the person assigned to hand me my secure iPad, which contained my morning briefing materials, including the very closely held PDB (the President's Daily Brief), and other items he or she selected for me to read. My briefer was there to answer questions, receive and respond to requests for follow-up information, and occasionally field my praise or criticism about the quality of the day's product. Not being a morning person, I was not especially talkative. Sometimes I had to make or receive a call, often with John Kerry, on the secure phone in my vehicle. Mainly, I focused on readying myself for the day ahead. Following the White House chief of staff's morning meeting, I scrambled to prepare for briefing the president—finishing my intelligence take, reading morning briefing notes prepared by the NSC staff, devouring the press, preparing my points for the president, and being armed in case he wanted to discuss any of the memos I sent him the night before.

Just before 10 a.m., our small NSC team would gather in the lobby outside the Oval. In addition to the president and vice president, the group consisted of: me; the deputy national security advisor (first Tony Blinken, and from January 2015 Avril Haines); Lisa Monaco, the president's counterterrorism and homeland security advisor; deputy NSA and speechwriter Ben Rhodes; Denis McDonough; and the vice president's national security advisor (first Jake Sullivan, then Colin Kahl). A senior leader from the office of the Director of National Intelligence would join at the top of the meeting, usually DNI Jim Clapper himself or one of his deputies.

When we heard the door from the Rose Garden colonnade to the outer Oval slam shut, we knew it was showtime. Obama was in the house. Sometimes Bo, the elder and more mellow of the Obamas' two large, very soft, white-shoed Portuguese Water Dogs, lounged lazily in a big leather chair to greet him. These meetings began with varying degrees of levity or trepidation, depending on the day. Bo's cheerful presence meant we collectively started in a better mood as we filed in to the Oval.

We each always sat in the same place. My spot was on the couch just to the left of the president's brown leather chair. That put me directly in the line of fire for whatever he was dishing that day—humor, frustration, firm direction, or a diversionary topic such as his perennial quest for a particular type of straw hat from Cuba. Like Ben and Denis, whose wardrobes the president regularly dissected, I occasionally endured a ribbing on things ranging from my shoes to the rationale for the weird holes in my suede jacket with a distinctive angular cut, a unique acquisition from a craft fair. And frequently, without impetus, Obama took the opportunity to remark on how short I am, as if he were noticing for the first time. His fascination with my height (or lack thereof) was a recurrent annoyance in our interactions. For my part, I gave as good as I got, although I confess to commenting approvingly on his notorious tan suit, which I actually welcomed as a respite from navy or gray.

Amidst all the seriousness and intensity of being in charge of the national security team, we made time for levity. Tony Blinken, my first deputy, was a wonderful colleague and friend who did an excellent job managing the Deputies Committee process with a hokey humor and smooth style that provided a kinder, gentler counterbalance to my own. He kidded me about my colorful language and my occasional feigned threat for someone who was getting on my last nerve to come and "kiss my black ass." For Christmas our first year, Tony gave me a small package. Inside was an ink stamp with four letters on it: "KMBA." I howled in laughter. Tony's advice was that I use it to display in shorthand my disapproval of certain memos that came across my desk.

A big day in the Obama White House, I would learn, was St. Patrick's Day, when each year the president would host the Taoiseach, Ireland's prime minister, in the Oval Office. The meeting was usually a festive affair complete with mandatory, leafy green boutonnieres, and green garb all around. Obama, with his part-Irish heritage, embraced this meeting and the celebration that followed on Capitol Hill. Given his typically excellent taste, I was surprised one St. Patrick's Day when he walked into the Oval looking his usual dapper self—but something was off. I realized his tie was all wrong. Rather than any discernible version of green, it was teal bluish and flecked with a strange pattern. It wasn't an ugly tie (but it was nothing special). It just plain as day was not green.

"Mr. President," I ventured, "your tie is not actually green."

"What are you talking 'bout Rice? Of course it's green."

"No," I held it closer to his face, "this is not green. It's a kind of blue."

"Give me a break. This is plenty green," he insisted.

I called for backup: "Ferial," appealing to the president's assistant, "does this look green to you?"

"No," she said, "not really."

Pete Souza, the president's photographer, agreed. Exasperated, Obama trudged back up to the residence and came back wearing a truly green tie. I was both amused and puzzled by this exchange, but when he returned I moved on to the daily briefing.

The next year, on St. Patrick's Day, I was taken aback when he came down again in that same bluish, flecked tie. I thought—*WTF?* With some trepidation, but determined, I started: "Mr. President, don't you remember we had this same conversation last year? That tie is not green."

"Yes it is!" he again insisted.

"No it's not. It wasn't green last year, and it isn't green this year," I braved.

This time, I didn't need to call for backup. It came swiftly, and the president retreated to the residence only to return again with the same correct green tie. I began to wonder if he was slightly color-blind.

Most mornings, our meetings began with less contention. And on some days, we just started with a celebration, like on August 4 when I typically led off with a (highly imperfect) rendition of Stevie Wonder's "Happy Birthday to ya'. Happy Birthday to ya'. Happy Biiirthday . . ." The first time I sang for his birthday, Obama smiled, turned to Biden and said, "See, that's what happens when you have a black national security advisor." After a few laughs and a couple more bars, we got down to work.

The DNI briefer typically departed after ten or fifteen minutes of field-ing the president's questions. Then it was my turn. For the next half hour or so, I updated, fireproofed, sought guidance, and offered the president whatever insight I thought he might need that day. On my trusty graph paper pad, I kept a daily list of items to raise with the president as well as my "to-do" tracker. My briefing would cover not only high-profile top-ics like North Korea, Syria, Russia, or China, but also matters of interest and importance ranging from political developments in West Africa to the long-term strategic implications of water scarcity or space technology and threats to undersea cables. After I exhausted my list, or occasionally triaged it because I sensed the president was running out of patience, I handed off to Lisa, Avril, and Ben for matters they wished to raise.

We didn't use these meetings to circumvent the Principals Committee process by trying to persuade the Boss of our preferred course before oth-ers could weigh in, and he would not have permitted that. But sometimes we did seek a sense of his gut instinct on tough topics in advance of a policy debate, so we would not be surprised, or surprise him, if our approaches were likely to diverge. This morning briefing time was a valuable oppor-tunity to ensure that we stayed closely attuned to the president's judgment and that he received daily the good, bad, and most often the ugly of what was going on around the world. Thankfully, Obama received bad news as we did—with equanimity rather than excessive emotion. His cool tem-perament and rationality enabled him to confront tough challenges with his formidable intellect, offering thoughtful direction and asking probing questions rather than shooting the messenger. Because President Obama is a voracious reader with huge capacity to retain information, our time was spent less on simply briefing him and more on collectively assessing the implications of key developments and considering potential paths forward.

Following the president's daily briefing, the balance of the day was usually mine to manage—barring a bolt from the blue that screwed every-thing up, like a terrorist attack, hostage scenario, coup, or threat to U.S. personnel overseas. Often, I chaired a staff meeting after the morning briefing: either a small, internal meeting of my deputies to plan our Prin-cipals Committee and Deputies Committee schedule, discuss personnel, or resolve internal differences; or a larger meeting of NSC senior directors representing each of the regional and functional offices—roughly thirty highly skilled, mostly career public servants (diplomats, intelligence analysts, military officers) crammed tightly into the Situation Room. Senior directors would flag issues that they anticipated would require senior-level involvement and sought quick guidance on pressing matters. These sessions enabled me to keep my fingers on the pulse of the staff and be readily accessible to them.

I devoted the afternoons to meetings with outsiders like visiting foreign counterparts, and to preparing either for NSC meetings with the president or, more often, to run Principals Committee meetings. The PC met roughly two to three times per week for approximately an hour and a half each meeting. The frequency and length of the meetings varied, depending on the topic and the press of events. When the Islamic State in Iraq and Syria (ISIS) was on the march or Ebola raging, when Syria negotiations were intense, or South Sudan was imploding and putting our embassy at risk, we would meet more frequently and sometimes with little advance notice.

Evenings were the only time available for reviewing and editing the thousands of memos my staff prepared in my name to send to the president. Briefing memos. Information memos. Decision memos. Thick binders of trip preparation materials. The volume of paper that we sent to the president, and which he read thoroughly, was all but overwhelming. Every night and weekend, I spent many hours ensuring that every page sent to the president was of uniformly high quality. A stickler for proper grammar and punctuation, I have a particular pet peeve about proper comma usage. (My chief of staff at USUN had to restrain me, in my own best interest, from giving an all-staff seminar on the comma.) I was not about to send garbage to any president, let alone the former president of the *Harvard Law Review*.

Occasionally, the tyranny of paperwork and tedium of the evenings were interrupted by a colleague dropping by before heading downstairs to go home. My favorite unannounced visitor was Vice President Joe Biden, whose office was just down the hall. Unlike President Obama, who rarely ambled into our suite and never without a purpose, the VP liked to pop in with no agenda and linger. He came to check on how we were doing, buck us up, tell a joke, shoot the breeze, or deliver a Bidenism—a family aphorism that never lost its value. In rare instances, the vice president surprised me by baring his soul, sharing his agony over his son Beau's cancer and later his tragic passing. Even when in pain, Joe Biden was warm and generous, always leaving me feeling better than when he walked in.

Evenings were when things typically loosened up at the White House. In the absence of a crisis, we had a moment to breathe, to laugh, and tend to the trivial—like the bizarre arrival of a snowy owl just blocks from the White House in McPherson Square. Jake, the avid birder, pinged my cell phone incessantly in January 2014 seeking my help in locating the snowy owl so that he could get a good photograph. My colleague in the front office, Anne Withers, volunteered to track sightings of the owl online for a few days (until it got injured by a Metrobus) so that, despite my work hours, I could still be of some use to my teenage son.

Rarely would I escape the office before 8 p.m., staying many nights past 10 or 11 to move the paper that had to go to the residence that night or out to the agencies. Avril, who as deputy NSA had the hardest job in government, was much more of a fiend. She almost never left the office before midnight and often much later. I had a small fridge and cabinets, in which I discreetly stocked the necessary provisions, including adequate supplies of beer, wine, and other necessities to keep me, my front office team, and any visitors tolerably disposed well into the night.

Too often, we ordered snacks or dinner from the White House Mess. By evening, my dietary restraint often lapsed, and I could be tempted by some of the best chicken fingers in the world as well as waffle fries, jalapeño poppers (Avril's favorite), or cheese and crackers. Being national security advisor, as I like to say, was "bad for my butt." In fact, it was worse than the U.N., where Madeleine Albright often quipped, the job is to "eat and drink for your country." In New York, I was usually able to leave the office in time to snag at least a late dinner at the residence, and there was no Mess. In Washington, I would graze on Mess food and then come home late and eat again with Ian, who had kindly prepared healthy dinners.

The job also wasn't good for my blood pressure, though neither was the U.N. When my dad was very ill in 2010, I went to the White House Medical Unit to have my back pain checked. As a matter of routine, the doctor took my blood pressure, which had always been excellent. I was shocked to see it was well over 150 systolic. It had never been an issue, but at forty-five, suddenly I developed a problem that had long plagued my dad. Medication controls my blood pressure well, and regular exercise helps, but the stress of the NSA job definitely exacerbated the challenge.

————

She kept slapping the table and yelling in Portuguese. *How could the U.S. have eavesdropped on my personal calls?*

For what felt like an eternity, Brazilian president Dilma Rousseff berated President Obama over allegations that the U.S. had tapped her personal phones. While the Brazilian foreign minister translated, I sat with the president at a small table in a quiet corner on the grounds of a Russian palace in St. Petersburg, where we were meeting for the 2013 G20 Summit. The hotter Dilma got, the cooler Obama became. He listened quietly at first, but I could tell his patience was running out. When it did, he interceded in a calm, low voice to explain antiseptically that he had not been aware of the reported eavesdropping. He had not directed the tapping of any friendly foreign leader's phone. Such surveillance would not continue. The U.S. and Brazil should address this challenge to the valued bilateral relationship in a measured and rational manner.

Dilma wasn't having it. She kept ranting until finally she ran out of steam. I watched half amused at this fascinating study in male-female dynamics. Obama failed utterly to meet Dilma where she was, to defuse her anger with reciprocal passion in his regret. This exchange reminded me of a scene between old-marrieds, when the wife is going berserk over her husband stepping out on her, and the husband is so icy in response trying to chill her out that it totally backfires. It would have been funny, if the whole thing were not so serious.

President Obama was royally pissed that he had to eat crap from foreign leader after foreign leader for a set of transgressions that he did not even know had been committed. It was only a few days after I started at the White House in early July that we learned from *The Guardian* that the massive cache of extraordinarily sensitive, highly classified documents—which a young, self-righteous intelligence contractor named Edward Snowden stole from the National Security Agency and selectively leaked to the press—alleged that the NSA was eavesdropping on the European Union and at least thirty-eight friendly countries. We later learned these targets purportedly included the personal communications of allied leaders.

Snowden's leaks did immeasurable damage to many aspects of U.S. national security, from our ability to detect and prevent terrorist attacks to revelations about how the U.S. allegedly conducts intelligence collection. To add insult to injury, after releasing vast quantities of stolen information, Snowden absconded to Vladimir Putin's Russia where he shared God knows what.

Particularly upset by the eavesdropping allegations was Obama's good friend and invaluable ally, Angela Merkel. In October 2013, she called so angry that she spoke the whole time in German for the first and only time I can recall in their many discussions. Her understandable fury (exacerbated by echoes of East Germany's Stasi past) was palpable from across the Atlantic, despite Obama's assurances that the U.S. "is not" and "will not" eavesdrop on her or other close allies' personal communications. Merkel was not mollified, and public opinion in Germany, where privacy protections are highly prized, turned sharply against the United States.

Obama was deeply concerned that this breach might ruin his closest foreign partnership. My own early dealings with my German counterpart, Christoph Heusgen, were also poisoned by the Snowden revelations, especially after I implied that we believed their reaction was somewhat overheated. For months, Christoph and I did not speak directly but conducted business through my very capable senior director for Europe, Karen Donfried. When Karen later departed the NSC, Christoph and I had no choice but to engage each other on pressing issues from Ukraine to counterterrorism. Necessity bred familiarity and, ultimately, a strong partnership and friendship between me and Christoph. But the Snowden allegations substantially set back the larger U.S.-German alliance, which took time and real effort on both sides to repair.

French president François Hollande also lodged a firm protest about the Snowden revelations, but France's objections were somewhat leavened by the tacit acknowledgment that the French are no boy scouts when it comes to spying, and their understanding of the importance of maintaining our joint counterterrorism cooperation. The Japanese and Mexican leaders were unhappy but less exercised.

For all the damage Snowden did to important bilateral relationships that is known to the public, the greatest harm was less visible. Suffice it to say, I spent much of my first six months as national security advisor trying to recover from and help clean up Snowden's mess. Rarely, if ever, did I see President Obama more frustrated and insistent on the urgency of resolving a major problem than on the Snowden disclosures. Obama almost never raises his voice in anger, and I never saw him display explosive rage. Yet on this issue, he was fit to be tied, as he quietly pressed his almost daily demands that we fully fix the flaws that we inherited, and fast.

For my part, I was furious and incredulous that unaccountable people years ago seemingly made hugely consequential decisions about how to target our collection capacity—without senior-level oversight or thorough consideration of the policy implications of getting caught. Equally, I felt nearly overwhelmed by the magnitude of the damage Snowden inflicted and its almost infinite implications. My nerves were close to fraying, as from one day to the next we never knew what new shoe might drop.

I led intense and sometimes contentious separate negotiations with my French and German counterparts on how to modify our security relationships. The president commissioned a five-person, outside review panel to offer expert advice. My team, colleagues in the various agencies, and I conducted a months-long, comprehensive interagency review of our intelligence collection policies, targets, and procedures. After painstaking and near constant work to bring this vast issue under control and ensure that the most sensitive collection decisions are carefully vetted, we implemented a wide range of reforms, including those the president codified in Presidential Policy Directive 28, "Signals Intelligence Activities," issued in January 2014.

Snowden's leak of classified programs and practices constituted one of the most difficult and serious problems I encountered in government. Congress and the American people were outraged by the (mis)perception that the NSA was spying indiscriminately on U.S. citizens' phone calls and emails. The European Union protested vehemently that U.S. intelligence agencies were vacuuming up vast quantities of E.U. citizen information without their knowledge or consent. American tech and telecom companies sought to put public and practical distance between themselves and the U.S. intelligence and law enforcement community, taking steps that made critical cooperation on terrorist and other threats far more difficult. Trust on all sides—domestic and international—was sorely strained, if not ruptured.

The damage Snowden caused to U.S. national security cannot be overstated. Those who praise him as a "whistle-blower" and a hero have no idea what they are talking about. Snowden deserves a full reckoning with the U.S. justice system, which I am confident would render the punishment he has earned. Instead, he remains coddled in Moscow, where he escaped to the warm embrace of our committed adversary and precipitated the sharp, ongoing decline in U.S.-Russian relations. Snowden's picture ought to be in the dictionary next to the definition of "traitor."

18

———

The Furies

"**Y**ou're shitting me, right?" I asked White House chief of staff Denis Mc-Donough on an evening in late August 2013.

"No, I'm serious. I was just on my nightly walk with the president, and he thinks we should pause and first go to Congress."

I was stunned. Denis, standing in my office doorway, repeated his news—that President Obama had suddenly decided not to strike Syria immediately, as planned, but first to get congressional approval for U.S. military action in response to Syria's horrific use of chemical weapons. Denis said a small group of us would soon gather in the Oval Office to discuss this further with the president.

As national security advisor for less than two months, I'd already chaired several Principals Committee meetings on our response to Syria's violation of the president's so-called "red line" on the use of chemical weapons. Nearly two thousand people, including many children, had been killed by the Syrian regime in a sarin gas attack on the Ghouta region. We almost all believed we needed to act militarily to demonstrate to Assad that he could not violate international law with impunity by using deadly gas against civilians without paying a price.

That afternoon, at an NSC meeting, the president agreed and approved appropriate military targets. We were very close to launching. Our primary impediment was the U.N., which needed time to move their personnel out of harm's way. We had lined up international partners to join our military operation, notably France and the U.K. But Prime Minister David Cameron decided to seek parliamentary approval for this action and, shockingly, he had lost the vote. This was a major setback, an "own goal" by Cameron, but France remained gung ho.

When we gathered that Friday evening in the Oval, President Obama laid out his thinking. He began with his description of the challenge he aimed to address. To start, he recounted, we did not have a clearly valid international legal basis for our planned action, but we could argue that the use of banned chemical weapons made our actions legitimate, if not technically legal. Domestically, we could invoke the president's constitutional authority to use force under Article II, but that would trigger the War Powers clock—meaning, if our actions lasted longer than sixty days, the president would need to obtain congressional approval. Therefore, before we used any significant force in Syria to address its chemical weapons use, the president thought it best to invest Congress in the decision, and through them the American people.

As usual, Obama was thinking several plays down the field—to the potential need for military action against Iran, if diplomacy failed, to force Iran to give up its still nascent nuclear weapons program. Once the precedent was established that Congress should act to authorize military action in Syria, we could insist on the same kind of vote, should we need to confront Iran—a much higher-risk proposition that he would want Congress to own with us.

I admired the president's logic but disagreed with his assumptions. As Obama polled his key aides assembled in the Oval for their individual views, all agreed with him. He called on me last, as he often did in my role as national security advisor.

The lone dissenter, I argued for proceeding with military action, as planned. We had signaled clearly and publicly (most recently that morning in a strong speech by Secretary Kerry) that we intended to hold Syria accountable through the use of force. Our military assets were in place. The U.N. was warned. Our allies were waiting. We needed to go. As Vice President Biden likes to say, "Big countries don't bluff." Finally, I invoked the painful history of Rwanda and predicted we could long be blamed for inaction.

Above all, I argued to the president, "Congress won't grant you the authority." That was my strong gut. I had come to believe from bitter experience that Republicans in Congress were so hostile to President Obama they would deny him anything of consequence he requested, even if they believed it was the right thing to do. I anticipated that congressional Democrats would splinter, as *many did not want to vote for what they feared might become another war of choice in the Middle East. The president listened closely to us all and acknowledged my concerns. He concluded his argument with characteristic aplomb, predicting that we would get the votes. Neither a political strategist, the legislative affairs director, nor twice elected president, I rested my case.*

The next morning, the president convened his whole national security cabinet to discuss Syria. Again, he laid out his thinking and polled the room. Everyone professed to agree with his arguments and proposed course of action, though I sensed some were not being fully forthcoming with their true opinion. When it was my turn at the end, I summarized with greater brevity the same concerns I had expressed the night before, for the other principals to hear: we would never get Congress on board; it was time to act. As the meeting ended, as anticipated, I was badly outvoted. So, figuratively, I saluted and moved out to implement the president's decision.

———— • ◆ • ————

President Obama later told me that he was not certain we would prevail in Congress but thought we had a fighting chance. He foresaw that a night or two of bombing might not change Assad's calculus and that a more sustained military campaign may be needed to achieve our objectives. Given that reality, Obama felt that even if we might fall short of the needed votes, it was important to try to vest Congress in such a consequential decision to use force. After Iraq, Afghanistan, and Libya, Congress needed to be on board with such critical choices; it had to own them alongside us—one way or the other.

In the meantime, sensing that Russia feared that the U.S. was on the verge of major military action, President Obama pigeonholed Putin on the margins of the G20 Summit in St. Petersburg in early September 2013. Obama told Putin he was prepared to use force to punish Assad for deploying chemical weapons, though he remained open to a more permanent negotiated solution, if one could be found, to address Syria's chemical stockpile. Intrigued, Putin agreed that Secretary Kerry and Foreign Minister Lavrov should discuss possible options. Obama later instructed me to alert Kerry to pursue this prospect with Lavrov.

The U.S. and Russia worked together to compel Assad to declare and relinquish his chemical weapons stockpile, subject to international verification. Russia vowed to exert the necessary pressure on Assad, and Kerry and Lavrov codified their agreement in a U.N. Security Council resolution, which threatened sanctions and, by implication, the use of force, if Syria failed to comply. The U.S. agreed to hold off bombing until we could see whether Assad would fulfill his commitments or not.

Ultimately, we would fail to garner the necessary support for a congressional authorization to use force. Republicans and Democrats had acted precisely as I predicted. Ironically, it turns out, I was right about the politics; but President Obama was right about the policy. Without the use of force, we ultimately achieved a better outcome than I had imagined. The bombing of some discrete chemical-weapons-associated targets (not actual stockpiles, for safety reasons) would have marginally set the Syrian regime back in the short term. It would have sent a message to Assad but would not have eliminated the vast bulk of his chemical weapons stockpile or changed the course of Syria's civil war.

Some months later, Syria did declare its stockpile, joined the Chemical Weapons Convention, and shipped out under international supervision all of its declared chemical weapons stockpile—some 1,300 metric tons. Israel, which was directly threatened by Syrian gas, hailed the action and stopped distributing gas masks throughout the country. The removal of Syria's declared stockpile could not have been accomplished through bombing. It was achieved through the *credible threat* of the use of force and painstaking U.S.-Russia diplomacy.

Unfortunately, this was not to be the end of the story. While we made considerable efforts to address any gaps and inconsistencies in Syria's declaration, including by raising such issues with the Organisation for the Prohibition of Chemical Weapons (OPCW), we were never fully satisfied that Syria had declared every element of their program. Ultimately, we were unable to point to anything sufficiently specific to prove this to the OPCW and, of course, Syria may have simply made new sarin gas. What we do know is that, in April 2017 and again in April 2018, Syria killed scores more in fresh chemical attacks. In both instances, President Trump dusted off the Obama-era military plans and target list and struck suspect facilities with cruise missiles and air strikes.

In my view, President Trump was right to act against Assad, who with Russian complicity had violated his agreement with the U.S. and the U.N. But the airstrikes were divorced from any strategy to leverage our use of force to catalyze a diplomatic solution. Senior Trump administration officials issued mixed public messages about the objective of the bombings, which further complicated matters. Ultimately, these U.S. strikes sent a message but failed to change any facts on the ground. The conflict persisted and Assad grew stronger, while continuing to kill innocents.

In both 2017 and 2018, the U.S. made clear too quickly that these were short-lived, limited packages of strikes. The Trump administration failed to keep Assad and Russia guessing, limiting their ability to again use the credible threat of force to pursue a diplomatic outcome that addressed our chemical weapons concerns or brought the conflict closer to conclusion. Syria's chemical weapons problem remains unresolved. So too does the larger Syria policy conundrum.

For six years, the Obama administration wrestled painfully and unsuccessfully with Syria, which I believe to be the hardest policy challenge we faced. Assad, the murderous dictator, remains hell-bent on regaining full control from rebels who once occupied significant swaths of Syrian territory. He uses whatever vicious means necessary—barrel bombs, chemical weapons, targeting hospitals—to kill hundreds of thousands and cause millions to flee as refugees.

The human costs of his slaughter burned our collective conscience and directly implicated U.S. interests by driving destabilizing refugee flows into fragile neighboring states like Jordan and Lebanon, as well as Turkey, and further afield to Europe, which has not recovered politically or socially from the shock of the inflow. The active intervention of Hezbollah, Iran, and later Russia dramatically exacerbated the conflict, aiding Assad but also threatening Israel. Terrorist groups, including Al Qaeda and ISIS, exploited the chaos to establish safe havens from which they planned attacks on the West. It was a complete horror show that only got worse with time.

At every stage, the dilemma for the Obama administration was how deeply to involve the U.S. in trying to topple Assad and stop the bloodshed and refugee flows. The gap between our rhetorical policy and our actions constantly bedeviled U.S. policymaking. In August 2011, several months

after the start of the Syrian uprising and in the midst of the Libya operation, President Obama joined our key European partners in declaring that
"the time has come for President Assad to step aside." But having learned
the lessons of regime change in Iraq and sobered by the complexity of
sustaining even an air campaign in Libya, no principal argued for direct
military intervention with U.S. ground troops to force Assad out, as President Bush had done to Saddam Hussein. The costs in blood and treasure
to the U.S. were massive in Iraq, and Syria would be at least as bad, if not
worse, given Iran's strong backing. Once Russia put its forces into Syria
in September 2015, any effort at regime change could have courted World
War III.

But we did consider and reconsider (again and again) many significant
steps short of direct war against Assad. At the same time, we imposed what
U.S. and European sanctions we could; but absent U.N. Security Council
authority, which Russia consistently blocked, comprehensive global sanctions were not achievable. We provided almost $6 billion in humanitarian
assistance to the victims of Syria's conflict and more to the neighboring
states coping with the burden. We spent untold amounts of senior-level
energy trying to negotiate with Russia, Syria, and other key players to end
the conflict peacefully. At various points, we tried to exploit potential diplomatic openings, but none ever came to fruition.

After over a year of intense internal debate, President Obama decided
in 2013 to join our Sunni Arab and Turkish partners in arming and later
training vetted Syrian rebels who were fighting Assad. The challenge we
continually faced, however, was that some of the rebels were genuine political opponents of the regime while others were members of lethal terrorist groups. Still others were in between. The terrorist groups, like the
Al Qaeda–linked al-Nusra Front, were the best anti-Assad fighters, but we
would never assist them. The difficulty was how to help the good guys,
and those in the gray area, without inadvertently providing sophisticated
weapons and training to terrorists.

We tried to walk that fine line but could never do so perfectly. The rebels were fractured and lacked a coherent, achievable political agenda. The
assistance we provided was significant but not as much as the rebels wanted
and arguably needed. We did not do the maximum, because we assessed

that the long-term risks of passing the most dangerous weapons to rebels in a murky war zone outweighed the benefits. While the U.S.-supported rebels fought as best they could and at times did increase military pressure on Assad, they were unlikely ever truly to threaten the regime's survival without direct U.S. military intervention.

The Principals fought over Syria longer and harder than on any issue during my tenure. John Kerry, John Brennan, and Samantha Power argued for the U.S. to do more—provide more lethal weapons to the rebels, take targeted strikes against Assad or his air force, and, perhaps, establish safe zones for civilians. Others, including me and Denis McDonough, Secretary Ash Carter, and Chairman of the Joint Chiefs Martin Dempsey and later Joe Dunford, were equally tortured by the suffering in Syria but opposed deeper U.S. military involvement.

I didn't see a feasible middle ground. If we took action that directly targeted Assad or his military, we were at war with him, Iran, and ultimately Russia. If we set up a no-fly zone or safe zones on the ground, we were buying a costly, dangerous, lengthy, and uncertain military commitment on top of Afghanistan and Iraq that put significant numbers of U.S. forces in harm's way. Could we have protected civilians in safe zones? Yes, had we deployed thousands of U.S. troops to take and hold the ground and committed roughly a hundred planes to provide an air-cap. Would that have toppled Assad in addition to saving lives? Unlikely, before Russia intervened in September 2015, and certainly not thereafter.

I believed, and continue to believe that, as pained as we felt, as much as our values were offended, and as amoral the decision not to intervene directly in Syria's civil war seemed, it was the right choice for the totality of U.S. interests. President Obama agonized over Syria constantly, but repeatedly reached the same conclusion. Many people I respect disagree strongly with that judgment, but in retrospect I cannot say that I would have done much differently—except perhaps to have avoided declaratory statements such as "Assad must go" or red lines as on chemical weapons that raised expectations for actions that may not have served U.S. interests. In the same vein, I question the wisdom of arming and training the Syrian rebels since the level of our support was not sufficient to create more than a temporary stalemate, before Russian intervention tilted the conflict in Assad's favor.

My heart and my conscience will forever ache over Syria. Since Rwanda, my bias has been in favor of action in the face of mass atrocities—when the risks to U.S. interests are not excessive. In contrast to Libya, in my view there was no version of U.S. intervention in Syria that we should have conducted except very limited strikes to respond to chemical weapons use. For instance, strikes against Assad's air force, as some advocated, would not have been one-off endeavors. To sustainably degrade his military capacity, given Assad's external backing and robust air defenses, would have required a long-term air campaign against a far-better-equipped and more sophisticated army than Qaddafi's. But even still, only U.S. ground forces deployed before Russia intervened could have reliably stopped Assad's deadly ground war against the rebels. This likely would have amounted to another Iraq-scale invasion. Although I acknowledge the very high costs of limiting our actions and am neither content nor proud to admit it, I believe we were correct not to become more deeply involved militarily in Syria.

———

Most days, the job of national security advisor seems infinite. Its weight feels like a huge slab of concrete constantly resting on one's torso. Fortunately, I could still breathe and function under that pressure, even as more and more bricks were piled on top of the original slab. In fact, in some strange way, the crush was both daunting and energizing. If one is doing the job of NSA thoroughly and conscientiously, there are more challenges to monitor and address, more opportunities to be pursued, than any one human being can manage, much less master. To survive and indeed thrive, I needed a first-class team alongside me: strong, capable deputies to divide and conquer the incoming challenges, plus highly motivated, exceedingly competent senior directors to seize strategic opportunities (such as pushing progress on global health security, climate policy, and cyber security) without needing my constant oversight and direction.

In my last two years as NSA, I was extremely fortunate to have the invaluable input, support, and counsel of my sisters, Avril Haines and Lisa Monaco. Avril replaced the wonderful Tony Blinken, who became deputy secretary of state in December 2014. A physicist, pilot, bookstore owner, lawyer, and former deputy White House counsel for national security and deputy director of the CIA, with years of additional work in the Senate and at the State Department, Avril is brilliant and brought deep knowledge and broad experience back to the NSC. Already well-known to the president and NSC staff, she adapted easily to her new role. Patient, wise, and calm, Avril helped soothe my sharper impulses with her uniquely disarming combination of love and reason.

Another accomplished lawyer, Lisa had served as a federal prosecutor, chief of staff to FBI director Robert Mueller, and most recently as assistant attorney general for national security when President Obama appointed her his homeland security and counterterrorism advisor in March 2013. Tough, plainspoken, with an acerbic wit and a well-buried soft streak, Lisa took no prisoners in all she did—from killing terrorists to punishing cyber criminals.

In the privacy of the Oval, President Obama dubbed his all-female senior national security team "The Furies." Avril, Lisa, and I—though all petite in stature—commanded significant power behind the scenes and were the three women President Obama most loved to tease. Never before, I am sure, had such small packages wielded such national security punch. Together, we led and managed the predominantly white male national security cabinet and deputies.

Lisa, Avril, and I laughed at being called "The Furies," but also feared that the Boss's nickname for us would leak. The Furies were known as "monstrous, foul-smelling hags," we would protest. "It's sexist," I insisted. "They were goddesses of vengeance and retribution who preyed on men. That is not us. We like men!"

President Obama countered that, "The Furies were not evil. They delivered justice and defended the moral and legal order, mainly by driving their victims mad. The moral and just had nothing to fear from The Furies, only the guilty and evil." And, his Furies were charming (some of us more than others), tough, smart, and fair. "It's perfect!" he declared. The president loved each of us individually, but especially the team.

One Saturday, we found ourselves in the Oval Office standing near the Resolute Desk. The Boss was looking at a *New Yorker* cartoon by Roz Chast that was entitled *Furies 2.0*. Lisa had found the cartoon and, to underscore our private joke, edited it—to depict "Ironia" as Avril, "Sarcasta" as Lisa, and "PassivAggressa" as me, except that Lisa had aptly crossed out

FURIES 2.0

IRONIA — SARCASTA — PASSIVAGGRESSA

R.Chst

"Passiv." As the three of us cracked up, our friend White House photographer Pete Souza, who was in on the secret, captured the moment in a well-known photo captioned: "A rare moment of weekend laughter with the President's key national security aides, from left, National Security Advisor Susan E. Rice, Homeland Security Advisor Lisa Monaco, and Deputy National Security Advisor Avril Haines as they joke about a cartoon in *The New Yorker* that resembled the three women." It didn't resemble us physically, of course, but we thought the personality labels were pretty spot-on.

The three of us were quite conscious of the rare gift we enjoyed of having two other strong, supportive women as our closest colleagues (plus Ben Rhodes, whom we also teased about being one of the girls, given his sensitive side). Between the three of us, there was always candor and trust. We always played straight with each other, even when we differed, as Lisa and I sometimes did over personnel and policy. Avril, ever the smooth and deft fixer, would help us forge common ground. Confident in ourselves and each other, we wouldn't let any outsider perceive, much less exploit, our differences. Woe unto anyone, especially any male counterpart, who tried to play one of us against another.

Often, Lisa, Avril, and I had to combine our collective efforts to tame a balky bureaucracy and deliver to the president the policy outcomes he sought. That variously entailed massaging, cajoling, pressing, and, if necessary, rolling certain agencies to achieve presidential objectives, which they initially resisted. These ranged from safely and responsibly but substantially increasing refugee admissions numbers and reducing the prison population at Guantánamo, to requiring public reporting by DOD and CIA of the number of civilians accidentally killed in counterterrorism operations, and to ensuring that as we reconfigured our military presence in Afghanistan, we did not fall back into the trap of having Americans directly fighting the Taliban, except in clear cases of self-defense.

On other occasions, the three of us ran interference to ensure that the president did not receive inadequately vetted proposals that we knew he would question and likely reject. On more occasions than I care to recall, like clockwork on a Friday evening, DOD would send over (with no prior notice) a time-sensitive proposal for a high-risk military operation, known as a "con-op" (concept of operations), and demand near immediate presidential approval. After cursing DOD—because we knew that any such proposal had taken at least a week to make its way up the DOD chain of command to the secretary of defense for his approval, yet now DOD was asking the president to bless it instantly—we got to work.

President Obama appropriately expected his NSC staff to employ the established national security decision-making process to give him well-considered recommendations as to whether to approve or reject a con-op. That meant we had to convene the Deputies and Principals on short notice to review the intelligence, operational plan, diplomatic implications, and risks/rewards of the proposal—all over a weekend—and preferably get a decision memo to the president within twenty-four hours. Remarkably, we repeatedly managed these fire drills swiftly and effectively, sometimes surfacing flaws in the proposal and prompting refinements to lower the risks and increase the odds of success. As fast as we obtained a decision, it often was not before someone at DOD had leaked to the press that the anal and micromanaging NSC was slow-rolling their urgent operational plan.

We didn't let those kinds of ploys knock us off our game or cause us to cut corners in giving the president the kind of analytical rigor and carefully considered recommendations he deserved. Together, Lisa, Avril, and I displayed fierce, loyal, and effective female leadership that was appreciated by the president and many on the NSC staff, if not all the agencies all the time. We cherished the fact that our collaborative women's leadership style was distinctive and rare, especially in our field.

When we left the White House in 2017, Lisa, Avril, and I gave a signed copy of the Roz Chast *Furies 2.0* cartoon to the Boss as a farewell gift. President Obama keeps it in his office at his foundation.

———

Given that we had to spend ridiculous hours together, I felt grateful to be part of a close-knit NSC leadership team that genuinely loved one another and also knew how to have fun. For starters, we decided to revolutionize the NSC Holiday Party. I led the dancing, which got funky and sweaty fast.

Ben Rhodes was a demon on the dance floor, flipping partners over his back and shoulders. Ben and I had worked closely together from the campaign through every foreign trip of my tenure, every tough press story, and every twist and turn in the Cuba and Iran negotiations. We also shared the experience of being vilified as scapegoats of the right wing, targeted by Fox, and blamed for Benghazi. Ben is funny, super-smart, and kind. Like another brother, Ben always had my back, and I will always have his.

Suzy George, the NSC chief of staff, tended to hang back and watch over the parties, making sure everyone else was having sufficient fun. I first met Suzy over twenty years before, back when she worked for Madeleine Albright at USUN and as deputy chief of staff at the State Department. Tough but sweet, funny but quietly ruthless, Suzy had been a partner at Albright Stonebridge, the highly successful firm Madeleine built after leaving government. With Madeleine's reluctant but generous blessing, Suzy came to help me whip the NSC into fighting shape—releasing weak players, hiring the best in class, guiding the "right-sizing" effort, and driving improved processes. Suzy had the extraordinary gift of firing somebody and making that person almost think the departure was his idea. I relied on her, like Salman Ahmed, to give me the hard advice straight, correct me when I was off-course, and tell me how to do it right—always with a disarming smile and deadly efficacy. I had learned from Howard Wolpe, when I was assistant secretary, the value of surrounding yourself with colleagues who have the courage and commitment to give you tough love.

Too late in my tenure, we added Wally Adeyemo to our team, a young lawyer of Nigerian descent whom National Economic Council director Jeff Zients and I brought over from Treasury to be our deputy for international economic affairs. Brilliant, polished, smooth, and effective, Wally helped us energize and empower the international economic team, which was responsible for everything from sanctions to trade policy, climate, energy, and preparations for the G7 and G20. Miraculously, he also made the economic aspects of my job far more enjoyable for me.

There is no team I'd rather be with in the trenches or on the dance floor than the extraordinary senior staff of Obama's second-term NSC.

———

"What's the sleep strategy?"

This was a standard Obama question predictably posed as we would fly past the Washington Monument on Marine One, the presidential helicopter, for the fifteen-minute ride to Joint Base Andrews at the start of an overseas trip. It was an especially pertinent question for long trips to Asia or Africa and the Middle East. The answer depended on the number of legs to the journey, time zones, and the schedule we faced when we arrived. Weighing the best approach to ensuring adequate sleep, work time, and readiness for the day ahead, we could usually reach a consensus view.

When the helicopter landed at Andrews, President Obama would bolt off and up the steps to Air Force One, with the press corps capturing his farewell wave. The small team aboard Marine One, who followed him up the front steps to the plane after he was out of sight, usually consisted of me, another senior staffer or two, the White House doctor Ronny Jackson, the president's lead Secret Service agent, his military aide, and the president's personal aide Joe Paulsen or Marvin Nicholson.

Once on board, we were wheels-up within a very few minutes, since the presidential aircraft takes priority and clears the airspace around D.C.

I always sat in the four-person senior staff cabin where I had a pull-down desk table by the window, an ample leather chair that swiveled but did not recline much, a pillow, and a blanket. Soon after takeoff, I hustled into one of the two forward bathrooms and changed into my comfy travel garb for the long journey ahead.

Air Force One has many cool features—a full office and comfortable bedroom with shower for the president, a conference room big enough to seat ten or more, secure airborne communications, a staff office, the ability to send and receive classified documents, a full kitchen, a doctor's cabin that can be converted into an emergency operating room, screens with live television and movies galore, and infinite quantities of food and drink.

But the two 747s that take turns flying the president of the United States and his staff are over thirty years old. They have prehistoric, if amply sized seats, but nothing approaching a lie-flat bed for anyone other than the leader of the free world. The bathrooms are cramped with no facilities for staff or press to wash up. It's always an honor and still a bit of an adrenaline rush to fly on Air Force One, but the glory is decidedly not in the aircraft itself.

Early in the flight, President Obama would usually saunter back from his cabin at the front of the plane on his way to the conference room, having changed into jeans or khakis, an open-collar shirt, and sometimes a cashmere sweater. He often poked his head into our cabin before walking farther back to greet the rest of the travelers, including the scheduling and advance team, NSC staff, stenographers, and any accompanying VIPs or members of Congress. Obama would then settle in at the far corner of the conference table where he spent the bulk of every trip reading briefing materials and memos, playing spades, eating his meals, and making phone calls, often to foreign leaders.

For me, the outbound journey on every trip was consumed by the need to review the briefing materials my team and I had provided to the president, prepare for every meeting he would conduct, review and edit speeches, press remarks, and talking points, and deal with whatever crisis du jour by fielding calls from the White House or cabinet colleagues. Sometimes I needed to support our frantic advance teams who were already on the ground struggling to resolve some last-minute hitch with the host government—like the Russians refusing to let Secret Service sweep the president's villa for listening devices, or Japanese officials making some entirely unreasonable demand about the president's schedule.

During the flight, I'd catch whatever rest I could on the only couch available to staff—in the hallway just outside our cabin. There was an unspoken hierarchy governing access to the couch. As the senior staffer on most foreign trips, it was mine. Occasionally, however, if someone who outranked me joined the trip, like the White House chief of staff, I'd tacitly relinquish the couch. I also deferred to White House senior advisor Valerie Jarrett when rarely she traveled with us. I'm not sure why I honored that convention, since on these foreign trips the demands on me far exceeded those on her, except that she is slightly older and a friend. Plus, she had owned the couch since the beginning of the administration, and I was a second-term late arrival. When I had no couch, I joined the other senior staff on the floor, each of us on a two-inch-thick, firm foam mat with pillow and blanket.

Inevitably, we arrived exhausted. The toughest trips for me were to Europe, because they were too short to enable me to complete my work and get anything close to enough sleep. Worse, we would usually leave early evening D.C. time and arrive in the wee hours of the morning to face a full day of meetings and a working dinner without any opportunity to do more than shower and, if lucky, exercise before the schedule began. Longer trips to Asia were better, because we usually landed at night and could get a full night's sleep after arrival, plus whatever we had snagged on the plane.

The trips themselves were intensely packed, as Obama would often complain, blaming me but to a far greater extent, Ben Rhodes, who planned most elements of the schedule beyond the obligatory official meetings and meals. Everywhere we went, the president would "meet and greet" U.S. embassy staff. He often sat down with private sector leaders and almost always with civil society activists to show U.S. support for democracy and human rights. Where possible, he held a town hall with selected young leaders from across the region. When time permitted, Obama liked to visit important historical or cultural sights like the Parthenon in Athens, the

Panama Canal, Bob Marley's house in Jamaica, the historic city of Luang Prabang in Laos, the impossibly tiny bones of Ethiopia's "Lucy"—believed to be the first humanoid—or World War II cemeteries in Belgium or the Philippines.

By day three, the president was almost always irritable. You could set your watches by the onset of his grumpy mood, due to a lack of sleep, jet lag, and his relentless schedule. By the fifth or sixth day of a long trip, as we could begin to see the light at the end of the tunnel, the president's mood usually lightened, and the trip home was like galloping back to the stables.

Despite the intensity, these trips had fun aspects. Ben, other senior staff, and I had a bounty of unscripted time with the president where we could joke, banter, or absorb his philosophical reflections, which he shared much more readily on long trips when we had a surplus of time in planes, helicopters, and automobiles. We enjoyed occasional drinks in his suite and regular meals prepared by his military valets, typically of salmon, chicken, or beef with broccoli and brown rice.

On the road, I was often asked to ride with President Obama in his limousine known as "the Beast." The large, armored car had two back-seats separated by a console with a secure phone and the presidential seal; these seats faced two other seats, allowing four people comfortably in the back, while two Secret Service agents manned the front. On these many car rides, I would sometimes brief him on important developments or late-breaking changes to the program, but more often we would talk about random subjects—our kids, politics, history, whatever he was reading, gossip from the staff's escapades the night before, or reflections from our youth. Just as often, we would sit quietly looking out the window, occasionally waving to people lining the streets, and absorbing the street scenes of Ho Chi Minh City, Kuala Lumpur, Panama City, Nairobi, or Havana. Obama would often play electronic scrabble, scour articles on his iPad, and frequently check his phone, while I read intelligence or paperwork and caught up on news and emails. Neither of us felt the need to fill the void; the silence between us was just as comfortable as conversation.

Occasionally, the trips got more interesting than planned.

When Nelson Mandela passed away in December 2013, President and

Mrs. Obama led the U.S. delegation to the memorial service in Johannesburg. The whole visit was something of a circus. The attendees constituted a who's who of global leaders, plus a massive U.S. congressional delegation, which flew on its own plane to South Africa, and the official U.S. party, which included two former presidents, George W. Bush and Bill Clinton, accompanied by Laura Bush and former secretary Hillary Clinton.

The Bushes, along with Hillary, flew seventeen hours with us to and from South Africa. The plane was unusually full, so most of the bigwigs shared the conference room during their waking hours. On the way down to South Africa, President George W. Bush (who turns out to be one of the funniest people I have ever met) regaled us with stories of his new passion as a painter and gave an iPad exhibition of his work, mostly colorful and commendable portraits of figures public and private. The rapport between the two Bushes and two Obamas is extremely friendly and relaxed, and with George Bush and Michelle Obama (who is also one of the funniest people I know) riffing off each other altogether unplugged, it made for a memorable flight.

Our time on the ground was less than twelve hours, just enough to get from the airport to the hotel (to shower and change) and then to the stadium, where Mandela's interminable memorial service was held in torrential rain. This brief stop in Johannesburg was a security nightmare. Rather than a normally smooth motorcade ride with streets blocked, police escort, and fast, unimpeded movement along the highways, we crawled in bumper-to-bumper traffic. The president's motorcade was stuck among cramped bush taxis, buses, and civilian cars. The drive into town was stressful, if ultimately uneventful for Secret Service, but it was only the beginning of a very long day.

While waiting hours at the hotel because the ceremony started late, we learned that the South African authorities had decided to let the massive crowds of citizens enter the stadium without the usual magnetic screening. In other words, Obama was going to be on stage in a football stadium with dozens of other heads of state surrounded by tens of thousands of people who could have been armed with anything, in a country known for having one of the highest crime rates in the world. Complicating matters, President Obama did not bring shirts or a suit that was sized to allow him to conceal a flak jacket underneath. The Secret Service wanted him to wear one; but having only a regularly sized suit in the clammy, humid rain, Obama demurred.

For several hours, the press focused on the sign language interpreter who mimed strangely behind Obama (and was later discovered to be a fraud), Obama's historic handshake with Cuban president Raúl Castro, the selfie taken by Helle Thorning-Schmidt, the very attractive blond prime minister of Denmark, of herself and the president laughing, and, to a far lesser extent, on Obama's truly moving tribute to Mandela. Meanwhile, those of us in the know worried that the president of the United States could be shot on the world's stage at Madiba's funeral.

Even though Africa was hardly the most dangerous place the president traveled, especially compared to Afghanistan or Iraq, it somehow accounted for a disproportionate share of our security-related stress. In July 2015, Obama visited Kenya for the first time as president. Predictably, the crowds were enormous, often pressing in on his motorcade as they densely lined the streets of Nairobi. The masses of people were uniformly friendly, but the enthusiastic crowds understandably concerned Secret Service. Once out of Kenya and on to Ethiopia, I assumed the collective blood pressure of the agents on the trip would drop precipitously.

So I was surprised to be summoned late in the evening to the Secret Service command post at the hotel just after I had returned to my room from the state dinner in Addis Ababa (still in my formal gown). I arrived to find the president's head of detail, several senior agents, and security officials from the U.S. embassy in Ethiopia all huddled in a secure tent talking anxiously. They reported that they had credible information that Al Shabab, a dangerous East African terrorist group, which had carried out successful attacks inside Ethiopia in the past, appeared to be planning to attack President Obama before he left the capital. Ethiopian security officials, who are both skilled and ruthless, claimed to have the plotters under surveillance and assured us that they had the threat in hand. Suffice it to say, these assurances did not assuage Secret Service (nor I, though I knew better how capable they were).

We talked through the information. I called back to Lisa Monaco in Washington to ensure that we were putting every effort into chasing down this plot and its alleged perpetrators. I also swiftly enlisted my old friend Gayle Smith, who was traveling with us in her role as a senior NSC staffer. Gayle knows Ethiopia as well as any (non-Ethiopian) American, so I grabbed her to work with me and the Secret Service late into the night, review their contingency plans, and ensure we were communicating with the Ethiopians at the highest level of government.

The plot was due to be executed the next day, reportedly, as the president's motorcade made its way from the African Union, where he was giving the final speech of his trip, to the airport. Only a very small handful of White House staff, in addition to Secret Service, knew about the plot. When the speech ended, the president was spirited into a holding room. Irritated and ready to go home, he kept asking what was delaying our departure for the airport. Anita Decker Breckenridge, his deputy chief of staff, and I explained that Secret Service was working through some security concerns related to a threat, and Gayle was trying to get the latest. The president waited, growing increasingly impatient.

I returned to Gayle, who was huddled in a closet-sized anteroom off the main hall of the new, Chinese-built African Union headquarters. With her were Ben Rhodes and Ethiopian prime minister Hailemariam Desalegn, whom we had flagged down right after the president's speech ended. "Mr. Prime Minister, we have a problem," I explained. "Our information indicates that the bad guy is still on the loose and is now positioned between here and the airport. Secret Service can't move the president until this is sorted out." Hailemariam took out his cell phone and called his chief of intelligence, Getachew Assefa. After a short conversation, he handed the phone to Gayle, who reiterated, "We have a real problem, here."

Getachew reassured her in half Tigrinya, half English, "Gayley, it's not a problem."

Gayle repeated, "No, it *is* a problem."

"Don't worry. There is not a problem."

Puzzled, Gayle explained that Secret Service can't rely on vague assurances that "there is no problem."

"No, it's not a problem," he said yet again.

Gayle said, "Do you know where he is?"

"Yes," Getachew replied. "He is with me. He is with me."

"Huh?" she said.

Getachew explained, "At the airport. I have him with me in the car."

"Okay. You've got him? Very good. Thanks." Gayle ended the call.

Images of a man stuffed in a trunk came to mind, but I didn't want to dwell on the details. After a Secret Service agent at the airport verified that the suspect was in custody, the president (still unaware) was hustled into the motorcade, and we sped to the airport. On the tarmac, we thanked the Ethiopian prime minister for his hospitality and the efficiency of his security forces. We took off on the steepest and most accelerated ascent I can recall on Air Force One (or on any military plane outside of a war zone).

Once airborne, Gayle, Anita, Ben, and I explained the whole story to the president, and we all had a good, if slightly nervous, laugh. Secret Service thanked me, and especially Gayle, for her critical assistance. There was no public evidence of the drama in Addis Ababa but perhaps some extra alcohol for the long ride home.

———

Foreign visits tended to be easier when the president was the host and the venue was the White House. There were some exceptions, such as the Chinese paranoia over protests targeting President Xi (which were in fact audible in the Rose Garden), the entitled Saudis, provocative Israeli prime minister Netanyahu, and the prickly Pakistanis. Generally, however, most foreign visits to the White House went according to our script.

State visits were a set-piece tradition, and Obama held thirteen during his presidency. Invitations were reserved for close partners or critical players, such as India, China, and our NATO or Asian allies. They followed a standard format beginning with a morning arrival ceremony on the South Lawn (notwithstanding sweltering heat or freezing cold) with full delegations on both sides ranging from the vice president and cabinet members to the mayor of Washington. This ceremony is one of my favorites, because of its unique pageantry, complete with a review of the troops, the military's fife and drum band in Revolutionary War costume playing "Yankee Doodle," and a twenty-one-gun salute.

Following the arrival ceremony, the president and visiting leader introduce each delegation to the other and then settle in for their intimate meeting in the Oval Office on more sensitive topics, often followed by an expanded meeting including more cabinet members and a broader set of issues in the Cabinet Room. Then there is the joint press conference in the Rose Garden or East Room, a luncheon hosted by the secretary of state in the ceremonial Benjamin Franklin Room on the top floor of the State Department and, later that evening, the state dinner.

Other rituals were equally obligatory but less fun. In particular, the White House Correspondents' Dinner was an annual root canal for cabinet officials and senior White House staff. On one level it is an important celebration of the free press and its crucial role in holding government accountable. At the same time, it is a pretentious mass gathering of the press, celebrities, current and former administration officials, members of Congress, and ambassadors, which traditionally featured a stand-up routine by a famous comedian that too often ended badly, and a carefully scripted, comedic speech by the president, which when Obama was in office was reliably funny as hell.

Nonetheless, the Correspondents' Dinner bequeathed me some of my least favorite memories. These included a night during which Charlie Rose, seated next to me, took every opportunity to put his hands all over my bare shoulders.

Worse, however, was at the next year's dinner, in 2015. During a break when people were mingling and moving around, I remained seated at my table. From behind me came a large and unexpected man. He summoned me from my chair. I looked for my husband, but Ian was engrossed in conversation some distance away and was oblivious to what was happening. Once I stood up, it was too late. It was Donald Trump who was looming. He surprised me by giving me an unsolicited hug.

Even though the hug was not too close, I was taken aback, given that I had never met him before. While holding me, Trump whispered in my ear that I had been "very unfairly treated" over Benghazi and was "doing a great job for the country." He then posed for a picture with his arm around me, in which we were both smiling too broadly, and left.

At the time, I was rattled and told White House correspondent April Ryan, who had snapped the photo of me and Trump, that I felt almost as if I had been molested. She asked if she could write that, and I said "please, no." Her blog post the next day skirted this characterization, reporting that she watched Trump "swarm" me "in an overly gregarious manner and hold a conversation. She [Rice] seemed shocked but said their conversation was pleasant and lasted several minutes."

I told my mother and family the story the next day, noting that I had not been this grossed out since the 2014 D-Day anniversary in Normandy when, in Obama's absence, Vladimir Putin puckered his lips and blew me a faux kiss while telling his colleague how good I looked, especially for a national security advisor.

I thought frequently during the 2016 campaign about making Trump's words public. He had accosted me just six weeks before he launched his presidential campaign, and I figured his praise of me would not sit well with Benghazi-crazed, Republican primary voters. Yet I resisted the urge, because I didn't want to be even a tangential part of another campaign-related story, however briefly.

Now, I kick myself.

19

Point Guard

My first meeting with the United States Secret Service came shortly be-fore I began as national security advisor. In a high-ceilinged, spacious transitional office in the Old Executive Office Building, I sat down with my lead-agent-to-be, Tim Lea, and the head of the president's protective detail, Robert Buster. They explained how their team would support me, shared a binder containing key information and protocols, and then asked me what I would like my call sign to be. This is the code name that the agents would use to identify me over radio and other communications and distinguish me from other protectees, each of whom has a unique moniker. In considering my answer, I knew I did not want to take on my predecessor's moniker, as is some-times customary. "Iron Hand" struck me as too hard. But I couldn't keep my Diplomatic Security call sign, which I quite liked but was reserved for the U.N. ambassador and passed down irrespective of the incumbent. So I asked if we could use "Point Guard," reflecting both the position I played in basketball and my view of the job I was about to begin. My request was granted.

The role of national security advisor is, in fact, much like that of point guard on a basketball team. Your job is to see the whole court, call the plays, execute the offense, pass to the big shooters, and lead the team to perform optimally as a unit. It's not the glory position. The point guard is rarely the showboat or high scorer (unless you're Steph Curry or Magic Johnson) but is essential to the cohesion and efficacy of the team. It's a position that requires strategic vision, leadership skills, effective ball-handling, and lots of selfless *assists. Point guard is the position I played in high school and at Oxford. Far from the best basketball player, I was still well-suited to the role.*

• ◆ •

As national security advisor, I aimed to help set up the plays we were running; dish the ball to the star players, like Secretary of State John Kerry, Secretary of Defense Ash Carter, Vice President Biden, and of course the president; and assist them to score. That's how I approached my responsibilities on major issues, ranging from Egypt, Snowden, and Syria, to Afghanistan, South Sudan, Ukraine, Ebola, Cuba, Iran, and the fight against ISIS. I provided similar assistance to the team who led our efforts to achieve the Paris Agreement on climate change and to Gayle Smith, who became USAID administrator, having crafted and implemented President Obama's signature development programs, including Power Africa, Feed the Future, and the Young Leaders initiatives in Africa, Southeast Asia, Latin America, and Europe.

In all our endeavors, whether we were responding to crises or advancing what I called the president's "affirmative agenda"—those opportunities we elected to embrace to effect positive change—my focus was to ensure that my senior colleagues had the support they needed, when they needed it. As a practical matter, that meant providing clear strategic direction through the Deputies' and Principals' decision-making process as well as prompt feedback and guidance from the president. When resources were a key constraint, I worked with the agencies and the Office of Management and Budget to help obtain what was required. If a cabinet official sought reinforcement from the White House, I would deliver the necessary letter or phone call from the vice president or president. To ensure that our negotiators met the president's expectations for success, I would provide my colleagues an unvarnished assessment as to whether what they had achieved was good enough, or they needed to do better.

I kept in close communication with my counterparts when they traveled, mainly through frequent calls and emails with members of the NSC staff who were embedded in our interagency teams or directly with John Kerry, to whom I spoke at all hours of the day and night when he was on the road. Kerry would call back frequently to provide updates and seek guidance, trying to assess if the outcome he was pursuing would pass muster. Sometimes, I would have to run the issue by the president, but mostly I had a strong sense of when a result would suffice, or when it would not, and gave it to John straight.

Kerry and I quickly developed a close and effective working relationship. John is dogged, relentless, and always willing to mount the hill ahead. He is a skilled and strong negotiator; still, to try to optimize the outcome, I sometimes encouraged him to go back into battle to gain a bit more. John might resist initially, explaining that he had gotten all that was possible and that a further push could upend the negotiation. We would parry back and forth, and then he invariably agreed to go back and try again. That is how Kerry eventually got Russian foreign minister Lavrov to accept that the 2013 U.N. resolution mandating the removal of Syria's chemical weapons must foreshadow sanctions or the use of force to punish Syria, if it reneged. It is also how John achieved the most elusive elements we needed in the Iran nuclear negotiation.

Literally, every time the president or I asked John Kerry to please go back and fight for more, whether on Syria, Iran, Afghanistan, or numerous other issues, he succeeded in obtaining a better outcome. *Every time.* Though I never confessed as much to John, I came to view this dynamic as almost a game. Even if what John had secured was not bad, I asked him to try for more, because I *knew* he could get it. Whatever the issue, whoever his interlocutor, I was confident he could take the outcome of the negotiation from minimally acceptable to exceptional, with more elbow grease, more cajoling, more pressure. And, he did.

John and I sometimes argued. He would often call at the start of the morning, with an update or creative proposal but occasionally with what I considered to be a half-baked idea. In those instances, I felt I had to serve as the wet blanket, a repetitive voice of tedious sobriety. On these mornings, John surely thought I was a major pain in his ass. But our relationship worked. We were a good team.

I admire John and supported him with those of our colleagues who occasionally worried that he seemed too hungry for a deal. John Kerry always strove to do his best and, despite being over seventy, he was fit, tireless, and never shied from the toughest assignments. Never did I hear John Kerry say "No, I will not" or "No, I cannot." I would not have traded him for another partner.

Most issues were not suited to be resolved solely between me, John, and even the president. They required the input and, preferably, the buy-in of the whole "interagency" team—those executive branch departments and agencies that play a significant role in national security affairs. Most matters have a diplomatic as well as military dimension and often an economic or law enforcement aspect. To make well-considered recommendations to the president on complex issues, the NSC needs to conduct a fair process in which every stakeholder has a voice and a vote.

In addition to the national security advisor and deputy NSA, the cast that makes up the NSC Principals Committee consists of the secretaries of state and defense, the director of national intelligence, CIA director, U.N. ambassador, chairman of the Joint Chiefs of Staff, White House chief of staff, often the attorney general and the secretary of the treasury, and sometimes the secretaries of commerce and homeland security, the USAID administrator, or the U.S. trade representative. The Principals Committee, which I chaired, was the vehicle through which we set policy, tracked implementation, and teed up decisions for the president. The Deputies Committee, consisting of the second-ranking officials at the key agencies, did the intense preparatory work of crafting and culling policy options, and usually joined the Principals as backbenchers as we wrestled with the issue at hand.

When President Obama convened the Principals for a National Security Council meeting, the sessions were always rigorous, and everybody was expected to be in top form, even if the subject was not their expertise. Having read every shred of paper carefully, he demonstrated an extraordinary grasp of detail and asked penetrating questions that generated new insights. The president wanted to hear the views of everyone at the table as well as the experts sitting along the walls. When satisfied that he had the necessary information, Obama carefully weighed but did not linger over tough decisions.

Obama's queries, taskings, and decision making had the effect of reminding all involved that, for better or worse, he was consistently the smartest guy in the room. Personally, I hated acknowledging that. But I knew the sooner I embraced this reality, the better prepared I would be.

At NSC meetings, I was always on guard, trying not to commit the sin Obama most criticized me for. Going back to my early days at the U.N., Obama occasionally gave me feedback aimed at helping me perform at the peak of my game. Consistently, his biggest complaint was: "You have no poker face! You can't reveal what you're thinking and feeling all the time."

My face unconsciously can speak volumes about what is running through my head. It is most problematic when I am irritated, angry, or thinking that what I am hearing is stupid. Obama stayed on my case about composing an impassive countenance (something he excelled at) and even hinted early on that he expected me to surmount this challenge, if I were named national security advisor. I did gradually improve, but I have never fully mastered the poker face.

The NSC and the Principals Committee met in the John F. Kennedy Conference Room in the White House Situation Room, the secure operations center in the White House basement that houses a twenty-four-hour watch. It places, receives, and transcribes presidential phone calls, provides alerts to staff, and connects national security personnel to one another across agencies and time zones. A wood-paneled conference room with the windows sealed and covered, JFK is the largest of three in the Situation Room, but still quite compact. With effort, we could fit twelve to fifteen people around the long oval wooden table.

As chair of the Principals Committee, I sat at the head of the table with NSC staff against the walls and my cabinet colleagues in assigned seats at the table, according to rough protocol order. If the secretaries of state and defense were each present (as opposed to their deputies), they would sit to my left and right, respectively, with others deliberately arrayed down the table. On the large video screen facing me was usually one or more principals participating remotely—often Samantha Power from New York, sometimes the VP or secretary of defense from aboard his plane, or Kerry from an embassy or makeshift secure tent in an obscure part of the world.

Knowing these meetings consumed a large quantity of the precious time of the most important policymakers in the world, I tried to ensure that they were well-prepared and well-executed. To start, I carefully reviewed and edited the papers written by NSC staff in advance of the meetings to make sure they were clear, comprehensive, and framed issues crisply for decision.

At the beginning of PC meetings, I sought to minimize posturing and lengthy intelligence presentations. I tried to walk the participants through the agenda in a linear fashion, aiming to elicit views, forge consensus or, failing that, clarify and encapsulate differences, so they could be represented precisely to the president. I also aimed, but too often failed, to start and end the meetings on schedule. My intent, that I hope to have met, was to leave participants with the sense that the issues and all perspectives had received a full airing.

Managing the PC is a tough challenge. The Principals, who are already leading large agencies, typically think they have better things to do than sit for up to two (or more) hours at the PC table. Yet, even when at USUN, I viewed effective participation in the decision-making process for the president as the Principals' most important responsibility. Everyone at the table is very tightly scheduled—with a foreign counterpart meeting, dinner to host, or plane to catch just after our meeting is set to end. Each principal also has a strong personality, healthy ego, and firm views.

During my tenure as NSA, the Obama principals mostly liked and respected each other, but not always and not every day. I didn't mind combat, either around me or involving me, but I tried to ensure the arguments didn't get too personal. Occasionally, the debate was barbed, and shots flew. Kerry and Defense Secretary Carter could get into it. Secretary Hagel might complain about the length and frequency of PCs or the granularity of the discussions. Brennan sometimes "got his Irish up." Power's presentations could veer into the heavy and high-minded. Clapper typically tried to offer some comic relief. Kerry sometimes delivered long, passionate arguments that left his colleagues more exhausted than moved. And, on rare occasions, Denis threw a curveball that upended the whole discussion.

I too could get impatient, even angry, with any or all of them and abruptly shift gears from a more open and collegial style to a more pointed and directive one. On occasion, if I sensed that one or more of my colleagues had failed to read the preparatory materials or was winging their commentary, I might uncharitably bombard them with a relentless interrogatory designed to elicit clarity in their position or reveal the weakness of their arguments. More often, I tried to employ humor to ease the tension or keep long meetings tolerable.

Most of the time, the Principals were able to reach consensus, and President Obama usually accepted their collective recommendation, but often only after pressure-testing their reasoning. At times, the Principals differed, and the debate would become robust. Starting from my childhood experiences at the family dinner table, I have always been comfortable with argument, even anger, so I did not shy from encouraging all to state their positions emphatically but respectfully. When the battle ended, it was my job to present the Principals' views fully and fairly to the president in a detailed memo without any "spin on the ball," and to close the memo with my own best recommendation as to how to proceed.

The range of issues with which the Principals Committee wrestled was broad and diverse, but certain matters, including Afghanistan and others I will highlight, consumed major shares of our time through the end of the administration.

———

I left the formal dinner incensed.

As we gathered back at the ambassador's residence to review what had just occurred, U.S. ambassador to Afghanistan Jim Cunningham and General Joseph Dunford, then our theater commander, seemed disheartened, even disgusted, but not shocked. They were accustomed to Afghan president Hamid Karzai being one of the most disagreeable leaders any of us had ever encountered.

In November 2013, I took my first solo trip after becoming NSA to Afghanistan. While I had visited Afghanistan as U.N. ambassador with the Security Council, this time I was there as President Obama's right hand to meet with U.S. forces, visit military outposts across the country, hear our ambassador's and commander's unvarnished assessments, and meet with Afghan officials.

Back home, the president would soon face critical decisions about the scope and scale of our post-2014 presence, the date after which the U.S. and NATO combat mission was set to end. Most urgently, we were also trying to obtain Karzai's signature on a Bilateral Security Agreement (BSA), which would govern the terms of America's military role after 2014. Without the BSA, U.S. forces would not have adequate legal protections and could not continue eradicating foreign terrorists or training and assisting the Afghan

Security Forces to fight the Taliban, which remained a serious threat to the Kabul government. Four billion dollars in annual international assistance to Afghanistan (from the U.S. and NATO partners) also depended on finalizing the BSA.

After painstaking negotiations and repeated brinkmanship, Karzai had finally agreed with Kerry on the text of the BSA. The Loya Jirga, a traditional Afghan decision-making conference, had just overwhelmingly approved the deal. So we expected the document would soon be signed.

My two-hour meeting with Karzai concluded with a small dinner at his residence. There, Karzai ruined what had been a relatively cordial discussion by suddenly insisting on new, capricious, and unachievable preconditions for signing the BSA. Worse, he broke into a typical but never tolerable rant about the alleged sins of the United States and the perfidy of U.S. forces.

Karzai plainly hated the U.S., and increasingly many of us (myself included) reviled his vitriolic nationalism, incorrigibly corrupt governance, and pompous leadership style. Above all, we resented his frequent disparagement of American servicemen and -women, including those who had died on Afghan soil. That night, Karzai accused U.S. forces of committing a litany of crimes . . . *busting into Afghan homes at night and terrorizing civilians for no reason . . . killing innocent Afghans indiscriminately . . . harboring a secret ambition to dismember the country.*

Despite U.S. and Afghan forces having fought the Taliban for over a dozen years to protect the Kabul government, Karzai even said he would happily accept a Taliban-led Afghan government, if that ensured a unified state. After several minutes of his bile, I couldn't take any more. Calmly, I told Karzai that I found his ingratitude for the service of American forces totally unacceptable: *Thousands of young Americans have made the ultimate sacrifice to enable Afghans to live in greater security and to build this fragile nation. American taxpayers have given Afghanistan tens of billions of dollars. Your denigration of our forces, the American people, and our leaders is deeply offensive. The Afghan people want us to stay. If you refuse to sign the BSA, you will find out what it is like for Afghans to have to fend entirely for themselves.*

Without a BSA, I warned, the U.S. and NATO will have no choice but to plan to withdraw all forces by the end of 2014. Karzai risked throwing his country's security down the drain. Thankfully, thereafter, the dinner ended swiftly and civilly, but I left convinced that Karzai aimed to force a U.S. withdrawal. On one level, I was disgusted and dismayed by his behavior, but on another I felt satisfied that he deserved what he would get, if America withdrew. The problem was: the people of Afghanistan did not.

Karzai ultimately refused to sign the BSA. It was only concluded after he left office and was replaced as president, in September 2014, by the far more sober, responsible, and gracious Ashraf Ghani.

After a run-off and U.N. vote audit, Ghani was deemed the winner of a close and bitterly disputed election against his rival Abdullah Abdullah. Questions over the legitimacy of Ghani's victory and the real risk of the country dividing along ethnic lines meant that a compromise was needed, however difficult and unpalatable. John Kerry, along with NSC senior director Jeff Eggers, a steady, experienced Navy SEAL and counterterrorism expert who saw combat in Iraq, patiently devoted many long days to trying to broker a solution that avoided new elections (which were neither feasible nor affordable), while enabling a new government to be formed and the BSA to be signed. President Obama spent hours on the phone talking repeatedly to both Ghani and Abdullah, finally getting them to agree to form a unity government, in which Abdullah served as chief executive under Ghani's presidency. It was a jury-rigged concept that neither liked but both reluctantly accepted.

Back in Washington, I stayed in close touch with Eggers and Kerry—offering guidance and ideas on the way forward, ensuring that the president utilized the background and core messages they had provided, and obtaining time on the president's schedule to make the series of calls to Ghani and Abdullah. Previously, during the negotiation over the BSA, my job had been to keep State and DOD on the same page, as both had critical interests at stake, and to backstop our negotiators as they wrangled with their Afghan counterparts.

Throughout this period, we faced another enduring challenge: how to gain the release of Americans taken hostage in Afghanistan. Sergeant Bowe Bergdahl had been captured and held as a prisoner of war by the Haqqani faction of the Taliban for almost five years, after walking away from his outpost under murky circumstances. It is the American creed not to leave a soldier on the battlefield, and Bergdahl, whatever his motives and mental disposition, was an American serviceman and POW.

After lengthy mediation through Qatar, in June 2014 we secured Bergdahl's release in exchange for the transfer to Qatar of five Taliban detainees held at Guantánamo Bay. As we anticipated, the trade sparked immediate Republican-stoked controversy. They questioned whether Bergdahl was worthy of the effort, having been accused by fellow soldiers of desertion. They proclaimed that the price paid was too high, that we wrongly negotiated with terrorists, and suggested that the administration inappropriately skirted the requirement to give Congress thirty days advance notice of transfers from Guantánamo. The furor was further fueled by announcing Bergdahl's release in a Rose Garden press event with the president flanked by Bergdahl's parents.

Then I made matters worse the next day on the ABC News Sunday show. Most of the interview went off unremarkably, until the end. In an effort to insist that Bergdahl was worthy of our efforts (which I still very much believe), and that any American who volunteers to serve in uniform deserves our gratitude and respect, I spoke unartfully and off-the-cuff. Responding to a question about the circumstances of Bergdahl's disappearance, I said, "He served the United States with honor and distinction. And we'll have the opportunity eventually to learn what has transpired in the past years."

As soon as we left the studio, my press aide said, "I think you will get hit for saying he served 'with honor and distinction.'" At first, I didn't take his point. I meant that Bergdahl's service shouldn't be denigrated (particularly at this moment) without a full investigation into why he left his base and whether he committed any crime or misdeed. In other words: innocent until proven guilty. Yet many had concluded already that he was a villain; and I had praised him excessively. Despite my benign intentions and that it is ingrained in me to show respect for all of our men and women in uniform, I misspoke. I wish I could take those words back and revise them. Instead, my mistake remains an exhibit in the right wing's bill of indictment against me as a "liar."

For the duration of the administration, from 2014 to 2016, we spent countless hours in the Situation Room debating the future size, role, and disposition of the U.S. and NATO military presence in Afghanistan. Originally, President Obama wanted to draw down U.S. forces to the minimum necessary in Kabul by the end of his term—enough to continue training Afghans at the ministry level, protect the U.S. embassy, and target foreign terrorists who threatened the U.S.

Our military has always resisted significant reductions in Afghanistan, arguing (every year for eighteen years) that more time and more troops are needed to build the Afghans' capacity to fight the Taliban effectively without us. The Intelligence Community and DOD consistently (and sometimes bitterly) diverged over the likelihood of ever reaching that point, with the Intelligence Community maintaining that we faced an eroding stalemate that gradually favored the Taliban, and DOD asserting that, with more U.S. support, the Afghan Security Forces could ultimately turn the corner.

In my view, the Intelligence Community and Vice President Biden (who from 2009 argued for only fighting foreign terrorists like Al Qaeda and not the indigenous Taliban) have proved more correct than DOD. I have long tended to favor a posture that would enable us to sustain counterterrorism efforts without perpetually propping up the Kabul government, which remains poor, weak, and ineffectual—unlikely to defeat or even hold back the Taliban without a continued, significant U.S. troop presence. Yet, risking the Afghan government's collapse, after years of U.S. sacrifice, is hard to contemplate. That is why, for years, we tried to pursue Afghan-led peace talks with the Taliban. Not surprisingly, given the Taliban's intransigence, the talks had yielded little progress.

Ultimately, President Obama heeded the pleas of most of his Principals, from Ghani and Abdullah, and from NATO leaders (especially Angela Merkel), to leave close to ten thousand U.S. troops in Afghanistan. President Obama also decided to give DOD more latitude to assist the Afghans with air and other tactical support without reengaging directly in fighting the Taliban.

Thus far, the Kabul government continues to hang on; the threats from Al Qaeda and the "Islamic State" emanating from Afghanistan and Pakistan endure even if they have been substantially diminished. President Trump approved a 50 percent increase in U.S. forces in 2017 (from roughly ten thousand to fifteen thousand), but the Taliban remains strong and increasingly threatens major population centers. Reversing course the next year, against the advice of his cabinet, Trump threatened unilaterally to halve the U.S. troop presence. It remains unclear for how long and with what mission a significant number of U.S. troops will stay in Afghanistan. Whatever reductions we make need to be careful, gradual, and conducted in close consultation with our allies and the Afghan government. At a significant cost, the U.S. could sustain indefinitely our presence in Afghanistan at current troop levels, which for the foreseeable future should suffice to prevent the Taliban from taking Kabul or other big cities. Yet, in doing so, we risk continually failing to wean the Afghan Security Forces off of critical U.S. and NATO support. Nearly twenty years after 9/11, I believe we need a rational and measured exit strategy from Afghanistan that preserves the political and security gains enjoyed by the Afghan people, particularly its women, and that limits our enduring commitment to preventing the resurgence of foreign terrorist organizations that directly threaten the United States.

———

South Sudan's corrupt and venal leaders never fail to disappoint.

In 2013, South Sudanese president Salva Kiir and his then–vice president, Riek Machar, were the Grinches who stole Christmas. A shootout in December between their respective security details escalated into a full-blown civil conflict with tribal overtones. Kiir accused Machar of attempting a coup, as Machar mustered a breakaway rebel group that aimed to replace the existing government. John Kerry spent hours on the phone trying to mediate between Machar and Kiir. I taped a message appealing to the people of South Sudan to unify to save their nascent country and also tried to talk sense into Kiir. As ever, they both were selfish and dismissive of the interests of their own people.

Street battles enveloped the capital, Juba, forcing aid workers and foreign embassies, including our own, to withdraw most personnel. The U.S. embassy, the largest and the anchor of the international community in South Sudan, was threatened by violent factions on both sides. President Obama ordered forty-five U.S. servicemen into Juba to protect and reinforce the embassy. He was prepared, if necessary, to close the embassy and withdraw all personnel, but this was an outcome we wished to avoid. If and when the U.S. were to leave South Sudan, we knew every other foreign government was likely to follow suit. Even the viability of the beleaguered U.N. peacekeeping mission would be in doubt. Without the U.S., South Sudan doesn't have a chance.

As clashes diminished in Juba, heavy fighting broke out in the north between the South Sudanese army, an undisciplined and abusive force, and Machar's equally nasty rebels. U.S. citizens, including dual nationals, were scattered around the country. To rescue stranded Americans, President Obama ordered U.S. military helicopters to fly north to Bor. As they descended, one Osprey helicopter was hit by ground fire, wounding four U.S. military personnel just days before Christmas and causing the mission to be aborted.

Fighting persisted, and the threat to U.S. personnel intensified to the extent that I had no choice but to convene the Principals every day from December 21 through December 27, 2013, including remotely on Christmas Day. That holiday summons made me especially unpopular with my colleagues and staff, but the American president has no higher priority than the safety and security of American citizens. We could not and would not risk leaving Americans in proximate danger—especially barely a year after Benghazi.

Neighboring Uganda intervened militarily to buttress Kiir's government, bringing needed security to the capital and helping the U.S. embassy and other foreign missions to remain operational. We got through the holidays with no more U.S. casualties.

Ongoing U.S. and regional diplomacy served to calm but not resolve the fundamental conflict. Neither an augmented U.N. force, regional leaders' negotiating efforts, the suspension of U.S. military assistance, nor President Obama's own personal involvement sufficed to persuade Kiir and Machar to resolve their differences in any lasting way.

To put muscle behind our diplomacy, the U.S. led the Security Council in imposing sanctions on individuals blocking peace efforts in 2015. We also threatened additional measures, including an arms embargo on South Sudan. But in a twist of irony, Russia and China, which historically had little interest in South Sudan and always favored Khartoum over Juba, became active protectors of Kiir's government at the U.N. As we sought to increase pressure on the South Sudanese government, they resisted any additional sanctions.

Inside the Obama administration, we differed over whether and when to impose an arms embargo. Samantha Power and John Kerry favored doing so earlier on. I didn't, reminding all that an arms embargo, which is always applied territorially, punishes one side disproportionately in a civil conflict (the government) and doesn't prevent rebels from acquiring weapons via neighboring countries where they take refuge. I also believed that once we imposed an arms embargo, we would lose any remaining leverage on the government. Those were rational arguments, but I was wrong to believe that, by husbanding our leverage, we could move Kiir's government to mitigate its behavior and accept a negotiated solution. Perhaps out of personal history, unrealistic hopes for the people of South Sudan, and an overestimation of U.S. influence, I was too slow to conclude that neither side had the will to end the conflict nor agree to a unity government.

It was not until 2016, when the specter of genocide appeared on the horizon, that I finally concluded we had to drop the hammer on South Sudan's hopeless leaders. It had been almost seventeen years since I first visited that often forgotten country. For so long, I had hoped that the people of South Sudan might at last enjoy the freedom and security they had long been denied. It pained me enormously to concede defeat of such a righteous dream as self-determination. But South Sudan's brutal leaders would not allow it to be fulfilled. That belated realization freed me to endorse the U.S. push in the Security Council for an arms embargo, which repeatedly failed to muster enough favorable votes. Only in July 2018, five years after the start of the civil war, did a U.S.-sponsored resolution to impose an arms embargo eventually gain the bare minimum number of votes to be adopted by the Security Council.

Despite yet another ceasefire agreement between Kiir and Machar, signed in September 2018, as of this writing, lasting peace and national unity remain elusive. Tribal and factional divisions within South Sudan persist, and hundreds of thousands of innocent South Sudanese have been displaced, raped, starved, and killed over the course of this continuing conflict. To date, South Sudan remains a stillborn state. Few things sadden me more, having put my heart and soul into such a worthy cause for so long.

———

There is no such thing as a short phone call with Vladimir Putin.

In the almost three years following Russia's illegal annexation of Crimea in March 2014 and its invasion of Eastern Ukraine, President Obama and the Russian president spoke over a dozen times by secure phone. A typical phone call lasted ninety minutes, prolonged by Putin's tedious monologues and the necessity of translation. The conversations typically began with a comical game of chicken, in which each side's communications staff tried to ensure their leader was last on the line. It was a game that Obama found ironic but not important, and he would simply busy himself with desk work or Scrabble on his iPad if Putin was slow to come to the phone.

Staffing presidential phone calls was a frequent responsibility. My team and I prepared a detailed briefing memo with background and recommended talking points. Prior to the call, the NSC experts (usually the relevant regional senior director and director) would join me in the Oval to provide the president any last-minute update or answer any questions he had after reading his memo. The team would stay with us in the Oval Office for the duration of the call, taking notes and scribbling down any additional arguments to hand to the president as the call progressed. An NSC staffer from the executive secretary's office, which handles administrative functions, oversaw the logistics from the Oval—communicating with the Situation Room downstairs, relaying when the president was ready to take the call, and ensuring that the translator at a remote location was ready to go.

"Introducing President Obama," the White House Situation Room announced. Obama picked up the secure phone on the Resolute Desk. My staff and I sat on the parallel couches or sometimes on the floor near the phone, if the other side of the conversation was hard to hear. "Hello, Vladimir," Obama began. Putin responded, "Hello, Barack, how are you?" Their conversations, while sometimes pointed and often unsatisfactory in substance, were always civil and mostly respectful.

Despite the number of times the two engaged, they were unable to resolve our stark differences over Ukraine. The crisis derived from Russia's enduring fear that Ukraine wanted to join the European Union and NATO, thus leaving the Kremlin's orbit. In November 2013, Russian pressure led the Moscow-backed government of Ukrainian President Viktor Yanukovych to back out of free trade and political agreements with the European Union. This decision sparked popular protests in Kiev against Yanukovych. The demonstrations were relentless, despite violent police repression, and culminated in February 2014 with Yanukovych fleeing the country. Russia angrily denounced his departure as a Western-backed "coup" and used it as an excuse to annex Crimea illegally, a strategic Ukrainian peninsula with historic ties to Russia.

Then, Russia massed troops on Ukraine's eastern border, threatening for months to invade, before eventually moving forces across their common border. Russia's invasion, which blatantly violated Ukraine's sovereignty as well as international law, spurred the U.S. and Europe to impose increasingly harsh, coordinated sanctions on Putin officials, crony oligarchs, Russian banks, and defense and energy entities.

President Obama spent untold hours on the phone and on videoconferences rallying our partners in the G7 and European Union to ratchet up economic sanctions on Russia. Our aim was not just to punish Russia for its actions but to pressure it to withdraw its military from Ukraine and restore its sovereign border. President Obama coordinated closely with France, Germany, Italy, and the U.K., to expel Russia from the G8 and to bolster NATO's military presence and readiness in Eastern Europe. After Russian-backed Ukrainian rebels shot down a Malaysian passenger airliner over Eastern Ukraine in July 2014, killing 298 innocents, Obama led the Europeans to crank up sanctions on Russia to near crippling levels.

At the same time, the president was careful to leave the door open to Russia. He continued his fraught communications with Putin, seeking to point him to an "off-ramp," and actively supported the diplomatic processes led by German chancellor Merkel and French president Hollande. Merkel and Hollande initiated a dialogue with Putin on the margins of the seventieth anniversary of D-Day in June 2014, which continued through the duration of the Obama administration with the elusive aim of achieving the withdrawal of Russian forces and restoration of Ukraine's control over its east.

My role was to support the president in his diplomacy by working with my national security advisor counterparts, especially the Germans and French, to prepare for and implement the decisions of our leaders. I also led the Principals Committee, aided invaluably by my deputies Tony Blinken and then Avril Haines—who both ran a relentless Deputies Committee process that enabled the Principals to propose to the president: the contours of successive sanctions packages designed to maximize pressure while keeping EU partners on board; increased U.S. military assistance to Ukraine; and billions in U.S. and IMF economic support to help stabilize the Ukrainian economy. We also recommended the establishment of the multibillion-dollar European Reassurance Initiative that ensured NATO countries maintained a rotating, continuous presence of forces and stockpiled equipment in Poland and the Baltics to deter future Russian aggression.

At Obama's behest, Vice President Biden took on primary responsibility for dialogue with Ukraine's leaders, investing large amounts of time in direct diplomacy. Assistant Secretary of State for European Affairs Victoria Nuland and NSC senior director Charles Kupchan spearheaded day-to-day U.S. efforts to support the diplomatic process, including through close coordination with their German, French, and Ukrainian counterparts and a painful series of meetings with key Putin advisors.

Biting sanctions worked to limit the extent of Russia's annexation of Ukraine. Yet, to date, no country, neither Germany, France, nor the U.S., has been able to move Putin to resolve the Ukraine crisis. Putin, for his part, has never forgiven the U.S. and Europe for imposing tough sanctions, which ultimately failed to force Russia to return what it stole from Ukraine. Appropriately, at the end of the day, the West would not resort to military power to reverse Russian aggression in Ukraine, since it is not a NATO member. To compound the challenge, President Trump has sent mixed messages by at once agreeing to provide lethal weapons to Ukraine and also hinting that he may be willing to accept Russia's illegal annexation of Crimea. Five years after Russia's initial aggression, fighting persists in Ukraine's east, sanctions remain in effect, diplomacy is dormant, and

Moscow has stepped up its pressure on Kiev and retains effective control over a sizable, stolen portion of Ukraine.

———

I couldn't stop staring at the hockey stick. It blew my mind.

Tom Frieden, director of the U.S. Centers for Disease Control and Prevention (CDC), passed a chart around the Situation Room table projecting the trajectory of the West African Ebola epidemic. It was late August 2014, and the line on the chart that resembled a hockey stick predicted that by the end of 2014, there could be *as many as 1.4 million people* in Guinea, Liberia, and Sierra Leone infected with this deadly disease that causes victims to bleed out of their orifices.

Knowing West Africa well and its extreme vulnerability to the rapid spread of disease, I was terrified by the implications of a potential Ebola pandemic on that scale. It could spread across the globe and kill hundreds of thousands, potentially millions, while sinking West Africa and much of the rest of the African continent under the weight of economic collapse, conflict, and massive refugee flows. The global economic implications were also mind-boggling—a halt to much international air travel and commerce, quarantines of whole regions, panic, and a Hobbesian inferno where no man helped another out of fear.

That chart shook up the Principals Committee like nothing I have seen before or since. Up until then, we had been scaling up civilian-led efforts to curb the epidemic as rapidly as possible. CDC and USAID had deployed teams to West Africa. Doctors Without Borders and other NGOs were on the ground. The World Health Organization had botched the initial response but finally seemed to grasp the gravity of the situation. None of it was enough. We had to do more.

For almost two months, the president had been pressing us hard to get the epidemic under control, to treat this as a national security crisis. If the United States did not lead, no one would. Despite our efforts, the virus was far outpacing our capacity to respond quickly enough. Despairing, late one night, my old friend Gayle Smith called me from Washington. She was leading the NSC's Ebola response effort, and I was in Wales with Obama at the NATO Summit. We talked through all that we were doing and where the gaps were. There weren't enough beds for the sick, not enough protective gear for health workers, not enough quality hospitals to treat medical workers who fell ill. It was a race to evade a tsunami, and we were losing.

I asked her what she thought we could do to try to get ahead of the curve. Gayle reported that our interagency team, led by CDC and USAID, would take one more look at whether they could further scale up the civilian response fast enough, but she doubted it. As we talked, I realized there was one option we hadn't yet discussed: utilizing the unmatched capacity of the U.S. military. They could bend the curve.

Recalling the Southern African floods we worked on together in 2000, I said, "What about deploying the U.S. military like we did during the Mozambique catastrophe and for other natural disasters?"

Gayle paused. "Do you think that's even an option?"

"You think it would make a major difference, don't you?" I asked.

"Hell, yes. No one can do it better or faster than the U.S. military."

"Okay, if you determine that the civilian side can't cut it, I'll see what we can do."

The president was open to using the military and told me to work it through the Principals Committee. It was a delicate proposition. No one could recall deploying the U.S. military to confront a disease. We would be sending U.S. servicemen and -women into a hot zone an ocean away. How would we handle the risks to them and, later, to Americans when our service members returned to the continental United States?

DOD swiftly quashed any notion of U.S. medics treating victims, which I understood, and was skeptical about where U.S. troops could add value. Yet, to his great credit, Joint Chiefs chairman General Dempsey decided to find a way to get to yes, rather than marshal a plethora of excuses to avoid action, as the Pentagon is adept at doing when it wants to avoid an unwelcome tasking. Dempsey went to work figuring out how we could bring uniquely American capabilities to bear to serve as a "force multiplier" for a stepped-up international response without the U.S. serving as "the pointy end of the spear."

The next day, General Dempsey came back with a proposal. The U.S. could airlift personnel and supplies to West Africa, establish a logistics staging area in Senegal, and stand up a military command center for the region in Monrovia, Liberia. U.S. military personnel could refurbish Roberts-field airport in Monrovia, distribute supplies, set up diagnostic labs, safely medevac Americans who fell ill in West Africa, and build Ebola Treatment Units (ETUs) across Liberia where the ill could be quarantined and safely treated. The military could also build a medical unit at the airport in Liberia, which would be staffed by the U.S. Public Health Service and serve volunteer health care workers from around the world. This facility was key to convincing volunteers to deploy, giving them confidence that they would receive quality medical treatment if they fell ill in the line of duty. In sum, the U.S. could lead the charge and use our commitment to galvanize others to contribute.

It was a gutsy move by Dempsey, and the president swiftly endorsed DOD's plan to deploy almost three thousand U.S. servicemen to save lives and help contain the epidemic before it became a global menace. Within three days, the U.S. commander of Operation United Assistance was on the ground in West Africa.

From there, my responsibility was to ensure we pressured every possible international contributor to do their part. President Obama, many members of the cabinet, and I made scores of calls to incredulous counterparts. "You want us to do what?" was a common refrain. President Obama convened a high-level session at the 2014 General Assembly with U.N. Secretary-General Ban Ki-moon. Few foreign leaders immediately grasped the gravity of the epidemic, the risk it posed beyond West Africa, and the urgency we attached to their contributions. We had to explain the hockey stick and its implications.

The whole of the U.S. government shamed, bludgeoned, and begged countries to join us. We got Britain to take charge in Sierra Leone and build ETUs and labs. The French did the same in Guinea. Japan provided protective gear and money. Germany contributed money and treatment expertise. Canada offered money and French-speaking health workers. China provided money and supplies. Above all, ten thousand volunteer health care workers came from across Africa to risk their lives to save others. In this way, we mustered a major global response that would eventually contain the disease to three countries in West Africa, causing the infection curve to flatten and eventually bend downward.

While we began to gain traction internationally, at home in the U.S. things were getting truly crazy. In late September, a Liberian visitor to Texas fell ill with Ebola, and the hospital in Dallas was unprepared to respond. He died. His contacts in Dallas were placed under quarantine and monitoring. Two nurses at the hospital that treated him contracted the disease, and one traveled by plane with a fever, prompting worry that other passengers might be at risk. Thankfully, both survived.

But not before Americans started panicking. Ebola is relatively hard to transmit. It's not like the flu, which you can easily get from airborne particles or a cough. To contract Ebola, you need to exchange bodily fluids with someone infected—blood, vomit, semen, saliva, sweat. In a hospital setting, at home caring for a victim, or burying a body, it is highly transmissible. Otherwise, it is not so easy to contract. Facts aside, Americans' fear was potent and palpable, if not always rational.

Domestic hysteria continued to mount in the media and across Washington. Certain governors refused to allow planes from Africa to disembark. Some members of Congress demanded that the Department of Homeland Security seal the border and threatened legislation to prevent anyone (American or African) from entering the country from West Africa. This was a particularly reckless idea, which would have deterred volunteers from helping stamp out the epidemic and effectively imposed an economic embargo on the already reeling region.

Meanwhile, the Islamic State in Iraq and Syria was beheading Westerners. Russia was chewing huge bites out of its neighbors' territory. And now this terrifying, hemorrhagic disease had touched down on American soil. We were in the eye of a storm.

Against this backdrop, President Obama wrestled with how to secure the American people against Ebola, while relying on facts, not fear. The U.S. domestic response started flat-footed. President Obama fumed privately that, "Our shit is not tight" (one of his more common refrains when he felt things were not well under control). For a spell, he seemed to be losing confidence in CDC director Frieden and perhaps others' ability to communicate with the public and manage the risks that Ebola posed here in the United States. Yet I also sensed the president was reluctant to change generals in the middle of battle.

Homeland Security Secretary Jeh Johnson and some others were leaning toward recommending that we stop issuing new visas to nationals from
the three affected countries and suspend existing visas. In a private discussion in the Oval with the president, Gayle and I argued strenuously against
curtailing visas. CDC said it wouldn't work. Only a third of travelers from
these West African countries were visa holders. The majority were Americans or permanent residents whom we could not keep out without raising
serious legal questions. Curtailing visas would encourage undetected, illegal entry, such as overland from Canada. It would serve as a sop to racially
stoked fears. It would stigmatize nationals from Liberia, Guinea, and Sierra
Leone already living in the U.S. It would sound the economic death knell
for West Africa, as other Western countries would follow suit, and the region would be cut off from the rest of the world. "There are better ways to
secure our citizens without using a nuclear weapon against a conventional
enemy," I pointed out, emphatically.

As the discussion ended, I wasn't sure where the president was going.
I worried that he and I might face a reckoning, if we found we had irreconcilable differences on an issue about which I felt so strongly. For the
first and only time in my tenure as NSA, I concluded privately, without
ever telling him, that if he decided to effectively close the border I would
have to resign. I never said so aloud. I wasn't interested in threats but the
consequences of our actions. I know Obama well enough to know that my
saying so would not have helped. Ever rational, the president relied on science and logic. Ultimately, despite the countervailing pressure, he made
the tough decision. The right decision.

Still, the challenge was: how best to protect Americans? In mid-October,
President Obama appointed Ron Klain—former chief of staff to Vice Presidents Gore and Biden and an experienced Washington fixer—as Ebola
Czar. Ron drew staff from the NSC and elsewhere to establish a White
House–based Ebola Task Force. Gayle remained a key player, as did Lisa
Monaco, Denis McDonough, and I, but Ron took on day-to-day leadership of the crisis and did a phenomenal job. His arrival enabled us to go
back to juggling multiple global crises simultaneously, rather than being
consumed by this enormous challenge.

To ensure Americans' safety without upending transatlantic travel, we continued having health care workers screen airport passengers for fever before all departures from West Africa. If those flying showed any symptoms, they could not travel abroad. In addition, inside the U.S., the CDC and Homeland Security officials devised a system where we funneled all passengers from the three Ebola-affected countries through five designated U.S. airports. Arrivals were medically screened before being admitted into the U.S. and then monitored daily by CDC for twenty-one days (the incubation period for Ebola). Hospitals across the country were trained and equipped to detect, test, safely isolate Ebola patients, and transfer them, if infected, to three specialized treatment centers across the country. As CDC and other agencies tightened up their "shit," Obama's ire abated.

It worked. Fear diminished.

In West Africa, the disease ultimately killed over 11,300 people and infected more than 28,500—too many, but far fewer than could have been the case. Over many months, new infections eventually fell to zero. Congress appropriated $5.4 billion in emergency funds to bolster our domestic and international health infrastructure. The U.S. border remained open. No U.S. troops fell gravely ill. CDC, USAID, and the U.S. Public Health Service Corps saved tens of thousands of lives. The National Institutes of Health invested in finding effective vaccines for Ebola (one of which demonstrated its efficacy in Congo in 2018). We revolutionized the readiness of our domestic health system to treat Ebola safely.

U.S. private donors, NGOs, and philanthropies made critical contributions. Our allies pulled their weight. (With the unusual exception of Australia, which tried to screen out any arriving passenger who had traveled recently to *any* of fifty-four African countries. When the U.S. delegation headed by President Obama landed in Australia in November for the G20 Summit, we refused to fill out their entry questionnaire, because it was so stupid and offensive.)

Over eleven thousand lives is a lot to lose. The death toll would have been exponentially higher had the U.S. not rallied the world once it became clear that this was no isolated Ebola hot spot but a fast-moving, potentially global epidemic that the World Health Organization and United Nations were unprepared to confront. By galvanizing the world to confront and contain a threat to us all, as only America can, we avoided the hockey stick scenario and demonstrated the power of U.S. global leadership at its best.

Months earlier, in February 2014, the Obama administration had launched the Global Health Security Agenda to encourage wealthier countries to help developing countries build their capacity to prevent, detect, contain, and treat deadly infectious diseases. Now this critically important initiative had real money from Congress and international impetus behind it. With air travel, deforestation, climate change, and humans' increased proximity to wildlife due to population growth, disease today can spread far more rapidly than at any time in human history. Experts agree that the resurgence of some form of global pandemic disease, whether Zika, Ebola, avian flu, or SARS, is all but inevitable. As national security advisor, this was (and remains) among my biggest fears. The loss of life, economic devastation, and the potential to spark armed conflict that would accompany a global pandemic—even one on half the (population-adjusted) scale of the 1918 Spanish Flu, which killed 3 to 5 percent of the world's population—overshadow many of the worst-case scenarios I was compelled to contemplate short of nuclear war.

———

It makes no sense that we have been stuck in the same situation all of my life. We have gotten nowhere. It's time for a change.

This was a snippet of private conversation, in which President Obama lamented the failure of U.S. policy toward Cuba over the last fifty-plus years. As we talked during a car ride late in his first term, I wholeheartedly agreed. Implied, but not stated, however, was that there would be no testing of the potential for change unless Obama won a second term.

Having tucked this insight away, after I became his second-term national security advisor, I hoped that we would get a chance to revisit America's bankrupt Cuba policy. Decades of diplomatic deep freeze with no formal relations and a legislatively mandated economic embargo had not ousted the Castros or meaningfully improved the human rights and living conditions of the Cuban people. Rather, the U.S. was reviled by much of Latin America as a Goliath trying in vain to squeeze the life out of a Davidian Cuba. Our dated Cuba policy was a ball and chain dragging down our broader efforts to strengthen U.S. ties to Latin America and the Caribbean and to bolster the wave of democratic progress that had washed over large swaths of the region.

Trying to change Cuba policy was a third rail of American politics. Even as the influence of Florida's aging, hard-line Cuban American community was starting to wane, and farm state representatives were eager to open the Cuban market to U.S. agriculture, many in Congress remained powerful and intimidating protectors of the status quo. Going against old-school Miami and the State Department's Western Hemisphere Bureau, which historically was a minefield of Cuba hard-liners, was a huge risk. If we failed, we'd look like fools. If we were exposed before negotiations were complete, the backlash in Congress would undermine the president's legislative agenda on multiple fronts. As a result, if we were going to explore the potential for any opening with Cuba, it would have to be done in absolute secrecy.

Early in 2013, President Obama assigned Ben Rhodes the task of negotiating with Cuba. It was a stealth pick—someone close to the president within the White House, who could move around with lower visibility than others, and whose communications role did not arouse suspicion of him serving as a special envoy. When I arrived midyear as national security advisor, Ben and Ricardo Zuniga, our extremely talented NSC senior director for the Western Hemisphere, had already held a preliminary meeting with the Cuban side. Cuban president Raúl Castro, who had taken over power from his ailing brother Fidel, assigned his son Alejandro, a military officer and trusted emissary, and Fidel's prized translator, Juana Vera, as their Cuban counterparts. The Canadian government agreed to facilitate quiet meetings in discreet locations near Ottawa and Toronto to enable the two delegations to come and go without detection.

Initially, apart from Ben and Ricardo, only a small handful of us at the White House knew this secret channel existed: Obama, Biden, Chief of Staff Denis McDonough, Deputy NSA Tony Blinken, the vice president's NSA Jake Sullivan, and me. It was highly unusual to operate so surreptitiously, but we could not risk leaks. The U.S. Interests Section in Cuba, members of Congress, and U.S. government agencies were not involved.

At first, the discussions focused mainly on the U.S. demand that Cuba free American Alan Gross, a USAID subcontractor unjustly imprisoned since December 2009. As a moral and practical matter, without Gross's release, there was no latitude for progress on any other front. For its part, Cuba wanted to be removed from the State Sponsor of Terrorism list, the release of some of its nationals from U.S. custody, and (of course) sanctions lifted. The two sides circled each other warily for months, stalled on these issues.

When I arrived at the NSC, I assured Ben that I would strongly support his efforts every step of the way. From the outset, we worked closely together on the strategy and tactics of his negotiation. In our early meetings, I was struck by the team's emphasis on getting Gross released as a predicate for negotiations on other matters. I believed that once it became known that we had negotiated directly with the Cubans on anything (even returning Gross), Congress would shut down the potential for further meaningful contacts. Moreover, it wasn't clear that we could even get Gross without cutting a larger deal. In my view, we shouldn't settle for one bite, if there was the potential for getting the whole enchilada.

Invoking one of the vice president's Bidenisms, "Don't die on a small cross," I proposed that we instead pursue a "Big Bang." The idea was to negotiate and announce the entirety of the agreed changes to U.S.-Cuban relations: Gross's release, Cuban prisoners' return, the terrorist list, sanctions easing, normalized diplomatic relations, talks between our leaders— all at once. The shock would be so great that our opponents would be paralyzed (at least temporarily) by the blast effects. By the time the dust settled, the deeds would have been done, and the silent majority of Americans and members of Congress who favored change would be free to support it at no political cost to them.

Over the next year and a half, that is how we proceeded—quietly toiling toward the Big Bang. Ben and Ricardo had multiple sessions with the Cubans, in locations ranging from Canada to Trinidad and Tobago, from New York to the Vatican. My former deputy at USUN, Ambassador Jeff DeLaurentis, ably managed bilateral engagement as our chargé in Havana. As we began to close the gaps and the potential for success came into focus, we started selectively to widen the circle of those in the loop. Understandably, no one was especially pleased to learn that this historic negotiation was happening without their knowledge, but all were good soldiers and quietly joined the team. As we neared agreement, we roped in appropriate additional officials at State, Justice, CIA, Treasury, and Commerce to execute those parts of the potential deal that fell uniquely within their purview. They all agreed to help do their part, happy to implement this momentous policy change.

By mid-December 2014, all the pieces were in place. It was time to bring Alan Gross home and ignite the Big Bang. This required careful orchestration—a last-minute heads-up to those in Congress who long favored a changed Cuba policy (especially Senators Patrick Leahy and Jeff Flake) and to the most powerful who opposed it.

Two planes—one carrying three former Cuban prisoners and another carrying Gross—passed in midair between Cuba and the U.S. President Obama signed an executive order directing the maximum amount of relief on commerce, travel, and other restrictions possible without legislation lifting the embargo. Both countries launched a process to establish normal diplomatic relations. Cuba publicly committed to release fifty-three political prisoners and improve internet access. President Obama and President Castro spoke for the first time by phone. And, on December 17, 2014, President Obama announced that he was turning the page on fifty-plus years of failed Cuba policy.

Miraculously, we managed to pull all this off with no leaks. NBC's intrepid Andrea Mitchell came dangerously close to getting the story and tried at a holiday party to wrench some insight out of me. I gave nothing. No one in the White House or the agencies let it slip, because all were invested in the new policy and understood its extreme sensitivity. When the president made the announcement, the press and public were stunned. The Big Bang blew exactly as planned.

The exhilaration of this historic policy change and its flawless roll-out was a highlight of my tenure as national security advisor. It also proved to be a welcome turning point. After a year and a half of relentless challenges and few obvious successes, we had a big one; and there would be more to come.

20

Putting Points on the Board

When I called down the hall, Ferial Govashiri, the president's personal aide, said he was on the phone but, "Come on down!"

On a small, three-by-five card with "The White House" printed on top, I wrote in all caps: WE HAVE AN IRAN DEAL. Card in hand, Avril, Ben, and I walked into the Oval Office and flashed the note before the Boss. The president knew that a deal might be close, but as we had learned repeatedly (and not just with the Iranians), nothing is done until it's done.

Obama's face lit up, and he ended the call. We all whooped and fist-bumped. Obama hugged me, and Ben jokingly suggested that Obama call the guy from the 2007 YouTube primary debate who asked if Obama would engage Iran.

John Kerry called in shortly thereafter to report the news officially and to receive well-deserved congratulations. He and a tireless team of U.S. negotiators led by Undersecretary of State Wendy Sherman, and including Energy Secretary Ernie Moniz, our extremely capable NSC coordinator for the Middle East Rob Malley, and an all-star cast of experts from NSC, State, Treasury, Energy, USUN, and the Intelligence Community, had spent nearly two years negotiating with Iran, the European Union, and the P5+1 (the U.S., Russia, China, France, and the U.K., plus Germany).

———•◆•———

Negotiations between the U.S. and Iran had begun in earnest in the summer of 2013. After years of painful sanctions and under the new leadership of the more pragmatic President Hassan Rouhani, Iran decided that it was time to stop stringing along the P5+1, as it had over the years, and to ascertain whether progress with the U.S. was actually possible. As President Obama stated as far back as the 2008 campaign, we were willing to test the same proposition.

Following a few rounds of secret negotiations in Oman between the U.S. team of Deputy Secretary of State Bill Burns and Jake Sullivan and their Iranian counterparts, we could begin to see the contours of an interim agreement. President Obama and President Rouhani both signaled publicly at the U.N. General Assembly in late September 2013 their cautious hope that discussions could yield progress. In a historic first since the severance of diplomatic relations in 1979, the two leaders spoke by phone, as Rouhani was heading to the airport in New York, to affirm their commitment to talks. Kerry and Iranian foreign minister Mohammed Javad Zarif met for the first time as counterparts at UNGA and launched a more formal and public negotiation in Geneva that would include the P5+1.

As with Cuba, the talks with Iran in the months leading up to the September 2013 conversation between Obama and Rouhani were very closely held within the U.S. government. Six months prior to that, the direct dialogue with Iran began in Oman, but it was not until Rouhani's election in June that it seemed our contacts might lead somewhere. We were concerned that any premature exposure of the talks would invite sabotage and poison the potential for progress.

Up through this early stage, my role was to liaise with the president and provide our negotiating team with strategic guidance and support, offering input on the parameters of what we could accept. Before late September 2013, we informed neither our European allies nor Israel of the first few rounds of talks, though we suspected the Israelis might know through their own means. Our allies were not happy to learn they had been left in the dark, especially the French, who like to be at the center of everything. Later, in November, the French demonstrated their enduring discontent by blocking P5+1 agreement on the initial version of the interim nuclear agreement.

It was Israel, however, that was most incensed and claimed to have been blindsided by the speed of events. I was meeting with my Israeli counterpart, Yaakov Amidror, in my White House office while, unbeknownst to us both, President Obama spoke by phone to Rouhani on September 27, 2013. The Israelis (and our Gulf partners) reported being shocked to learn of the call. Netanyahu was scheduled to meet with Obama at the White House three days later, and it was then that the president laid out the state of our engagement with Iran and our intention to try to resolve the nuclear issue through diplomacy. The day after their meeting, Netanyahu color-fully blasted the nuclear talks and Rouhani in his UNGA speech, saying, "He fooled the world once. Now he thinks he can fool it again. You see, Rouhani thinks he can have his yellowcake and eat it too."

By November 2013, after painstaking negotiations, we reached an in-terim agreement to freeze the progress of Iran's nuclear program in ex-change for modest sanctions relief—in order to create time and space for negotiations toward a full, final deal. Once the interim Joint Plan of Action (JPOA) was signed by the U.S., Iran, and the P5+1, the difficult conten-tious negotiations toward a comprehensive agreement got under way. The JPOA was set to last six months but had to be renewed twice due to the political and substantive complexity of the negotiation.

Over this period, the Principals Committee met on numerous occa-sions, as did the NSC with the president, to define the limits of our negoti-ating posture and decide how to surmount various obstacles. Throughout, our bottom line was that any deal must fully and verifiably eliminate every potential pathway for Iran to acquire a nuclear weapon. We were also de-termined to extend the time it would take for Iran to acquire enough nu-clear material to make a bomb (if it decided to violate the deal)—from two or three months to over one year. That increased "breakout time" would give the U.S. plenty of opportunity to respond, including militarily, before Iran developed any weapon.

One important concern we faced was how to reimpose U.N. sanc-tions swiftly if Iran broke the deal. We could not allow Russia or China to veto renewed sanctions, should they differ with us on whether Iran was to blame and how to react. In response to a question about how to address this challenge during an interview on *60 Minutes* that aired in December 2013, I replied (speaking as a former U.N. ambassador) that I believed we could craft some kind of "automatic triggers" that would reimpose sanc-tions "for failure to comply" and avert a Russian or Chinese veto. We could insert unorthodox language into the U.N. resolution, which would codify any eventual deal, that allowed sanctions to be reinstated by any permanent member of the Security Council if there were a significant violation.

In other words, I felt confident there was a way to ensure we could "snap-back" sanctions, as I told my colleagues at the next Principals Committee meeting on Iran, even though I had not yet figured out exactly how. My off-the-cuff answer on TV put "snap-back" into the sanctions lexicon and inspired us to devise effective UNSC resolution language and then work with the Russians to embed it in the implementing resolution. The "snap-back" assurance became a core element of the final deal and our ability, ultimately, to sell it to Congress.

Kerry and Foreign Minister Zarif were the lead diplomatic negotiators. Energy Secretary Ernie Moniz and Ali Akbar Salehi, the head of Iran's nuclear enterprise, were nuclear physicists with shared ties to MIT who together chaired the technical nuclear discussions. There were numerous fits and starts, near collapses, and efforts at sabotage—on both sides. At times, their meetings became so testy that John Kerry once slammed his fist on the table so hard that he propelled a pen and directly hit Zarif's deputy Abbas Araghchi. At any point, we knew the whole deal could fall apart and, sure enough, on the final day of negotiations, an exasperated and dramatic Zarif moved to walk out. For all intents and purposes, the negotiation appeared to be collapsing—until the very last moment when the walkout was blocked by a hobbled John Kerry, recovering from surgery on a badly broken leg, who used his crutch to bar the door.

Throughout, hard-liners in Iran opposed any restraint on its nuclear program and completely distrusted the U.S. Meanwhile, hard-liners in Washington—mainly Republicans but also some Democrats—decided well in advance of any agreement that the only good deal with Iran was no deal; and they made every effort to force us to fail. Their devious tactics ranged from Senator Tom Cotton's "open letter" signed by forty-six other Republican senators to Iran's leaders aimed at undermining their confidence in the durability of any deal; to House Speaker John Boehner's secret invitation to Prime Minister Netanyahu to deliver a joint address to Congress in March 2015, during which Netanyahu roundly condemned the "bad deal" with Iran.

Inside the White House, we seethed at the Israeli prime minister's machinations to orchestrate a joint session invitation behind the back of the administration and Democrats in Congress. In my view, this marked a new low in the already strained U.S.-Israel bilateral relationship, removing it from the customary protection of bipartisanship. As I said at the time in an interview, Netanyahu's gambit "injected a degree of partisanship, which is not only unfortunate, I think it is destructive of the fabric of the [U.S.-Israel] relationship."

One month later, in early April 2015, we agreed with Iran on the framework for a comprehensive deal. Negotiations continued through the evening of July 13, when our team in Vienna sent back the final draft text for one last review by Washington. It was a 150-plus-page tome full of technical complexities. Reviewing it line-by-line and providing timely feedback to our exhausted and impatient negotiating team was a challenge.

Avril assembled a cadre of NSC lawyers and experts in the Situation Room. We plugged in Vienna via secure video so we could seek clarifications in real time from the negotiating team and give rolling responses as we plowed through the text. Avril and the NSC team worked through the night and woke me several times to obtain guidance on our proposed amendments. By morning, we thought we might have the makings of a deal, pending the agreement of the other parties. Indeed, on July 14, 2015, Secretary Kerry signed the final agreement known as the Joint Comprehensive Plan of Action (JCPOA).

As soon as the ink dried, the truly hard work began: persuading Congress not to torpedo the deal. Again, sadly, it was the Obama administration vs. Netanyahu. Congress had recently passed the Iran Nuclear Agreement Review Act, which required the president to submit the full, final agreement to Congress. The law prevented the president from waiving or suspending nuclear-related sanctions against Iran (as the deal required, if Iran fulfilled its commitments) until congressional review was complete and no resolution of disapproval had been enacted. In other words, if sixty days after signing the deal, Congress did not vote to disapprove it (or, thereafter, if Congress failed to override an Obama veto), the sanctions could be suspended, and the deal could go into effect—pending full Iranian compliance.

As a practical matter, this meant the administration had to gain support from at least thirty-four Democratic senators and, ideally, one-third of all House members to sustain a veto. But we sought to gain the support of at least forty-one senators so that Democrats could successfully filibuster any Republican attempt to pass a resolution of disapproval in the first place. This might seem like an easy lift since we only needed Democrats, but it was not, given widespread misunderstanding about the complicated terms of the deal and Israel's heavy-handed efforts to sink it.

I spent hours on the phone arguing, reasoning with, and cajoling friendly members of Congress, including Congresswoman Terri Sewell, my buddy from Oxford; Senators Mark Warner and Claire McCaskill; and Senator Michael Bennet, my friend since nursery school. While we shared their concern that Iran could not be trusted, we argued that this deal was based not on trust but on the strictest and most intrusive verification regime. As many former officials in Israel's security establishment acknowledged, if not the country's current political leaders, the agreement would benefit Israel's security rather than diminish it. Ultimately, after a summer of sustained personal engagement by the president, vice president, Kerry, Moniz, Sherman, and many others, we obtained more than the necessary support. The congressional review period expired without a vote of disapproval. The deal was done!

The Iran agreement is proof of the value of tough sanctions, when combined with skillful, relentless diplomacy, to accomplish the seemingly unachievable in international affairs. The JCPOA was a finely detailed agreement that effectively closed all pathways to Iran developing a nuclear weapon and ensured Iran would face the most rigorous, intrusive international inspections regime ever established. It was never able, nor was it intended, to halt all of Iran's nefarious behavior—its support for terrorism, its destabilization of neighboring states, its hostility toward Israel, or its ballistic missile program. Still, it effectively addressed our biggest concern and that of the international community—preventing Iran from posing a far more dangerous threat to the region and the world through its acquisition of nuclear weapons.

Understandably, Israel always said it viewed Iran's nuclear program as an existential threat. So, surely, the removal of that threat would be welcome news to Israel, our Gulf partners, and their backers. In reality, we discovered that removing the nuclear threat was not in fact their principal motivation. Rather, Israel and the Gulf Arab countries aimed to put permanent and crippling economic and military pressure on Iran such that either the regime collapsed, or it was too weak to wield meaningful influence in the region. The nuclear deal, which allowed Iran to access much of its *own* frozen assets held abroad under sanctions, in exchange for full and verifiable compliance with the terms of the agreement, was deemed worse than no deal at all by those who prioritized keeping the international community's boot on Iran's neck above halting its nuclear program. It turns out, the whole Likud-led campaign against a nuclear-armed Iran was never on the level.

Indeed, as the U.S. Intelligence Community and International Atomic Energy Agency repeatedly validated, the Iran deal was working exactly as intended when later President Trump decided to withdraw from the agreement in May 2018. Iran had fully complied with its obligations to constrain its nuclear activities—relinquishing 97 percent of its uranium stockpile, dismantling its plutonium facility and two-thirds of its centrifuges, forswearing ever producing nuclear weapons, and submitting to the most stringent verification regime ever established.

Unfortunately, the U.S. withdrawal from the nuclear deal put Iran's continued compliance in jeopardy, did nothing to address our other concerns about Iran's behavior, placed us at odds with our closest European allies with whom we negotiated the deal, and called into question why any adversary would agree to strike a deal with a self-evidently fickle America. The Iran deal wasn't perfect, but it was a damn good way to resolve a grave and growing threat to international peace and security while avoiding resort to a highly costly and deadly war. With the U.S. abrogation, reimposition of crushing sanctions, and America's military buildup in the region, Iran has resumed its nuclear program and stepped up its destabilizing actions in the region. Moreover, the risks of a direct U.S.-Iran conflict are much increased, as Israel, Saudi Arabia, and many in the Trump administration appear intent on embarking on a foolhardy and unnecessary military operation to try to effect regime change in Iran.

Of all the vindictive and shortsighted actions President Trump has taken only to undo President Obama's legacy—from abandoning the Paris Climate Agreement to withdrawing from the Trans-Pacific Partnership (TPP) trade agreement—jettisoning the Iran nuclear deal is the most dangerous and dispiriting to me. We and our allies expended years of painstaking diplomacy to reach an agreement that was fully meeting its objective. The sheer stupidity of withdrawing without an alternative strategy to accomplish their ill-defined objectives, the wasted effort, and the poisoned relationships amount to mind-boggling recklessness. While we can potentially rejoin Paris and the successor to TPP, it's very hard to imagine how we will ever again verifiably dismantle Iran's nuclear program short of war—and even then only temporarily.

———

The president was pissed off, or, as he often said when he was most annoyed, "I'm aggravated."

How come we have ISIS in Mosul practically overnight and virtually no warning that the Iraqi security forces would fold like a cheap tent? In the midst of (rather gently) chewing out Jim Clapper, the director of national intelligence, Obama pressed Jim to explain why the Intelligence Community had failed to warn him and senior policymakers that the terrorist group known by various names, but most simply the Islamic State in Iraq and Syria (ISIS), was about to conquer a large swath of northern Iraq.

It was a fair question. Prior to June 2014, we had not been warned of the likelihood that ISIS, a reincarnation of Al Qaeda in Iraq, which had gained strength in Syria and seized the Iraqi city of Fallujah, would move across the Syrian border and swiftly take Mosul, Iraq's second largest city. More significantly, it had not been predicted that ISIS's roughly one thousand fighters would easily overrun thirty thousand Iraqi security forces (ISF) soldiers who abandoned their positions, dropped their weapons, and fled. As director of national intelligence, Jim Clapper readily acknowledged the Intelligence Community was surprised by the Iraqis' lack of will to fight.

As policymakers, we too failed to anticipate and react swiftly enough to ISIS's march and the Iraqis' ineptitude. We knew Iraqi prime minister Nouri al-Maliki was a venal Shia sectarian whom we did not trust to govern in the interests of all Iraqis. But we did not fully appreciate the extent to which he had allowed the Iraqi army to atrophy in both will and capacity. Before 2014, we had viewed ISIS as more of a concern in Syria than Iraq and as a lure for foreign fighters who might return home to conduct attacks. Most of my colleagues and I underestimated ISIS as an occupying army that would seize and hold territory, much less try to establish a caliphate. Until Mosul.

As soon as Mosul fell, and ISIS elements started heading south toward Baghdad, we knew we were living in a different world. ISIS and its so-called "caliphate," at this point spanning large portions of both Syria and Iraq, could not be allowed to stand. Prime Minister Maliki wanted American air combat support against ISIS, but his corrupt, anti-Sunni tyranny had facilitated ISIS's advance. President Obama rightly determined that we weren't going to be Maliki's air force against the Sunni. For the Iraqis themselves to defeat ISIS, as they had to do, they needed to be unified in their cause—Sunni, Shia, Kurd. Maliki was a force for division and defeat; he needed to resign and, until he did, the United States would not intervene militarily to help the Iraqi army.

As Maliki clung to power, ISIS advanced on the predominantly Kurdish city of Erbil, seized the Mosul Dam, and threatened Baghdad. Erbil was an important city that housed a U.S. consulate and U.N. agencies. To protect Americans in Erbil and regain control of the Mosul Dam, President Obama authorized limited air strikes in early July to support mainly Kurdish forces who were fighting ISIS in the north.

In early August, confronted with a major humanitarian crisis, Obama ordered the U.S. military to strike ISIS targets and air-drop critical relief supplies to assist thousands of displaced people from the Yazidi sect who were stranded on Sinjar Mountain and facing potential genocide. The president, nonetheless, rightly continued to resist directly aiding the Iraqi government until Maliki resigned. By mid-August, Maliki relented and relinquished power to Prime Minister Haider al-Abadi, a rational, responsible Shia leader who sought to unite the country. This transition enabled the U.S. to deploy military trainers and combat aircraft to fully join the Iraqi-led campaign against ISIS.

Over months of meetings in the Situation Room, we crafted, refined, and implemented an integrated campaign plan designed to degrade and ultimately defeat ISIS in Iraq and Syria. We deployed over 5,200 U.S.

forces to train, advise, and equip the Iraqi security forces so that, once sufficiently regenerated, they could take the ground fight to ISIS. The U.S. also employed extensive air strikes against ISIS command facilities, forces, bases, banks, oil infrastructure, and leaders. In Syria, we trained, advised, and equipped Kurdish and Arab opposition elements, known as the Syrian Democratic Forces (SDF), to fight ISIS and provided air support for their battles to retake strategic territory in the far south as well as in the north— from Kobane to Manbij and, eventually, Raqqa.

Led by Special Envoys General John Allen and Brett McGurk, the Obama administration assembled a coalition of over sixty-five partner countries from NATO, the Gulf, and Asia to wage war against ISIS. Through intensified, targeted strikes, the U.S. military hit both ISIS and Al Qaeda (Khorasan Group) targets across Syria. The strategy also entailed cutting off financial pipelines to ISIS, restricting the flow of foreign fighters into Syria, assisting the Iraqi government to stabilize its finances and to govern more inclusively, and countering the ISIS propaganda machine, which recruits soldiers and spreads venomous propaganda through the internet and social media.

We faced many gut-wrenching and white-knuckle moments over the course of the counter-ISIS campaign, particularly the horrific terrorist attacks in Paris in 2015, the subsequent brutal bombings on the subway and airport in Brussels, and the ISIS-inspired massacre in San Bernardino, California. Most personally painful was the killing of Kayla Mueller, an American human rights activist and humanitarian, and the brutal beheadings by ISIS of American journalists Steven Sotloff and James Foley, and humanitarian aid worker Abdul-Rahman Kassig. At the White House and throughout the U.S. government, led by Lisa Monaco, our colleagues and I worked tirelessly to win the freedom of Americans held hostage abroad, especially in Syria. I got to know James Foley's mother, Diane, who visited me at USUN and later the White House as she pursued every avenue to bring her son home safely. As a mother, my heart broke for the Foley family, and I grew emotionally invested in James's fate.

In the summer of 2014, we received information about the location where we believed Foley and other captives were being held. President Obama swiftly ordered Special Forces to conduct a high-risk nighttime rescue operation. Anxiously, I waited late in my office for the results of the raid, praying that I would have the opportunity finally to give Diane Foley good news. I was crushed when word came back that the compound where the hostages had been held was empty. There was nobody left to rescue.

In the U.S., fear of ISIS reached irrational, near fever levels by the fall of 2015. When I visited senior executives at NBC headquarters in New York, I was shocked to be asked by a smart and very well-informed executive whether she should still allow her children to walk to school in New York City, given the risk that ISIS might behead them. As a parent, I could relate to her concern, but as national security advisor, I found such outsize fear to be baffling. So too did President Obama, whose ever-rational, calm cool threatened to lead him to downplay the degree of public fear.

At a November 2015 press conference in Turkey shortly after the Paris attacks, President Obama was peppered with questions on ISIS, including by CNN's Jim Acosta, who asked breathlessly, "Why can't we take out these bastards?" By this point, the president had reached his limit. This last question was so over the top that an exasperated Obama dismissed it, saying he "just spent the last three questions answering that very question, so I don't know what more you want me to add."

I shared President Obama's frustration with those journalists and political opponents who were irresponsibly hyping the ISIS threat, but I worried that he risked sounding out of touch with the popular mood. Before each press availability over the duration of that trip, the traveling senior staff and I joined forces to remind the president that, when it comes to ISIS, like Ebola, he needed to "meet the public where they are," however out of proportion their alarm may seem. Grudgingly and gradually, the president calibrated his public comments to acknowledge popular concerns without stoking panic. Our focus, however, remained on steadily executing our strategy to degrade and ultimately defeat ISIS, while preventing terrorist attacks on Americans and our allies. Meanwhile, as the 2016 election approached, others cravenly used ISIS as a cudgel to demonize refugees, immigrants, and Muslim Americans for political benefit.

On a separate issue related to ISIS, our fears were in no way overblown. The Mosul Dam in northern Iraq was, and is, a disaster of biblical proportions waiting to happen, causing the president, me, and our team significant stress. The foundation of the dam is profoundly damaged and precarious. For years, the dam was expertly grouted to mitigate its degradation, but war and ISIS's proximity to the dam resulted in long periods without maintenance so that the dam's deterioration accelerated.

If and when the Mosul Dam breaks, the mighty Tigris River will nearly instantly destroy hundreds of thousands of lives, countless acres of critical agricultural land, and spread death and disease from Mosul to Baghdad. Experts predict the city of Baghdad, including the U.S. embassy compound, will be inundated within three to four days. Iraq as we know it will be gone. Our Intelligence Community prepared a video simulation of the destruction that the dam's collapse would wreak. When it was shown to the Principals in the Situation Room, there was utter silence. The U.S. government repeatedly sounded the alarm, struggling to animate the Iraqi authorities with the necessary urgency, and pressed them to fund and deploy security personnel for an international grouting operation that would work to stave off the dam's potential collapse. Of all the terrifying scenarios I lost sleep over—pandemic flu, a terrorist attack employing weapons of mass destruction, a North Korean nuclear strike—the collapse of the Mosul Dam remained in the top five of my recurring nightmares.

Throughout the duration of the administration, the intensity of our efforts to defeat ISIS never waned. The president convened his NSC on ISIS over and over again. I chaired countless Principals Committee meetings, and Avril held scores of Deputies sessions, to sustain the interagency focus that the president demanded. Obama tasked my NSC colleague Rob Malley with coordinating the counter-ISIS campaign day-to-day from the White House and directed that we provide weekly updates and assessments of the campaign's progress. In December 2015, Obama internally mandated that his administration "put ISIS in a box" by the end of his term.

Defense Secretary Ash Carter, a cerebral, self-assured academic with long and deep policy experience, worked with Joint Chiefs chairman Martin Dempsey and later Joseph Dunford, alongside Central Command Generals Lloyd Austin and, subsequently, Joe Votel, to devise and continuously improve an intensified military campaign to fulfill the president's directive. Their plan entailed retaking Raqqa and Mosul and then cleaning up remaining pockets of ISIS in Syria's south and east as well as the seam between Iraq and Syria.

Throughout, we wrestled with persistent challenges, including deconflicting our operations with those of the Russians deployed inside Syria, and balancing Turkey's contributions to the counter-ISIS campaign with the imperative of supporting the Kurds. The Turks viewed the Kurds as terrorists, but the Kurds formed the backbone of our Syrian force fighting ISIS. This tension was extremely difficult to manage, but President Obama was able to massage Turkish president Erdoğan enough to keep the campaign on track. By the time President Obama left office, the coalition had retaken over 60 percent of territory controlled by ISIS in Iraq and almost 30 percent in Syria. Raqqa was under mounting pressure, and preparations for the campaign to retake Mosul were well-advanced.

Through intensive, coordinated interagency effort, we did indeed manage to "put ISIS in a box" by the end of the administration, placing it securely on the path to defeat and neatly packaged for Obama's successor to finish off. We knew from the outset that the fight against ISIS would take time and entail setbacks as well as successes. To its credit, for two years the Trump administration pursued our very war plan to continued positive effect, retaking Raqqa and Mosul, eliminating the so-called "caliphate" and, eventually, ISIS's sole remaining stronghold along the Iraq-Syria border.

Then, in December 2018, President Trump shocked his closest advisors, Congress, and the world by declaring that he would rapidly withdraw all two thousand U.S. forces from Syria, putting in jeopardy the painstaking gains made against ISIS and abandoning meaningful efforts to assist battle-damaged, liberated portions of Syria. Trump later decided to leave only four hundred U.S. military personnel—fewer than needed to keep ISIS and the Syrian regime in check, much less Iran and Russia, or to protect the Kurd and Arab forces who bore the brunt of the fighting against ISIS. Thus, the risk that ISIS will revive and reinvent itself remains.

———

Over a year after I left the White House, with the stresses of being national security advisor behind me, my cell phone rang. Answering, I was surprised to hear a familiar voice start without even a hello, "Boy, do I miss that micromanaging bitch!"

I laughed uproariously, delighted to hear from a still serving senior general with whom I worked closely in the Obama administration, calling to say "Hi" and commiserate. The general was jokingly referring to the public rap on the Obama White House and his NSC that we, and especially I, micromanaged the agencies and the policy process. The bill of indictment included such dings as: 1) The Principals Committee met too frequently; 2) Meetings went too long; papers were late; and discussion went too much in the weeds; 3) We got too deeply into the agencies' knickers; and 4) We were overly directive.

There is some validity to these criticisms. Several of these shortcomings we could and did address, making improvements at least on the margins, if not always to the satisfaction of every principal. After establishing a system to track weekly the number and topics of PCs, we worked to reduce their frequency to the extent events permitted as well as to start and end them more promptly. We increased the timeliness of preparatory paper for PCs, but not uniformly, and tried to focus Principals meetings on the most consequential decisions.

Almost all of my predecessors, most experts, and I laud the "Scowcroft model" of running the NSC—that of the legendary Lieutenant General Brent Scowcroft when he served his second tour as NSA under President George H. W. Bush. In his day, the NSC was viewed as lean and efficient—far smaller, more nimble, and playing a simple coordinating role while generally refraining from involvement in the operational work of the State Department and other agencies. However, the advent of email, the 24/7 cable news cycle, and social media have fundamentally changed the pace and the pressures of national security decision making. The enormous range of national and homeland security issues weighing on any modern president in the post–Cold War world, the incessant demands for immediate response, the intractable reality that the toughest problems, by definition, have no satisfactory solutions, combined with the politicization of foreign policy have largely rendered the Scowcroft gold standard of NSC management obsolete.

In any event, President Obama's own approach to governing was not well-suited to a hands-off NSC. He delved deeply into issues, demanded stringent analysis and options, confronted the hardest problems squarely, and to the greatest extent possible made tough decisions on the merits rather than based on political considerations. With his formidable intellect and vast ability to absorb information, Obama was a detail-oriented commander-in-chief who expected that the national security process match his standards of rigor and comprehensiveness. Equally, he required me and his national security team to mirror and support his style of governing. Any less would have been wholly unsatisfactory to him.

I and my deputies, therefore, worked to the best of our abilities to serve a hands-on president with an ambitious agenda, who took decision making very seriously. President Obama did not want to own responsibility for what he called "stupid shit," or dangerous choices that he didn't make, even as he would readily take the blame for those he did. Whether regarding drone policy, if and when to execute a risky hostage rescue operation, or how many troops to deploy and with what mission to Iraq or Afghanistan, President Obama was determined to make, rather than delegate, those most consequential decisions. His was a management style that matched my own temperament and instincts, and I was comfortable driving a policy process that best suited him. That engendered some frustration, particularly at DOD and to some extent at State, and surely inspired some sniping in the press about how we did our jobs.

Neither at the time, nor in retrospect, however, do I regret the president's hands-on approach and the assiduous work we did to support it. I will gladly take criticism for micromanaging, since the alternative (as we have seen of late) too often is chaos. When the nation's security is at stake and the costs of failure are so high, I would always rather err on the side of thorough analysis and careful consideration of the risks and benefits— even when we must run the policy process at warp speed.

By contrast, I do not think it wise to grant unlimited discretion to theater commanders to prosecute military campaigns without any high-level civilian oversight, which enables senior leaders to weigh the consequences of discrete operations for our broader national security. Equally, I strongly prefer that the U.S. president govern with intellectual rigor, clear accountability, and a disciplined policy process rather than with loose, uncoordinated pronouncements based on ideology, whim, or political expediency, which often fail to align with U.S. interests. But I may be old-fashioned.

21

The Fourth Quarter

WE ARE ENTERING
THE FOURTH
QUARTER AND
REALLY IMPORTANT
THINGS HAPPEN IN
THE FOURTH
QUARTER.
—PRESIDENT BARACK OBAMA

These were the exact words printed in black ink vertically on small, white three-by-five cards embossed with "THE WHITE HOUSE" in blue across the top. Chief of Staff Denis McDonough personally delivered these cards to White House staff in early January 2015. A tall, lean, chiseled former football player from Minnesota with close-cropped, silver hair (despite his relative youth), Denis has something of the coach in him—complete with sometimes hokey team-building techniques.

When he came by my office to hand me my card, I probably offered a perfunctory thank-you and kept on working. Rather than toss it into the trash, for some reason I placed it on my desk next to my computer, where I kept it and saw it multiple times a day for the next two years.

We still had a lot to get done, and no one was taking their foot off the gas, least of all the president of the United States. As evidenced by his campaigns,

Obama is the classic closer—a fourth quarter player. That's when he ups his game to even higher levels, pulling off the win, sometimes after coming from behind. That's how 2008 felt through the primary and early general election. That's how 2012 felt after Benghazi and a poor first debate performance.

That's how it felt to me as I managed Obama's second-term national security agenda. Two thousand thirteen and 2014 were unrelenting, crisis-filled years with little to celebrate. But after Cuba in December 2014, we started racking up wins—from the Iran deal to the Paris Climate Agreement that enabled us to close with an Obama-strong fourth quarter.

The same was true on the domestic front. One of the most joyous days at the White House was June 26, 2015, when we learned the Supreme Court had validated the right to same-sex marriage. There were hugs and whoops and tears of joy throughout the building when the president spoke in the Rose Garden, as colleagues heralded this landmark decision and friends for whom this issue was deeply personal saw their lives transformed. That evening, I celebrated with staff on a balcony of the Old Executive Office Building, watching as the White House was lit up in the colors of the rainbow when night fell. Ian and I cherish a picture of the two of us outside the colorful White House taken as we joined tourists and passersby in affirming that love is love. Two days later, we rejoiced again as the Supreme Court upheld the Affordable Care Act ensuring that millions of Americans could retain their newly accessible health insurance. We were "getting shit done."

———•◆•———

Behind the scenes at the NSC, we would continue full throttle until the moment we were asked to turn in our badges and cell phones. Our aim was to leave to our successors the best possible security landscape for the American people. A tall order in a tough and unforgiving world.

Even though, for the most part, I performed the traditional role of point guard who calls the plays, runs the offense, and passes the ball, on occasion I also played the position of shooting guard—the player on the team most expected to drive to the basket and score.

One of my most gratifying initiatives was leading the NSC Principals' push to diversify the national security workforce. Ever since I entered government as a twenty-eight-year-old staffer, I had been mindful that there were few like me at any given policymaking table. Few women, few minorities, and even fewer women of color. There were also few Muslims, few Chinese and Farsi speakers, too few Latinos, and almost no Native Americans. This diversity deficit didn't concern me simply because I was outnumbered and likely more misunderstood than I appreciated.

It troubled me mainly because I found that people from similar backgrounds—for instance, white male graduates of the Ivy League—tend to approach complex issues in similar ways. They might miss nuances of language and gender, while dismissing insights that others from different backgrounds might more readily embrace. On a wide span of issues—ranging from how many refugees to admit from each region of the world, to sexual assault in the military, how best to counter violent extremism, and the kind of support we provide families of Americans held hostage overseas—I saw firsthand the benefits of incorporating the sometimes divergent perspectives of female, LGBT, Muslim, and other minority voices in the policy debate.

We are the most diverse nation on earth, and it benefits the U.S. to model that diversity to the world; yet all too often we fail to leverage our greatest strength. By choice, we are battling to defend our people and our interests in a complex world with the equivalent of one hand tied behind our back. It makes no sense to me. Meanwhile, numerous recent studies have validated that, whether in the private sector, nonprofit world, or government, more diverse teams make better decisions and achieve measurably better outcomes.

The fundamental equality of all human beings is the closest thing I have to a life's creed. My parents taught me and my brother that it is our sacred obligation to pave the pathways for those who have had fewer advantages than we. Lifting others up, diversifying opportunity, has been my family's enterprise—from my great-grandfather's founding of the Bordentown School in the late nineteenth century to my mother's work to establish and sustain the Pell Grant program and my brother's founding of Management Leadership for Tomorrow. I carry that same responsibility with me wherever I go, including to the White House—where, as an African American woman, I had the privilege of serving as national security advisor to the first African American president of the United States. How

fitting and right it felt when I had the chance to tackle the diversity challenge head-on, with the full backing of my boss. I could not have slept well
at night if I didn't try.

Back in 2011, President Obama issued an executive order prioritizing
diversity and inclusion throughout the federal workforce. From the outset
of the administration's efforts, we were mindful that one area of government lagged behind the rest: the national security agencies. Frustrated by
the persistently lower levels of racial, ethnic, religious, sexual orientation,
and gender diversity in the national security workforce, I decided to elevate
the issue to the attention of NSC Deputies and Principals.

Though nearly 40 percent of Americans are people of color and, by
2044, it is estimated that the U.S. will be "majority minority," the national
security workforce (especially its senior ranks) does not reflect America.
Minorities collectively comprise well under 20 percent of senior foreign
service officers and under 15 percent of senior military and intelligence
officers. Neither I nor President Obama saw this as a human resources
challenge; improving workforce diversity is a "national security imperative." I consistently stressed the national security rationale for a diverse
workforce, arguing that a collection of leaders from diverse backgrounds
can often come up with more creative insights, proffer alternative solutions, and thus make better decisions.

The best part of leading this initiative was that I met zero resistance;
at every stage, I was pushing on a wide-open door. My cabinet-level colleagues were each deeply committed to this effort, and several had already
taken important steps to increase diversity and inclusion. Not one cabinet
secretary or agency head offered excuses. Not one delayed or deflected
responsibility. In fact, they competed with each other around the Situation Room table for who could boast the most progress. Jim Clapper and
John Brennan proudly detailed the strides the Intelligence Community
had made in promoting the advancement of LGBT officers. Ash Carter
heralded the recent advances for women, gay, and transgender people in
the military, starting with the repeal of the "Don't Ask, Don't Tell" policy
in 2011 and culminating in the decision in 2016 to lift the ban on transgender people serving openly in the military. John Kerry lamented the State
Department's long-standing shortcomings and pledged personally to pri-

oritize diversifying the foreign service. These were by far the easiest and most enjoyable Principals Committee meetings I chaired.

In October 2016, President Obama issued a presidential memorandum codifying the U.S. government's commitment to promoting diversity and inclusion in the national security workforce. The memo, which was the product of the NSC Deputies' and Principals' efforts, required all national security agencies to: collect, analyze, and publicize demographic data, including on recruitment and retention; to enhance professional development opportunities consistent with merit; and to hold senior leaders accountable for their results. One of the last memos I sent to President Obama, in January 2017, was a ninety-day report on progress in implementing this new policy. Given the scope of our work over eight years, promoting diversity in the national security workforce was a relatively small effort, but it was one that I pursued with pride and personal passion.

———

In the last year of the administration, I took on another responsibility for the sake of posterity—negotiating the memorandum of understanding (MOU) that would determine the specific terms and the value of the next ten-year security assistance agreement with Israel. In lengthy sessions over almost a year with my Israeli counterpart, Jacob Nagel, and many intervening engagements very ably led by NSC senior director Yael Lempert, we reached an agreement in September 2016 to provide Israel with $38 billion in military assistance over ten years (starting in 2018) and to modernize our security assistance relationship so that American defense suppliers, and no longer just Israeli defense companies, would fully benefit from this largesse.

Our commitment provided a hugely beneficial package for Israel—the largest in history—but, of course, Netanyahu wanted more and strongly resisted changes to the traditional terms of the grant. In what was then a budget-constrained Washington, we were constantly reminded that $38 billion is a huge sum for a developed country, even one as important as Israel, and that this money might have been used for pressing domestic purposes like Pell Grants or making community college accessible to every American who wanted to attend.

Nonetheless, President Obama gave me great latitude to do the right thing for the U.S. and Israel, even at a time when his personal relationship with Prime Minister Netanyahu was sorely strained. With his support, we concluded a mutually beneficial MOU that emphatically underscored President Obama's unshakable commitment to the security of Israel. This unprecedented package ensured that Israel will maintain its "qualitative military edge," thus enhancing Israel's ability to defend itself by itself.

Despite this and other achievements, I was disappointed to find after I returned to Washington to become national security advisor that some of Israel's staunchest advocates came to cast me as a grudging partner, at best, and, at worst, as hostile to Israel. In the wake of the Iran negotiations and nuclear deal, the relationship between Obama and Netanyahu deteriorated, and supporters of Netanyahu's right-wing Likud party increasingly leveled dishonest ad hominem attacks against the president and his closest advisors, including me. I found these charges frustrating and unfair, particularly in light of the work I did every day to defend and support Israel at the U.N.

Nevertheless, when we gathered on September 14, 2016, in the Treaty Room at the State Department to sign the MOU, I spoke from my heart:

> *For as long as the state of Israel has existed, the United States has been Israel's greatest friend and partner. That ironclad bond has endured l'dor v'dor—from generation to generation—across parties and administrations.*
>
> *This is the single largest pledge of military assistance to any country in U.S. history. At a time when we're tightening our belts across the board . . . this MOU nonetheless greatly increases our military assistance commitment to Israel. And that's not an accident. It's a reminder of the United States' unshakeable commitment to Israel's security.*
>
> *. . . I'll note that this MOU is not just good for Israel, it's good for the United States. Our security is linked. When allies and partners like Israel are more secure, the United States is more secure. Moreover, our Israeli friends will be able to buy more of the advanced capabilities produced by the United States, which will support American jobs. Like so many aspects of the U.S.-Israeli relationship, this MOU is a win-win.*

At the signing ceremony, I was also proud to offer tribute, one last time, to my friend and hero Shimon Peres. He had recently fallen gravely ill at ninety-three, and his prognosis was not good.

Twelve days later, on September 28, 2016, Shimon Peres passed away. I was honored to join President Obama in paying our last respects at his funeral in Jerusalem and took some small measure of comfort from knowing that the MOU had come to fruition on his watch.

Sadly but not unexpectedly, Peres's life dream of achieving two states for two peoples—a secure Jewish state of Israel living in peace alongside a viable, contiguous Palestinian state—never came to pass during his lifetime. This long-standing, bipartisan objective of U.S. policy remains in my view the only way to resolve the conflict, meet legitimate, long-deferred Palestinian aspirations, and preserve Israel as both a Jewish state and a democracy.

For five years, until 2014, the Obama administration expended great effort and political capital trying to achieve this goal, hoping that both sides would view the U.S. as a committed, honest broker. It was deeply disappointing, if not surprising, to find yet again that neither party was interested in making the hard compromises necessary for peace. President Abbas of the Palestinian Authority consistently lacked the will and the confidence to make a deal, despite knowing that he would likely not again find a more fair or sympathetic American partner. Prime Minister Netanyahu of Israel never seemed interested in a two-state solution, but rather spent eight years thwarting any progress toward peace.

In late 2016, following years of intensified and accelerated Israeli settlement activity that rendered the prospect of a viable Palestinian state ever more remote, the Obama administration decided to take a different approach. At the U.N., Ambassador Power was instructed to abstain on a British-drafted security council resolution, allowing to pass by 14–0 a text that condemned settlements and reaffirmed that their establishment "has no legal validity and constitutes a flagrant violation under international law and a major obstacle to the achievement of the two-state solution." In a significant rebuke to the Palestinians, the text also condemned "all acts of violence against civilians, including acts of terror, as well as acts of provocation, incitement and destruction."

The Obama administration's decision to abstain was harshly criticized by Israel, some American Jewish organizations, and by the incoming Trump team, which worked improperly behind the scenes during the transition to try and thwart adoption of the resolution. Despite the negative reaction our abstention engendered in some quarters, I thought it was appropriate to demonstrate that America would not continue to defend at all costs an eroding status quo. Clearly, neither party was interested in peace; meanwhile the Netanyahu government continued to build settlements with abandon and take other steps that dim any prospect for peace through a two-state solution.

———

The U.S.-China relationship, as President Obama often said, is the "most consequential bilateral relationship in the world." And, as a matter of history, custom, and efficacy, it fell to me as national security advisor to manage it on behalf of the president. Ever since 1972, when Henry Kissinger occupied my NSC office, U.S.-China relations have been led from the White House. State, DOD, and Treasury, of course, play vital roles, but China has long preferred dealing directly with the White House on bilateral affairs. More importantly, from the U.S. point of view, given the complexity of the relationship, its many economic and strategic facets, and the need to ensure that multiple, disparate agencies sing from the same hymnal, strong White House leadership makes sense.

As NSA, I embraced this responsibility. Having dealt intimately with China as U.N. ambassador, I had gained a good understanding of their interests and idiosyncrasies. In that period, at least, played correctly, the U.S.-China relationship need not have been dangerously adversarial, nor zero-sum, but rather more of a potentially combustible mix of competition and cooperation. The challenge, as President Obama and I viewed it, was to manage our economic and strategic competition effectively—gaining advantage for the U.S. wherever possible while avoiding unnecessary conflict—and, at the same time, maximizing our cooperation.

We had vigorous disagreements with China over its trade policy, currency manipulation, theft of intellectual property, and the disadvantageous restrictions it places on U.S. businesses operating in China. The U.S. strongly opposed China's aggressive acquisition of and construction on disputed land in the South China Sea, its cyber-enabled theft of proprietary American commercial information, its pressure on Taiwan and Hong Kong, its crackdown on NGOs and religious freedom, and its myriad human rights abuses. We also sought closer Chinese cooperation and stepped up economic pressure to address the North Korean nuclear and missile threat. These were among the most contentious issues in the bilateral relationship that risked conflict, if not managed effectively.

In 2011, President Obama implemented the "rebalance" to Asia, shifting more of our strategic assets and focus to optimize U.S. influence in the Asia-Pacific region. Under this policy, the U.S. augmented its military presence. We reinforced our alliances with Australia, Japan, South Korea, and the Philippines (until the May 2016 election of President Rodrigo Duterte whose erratic and authoritarian leadership limited the potential to do more). We strengthened ties to the countries of Southeast Asia, especially Indonesia, Singapore, Malaysia, and Vietnam, joined the annual East Asia Summit, and secured the Trans-Pacific Partnership Agreement to establish a high-standards free trade network among a dozen of the world's economies. The objective of these combined efforts was to advance U.S. interests and check China's expanding role in Asia. Our approach to China was not reactive but rather embedded in a far-sighted and multifaceted strategy for the Asia-Pacific region and India.

Even as we directly confronted the various areas of competition and concern with China, President Obama and I believed that expanded cooperation was not only important but possible to achieve. From 2013 to 2017, I held numerous meetings in Washington, New York, and Beijing with my Chinese counterpart, State Councilor Yang Jiechi, as well as China's foreign minister, senior military leaders, economic advisors, and party chiefs. These discussions were invaluable to forging progress on a wide range of issues. I traveled five times to Beijing as national security advisor, making it a habit to visit in the summers to prepare for upcoming summits between our presidents.

On each of my solo trips to Beijing, I was greeted with senior-level access and exceptional protocol arrangements, which to the Chinese are particularly important. Each time I arrived, whether in Beijing or Shanghai, the Chinese would shut down the highways and provide a police-escorted motorcade, which is usually a gesture reserved for visiting heads of state. I met for hours on each visit with my Chinese counterpart and other senior leaders. They hosted elaborate lunches and intimate dinners and, most importantly, I was always accorded a meeting with President Xi Jinping in a cavernous state room in the Great Hall of the People. These roughly forty-five-minute meetings, which began with brief comments before the international and Chinese press, were meant to underscore the importance the Chinese assigned to the U.S.-China bilateral relationship and their understanding of my proximity to the president of the U.S. The Chinese also always sought to ensure that their leaders were accorded the utmost respect, proper protocol, and unfailing security in the U.S., so they treated me with the expectation of reciprocity.

While the Chinese tend to emphasize form, Americans like to focus on substance. On each of my visits, I came with a detailed set of topics that I did not just want to discuss but to make real progress on and, ultimately, reach agreement. On areas of divergence, my aim was to deepen mutual understanding, plainly lay out U.S. concerns, explore ways to narrow our differences, but always to make clear where we would not bend and what the adverse consequences of their oppositional policies might be.

My first visit to China as NSA came at a low point in bilateral relations. In asserting a new style of bold, unchallenged leadership, President Xi had tried to constrain U.S. and international flights over the South and East China Seas. Weeks before my arrival, there had been a near disaster when a Chinese fighter jet buzzed a U.S. P-8 reconnaissance plane flying in international airspace, coming within thirty feet of the U.S. aircraft. In my meeting with Chinese military officials, I insisted, "We will continue to fly where we choose in international airspace," even if close to Chinese territory (which they hated). But I also revived an earlier proposal by President Xi that we reduce mutual risk by negotiating formal confidence-building mechanisms (CBMs)—rules to govern our encounters in air and sea to minimize the potential for unintended conflict. We were later able to sign detailed CBMs.

On the same trip, I emphasized the importance of increasing pressure on North Korea to abandon its nuclear weapons and ballistic missile program and of coordinating policy approaches between the U.S. and China. We subsequently established and sustained a bilateral dialogue on Northeast Asia, which helped shape our shared thinking about future contingencies in the region.

I also stressed the value of the U.S. and China leading the international community on climate change by each setting ambitious new targets for the reduction of carbon emissions, and thus smoothing the path to the Paris Climate Agreement. This was an initiative that Secretary Kerry and White House counselor John Podesta conceived and ably pursued. With pushing and prodding, we were able to get the Chinese to agree to announce our joint targets and unprecedented collaboration during President Obama's Beijing summit with Xi in November 2014. Similarly, I pressed collaboration between the U.S. and China on global health, Ebola, nonproliferation, development cooperation, nuclear security, the campaign against ISIS, and peacekeeping—all areas where, ultimately, we were able to make progress. Our efforts were driven by President Obama's conviction that, "When the U.S. and China are able to work together effectively, the whole world benefits."

In other areas, confrontation was more appropriate than cooperation. This was true, of course, on key aspects of the economic relationship as well as China's aggressive and unlawful assertion of its claims in the East and South China Seas. The U.S. continued to insist on our right to fly, sail, and operate wherever international law allows. We underscored that policy in 2015 by resuming regular "freedom of navigation operations." On these missions, the U.S. Navy would sail within twelve nautical miles (the legal nautical boundary) of land features—occupied by China or other countries—in order to emphasize that we do not recognize the legality of their claims. President Obama also made plain to President Xi that any Chinese effort to take or build on land occupied by a U.S. ally would activate our treaty obligations regarding mutual defense and could escalate into U.S.-China conflict. That message was received and respected, at least through the duration of the Obama administration. At the same time, the Defense Department made deliberate enhancements to our Pacific posture to improve our readiness to defend U.S. interests and that of our Asian allies and partners.

One of the biggest disputes in the U.S.-China relationship involved China's cyber-enabled theft of American intellectual property to give their companies a commercial advantage. For years, the Chinese government, military, and private entities have hacked into U.S. companies' proprietary systems and stolen information that they have then used for competitive gain. Over years, this unabated theft has cost U.S. companies billions of dollars, despite Justice Department indictments of Chinese military personnel and vigorous demands that China stop.

The issue is not about spying; frankly, we know (and they know) that we spy on each other as best we can through cyber and other means. In my business, espionage is fair game. What is utterly unacceptable to the U.S. is cyber theft of private company information for commercial gain. China had grown adept at stealing American companies' intellectual property and using it to make advanced products that compete against our own.

By August 2015, when I visited Beijing alone for the second time as NSA, the U.S., as my dad used to say, had already had "a bellyful" of their behavior. Diplomacy had not yielded results. Repeated warnings had failed. I came to Beijing with a strong and clear message: *If China doesn't stop stealing our stuff, we will sanction you on the eve of President Xi's first state visit to the U.S.*, which was scheduled for late September. I repeated our position privately at every opportunity, including more diplomatically with President Xi. We meant it and, as I reminded my Chinese interlocutors, the president had already signed an executive order giving us the tools to swiftly sanction any foreign actor for malign cyber deeds.

I delivered our points clearly. Knowing how sensitive the Chinese are to any potential embarrassment, much less serious turbulence surrounding their president's foreign travel, I hoped our message had been received. So, at first, I was chagrined to read, as I was leaving China, an unsourced *Washington Post* article reporting that the administration was preparing to impose sanctions on China. I hate all leaks and was pissed in principle. In this case, specifically, I worried initially that the Chinese would perceive bad faith on our part by going to the press before our final efforts at diplomacy had played out. Yet by the time we were wheels-up from Beijing, my concern about the leak quickly and cynically turned to appreciation for the prospect that the article might serve to amplify the seriousness of my message.

Within a few days of my return, the Chinese system kicked into gear. Worried that sanctions would upend Xi's visit, China asked to send a very high-level delegation immediately to Washington to try to resolve the issue. The proposed visit was scheduled to start on September 9, the precise day we had planned internally to announce sanctions against Chinese individuals and entities. Inside the White House, we had a robust debate as to how to proceed. I argued that we should wait to see what the Chinese delegation had to say before pulling the trigger on sanctions. We could still implement the sanctions before Xi arrived if we were unsatisfied. Several of my colleagues wanted to sanction China preemptively and then double down with additional measures if China's envoys failed to meet our demands.

Though we all doubted these discussions would yield any progress, President Obama decided that we would hold off on sanctions and receive the Chinese delegation. Lisa, Avril, and I, though not originally in agreement on when to levy sanctions, came together (as always) to press the divided agencies to fall in line behind the president's decision to give diplomacy one more serious try.

The Chinese side, led by Politburo member and senior security czar Meng Jianzhu, met with Secretary of Homeland Security Jeh Johnson, Attorney General Loretta Lynch, and FBI director James Comey, before coming to see me in the Roosevelt Room at the White House. Their posture was respectful, but they recited the usual complaints about U.S. misdeeds and denied Chinese bad behavior. I laid out our terms pointedly: absent a groundbreaking new understanding to halt their commercially motivated cyber theft, we were headed to a bad place on the eve of Xi's visit. I outlined the terms of what we needed in any potential agreement.

Later, I held a private follow-on conversation with another member of Meng's delegation—Deputy Foreign Minister Zhang Yesui, my former Chinese counterpart during my first year at the U.N., with whom I had always had a collegial relationship. I told Yesui that, "We are really at a critical point. We are not bluffing, and I have no room for maneuver. If you don't agree to our proposal, we are in for a rough ride." Following our discussion, our staffs met for over thirty-six hours of nearly continuous negotiations at the White House and Chinese embassy. In the end, they reached an understanding, subject to ratification by Beijing and President Obama.

Nonetheless, early Saturday morning, after an all-night negotiating session and as the Chinese delegation was flying home, I received an alarming report from my team that the Chinese side had torpedoed the deal. At once, I called the Situation Room and asked them to rouse the Chinese ambassador to Washington, Cui Tiankai. After initial protests from his staff that he was unavailable, we were connected. I lit into him, telling the normally very calm but now quite agitated ambassador, "You need to fix this mess by Monday morning or be prepared to explain to your president why Washington will be his worst state visit to date."

By Monday morning, the Chinese had reconsidered, and we had a deal that satisfied our concerns. To the shock of informed observers, the two presidents announced on September 25 in the Rose Garden: "Neither country's government will conduct or knowingly support cyber-enabled theft of intellectual property, including trade secrets or other confidential business information, with the intent of providing competitive advantages to companies or commercial sectors." The U.S. side also made plain that, if we saw evidence that China was violating the deal, we stood ready to impose sanctions.

This agreement between the U.S. and China largely held through the duration of the Obama administration, and seemingly until U.S.-China relations deteriorated markedly under President Trump, when aggressive theft resumed.

In our time, the U.S. Intelligence Community and the private sector consistently reported to us that they detected a marked reduction in Chinese commercial-related cyber theft (if not its complete elimination), assessing that continued suspicious behavior largely fell in the gray area abutting espionage. We also worked with China to translate our bilateral agreement into multilateral understandings at the G20, U.N., and other international venues to induce more countries to adhere to cyber norms. Progress on tough issues like cyber theft and currency manipulation, the unprecedented cooperation we achieved in a range of new areas, plus the growing personal ease between President Obama and President Xi, enabled us to leave the potentially antagonistic U.S.-China bilateral relationship on a stable footing for our successors.

Vividly, I recall President Obama's last trip to China in September 2016, when President Xi, as host of the G20, took the floor at the conclusion of the summit in Hangzhou to give one final, lengthy statement. Before the assembled leaders of the world's most powerful countries, President Xi warmly praised President Obama for helping guide the world away from the brink of financial collapse in 2009, for his wisdom as a leader, his contributions as a valued partner to each of them on all issues of global consequence, and as a man of vision, patience, and integrity. It was a remarkable tribute from a competitor, as unexpected as it was personal and seemingly genuine.

Xi's comments also stood in sharp contrast to how our visit to Hangzhou began. When we arrived on Air Force One, the Chinese—who by now we knew to be notoriously heavy-handed and imperious hosts—were at their finest.

First, a tarmac dispute between the airport authorities and the U.S. Secret Service over who would drive the mobile staircase up to the side of the plane resulted in the Chinese refusing to allow the full-length staircase to be used by the president to disembark. With time wasting, the U.S. side decided to take matters into their own hands. Unwitting of any issue, and by nature unpretentious, the president walked off the plane using the short internal steps from the base of Air Force One, which made for a less grand descent than is customary. The traveling White House press corps erupted in outrage as if hell had just frozen over and started their reporting of the trip heralding a monumental snub by the Chinese of President Obama.

Their frenzy was heightened when a six-foot-three-inch goonish Chinese security guard abruptly body-blocked me as I tried to pass under a tape barrier to join the president in his limo waiting plane-side. Initially, I plowed ahead without paying him much heed, but he kept stopping me. When my explanation of who I was and where I was going failed to satisfy the guard, my lead Secret Service agent, Tom Rizza, nearly came to blows with my Chinese barrier. To ensure I reached the vehicle before the motorcade moved out, I imagine Rizza spoke into his wrist giving his fellow agents a heads-up, *Point Guard moving to join Renegade in the Beast.*

All this drama happened under the noses of our traveling press corps assembled beneath the plane's wing, reinforcing their commitment to the narrative that we were being bullied even before the first meeting began. It was a bogus story, not least because it was one of Xi Jinping's staff who recognized me and helped me join the president in his vehicle, overruling the ignorant local security guard. And "stair-gate" was an equal exaggeration, having nothing to do with official intent on either side but rather a staff-level skirmish. Still, our press had already decided that the visit was off to a bad start, but in this case their overheated reporting failed to sabotage it.

Through eight years of deep engagement with the Chinese on various issues, I found that with vision and tenacity, the U.S. has the capacity to broaden areas of cooperation with China while at the same time directly confront our profound differences with the appropriate combination of fortitude, firmness, and care. China's power and global influence will continue to grow. So too will its transgressions and provocations. In the last few years, China has intensified abuse of its own citizens and doubled down on construction in the South China Sea and its pursuit of nefarious trade and technology policies. How the U.S. manages this dynamic—alone or with allies, with confidence and calm, or with fear and fatalism—will substantially define the global landscape in the twenty-first century.

———

"Susan, do you have a few minutes to stay back and talk privately?" I heard John Brennan asking me, as fellow members of the PC quickly departed the meeting we had just concluded on a busy day in early August 2016.

John, a tough, loyal, burly man of Irish descent who had devoted his whole career to keeping America safe by ably defeating terrorists and other adversaries, was one of my favorite colleagues. Sometimes irascible, but always a straight shooter with a generous heart, I trusted John's judgment and experience implicitly.

We had the Situation Room to ourselves. He pulled a paper out of his lock bag and said without drama, "We have strong evidence that Putin himself is trying to interfere in our election. This is not a low-level operation. It comes from the top." He showed me the smoking-gun report and detailed the credibility of its sourcing.

I took a couple of seconds to collect my thoughts and said, "We gotta go upstairs and tell the Boss."

On the way into the Oval, we rounded up White House chief of staff Denis McDonough. Ferial directed us back to the president's private dining room at the end of a small hallway off the side of the Oval Office. Obama, sitting at the table reading, looked up. Brennan repeated the same message he had given me and handed the president the report. The president read over the paper and instructed us to convene a select group of Principals as soon as possible.

From that moment in early August through Election Day, President Obama and a tight circle of senior officials wrestled with how to counter a Russian threat that far exceeded anything we had seen to date. Russia had previously hacked into U.S. government and private entity systems. It had spread disinformation. Since the Cold War, it had employed propaganda and other means to influence U.S. elections. It had messed with elections in European countries, but we had not previously experienced this particular variety of Russian cyber espionage in the U.S., which combined hacking into party systems, official propaganda, social media manipulation, and attempts to penetrate state electoral systems. The Russians coordinated all these hostile elements in a concerted effort to interfere in a U.S. presidential election. Nor had we before possessed such strong evidence that the order came directly from the top. For weeks, my stomach churned with a low-grade, intermittent nausea.

It was not immediately clear what Russia's motives were. A range of possibilities included: 1) to help Trump; 2) to discredit Clinton; 3) to hamper Clinton's ability to govern effectively if elected; 4) to sow domestic discord and distrust in the results of the election; 5) to discredit democracy globally; or, 6) all of the above. Regardless of the motive, what worried us most was that Russia might gain access to state electoral systems and manipulate the voter rolls by excluding voters or adding ineligible voters, or even try to falsify the vote count in strategic jurisdictions. We also feared that Russia might not only steal and release hacked emails, as they had done with the Democratic National Committee and later would do with Clinton campaign chairman John Podesta's personal emails, but that they might also doctor stolen messages to embed false, derogatory information and make it look real.

In our initial meetings, we quickly determined that we had to pursue a multitrack counterstrategy.

First, we asked the Intelligence Community to increase collection and accelerate efforts to produce a unified assessment of what exactly the Russians were doing and why, so that we could share the findings with the

American people. Given the gravity of the issue, it was important that the conclusions of the IC be agreed to by all its components and that they could collectively affirm "high confidence" in their validity. This impartial IC assessment was a prerequisite to informing the American people, which we deemed urgent and essential, and we hoped it would be backed publicly by the bipartisan leadership of Congress. Unfortunately, it took the IC until the end of September to reach a sufficient level of confidence and unity in their assessment, and we were unable to get congressional agreement on a bipartisan statement, which would have underscored that what we were announcing was not motivated by partisan politics.

Finally, on October 7, we were able to issue an unprecedented, flashing-red public warning from the director of national intelligence and the secretary of homeland security, the senior officials we believed were best placed to deliver such a finding. Some have wondered why President Obama or the White House did not issue the statement, given its significance. Since the president and the political arm of the White House were engaged in the campaign, we thought that any announcement from the White House would muddy the message that the warning was to be understood as a purely nonpartisan, national security matter. The October 7 statement revealed:

> *The U.S. Intelligence Community (USIC) is confident that the Russian Government directed the recent compromises of e-mails from U.S. persons and institutions, including from U.S. political organizations. . . . These thefts and disclosures are intended to interfere with the U.S. election process. . . . We believe, based on the scope and sensitivity of these efforts, that only Russia's senior-most officials could have authorized these activities.*

News of this high-level U.S. government warning about Russian interference in our national election was quickly overtaken by other events. Not long after I had sent Russian ambassador Sergey Kislyak packing from my office, having informed him we were about to call out publicly Russia's intervention in our election, Denis walked into my office.

He said, "Have you seen the video?"

"What video?"

"Just go online and you will see."

Holy shit, I thought, as I watched the *Access Hollywood* tape of candidate Trump boasting about sexually abusing women. *How in the hell can he survive this? How can such a misogynist be president?*

And then came, almost right away, the curiously timed WikiLeaks release of John Podesta's hacked emails.

Suffice it to say, these two dramas knocked our stark announcement of Russian electoral interference down "below the fold" on the front pages of our national newspapers. The impact that we hoped the DNI statement would have on public understanding was more than diluted by the subsequent news of the day.

Second, in early August, the president ordered Secretary of Homeland Security Jeh Johnson to convene the secretaries of all fifty states urgently to inform them of the threat and enlist their cooperation to harden their states' electoral systems so that hackers could not penetrate them effectively. Johnson did so but was surprised to find that many Republican secretaries of state forcefully rejected Johnson's suggestion that DHS designate their state electoral systems as "critical infrastructure," which would have given the federal government greater latitude to assist the states. Numerous "red states" viewed this proposal as an infringement on their sovereign rights and pushed back with such force that Johnson relented, calculating that it was better to get as much voluntary cooperation as possible, rather than engender additional resistance by pressing the "critical infrastructure" designation, even though it would have helped.

Third, President Obama directed John Brennan to brief bipartisan congressional leaders (the so-called "Gang of Eight") as soon as possible on the same threat report he had received. We needed not only congressional leaders' awareness but their cooperation to convey to the American people that we faced a serious threat to the integrity of our democracy that could affect all voters and candidates in both parties up and down the ballot. We wanted Congress's help to underscore the truth that Russian interference was not a partisan concern but a serious national security threat.

It took over a month for all eight leaders to make themselves available to receive Brennan, who was ready to fly to meet them anywhere over the August congressional recess. Certain Republican leaders were not willing to be briefed until after Labor Day. When finally informed, Senate Majority Leader Mitch McConnell cast doubt on the credibility of the reporting and deliberately downplayed the threat. McConnell's motivations appeared plainly partisan, as he somehow sensed this revelation might harm candidate Trump.

In early September, President Obama personally asked the four bipartisan leaders of the House and Senate to coauthor a letter underscoring their shared concern with the Russian threat and advising states to take it seriously, but McConnell continually blocked the effort to issue a timely bipartisan warning to the American people. We also requested a public bipartisan statement regarding Russian interference that would serve to make clear to the American people that this was not and should not be construed as a partisan issue. For weeks, Senator McConnell refused to budge. When, finally in late September, he relented, McConnell would only affix his name to an anodyne, hard-to-decipher letter that didn't even mention Russia.

Fourth, we set out to deter Russia from taking actions that went beyond their activities to date (the previous hacking, the strategically timed release of hacked information, and propaganda activities) and to prepare an appropriate response to their egregious conduct. We knew there was much more Russia could do—falsely smear a candidate; release faked versions of stolen information; penetrate the election systems to disenfranchise voters; or more difficult, but not impossible, attempt to alter the vote count in certain places. We assessed that much of what Russia had stolen they had already transferred to third parties, including WikiLeaks. Those cats were likely already out of the bag.

Our aim *now* was to prevent a worst-case scenario. Brennan delivered a stark warning to his Russian counterpart making plain that we knew what they were doing. President Obama cornered Putin for a one-on-one conversation after their formal meeting at the G20 on September 5, in Hangzhou, China. Obama delivered a carefully crafted, forceful message telling Putin, in essence—*We know exactly what you are doing, we will be watching carefully, and, if you do anything further, we will punish Russia in ways you have not experienced before.* While deliberately ambiguous about the nature of the consequences, Obama left no doubt that he was serious. As expected, Putin denied and deflected, falsely trying to shift blame to the U.S. for stoking the so-called "color" revolutions in former Soviet states. A month later, Obama reiterated and amplified his warning in a private, written message to Putin, which I delivered through Ambassador Kislyak.

Meanwhile, a subset of the NSC Deputies and Principals, along with a very few staff experts, readied the economic, diplomatic, cyber, and other measures to punish Russia not only for what they had done but also in the event they went further and, for example, tried to affect the vote. These measures were prepared so that they could be deployed when the president determined the time was right. It is not the case, as has been reported, that I quashed further work on cyber options. That work proceeded. Rather, I insisted that knowledge of this highly sensitive effort be restricted to a very small group of senior officials and that it be considered along with other punitive response options, not in isolation.

Since our aim, in the first instance, was to deter more detrimental Russian interference, President Obama did not deem it wise or necessary to preemptively punish Russia for what they had already done before the election, unless we saw evidence that Russia had crossed the line the president had drawn. Preemptive U.S. penalties on Russia might well have provoked precisely the kind of more hostile actions we were trying to deter. We assumed that part of Russia's aim was to sow public doubt about the integrity of the election process. At the same time, we were mindful that candidate Trump's repeated, unfounded allegations that the election would be rigged only fed such doubts. We did not want to do the Russians' dirty work for them. Therefore, the administration sought to avoid steps that could unintentionally cast doubt on the credibility of the election, unless Russian escalation forced us to do so.

President Obama was deeply determined to act and be seen to be acting in an apolitical, unbiased manner in dealing with the Russian threat, even as he served simultaneously as the leader of one political party. Above all, he did not want to put any weight on the scales of our electoral process; equally, he prioritized maintaining public confidence in the integrity of our democracy.

Inside the administration, we studied Russian actions closely, looking particularly for evidence that they were trying to manipulate the mechanics of the voting process. All the while, we remained locked and loaded, ready to retaliate before the election, if necessary.

Prior to the election, the Intelligence Community did not in fact detect evidence that Russia was corrupting the mechanics of the voting—by fouling voter rolls or vote tallies. Nor did we see Russia falsify stolen information. What we all did see was the continued, strategically timed release of stolen emails that had been handed over to WikiLeaks and others in the spring and summer of 2016. We also observed sustained efforts by the Russian outlets, RT television and Sputnik news service, to publish content favorable to Trump and unfavorable to Clinton.

However, both the Intelligence Community and administration policymakers were less focused on the potential impact of Russia's ongoing manipulation of social media—its use of bots, troll farms, and fake personas—to plant false or misleading content aimed at biasing voter opinions. In retrospect, we substantially underestimated the pervasiveness and severity of Russia's social media manipulation in the run-up to the 2016 election. Only after we left office, when further information reached the public domain, did I and others fully appreciate the influence of Russian social media activities on shaping public sentiment.

After the election, the Principals Committee reconvened to take stock and revisit the punitive options we had formulated in August and September. The IC provided an updated, far more stark assessment of the purpose of Russia's interference, which they concluded was to harm Secretary Clinton's electoral prospects and to advantage Donald Trump. President Obama tasked the IC to compile a comprehensive assessment of all available information about Russia's role in the 2016 election and to provide a classified version to him, the president-elect and his team, and Congress by early January, as well as to prepare an unclassified report for the American people.

The Principals refined and sharpened the menu of potential punishments to levy against Russia. In late December, the president announced that we would punish Russia by: sanctioning two Russian intelligence services as well as malicious entities and individuals; publicly exposing the cyber tools and tricks Russians used to infiltrate our systems; closing two Russian compounds, or "dachas," in Maryland and New York used by Russian diplomats for vacationing and clandestine activities; expelling thirty-five Russian "diplomats" who we believe acted as spies; and continuing "to take a variety of actions at a time and place of our choosing, some of which will not be publicized."

We knew at the time that these sanctions and other punitive actions, while serious, were not the maximum measures the U.S. could take. The toughest sectoral sanctions we considered would have adversely impacted our European allies, not just Russia. We were reluctant to harm our allies, particularly as we sought to solidify their fragile support for sustaining strong European Union sanctions on Russia for its actions in Ukraine. In addition, we were mindful that President-elect Trump remained dismissive of Russian interference in the election and seemed open to lifting previous U.S. sanctions on Russia for Ukraine and other misbehavior. Recognizing the risk that, if we imposed maximum penalties, Trump might turn around and lift them soon after his inauguration, I and others sought to avoid a potential reversal that would be detrimental to U.S. credibility.

Indeed, we were surprised that soon after our sanctions announcement, President-elect Trump publicly congratulated Putin on refraining from immediate retaliation. This strange tweet raised questions as to whether the Trump transition team had suggested to Russia that they may later undo our sanctions. Our worries were later validated.

In early January, President Obama and select senior advisors received the highly classified findings of the Intelligence Community assessment of Russian interference in U.S. elections. It was in this context that we received for the first time a highly classified, brief summary from the IC of the so-called "Steele Dossier," named for the British former intelligence officer who compiled the report containing salacious allegations about Trump's behavior in Russia. President Obama, like the rest of us, was revolted by this information and protested even hearing about it. I insisted he receive at least the bare minimum, because President-elect Trump was to be briefed on it, and there was always the possibility that it could become public knowledge. This exchange was one of my most uncomfortable with President Obama in the Oval Office.

In retrospect, I wish that in December 2016 we had hit the Russians harder with powerful sectoral sanctions that shook the foundations of the

Russian economy. We refrained in order to spare our European allies and to avoid any adverse boomerang effects on the U.S. economy. Nevertheless, given continued Russian interference in our democracy, I believe we must still impose maximum costs to try to prevent future interventions. Regrettably, neither Congress nor the Trump administration has yet wielded nearly the full force of our economic power against Russia.

Dealing with Russian interference in our 2016 presidential election was a uniquely challenging policy problem. Each judgment we faced was difficult—when to go public; who should announce the Intelligence Community's findings; how to deal with a divided and suspicious Congress; how to inform the public without scaring them unduly; when and how to punish Russia; how to deal with a candidate who was stoking fears of voting fraud, praising WikiLeaks, and encouraging Russian hacking of his opponent's systems? We were operating in substantially uncharted territory where the stakes couldn't be higher. To my knowledge, no one in the Obama White House was ever informed by the FBI or Justice Department that they had opened an investigation into whether anyone affiliated with the Trump campaign coordinated with Russia on its election interference. I learned of the fact of the investigation only after leaving office, when FBI director James Comey testified before Congress to that effect. Still, the pressure we faced through the late summer and fall of 2016 in confronting the unprecedented scope of Russian electoral interference was enormous. Each step of the way, we made the best decisions we could for the right reasons. Yet we knew at the time we could never make every judgment flawlessly, and we did not, as is evident with the benefit of hindsight.

———

As I reflect on the course of President Obama's eight-year tenure, I am struck by the degree to which he largely adhered to the principles and priorities he laid out at the start of his presidency. His consistency defied the range of unforeseen challenges we faced—from the Arab Spring to the rise of populist nationalism and elected authoritarians, from the emergence of an ISIS "caliphate" to Brexit, from Russian aggression in Ukraine to its interference in our election. Through an active national security decision-making process, the Obama administration was able largely to manage such complex crises, while at the same time, "put points on the board" by accomplishing important goals that we *opted* to pursue.

I remain convinced that President Obama's foreign policy agenda was strategically sound. Ultimately, if inevitably, our record was mixed—though I would argue, on balance, positive. Though I am very proud of what the administration accomplished, my pride is tempered by recognition of what we may have done better.

We fell short of achieving several important objectives, including closing Guantánamo, even though we reduced the prison population dramatically. To our lasting frustration, Congress consistently blocked Guantánamo's closure by preventing the transfer of those remaining inmates to maximum security U.S. facilities. We were also unable to resolve the conflict in Syria, stabilize Libya, or move the needle on intractable, inherited challenges such as brokering Israeli-Palestinian peace or eliminating North Korea's nuclear and missile programs.

Our failures had various roots. In some cases, we suffered from a mismatch between our stated objectives and the means we were prepared to employ to achieve them—as in Libya, Syria, Ukraine, and, arguably, Afghanistan. During the Arab Spring and in the president's 2009 Cairo speech, we inadvertently raised expectations about the speed and ease with which major change could occur in the Middle East and the role that U.S. policy could play. Elsewhere, we remained reluctant to exert maximum pressure on our partners to take steps they resisted—whether on the Saudis to end the war in Yemen or the Israelis and Palestinians to negotiate in good faith. Finally, short of using force, we were unable to persuade or compel determined dictators—from Vladimir Putin to Kim Jong Un—to abandon hostile policies that bolstered their domestic power and international standing.

I also believe we underestimated the extent to which growing domestic partisan divisions were hampering America's ability to lead on the world stage. Opposing political parties too often consider withholding or blocking congressional support for a presidential foreign policy initiative that could advance U.S. interests, simply out of a desire to deny the sitting president a "win." That calculus appears to have animated many Republicans in Congress who withheld support for Obama's plan to use force to confront Syrian chemical weapons, sought to thwart the Iran deal, ridiculed the Paris Climate Agreement, and (like McConnell) failed to condemn Russian interference in the 2016 election in a forceful and timely way. Similarly, traditional GOP supporters of free trade (unlike most Democrats) who normally would have been inclined to support the twelve-nation Trans-Pacific Partnership to promote American exports and balance an economically rising China, could not countenance handing the administration even that foreign policy success.

Despite such headwinds, President Obama and his team succeeded in many important respects, starting with taking the necessary actions domestically and internationally to prevent a global economic catastrophe. We responsibly brought home the vast majority of our troops from Iraq and Afghanistan, while taking bin Laden off the field and decimating core Al Qaeda. Though we did not anticipate quickly enough the gathering threat ISIS posed in Iraq and Syria, we adjusted and devised a sound strategy that resulted in its battlefield defeat. The Obama administration fully and verifiably rolled back Iran's nuclear program and thus averted another potential major war in the Middle East through the skillful mix of diplomacy, economic sanctions, and the threat of force. Following the bitter acrimony over the Iraq War, we managed crucially to heal deep wounds with our European allies, despite the tensions reignited by the Snowden disclosures.

We positioned the U.S. to lead more effectively in the Western Hemisphere, particularly by normalizing relations with Cuba. In Asia, the Obama administration invested new resources and attention toward building our relations with India and Southeast Asian countries along with our treaty allies in Japan, Australia, South Korea, and the Philippines. We demonstrated the ability of the U.S. to simultaneously compete and cooperate with China, as most vividly illustrated by the understandings we reached on climate change. In Africa, President Obama hosted the first-ever U.S.-Africa Summit and implemented numerous initiatives to bolster economic development and security sector capacity.

The landmark 2015 Paris Climate Agreement grew out of years of relentless personal diplomacy by President Obama, starting at the U.N. climate conference in Copenhagen in 2009 and culminating in groundbreaking agreements with China, and later India, which were critical to achieving international consensus. Further, he demonstrated the power of effective U.S. leadership on numerous other global challenges from combating ISIS and global health security threats like Ebola to spearheading historic advances in arms control and nuclear security as well as landmark development initiatives to reduce poverty, boost food security, increase access to electricity, and empower girls and young leaders.

Our most notable successes were born largely of President Obama's willingness to take risks and our collective determination to be proactive and persistent in pursuit of an affirmative agenda rather than simply manage the in-box of proximate threats and challenges. There was also the intangible persuasive power of an unlikely and inspirational American president whose election, reelection, and steady leadership reminded the world both of America's ability to grow and change and of our collective potential to rise to meet even the most daunting challenges. On the international scene, as on the domestic front, progress resulted substantially from careful orchestration and coordination of effort among leaders in the Obama administration, who envisioned, pursued, and successfully implemented a wide range of initiatives that benefited the American people and countless others around the world.

Many of these important gains, along with the world's faith in the constancy of American leadership, would later be sorely challenged, and in some cases undone, by what would come next—a new president with a very different temperament, principles, and priorities, as well as a dysfunctional national security decision-making process.

22

"He F#%@ing Won?"

—Eddie Murphy

I *can't say I didn't see it coming.*

---•◆•---

Like most in the Obama administration, I was hopeful that Secretary Clinton would win the 2016 presidential election. I just wasn't as sure as some that she would. Partly, that was because I never forgot how, in 2008 against Obama, Clinton seemed at least initially to have taken victory for granted and squandered her advantages. In addition, I found her 2016 campaign to be workmanlike, despite being as invested in her victory as any Democrat. Mainly, I long had a nagging feeling that Trump could tap into a nasty vein of populist nationalist American politics that was potent, if seemingly latent.

I first ventured this argument in August 2015, during a small dinner with President Obama and a couple of his senior political aides in his hotel room during a visit to Alaska. This discussion preceded any primaries but came after Trump had declared his candidacy. As we bantered about the coming primary season, I said that I could see a way for Trump to gain the nomination.

"No way, NO WAY," the others said. "That will never happen."

For a short while, I persisted, saying, "There is a lot of hate out there. You know some people just can't get over where we are now"—meaning

453

but not saying: the fact that we have an intelligent, successful, squeaky-clean, still popular, two-term African American president with a beautiful wife and kids. I was not suggesting then that Trump would be president, but I didn't think the nomination was out of his reach. In response, I was sufficiently ridiculed that I dropped the argument, comforted that the political experts thought I was crazy.

In the two weeks before the 2016 election, I started to get that nagging feeling again. The unexpected, eleventh-hour announcement that FBI director Comey had reopened the Clinton email investigation reignited the media's obsession with Clinton's server. Popular energy for Clinton's candidacy seemed underwhelming, despite her inner strength, deep experience, and commanding debate performances. It all left me uneasy. Trump was acting as wildly as ever but maybe, like my dad used to say, "crazy like a fox."

The French government sent a couple of President Hollande's senior advisors to Washington the week before the election. They were trying to get a feel for what was going to happen. They met with several administration officials before they got to me. Each of us was asked about his or her expectations for the election outcome. All my colleagues had said they were confident Clinton would win; so, the French were surprised and concerned to hear me say, "I'm not so sure." Still, I tried to reassure them by stressing—*I'm the national security advisor, not the political director, and this assessment falls outside my area of expertise.*

I had a similar exchange with Emirati Crown Prince Mohammed bin Zayed (MBZ) during my visit with him in Abu Dhabi the weekend before the election. He asked me what I thought was going to happen. Most people thought Clinton would win, I reported, but I believed Trump had a decent chance. "*Really?*" he said, leaning forward in his seat with deep interest and anticipation. He was genuinely shocked by my assessment, but I wasn't sure at the time whether he took that as good news or bad. (In retrospect, it's clear that it was the former.)

The day before the election, I traveled with President Obama on his last campaign swing. I rarely went on domestic trips with him, but this seemed historic and final, and I was curious to get a feel for the mood in the country. Obama held rallies in Michigan, New Hampshire, and Pennsylvania, the last one jointly with Clinton. Hillary's closest aides seemed pretty confident but by no means cocky. That we were even asked to go to Michigan concerned me. Then, in Philadelphia, the Obama team got wind that the Clinton team intended to play Fleetwood Mac's "Don't Stop Thinking About Tomorrow," a staple of the 1992 Bill Clinton campaign, at their joint rally. Our folks said, "Not happening" and nixed the idea, but several of us could not help thinking privately that this too did not bode well. Still, Obama's political advisors appeared confident Clinton was going to win. So much so that I slept well on election eve.

On election night, I planned to stop by two parties before heading home to share the election of the first woman president with my daughter, Maris. This was a moment I needed to be with her. By eight o'clock at the first party, things were starting to seem dicey. I called the White House political director for reassurance, but he had none to offer. It was looking like this could be a very bad night. My stomach started to churn, so I left quickly, not wanting to be far from my own bathroom. Ian and I made a quick appearance at the second party. By the time we got home, it was clear Clinton was done.

Donald Trump was going to be president.

Maris went to bed early, without knowing the final result. When I woke her in the morning with the news, she thought I was joking. As soon as she grasped that I was dead serious, she melted. Maris believed in Hillary but even more so in the power of her example for all young women. I tried to reassure Maris that what Hillary had done will pave the way for women who will ultimately fulfill our collective dream.

As I said goodbye, I knew, as in my favorite children's book, that it was going to be a "Terrible, Horrible, No Good, Very Bad Day." Maris's emotion was merely a harbinger of the devastation and raw pain of the young White House staffers I encountered throughout the day. I worked hard to maintain a brave face for them and my own shocked NSC staff, just as I had for Maris. I reminded the NSC senior staff that the president and I remained fully committed to executing a thorough and responsible transition.

"We're all patriots and professionals," I told my staff, and we will do our best to assist the incoming team. I urged those who were career professionals to commit to staying at the NSC as long as needed. I explained that we had seen radically different administrations succeed one another before, and our country and its institutions were strong enough to manage such change seamlessly. This should be no different. That was my mantra, and I was sticking to it.

Throughout the day, President Obama played consoler-in-chief, bucking up the White House team as best he could with the same stiff upper lip. I was starting to believe my own rhetoric. It would be okay. I kept up my reserve and resolve all through Wednesday and well into Thursday, when Obama met with Trump in the Oval. That evening, Obama hosted a reception for senior staff and cabinet members and their spouses. He was still bucking people up, and I was still sounding painfully rational refrains, even with colleagues who were confidently predicting that the Trump administration would be an utter disaster.

When Ian and I returned to my office in the West Wing to gather my stuff, I sat down at my desk. And . . . just . . . lost . . . it. I was almost gasping for air, as the tears rushed, and I finally let the enormity of this loss and its inestimable consequences hit me. Trump's election felt like a stinging rebuke of all we believed in—unity, equality, dignity, honesty, hope, and progress. It presaged the wholesale unraveling of the accomplishments we had worked hardest to achieve and that would have the most lasting, positive impact on America and the world. His crude, zero-sum "America First" mantra also signaled a retreat from America's allies, the post–World War II international institutions that had facilitated peace and growing prosperity for some seventy years, and the abdication of traditional American leadership in accordance with both our values and our interests. The more I thought about it, the worse I felt. To lead my team, effect a responsible transition, and finish the job, I had to focus on the present and not speculate about the ominous future. So resolved, after ten minutes I pulled myself together and held it together until January 20.

President-elect Trump began to announce his national security team during President Obama's final foreign trip of his presidency. In mid-November, Obama traveled to Greece to pay respect to the birthplace of democracy; to Germany to say an emotional goodbye to his good friend Angela Merkel and to meet with other key European allies; and to Peru for his last APEC (Asia-Pacific Economic Cooperation) Summit, where he held final bilateral meetings with President Xi of China, Prime Minister Justin Trudeau of Canada, and Prime Minister Malcolm Turnbull of Australia.

The trip was depressing. Trump named Michael Flynn as his national security advisor, a choice Obama had warned Trump against, and appointed Jeff Sessions as attorney general, whose old-school Dixie, conservative credentials rendered his selection frightening on its face. We found all of America's allies apprehensive, to put it mildly, about what a Trump administration would portend.

President Xi warned that China did not want a trade war with the U.S., but if one were foist upon it, China would play to win. The Trans-Pacific Partnership trade agreement, which had been concluded with eleven other APEC countries, seemed set to be an early casualty of Trump's reckless protectionism.

Against this backdrop, it was hard to muster much in the way of a silver lining. Yet, in the best Obama team tradition, we found one anyway. On the last night of the trip in Lima, the traveling staff—NSC, scheduling and advance, the president's personal staff, and many others—commandeered the top floor of a popular Peruvian nightclub. We drank pisco sours and danced like fiends to R&B and hip hop. It was the party to end all Obama team parties. Finality and frustration, friendship and camaraderie made for potent fuel that drove us long into the night.

Unlike most others, I had to wake up early to join Obama in his first meetings. When I stood up in the morning at my bedside, my legs buckled in pain. I was only tolerably hungover, so the problem was elsewhere. My fifty-two-year-old knees were shot from raucous dancing, complete with many gravity-defying moves, such that I struggled to make it to the shower.

When I hobbled into the Beast to accompany Obama, he quizzed me as usual on the prior night's exploits. His desire for detail belied a tacit tinge of regret that he could never join in the fun. As always, I gave it to him straight: "Mr. President, you missed a hell of a party, and none of us is going to be in top form today."

The day after we returned from Lima, I called Michael Flynn to congratulate him and offer unlimited amounts of my time before Inauguration Day. President Obama was determined to execute a transition at least as professional and generous as the one he was grateful to have received from President George W. Bush. Our marching orders were clear: give them all they needed and then some.

While Flynn was cordial on that first call, I had a hell of a time nailing down meetings with him. We had prepared over one hundred carefully crafted briefing memos on every conceivable important topic from the administrative (like how to hire and budget for NSC staff) to hot policy issues like North Korea and the counter-ISIS campaign, to bad scenarios that could unfold early in the new administration (e.g., the collapse of Mosul Dam), complete with our suggestions as to how to approach each potential challenge. In the early weeks of the transition, Flynn seemed to spend the bulk of his time meeting with visiting foreign officials at Trump Tower and betrayed little interest in the policy advice of his predecessor or in hiring staff to fill key vacancies.

After two or more weeks of my persisting, Flynn and I met for the first time in early December and then three times thereafter for a total of over twelve hours. I walked him through the major issues he would encounter and encouraged him to digest the binders of written materials we prepared. Alas, the many memos we wrote did not get much attention during the transition, and it is unclear if they were ever read.

In our meetings, I found Flynn to be civil and respectful, but bizarrely focused on exotic, highly compartmented, classified matters, which I did not think he needed to know until after he took the job. As I shared privately with a couple close members of my team, I instinctively doubted whether Flynn would actually make it to become national security advisor and, if he did, I suspected he would not last long. I had no concrete basis for that doubt beyond cumulative clues that left me dubious about his interests and capacity.

Flynn did not seem very focused on the nuts and bolts of running the NSC staff and the Principals Committee process, nor on how best to support the president. We had perfectly professional and pleasant interactions, but I was not very impressed by Flynn's intellect, strategic vision, or his perspective on the world and key threats. Russia, in his view, is not a significant adversary, but a declining power of limited consequence. China is the greatest enemy we face, a huge bogeyman that's already eating America's lunch, and we would be wise to fight her sooner rather than later. Erdoğan's Turkey and the Sunni Gulf Arab states deserve America's deference and unqualified support, given the threat of "radical Islamic extremism," while our European allies barely rate mention.

During a couple of our meetings, we were joined by Flynn's deputy NSA-designate, K. T. McFarland, and deputy NSA, Avril Haines. K.T., a former Fox News personality, shocked us by raising in our first encounter the question of whether it might be possible for them to work in shifts, so that Flynn, for example, might do mornings, and she would be there in the afternoon to cut down on the hours. Avril and I sputtered in response that there was no way that kind of arrangement would work, and I stressed to K.T. my view that the job of deputy national security advisor (when done right) is the toughest in government. She seemed surprised by that insight.

K.T. also made an impression with the full-length mink coat she wore to transition meetings in the White House. One day, when she walked into the Situation Room wearing it, I said (sincerely) that I imagined this was the first time such a garment had ever seen the inside of the Sit Room. She protested that, of course, it must have happened in the Reagan administration. I said, "I really doubt it," thinking that the only woman who would have been invited into Reagan's Sit Room was Jeane Kirkpatrick, the former U.S. ambassador to the United Nations, and she didn't strike me as the mink-coat-wearing type.

At our final meeting just days before the inauguration, Flynn expressed appreciation for my efforts to ensure an effective NSC transition. Indeed, ours turned out to be the *only* national security transition in the entire U.S. government, because Trump's designated successors to the secretaries of state and defense refused or were prohibited from meeting with their predecessors. Trump's team seemingly had no interest in learning anything from their Obama counterparts, even if it meant entering the most important jobs in government in near perfect ignorance about what awaited them.

And then came that moment when, instead of shaking my outstretched hand, Flynn accepted my good wishes and offer to help him subsequently, if ever I could, and asked for a hug. After the hug was granted, we parted that afternoon. It was the last time I saw him and have never heard from him since. It turned out I was twenty-four days off on the over/under for how long he would make it in the job.

———

Those last days of the Obama administration were both joyful and painful. Joyful because we had maintained a strong sense of team, a camaraderie among veterans who had each other's backs, played our hearts out until the final buzzer, and ended an eight-year-long season with a winning record. Yet painful because of Clinton's devastating electoral loss and the foreboding we all felt about the future. Could Trump prove as dangerous and ill-suited for the presidency as he seemed? Could it be far worse than any of us imagined?

On January 20, 2017, as I witnessed the literal dismantling of the Obama presidency—his Oval Office desk, carpet, and drapes being removed and refitted for a successor who could not have had more different taste—in decor, policy, or patriotism—I doubted whether any among the incoming Trump team would even care to try to bend "the arc of the moral universe toward justice."

When I reflect back on the myriad crises and pressures I faced, particularly in my first two years as national security advisor, I marvel that I did not lose my composure or crumble in exhaustion. The job was brutal, however much I enjoyed it and felt privileged to have it.

Still, family always came first. With the unequivocal backing of President Obama, and in order to model to my team that they should do the same, I never skipped a child's doctor's appointment, a back-to-school night, or a parent-teacher conference. To ensure I would not miss a potentially urgent call from my mother or one of her caregivers, I asked my assistant to listen out for my personal phone when I was in the Situation Room, the Oval Office, or my own office—all secure spaces where one cannot take a cell phone. If the call was important or time-sensitive, they would send a note to me so I could step out and respond.

While I mostly managed to separate my personal life from the pressures of the job, at times work and family merged, if only to enable me to be with my kids when it mattered most to them. I tried hard to catch Maris's weekend soccer games, if they were not too far away. Never untethered from email, the phone, or secure communications, I often found myself multitasking on the sidelines, talking to one of my colleagues while watching the games intently and apologizing when loud cheers (including my own) interrupted our discussions.

Potentially a more fraught occasion, the December 2015 night when Jake was set to hear whether he would gain admission to his preferred college coincided with our NSC Christmas party for staff and families. As host, I had to attend, but Jake, Ian, and I stayed behind in my White House office until the decisions were released so Jake could be with us when he got the news. When he logged on and saw the word "Congratulations," we whooped and danced and popped champagne before heading over together to join the real party.

Over the years, I demonstrated an odd capacity to compartmentalize. Throughout my time in government, I managed to sleep well most nights. Able to bound my work-related responsibilities, I did not allow the stress they engendered to consume my family life or adversely affect my overall state of mind, and vice versa. Perhaps I first developed that skill early when I had to keep the difficulties in my family life and my parents' divorce from stunting my academic and personal development.

Yet I worried sometimes that this detachment, this strange separation of my work from the emotional side of my life, was unnatural, if not unhealthy. It enabled me, for instance, to endure the psychic pain of making difficult decisions without them eating away at my soul. Rather than dwell on my strange ability to separate my emotions from my intellect, and my passions from policymaking, however, I was just grateful to be able mostly to keep the pressures of the job in a workbox and to spare my family from after-hours agonizing.

Throughout my tenure in the Obama administration, the biggest source of stress in my life was actually never my job, either as U.N. ambassador or national security advisor. It was worrying about my parents, especially my mom in her later years.

While my dad was recovering from his stroke and surgeries in 2010, and before he passed away in 2011, my mom experienced a recurrence of her prior cancers of the epiglottis and surrounding lymph nodes. A mass was discovered in her lung. I attended her surgery and recovery at Massachusetts General Hospital in Boston, after which she was able to continue to live independently in Washington for another eighteen months, before a second lung cancer required yet another surgery in June 2012. Mom came through this subsequent surgery at Mass General but then suffered a post-operative stroke, which impaired her physical strength and diminished her executive functioning (including her capacity to keep a schedule), dulled just slightly her incredibly sharp mind, and changed her personality, rendering her somewhat less argumentative and more persuadable.

Following her stroke and long recovery, Mom required 24/7 home care. I took on the task of hiring, firing, and scheduling round-the-clock caregivers. Sitting alone in my spacious West Wing office, I often had to make evening calls in between reviewing piles of paperwork to ensure that Mom always had continuous, quality support in her own home. Too often, I had to scramble, beg, and plead with various caregivers to fill gaps in her coverage especially over weekends and holidays, which I tracked carefully using a printed-out monthly calendar. Yet, to concentrate on my job, I desperately needed the peace of mind of knowing that Mom was in safe, kind hands.

My mother hated being minded and longed for her independence. She balked at having someone around her constantly, but she loved her extraordinary caregivers, especially the incredibly diligent, devoted Kadiatou Touré and deeply experienced and hilarious Missy Moore. Without their care and friendship, Mom would not have lived her final years as fully and happily, and I could not have continued serving at the highest levels in government.

After the stroke, for the next five and a half years Mom gradually continued to weaken, her voice fading almost to a whisper as scar tissue from radiation ruined her vocal cords and made swallowing difficult. She had two more recurrences of lung cancer.

Despite her deteriorating condition, Mom remained emotionally strong, never giving up, never doubting her ability to endure, and ever devoted to her children and grandchildren. Almost every Sunday, we hosted Mom for dinner at our house with the kids, and with Johnny's family whenever possible. It was a ritual I clung to desperately, as I worried our remaining time with Mom was diminishing. Those family dinners afforded us all cherished quality time with her.

Ever the matriarch, Mom used the occasions to ensure her children and grandchildren were meeting her standards of excellence—critiquing the kids' table manners, college options, political views, and sports performance. She also never spared me and Johnny her unvarnished views of how we were executing our professional, spousal, and parenting responsibilities.

Mom's toughness was legendary. No challenge was too difficult to surmount—not six cancers, not a worsening swallowing disorder, not a stroke nor pneumonia. One Friday night in November 2014, the day before my fiftieth birthday party, Mom fell in her dining room. She had been left alone for a few minutes between caregiver shifts. When the next caregiver arrived, she found Mom lying on the slate floor conscious but bleeding from the back of her head. It wasn't clear what her head had struck or how badly she was injured.

Rushing to her from the White House, I arrived just as the ambulance was preparing to take her to Georgetown University Hospital. The MRI showed no head trauma, but a laceration on the back of her scalp needed stitches. Mom spent the night in the hospital for observation but was determined to escape the next morning in order to get ready for the party. On Saturday night, Lois showed up at Union Station, where Ian hosted the best party since our wedding, looking fly. Mom's hair was perfectly done and her outfit impeccably chic.

Ian had arranged the best birthday present ever: Aretha Franklin performed at my fiftieth birthday party! After hosting my U.N. Security Council colleagues in 2009, Aretha had kept in touch with us. She seemed to take a special liking to Ian, and they exchanged friendly text messages over the years. In fine form, she rocked the house full of friends from every stage of my first half century. The only momentary glitch was when Aretha lost an emerald earring and the whole party stopped to scour the floors to find it. After a few minutes, Aretha discovered the gem in the pocket of her own gown. Crisis ended. Mom joined family and friends on the dance floor in a series of righteous boogies. That night, I was bursting with gratitude—for Ian, my beloved friends and family, Aretha, and above all the woman who brought me into this world fifty years before.

The support Mom provided never ebbed. I counted on her every day. Even as her health deteriorated and she shrank physically, Mom's centrality in my life never diminished. I depended on her encouragement, wisdom, and support. When I called her from the office or in the car on the way home, no words meant more, even when she could only whisper them, than when she told me, "I adore you." Her potent love helped sustain me through all of the toughest times and buoy me in my greatest triumphs. In many ways, we valued our relationship more for having struggled to find mutual peace over so many years.

When we spoke each night, she often ended by reiterating how proud she was of me and Johnny. After major news events, like an Obama State of the Union speech or a legislative defeat, she dialed me within seconds to celebrate or commiserate. To this day, if the home phone rings after a consequential television moment, like the end of the riveting Blasey Ford/Kavanaugh hearing, I expect it to be Mom calling.

By 2016, I sensed that Mom's time was limited. She was tolerating immune-therapy treatment for her last cancer, and it seemed to have slowed the cancer's growth. But Mom's weakness was increasing, and her weight stayed stubbornly under one hundred pounds. I brought Mom, her caregiver Kadi, and a dear friend of Mom's from her college days to the White House for one of the last Christmas parties of the Obama era. She was able to see President Obama again and hold court at the party. Mom was equally a hit at the family holiday party my husband and I throw where, as usual, she stayed to the end, charming friends and neighbors.

At Christmas dinner at Johnny's, Mom was suffering from a bad cold and struggling with excessive quantities of mucus. But it seemed like she would overcome it. After Ian, the kids, and I left on December 26 for Anguilla, we didn't expect to get that call from Johnny on New Year's Eve, saying, "You need to come home. As soon as possible."

Mom was in the hospital with her second bout of pneumonia, and it was serious. When I arrived, Mom was in the ICU on breathing support. She was conscious and able to communicate with difficulty, and we hoped she might pull through yet again. The next night, Johnny's family and mine, our closest cousins, and Mom's caregivers gathered at her bedside to offer her encouragement and affirm our love. She couldn't speak. Her breathing, even with support, was very labored. But when Mom's doctor, who had been a classmate of mine at Stanford, showed up to check on her, looking fine in a smart leather jacket, she perked up, managed to talk, and put her best face on. It was classic Lois.

Mom passed quietly the next morning, January 4, 2017, with Johnny and me crying while holding her hands. It all ended sooner than I had anticipated. I figured we likely had only months left with her, a year max. For a long time, I'd been working to prepare myself for this loss, and when it came I was grateful that she didn't suffer long. Johnny, who takes the opposite approach to death—fighting its inevitability until it can no longer be denied—was devastated. Losing our last parent was unmooring and profoundly painful. Since she passed, I have felt a huge sense of loss, tempered by tremendous gratitude for all she has given me and my family and so many others whom she powerfully touched.

I miss my mom and dad mightily.

Knowing Mom, I believe she timed her passing strategically—to leave this world while her beloved Barack Obama was still president and when predictions even about the near future could only be speculative.

23

Bridging the Divide

Sitting alone at our kitchen table, now my makeshift office, on the second day after the end of the Obama administration, I am trying to adjust . . . to the feeling of having no huge stack of paper awaiting my review, no government-issued cell phone alerting me to the next crisis. Exhausted, proud, and done, following eight years of long hours and intense pressure, I am relieved to be through with government—at least for now. It has been a tremendous experience and an unmatched privilege to serve. At this point, however, I want nothing more than to sleep, vacation, and spend time with my family and friends.

Unburdened and untethered, liberated and lonely, I am befuddled by the recognition that there is nothing I have to do right then and there. Email offers a familiar distraction, even if it will not contain any issues of urgency or national security import, much less a matter of life and death. Opening my mailbox, I find a series of kind messages from former colleagues and friends thanking me for my service and wishing me well in the "afterlife" and more notes of condolence for my mother's passing three weeks earlier.

In my crowded inbox, one email immediately jumps out, because it is entitled "Love You." It's from Jake, then a freshman at Stanford University, and his message is characteristically direct:

> **Hey Mommy,**
>
> I have been thinking about you this week, and about how proud I am of you. You are truly a massive source of inspiration

for me in life, and I look up to you in everything that I do. I will always be proud to identify myself as your son. You have done amazing work for our country, and I will forever be grateful for that.

...Look forward to talking to you tomorrow. I am going birding but will try to call you in the afternoon.

Love,

Jake

Jake's email leaves me briefly buffeted by emotion. No one has sacrificed more than my family, especially my two children and my husband, to enable me to serve another eight years in government. It is gratifying to be reminded that Jake neither resents the tradeoffs my service entailed nor the lost time.

His pride moves me enormously, especially since Jake has long since declared his political independence from our family and adopted a classic conservative philosophy. At Stanford, he would grow more active and vocal, eventually becoming the high-profile president of Stanford College Republicans and, as my son, a darling of right-wing media. Given our strong differences—including over key issues that define the Obama administration's foreign policy legacy—I am touched all the more that my son emphasized his admiration for me and my service, appreciating that I had done my best for our country.

Jake's message is a timely reminder of how much we share and how bound we remain. Jake and I agree that we cannot allow our differences to overshadow what we have in common—an abiding bond of family and country—even in the most testing times.

---•◆•---

Initially, my return to private life was refreshing—a time to focus on my health, relax and catch up on sleep, and start to think about what I wanted to come next. Struggling against sensory overload, I tried my best not to despair over early indications of how disruptive and dishonest Trump's presidency would prove to be.

Then, barely ten weeks after Trump took office, a new assault began, which I could not tune out.

Step one of their play was run the night of Sunday, April 2, 2017. Ian alerted me by texting a link to Mike Cernovich, the alt-right conspiracy theorist who had accused Hillary Clinton of running a child sex ring out of a pizza parlor in Northwest Washington. Cernovich had tweeted: "I just published 'Susan Rice Requested Unmasking of Incoming Trump Administration Officials.'"

Within minutes, I was trending on Twitter. Shortly thereafter, I again became a constant story on Fox. The right-wing media machine, and many Republican members of Congress, including of course Senator Lindsey Graham, accused me of "improperly" or "illegally" "unmasking" Trump campaign and transition officials "for political purposes." *The Wall Street Journal* editorialized: "All this is highly unusual—and troubling. Unmasking does occur, but it is typically done by intelligence or law-enforcement officials engaged in anti-terror or espionage investigations. Ms. Rice would have had no obvious need to unmask Trump campaign officials other than political curiosity."

I'd seen it coming but hadn't anticipated the full force of the hit. After leaving government at the end of the Obama administration and free from the public spotlight, I was briefly under the illusion that I would no longer be a favorite target of the right wing, a recyclable bogeyman. Certainly, I never expected to be personally and publicly targeted by this (or any) president of the United States.

Thankfully, I had already heard rumors that the White House and then-chairman of the House Permanent Select Committee on Intelligence, Representative Devin Nunes, were gunning for me. Friends confided that, to reduce the pressure President Trump was feeling from the investigations into Russian interference in the 2016 election, the White House wanted to change the subject. Trump's March 4, 2017, tweet storm of lies accusing President Obama of having put a "tapp" on Trump Tower had been thoroughly discredited. The Trump team needed somehow to justify those false tweets and divert attention from Attorney General Jeff Sessions's recusal from the Russia investigation, just after it became clear he made false statements to the Senate Judiciary Committee about his campaign contacts with Russians.

Their fabricated allegation was that I had asked the Intelligence Community to reveal to me the names of Trump associates who were caught in intelligence collection on foreign targets, and that my motives for doing so were political (though no one has ever explained what that meant). Worse, they claimed that once the names were provided to me, they were widely disseminated within the U.S. government, and thus, directly or indirectly, I was responsible for the leaking of those names to the press.

The truth is far different. So-called "unmasking" and leaking are two very different things. "Unmasking," or requesting the identity of a U.S. person or entity who is not named in a particular intelligence report, is something that I and other senior officials did when necessary to understand the report's importance. As national security advisor, my job—like that of other cabinet-level national security officials—was to protect the American people and the security of our country. To help me do that, every morning the Intelligence Community gave me a carefully selected compilation of some twenty to thirty intelligence reports chosen to provide the best current information on what was going on around the world. I read them faithfully. On occasion, I received a report in which a "U.S. person" was referenced but no name was provided (as is customary to protect privacy). If, in order to assess the significance of the report, I needed to know who that "U.S. person" was, I would ask through my IC briefer whether the agency that produced the report could reveal the identity to me.

To give a hypothetical: if I received a report about a conversation involving an unnamed American proposing to sell an adversary high-tech bomb-making equipment, clearly, as national security advisor, I would want to know who that American person was and whether he had the capacity to follow through. Was this some pretender on the internet flacking something he didn't have, or was this a serious person with the will and the means to provide dangerous technology to an adversary? In such a case, the identity of the U.S. person is essential to assessing the importance of an intelligence report revealing a potential threat.

There is a long-standing process by which such requests for the identity of U.S. persons are made to the Intelligence Community, and there are guidelines for the access and use of such information consistent with the law. Assuming the IC provides the identity of a "masked" U.S. person, it would come to me personally and directly from my briefer. The identity is not broadly disseminated throughout the national security community or the government. It is completely false to suggest that asking for the identity of an American person is the same as leaking it. Leaking classified information is a serious crime. I have not and would not leak classified information.

As another example, if I saw information indicating Russia or any adversary were interfering in our electoral process, it would be my responsibility to understand its significance and initiate an appropriate policy process at the direction of the president. For me not to try to understand that information would be dereliction of duty. The much hyped and bogus "unmasking" charge was a case of being assailed for doing my job responsibly.

But the truth be damned.

President Trump told *The New York Times*, without a shred of evidence, that he thought I had committed a "crime." To further hype the distraction, Trump said: "I think the Susan Rice thing is a massive story. I think it's a massive, massive story."

Calling me a criminal from the Oval Office was so baseless that few in the mainstream media gave it credence. Trump sounded manic in defaming me, but he succeeded briefly in changing the subject from the Russia investigation, while firing up his base. The "unmasking" faux-scandal didn't last that long, and it was such a bogus hit that it soon lost much steam even on the right. But more helpful than the power of the truth in refocusing public attention was President Trump himself, who continued generating an endless stream of juicier, fresher, and more deceitful distractions.

Trump's attacks on me have proved tame in comparison to those he has since leveled against many other loyal, principled public servants in both the Obama administration and his own. Tame as they are, I wear them as a badge of honor.

———

My main comfort was that my mom was not here to see this happen again. Moreover, Maris, fourteen at the time, was old enough to understand the attacks in ways she could not five years earlier during Benghazi. Well-informed and a critical thinker, my daughter recognized that I was being vilified by the right wing to distract from concerns that the Trump team may have colluded with Russia during the 2016 election. This time, she was able to support *me* and urge me to stay strong.

Similarly, Jake, who brooks no assault on his mother, was sympathetic and supportive throughout. By virtue of my experience, Jake has seen first-hand how dishonest and defamatory the right-wing media can be, even as he remains an all too avid consumer.

Perplexing as such cognitive dissonance is to us, Ian and I love Jake as deeply and surely as any parents can love their child. We are thankful that he is a smart, self-disciplined, and responsible kid, who has given us few headaches apart from politics. We talk and text frequently when he is away, and he continues to seek his parents' advice and crave our approval.

Drawn academically to economics, political science, and history, Jake professes no interest in running for political office, favoring the private sector and finance. Ever quirky, his greatest passion remains birdwatching. Jake knows the sight and sound of most every bird in North America and continues to study the roughly ten thousand species worldwide. By his twenty-first birthday, Jake had recorded more than one thousand species of birds on six continents.

As close as Jake and I are, we know exactly how to push each other's buttons. Like every good Dickson and Rice, he is not shy about advocating, even aggressively, for what he believes. Our arguments *can* be calm and rational—when we try hard to reason deliberately and exercise maximum restraint.

More often, a phone call or casual conversation in the car or around the dinner table can escalate into an explosive, sometimes profane argument. Occasionally, after a heated debate, Jake will muse aloud, "Maybe we should just stop talking about politics." Truthfully, I'm sometimes sorely tempted to do so. But my response is, "Jake, if you and I can't manage to discuss this stuff, I don't know who can. Painful as it can be, we have to keep talking."

In reality, Jake and I differ more on policy means than ultimate ends; and, on some issues, we find our way to acknowledging that we don't ac- tually disagree that much, if at all. Indeed, we agree on: the importance of strong national defense and principled American global leadership; sup- porting democracy, human rights, and the rule of law; protecting the liberty and equality of every individual; free, fair trade and robust economic growth that enables many to thrive; the severity of the Russian threat; the value of our alliances; and a passion for Africa. Yet, we strongly differ on other foreign policy matters, such as Cuba, the Iran nuclear deal, and Middle East policy.

We argue energetically over domestic policy. Jake typically takes a libertarian, constitutional conservative view of most social and economic issues, and I favor pragmatic progressive solutions. He is pro-life, while I am pro-choice. He favors shrinking the state, and I believe the state has an important role to play. He opposes the Affordable Care Act, while I am deeply committed to ensuring that quality health care is accessible to all. Jake is not exercised about climate change; to me, it is an urgent, existential threat.

Even when most frustrated, I'm proud that Jake cares deeply about public issues and is an effective leader. It takes guts to get in the arena, especially at a place like Stanford where his views have earned him many dedicated detractors. Still, I confess it can be deeply painful to love someone so powerfully with whom I disagree so profoundly. As much as Ian and I have struggled to understand Jake's ideological evolution, chastising ourselves—what did we do or not do?—to this day, we're not sure when or why his views shifted so far to the right. The facts belie Jake's claim that he has always been a conservative. Yet his posture seems more than a phase of youthful rebellion, given its intensity and duration—although a swing from one end of the spectrum to the other has been a pattern in Jake's intellectual development. He moved from supporting the far-left Dennis Kucinich early in the 2008 campaign to center-left Obama, and then to conservative Rick Perry in 2012 and Tea Party ideologue Ted Cruz in 2016. Political views aside, Jake still personally likes and respects President Obama, who has always been extremely kind to him.

As far to the right as Jake has moved, Maris—as warm and easygoing as ever—is almost an equal distance to the left. Brilliant and beautiful, an excellent high school student fascinated by science, math, and literature, a three-sport Varsity athlete, and saxophone player, she is deeply committed to celebrating diversity and demanding inclusion of all people without exception. Ian and I agree with Maris on social issues, even as she leans more left on economic policy than we do. Frugal to a fault, Maris rails against "entitlement" and is critical of excessive wealth.

Rarely having met a progressive cause that she didn't wish to champion, Maris rallies (often with us) for: civil rights; Black Lives Matter; March for Our Lives; gay pride; the Women's March; Earth Day. Unfailingly light-hearted, tough-minded, and strong, Maris has wanted since age nine to serve her country in what she believes to be the most demanding possible way—in the armed forces. A better version of Mom and me, Maris is proof (at least in our family) that Darwin was onto something.

Jake and Maris truly love each other, but given their extreme differences, as older children they have struggled to get along. Ian and I tried to mediate and defuse their battles—a thankless task. Imploring them to recognize what's at stake, Ian once bluntly told the kids, "Just stop it. You guys need to listen and consider the other's point of view. Pause ten seconds before responding to what the other said. Remember," he stressed, "you two only have each other. Long after we're gone, you will have to get along, or be alone." It worked. In recent years, our children have mostly honored a mutual commitment to be more kind and try to understand each other's perspective.

In that spirit, unbeknownst to us, Maris invited Jake to come to speak at Maret, her school and his alma mater. She wanted her brother to share with the overwhelmingly liberal student body the foundation of his conservative views and then answer questions. Proud and at the same time nervous that the two might publicly combust, or that Jake would say something to offend Maris and other students, I anxiously awaited news of how the event unfolded.

Maris happily reported, "Jake answered questions openly and respectfully. He offered a good explanation of his core values as a conservative, opening many eyes." Fellow students told her that his views were internally consistent and made sense to them.

While I privately wished Jake might have been less persuasive, I was thankful that both kids viewed the event as a success. In our household, we have tried to instill deep respect for free speech and the necessity to try to understand and debate (hopefully civilly) those with whom we differ. Jake usefully affords us firsthand insight into the perspectives of many fellow Americans, which we would otherwise lack. Without him and our inescapably contrasting views, I doubt I would fully appreciate the urgency and importance of bridging our increasingly deep domestic political divide.

———

In the process of reflecting on the Washington in which I was raised and the world in which I am raising my kids, I am affirmed in my faith that, as a family and as a body politic, our divisions need not be fatal. We have the ability to heal.

Personally, I still worry there could come a day when Jake and I determine that our disagreements have become so profound, that we are irreconcilable. Not only do I pray that never happens, but I am committed to doing everything in my power to prevent and repair any rupture. Love and respect, however tough, are the most powerful salves to heal wounds, and we can't be afraid to use them—whether with family or, as I was reminded, with our compatriots.

The distressing news of Senator John McCain's terminal illness in 2017 prompted me to reflect on what Americans owe each other as fellow citizens, reminding me that to heal, we must be willing to forgive. Confronting that imperative, I struggled to reconcile my complicated feelings toward McCain. Though he had continuously assailed me and disdained many of the policies I helped craft, I could never bring myself to dislike him in return. He was often wrong on national security issues, in my view, and in particular too quick to favor using military force. Yet McCain consistently championed strong and principled U.S. global leadership, our alliances and universal values, while seeing clearly the threat we face from Russia and other totalitarian regimes.

Above all, I admired John McCain's guts, his fearlessness, and his readiness to stand up for what he believed. From his brave service in Vietnam and the torture he sustained as a POW to his firm rebuke of a supporter on the campaign trail who said she "can't trust Obama . . . he's an Arab," from his gracious concession speech in 2008 to his principled vote to save the Affordable Care Act and his sustained critique of President Trump, Senator McCain was a patriot and a decent man. McCain also had a remarkable capacity to forgive—whether his Vietnamese captors or his political opponents whom he invited to speak at his funeral. His loss dealt a blow to our democracy and our global leadership.

When he died, I was saddened but also deeply torn. I had long regretted my comments about McCain on the 2008 campaign trail, which were fairly construed as disrespectful. My aim had been to draw a contrast on policy but not to engage in an ad hominem attack. Much as I wanted to pay my respects and honor his service, knowing how he felt about me, I didn't want to seem a hypocrite or the classic Washington poser who cares mainly about being seen. Wrestling with the question of whether to attend his funeral, I had decided to stay home and watch it on television.

Then I received an email that made me laugh so hard I cried. It was from Ambassador Deborah Jones, whom I had not heard from since I left government. A career foreign service officer who had succeeded Christopher Stevens as U.S. envoy to Libya, she wrote to me days after McCain's passing but before his memorial service at the Washington National Cathedral:

> Dear Susan,
>
> Just wanted to share this private anecdote with you because it was so typical of John McCain, God rest his soul, and involved you.
>
> As you know only too well, McCain was obsessed with Libya, even more so following Chris Stevens' death in Benghazi. He loved the romantic notion of dealing with "the war" (revolutionaries) and he also had a great fondness for Chris and believed the Obama Administration had covered up the "real [AQ] story" on Benghazi. He'd come to Tripoli for a whirlwind visit—naturally flying milair—and we'd ensured he'd gotten to see some of "the war" and to visit his favorite shawarma stand (security be damned) and were heading back to the airport. He asked me what Libyans currently thought of America (this was late 2013 I recall) and before I realized what I was triggering in him, the words were leaving my mouth to recount that Libyans had told me: "When she raised her right hand at the UN to support the Libyan people against Qaddafi,

Susan Rice became our Statue of Liberty!" He erupted, nearly leaping across the seat at me, yelling "well that was before she lied, LIED about Benghazi!" I replied "Senator, we're just going to have to agree to disagree on that point," which only served to infuriate him further. "Madame Ambassador," he began—which as you know is what happens when Senators are irritated; they resort to formal title—and continued facetiously "I'm sure you know Libya much better than I do [here I interjected, "oh Senator, I'm sure I do not"] but you can't tell me that large groups of young men go around carrying RPG's and the sort of weapons those groups who attacked our facilities in Benghazi were carrying!" Just then a bunch of heavily armed militia members drove by. "Senator, they do," I replied. We rode in silence the rest of the way. (I should mention that his accompanying staff, unaccustomed to hearing anyone push back on the great man were smiling ear to ear in the rear seat of our armored SUV.)

I've never forgotten this. I actually found it rather amusing.
Hope all is well with you and yours,
Best,
Deborah Jones

Once I collected myself, I forwarded the email to a few family members and to my good friend since Oxford, Lance Bultena, for their amusement. A South Dakota Republican, Lance had worked for McCain in the Senate and tried to advise me in the wake of Benghazi on how best to defuse McCain's ire. Lance loved Ambassador Jones's message and opined on how McCain would have approached my funeral, "Were he you, he would have attended the funeral to get the attention and make the type of generous comment with a slight 'but'—without using the word 'but'—to trigger the press awareness of what was being said." Hearing my explanation as to why I would not attend, Lance deftly persuaded me that going was the right thing to do, subtly suggesting that it would be a gesture of forgiveness and healing. Lance secured me a ticket as his guest at the invitation-only ceremony, after alerting the organizers whom he intended to bring. Hearing no objection, which I took as a reciprocal measure, I sat discreetly in the back row of the long Cathedral Nave. It felt appropriate to be present and personally give the "great man," as Ambassador Jones called him, his due.

———

At a time when the president and many political leaders govern deliberately in a manner designed to exacerbate our divisions, the challenge of overcoming them is greater than ever. Tragically, we have entered an unprecedented era in which the president of the United States tells bald-faced lies on a near daily basis, while attacking unpleasant truths as "fake news," the free press as "the enemy of the people," and loyal career public servants and critical government institutions as "the Deep State." His demonization of our fellow Americans—from Muslims to Latinos, refugees, immigrants, women, transgender persons, African Americans, and other minorities, while excusing or even praising anti-Semitic, racist white supremacists—has become so commonplace as to be nearly numbing. At the same time, President Trump lauds adversaries like Vladimir Putin and Kim Jong Un, embraces autocrats from Turkey to Saudi Arabia, dismisses scores of nations as "shithole countries," and degrades our treaty allies who share our values.

Up is down, and down is up.

What this all reveals about the character, motives, and loyalties of the American president cannot be dismissed. Nor can the inaction of the president's party in Congress in the face of direct, daily assaults on the integrity of our core values and national institutions. Together, they are systematically rending the fabric of our national democracy purely for partisan political gain.

The key questions that remain are whether our democratic institutions can withstand this sustained assault, and whether the American people will hold leaders accountable at the ballot box for placing party over country. I believe the answer to both questions is yes, but only if Americans fully understand what's at stake.

Today, our domestic political divisions constitute the greatest threat to our national security. Healing them is critical to the survival of our democracy and the preservation of America's global leadership.

America's polarization along socioeconomic, geographic, racial, religious, and political lines appears only to be deepening. We are too often suspicious of "the other"—those who don't look, worship, or think like us—and assume that our interests are more likely opposed than common. In an era when the benefits of wealth, economic growth, and our global leadership are so unevenly distributed, Americans often perceive that they are competing with each other for their share of a static or shrinking pie. Rather than expecting to grow the national pie and thus, potentially, our respective shares, too many Americans are locked in a zero-sum mentality, in which what is good for me and mine cannot be good for others; or, when I win, someone else must lose. As our country changes demographically—growing more racially and ethnically diverse, on course to becoming "majority minority" in the 2040s—this fear, this presumption of *us vs. them*, is becoming more pervasive and pernicious.

Not only do these divisions, exacerbated by self-interested leaders, weaken our national cohesion, they threaten our national security by keeping us from tackling urgent problems and by creating openings for our adversaries to exploit. Extreme political polarization prevents leaders in Washington even from taking actions that members of both parties agree are necessary—from repairing and replacing aging infrastructure, like bridges and airports, and expanding broadband access, to ensuring that government does not shut down over minor budgetary disputes, enacting comprehensive immigration reform, and passing paid family leave.

Washington is broken, and our democracy is increasingly dysfunctional.

Even more dangerously, our vulnerabilities are not lost on our adversaries, who seek to weaken America from within and strengthen their global position at our expense. Russia, above all, has intervened to manipulate and discredit our electoral process, most blatantly in 2016, but its nefarious actions are not tied solely to our political cycle. They continue and are constant. When a Ferguson, Charlottesville, Parkland, or massacre at the Tree of Life Synagogue in Pittsburgh occurs, Russian propaganda engines from RT television to thousands of coordinated social media bots light up to magnify suspicion and anger among Americans on both sides of contentious issues. Our divisions afford our adversaries easy openings through which to pit Americans against one another—to distrust, discredit, and ultimately, detest each other.

If Russia, China, North Korea, Iran, or any adversary can corrode our confidence in our national institutions—the media, Congress, the Intelligence Community, law enforcement, the presidency—as well as our faith in each other's motives and loyalties as Americans, then they need never fire a bullet to defeat us and our democratic way of life. We will have done the equivalent of putting a bull's-eye on our own back, handing our enemy a loaded rifle, and standing still waiting to be shot.

Terrorists, too, now get more bang for each blast. After 9/11, Americans largely came together, united in their resolve to defeat the Al Qaeda terrorists that struck us and to recover from our losses. Yet, not even a dozen years later, by Benghazi, politicians had learned to demagogue terrorist attacks for political gain and have done so repeatedly since—from Paris to San Bernardino to Niger. Terrorists now know that a successful attack is more likely to further divide Americans than to unite us, which makes us a more attractive target. Not only do terrorists reap the propaganda gains of killing and maiming, they also benefit from the lasting consequences of a more fragmented and fractious America.

At the same time, our adversaries are working to erode that which at our core makes us American—our faith in democracy. Democracy can only endure if citizens believe that their vote counts, their voice can be heard, and their will is respected. In magnifying our divisions, our opponents seek to cause as many Americans as possible to doubt the legitimacy and utility of our democratic institutions, to lose faith, disengage, and to denigrate the process and each other. Even if our adversaries fall short of provoking domestic conflict, they will surely still succeed in devaluing the democratic model globally and boosting the attractiveness of authoritarianism.

The risks to our survival as a strong, influential, and cohesive nation cannot be underestimated. It's mind-boggling and alarming to hear some right-wing commentators predict, almost with relish, a coming "civil war." Yet America has been divided before—far more deeply than today. Recall the actual Civil War and Reconstruction, the pull of the isolationist movement of the 1930s, McCarthyism, the civil rights era riots and destruction in our major cities, Vietnam. We emerged from each of these periods whole and, arguably, if not immediately, stronger.

What is different today is that our adversaries have demonstrated both the will and capacity to weaponize our divisions for use against us, and they are aided and abetted, whether deliberately or not, by nativist leaders who seek political benefit in pitting groups of Americans against each other—on the basis of race, class, religion, or national origin.

In tandem, our political system has evolved in ways that make it easier and far more beneficial to pursue zero-sum partisan outcomes. From the nearly unlimited role of money in politics (particularly from "dark" and unaccountable sources) and our relentlessly gerrymandered congressional districts, to a primary system that rewards extremes on both sides, we face real structural impediments to compromise and cooperation across party lines.

Concentrated ownership of local news stations, the influence of cable television, which offers a network for every political disposition while demonizing opposing views, the decline of traditional newspapers and local coverage, and a social media revolution that enables individuals to choose what information they consume all make things far worse. No child today knows the simplicity I enjoyed of receiving my nightly news courtesy of a venerable man anchoring one of the three original networks.

Civil discourse has suffered further from Americans' growing penchant to filter out information we prefer not to hear—whether through the issuance of "trigger warnings" in classrooms, efforts to constrain conservatives or pro-Israel groups on college campuses, or the right's reactionary dismissal of progressive views as "un-American" or "socialist" or "identity politics."

We can now select what "facts" we want to believe and discount those we do not. This danger will only worsen as technology enables the perfection of "deep fakes," like manipulated videos that make it authentically appear a politician has done or said something he has not, or improved algorithms that further skew the information we are fed. If citizens cannot agree on the realities we are facing, how can we rationally debate challenges, much less devise common solutions?

Americans are more and more segregated along ideological lines—not just racial and socioeconomic. Liberals and conservatives tend to live in different zip codes and don't encounter each other on a routine basis.

Washington has changed too, as members of Congress rarely move their families to town, and instead sleep two or three nights a week on cots or in group houses on Capitol Hill. Democrats and Republicans in Congress do not know each other as they once did. The ties of school, friendship, and shared personal struggle that bound families across party lines, like mine with the Brock family—Republicans from Tennessee who embraced me almost as their own child—barely exist.

We live apart, in our own bubbles, and resist any disturbance to the comfort of our self-imposed cocoons. It's hard to trust someone you have never met, to respect someone you know little about, to hear someone who doesn't even see you.

———

The good news is: our domestic divisions are a problem of Americans' own making, and thus we can fix it. From the personal to the national level, every one of us can contribute. Within our families, at work, and in our communities, we can listen, learn, and try to understand what animates those with whom we disagree. Yet we also need to reach well beyond the confines of the familiar and challenge ourselves to know those we don't, those we think we won't like, even those we fear.

When our differences feel too vast to bridge, we need to step back, cool off, and try again. That may sound facile, but the alternative is too dire not to try.

Each of us, not just our leaders, has agency and responsibility. Each of us can contribute to catalyzing our national healing. We have the tools, if only we have the will.

For instance, one year of mandatory national service would compel Americans to get to know each other and work together. Universal civics education—with a curriculum focused on the Constitution, our electoral and legislative process, our democratic institutions, the rule of law, and how to distinguish fact from fiction—would make for more competent and engaged citizens. Truth in advertising on social media, a revival of apolitical local news, and the genuine, not selective, application of norms of free speech and free assembly, would better inform our citizens. Limiting the role of money in politics, implementing nonpartisan redistricting and measures like rank-choice voting of candidates from all parties as in Maine, while making it far easier for *all* citizens to vote, are steps that would strengthen our democracy and constrain the role of extreme partisans and special interests.

America's potential to continue to grow and thrive, to innovate and contribute is almost limitless, if and when we pull together—as a people, a nation, a body politic. We are at a crossroads where Americans will either heal, remake, and renew ourselves as a nation; or we will tear ourselves apart, ensuring our national rot and international decline, due to fear, division, and our inability to care for and learn from each other. We are testing the strength of our national cohesion and our democratic institutions; and the jury is out.

Will we demand leaders who put country over party? Leaders who put our shared national mission first?

That mission remains to champion the worth, dignity, and well-being of every American—regardless of what they look like, when they came here, how they worship, or who they love. It is to expand opportunity and revive the American Dream rather than restrict access to it. Ultimately, it is to lift up the coming generations, so that like my parents and me—the descendants of immigrant laborers and slaves—they too can rise and thrive and claim this country fully as their own.

The choice is ours.

I believe, as always, that we must choose each other. Individually and collectively, we can and must bend the arc of the moral universe—toward both justice and unity. We do not live in a zero-sum America. Your failure can never be my success. Our national creeds, of equality and "Out of Many, One"—*E Pluribus Unum*—must still guide us.

For better, for worse, we are in this together. And we cannot *afford* to part.

That's why I remain fundamentally optimistic about America. We have overcome far greater challenges as a people, a nation, and a global leader.

No one has ever won by betting against America's long-term capacity for growth, change, and renewal.

It would be foolish to start now.

Afterword to the

Paperback Edition

*S*igning off yet another Zoom meeting, I felt comforted, steadied. It was
wonderful to collaborate again with Dr. Anthony Fauci, director of the
National Institute of Allergy and Infectious Diseases. During the Obama
years, we spent countless hours together in the Situation Room combating the
Ebola and Zika viruses. I know Tony Fauci to be one of the smartest, most
experienced and honest public servants I have ever encountered. Plus, he's a
sweetheart—as endearing in reality as he looks on TV.

I last saw Tony a couple of years back, when our families collided at a neighborhood restaurant, and we exchanged a warm hug. Now, in May 2020, we
were discussing the coronavirus on a video call convened by Washington, D.C.,
mayor Muriel Bowser. Four weeks earlier, the mayor had asked me to co-chair
her ReOpen DC Advisory Group. Meanwhile, Dr. Fauci had been struggling
for months to infuse facts and expertise into the Trump administration's handling
of the COVID-19 pandemic. Still, he was generous enough to provide feedback
on our proposals to reopen D.C. as safely as possible. For a brief moment, Fauci's
measured demeanor and his signature raspy voice took me back to better days,
when science guided U.S. public health policy.

———◆———

"Nobody knew there'd be a pandemic or an epidemic of this proportion," said President Trump on March 19, 2020.

In truth, many of us knew another pandemic was a virtual certainty. I wrote in chapter 19 of this book, published in October 2019:

> *Experts agree that the emergence of some form of global pandemic disease,*
> *whether Zika, Ebola, avian flu, or SARS, is all but inevitable. As national*
> *security advisor, this was (and remains) among my biggest fears. The loss*
> *of life, economic devastation, and the potential to spark armed conflict that*
> *would accompany a global pandemic . . . overshadow many of the worst-case*
> *scenarios I was compelled to contemplate short of nuclear war. [page 407]*

That is why the Obama administration tried to prepare the nation and the incoming Trump team for a potential pandemic. Following the Ebola crisis (2014), I created a new office for "Global Health Security and Bio-defense" within the National Security Council. Its purpose was to provide early warning, prevent diseases from spreading, and support a rapid response when outbreaks occur. We also sustained a USAID program in China called PREDICT to help scientists identify deadly pathogens that could spread from animals to humans.

During the transition, my colleague Lisa Monaco and I provided my designated successor, Michael Flynn, and his deputies with a detailed briefing on key global threats, including pandemic disease. We hosted a tabletop exercise with Trump's cabinet appointees predicated on the scenario of a SARS-like infectious disease emerging in China. Afterward, my staff left the Trump team a sixty-nine-page playbook, which I call "Pandemics for Dummies," to guide their response to any such outbreak.

Tragically, President Trump dismissed our warnings and later those of his own team. My stomach sank in 2018, when Trump and his third national security advisor, John Bolton, disbanded the NSC Global Health office—yet another reckless effort to undo anything Obama. Later, after effectively trashing our pandemic playbook, Trump let funding expire for the PREDICT program and cut the federal budget for pandemic preparedness.

Then came early January 2020, when Trump was first warned about the emergence of a novel coronavirus in Wuhan, China. Instead of jumping into action, Trump ignored, then denied, and later downplayed the severity of the coronavirus threat to the U.S. In those crucial early weeks of January and February 2020, a competent White House would not only have launched work on vaccines but also swiftly taken several key steps, consistent with our playbook, to prepare the nation for the impending pandemic. These include:

- Communicating soberly and honestly with the American people
- Ordering mass production of coronavirus testing kits, utilizing the U.S. government, universities, private sector, and international partners
- Procuring huge stocks of personal protective equipment (masks, gloves, gowns) and ventilators
- Coordinating the purchase and distribution of critical supplies using the Defense Production Act, rather than leaving states to fend for themselves in competing for scarce, overpriced equipment
- Expanding hospital capacity and surging medical personnel to meet anticipated demand
- Urging all states to maintain broad stay-at-home orders long enough to curb the disease
- Rallying the world to confront the virus collectively

Instead, Donald Trump again prioritized his political interests over the security and well-being of the American people. He began by willfully misleading the public to preserve his prized, if flimsy, trade deal with China signed in January 2020, and to keep the stock market humming in an election year. For more than two critical months, Trump repeatedly likened COVID-19 to the seasonal flu, falsely assuring Americans that it was "totally under control" and that "when it gets a little warmer, it miraculously goes away."

Trump's much-touted, late January travel ban on China actually accomplished very little. It came after twenty-nine countries had already done the same, and it still permitted over four hundred thousand travelers to enter the U.S. from China between December and March 2020. However, the travel ban briefly gave Americans a false sense of security and conveniently launched Trump's "blame China" campaign, while fueling the demonization of Asian Americans.

Then, in mid-March, Trump abruptly halted travel from Europe—the major source of U.S. infections—causing a chaotic crush at U.S. airports that accelerated the spread of the virus. On March 13, the president was asked whether he accepted responsibility for the myriad failures in coronavirus testing. Standing in the Rose Garden, Trump replied flatly, "No, I don't take responsibility at all." Watching at home on my small kitchen TV, even I was stunned.

American presidents take responsibility. They lead. Especially in times of crisis.

When national unity and shared resolve were needed more urgently than at any moment since World War II, Donald Trump chose to pit Americans against each other. He silenced or fired officials who dared tell the truth. He assailed journalists and punished governors who did not pay him public homage. He prescribed dangerous drug therapies and even the physical injection of bleach—serving up daily diversions to distract the electorate from his own colossal failings. Finally, Trump's election-driven rush to "reopen America" turbocharged the disproportionate toll the coronavirus has taken on the most vulnerable in our society—the elderly, people of color, factory and frontline workers, meat packers, the incarcerated, health-care providers, and first responders.

Had President Trump acted responsibly, like his counterparts in New Zealand, Germany, and South Korea, many thousands fewer Americans would be dead today. Our economy would not have suffered such extreme devastation, with tens of millions out of work and thousands lining up daily at food banks. By prioritizing the health of all Americans through gradually and safely reopening our economy, we would have reduced the risk of disease resurgence and launched a more sustainable economic recovery. But Trump put Trump first.

Honestly, like so many of you, I find it exhausting and difficult to remain hopeful in the face of such immoral and incompetent leadership. It's harder still when Donald Trump seems willing to do *anything*—enlist foreign adversaries, inflame racial tensions, demand the use of brute force against protesters, smear his opponents with outrageous lies, thwart mail-in balloting, suppress the vote, and much more—to ensure his reelection. Worse, congressional Republicans and even some jurists eagerly legitimize Trump and his drive to dismantle every element of our democracy that could check his push for unbridled power. Above all, it's hard to remain hopeful when so many Americans are dying and suffering such profound loss and pain.

In the year since I finished writing *Tough Love*, more has changed than I could ever have imagined. The coronavirus pandemic has transformed our society in ways permanent, if immeasurable. The long-suppressed agony of the African American community over never-ending police brutality has exploded in widespread, extremely diverse, peaceful protests, which in some places were marred by looters and vandals, perhaps fanned by foreign adversaries. Civil conflict is conceivable. And, just when we need them most, America's democratic institutions are failing us. Witness the Republican-led Senate's abdication of its constitutional duty during the impeachment inquiry, underscored by those senators' refusal even to call witnesses or demand documents. Recall their continued corruption of the congressional oversight process, using it to target Trump's political opponents.

These and other distressing events have left me wrestling with whether the optimistic ending to *Tough Love* remains valid, even for me. Honestly, it's not an easy call. To answer, I had to draw on all that I have learned and shared in the story that I've told—my upbringing, my study of history, my professional experience.

My judgment is that we are facing a profound *tough love* moment for our nation—a time when we must love America fiercely but not uncritically.

America has been knocked down, arguably as never before in our lifetimes. Our vast racial, health, and economic inequities have been laid bare, our vaunted "exceptionalism" exploded, our global leadership squandered. We've dealt ourselves a series of self-inflicted blows.

Yet, as my remarkable parents taught me, as prejudice and injustice have taught me, as the relentless attacks on my own integrity have taught me: when you get knocked down, there are only two choices—stay down or get back up.

Where I come from, giving up is not an option. Staying down means conceding defeat. The *only* option is to get back up, to rise again, however battered and bruised, to keep battling for what is right and just. It is also to hoist up those so badly hurt they need your arms, your strength, to regain their footing.

That's the moment we are in now. America is down, but we can—and we must—get back up.

I must, you must, *we must* remain hopeful and determined.

I still firmly believe that Americans have the strength, if only we can find the unity and resolve, to reclaim our sense of collective purpose. Our sense of decency, empathy, and fairness. Our recognition that we sink or swim together.

It's not enough to get back to normal. Normal is too costly and deadly for *all* Americans. As the pandemic has made plain, we all pay an enormous price when suffering pervades a large swath of our society. Disease—catalyzed by poverty, inequality, racism, interdependence, and a culture of self-absorption—is the ultimate disrupter. None of us is immune. Not the healthy. Not the wealthy. Not the educated. Not the powerful. We each suffer to a greater or lesser degree.

It's long past time to build a more just and equitable America.

Historically, a hallmark of our national strength has been our ability to forge opportunity out of crisis. After the Civil War, we ended slavery and enshrined the concept of "equal protection" under the law. In the Great Depression, we established the Works Progress Administration and Civilian Conservation Corps to improve American land and infrastructure. After World War II, we enacted the G.I. Bill of Rights to help veterans afford education and housing. In the 1960s, we abolished segregation, established full voting rights, and enacted the Great Society reforms.

My vision for our future is expansive but eminently achievable: America must finally become the place where every child, from the Bronx to Brownsville, from the Sioux Nation to rural West Virginia, has the ability to dream without limits and the opportunity to make her dreams come true.

To realize her dreams, every American child needs a solid foundation—early childhood education, good nutrition, affordable health care, decent housing, schools and neighborhoods that are safe from guns, internet access, quality secondary education, and the opportunity to attend college without going into debt. All our children depend on having parents who can earn enough to provide for their families and secure a dignified retirement. Each child needs truly equal protection under the law and a criminal justice system that respects his humanity. Everyone requires a healthy environment and a livable planet that will sustain future generations.

These are not pipe dreams or liberal fantasies. They are practical necessities that are within our reach. If we can fund trillion-dollar tax breaks for those who need them least, we can instead invest in the most important, yet vulnerable among us—our children. That is the only way to build a better future.

Yet, to do so, we must first fix our broken politics. When we are so polarized and poisoned, when we view each other through an us-versus-them prism, we remain paralyzed. Like a society afflicted by a flesh-eating disease, we are devouring ourselves from within.

We have now reached the tipping point where our democracy can only be salvaged by the rapid and resounding restoration of selfless leadership to the White House, our statehouses, and to Congress. Leadership that values our common humanity and our national unity over any party or ideology.

We must invigorate our checks and balances, the rule of law, and unfettered oversight. We must establish the primacy of facts and truth over opinion and dogma. We must finally reckon with the hate and injustice that flows from our nation's original sin, slavery, and centuries of oppression. We must purge foreign interference from our politics and dismantle domestic terrorist groups.

It's now or never.

Now we must harness the energies and marshal the determination of a frightened yet fearless electorate that refuses to allow the America we love to self-destruct.

Lest we come apart, we must come together.

Our collective fate depends on enough of us, individually, making the calculation that our sum remains greater than our parts.

I won't stop betting on you and on our America.

In fact, I'm doubling down.

Susan E. Rice
Washington, D.C.
July 1, 2020

Acknowledgments

From childhood, I have used a cylindrical wooden wine barrel my dad brought home from Europe as a bedside table. It has a removable top, and into it I threw every important piece of paper I ever wanted to keep—letters, event programs, the occasional report card, notes to myself. I never bothered to unearth what it contained. I just kept chucking stuff in. That barrel, which I still keep in my bedroom today, amounts to an archeological dig of my life before email. In the process of excavation, I found a handwritten note to me from my paternal grandmother, who died when I was four; virtually all of Ian's letters to me; and loads of correspondence from secondary school, Stanford, and Oxford.

After my mother passed away in 2017, we discovered dusty, mite-infested trunks in her attic filled with family history, newspaper clippings, and photographs. It was a treasure trove. Years earlier, my brother, Johnny, did the painful work of cleaning out my father's house in Camas, Washington, after he died in 2011. Unable emotionally or practically to sift through all of Dad's papers, he stashed them in his basement. Prompted by my pleas to assist with the book, Johnny dug them out, and I have benefited enormously from what we have found—from the ugly, such as depositions from my parents' divorce proceedings, to the mundane, like tax records, to the amazing, including photographic portraits of my father's relatives, official Air Force pictures of Dad's service in World War II at Tuskegee, and personal photos from his days in India and Berkeley.

I have truly enjoyed writing *Tough Love*. A large part of the personal purpose behind this endeavor was to explore my family history, to revisit unflinchingly the painful aspects of my childhood that I had sped through in order to cope in the moment, and to ask myself the hard questions of where and why I have succeeded and failed and what I have learned in the process.

I needed to unbury my own life—literally and figuratively. No one else could do that for me. Thus, when some suggested at the outset that I partner with a ghostwriter or coauthor to help me produce this book, I resisted.

That said, as at every stage and in every aspect of my life, I could never have completed this project nor had this story to tell without the extraordinary help and support of so many others.

My agents at Creative Artists Agency, Mollie Glick, David Larabell, Christine Lancman, Kate Childs, Craig Gering, and Michelle Kydd Lee, believed in the importance of my story, offered valuable feedback, and supported me every step of the way.

I am grateful to Simon & Schuster for enabling me to tell this story, especially my dedicated, diehard editor Dawn Davis, who made this journey fun as well as a humbling learning experience. Chelcee Johns, Mark LaFlaur, Christina Zarafonitis, Min Choi, Amanda Lang, Cary Goldstein, and Jonathan Karp have also been great partners.

I am extraordinarily indebted to Alexander Cox, my special advisor and research coordinator, who joined me at the start, contributing extraordinary research, painstaking editing, unvarnished and consistently thoughtful feedback, logistical and administrative support, and invaluable encouragement. In addition, Elizabeth Pan supported my transition from government to private life and helped me get this project launched.

Mim Eichler Rivas taught me more than anyone in this process—about structure, storytelling, language, and the world of commercial publishing. Mim originally offered to help me to "rearrange the furniture" but did so much more, pushing me to grow as a writer, to dig deeper, to revise relentlessly, and not to get overly frustrated in the process. I cannot thank her enough.

I am blessed with extraordinary friends from all corners of my life, many of whom read and commented thoughtfully and extensively on drafts of the book. While the flaws are all mine, without their wise and candid input, their "tough love," this would be a lesser endeavor by far. My deepest thanks to Salman Ahmed, Brooke Anderson, Erica Barks-Ruggles, Alex Butcher-Nesbitt, Richard Clarke, Suzy George, Avril Haines, Zev Karlin-Neumann, Vernon Lobo, Courtney O'Malley, Erin Pelton, Ben Rhodes, Priya Singh, Gayle Smith, Bonnie St. John, and Dan Wilhelm.

I am forever grateful to Kathy Ruemmler, Nick McQuaid, and the Latham and Watkins team for their extraordinary and generous support in this and too many other endeavors.

Anne Withers and Mike Smith at the National Security Council expeditiously read and reread the manuscript, shepherding it expertly through the interagency clearance process and generously offering valuable insights along the way.

I am thankful to Jim Goldgeier, Christine Chin, and Sylvia Burwell for embracing and supporting me so enthusiastically at American University's School of International Service.

As I struggled mightily with my title, my friend and poet Tom Healy never grew tired of bantering and ultimately led me to discover that *Tough Love* summed it all up.

Nothing forges strong bonds of friendship like being in the trenches together, especially when the figurative bullets are flying. Some of my closest friends and most valued colleagues are those with whom I worked in the Clinton and Obama administrations at the NSC, the State Department, and the U.S. Mission to the U.N. It was my fortune to work with several of these colleagues in multiple capacities over the years, but I will name each only once, usually in the context of where we first collaborated.

From my Clinton era stints at the NSC and State, I want to thank in particular Madeleine Albright, Erica Barks-Ruggles, Randy Beers, the late Sandy Berger, Annette Bushelle, Prudence Bushnell, Johnnie Carson, Richard Clarke, Ted Dagne, the late MacArthur DeShazer, David Dunn, Grant Harris, Vicki Huddleston, Howard Jeter, Don Kerrick, Anthony Lake, Shawn McCormick, George Moose, Eric Pelofsky, Tom Pickering, Nancy Powell, John Prendergast, Joann Rice, Witney Schneidman, Eric Schwartz, the late Michael Sheehan, Wendy Sherman, Elaine Shocas, Gayle Smith, Nancy Soderberg, Jim Steinberg, Strobe Talbott, John Underriner, Joe Wilson, and the late Howard Wolpe.

I am also thankful for my friends and colleagues from McKinsey & Company in Toronto, many of whom have stayed close over years and distance, and at the Brookings Institution. I wish to thank especially Corinne Graff and Carlos Pascal for their support, along with many fellow Brookings scholars whom I am proud to call friends.

I am indebted to the entire U.S. Mission to the United Nations team, and especially Salman Ahmed, Brooke Anderson, Amar Bakshi, Ana Barahona, Rick Barton, Warren Bass, Anya Benenson, Josh Black, Dorothy Burgess, Elizabeth Cousens, Jeff DeLaurentis, Rosemary DiCarlo, Susan Din, Ravi Gupta, Alex Hughes, Mark Kornblau, Colleen King, Katie Lillie, Kathleen McGlynn, Alex McPhillips, Michael Pan, Alex Pascal, Erin Pelton, Taara Rangarajan, Maria Riofrio, Rexon Ryu, Hillary Schrenell, Lindsay Scola, Jennifer Simon, Mark Simonoff, Priya Singh, Caroline Tess, Stanton Thomas, Joe Torsella, Meridith Webster, Alex Wolff, and all of the wonderful Diplomatic Security agents who served on my detail. I am also grateful for the collegiality and support provided by Secretary of State Hillary Clinton and her team.

Upon my return to the White House as national security advisor, I was deeply fortunate to have led so many talented professionals in every NSC directorate. I also remain grateful for my enduring friendships with and immeasurable support from NSC colleagues in the West Wing, particularly Wally Adeyemo, Tony Blinken, Suzy George, Avril Haines, Colin Kahl, Lisa Monaco, Denis McDonough, Michael Ortiz, Ben Rhodes, Curtis Ried, Loren DeJonge Schulman, Dilpreet Sidhu, Adam Strickler, Jake Sullivan, Anne Withers, and the amazingly talented and collegial White House senior staff. I am deeply thankful for the invaluable support of the NSC Systems team who kept me connected 24/7 from literally every corner of the globe, especially Gary Bresnahan, the late Allen Jones, Will Reynolds, and Phillip Abenes, as well as all the extraordinary U.S. Secret Service agents on Point Guard detail.

I am very appreciative of the camaraderie, commitment, and invaluable contributions of the NSC Principals with whom I served as national security advisor, including Vice President Joe Biden, John Brennan, Bill Burns, Ash Carter, James Clapper, Martin Dempsey, Joseph Dunford, Michael Froman, Chuck Hagel, Eric Holder, Jeh Johnson, John Kerry, Jack Lew, Loretta

Lynch, Samantha Power, Penny Pritzker, Raj Shah, Gayle Smith, and their immensely talented, hardworking deputies who made all our work possible.

I remain deeply grateful to President Barack Obama for his confidence in me, his remarkable leadership of our country and the world, his calm, rational, and steady hand at the helm, and his enduring friendship.

At every juncture of my life, I have been blessed with the love and support of dear friends whom I will always cherish. In particular, I want to thank Hutchey Brock, Laura Richards Coleman, Trinka Roeckelein, Sarah Whitehouse, and Andrea Worden whom I first met in my early school days and who have stuck by my side every year since. Several other good friends from high school, college, and graduate school are mentioned in *Tough Love*, but there are many others too numerous to name who were powerfully influential and remain important to me.

From Beauvoir to National Cathedral School, from Stanford to Oxford, I salute the teachers and coaches who taught me not only vital knowledge and skills but also to adhere to the core values and high standards they instilled.

Tough Love has truly been a collective endeavor. My first cousins, Caroline Dickson and her husband Taft Broome, Valerie Dickson Horton, family historian Daryl Dickson, as well as my mother's friends from Radcliffe, Kathy Sreedhar and Ellie Fuchs, and cousins and friends Cliff and Adele Alexander, were generous in sharing their recollections. My stepsiblings— Ben, Cate, and Craig Fitt—provided helpful memories and perspective. I discovered more distant relatives in this process who have also been generous with family history, notably Mildred Rice Jordan and Michelle Forrester Covington.

Tennis coach Karim Najdi and my trainer Aaron Gamble encouraged me every step of the way, offering unique insights while kicking my ass on a consistent basis.

For over twenty years, Adela Jimenez and Bertha Montiel have given our family their love, support, and invaluable assistance, and I could not have managed without them. Kadiatou Touré, Missy Moore, and Ticey Westbrooks kept *both* my parents going strong, providing me the confidence, strength, and sanity to keep serving to the best of my ability. I am eternally grateful to them as well as to each of my parents' other caregivers.

In very different but vital ways, Elizabeth Jennings and my beloved late godmother, Peggy Cooper Cafritz, helped raise me and make me who I am.

My greatest debt, of course, is to my mother, Lois Dickson Rice, and father, Emmett John Rice, who gave me all the tools I needed to grow, thrive, and serve. Their unconditional love and support, their wisdom and example shaped me and guided my journey more than anyone else. My love for them is infinite and my debt to them immeasurable.

Above all, I must thank my devoted family. My brother, Johnny, traveled this journey every step of the way with me, as he has every stage of my life, contributing his far better memory than mine as well as his advice, criticism, and support. Andrea, Mateo, and Kiki Rice were wonderfully supportive as readers and cheerleaders.

I could not have written this book without the indulgence, selflessness, unrelenting support, and careful reading that my children Jake and Maris provided throughout this process. They were deeply generous in letting me tell a good deal of their personal stories. Each has made this a better book, as they have from the outset made me a much better person.

Finally, I could not do what I do or be who I am without Ian, my life partner, my forever love, and my best friend. Ian read every word of every draft and offered invaluable feedback. For two years, he gave me, as always, the space and the support—emotionally and practically—to live this project and complete it with him. No one deserves more credit for *Tough Love* and what comprises its ingredients than Ian. I can never thank you enough.

Notes

CHAPTER 1: SERVICE IN MY SOUL

23. *Mother has a quiet:* Lois Ann Dickson, "Her Home Is Her Castle, Her Children Her Pride," *Portland Sunday Telegram*, May 14, 1950.

24. *"They were Republican in politics":* David W. D. Dickson, *Memoirs of an Isolate* (Ormond Beach, FL: Corporate Images Publishing Co., 1995), p. 14.

24. *Sturbridge's clothing store:* Ibid., p. 8.

25. *arrived in New York on May 16, 1911:* Declaration of Intention, David Augustus Dickson, June 16, 1913, Portland, ME. "Petitions and Records of Naturalization, 1790–11/1945," *Records of District Courts of the United States, 1685–2009*, Record Group Number 21. Waltham, MA: National Archives at Boston.

26. *Maine has long had very few blacks:* Maureen Elgersman Lee, "What They Lack in Numbers: Locating Black Portland, 1870–1930," in *Creating Portland: History and Place in Northern New England*, Joseph A. Conforti, ed. (Durham, NH: University of New Hampshire Press, 2005), p. 236.

27. *David was active in the local NAACP:* Dickson, *Memoirs of an Isolate*, p. 22.

27. *Bowdoin's record on integration:* Kenneth Chenault, "The Blackman at Bowdoin," an Honors Paper for the Department of History. Bowdoin College, 1973, pp. 3, 6. Courtesy of the Bowdoin College Library.

28. *"mixed, Jim Crow facilities":* Letter from Leon A. Dickson to his parents sent from Tuskegee Army Airfield, Alabama, July 6, 1945. Copy in possession of author.

29. *"psychological impact of that kind":* Dickson, *Memoirs of an Isolate*, p. 16.

31. *"Colored girls of beauty":* Ibid., p. 25.

32. *born a slave in South Carolina in 1845:* Mildred L. Rice Jordan, *Reclaiming African American Students: Legacies, Lessons, and Prescriptions: The Bordentown School* (Bloomington, IN: iUniverse, 2017).

32. *Upon his return to Laurens County:* Ibid., p. 4.

33. *Rev. Walter Rice spent ten years:* Ibid.

33. *Its ranks gradually filled:* "Report of the Manual Training and Industrial School Located at Bordentown—1894–95," Annual Report of the Board of Education and of the Superintendent of Public Instruction of New Jersey, 1895 (Trenton, NJ: The John L. Murphy Publishing Company, 1896), p. 337, in Jordan, *Reclaiming African American Students*, p. 6.

33. *ranging from Latin to physics:* Ibid.

33. *Great-grandfather Walter Rice died in 1899:* Report of Death, Walter A. S. Rice, January 4, 1899, New Brunswick, NJ. New Jersey State Archives, Trenton, NJ. Copy in possession of author.

34. *first to teaching and later to the ministry: Centennial Encyclopedia of the African Methodist Episcopal Church,* Vol. 1, Richard R. Wright, ed. (Philadelphia, PA: Book Concern of the AME Church, 1916), p. 281.

34. *Chairman of the Laurens County Republican Party:* "Abstract from the Election Returns for 1870," Reports and Resolutions of the General Assembly of the State of South Carolina, Regular Session, 1870–1871 (Columbia, SC: Republican Printing Company, 1871), p. 499; "List of School Commissioners," p. 416.

34. *In 1880, he was badly beaten:* "Exhibit E," Papers and Testimony in the Contested Election Case of C. J. Stolbrand vs. D. Wyatt Aiken from the Third Congressional District of South Carolina, House of Representatives, Forty-seventh Congress, First Session, Miscellaneous Document No. 23 (Washington, D.C.: U.S. Government Printing Office, 1882), p. 85.

34. *Emmett enjoyed a comfortable early childhood:* Emmett J. Rice, "Education of an Economist: From Fulbright Scholar to the Federal Reserve Board, 1951–1979," an oral history conducted in 1984 by Gabrielle Morris. Regional Oral History Office, The Bancroft Library, University of California, Berkeley, 1991, p. 4.

35. *"There was a great deal of prejudice":* Ibid., p. 11.

36. *"a child of the Depression":* Ibid., p. 13.

37. *"Many black pilots thought":* Interview of Emmett J. Rice conducted by John "Jake" Rice-Cameron, Washington, D.C., February 2010. Transcript in possession of the author.

37. *"consciousness of being black":* Rice, "Education of an Economist," p. 64.

38. *I concluded that I am only one person:* Ibid., p. vi.

CHAPTER 2: COMING UP

41. *"the forbidden six": Red Book: Students' Handbook of Radcliffe College, 1951–52,* Issued by the Student Government Association of Radcliffe College, p. 84.

41. *"Cambridge is a well-stocked hunting ground":* Ibid., pp. 97, 99.

42. *She ultimately won a hotly contested battle:* "Dickson Wins Radcliffe Race for SGA President Position," *The Crimson,* March 19, 1953.

45. *"Both foreign and American friends":* Emmett J. Rice, "Education of an Econo-

mist: From Fulbright Scholar to the Federal Reserve Board, 1951–1979," an oral history conducted in 1984 by Gabrielle Morris. Regional Oral History Office, The Bancroft Library, University of California, Berkeley, 1991, pp. iv–v.

45. *"It was the first living experience":* Ibid., p. 39.

45. *"It was much harder to get a job":* Ibid., p. 42.

45. *"making statements like that to foreigners":* Ibid., p. 43.

46. *"They did not like the idea":* Ibid., p. 55.

46. *"It was my job," Dad said:* Interview of Emmett J. Rice conducted by John "Jake" Rice-Cameron, Washington, D.C.: February 2010. Transcript in possession of the author.

46. *"I could not have worked in the [U.S.] Treasury":* Rice, "Education of an Economist," p. 60.

47. *"It was possible for a black person":* Ibid., p. 41.

48. *On takeoff, the Boeing 707's:* Aviation Safety Network Accident Report, TWA Boeing 707-331 N761TW, May 29, 1964, Paris-Orly Airport, France. Flight Safety Foundation, http://aviation-safety.net/database/record.php?id=19640529-2.

CHAPTER 3: GROWING UP TOO SOON

68. *Named senior vice president for planning:* "Rice Named to High Post with NBW," *Washington Post,* January 11, 1973, p. D7.

73. *Americans to attend college since 1973:* Email to Alexander Cox from Ed Pacchetti, U.S. Department of Education dated April 24, 2019, in which it is confirmed: "The number of unduplicated BEOG/Pell Grant recipients from the 1973–74 award year to present is approximately 80 million. This number has been validated by *multiple teams* at FSA using student-level data from our archived data and the current origination/disbursement system . . ." Email in the possession of the author.

CHAPTER 6: BUSTING OUT

123. *collection of the best African American Art: Fired Up! Ready to Go! Finding Beauty, Demanding Equity: An African American Life in Art. The Collections of Peggy Cooper Cafritz.* Peggy Cooper Cafritz and Charmaine Picard, eds. (New York, NY: Rizzoli Electra, 2018).

CHAPTER 7: ROOKIE SEASON

146. *"saved at least a third":* Interview of President Bill Clinton, CNBC, March 13, 2013.

147. *"jamming is an ineffective":* "Memorandum for Deputy Assistant to the President for National Security Affairs, National Security Council," U.S. Department of

Defense. May 5, 1994, https://nsarchive2.gwu.edu/NSAEBB/NSAEBB53/rw 050594.pdf.

148. *"If there's any particular magic":* State Department Briefing, Federal News Service, June 10, 1994.

149. *"protect threatened civilians":* Marlise Simons, "France Is Sending Force to Rwanda to Help Civilians," *New York Times*, June 23, 1994, https://www.nytimes.com /1994/06/23/world/france-is-sending-force-to-rwanda-to-help-civilians.html.

150. *decided to deploy the U.S. military:* Ray Wilkinson, "Heart of Darkness," *Refugees Magazine*, Issue 110, UNHCR, December 1, 1997, http://www.unhcr.org/en-us /publications/refugeemag/3b6925384/refugees-magazine-issue-110-crisis -great-lakes-cover-story-heart-darkness.html.

CHAPTER 9: STORMING STATE

179. *Indeed, in 1999, Ethiopian forces:* "Ethiopia Admits Killing European Nationals in Plane Shooting," *The Guardian*, September 1, 1999, https://www.theguardian .com/world/1999/sep/01/ethiopia.

CHAPTER 10: "I REMEMBER WHEN I TOO WAS A YOUNG ASSISTANT SECRETARY"

189. *Susan Bartley lost both:* My American colleagues killed in the Al Qaeda attack on Embassy Nairobi were: Jesse Nathan Aliganga Jr., Julian Bartley Sr., Julian Bartley Jr., Jean Rose Dalizu, Molly Huckaby Hardy, Kenneth Ray Hobson, Prabhi Guptara Kavaler, Arlene Kirk, Mary Louise Martin, Ann Michelle O'Connor, Sherry Lynn Olds, and Uttamlal T. Shah, https://1997-2001.state .gov/regions/africa/board_victims.html.

190. *It was selected largely because:* Tim Weiner and James Risen, "Decision to Strike Factory in Sudan Based on Surmise Inferred from Evidence," *New York Times*, September 21, 1998, https://www.nytimes.com/1998/09/21/world/decision-to -strike-factory-in-sudan-based-on-surmise-inferred-from-evidence.html.

CHAPTER 11: GOING GLOBAL

207. *September 11 might have been prevented:* David Rose, "The Osama Files," *Vanity Fair*, January 2002, http://www.vanityfair.com/news/2002/01/osama200201/, accessed July 15, 2017.

208. *The fact is members of the Clinton Administration:* Letters to the Editor, *Vanity Fair*, March 2002, pp. 94–96.

209. *The article exposed the biases:* Ruth Shalit, "J'Accuse!," *Elle*, Number 201, May 2002, p. 226.

209. *She had dreams of becoming the first:* Ibid.

210. *"You have got people saying":* Ibid., p. 227.

210. *In the* Post, *they again targeted me:* Tim Carney and Mansoor Ijaz, "Intelligence Failure? Let's Go Back to Sudan," *Washington Post*, June 30, 2002, https://www.washingtonpost.com/archive/opinions/2002/06/30/intelligence-failure-lets-go-back-to-sudan/1b8e47a7-a603-4657-aef9-ffb4c4b83276/?utm_term=.df65d75f043c.

210. *"after many interviews":* Statement by Daniel Byman, Professional Staff Member and Leader of the "Lookback" Team, Joint Inquiry into Intelligence Community Activities before and after the Terrorist Attacks of September 11, 2001. May 20, 2019 email in the possession of the author.

222. *"Jesse Jackson won South Carolina":* David Catanese, "Bill Clinton's 2 a.m. Phone Call to Jim Clyburn," *U.S. News & World Report*, February 11, 2014, https://www.usnews.com/news/articles/2014/02/11/bill-clintons-2-am-phone-call-to-jim-clyburn/, accessed October 27, 2018.

222. *"working, hard-working Americans":* May 7, 2008: "I have a much broader base to build a winning coalition on," she said in an interview with *USA Today*. As evidence, Clinton cited an Associated Press article "that found how Sen. Obama's support among working, hard-working Americans, white Americans, is weakening again, and how whites in both states who had not completed college were supporting me." "There's a pattern emerging here," she said. https://usatoday30.usatoday.com/news/politics/election2008/2008-05-07-clintoninterview_N.htm; https://thecaucus.blogs.nytimes.com/2008/05/08/clinton-touts-white-support/.

CHAPTER 12: REPRESENT

238. *"As in previous administrations":* "Remarks of President-elect Barack Obama, Announcement of National Security Team," The Office of the President-elect, December 1, 2008. https://webarchive.loc.gov/all/20090501163714/http://change.gov/newsroom/entry/key_members_of_obama_biden_national_security_team_announced/.

239. *"The people of Maine are proud":* Nomination of Hon. Susan E. Rice to Be U.N. Representative. Hearing Before the Committee on Foreign Relations, United States Senate, One Hundred Eleventh Congress, First Session, January 15, 2009, pp. 1–3.

242. *"the peace and security":* https://obamawhitehouse.archives.gov/the-press-office/remarks-president-barack-obama-prague-delivered.

245. *"We need the United Nations":* "Obama's National Security Team Announcement."

251. *Only several years later:* Matthew Rosenberg, "Obama Won't Stay at Waldorf Astoria for U.N. Event; Security Concerns Are Cited," *New York Times*, September 11, 2015, https://www.nytimes.com/2015/09/12/us/politics/white-house-spurns-waldorf-astoria-out-of-security-concerns.html.

254. *"Our opposition to the resolution":* Explanation of Vote by Ambassador Susan E. Rice on the Resolution on the Situation in the Middle East, including the question of Palestine, in the Security Council Chamber, February 18, 2011.

255. *"Todah rabah. Erev Tov":* "The Responsibility We Share for Our Common Future," remarks by Ambassador Susan E. Rice, U.S. Permanent Representative to the United Nations, at the Israeli Presidential Conference 2009, Facing Tomorrow, Jerusalem, October 21, 2009.

CHAPTER 13: HIGH-STAKES DIPLOMACY

262. *U.S.-Iran military-to-military hotline:* Jay Solomon, "Iran Rejects Proposed U.S. Military Hot Line," *Wall Street Journal*, October 4, 2011, https://www.wsj.com/articles/SB10001424052970203791904576609093178338996.

264. *Next, in September, the U.S. revealed:* David E. Sanger and William J. Broad, "U.S. and Allies Warn Iran over Nuclear 'Deception,'" *New York Times*, September 25, 2009, https://www.nytimes.com/2009/09/26/world/middleeast/26nuke.html.

270. *On the record, I sharply condemned:* "Rice Arrival Statement in Nairobi, Kenya," U.S. Department of State, accessed on Reliefweb, November 21, 2000, https://reliefweb.int/report/sudan/rice-arrival-statement-nairobi-kenya-assesses-humanitarian-conditions-southern-sudan.

272. *"We have got to think about giving out cookies":* Stephanie McCrummen, "U.S. Envoy's Outreach to Sudan Is Criticized as Naïve," *Washington Post*, September 29, 2009, http://www.washingtonpost.com/wp-dyn/content/article/2009/09/28/AR2009092802336.html.

CHAPTER 14: THE ARAB SPRING COMES TO NEW YORK

279. *The Libyan army fired directly:* https://www.nytimes.com/2011/05/05/world/africa/05nations.html?ref=world.

281. *"Prepare yourselves":* David D. Kirkpatrick and Kareem Fahim, "Qaddafi Warns of Assault on Benghazi as U.N. Vote Nears," *New York Times*, March 17, 2011, https://www.nytimes.com/2011/03/18/world/africa/18libya.html.

291. *"Many Libyan parents":* Rod Nordland, "In Libyan Rebel Capital, Shouts of Thanks to America and the West," *New York Times*, May 28, 2011.

CHAPTER 15: *STAR WARS* CANTINA

298. *"The U.S. is disgusted":* Colum Lynch and Alice Fordham, "Russia, China Block U.N. Vote," *Washington Post*, February 5, 2012.

299. *"Sometimes it's a little bit":* Karen Tanabe, "Susan Rice Talks United Nations and 'Star Wars,'" *Politico*, August 16, 2011, https://www.politico.com/blogs/click/2011/08/susan-rice-talks-united-nations-and-star-wars-038408.

CHAPTER 16: BENGHAZI

308. *"It's disgraceful that":* "What They Said, Before and After the Attack in Libya," *New York Times*, September 12, 2012, https://archive.nytimes.com/www.nytimes .com/interactive/2012/09/12/us/politics/libya-statements.html?hp.

308. *The currently available information:* "Benghazi Talking Points Timeline," ABC News, page 8, http://abcnews.go.com/images/Politics/Benghazi%20Talking% 20Points%20Timeline.pdf.

309. *"a widespread cover-up":* Hannity, Fox News, September 20, 2012.

310. *"She [Ambassador Rice] goes out":* The Five, Fox News, September 21, 2012.

310. *"You made several troubling statements":* Letter from Senators McCain, Graham, Johnson, and Ayotte to Ambassador Susan Rice, September 25, 2012.

310. *"I believe she should resign":* Rep. Peter King on CNN, speaking to Wolf Blitzer, September 28, 2012.

311. *We later learned:* U.S. Senate Select Committee on Intelligence, "Review of the Terrorist Attacks on U.S. Facilities in Benghazi, Libya," pp. 40–41.

311. *"It remains unclear if any group":* Ibid.

311. *"Madam Ambassador, he [the Libyan president]":* Face the Nation, CBS News, September 16, 2012, https://www.cbsnews.com/news/face-the-nation-transcripts -september-16-2012-libyan-pres-magariaf-amb-rice-and-sen-mccain/2/.

312. *As the Intelligence Community collects:* Shawn Turner, "Statement by the Director of Public Affairs for ODNI on the Intelligence Related to the Terrorist Attack on the U.S. Consulate in Benghazi, Libya," Office of the Director of National Intelligence, September 28, 2012, https://www.dni.gov/index.php/newsroom /press-releases/press-releases-2012/item/731-statement-by-the-director-of -public-affairs-for-odni-shawn-turner-on-the-intelligence-related-to-the-ter rorist-attack-on-the-u-s-consulate-in-benghazi-libya.

313. *the Intelligence Community again adjusted:* Michael Morell, *The Great War of Our Time: The CIA's Fight Against Terrorism from Al Qa'ida to ISIS* (New York: Twelve, 2015), pp. 206–9. Also Eric Schmitt, "After the Benghazi Attack, Talk Lagged Behind Intelligence," *New York Times*, October 21, 2012.

313. *"not a highly coordinated plot":* U.S. Senate Select Committee on Intelligence, "Review of the Terrorist Attacks on U.S. Facilities in Benghazi, Libya," p. 40.

313. *"The U.S. ambassador":* "Libyan President Says 50 Arrested in U.S. Consulate Attack," Reuters, September 16, 2012.

313. *"But in the days after":* David Kirkpatrick, "Election-Year Stakes Overshadow Nuances of the Libya Investigation," *New York Times*, October 15, 2012.

313. *What I repeatedly said:* Morell, *The Great War of Our Time*, pp. 205–6.

314. *Our current assessment: Meet the Press,* NBC News, September 16, 2012, http:// www.nbcnews.com/id/49051097/ns/meet_the_press-transcripts/t/september -benjamin-netanyahu-susan-rice-keith-ellison-peter-king-bob-woodward -jeffrey-goldberg-andrea-mitchell/#.W-XUt5NKhPZ.

314. *Subsequent investigations:* David Kirkpatrick, "Deadly Mix in Benghazi: False

Allies, Crude Video," *New York Times*, December 28, 2013. Also Morell, *The Great War of Our Time*, pp. 205–6.

314. *Among those who reportedly:* Spencer Hsu and Ann Marimow, "Accused Benghazi Ringleader Convicted on Terrorism Charges in 2012 Attacks That Killed U.S. Ambassador," *Washington Post*, November 28, 2017. Also Morell, *The Great War of Our Time*, p. 206.

314. *"if any Administration official":* Patrick Kennedy, "Testimony to the House Oversight Committee," October 10, 2012, https://oversight.house.gov/wp-content /uploads/2012/10/2012-10-10-Kennedy-testimony-Final1.pdf, as cited in Noah Schachtman and Robert Beckhusen, "State Department: We Monitored Libya Attack 'In Almost Real Time,'" *Wired*, October 10, 2012.

315. *"This latest assault":* Mitt Romney speech at Virginia Military Institute, October 8, 2012, https://foreignpolicy.com/2012/10/08/mitt-romneys-remarks-at -virginia-military-institute/.

315. *"either incompetent or untrustworthy":* Sen. Lindsey Graham interview with Charles C. W. Cooke, *The National Review*, October 12, 2012, https://www.national review.com/corner/senator-graham-secretary-state-susan-rice-impossible -charles-c-w-cooke/.

315. *"I'm particularly troubled":* John Kerry, "Kerry Defends Ambassador Rice Against Attacks," United States Senate Committee on Foreign Relations, September 28, 2012.

315. *"In order to inform":* Elizabeth Titus, "Reid Defends Rice, W.H. on Libya," *Politico*, September 29, 2012, https://www.politico.com/story/2012/09/reid-defends -rice-wh-on-libya-081813#ixzz2CETukEqe.

316. *"Secretary Clinton has done":* Commission on Presidential Debates, "October 16, 2012 Debate Transcript," October 16, 2012, https://www.debates.org/voter -education/debate-transcripts/october-16-2012-the-second-obama-romney -presidential-debate/.

316. *"There was no demonstration":* Ibid.

316. *"The suggestion that anybody":* Ibid.

319. *"Susan Rice should have known better":* *Fox and Friends*, Fox News, November 14, 2012. Also Luke Johnson, "John McCain: I Would Block Susan Rice for Secretary of State," *Huffington Post*, November 14, 2012, https://www.huffing tonpost.com/2012/11/14/john-mccain-susan-rice_n_2128940.html.

319. *"not being very bright":* Sen. John McCain in conversation with Charlie Rose and Norah O'Donnell, *CBS This Morning*, November 14, 2012. Also Kevin Robillard, "McCain: Rice 'Not Qualified' for State," *Politico*, November 14, 2012, https://www.politico.com/story/2012/11/mccain-rice-not-qualified-for -state-083824.

319. *"I don't trust her":* Adam Beam, "Embattled UN Ambassador Susan Rice Has SC critics, Support and Roots," *The State*, November 15, 2012.

319. *Well first of all I'm not going to comment:* "President Obama's news conference in the East Room of the White House on Nov. 14, 2012 (Full Transcript)," *Washington*

Post, November 14, 2012, https://www.washingtonpost.com/politics/president-obamas-news-conference-on-nov-14-2012-running-transcript/2012/11/14/031dfd40-2e7b-11e2-89d4-040c9330702a_story.html?noredirect=on&utm_term=.cbd932a36f69.

320. *Though Ambassador Rice has been:* Letter to President Obama from Republican members of the House of Representatives, November 19, 2012, https://jeffduncan.house.gov/sites/jeffduncan.house.gov/files/Rep.%20Duncan%20Letter%20to%20President%20Obama%20on%20Ambassador%20Susan%20Rice%20(11.19.12).pdf.

320 *Democrats decided they had enough:* Michael McAuliff, "Susan Rice Libya Remarks Defended By Democrats Deploring Efforts To 'Pillory' UN Ambassador," *Huffington Post*, November 16, 2012, https://www.huffpost.com/entry/susan-rice-libya-remarks_n_2145778; and Eleanor Holmes Norton, "Opening Statement of Congresswoman Eleanor Holmes Norton Press Conference Supporting Ambassador Susan Rice As Prepared for Delivery," November 15, 2012, https://norton.house.gov/media-center/press-releases/norton-democratic-colleagues-defend-ambassador-susan-rice-at-press.

321. *This had nothing to do with Susan Rice:* Interview of Rep. James Clyburn with Dana Bash, CNN, November 20, 2012.

322. *"Explain your view of the controversy":* "Remarks by Ambassador Susan E. Rice, U.S. Permanent Representative to the United Nations, at the Security Council Stakeout," U.S. Mission to the United Nations, November 21, 2012.

323. *"it seems to me that everything":* Interview of Sen. Joe Lieberman by Andrea Mitchell, MSNBC, November 28, 2012.

324. *"I regret that the talking points":* "Statement by Ambassador Susan E. Rice, U.S. Permanent Representative to the United Nations," U.S. Mission to the United Nations, November 27, 2012, https://2009-2017-usun.state.gov/remarks/5596.

324. *"very disappointed with":* Interview with Republican senators on Benghazi terrorist attack, C-SPAN, November 27, 2012, https://www.c-span.org/video/?309645-1/republican-senators-benghazi-terrorist-attack.

324. *"I don't think people around here":* William Douglas, "Susan Rice—No Stranger to Confrontation," McClatchy, December 5, 2012.

325. *"Frankly, I found her to be":* Ibid.

325. *"I am concerned that":* Interview of Sen. Susan Collins by Wolf Blitzer, *The Situation Room*, CNN, November 28, 2012, http://transcripts.cnn.com/TRANSCRIPTS/1211/28/sitroom.02.html. Also Ben Armbruster, Hamed Aleaziz, and Hayes Brown, "Updated: What Everyone Should Know About the Benghazi Attack," *ThinkProgress*, October 15, 2012.

325. *"What troubles me so much":* Joshua Hersh, "Susan Rice Role in Lead-up to Africa Embassy Bombings Recalled as Minimal," *Huffington Post*, November 29, 2012.

326. *"personality disorder":* Lloyd Grove, "Susan Rice's Personality Disorder," *The Daily Beast*, December 12, 2012.

326 *"ambitious and aggressive":* "Russia wants John Kerry, not Susan Rice as US Secretary of State," *The Telegraph*, November 8, 2012, https://www.telegraph .co.uk/news/worldnews/us-election/9663613/Russia-wants-John-Kerry-not -Susan-Rice-as-US-Secretary-of-State.html

327. *"What you don't want to do":* Interview of Sen. Johnny Isakson by Soledad O'Brien, CNN, November 28, 2012.

327. *leaders of the American Jewish community:* Abraham Foxman, as quoted in Nathan Guttman, "Susan Rice Wins Over Israel Supporters," *Forward*, November 28, 2012, https://forward.com/news/israel/166816/susan-rice-wins-over-israel-sup porters/; and David A. Harris, "It's Time to Throw the Obama Smears 'Under the Bus,'" *Jerusalem Post*, December 9, 2012, https://www.jpost.com/Opinion /Op-Ed-Contributors/Its-time-to-throw-the-Obama-smears-under-the-bus.

327. *Secretary Clinton came to my defense:* "Clinton Defends UN Envoy Rice as 'Stal-wart Colleague,'" Agence France-Presse, December 7, 2012.

329. *"I do believe so":* Meghashyam Mali, "Durbin: Rice Could Win Senate Confir-mation for Secretary of State," *The Hill*, December 9, 2012.

329. *I am honored to be considered:* Letter from Ambassador Susan E. Rice to President Barack Obama, December 13, 2012.

330. *For two decades, Susan has proven:* "Statement by the President on Ambassador Rice," The White House, December 13, 2012.

331. *"America is fortunate that":* Daniel Halper, "Susan Rice: 'America Is Fortunate That Senator John Kerry Will Be Our Next Secretary of State,'" *The Weekly Standard*, December 21, 2012.

337 *"even the longest and most politicized investigation":* Benjamin Siegel, "Benghazi Committee Report: What to Know," ABC News, June 28, 2016, https://abc news.go.com/Politics/benghazi-committee-report/story?id=40195924.

CHAPTER 17: RUNNING THE TABLE

344. *"She is fearless; she is tough":* "Remarks by the President in Personnel Announce-ment," The White House, June 5, 2013, https://obamawhitehouse.archives .gov/the-press-office/2013/06/05/remarks-president-personnel-announcement.

348. *"is not taking direction":* Memoranda of telephone conversations with Morsi, July 1, 2013, and El-Haddad, July 1, 2013, National Archives and Records Admin-istration.

351 *the upcoming major annual U.S.-Egypt:* "His Options Few, Obama Rebukes Egypt's Leaders," by Mark Landler and Peter Baker, *New York Times*, August 15, 2013. https://www.nytimes.com/2013/08/16/world/middleeast/obama-statement -on-egypt.html.

359. *We later learned these targets:* Alison Smale, "Anger Growing Among Allies on U.S. Spying," *New York Times*, October 23, 2013, https://www.nytimes

.com/2013/10/24/world/europe/united-states-disputes-reports-of-wiretap
ping-in-Europe.html.

CHAPTER 18: THE FURIES

367. *"the time has come":* Scott Wilson and Joby Warrick, "Assad Must Go, Obama
Says," *Washington Post,* August 18, 2011, https://www.washingtonpost.com
/politics/assad-must-go-obama-says/2011/08/18/gIQAelheOJ_story.html
?utm_term=.c694833fbb8a.

367. *After over a year of intense:* Peter Baker, "Heavy Pressure Led to Decision by
Obama on Syrian Arms," *New York Times,* June 14, 2013, https://www.nytimes
.com/2013/06/15/us/politics/pressure-led-to-obamas-decision-on-syrian-arms
.html; "Statement by the President on Congressional Authorization to Train
Syrian Opposition," The White House, September 18, 2014, https://obama
whitehouse.archives.gov/the-press-office/2014/09/18/statement-president
-congressional-authorization-train-syrian-opposition.

CHAPTER 19: POINT GUARD

393. *"He served the United States":* Interview of Susan Rice by George Stephanopou-
los, *This Week,* ABC News, June 1, 2014, https://abcnews.go.com/ThisWeek
/week-transcript-ambassador-susan-rice-sen-ted-cruz/story?id=23942676.

400. *enabled the Principals to propose to the president:* "Fact Sheet: U.S. Assistance to
Ukraine," The White House, November 21, 2014, https://obamawhitehouse
.archives.gov/the-press-office/2014/11/21/fact-sheet-us-assistance-ukraine;
"Fact Sheet: European Reassurance Initiative and Other U.S. Efforts in
Support of NATO," The White House, June 3, 2014, http://go.wh.gov/NB
2Rmr; "Ukraine and Russia Sanctions," U.S. Department of State, https://
www.state.gov/e/eb/tfs/spi/ukrainerussia/.

400. *President Trump has sent mixed messages:* Christian Caryl, "Donald Trump's
Talking Points on Crimea Are the Same as Vladimir Putin's," *Washington
Post,* July 3, 2018, https://www.washingtonpost.com/news/democracy-post
/wp/2018/07/03/donald-trumps-talking-points-on-crimea-are-the-same-as
-vladimir-putins/?utm_term=.5ae96909ff3f.

CHAPTER 20: PUTTING POINTS ON THE BOARD

413. *"He fooled the world once":* "PM Netanyahu addresses UN General Assembly,"
General Assembly of the United Nations, October 1, 2013, https://gadebate
.un.org/sites/default/files/gastatements/68/IL_en.pdf.

414. *At times, their meetings became so testy:* Ambassador Wendy R. Sherman, *Not for
the Faint of Heart: Lessons in Courage, Power, and Persistence* (New York: Public-
Affairs, 2018), p. 160.

414. *the negotiation appeared to be collapsing:* Ibid., p. 186.

415. *"injected a degree of partisanship":* Peter Baker and Jodi Rudoren, "Talk Toughens as U.S.-Israel Relations Fray," *New York Times*, February 25, 2015, https://www.nytimes.com/2015/02/26/world/middleeast/talk-toughens-as-us-israel-relations-fray.html.

416. *As many former officials:* https://armscontrolcenter.org/many-former-israeli-national-security-officials-support-the-iran-deal/; https://www.newyorker.com/news/daily-comment/why-israeli-nuclear-experts-disagree-with-netanyahu-about-the-iran-deal.

421. *"Why can't we take out these bastards?":* Katherine Kruger, "CNN Reporter Asks Obama: 'Why Can't We Take Out These Bastards?,'" *Talking Points Memo*, November 16, 2015, https://talkingpointsmemo.com/livewire/jim-acosta-obama-isis-g20.

422. *If and when the Mosul Dam breaks:* Fact Sheet from "Statement on Mosul Dam Emergency Preparedness," U.S. Embassy in Baghdad, February 28, 2016, https://photos.state.gov/libraries/iraq/231771/PDFs/mosul_dam_overview_english.pdf.

422. *Our Intelligence Community prepared:* Unclassified version of video: *Mosul Dam*, National Geospatial-Intelligence Agency, September 7, 2018, https://www.youtube.com/watch?v=TDrIcsajyPU.

424. *public rap on the Obama White House:* Helen Cooper, "Fraying Ties with Trump Put Jim Mattis's Fate in Doubt," *New York Times*, September 15, 2018, https://www.nytimes.com/2018/09/15/us/politics/jim-mattis-trump-defense-relationship.html?action=click&module=Top%20Stories&pgtype=Homepage.

CHAPTER 21: THE FOURTH QUARTER

428. *Meanwhile, numerous recent studies:* https://www.glassdoor.com/employers/blog/diversity-inclusion-research-roundup-top-studies-you-need-to-know/; https://www.monstergovernmentsolutions.com/docs/win/MON_DIwhitepaper_monster_0523.pdf.

430. *In October 2016, President Obama:* https://obamawhitehouse.archives.gov/the-press-office/2016/10/05/presidential-memorandum-promoting-diversity-and-inclusion-national; https://obamawhitehouse.archives.gov/the-press-office/2016/10/05/fact-sheet-presidential-memorandum-promoting-diversity-and-inclusion.

430. *In lengthy sessions:* "Fact Sheet: Memorandum of Understanding Reached with Israel," The White House, September 14, 2016, https://obamawhitehouse.archives.gov/the-press-office/2016/09/14/fact-sheet-memorandum-understanding-reached-israel.

431. *For as long as the state of Israel:* Susan Rice, "The U.S. Is Making a Historic Investment to Protect the Security of Israel," The White House, September 14, 2016, https://obamawhitehouse.archives.gov/blog/2016/09/14/us-making-historic-investment-protect-security-israel.

432. *"has no legal validity"*: U.N. Security Council Resolution 2334, adopted December 23, 2016.

432. *worked improperly behind the scenes*: Katie O'Keefe and Farnaz Fassihi, "Inside the Trump Team's Push on Israel Vote That Mike Flynn Lied About," *Wall Street Journal*, January 5, 2018, https://www.wsj.com/articles/inside-the-trump-teams-lobbying-blitz-on-2016-u-n-israel-vote-1515153600.

436. *"When the U.S. and China"*: Mark Landler, "U.S. and China Reach Climate Accord After Months of Talks," *New York Times*, November 11, 2014, https://www.nytimes.com/2014/11/12/world/asia/china-us-xi-obama-apec.html.

437. *So, at first, I was chagrined to read:* https://www.washingtonpost.com/world/national-security/administration-developing-sanctions-against-china-over-cyberespionage/2015/08/30/9b2910aa-480b-11e5-8ab4-c73967a143d3_story.html?utm_term=.350dae3fd784.

439. *"Neither country's government will conduct"*: David E. Sanger, "Limiting Security Breaches May Be Impossible Task for U.S. and China," *New York Times*, September 25, 2015, https://www.nytimes.com/2015/09/26/world/asia/limiting-security-breaches-may-be-impossible-task-for-us-and-china.html.

439. *when aggressive theft resumed:* David E. Sanger and Steven Lee Myers, "After a Hiatus, China Accelerates Cyberspying Efforts to Obtain U.S. Technology," *New York Times*, November 29, 2018, https://www.nytimes.com/2018/11/29/us/politics/china-trump-cyberespionage.html.

443. *The U.S. Intelligence Community (USIC) is confident:* "Joint Statement from the Department of Homeland Security and Office of the Director of National Intelligence on Election Security," U.S. Department of Homeland Security, October 7, 2016, https://www.dhs.gov/news/2016/10/07/joint-statement-department-homeland-security-and-office-director-national.

447. *In late December, the president announced:* "Statement by the President on Actions in Response to Russian Malicious Cyber Activity and Harassment," The White House, December 29, 2016, https://obamawhitehouse.archives.gov/the-press-office/2016/12/29/statement-president-actions-response-russian-malicious-cyber-activity.

CHAPTER 23: BRIDGING THE DIVIDE

468. *"All this is highly unusual"*: "Susan Rice Unmasked," *Wall Street Journal*, April 3, 2017, https://www.wsj.com/articles/susan-rice-unmasked-1491262064.

470. *President Trump told* The New York Times*:* "Partial Transcript: Trump's Interview with the Times," *New York Times*, April 5, 2017, https://www.nytimes.com/2017/04/05/us/politics/donald-trump-interview-new-york-times-transcript.html.

Index

Key to abbreviations: NSA = National Security Advisor; NSC = National Security Council; SR = Susan Rice; WH = White House

Abacha, Sani, 166, 200, 202
Abadi, Haider al-, 419
Abbas, Mahmoud, 432
ABC News, 107–8, 206
 SR interview on Bergdahl, 393
 This Week, 240–41, 287, 308
Abdel Rahman, Omar, 156, 206
Abdullah, Abdullah, 392
Abernethy, David, 101
Abiola, Moshood, 166–69
Abramowitz, Mort, 112
Abramowitz, Sheppie, 112
Abubakar, Abdulsalami, 166, 167
Abu Ghraib scandal, 40
Abu Khattala, Ahmed, 314
Abu Nidal, 157
Acosta, Jim, 421
Adeyemo, Wally, 374
affirmative action, 91, 93
Affordable Care Act (Obamacare), 427, 472, 474
Afghanistan, 4, 212
 Bergdahl release, 392–93
 Bilateral Security Agreement (BSA), 390–91
 Clinton bombing of, 189
 international assistance, 391
 Karzai and, 390–92
 Loya Jirga of, 391
 Obama and, 242, 390–95, 450, 451
 Taliban and, 391, 392, 394–95
 Trump policy, 394
African Center for Strategic Studies, 202
African Crisis Response Initiative, 152
African Growth and Opportunity Act (AGOA), 176, 201
African Methodist Episcopal (AME) Church, 32, 34
Ahmadinejad, Mahmoud, 264, 269, 301
Ahmed, Salman, 241, 346, 374
Aidid, Mohammed, 137–38, 140
Air Force One, 374, 375, 381
Albright, Joe, 56
Albright, Madeleine, 56, 57, 76, 118, 130, 190, 327, 373
 Africa and, 171
 Algiers Agreement, 183
 Congo Summit, 197–99
 Ethiopia-Eritrea conflict, 177
 Lois Rice and, 161, 162
 Rwanda genocide and, 147
 as secretary of state, 159, 161, 175
 Somalia conflict, 137

Albright, Madeleine (*cont.*)
SR and, 161–63, 172–73, 188–89, 198, 204
as U.N. ambassador, 134, 137, 161, 357
Vanity Fair article and, 207–9
Aldrin, Buzz, 53
Alexander, Clifford, 42
Algeria, 181, 182, 183
Algiers Agreement, 183
Aliganga, Jesse Nathan, Jr., 492n189
Allen, John, 420
Al Qaeda, 135, 187, 206, 207, 212, 242, 366, 394, 418
Benghazi attack and, 311, 313
embassy bombings, 481–82
Khorasan Group, 420
Syria and, 297, 367
Al Shabab, 379
Amidor, Yaakov, 412–13
Anderson, Brooke, 241
Angola, 136, 156, 161, 172, 193, 194, 200
Apollo 11 moon landing, 53
Arab League, 281
Arab Spring, 278–82, 449, 450
Araghchi, Abbas, 414
Araud, Gérard, 264–67, 274, 284, 285
Armstrong, Neil, 53
Arneil, Barbara, 125
Ashcroft, John, 163–64, 165
Asia-Pacific Economic Cooperation (APEC) Summit, 456–57
Aspen Strategy Group, 212, 239
Aspin, Les, 138–39
Assad, Bashar, 264, 279, 297, 364–69
"Assessing Russian Activities and Intentions in Recent US Elections" (ICA), 5
Audacity of Hope, The (Obama), 19
Austin, Lloyd, 422
Australia, 110, 212, 252, 345, 406, 434, 451, 457
Axelrod, David, 229
Ayotte, Kelly, 310, 319, 323, 324

Bahrain, 279
Bailey, Michael, 177
Balkan conflict, 184
Ban Ki-moon, 245, 252–53, 273, 403

Barber, Simon, 172
Barks-Ruggles, Erica, 241, 246
Barr, Michael, 119
Bartley, Edith, 189
Bartley, Julian, Jr., 189, 492n189
Bartley, Julian, Sr., 189, 492n189
Bartley, Susan, 189
Bashir, Omar al-, 271–72
Bayh, Evan, 239
BBC-TV, 352
Bearden, Milton, 210
Beauvoir School, 50–51, 54–56, 212, 214–15
SR at, 51, 54, 55, 56, 82
SR on Board of Trustees, 55
Beers, Randy, 76, 134–35, 142, 220
Benghazi, Libya, 281
NATO air strikes and, 291
Qaddafi assault on, 281, 283, 284, 287, 292
SR visit, 2011, 292
UNSC resolution, SR, and, 286
Benghazi terrorist attack, Sept. 11, 2012, 293, 306–7, 479
CIA's talking points, 308
Clinton, Hillary and, 247
Congress investigates, 337
DNI's update on, Sept. 28, 315
McCain and, 475–76
SR and 10–12, 87, 247, 307–37
SR press statement, 322
SR's family and, 316, 334
SR's staff and, 317–18, 334
SR's support, 319–20, 326–27, 331–32
Bennet, Douglas, 56
Bennet, Michael, 416
Bentsen, Lloyd, 119
Bergdahl, Bowe, 392–93
Berger, Sandy, 6, 17, 60–61, 76, 161, 327, 347
award for SR and, 183–84
Rwanda genocide and, 147
SR, death of Abiola, and, 168
SR, Holbrooke, and, 198
SR hired for assistant secretary of state, 161–63

SR hired for NSC, 131, 132
Vanity Fair article, 207–9
Berman, Howard, 268
Bernstein, Barton, 101
Bethune, Mary McLeod, 33
Biden, Jill, 250
Biden, Joe, 4, 232, 250, 271, 343, 354, 405, 409
　Cuba and, 408
　Mubarak and, 279
　Qaddafi and, 281
　son Beau's death and, 357
　SR and, 165, 356–57, 385
　on Syria, 363
　Ukraine and, 400
　WH briefing, Jan. 5, 2017, 5–6
bin Laden, Osama, 157, 187, 190, 207–9, 242, 451, 295–97
Black Student Fund, 100–101
Blaisdell, Allen, 45
Blinken, Tony, 279, 282, 343, 352, 353, 369, 400, 408
Boehner, John, 414
Bollettieri, Nick, 12
Bolling, Eric, 310
Bolton, John, 241, 243, 245, 259
Booker, Cory, 223
Bordentown School, 33, 227, 428
Borders, Frances, 50–51
Bosnia, 136, 142, 160, 183, 184, 196
Botswana, 172, 176
Boulé (black fraternity), 225
Boutros-Ghali, Boutros, 146, 148
Bowdoin College, 27–31, 44
　Mary M. and David A. Dickson Scholarship Fund, 30
Boxer, Barbara, 321
Brazil, 268–69, 358
Brazile, Donna, 225
Breckenridge, Anita Decker, 3, 4, 8, 380, 381
Brennan, John, 295–96, 350, 368, 389, 429
　Russian election interference and, 441–42, 444–45
Brock, Bill, 82

Brock, Hutchey, 57, 88
Brock, Muffett, 57
Brookings Institution, 17, 76, 94, 96, 211–12, 214, 217, 219, 221, 226, 327
Brown, Gordon, 95
Brown, James, 125
Brown, Ron, 54–55, 161
Browne, Tom, 225, 289
Brown v. Board of Education, 33, 43
Brussels terror attacks, 420
Bultena, Lance, 111, 476
Bunche, Jane, 42
Bunche, Ralph, 42
Burgess, Dorothy, 250
Burkina Faso, 180–81
Burns, Bill, 412
Burton, John, 84
Burundi, 143–44, 152, 155, 161, 195, 199, 200, 202
Bush, George H. W. (Bush 41), 19, 119, 121, 131, 135, 136, 246, 424
Bush, George W. (Bush 43), 40, 130, 216, 246, 351
　blame for 9/11 attacks, 207
　Clarke's criticism of, 135
　Iraq War and, 230
　Mandela funeral, 378
　North Korea and, 255, 266
　Obama transition and, 458
　PEPFAR and, 202
　reelection 2004, 220
　Saddam Hussein and, 367
　Somalia, Operation Restore Hope and, 136
　Sudan and, 209, 271
　U.N. and, 243
Bush, Laura, 378
Bushelle, Annette, 169
Bushnell, Prudence "Pru," 169, 186, 189
Buster, Robert, 384

Cafritz, Peggy Cooper, 73–74, 92, 115, 125
Camas, Wash., 224–25, 288
Cambodia, 136, 142
Cameron, David, 95, 287, 292, 362–63

Cameron, Ian O. (husband), 3, 4, 6, 7, 9, 99, 107–8, 309
  at ABC, 107–8, 206, 240–41, 287
  Africa and China backpacking with SR, 116–17, 120–21
  Benghazi postmortem, 335–36
  at CBC, 121, 123, 133, 212–13
  children's politics and, 472–73
  Churkin and, 299
  engagement to SR, 122–23
  at London School of Economics, 117
  in Ottawa, 99
  as parent, 219, 287–88
  parents of, and SR, 122
  SR and, 97–100, 102, 108, 117, 122
  SR and married life, 212–19, 232, 241
  SR as NSA, 461
  SR as U.N. ambassador, 240, 249–50, 265, 287–88, 300
  SR in Clinton's NSC, 133
  SR in Clinton's State Department, 163
  SR's fiftieth birthday party, 463–64
  SR's withdrawal as secretary of state candidate, 328–29
  as TV producer, 121, 212, 240–41, 287
  wedding to SR, 124–25
Cameron, Newton (father-in-law), 122–23
Campbell, Kurt, 212
Camp David Accords (1978), 89
Camp David Summit (2015), 7
Canada
  Ian Cameron, family, and, 98, 122–23, 326
  Ebola epidemic and, 403, 405
  TransCanada pipeline, 326
  U.S.-Cuba back channel and, 408, 409
Canadian Broadcasting Company (CBC), 121, 123, 133, 212–13
Carlos the Jackal, 157
Carlson, Tucker, 229–30
Carney, Jay, 332, 333
Carney, Tim, 157–58, 209–10, 326
Carson, Clayborne, 101

Carson, Johnnie, 162–63, 169, 186, 190, 286
Carter, Ash, 368, 385, 389, 422, 429
Carter, Jimmy, 68, 82, 118, 345
Castro, Alejandro, 408
Castro, Fidel, 408
Castro, Raúl, 379, 408
CBS, *Face the Nation*, 308, 311–12
Ceadel, Martin, 111
Cernovich, Mike, 468
Chad, 273
Chast, Roz, 370, 373
Chatham House-British International Studies Association Award, 120
Cheney, Dick, 130
China, 266, 445
  climate change and, 436, 451
  confidence-building mechanisms (CBMs), 435
  Ebola epidemic and, 403
  global health and, 436
  intellectual property theft, 436–39
  Iran sanctions and, 267, 413
  Libya, Qaddafi, and, 285
  North Korea and, 435
  Obama and, 243, 433–41, 451
  Obama at Beijing Summit, 2014, 436
  Obama at G20 in Hangzhou, 2016, 439–41, 445
  South Sudan and, 396–97
  SR backpacking trip, 116–17
  SR in, as NSA, 434–35, 437
  Sudan and, 270, 272
  Syria and, 297–98
  Trump and, 439, 457
  UNSC North Korean sanctions and, 256, 257–60
  U.S. areas of confrontation and progress with, 433–34, 436
  U.S. sanctions and, 437–38
Chissano, Joaquim, 172
Christopher, Warren, 138–39, 148, 149, 157–58, 161
Churkin, Irina, 299
Churkin, Vitaly, 257, 259, 264, 274–75, 277, 285, 297–98

City College of New York, 35
Civil Rights Act of 1964, 52
Civil War, SR's ancestor in, 32
Clapper, James, 352, 418, 429
Clark, Wesley, 231
Clarke, Richard, 76, 134, 135, 142, 155, 207
  counterterrorism responsibility, 156, 187, 189
  criticism of Bush 43, 135
  Rwanda and, 147, 149
  Somalia and, 137, 138
  as SR's boss, 133–35, 155, 347
climate change, 218, 242, 244, 385, 427, 436, 451–52
Clinton, Bill, 8, 13, 19, 189, 222, 378, 455
  Africa agenda, 156, 160–61, 171, 176, 200–203
  African Growth and Opportunity Act, 176, 201
  Africa trip, 1998, with SR, 174–76, 200
  Africa trip, 2000, 203
  Albright as secretary of state, 130, 159, 161, 171, 175
  Berger as NSA, 161
  blame for 9/11 and, 207–11
  Bosnia and, 160
  Christopher as secretary of state, 138–39, 148, 157–58
  East Africa embassy bombings, reprisals for, 189–90
  Ethiopia-Eritrea conflict and, 180, 183
  Fox News and, 333
  Hillary's presidential bid, 2007–8 and, 222
  HIV/AIDS crisis and, 202
  Jesse Jackson and, 168
  Lake as NSA, 17, 136
  "New African Leaders" and, 160, 177
  "Partnership for Economic Growth and Opportunity in Africa," 176, 200
  PDD-25 and, 142–43
  reelection, 1996, 161
  Rwanda and, 144–46, 150
  Soderberg on NSC, 119, 131

  Somalia and, 138, 139, 140
  SR's relationship with, 60–61, 79, 131, 332
  Sudan and, 156–60, 270
  U.N. and, 141–42, 245
  World Trade Center bombing, 1993, and, 156
Clinton, Chelsea, 332
Clinton, Hillary, 378
  Benghazi terrorist attack and, 247, 316, 332
  fake news about, 468
  FBI email investigation, 454
  Mubarak and, 279
  as Obama's secretary of state, 130, 238, 245, 247
  presidential bid, 2007–8, 59, 76–78, 222–23, 230, 453, 493n222
  presidential campaign, 2016, 453, 454–55
  Qaddafi, Libya, and, 281–83, 286–87
  on revenge, 337
  Russia and, 267, 268
  Russian election interference and, 442
  solo trips to Africa, 161
  SR and, 239, 246–47, 332
  SR appears in TV interviews in place of, on Benghazi attacks, 307, 325, 334
  SR defended by, 327
  Sudan issue and, 272
  as U.S. senator, 271
Clinton Foundation, 146
Clyburn, Jim, 223, 321
CNN, 316, 421
  Isakson defends SR on, 327
  Obama-Romney debate, 316–17
  SR on Benghazi and, 318
  State of the Union, 308
Colbert, Stephen, 299
College Entrance Examination Board (CEEB), 44, 57
Collins, Michael, 53
Collins, Susan, 239–40, 325
Color Purple, The (Walker), 101
Comey, James, 5, 438, 449, 454
  WH briefing, Jan. 5, 2017, 5–6

"Commonwealth Initiative in Zimbabwe, 1979–1980" (Rice), 120
Congo (formerly Zaire), 150, 152, 160, 172, 177, 202, 269
　Congo War, 193–99
　Kinshasa, capital, 193
　Lusaka Ceasefire Agreement, 195, 198, 199
　Rwanda and, 150–51, 193
　Security Council Summit, 197–99
　SR's and team's tour, 193–94
Congressional Black Caucus (CBC), 223
Control Data Corporation, 73, 226
Conway, Kellyanne, 9
Cook, Lisa, 113
Cooper, Casey, 73
Corker, Bob, 324
Cornell University, 47
Cornwell, Edward, 55
Cornwell, Michael, 55
Cornwell, Shirley, 55
Côte d'Ivoire, 121, 269–70
Cotton, Tom, 414
Cousens, Elizabeth, 241
Cousin, Ertharin, 79
Cressey, George, 25, 27
Crimea, 299, 398, 399, 400
Cronkite, Walter, 53
Crowley, Candy, 317
Cruz, Ted, 472
Cuba, 341, 407–10, 427, 451
Cui Tiankai, 439
Cunningham, Jim, 390

Dabbashi, Ibrahim, 280
Daily Show, The (TV show), 334
Daley, Bill, 281, 289–90
Dalizu, Jean Rose, 492n189
Dayton Peace Accords, 183, 196
Dean, Dorothy, 42
Dean, Howard, 219–20, 326
de Koonig, Willem, 6–7
Democrats/Democratic Party
　CBC and, 223
　Chicago DNC riots, 1968, 53
　Bill Clinton's election, 1992, 131

Hillary Clinton's presidential bid, 2007–8, 59, 76, 77, 78, 222, 230, 231
　Dukakis campaign, 1988, 118–19, 132
　Obama's DNC speech, 2004, 18
　Obama's presidential campaign and election, 2008, 40–41, 59, 76–79, 94–97, 107–8, 129, 221–24, 226, 228–33
　partisan divisions and, 450, 480–81
　Russian email hacking, 442
　Southern Democrats, 34
　SR defended by, 315, 320–21, 326–27
　Trump's election and, 453–54
　U.S. in Syria and, 363–64, 365
Dempsey, Martin, 350, 368, 402–3, 422
DePauw University, 43
Dickson, Audley, 28–29
Dickson, David A. (grandfather), 20, 23–28, 31, 70
Dickson, David W. D. (uncle), 24, 29, 31, 36, 70
Dickson, Frederick (uncle), 29–30, 44
Dickson, Leon (uncle), 27, 28, 36, 66, 70
Dickson, Mary Marguerite Daly (grandmother), 23–25, 26, 30–31, 70, 72
Dickson, Val (aunt), 28
Dickson, Vera (aunt), 29
Dickson-Horton, Valerie (cousin), 120
Doherty, Glen, 306–7
Donfried, Karen, 359
Donilon, Tom, 6, 281, 303
　as NSA, 279, 315, 332, 334, 343, 344–45
"Don't Stop Thinking About Tomorrow" (song), 455
dos Santos, José, 160, 171
Dukakis, Michael, 118–19, 131, 220
Duke Ellington School for the Arts, 73
Dunford, Joseph, 368, 390, 422
Dunn, David, 177
Durbin, Dick, 321, 328
Duterte, Rodrigo, 434

East Africa embassy bombings, 4, 186–91, 306–7, 325

East Asia Summit, 434
Ebola epidemic, 401–7, 452
  Ebola Task Force, 405
  Global Health Security Agenda and, 407
  Operation United Assistance, 403
Edwards, Bob, 206
Edwards, John, 17, 18, 77
Eggers, Jeff, 392
Egypt, 282
  Arab Spring in, 279
  Morsi coup, 347–51
  Mubarak deposed, 279
  Obama's Cairo speech, 2009, 450
  SR's family trip to (1979), 88–89
  U.S. aid to, 349
  U.S. embassy, Cairo protests and, 307, 308, 309, 313–14
Egypt-Israel Peace Treaty, 82, 89
Einstein, Albert, 33
Eisenhower, Dwight D., 246
Elle magazine, "J'Accuse!" (Shalit), 209–10
Ellington, Duke, 33
Erdoğan, Recep Tayyip, 268, 423
Eritrea, 159, 160
  Algiers Agreement, 183
  Ethiopia conflict and, 177–85
  Holbrooke and, 182
  SR in Asmara, 178, 179, 184
Erwa, Elfatih, 172
Ethiopia, 159, 160, 172
  Addis Ababa, 379–80
  Algiers Agreement, 183
  bombing of Mekele, 180
  Eritrea conflict and, 177–85
  OAU Summit, 157
  Obama threatened in, 2015, 379–81
  SR in Addis Ababa, 177–78
European Reassurance Initiative, 400
European Union (EU)
  Iran nuclear deal and, 411
  Iran sanctions and, 269
  Russian sanctions, 399–400
  U.S. surveillance of foreign citizens and, 360–61

Federal Bureau of Investigation (FBI), 45, 156, 187, 263, 370
  Benghazi attack and, 309, 312, 323, 324
  SR, the Iranians, and, 262
  Trump investigation, 449
  See also Comey, James
Feed the Future, 385
Feinstein, Dianne, 320, 321
Ferraro, Geraldine, 222
Fisher, Paul, 98
Fitt, Alfred, 63, 66, 67, 69–71, 73, 91, 105, 125, 226
Fitt, Ann, 70
Fitt, Ben, 70
Fitt, Cate, 70
Fitt, Craig, 70
Fitzpatrick, John, 7
Flake, Jeff, 410
Fleetwood Mac, 455
Flynn, Michael, 4, 6, 457–60
Foley, Diane, 420–21
Foley, James, 420–21
For Colored Girls Who Have Considered Suicide/ When the Rainbow Is Enuf (Shange), 113
Ford, Christine Blasey, 90
Fox News, 11, 248, 249
  Benghazi coverage, 309–10
  McFarland from, 459
  SR on *Sunday*, 308
  SR targeted by, 317, 332–34
France
  Africa and, 161, 177
  Ebola epidemic and, 403
  Iran sanctions and, 266–67
  Libya, Qaddafi, and, 280, 281, 284–85, 291, 292
  Obama's Iran negotiations and, 412
  Obama trip to (2008), 95
  Paris bombings, 420, 421
  Rwanda "Opération Turquoise," 149–50
  Snowden's leaks and, 359, 360
  Syria and, 297, 362
  U.N. ambassador, 264–65
  U.S. election, 2016 and, 454

Frank, Barney, 333
Franklin, Aretha, 300, 463–64
Frasure, Robert, 184
Frazer, Jendayi, 327
Frieden, Tom, 401, 404
Frontline States Initiative, 159
Frum, Barbara, 123–24
Fudge, Marcia, 321
"Funkin' for Jamaica" (song), 225, 289

Gabon, 285, 286
Garang, John, 271
Gates, Robert, 238, 279, 281
Gatkuoth, Ezekiel, 276
Gbagbo, Laurent, 270
George, Suzy, 9, 373–74
Germany, 456
    Ebola epidemic and, 403
    Iran sanctions and, 266–67
    Obama speech (2008), 95
    Snowden's leaks and, 359, 360
    UNSC and, 264
Getachew, Assefa, 380–81
Ghana, 120, 149, 172, 175
Ghani, Ashraf, 392
Ginsburg, William, 335
Giovanni, Nikki, "Resignation," 125
Global Health Security Agenda, 407
Godman Field, Ky., 36
Goldman Sachs, 131
Goldstone, Richard, 253
Gore, Al, 196, 202, 405
Govashiri, Ferial, 3, 354, 411, 441
Gowdy, Trey, 337
Graceland (Paul Simon album), 115
Graham, Lindsey, 310
    SR and Benghazi, 11, 315, 316
    SR as secretary of state opposed, 319–21,
        323–25
    SR unmasking charge, 468
Gramm, Phil, 141
Gration, J. Scott, 272, 273
Great Depression, 36
Great Lakes Justice Initiative, 152
Great Recession (economic crisis, 2008),
    237, 242

Greece, 456
Gregory, David, 314
Gross, Alan, 408–9, 410
Guantánamo Bay detention facility, 237,
    243, 450
    detainees-Bergdahl swap, 393
Guinea, 401, 403, 405

Haddad, Essam el-, 348
Hadley, Robyn, 113–14
Hadley, Steve, 6
Hagel, Chuck, 350, 389
Haggar, Anis, 210
Hailemariam, Desalegn, 380, 381
Haines, Avril, 352, 355, 357, 369–73, 400,
    411, 415, 422, 438, 459
Haiti, 136, 142, 160
Ham, Carter, 275, 276
Handley, Bill, 104
Hannity, Sean, 309–10
Hardy, Molly Huckaby, 492n189
Hargadon, Fred, 91
Harvard Business School, 227
Harvard University, 28, 29, 41–42, 91, 92
Hawkins, Augustus "Gus," 85
Heusgen, Christoph, 359
Hezbollah, 366
HIV/AIDS crisis, 199, 202
    PEPFAR and, 202
Hobson, Kenneth Ray, 492n189
Holbrooke, Richard, 76, 184, 195–99, 336
    animosity of, 182, 196, 199–200, 326
    Congo Security Council Summit,
        197–99
    Congo War and, 195–99
    Dayton Peace Accords and, 183, 196
    To End a War, 183
    Ethiopia-Eritrea conflict and, 182–83,
        199
    HIV/AIDS campaign, 199
    SR confrontation with, 197–98
    as U.N. ambassador, 182, 195, 197
Holder, Eric, 223, 238
Hollande, François, 359, 399, 454
Holmes Norton, Eleanor, 117–18, 120
Hoyer, Steny, 320

Huddleston, Vicki, 169
Hu Jintao, 267
Humphrey, Hubert H., 53
Hurricane Katrina, 40

"I Feel Good" (song), 125
Ijaz, Mansoor, 209
India, 24, 46, 265–66, 286, 345, 381, 434, 451
Innocence of Muslims (video), 309, 313–14
International Atomic Energy Agency (IAEA), 253, 264, 417
International Criminal Court, 271, 279, 280
International Monetary Fund for the Heavily Indebted Poor Countries initiative, 201
Iran, 411
  American hikers captured, 262
  Islamic Revolutionary Guard Corps, 269
  Levinson missing in, 262
  nuclear deal (JCPOA), 269, 386, 411–18, 451, 472
  nuclear program, 262, 263–64
  P5+1 nuclear deal and, 412
  sanctions on, 260, 264, 266–69
  Sudan and, 157
  Syria and, 366, 367, 368
  terrorism supported by, 264
  U.N., SR, and, 261–64
  U.N. Mission, N.Y., 261–62
  U.S. back channel to, 261–63
  U.S. Embassy hostages, 82
  U.S.-Iran conflict threat, 417
  U.S. relations with, 415
Iran-Contra affair, 19
Iraq, 40, 243, 367
  Erbil and, 419
  ISIS and, 418–19, 422–23, 451
  Mosul and, 418–19, 422
  Mosul Dam, 421–22, 458
  Obama and Iraq War, 222, 230
  Obama policy, 242, 418, 451
  SR and, 212, 219–20, 326
  urban counterinsurgency, 140
Irish, James Theodore "Ted," 44
Isaias Afwerki, 160, 177, 178–79, 182, 184

Isakson, Johnny, 326–27
ISIS, 301, 421, 449
  beheadings by, 404, 420
  Libya and, 293
  in Mosul, 418
  Obama's counter-ISIS campaign, 4, 418–23, 451, 458
  Syria and, 297, 366
  U.S.-led coalition and, 420
Israel
  Goldstone Report and, 253
  Iran and, 307
  Iran nuclear deal and, 412–17
  memorandum of understanding (MOU), 430–32
  nuclear program, 253
  Obama trip (2008), 95
  Palestinian negotiations, 450
  Peres and SR, 254–55
  Peres funeral, 432
  Sderot, 95
  SR at U.N. and, 252–54
  SR's family trip to (1979), 88–89
  Syria and, 365, 366
  Trump and, 432–33
  Turkey conflict, 253
  two-state solution, 253–54, 432
  U.S. abstains on U.N. anti-settlement vote, 432–33
  U.S. aid to, 349, 430
  Yad Vashem, 95

"J'Accuse!" (Shalit), 209–10
Jackson, Jesse, 168, 222
Jackson, Ronny, 374
Jamaica
  SR's childhood visit to, 51–52
  SR's grandparents and, 24–25
Japan, 37, 227, 252, 345, 376, 434, 451
  Ebola epidemic and, 403
  North Korean sanctions and, 258, 259
  North Korean threat to, 256
  Snowden's leaks and, 359
Jarrett, Valerie, 229, 250, 290, 376
Jennings, Elizabeth, 57–58, 67
Jimenez, Adela, 206, 241

Johnson, Bob, 222
Johnson, Jeh, 387, 405, 438, 444
Johnson, Lyndon B., 53
Johnson, Ron, 310
Joint Base Andrews, 7, 8–9, 306, 374
Jones, Deborah, 475–76, 477
Jones, James, 130, 238
Jordan, 95, 366
Jordan, Vernon, 43–44

Kabila, Laurent, 193, 195
Kagame, Paul, 149, 151, 160, 172, 178, 326
Kahl, Colin, 352
Karl, Jon, 319
Karzai, Hamid, 390–92
Kassig, Abdul-Rahman, 420
Katzman, Julie, 232
Kavalar, Prabhi Guptara, 492n189
Kavanaugh, Brett, 90
Kennedy, Donald, 105
Kennedy, Patrick, 314–15
Kennedy, Robert F., 52
Kenya
    bombing of U.S. Nairobi embassy, 186–91, 492n189
    Bushnell as ambassador, 186
    Lokichoggio, 270
    Nairobi, 270
    Obama trip, 2015, 379
    U.S. Sudan embassy in, 157, 158, 209
Kerry, John, 231, 239–40, 335, 368
    Afghanistan BSA and, 391, 392
    China's climate change policy and, 436
    diversifying State Department workforce, 429–30
    Iran nuclear deal and, 386, 411, 412, 414, 415, 416
    on Morsi's deposing, 350
    as Obama's secretary of state, 318–19, 327, 331, 363, 364, 411
    presidential campaign, 2004, 17–18, 40, 107, 220–21
    Principals Committee and, 389
    South Sudan and, 395, 397
    SR and, 1, 315, 321, 331, 352, 385–87

U.N. resolution on Syria's chemical weapons, 386
Khalilzad, Zalmay, 241
Khazaie, Mohammed, 261–63
Kiir, Salva, 276, 277, 395–98
Kim Jong Un, 450, 477
King, Martin Luther, Jr., 52, 101
    quotation on Oval Office carpet, 4, 14, 460
King, Peter, 310
Kingibe, Baba, 168
Kirk, Arlene, 492n189
Kirk, Ron, 250
Kirk-Greene, Anthony, 120
Kirk-Greene, Helen, 120
Kirkpatrick, Jeane, 459
Kislyak, Sergey, 443, 446
Kissinger, Henry, 6, 433
Klain, Ron, 405
Kruzel, Joe, 184
Kucinich, Dennis, 78, 472
Kupchan, Charles, 400

Ladysmith Black Mambazo, 115
Lake, Julie, 19
Lake, Anthony "Tony," 6, 17, 19, 216
    as Clinton's NSA, 17, 136, 147, 148, 154, 156, 161
    Holbrooke and, 182
    Obama's policy and, 242
    Obama's presidential campaign and, 59, 76–77, 94, 232
    Rwanda and, 143, 147, 148
    as special envoy for Ethiopia and Eritrea, 181–84, 193
    SR interviewed by, 131, 132
    as SR mentor, 186, 347
    SR's promotion and, 154–55
    U.S.-Africa partnership and, 161
Lavrov, Sergei, 267, 268, 364–65, 386
Lea, Tim, 341–42, 384
Leahy, Patrick, 410
Lebanon, 187, 269, 281, 284, 366
Lee, Charles F., 32
Leland, Mickey, 179
Lempert, Yael, 430

Levertov, Denise, 101
Levi, Peter, 101
Levin, Carl, 321
Levinson, Robert, 262
Lew, Jack, 318
Lewinsky, Monica, 189, 335
LGBT rights, 244, 429
Li Baodong, 266
Liberia, 156, 269
    Ebola epidemic, 401, 403–5
    Monrovia, drawdown of U.S. embassy
        staff, 200
Libya, 4, 450
    Arab Spring and, 279–82
    girls named Susan, 291
    ISIS in, 293
    McCain and, 475–76
    NATO air strikes in, 289, 291, 298, 367
    no-fly zone and, 280–81
    post-Qaddafi problems, 292–94
    regime change in, 291, 297
    sanctions and, 260
    SR and, 153, 279–83, 369
    SR and U.S. position, 283–84
    SR visit, 2011, 291–92
    Sudan and, 272
    UNSC sanctions and, 278, 280
    U.S. embassy, Tripoli, 280
    See also Benghazi, Libya; Benghazi
        terrorist attack
Liddy, G. Gordon, 54
Lieberman, Joe, 323
Lincoln University, 32, 34
Lippert, Mark, 77
Livni, Tzipi, 252
Lodge, Henry Cabot, 246
Lovell, Whitfield, 249
Lula da Silva, Luiz Inácio, 268
Lyall Grant, Sir Mark, 265
Lynch, Loretta, 438

Macdonald, Anne, 81
Machar, Riek, 277, 395, 396, 397
Magruder, Jeb, 54
Maliki, Nouri al-, 418–19
Malley, Rob, 411, 422

Management Leadership for Tomorrow
    (MLT), 227, 428
Mandela, Nelson, 105, 175–76, 214, 377,
    379
Maret School, 216, 473
Martin, Mary Louise, 492n189
Marton, Kati, 197
Mathews, Sylvia (Burwell), 119
Mauritius, 159
Mazimhaka, Patrick, 178–79, 180
Mbeki, Thabo, 202
McCain, John, 141, 230, 231, 310, 350
    Jones's anecdote about, 475–76
    SR and, 231, 323–24
    SR as secretary of state opposed, 319,
        320, 322, 325–26
    SR's reflections on, 474–77
McCaskill, Claire, 416
McClellan, Whalen, 124
McConnell, Mitch, 445, 451
McCormick, Shawn, 327
McCoy, Van, 54–55
McDonough, Denis, 77, 250
    Cuba negotiations and, 408
    as deputy national security advisor, 296,
        323
    Ebola epidemic and, 405
    Russian interference in 2016 election
        and, 441, 443
    Syria and, 362, 368
    as WH chief of staff, 9, 343, 352, 353,
        389, 426
McFarland, K. T., 459
McFaul, Michael, 104
McGurk, Brett, 420
McKinsey & Company, 121–22, 131, 132,
    133
Medvedev, Dimitri, 267, 285, 286
Meles, Zenawi, 160, 172, 177, 178–80,
    182–83, 216
Menendez, Robert, 158–59
Meng, Jianzhu, 438
Merkel, Angela, 95, 359, 394, 399, 456
Mexico, 304–5, 345, 359
Mikva, Abner, 17
Millet, David, 249

Mitchell, Andrea, 323, 410

Mobutu Sese Seko, 160, 193

Mogae, Festus Gontebanye, 172

Mohammed bin Zayed (MBZ), 454

Monaco, Lisa, 353, 355, 369–73, 379–80, 387, 405, 438

Moniz, Ernie, 411, 414, 416

Moore, Missy, 462

Morell, Michael, 323–24, 325

Morsi, Mohamed, 348–51

Moscone, George, 84

Moscone, Rebecca, 84

Mozambique, 136, 161, 172

MSNBC, 12, 323
  Morning Joe, 352
  Tucker Carlson Show, SR on, 229–30

Mubarak, Hosni, 157, 279, 348

Mueller, Kayla, 420

Mueller, Robert, 370

Mugabe, Robert, 119, 160, 171, 174, 199

Murphy, Eddie, 453

Museveni, Yoweri, 172

Muskie, Edmund, 118

NAACP, 27, 28

Nagel, Jacob, 430

Najdi, Karim, 342

Namibia, 193, 194–95

Napolitano, Janet, 238

National Cathedral School (NCS), 50, 81, 88, 92–93
  SR attends, 79–82, 86–93, 99

National Child Research Center (NCRC), 50

National Democratic Institute, 212

National Economic Council (NEC), 131–32, 133, 347

National Scholarship Service and Fund for Negro Students (NSSFNS), 32, 43

National Security Advisor (NSA)
  Donilon as, 279, 315, 332, 334, 343, 344–45
  Jones as, 130, 238
  Lake as, 17, 136, 147, 148, 154, 156, 161
  SR as, 13, 344–452
  SR's appointment, 342–44

National Security Agency (NSA), 358–59
  PPD 28, "Signals Intelligence Activities" and, 360
  Snowden's leaks and, 358–61

National Security Council (NSC), 2, 13
  Berger and SR, 131, 132
  budget, 135
  Clarke and SR, 134, 135
  collegiality at, 135–36
  daily presidential briefings, 354–55
  Deputies Committee, 387
  Egypt and Morsi coup, 348–49
  Holiday Party, 373
  Lake and SR, 131, 132
  National Security Staff, 347
  Obama-era records, 7
  Obama's approach to governing and, 424–25
  office of, 348
  operations of, 136
  Prendergast and, 178
  Rwanda genocide and, 143–53
  "Scowcroft model," 424
  size of staff, 135
  Soderberg as staff director, 119
  Somalia and, 136–41
  SR hired for director for international organizations and peacekeeping, 132–34
  SR mentored by Beers at, 134–35
  SR on Somalia and lessons of, 139–41
  SR's mantra, 135
  SR's U.N. portfolio, 136
  staff of, 346, 347
  Trump team and, 455–60
  U.S. policy on U.N. peacekeeping and, 142

National Security Council (NSC),
  Principals Committee, 130, 246, 247, 272–73, 343, 345, 356, 387–90, 424
  Ebola epidemic and, 401, 402
  Iran nuclear deal and, 413–15
  ISIS and, 419–20, 422
  Libya and, 281, 283
  Mosul Dam threat and, 422
  Russian election interference in 2016 and, 442, 447–48

Somalia decisions and, 140
South Sudan and, 396
Sudan and, 158
Syria decisions, 368
NATO, 381
  in Afghanistan, 390, 391, 393, 394,
    395
  European Reassurance Initiative and,
    400
  Libyan air strikes, 291, 298
  Somalia conflict and, 146
  Summit in Wales, 401
  U.K. and, 103
  Ukraine and, 399, 400
  war against ISIS and, 420
NBC
  ISIS fears and, 421
  Meet the Press, 308, 314
  Obama's Cuba policy and, 410
  Williams's SR interview, 330
Netanyahu, Benjamin, 95, 252, 265, 307,
    381, 412, 413
  Israel-U.S. MOU and, 430–31
  Obama's Iran negotiations and, 414–15
  settlements and, 432, 433
New Yorker, Roz Chast cartoon *Furies 2.0*,
    370–71, 373
New York Times, 44, 291, 326
  on cause of Benghazi attack, 313, 314,
    318, 321
  Rwanda genocide and, 148
  Trump on SR in, 470
Nicholson, Marvin, 374
Niger, 120
Nigeria, 47, 156, 172, 285, 286
  Abiola death and SR, 166–69
  debt relief and, 201
  transition to democratic rule, 200,
    202–3
9/11 Commission, 207, 210
9/11 Commission Report, 18
9/11 terrorist attacks, 135
  SR and, 206–11, 326
  Sudan and, 207, 208, 326
Nixon, Richard, 53, 54
North, Oliver, 144

North Korea, 4, 450, 458
  ballistic missile launch, 255
  China's role with, 435
  "New York channel" to, 263
  nuclear weapons and, 256, 263
  Six Party Talks, 256
  U.N. sanctions, 255–60, 266
Norton, Eleanor Holmes, 320
NPR, *Morning Edition*, 352
Nuclear Non-Proliferation Treaty, 244
Nuland, Victoria, 400
Nunes, Devin, 468

Obama, Barack
  The Audacity of Hope, 19
  background and family, 41
  character and personality, 353, 355, 358,
    360, 377, 387–88
  criticism of, 222
  DNC speech, 2004, 18
  Hope Fund, 19
  Iraq War opposition, 222, 230
  as junior senator, 19, 95, 271
  overseas trip, summer, 2008, 95–96,
    231
  presidential campaign and election, 2008,
    40–41, 59, 76–79, 94–97, 107–8, 129,
    221–24, 226, 228–33
  as role model, 18
  Russia and, 267
  senate race, 2004, 17–18
  SR's relationship with, 2, 8, 17–19, 41,
    60, 130–31, 221, 229, 245, 246, 289,
    290, 303, 315–17, 319–20, 330, 344,
    350, 353, 377
  supporters, 222
  values and principles, 19
Obama, Barack, presidency of
  Affordable Care Act, 427, 472
  Afghanistan and, 242, 390–95, 450
  Africa agenda, 201, 385
  Africa Summit hosted by, 451
  Africa trip, 2013, 348
  Africa trip, 2015, 379–81
  Al Qaeda and, 242
  American values of, 243

Obama, Barack, presidency of (*cont.*)
  America's global leadership and, 242–43, 407, 471–72
  Asian policy, 242–43, 434, 451
  banning torture, 237, 243
  Benghazi attack and, 309–10, 315, 316–17, 319–20, 322
  bin Laden's killing and, 295–97, 310, 451
  Cairo speech, 2009, 450
  campaigning in 2012, 315
  campaigning in 2016, for Hillary, 454–55
  challenges and objectives, 241–42
  China and, 243, 267, 433–41, 451
  China and, Xi's state visit, 437–39
  China Summit, 2014, 436
  China Summit, 2016, 439–41
  climate change, Paris Agreement, 242, 244, 385, 427, 436, 451–52
  Hillary Clinton as secretary of state, 130, 238, 245, 247
  Cuba and, 341, 407–10, 427, 451
  cyber defenses, 242
  daily briefing, 1, 350–51, 352, 354, 355
  daily schedule, routine, 351–55
  diversifying federal workforce, 427–30
  dogs of, 353
  Ebola epidemic, 401–7, 452
  economic recovery, 237, 242
  farewell at Andrews, 8–9
  final APEC Summit, 456–57
  final meetings with Xi, Trudeau, and Turnbull, 457
  final overseas trip, 2016, 456–57
  foreign dignitaries at WH, 381
  foreign policy, 19, 237, 450 (*see also specific issues*)
  "Fourth Quarter" quote, Jan. 2015, 426–27
  "The Furies" and, 370–71, 373
  G20 Summit, 2013, 358, 364
  global goodwill toward, 245
  global health issues, 242, 407, 452
  Guantánamo Bay and, 237, 243
  Holder as attorney general, 238
  Iran Nowruz message, 263–64

  Iran nuclear deal and, 269, 341, 386, 411–18, 427, 451
  Iran nuclear program, 263–64
  Iran sanctions, 267
  Iraq War and, 242
  ISIS and, 418–23, 451, 452
  Israel and, 430–33
  Israel trip, Peres funeral, 2016, 432
  Jones as NSA, 130, 238
  Kerry as secretary of state, 318–19, 327, 331, 363, 364, 411
  Latin America visit, 287
  leaving office, 3–4, 8–9
  Libya, Qaddafi, and military intervention, 279–84, 286, 289, 291, 292, 298, 367
  limousine, "the Beast," 377, 440, 457
  management style, 424–25
  Martha's Vineyard vacations, 350–51
  Middle East policy, 341
  Mubarak and, 279
  national security challenges, 237–38
  national security team, first term, 237, 238
  North Korean sanctions, 255
  nuclear weapons and, 242, 244, 255, 301
  Oval Office of, 3–4, 460
  overseas trips: routines and protocols for, 374–77
  Peres and, 255
  Principals Committee meetings and, 387–90
  Putin and, 398–99, 445–46
  Republican obstructionism and, 450–51
  Russia and, 243
  Russian election interference and, 441–49, 451
  St. Patrick's Day at WH, 353–54
  same-sex marriage, 427
  second term team, 2, 343, 374
  signature development programs, 385
  Snowden and, 358–60, 451
  South Africa trip, Mandela's funeral, 377–79
  South Sudan and, 395–96

SR as NSA, 13, 342–452
SR as secretary of state candidate, 319–31
SR as U.N. ambassador, 129–30, 200,
    237–337
SR asked if wants World Bank
    presidency, 303
SR's reflection on eight-year tenure of,
    449–52
state visits at WH, 381–82
successes of, 451–52
Sudan, 270–77
Syria, 341, 362–69, 450–51
TPP, 242–43, 418, 434, 451
Trump transition and, 458
UN and, 243, 245
UNGA speeches, 273, 412
UN rituals, 301, 302–3
WH briefing, Jan. 5, 2017, 5–6
WH Correspondents' Dinner, 382
Obama, Malia, 349, 350
Obama, Michelle, 8–9, 78, 232, 250, 378
Obasanjo, Olusegun, 172–73, 202–3
    wife Stella, 203
O'Connor, Ann Michele, 492n189
O'Hanlan, Michael, 327
Olds, Sherry Lynn, 492n189
Olmert, Ehud, 95
Oman, as U.S.-Iran back channel, 412
Organisation for the Prohibition of
    Chemical Weapons (OPCW), 365
Organization of African Unity (OAU),
    180–81, 183
"Osama Files, The" (Rose), 207–9,
    210–11
Ottinger, Richard, 82
Ouyahia, Ahmed, 181
Oxford, England, 101–2
Oxford University, 110, 111, 113–14
    New College, 109–11, 114
    SR and anti-apartheid movement at,
        115
    SR as Rhodes Scholar, 108–17
    SR's lost passport and, 111–13
    SR's M.Phil degree, 111, 113
    SR's PhD, 118, 119
    SR's thesis and award, 120

Palestinian state, Palestinians, 157, 432,
    450
Panetta, Leon, 332
Paris Climate Change Agreement, 385, 418,
    427, 436, 451–52
Paulsen, Joe, 374
Payne, Donald, 223, 275
Pell, Claiborne, 73
Pell Grants, 73, 428, 430, 489n73
Pelosi, Nancy, 320
Penobscot Bay, Me., 226
Peres, Shimon, 254–55, 431–32
Perino, Dana, 310
Perry, Rick, 472
Persons, Michael, 112
Peru, 456
Petraeus, David, 321, 332
Philippines, 377, 434, 451
Pickering, Tom, 166–68, 191, 201, 208
Plouffe, David, 229
Podesta, John, 436, 444
Portland, Me., 14, 20–23, 25, 26, 27, 30
Portnoy, Elliott, 104, 111
Powell, Colin, 271, 275, 276
Power, Samantha, 251, 279, 282, 351,
    368
    gaffe by, 230
    Principals Committee and, 389
    A Problem from Hell, 152
    South Sudan and, 397
    SR and, 152–53, 344
    as U.N. ambassador, 344, 388, 432
Power Africa, 385
Prendergast, John, 178, 182, 198, 327
Presidential Decision Directive 25 (PDD-
    25): "U.S. Policy on Reforming
    Multilateral Peace Operations,"
    142–43
Presidential Policy Directive 28 (PDD-28),
    "Signals Intelligence Activities,"
    360
Problem from Hell, A (Power), 152
Pryor, Richard, 55
    Bicentennial Nigger album, 55
Puerto Vallarta, Mexico, 304–5
Pullman, Amy, 215, 217

Putin, Vladimir, 286, 291, 297, 359, 383, 450
  election interference and, 441–49
  Obama and, 364
  Obama and, G20 meeting, 2016, 445–46
  Obama phone calls, 398–99
  Trump and, 477
  Ukraine and, 400

Qaddafi, Muammar, 279–80, 369
  Benghazi assault by, 281, 283, 284, 287
  capture and killing of, 291
  at the U.N., 301–2
Qatar, 287, 393

race, racial issues
  British/Caribbean racial caste system, 26
  Civil Rights Act of 1964, 52
  discrimination in education, 27, 28, 29, 35, 43, 100–101
  discrimination in employment, 25, 45–47
  discrimination in the military, 21, 36–37
  Obama and equality, 41
  psychological impact, 29, 35, 37
  social discrimination and segregation, 31–32, 35, 36, 38–39
  "Southern prejudicial practices," 28
  SR as anti-apartheid activist, 102, 104–5, 115, 176
  SR in England and, 114–15
  SR's experience with, 86, 88, 102–3, 124
  SR's family's experiences and, 25–26, 29, 31–32, 34, 35, 36–37, 38–39, 45
  Tuskegee Airmen as vanguard of black achievement, 36–37
  Washington, D.C. riots, 52
Radcliffe College, 31, 41–42, 39
  SR's mother and, 31–32, 41–44
Ramos, Wilson, 342
Rangarajan, Taara, 346
Rawlings, Jerry, 172, 175
Reagan, Ronald, 19, 82–83, 104, 135
Reid, Harry, 315

Republicans/Republican Party
  Benghazi attacks, SR, and, 11–12, 308, 315–17
  Bergdahl release and, 393
  domestic partisan divisions and, 450–51, 480–81
  freed blacks and, 34
  Iran nuclear deal opposition, 414, 416
  opposition to Obama policies, 450–51
  opposition to SR as secretary of state candidate, 319–31
  Romney as presidential candidate, 2012, 308
  SR as target of, 11–12, 87, 247, 309–11, 315–17, 319–37, 468
"Resignation" (Giovanni), 125
Rhodes, Ben, 3, 77, 279, 282, 302, 322–23, 350, 352, 355, 371, 373, 376, 380, 381, 408, 409, 411
Rhodes Scholarships, 104, 108, 109
  SR and, 103–4, 108–17
Rice, Andrea Williams (sister-in-law), 102, 227–28, 342
Rice, Condoleezza "Condi," 6
Rice, E. John Jr. "Johnny" (brother), 5, 12, 14, 20–21, 23, 33, 89, 250–51, 344
  on Benghazi, 335–36
  birth of, 49–50
  Cafritz and, 115
  career, 227
  childhood, 51–52, 54, 55, 57, 61–75
  father's death, 289
  at Harvard, 227
  jazz and, 45
  lessons of childhood, 38, 39
  Management Leadership for Tomorrow (MLT), 227, 428
  marriage of, 102, 227–28
  mother's relationship with, 226–27, 228, 462–63, 464
  Obama's election and, 232
  parental discord and divorce, 62, 64, 66
  at St. Albans School, 102
  SR's relationship with, 64, 102, 105, 109, 124–25, 342

SR's withdrawal as secretary of state
candidate and, 328–29
TWA's Board of Directors' trip to Egypt
and Israel, 88–89
upbringing and values, 80, 428
at Yale, 102, 227
Rice, Emmett J. (father), 31, 34–39, 89
advice for SR upon leaving home, 96–97
Albright family and, 56
in the Army Air Force, World War II, 36
background and family, 32, 34–35
in Berkeley Fire Department, 46
blood pressure problems, 250, 357–58
in Camas, Wash., 224–26, 289
Ian Cameron and, 122
career of, 68
Carter appoints to the Federal Reserve
Board, 68
at CCNY, 35
character and personality, 45, 53, 58, 68,
69, 224
core doctrine, 14
death of, 289
degrees of, 32, 35–36
détente with ex-wife, 250–51
favorite dance song, 225
as Fulbright Scholar, India, 46
as grandfather, 250–51, 288
growing up in New York, 35
health decline of, 288, 461
"life lessons" taught to SR and her
brother, 37–38, 69
living in Shepherd Park, Washington,
D.C., 54–55
marriage and divorce, 41, 47, 58, 61–68,
73–75
at the N.Y. Federal Reserve, 47
Obama campaign and, 223–24, 226, 232
parental role of, 58, 65, 67–68, 69, 80, 91,
92–93, 96–97
PhD at UC Berkeley, 32, 41, 44–45
philosophy about race in America, 38–39,
46, 80, 93
segregation in the military and, 36–37
SR's adult relationship with, 224–26,
250, 288

SR's childhood and, 20
SR's Stanford graduation and, 105
SR's wedding and, 124–25
teaching positions, 47
TWA's Board of Directors, 65
TWA's Board of Directors, trip to Egypt
and Israel, 88–89
with USAID, Nigeria, 47
with U.S. Treasury, 49
workplace discrimination and, 45–47
World Bank and, 303
Rice, Gladys Clara (aunt), 34
Rice, Kiki (niece), 232, 342
Rice, Lois Dickson (mother), 11, 14, 23,
30, 43, 89
academic excellence, 30, 32, 42–43
Madeleine Albright and, 161, 162
Benghazi controversy, impact of, 316
birth of John, 49
birth of SR and stillborn twin, 48–49
on Board of Trustees, Beauvoir School,
55–56
Brookings Institution and, 226
Ian Cameron and, 122
cancer of, 11, 71, 228, 461–64
career of, 32, 39, 43, 72–73
at College Board, 44, 47, 57, 73
character and personality, 42, 71, 72, 463
at Columbia University, 43
at Control Data, 73, 226
death of, 5, 464–65
détente with ex-husband, 250–51
Fitt's death and, 124
as grandmother, 228, 241, 250–51, 462–63
housekeeper for, 57–58, 67
Jamaican heritage, 23
Vernon Jordan and, 43–44
marriage, to Alfred Fitt, 69–71
marriage, to Emmett Rice, and divorce,
41, 58, 61–68, 73–75
marriage, to Ted Irish, 44
MLT and, 227
in Nigeria, 47
at NSSFNS, 43
Obama and, 226, 464, 465
Pell Grants and, 73, 428, 489n73

Rice, Lois Dickson (mother) (*cont.*)
  Penobscot Bay, Me., home, 226
  pregnancy with SR, 47–48
  race, racial issues and, 39
  at Radcliffe, 31, 39, 41–44
  as role model, 56–57
  scholarships for, 32
  SR's Benghazi TV interviews, warning
    by, 307, 308, 334
  SR's childhood and, 20
  SR's children and, 216
  SR's lost passport, 112, 113
  SR's relationship with, 11, 47–50, 56–57,
    71–73, 74, 90, 91, 92, 97, 211, 226–28,
    461–65
  SR's Stanford graduation and, 105
  SR's wedding and, 124–25
  SR's withdrawal as secretary of state
    candidate and, 328–29
  Stevenson campaign and, 43
  tribute to her mother, 23
  visiting SR at the WAT apartment, 250
Rice, Mateo (nephew), 232, 304–5, 342
Rice, Pansy Victoria (aunt), 34, 66, 79, 225
Rice, Sue Pearl Suber (grandmother),
  34–35
Rice, Susan
  on America's polarization, 477–81
  appearance, 2, 116, 161
  character and personality, 3, 12–13, 14,
    38, 54, 56, 61, 62–63, 72, 74–75, 86,
    87, 117, 170, 210, 224, 337, 342
  compartmentalizing by, 461
  competitiveness, 12, 21
  on democracy in jeopardy, 479
  family as priority of, 460–61 (*see also*
    Rice-Cameron, Jake; Rice-Cameron,
    Maris)
  father, Emmett, 96–97, 105, 224–26, 288
  father's death, 289
  fiftieth birthday party, 463–64
  friends, closest, 19, 76, 87–88, 110–13,
    116–17, 125, 195
  husband and marriage, 3, 4, 6, 7, 9, 154,
    163, 212–19 (*see also* Cameron, Ian)
  jazz and, 45

  life after government service, 466–67
  mother, Lois, and, 11, 47–50, 56–57,
    71–73, 74, 90, 91, 92, 97, 105, 112,
    113, 211, 226–28, 461–65
  mother's death, 5, 464–65
  opinion of Trump, 8, 468, 477
  as parent, 205, 212–19, 241, 287–88,
    460–61
  philosophy about race, 38, 80, 93, 103
  role models and mentors, 56–57, 80–81,
    82, 85, 118, 130, 161, 204, 347
  signature mantra, 7
  solutions for healing America's divides
    by, 481–82
  tennis and, 2, 12, 224, 289, 342
  values, 13, 14, 19, 21–22, 33, 37–38, 39,
    59, 69, 80, 100, 227, 428
  —1964–82, early years, 20–22, 49–58,
    61–75
  college acceptances, 90–92
  conception and birth, 47–49
  events of the 1960s–70s, 52–54
  family and heritage, 19–39, 41–50, 239
  middle school and high school, 79–82,
    86–90, 99
  as page, U.S. House of Representatives,
    83–86
  parental discord and divorce, 58, 61–68,
    88
  politics, early interest in, 81–86
  preschool and elementary school, 50–51,
    54, 55, 56, 82
  religious ties, first church, 79–80, 89, 124
  teenage recklessness, 89–90
  TWA's Board of Directors' trip to Egypt
    and Israel, 88–89
  —1982 to 1993, as young adult
  Africa, China backpacking, 116–17,
    120–21
  anti-apartheid movement and, 102,
    104–5, 115
  Ian Cameron and, 97–100, 102, 108,
    116–17
  Ian Cameron, engagement, 122–24
  Ian Cameron, wedding, 123–25
  colleagues of, 119

Dukakis campaign, 1988, 118–19, 131, 132, 220
at McKinsey & Company, 121–22, 131, 132, 133
NEC position offer, 131–32
Oxford M.Phil, 111, 113
Oxford PhD, 117–18, 119
Rhodes Scholarship, 103–4, 108–17
role in *For Colored Girls Who Have Considered Suicide/ When the Rainbow Is Enuf*, 113
Soviet Union trip, 116
at Stanford, 91–92, 96–106
thesis and award, 120
Zimbabwe research, 119–20
—**1993–97, Clinton's NSC staff,** 13, 59, 131–65
Albright and, 134
Angola and, 156
Beers and, 76, 134–35, 142, 220
Berger and, 131, 132, 133
Burundi and, 155
Clarke and, 133–34, 155
hiring of, 132–34
husband Ian and, 133, 154
Lake and, 17, 131, 132, 154–55
Liberia and, 156
New African Leaders, 160, 177
Nigeria and, 156
PDD-25 and, 142–43
Rwanda genocide and, 143–53
as senior director for African affairs, 154–65
Somalia and, 136–41
South Africa and, 155–56
status at, 150
Sudan policy and, 156–60
as U.N. director, 136, 154
U.S. policy on U.N. peacekeeping operations, 142
—**1997–2001, Clinton's assistant secretary of state,** 13, 59, 152
African Crisis Response Initiative, 152
African debt relief, 200–201
African education initiatives, for girls, 201–2
age and appearance, impact of, 171–72
Albright's official African visits and, 161, 172–73
Carson as deputy, 162–63
Chiefs of Mission serving in Africa conference, 170, 171
Clinton appoints, and Senate confirmation, 161–65, 204
Clinton's Africa trip and, 174–76, 200
Congo War, 193–99
Congo War regional tour, 193–95
direct reports to, 169–70
East Africa embassy bombings and, 186–91, 206, 307, 325
East Africa trip, following embassy bombings, 188–89
goals, Clinton's agenda, and, 170–71
Great Lakes Justice Initiative, 152
Holbrooke and, 196–200
Lake as advisor, mentor, 186
leaks and, 172–73
maternity leave and, 164, 165
"New Partnership with Africa for the 21st Century," 170
in Nigeria, Abiola's death and, 166–69
Nigeria's Obasanjo and, 202–3
office of, 169
personal mantra of, 171
Pickering's anger at, 191
press attacks on, 326
professional growth and lessons learned, 203–4
reputation from NSC, 170
Samuel Nelson Drew Memorial Award, 183–84
Sudan trip, 270–71
Summers's animosity, 201
team, 169
Wolpe's criticism, advice, 192
—**2001–8, between Democratic administrations,** 205–37
Asia and Middle East travel, 212
Aspen Strategy Group and, 212
Brookings Institution and, 17, 76, 94, 96, 211–12, 214, 219, 221, 226

Rice, Susan—2001–8, between Democratic administrations (*cont.*)

career goals and, 211

Hillary Clinton's presidential bid and, 59–60

Howard Dean's primary campaign and, 219–20

Elle magazine article and vindication, 209–10

Kerry/Edwards presidential campaign, 17–18, 220–21

leaves government, 205

9/11 terrorist attacks and, 206–11

on nonprofit boards, 212

Obama's election and, 107–8, 232–33

Obama's first contacts with, 17, 18–19

Obama's presidential run, 2007–8 and, 59–61, 76–79, 94–97, 108, 221–24, 228–32

Obama transition team and, 231–32, 233, 237

public assault on integrity and competence, 210

TV appearances, 228–30

Vanity Fair article and false accusations, 207–10

—2009–13, Obama's U.N. ambassador, 13, 200, 237–337

Africa trips, 269

appointment and Senate confirmation, 129–31, 237–40

Ban Ki-moon and, 252–53

Benghazi embassy attack, 2012 and, 10–12, 87, 247, 293

Benghazi political fallout, 309–31

Benghazi postmortem, leadership lessons, 334–37

bin Laden's killing, 295–97

bringing Jake to sessions, 257

as chair, UNSC, 300

championing of human rights, fighting global poverty, 244

China and, 256–58

Churkin and, 257, 259, 264, 274–75, 277, 285, 297–98

climate change and, 244

Hillary Clinton and, 239, 246–47

on *The Colbert Report*, 299

commuting to N.Y. and, 240

on *The Daily Show*, 334

D.C. office and staff, 246

DS agents for, 240, 247–49, 258, 262, 289, 295, 305, 330

duties, 241, 243

eating habits during tenure, 357

"To enhance our common security, we must invest in our common humanity," 238–39

family life and, 241, 249–50, 287–90

farewell party, 298–99

FBI and, 262

hosts UNSC party, 265–66

husband Ian's participation, 300

inclusion in the cabinet, 246

Iran back channel, 261–63

Iran sanctions and, 263–64

Israel supported by, 252–54

job protocol, rituals, 299–301

learning negotiation, 259–60

LGBT rights and, 244

Libya, Qaddafi, and military intervention, 153, 279–94

Libya trip, 2011, 291–92

love for the job, 303–4, 343–44

member, NSC Principals Committee, 130, 246, 247, 272–73

Mexico trip and cactus mishap, 304–5

Mubarak's resignation and, 279

North Korean sanctions, 255–60

Obama's management style, 245

Obama's objectives, 241, 243

Obama's view of role, 238

P5 members and, 264–66

Palestinian status at U.N. and, 253

Peres's friendship, 254–55, 431–32

principal deputy Wolff, 241

relationship building with member states and, 251–52

"right to food" issue, 244

Russia and, 255–57
as secretary of state candidate, 318–31
successor for, 344
Sudan conflict, 270–77
Sudan trips, 273–77
Syria and, 153, 297–98
team for, 241, 317–18
UNSC members and, 252
WAT apartment, 249–51, 302, 328
women's advancement and, 244
World Bank presidency offer, 303
—2013–17, Obama's National Security
    Advisor, 13, 344–452
in Abu Dhabi, 2016, 454
accompanying Obama to Martha's
    Vineyard, 350–51
Afghanistan policy, 390–95
Afghanistan trip, 2013, 390–92
appointment of, 342–44
Bergdahl release and, 392–93
bias for action and, 369
Blinken as deputy, 343, 352, 353, 369,
    408
brutal demands of the job, 460
China and, 433–41
China-Hangzhou Summit, 2016 and
    "stair-gate," 439–41
classified iPad, 1, 352
counterterrorism operations, 372
criticism of, 424
Cuba and, 407–10, 427
daily schedule and routines, 351–57
diversifying the national security
    workforce, 427–30
DOD and, 372
eating habits during tenure, 357
Ebola epidemic and, 401–7
Egypt, Morsi, and, 347–51
end-of-administration responsibilities,
    4–5
family demands and, 460
FBI investigation into Trump campaign
    and, 449
final APEC Summit, Peru, 457
final overseas trip with Obama, 8
Flynn and, 4, 6, 457–60

Foley killing by ISIS and, 420–21
"The Furies" and, 370–71
G20 Summit, 2013, 358, 364
Haines as deputy, 369–70 (*see also*
    Haines, Avril)
health affected by job, 357–58
intelligence briefer for, 1, 2
Iran nuclear deal and, 386, 411–18, 427
ISIS and, 418–23
Israel MOU and, 430–32
Kerry and, 352, 385–87
leaking accusations, 469, 470
leaving office, 1–9, 460
Libya policy decisions and, 293
NSC Holiday Party and, 373
Obama at Mandela's funeral and,
    377–79
Obama in Ethiopia, 2015, threat against,
    379–81
Obama's "affirmative agenda" and, 385
Obama's approach to governing and, 425
Obama's Fourth Quarter quote, Jan.
    2015 and, 426
Obama's overseas trips, routine and
    protocol for, 374–77
office of, 4–7, 348
opening pitch, Nationals Park, 341–42
Paris Climate Change Agreement, 385,
    427
PDB and, 352
preparation for role, 345–46
as Principals Committee chair, 348–49,
    356, 362, 387–90, 400
Putin and, 383
responsibilities of, 345, 346, 369, 384–86,
    398
Rose and, 382
Russia, Ukraine, and, 398–401
Russian election interference and,
    441–49
Secret Service agents and, 1, 2, 7, 9,
    341–42, 384, 440
Secret Service call sign, 384
"snap-back" and sanctions lexicon,
    414
Snowden's leaks and, 358–61

Rice, Susan—2013–17, Obama's National Security Advisor (*cont.*)
South Sudan and, 395–98
staffing president's phone calls, 398
Syria and, 153, 362–69
team for, 346–47, 352, 369–74
Trump and, 382–83, 453–60
unmasking accusation, 468–70
WH briefing, Jan. 5, 2017, 5–6
Rice, Ulysses Simpson (grandfather), 34
Rice, Ulysses Simpson, Jr. ("Suber," uncle), 34, 35, 36
Rice, Walter Allen Simpson (great-grandfather), 32–33, 227, 428
Rice-Cameron, John "Jake" (son), 11, 18, 77–78, 107, 213–18, 228, 232
birth of, 164, 213
college acceptance, 461
interests of, 265–66, 471
at Maret School, 216
mixed-race heritage of, 219
Obama and, 472
politics of, 471–74
prekindergarten school, 214–15
SR as NSA and, 357
SR as parent and, 205, 471
SR away from family, 287–88
SR's Africa trip and, 173, 174
SR's withdrawal as secretary of state candidate and, 328–29
Sudan trip (2011), 275–77
unmasking controversy and, 471
U.N. sessions and, 257
Rice-Cameron, Maris (daughter), 7, 107, 216–19, 228, 232, 287, 309, 461
Benghazi controversy and, 10, 11, 316, 334
mixed-race heritage of, 219
political opinions of, 472–73
SR as U.N. ambassador and, 239, 240, 266, 287–88
SR's withdrawal as secretary of state candidate and, 328–29
Trump election and, 455
unmasking controversy and, 470–71
Richards, Laura, 87, 90, 112, 125

Ried, Curtis, 7
Rivlin, Alice, 57
Rizza, Tom, 7, 440
Robinson, Mary, 172, 173
Roecklein, Trinka, 87, 125
Romney, Mitt
Benghazi and SR, 308, 315–17
presidential bid, 2012, 308
Roosevelt, Eleanor, 33
Rose, Charlie, 382
Rose, David, "The Osama Files," 207–9, 210–11
Rouhani, Hassan, 269, 411, 412, 413
Rousseff, Dilma, 358
Rubin, Robert, 131–32, 133, 200
Russia
"Assessing Russian Activities and Intentions in Recent US Elections" (ICA), 5
Côte d'Ivoire and, 269–70
Crimea and, 299, 398, 399, 400
cyber espionage by, 442
election interference by, 441–49, 478
expelled from the G8, 399
G20 Summit, 2013, 358, 364
invasion of Ukraine, 299
Iran sanctions and, 267, 413
Libya, Qaddafi, and, 284, 285–86, 291
Obama presidency and, 243
sanctions on, 399, 400, 447–48
Snowden in, 359, 361
South Sudan and, 396–97
SR's travel and, 116
Sudan and, 270, 272, 274
Syria and, 297–98, 299, 364–65, 367, 368, 369, 423
Trump and, 400, 448, 449
Trump-Russia collusion allegations, 5–6
Ukraine and, 398–401, 448, 449
UNSC, North Korean sanctions and, 255–56, 257
U.S. relations with, 291, 299, 361, 364–65, 366
See also Churkin, Vitaly

Russwurm, John Brown, 27
Rwanda, 136, 142, 160, 172, 326
   Belgian U.N. peacekeepers killed, 144, 145
   Clinton Foundation in, 146
   Clinton visit, with SR, 175
   Congo War and, 193, 195
   evacuation of U.S. citizens, 144
   French forces in, 149–50
   genocide in, 143–53, 195
   International Criminal Tribunal for Rwanda, 152
   Kigali, 143, 144
   president's plane shot down, 143–44
   Radio Mille Collines, 144, 147
   recovery from genocide, 151
   refugees from, 150–51, 193
   SR affected by, 151–53
   SR witnesses genocide in, 143
   UNAMIR, 145, 147
   UNAMIR II, 148
   U.S. Operation Support Hope, 150
   U.S. policy in, 146–47, 152–53
Ryu, Rexon, 246

Sadat, Anwar, 82
Saddam Hussein, 367
St. Albans School, 50, 84, 92, 102, 342
   the Little Sanctuary, 123
St. John, Bonnie, 113
Salehi, Ali Akbar, 414
San Bernadino massacre, 420
Sanqcu, Baso, 278
Sarkozy, Nicolas, 95, 287, 292
Saudi Arabia, 279, 381, 417, 450, 477
Schieffer, Bob, 311–12, 314
Schiff, Adam, 320
Schneidman, Witney, 169, 201
Scotsman, The, 230
Scowcroft, Brent, 424
Senegal, 120, 161
   Goree Island, 176
Sessions, Jeff, 457, 468
Sewell, Terri, 113, 416
Shah, Uttamlal T., 492n189
Shalev, Gabriela, 252

Shalgham, Abdurrahman, 280, 302
Shalit, Ruth, "J'Accuse!," 209–10
Shange, Ntozake, *For Colored Girls Who Have Considered Suicide/When the Rainbow Is Enuf*, 113
Sherman, Wendy, 159, 411, 416
Sidwell Friends, 214
Sidwell Tennis Camp, 73
Sierra Leone, 200, 401, 403, 405
"Signed, Sealed, Delivered" (song), 232
Simon, Paul, 115
   Graceland, 115
Singh, Priya, 292
Sisi, Abdel Fattah el-, 348, 351
60 Minutes, SR interview, Dec. 2013, 413–14
Smith, Adam, 320
Smith, Gayle, 19, 76, 177, 178, 195, 203, 216, 380
   NSC's Ebola response effort and, 401–2, 405
   as NSC senior director for African affairs, 181, 201
   Obama's development programs and, 385
   SR and, Congo War regional tour, 193–95
   threat against Obama in Ethiopia and, 380, 381
Smith, Sean, 306–7
Snowden, Edward, 341, 358–61, 451
   PPD 28, "Signals Intelligence Activities" and, 360
Soderberg, Nancy, 119, 131
Somalia, 136–42, 160, 177, 269
   Black Hawk Down, 138, 140
   influence on U.S. Rwanda response, 144, 145, 146, 147
   Mogadishu, 137, 138
   Operation Restore Hope, 136
   U.N. peacekeepers in, 137
   U.S. and U.N. casualties, 136, 137, 138, 139
   U.S. Congressional response, 138–39
   U.S. policy, 137–38
Sotloff, Steven, 420

South Africa, 105, 172, 194
   anti-apartheid movement and, 102,
      104–5, 115
   ARMSCOR case, 202
   Clinton administration and, 202
   Clinton visit, with SR, 175–76
   cultural boycott of, 115
   Libya, Qaddafi, and, 285, 286
   Mandela government, 155–56
   Mandela's prison cell and, 175
   Obama's and SR's trip, Mandela's
      funeral, 377–79
   U.N. ambassador Sanqcu, 278
   U.S.-South Africa Binational
      Commission, 202
South Korea, 252, 256, 258, 259, 345, 434,
      451
Souza, Pete, 354, 371
Sperling, Gene, 119, 131
Stanford Business School, 228
Stanford University, 102, 106
   "America in the 1960s," 101
   Amy Biehl Foundation, 105
   Free South Africa Fund, 105
   "Group Communication," 102–3
   King's papers at, 101
   Oxford University vs., 110
   Rhodes Scholars, 1986, 104
   SR and campus anti-apartheid
      movement, 102, 104–5
   SR attends, 96–106
   SR meets Ian Cameron, 97–98
   SR receives scholarship, 103
   SR's decision to attend, 91–92
   SR's graduation from, 105
   SR's Oxford quarters, 101–2
   Jake Rice-Cameron at, 472
   Stanford-Berkeley game, 1982, 94, 98–99
   Ujamaa at, 102
   victory song, 296
Stevens, J. Christopher, 10, 293, 306–7,
      308, 322, 475
Stevenson, Adlai, 43
Stewart, Jon, 334
Strickler, Adam, 7
Suber, Pratt (great-grandfather), 34

Sudan, 156–60, 161, 177
   Al Shifa factory bombed, 189–90
   atrocities in, 270–71
   bin Laden in, 190
   Clinton administration and, 156–60,
      270
   Comprehensive Peace Agreement
      (2005), 271, 273
   Darfur genocide, 271–74
   gum arabic exports, 158–59
   human rights violations in, 158
   Lui (hospital), 270
   Marial Bai (village), 270
   Mubarak assassination attempt, 157
   National Islamic Front government,
      158
   NGO expulsions, 273
   9/11 terrorist attacks information, 207,
      208, 326
   Obama policy and, 270–77
   Rumbek (town), 270
   Russia, China, and, 270, 274
   sanctions against, 158
   South Sudan, 270–77, 395–98
   SR trips, 270–71, 273–77
   Sudan People's Liberation Movement
      (SPLM), 159
   terrorism and, 156–57, 207–8, 210–11
   U.N. ambassador, 172
   U.S. embassy in Khartoum, 157–58
   war and famine in, 200
Sullivan, Jake, 352, 357, 408, 412
Summers, Larry, 200, 201
Sumter, S.C., 34
Swing, William, 198
Syria, 4, 265, 279, 341
   chemical weapons and, 297, 362,
      364–66
   Chemical Weapons Convention and,
      365
   civil war in, 297
   Iran and, 366, 367, 368
   ISIS and, 297, 366
   Kurds and, 423
   al-Nusra Front, 367
   Obama and, 341, 362–69, 450–51

Russia and, 297–99, 364–65, 367, 368,
  369, 423
SR and policy decisions on, 153, 297–98,
  362–69
Trump and, 365–66, 423
U.N. resolution on chemical weapons
  removal, 365, 386
U.S. humanitarian aid, 367
U.S. operations against ISIS in, 420,
  422–23, 451
Syrian Democratic Forces (SDF), 420

Talbott, Strobe, 214
Taliban, 391, 392, 394–95
Talwar, Puneet, 261–62
Tanzania, 348
  U.S. embassy bombing, 186–91
terrorism
  Afghanistan and, 394–95
  Africa and threat of, 171
  Africa's Sahel and, 282, 293
  Al Qaeda and 9/11 terrorist attacks, 135,
    206–11
  Al Shabab, 379
  Benghazi attack, 311, 312–13
  in Brussels, 420
  Counter-terrorism Support Group,
    187
  East Africa embassy bombings, 4,
    186–91, 306–7, 325
  ISIS and, 293, 297, 404, 418, 420
  Paris bombings, 420, 421
  San Bernadino massacre, 420
  Sudan and, 156–57, 208, 326
  Syria and, 366
  U.S. political division and, 479
  World Trade Center bombing, 1993,
    156
Thomas, Mickalene, 249
Thomas, Stanton, 250, 302
Thorning-Schmidt, Helle, 379
Tibbetts, Jim, 80–81
To End a War (Holbrooke), 183
Torsella, Joe, 104, 111
Toulmin, Catherine, 93
Touré, Kadiatou, 462

Trans-Pacific Partnership Agreement
  (TPP), 242–43, 418, 434, 451, 457
Trudeau, Justin, 457
Trump, Donald, 5, 298, 453–60
  Access Hollywood tape, 444
  Afghanistan and, 394–95
  briefing of, queries about by Obama
    administration, 5
  China and, 439, 457
  domestic policy divisions and, 477–78
  FBI investigation and, 449
  Flynn appointment, 457–60
  Inaugural Address, 8
  inauguration of, 1, 2, 7
  Iran nuclear deal and, 417–18
  ISIS and, 423
  Israel and, 432–33
  Kim Jong Un and, 477
  McCain as critic, 474
  national security decision-making
    process, 452
  national security team, 456
  Oval Office of, 460
  Paris Climate Change Agreement and,
    418
  Putin and, 477
  Russia and, 400, 448, 449
  Russia collusion allegations, 5–6, 468,
    470–71
  Russian election interference and, 442,
    445, 447, 448
  Sessions appointment, 457
  South Sudan and, 397
  spying on, 468
  SR accused by, 470
  SR and, 382–83
  SR and NSC transition team, 455–60
  SR's opinion of, 8, 468, 477
  SR unmasking controversy, 468–70
  "Steele Dossier" and, 448
  Syria and, 365–66, 423
  TPP and, 418, 457
  Ukraine and, 400
Tunisia, 279, 282
Turabi, Hassan al-, 158
Turkey, 253, 268–69, 366, 421, 423, 459, 477

Turnbull, Malcolm, 457
Tuskegee Airmen, 36–37
Tuskegee Army Air Field, 21, 29
Tuskegee Veterans Hospital, 28
Tutu, Desmond, 104
Twaddell, Bill, 166–68

Uganda, 159, 160, 163, 172, 396
    atrocities in, 173
    Bill Clinton visit, with SR, 175
    Congo War and, 193, 195
    LRA, 158, 173
    SR and Albright's visit to, 173
    U.S. embassy threatened, 187
Ukraine, 398–401, 449
Underriner, John, 193–94
UNICEF, 212
United Kingdom, 114–15, 449
    Ebola epidemic and, 403
    Iran sanctions and, 266–67
    Libya, Qaddafi, and, 280, 281, 284, 291,
        292
    Obama trip to (2008), 95
    SR as Rhodes Scholar in, 103–4, 108–17
    Syria and, 297, 362–63
    as UNSC P5 member, 259
United Nations (U.N., UNGA), 136
    Albright as U.S. ambassador, 134, 137,
        161, 357
    anti-Israel bias, 252, 253, 254
    Bolton as U.S. ambassador, 241, 243,
        245, 259
    Clinton administration policy on
        peacekeeping, 141–42
    convention to support disabled persons,
        244
    Correspondents' Dinner, 334
    Ebola epidemic and, 403
    General Assembly opening, 300
    Goldstone Report and, 253
    Holbrooke as U.S. ambassador, 182, 195,
        197, 199
    hot conflict issues, Clinton era, 136
    Human Rights Council, 244, 245, 246,
        253
    Iran nuclear deal and, 412, 413

ISIS and, 301
LGBT rights and, 244
"the month of Africa," 197
Obama and building diplomatic
    coalitions, 243
Obama's approach to, 245
Open Government Partnership, 301
Palestine's status and, 253
PDD-25 and, 142–43
Qaddafi at, 301–2
"right to food" issue, 244
Rwanda genocide and, 148–49
Soderberg and, 119
Somalia conflict and, 136–41
SR as U.S. ambassador, 10–12, 13, 87,
    237–337
SR's analysis of role in Somalia, 140
SR's NSC position under Clinton,
    132–34, 136, 154
Sudan and, 159, 301
United Nations Assistance Mission for
    Rwanda (UAMIR, UNAMIR II), 145,
    147, 148
U.N. Millennium Development Goals,
    244
U.S. Mission building, 259, 261, 262,
    276, 281, 290
U.S. president's meetings, speeches,
    receptions, 300–301
U.S. status in, 2009, 243–44
women's advancement and, 244
World Conference on Racism, 253
United Nations Security Council
    (UNSC), 259
    African affairs, 196, 269–77
    African trips, 269
    Brazil and Turkey on, 268–69
    Côte d'Ivoire and, 269–70
    Ethiopia-Eritrea conflict and, 181, 183
    EU-3, 266–67
    Goldstone Report and, 253
    Holbrooke and, 196–98, 199
    Iran sanctions, 264, 266–69, 413–14
    Israel-Turkey conflict, 253
    Libya as member, 301
    Libya resolution, 278, 280, 282–87

nonpermanent members, 252
North Korea sanctions, 255–60, 266
Obama summit on nuclear proliferation, 301
P5, 259, 264–66, 285
P5+1, 264, 411
presidential statement (PRST) and, 254, 256
rotating African seats on, 159
rotating presidency, 299–300
Russia, China "double-veto" on Syria, 298
Rwanda genocide and, 146–47
Somalia conflict and, 137–38
South Sudan and, 396–97
SR and Obama's agenda, 241–42, 243
SR as chair, 300
SR at sessions, 240
Sudan and, 157, 270–77
Syria and, 264, 297, 367
Syria chemical weapon removal and, 365, 386
U.S. abstains on anti–Israeli settlement vote, 432–33
University of California, Berkeley, 36, 44
International House, 44–45
SR's father's PhD, 32
Stanford-Berkeley game, 1982, 94, 98–99
University of Chicago Law School, 17
U.S. Agency for International Development (USAID), 56, 192, 346, 387
Ebola epidemic, 401, 402, 406
Gross imprisoned in Cuba and, 408–9
Emmett Rice and, 47
Gayle Smith and, 177, 195, 385
U.S. Centers for Disease Control and Prevention (CDC), Ebola epidemic and, 401–7
U.S. Congress
African Growth and Opportunity Act, 176, 201
Benghazi investigations, 311, 313, 337
Biden and Senate Foreign Relations Committee, 165
constraining the President, 139

Ebola epidemic appropriations, 406
embassy appropriations, 190
"Gang of Eight," 444–45
Iran nuclear deal and, 415–16
Iran sanctions, 267–68, 269
Joint Congressional Inquiry into 9/11, 210
Menendez and Senate Foreign Relations Committee, 158–59
Netanyahu joint address, Mar. 2015, 414–15
Obama as junior senator, 19, 95
Obama's Cuba policy and, 408, 409, 410
policy on U.N. peacekeeping, 154
Somalia and, 138–39, 141
SR as page, 83–86
SR's confirmation as assistant secretary of state, 163–64
SR's confirmation as U.N. ambassador, 239–40
SR's secretary of state candidacy and, 323–25
Sudan sanctions and, 158
Thompson-Markward Hall, 84
U.N. debt appropriations, 199
U.S. military action in Syria and, 362, 363–64, 365
U.S. Department of Defense (DOD)
African Center for Strategic Studies (war college), 202
China and, 436
Ebola epidemic and, 402–3
Rwanda genocide, 147, 149
SR and proposals from, 372–73
U.S. in Afghanistan and, 394
U.S. Department of Homeland Security (DHS)
Chinese cyber theft and, 438
Ebola epidemic, 404–6, 406
Russian interference in 2016 election and, 443, 444
See also Johnson, Jeh; Monaco, Lisa
U.S. Department of Justice (DOJ), 156, 437
Obama and, 5, 6
Trump-Russia collusion allegations, 5, 449

U.S. Department of State (DOS)
Africa Bureau, 144, 157, 169, 190, 191, 198, 201–2
African debt relief and, 200
African embassies threatened and SR's closing of, 190–91
Art in Embassies program, 249
diversifying workforce, 429–30
East Africa embassy bombings, 186–91, 206
evacuation of U.S. personnel from Rwanda, 144–45
Foundation for Art and Preservation in Embassies, 249
leaking by, 246
Medical Unit psychiatrist, 188
Monrovia, drawdown of U.S. embassy staff, 200
Operations Center, 186, 187, 188
risks taken by Foreign Service Officers, 184
Rwanda conflict as genocide, 148
South Sudan and, 395–96
SR and Ethiopia-Eritrea conflict, 177–84
SR as assistant secretary of state for African affairs, 13, 59, 152, 162–65, 166–204
SR in Nigeria and death of Abiola, 166–69
SR's AF Front Office and direct reports, 169–70
Sudan embassy closing, 157–58
as supportive of SR as U.N. ambassador, 245
U.S.-Nigeria Bilateral Commission, 203
U.S. policy on U.N. peacekeeping operations and, 142
vulnerable embassies of, 187
U.S. Department of the Treasury (USDT), African debt relief and, 200–201
U.S. Department of Transportation (DOT), 201–2
U.S. Intelligence Community (IC), 332
agencies of, 309
Benghazi attack talking points by, 11, 308–15, 318, 323, 324, 332, 335

Benghazi update, 315
Chinese cyber theft and, 439
diversifying workforce, 429
DNI (director of national intelligence), 309
DNI Oct. 7 statement on Russian email hacking, 443, 444
Iran nuclear deal and, 417
ISIS in Iraq and, 418
Mosul Dam threat and, 422
Russian election interference and, 442–43, 447, 449
SR's unmasking requests, 469–70
"Steele Dossier," 448
U.S. in Afghanistan and, 394
U.S.-Nigeria Bilateral Commission, 203
U.S.-South Africa Binational Commission, 202
U.S. Supreme Court
Affordable Care Act and, 427
same-sex marriage and, 427

Vanity Fair
"The Osama Files" (Rose), 207–9, 210–11, 326
SR rebuttal to Rose article, 208
Vera, Juana, 408
Vietnam War, 53
Votel, Joe, 422

Waldorf-Astoria Towers (WAT) apartment, 249–51
Walker, Alice, 101
The Color Purple, 101
Walker, John T., 89
Wall Street Journal, 318
SR and unmasking, 468
Warner, Mark, 416
Washington, Booker T., 33
Washington, D.C., 52–53, 83
Black Student Fund, 100–101
Boulé in, 225
Forest Hills neighborhood, 50
Rock Creek Park, 54
SR and July 4th in, 349
SR's family in Shepherd Park, 54–55

SR's home in Adams Morgan
  neighborhood, 137, 206
SR's home in Kent neighborhood, 206
as SR's hometown, 13, 41, 49, 52–53,
  82–83
Washington National Cathedral, 50, 79–80,
  89
Washington Post, 321
  Carney op-ed in, 210
  leaked story on Chinese sanctions, 437
Webster, Meridith, 330
Weems, Carrie Mae, 249
Weinstein, Jeremy, 327
Westbrooks, Ticey, 226, 288, 289
White House Correspondents' Dinner, 381
White House Situation Room, 143, 157,
  388, 401, 415, 419, 422, 429, 439, 441,
  460
  Afghanistan and, 393–94
  Brennan meets SR on Russian election
    interference, 441
  John F. Kennedy Conference Room, 388
  K. T. McFarland and, 459
  Morsi coup meeting in, 348–49
  Principals Committee meetings in, 283,
    356, 388, 415, 419–20, 422
  Putin phone calls and, 398–99
  Reagan and, 459
  Somalia crisis and, 137, 138
  SR and, 1, 6, 161
WikiLeaks, 444, 445, 449
Williams, Brian, 330

Williamson, Ruth Ann, 81, 93
Wisner, Frank, 147
Withers, Anne, 357
Wolff, Alejandro, "Alex," 241, 248, 253, 262
Wolpe, Howard, 191–99, 374
  advice to SR, 191–92
  Congo war and, 193–99
  Lusaka Ceasefire Agreement, 195, 199
Wonder, Stevie, 232, 354
Wood, John, 81
Woods, Tyrone S., 306–7
Worden, Andrea, 87–88, 116–17, 125
World Bank, 303

Xi, Jinping, 381, 435, 436, 437–39, 440,
  457

Yale University, 91, 92, 102, 227, 228
Yang, Jiechi, 434
Yanukovych, Viktor, 399
Yates, Sally, WH briefing, Jan. 5, 2017, 5–6
Yemen, 279, 450
Young Leaders initiatives, 385

Zarif, Mohammed Javad, 412, 414
Zhang, Yesui, 257–58, 266, 438
Zients, Jeffrey, 374
Zimbabwe, 118, 119–20, 132, 160, 163, 172,
  173–74, 193
Zoellick, Robert, 303
Zuma, Jacob, 286
Zuniga, Ricardo, 408, 409

About the Author

Ambassador Susan E. Rice is currently Distinguished Visiting Research Fellow at the School of International Service at American University, a Non-Resident Senior Fellow at the Belfer Center for Science and International Affairs at Harvard's Kennedy School of Government, and a contributing opinion writer for the *New York Times*. She serves on the board of Netflix and previously served on several nonprofit boards, including the U.S. Fund for UNICEF and the John F. Kennedy Center for the Performing Arts.